VIL CO LGE

work
organisations

KEY ISSUES IN WORK AND ORGANISATION ■
CONTEMPORARY CHANGES IN WORKING LIFE ■
UNDERSTANDING ORGANISATIONAL BEHAVIOUR:
ISSUES AND AGENDAS ■ THEORISING ORGANISATION

work
organisations

a critical approach

Fourth edition

Paul Thompson
and
David McHugh

palgrave
macmillan

First edition 1990
Second edition 1995
Third edition 2002
Fourth edition 2009

Published by
PALGRAVE MACMILLAN

Palgrave Macmillan in the UK is an imprint of Macmillan Publishers Limited,
registered in England, company number 785998, of Houndmills, Basingstoke,
Hampshire RG21 6XS.

Palgrave Macmillan in the US is a division of St Martin's Press LLC,
175 Fifth Avenue, New York, NY 10010.

Palgrave Macmillan is the global academic imprint of the above companies
and has companies and representatives throughout the world.

Palgrave® and Macmillan® are registered trademarks in the United States,
the United Kingdom, Europe and other countries.

ISBN: 978–0–230–52222–0

This book is printed on paper suitable for recycling and made from fully
managed and sustained forest sources. Logging, pulping and manufacturing
processes are expected to conform to the environmental regulations of the
country of origin.

A catalogue record for this book is available from the British Library.

A catalog record for this book is available from the Library of Congress.

10 9 8 7 6 5 4 3 2 1
18 17 16 15 14 13 12 11 10 09

Printed and bound in Great Britain by
CPI Antony Rowe, Chippenham and Eastbourne

contents

list of tables and figures

Tables

Figures

acknowledgements

Once again this new edition has taken us a lot longer than we intended. We thank family, colleagues and especially Ursula Gavin and Mark Cooper at Palgrave Macmillan for their patience and support. Keith Povey is owed our thanks once again for his sterling work on the proofs.

Paul Thompson writes:

Writing this edition while being Head of Department (of Human Resource Management at Strathclyde) has, predictably, not been easy. Thanks then to my colleagues for making that job tolerable enough to do a few other things, including this book. Teaching is always a challenge and inspiration for writing and I've benefited from working with colleagues, particularly Kirsty Newsome and Charlie Ford. As with previous editions, the main source of material is always the research and scholarly collaborations with colleagues in the UK and across the globe. I'd like to thank everyone I collaborated with for stimulating my ideas and tolerating me utilising things we've done together for this new edition. In particular, thanks to co-editors on the *Oxford Handbook of Work and Organization*, Stephen Ackroyd, Rose Batt and Pam Tolbert; Jeff Hyman and Bill Harley similarly for *Participation and Democracy at Work*; Paul Boreham, Rachel Parker and Richard Hall, my co-authors on *New Technology@Work*; Chris Warhurst, Abigail Marks, Chris Smith and (again) Bill Harley for our ongoing work on knowledge work, identity and labour process theory respectively. I have occasionally managed to sneak away to spend some time abroad and to be freer to write. Colleagues at the University of Sydney, particularly Diane van den Broek, have made me very welcome. Finally, thanks to Kerry Ann Boyle for looking at Chapter 10 and Gillian Pallis for looking after my well-being.

Dave McHugh writes:

In memory of my father John Patrick McHugh (1926–2001). He lived it so that I could write about it, my eternal thanks.

preface to the new edition

Our aim in writing the first edition of *Work Organisations* was to provide a critical alternative to the standard, often American, texts that still predominated in the 1980s, as well as to some of the derivative British versions. These 'standard' texts tended to combine a narrow and prescriptive orientation to issues of management, structure and organisational design, with a behavioural agenda dealing with issues such as personality and perception, where a focus on the individual appeared to have little relationship to the more 'structural' material. Since that time, more alternative texts have followed us into that gap in the market, to say nothing of regular conferences and journal on 'critical management studies'. All this is to be welcomed, but we still think this book has something distinctive to say. By the time you get to a fourth edition the stall is pretty much set out, but another go gives a further opportunity to bring materials up-to-date, sharpen arguments and address new issues.

'Critical' has become a bigger, if not always better brand. For us it has meant aiming to balance exposition and evaluation of mainstream writing and research with an attempt to bring together the large, but often fragmented, body of writings from, among other sources, organisation and management theory, labour process analysis, feminism, industrial sociology and social psychology – where they are radical and relevant to the study of work organisations. Any orientation of this sort by definition has to be interdisciplinary, pluralistic and pragmatic in the choice of sources it draws on for inspiration. That is not to say this book is just neutral exposition. We make our and other views clear, but the emphasis is on what the weight of evidence is telling us about key trends.

One of the distinctive problems we have grappled with across the various editions has been the question of how to link the broadly sociological and more behavioural material. We have never pretended that any form of grand integration was possible. Our aim has been to ensure that the discussions in the main parts of the book were complementary in the kind of analysis used and issues discussed. We feel strongly that organisations are places in which attempts to shape the subjectivity and identity of employees are central to the purposes of management, and that this provided an important bridge and common focus between debates in the different chapters. We have continued to look for ways of integrating material, a result of which the third edition had two new chapters on teams and on learning and that provided opportunities to bring debates and approaches together, and in this edition a new chapter on knowledge management fulfils the same function.

This new edition also gives us the opportunity further to enhance the accessibility of the book for readers. In the previous edition, we broke the material into more easily digestible chunks, increasing the chapters from 12 to 26. To further aid the process, we have added chapter aims at the beginning and clearer summaries, key points and key readings at the end. As for the content, we are still trying to balance an introduction to key debates, with sufficient depth and reflection to engage with issues and ideas in a meaningful way. All chapters have been updated to take account of new studies and insights, though clearly some have more additions than others for the simple reason that either the world or our accounts of it have changed. Examples of substantial additions include the burgeoning debates about resistance that are covered in Chapters 8 and 9, and the addition of a completely new chapter (16) on knowledge and its management. The biggest change to structure and content is, however, what is now Part II. It's always difficult to know how to deal with those territories that are tied most closely to contemporary changes in work and employment, given that they overlap and suffer from the most rapidly shifting theories and practices. In the previous edition we handled this by putting claims of major change (new economy, new organisations) in one chapter and research that showed greater continuity as well as change in another. Like any format, it had its merits, but risks repetition. This time we have broken down the contemporary changes into five main areas and chapters. Each has had substantial new material added.

So, the structure of the book is now organised through four parts. Part I – Key Issues in Work and Organisation – focuses on the areas traditionally dealt with by organisation theory and the predominantly sociological contributions to theory and research. The chapters are a combination of accounts of some of the classic contributions in their historical context from Taylor, Weber and the Human Relations tradition, and more modern issues and literatures such as power, control, gender and culture. Part II is the addition as described above and moves from the big picture – general accounts of change in economy, society and organisation – to particular spheres: corporate structures, labour markets and flexibility, labour processes and managing knowledge. The latter chapter is a little different from the others. Given the relative newness of much of the theory and practice it is more speculative and also acts as a link to the behavioural material in Part III. In Part II the format changes slightly. Because of the close connections between each sphere, the objectives and key points/key reading is for the whole Part II rather than each individual chapter.

Part III focuses as before on predominantly psychological material traditionally described as the study of *organisation behaviour* or OB. The overall theme as before is to assess the nature and adequacy of the mainstream agenda for an understanding of our experience of organisational life, and how this shapes the construction of the identities through which we face it. At the same time we have tried to shift emphasis somewhat to focus more on how we use organisations for our own purposes as distinct from how organisations dominate subjectivity. Although readers can use the chapters separately, we still recommend that they take on board the contextual discussion of what we term the 'subjective factor', which has now been gathered into Chapter 17. The structure and sequencing of Part III has changed somewhat, sometimes as with the chapter on personality, because the old chapters were getting too large when revised, and others, such as those on motivation and stress, swap in sequence because there is more discussion of contextual and HRM issues in the latter. We have removed sections on communication, interpersonal influence, innovation and creativity mainly because they did not fit with the new structure and overall argument. They are still there in the 3rd edition! We have expanded the material on stress to focus more on issues of well-being and the coverage of emotions now includes a brief exposition and critique of emotional intelligence. As previously we do not apologise for overlap between issues in Parts I and II and Part III, the areas of commonality are there in the real world and are reflected in our account.

Part IV deals with more complex theoretical issues. The discussion draws on and links to some of the substantive issues explored in previous chapters, such as bureaucracy and rationality, but locates them in the underlying theoretical resources that particular research and concepts draw from, as well as introducing additional themes that reflect conflicts between rival paradigms. The final chapter ends the book with a wider discussion on the nature and uses of organisational knowledge. How do theorists using different paradigms speak to each other? How do managers use theory in practice? How can participants at work learn from past and present to create more democratic, as well as more efficient, organisations? Because this chapter works as a kind of conclusion to Part IV, no additional summary and key points are provided, but there is a Key Reading section.

Within Parts I and III, chapters have been designed to be read as stand-alone expositions and commentaries on theory and practice. We have tried hard to always signpost links backwards and forwards from chapter to chapter. It is worth reminding readers at the outset that a textbook is not like a novel. There is no narrative that requires you to start at the beginning and work through chapter by chapter until you find out 'who done it?' However, it makes some sense to read Chapter 1 first, mainly because it tries to give a basic picture of the kind of approach taken in the book as a whole. It seeks to explore three main questions. Why are we interested in studying organisations? How should they be studied? And what are the general concepts and principles available to do so? The more adventurous reader could go directly to Part IV and follow some of the more theoretical issues through, but it is not necessary to do this in order to follow the substantive discussions found in the intervening chapters, where we build up an understanding of theory and research in a more incremental way. As we have added chapter or Part aims, setting out the content and purposes of each in this introduction seems superfluous. So, happy reading.

part I

key issues in work and organisation

1 studying organisations: an introduction

Organisations and organisation society

> " Pouring in doctors, nurses and medicines without the administrative infrastructure to deploy them where they're needed, is merely to leave hope piled in opened boxes at some bemused local airport. ... Success or failure, life or death – they don't depend on cash alone, but on organization. (Peter Preston reflecting on the Asian Tsunami, *The Guardian*, 3 January 2005)

This should be a happy, or at least pertinent judgement for those of us who make a living studying organisations. Yet, as citizens of society we tend to have a love–hate relationship with large-scale organisations. We frequently berate them for being bureaucratic, wasteful and placing us under the shadow of big brother. As Peter Preston says elsewhere in the above article, too many administrators is often the explanation for the failure of anything from policing to health service reform. Yet we take organisations for granted as providers of employment, public welfare, private services, and even charity or other voluntary activities. In the not so distant past, information, leisure, economic needs and other basic life processes were more likely to be directly and locally produced or consumed. Now, complex economic, social and political organisations provide a network of individual and social relationships through which we participate in society at local, national and global levels (Morgan, 1990b).

Such organisations have therefore become a focus for academic analysis, often under the heading of organisation studies (OS). This is not a discipline with clear sources and boundaries in the manner of economics or political science. Rather it is constructed from a variety of disciplines and sub-disciplines including industrial sociology, management theory, organisational sociology and psychology, and industrial relations. This is not the place to provide detailed descriptions or historical explanations of such disciplines (see M. Rose, 1986; Hyman, 1981). What we can observe is that a common field of study around organisations has facilitated a welcome overlap in subject matter and conceptual frameworks. Though different strands will have their own more specific interests such as motivation or skill and work satisfaction, there are a growing number of common interests and frameworks. If we take management strategy, for example, it is clear that a considerable amount of research has been done from an industrial sociology perspective, within an industrial relations framework and by management studies. Similar points could be made with respect to job design, labour markets and a range of other issues. We welcome this interdisciplinary framework and its effect on OS and hope that this book reflects and encourages it.

However, it would be misleading to give the impression that all is sweetness and light in this field of study. For a start, the same paradox that affects public attitudes is often reproduced intellectually. Indeed, from popular management writers to postmodernists, organisation – at least in the sense of action to create order – has become something of a dirty word. The fashion instead is for decentralisation, disorganisation and even chaos (Peters, 1989). Big and bureaucratic is bad; but we are running ahead of the story.

The past fifty or a hundred years have seen a remarkable growth in the number, size, and power of organizations of many kinds, ranging through all areas of life. The extent of this change in the character and atmosphere of society can be visualized if we contrast the situation of 1952 with, say, that of 1852. In 1852 labour unions were practically nonexistent. There were practically no employers' associations or trade associations. There were practically no professional associations. There were no farm organizations of any importance. National governments absorbed – by present standards – an almost infinitesimal part of the total national product. There was no Department of Agriculture, no Department of Labour, in Washington. There were few corporations and few large businesses. Organizations outside government itself were largely confined to the churches, a few local philanthropic societies, and the political parties. There were, of course, many sporadic attempts at large-scale organizations, in almost all fields, in the first half of the nineteenth century. None of these attempts, however, resulted in the establishment of stable, continuing organizations such as we see today.

(Kenneth Boulding, *The Organizational Revolution*, 1953)

The theory and practice of organisation has developed around bureaucracies, deriving partly from the work of Max Weber, who, at the turn of the last century, was most responsible for drawing our attention to the significance of large-scale organisations. As the division of labour in society and at work became more complex and difficult to manage, the responsibility and means of co-ordination of core activities became focused on specialised units. The essence of organisation is the creation of regular, standardised behaviour and orderly structure. For Weber the characteristic feature of society would be complex and highly developed administrative structures governed by rules, hierarchy and experts. Most people would work for or become clients of such bureaucracies. In current discourse, such developments are linked to the wider growth of *modernism*, in which planning, calculation and a hierarchy of authority spread to most areas of social and cultural life.

As the extract above indicates, some modern writers came to believe that such an *organisation society* reached fruition in the post-1945 period (Kerr *et al.*, 1960; Bell, 1960; Prethus, 1962). The dominant themes were that private and public corporations had helped to usher in a new era where politics, ideology and conflict had been superseded by rational, scientific decision-making, guided by a new enlightened, though powerful, administrative élite. Standardised mass production and consumption went hand-in-hand with central direction of the economy and state by professional managers and politicians. A special sort of person – organisation man – was even evoked, who could be relied on to be one of the vehicles of such techniques, given that his personality and commitment was subordinated to the corporation (Whyte, 1956). As Biggart comments, Whyte was describing 'a generation of organisational workers who had been moulded by the needs of the corporation ... conservative, impassive little grey men. Their lives in the organisation were routine and largely unemotional' (Biggart, 1989: 4). The emphasis on 'man' is not accidental. An organisation society was predicated on the assumption of male corporate warriors, sustained by women at home providing the practical and emotional support.

It was pointless to desire significantly different arrangements, as all industrial societies were destined to converge into a single, similar type. The hierarchical and bureaucratic large-scale organisation, with its particular form of technology, was placed at the centre of mature industrial society. In retrospect this kind of perspective is more of an ideology masquerading as science than an accurate description of social trends. Organisation society and 'man' are part of an imagery where:

> all the major institutional landmarks of modern industrial society – the factory, the welfare state, the
> business corporation, representative democracy, an independent civil service, universal education and

> medical care – were firmly set in place and equipped to manage any new problems which were likely to emerge in the foreseeable future. Institutional fine-tuning and technical adjustment were all that was necessary to maintain social stability and economic development. (Reed, 1985: 99–100)

At a time when there is considerable public scepticism about corporations, government and, indeed, science, this all now seems over-optimistic. It was always misguided. Grouping developments under a catch-all label of organisation society or 'complex organisations' became a means, however unintended, of stopping questions being asked about how such arrangements had come into being, how they were maintained, and whether they were necessary. In particular it obliterated real differences between organisational experiences such as being a worker and consumer of public or private services, organisations in a capitalist or non-capitalist society, and the origins and effects of different types of technology in varied cultural settings. In other words, such frameworks obscured the social contexts and social choices made about the nature of organisations – how they are structured, managed and experienced.

So far we have established that studying organisations is important, but contentious. What else does this introductory chapter set out to achieve?

- To define what organisations and what territories they operate on, making case that we should focus on *work* organisations.
- Map out some of the disputed things that go on under the heading of organisation theory or analysis,
- Elaborate some of the questions and issues that divide mainstream and critical approaches.
  - Can we talk of organisational goals?
  - Is there a rational, efficient 'best way' of organising?
  - Is hierarchy inevitable?
  - Is studying management synonymous with organisation?
  - Can there be a science of organisational behaviour?
- Set out the basic principle that underlies a critical and hopefully more persuasive approach to studying organisations.

Defining the scope and purpose of organisations

Whether existing organisational structures and practices are necessary and efficient and regardless of which forms are dominant, it is demonstrably the case that greater power over our lives is exerted through such processes. Organisations mediate between the wider society and the individual, and joining an organisation as an employee exposes the individual to substantial direction and control. Despite the self-activity of their members, organisations as corporate bodies do have economic and political powers above and beyond those of the particular individuals that comprise them. In fact, there is every indication of a concentration of those powers in a small number of organisations, which is far from enlightened in its effects on us as workers or citizens. This was a perspective raised decades ago by C. Wright Mills (1959), who dubbed those who commanded major organisations the 'power élite'. Today, takeovers and mergers continue unabated, whether the beneficiaries are tycoons such as Rupert Murdoch or faceless financial institutions.

So, despite the limits to the idea of an organisation society, there is a case for studying organisations. But, there remain a number of unanswered questions as to *how*? The orthodox approach is to define organisations as purposeful systems characterised by co-ordinated action towards an objective. By defining organisations in this way, Donaldson (1985: 7) can link together corporations, schools, families or neighbours fixing a fence. But though work may take place within a charity or a political party, its nature and purposes are different from those that operate under market discipline. Organisation may be necessary to ensure that co-ordinated action of any kind takes place, but actions vary enormously with the type of objective. Take Buford's account of his time among extremely well-organised football hooligans:

> Extensive preparations had gone into Manchester United's last meeting with West Ham – coaches had been hired, with complex routes into the city to evade the police, the arrival times staggered so that everyone did not appear *en masse*. ... Problems of leadership, organisation, and 'big numbers', and a hierarchical command structure: the technocrat phrasing did not obscure that what Steve was describing was a civil disturbance involving several thousand people. (Buford, 1991: 119–20)

The problem is that only by operating at an excessive level of generality and abstraction is it possible to treat things as diverse as hooligans, scout troops and transnational companies within the same analytical framework. As Nelson and Winter note, 'There are a great many different sorts of organisations, and it is implausible that a given collection of concepts and propositions would apply uniformly, or even usefully, to all of them' (quoted in Rowlinson, 1997: 70). Salaman makes a similar point:

> a genuine sociology of organisations is not assisted by the efforts of some organisation analysts to develop hypotheses about organisations in general, lumping together such diverse examples as voluntary organisations, charities and political organisations. ... It also obstructs the analysis of those structural elements which are dramatically revealed in employing organisations, but not necessarily in all forms of organisation. (Salaman, 1979: 33)

We agree with Salaman here, that organisations as such are not a coherent category of objects capable of being studied in a distinctive way. This is implicitly recognised in orthodox writing, which, most of the time, is *not* about organisations *per se*. Though comprehensive formal definitions may be retained, the overwhelming amount of writing and research is about business. Why then even refer to *work* organisations? Work organisations remain a crucial meeting place of contending social forces – owners, managers, professions, and workers – which generate and reflect contradiction and change. It is also the case that it is the profit-seeking nature of business organisations that creates their distinctive forms of management, control or other social relations. Such forms of organisation remain the structural core of advanced societies, even allowing for the decline in the proportion of those engaged in manufacturing activities. It is primarily for these reasons that the bulk of this book is geared towards those events and experiences.

But in the end it is neither possible nor desirable to maintain a complete distinction between business and other forms of work organisation. Parts of the public sector have always operated in a market environment, and this tendency has rapidly increased in parts of the health service, local government and other public spheres in recent years. In addition, management methods or technologies may arise in a specific sector, but are frequently applied in modified forms in others. Finally, as Weber recognised, there are continuities of structure and practice deriving from the bureaucratic forms present within all large-scale organisations. For these reasons, while recognising the limitations, we prefer to retain work organisations as a broad framework. However, this does not mean that they are studied in isolation. Families and state structures are just two of the forces that interact with work organisations and whose links need to be examined.

Organisational analysis: problems and problematics

Even if we can settle some of the issues of the scope of organisational analysis, many unresolved problems remain which are essentially theoretical in nature. Since the 1950s, a particular approach, normally labelled organisation behaviour (OB), or sometimes organisation theory (OT), has become dominant. It is drawn mainly from management writings and organisational psychology, but enthusiastically borrows from sociology, economics, anthropology and other areas; thus laying claim to be genuinely interdisciplinary. While the borrowing of concepts may be eclectic, it is not random. Rather it is structured by specific problematics (a network of concepts oriented towards a core idea). OB focuses on social behaviour in the enterprise, directed chiefly towards problems of motivation and the performance of individuals and groups in relation to different structures and practices. OT is, according to Donaldson, primarily concerned with the trivariate relationship between structure, contingency and performance; or put another way it is 'mainly about the analysis of different designs, and their contingencies and their outcomes' (1985: 121). When both are taken into account, the result is that, 'These writers have attempted to draw together and distil theories of how organisations function and how they should be managed. Their writings have been theoretical in the sense that they have tried to discover generalisations applicable to all organisations' (Pugh, 1971: 9).

This approach is found in most American and some British textbooks and business schools. Therefore, though OS has always been by its very nature interdisciplinary, this has often been on a narrow, management plus psychology basis. One of the limiting factors has been the gradual split from sociology. Organisational sociology has had a less than peaceful coexistence with orthodox approaches. In the last 25 years there has been a shift in the study of organisations from sociology departments to business and management schools (Hinings, 1988). The orientations of OB and OT have become narrower and more prescriptive. Donaldson (1985: 71–2, 119–20) defends this by reference to different levels of analysis. Issues of class and power, ideology and social stratification, and economic contradictions are the province of sociology. OT concentrates on the problems of people working inside organisations. Advocates of this approach thus seek to deflect criticism of neglect of wider concerns by moving the analytical goalposts. It is impossible satisfactorily to study something like the division of labour or hierarchy of groups in a business without an understanding of the broader social division of labour and power structure.

This is not the only or main problem with 'organisation theory' that Donaldson (1985) attributes to North American business and management schools. Despite his spirited defence, this literature continues to reproduce a largely taken-for-granted view of organisations with respect to both their structures and processes, and notions of effectiveness and rationality. The rest of this chapter seeks to open up this discussion by examining some of the basic theoretical assumptions of orthodox or mainstream approaches, before going on to outline some alternatives that inform the way we have attempted to understand work organisations in this book. So as to avoid the discussion getting too complex at this stage, we have not dealt with the theoretical resources that mainstream or critical approaches draw from. These are outlined in Part III.

Goals, diversity and interests

If organisations are consciously created instruments, then their purpose tends to be defined in terms of goal seeking. This is unexceptional and, in fact, provides a means of distinguishing organisations from social institutions (for example, families) or movements (such as feminism), which do not manifest systematic structures and processes for controlling relations between means and ends. But further definition is more controversial. Goals are seen as preferred states which organisations and their members attempt to achieve through collective and co-ordinated action: 'the planned co-ordination of the activities of a number of people for the achievement of some common, explicit purpose or goal' (Schein, quoted in Mullins, 1985: 2). In this 'goal model', action and values are seen in consensual terms. Goals are formulated, policies

CULTURE, COMPANIES AND COUNTRIES IN A GLOBALISING ERA ▪ MANAGEMENT ▪ CONTROL AND RESISTANCE ▪ POWER IN ORGANISATIONS ▪ GENDER, SEXUALITY AND ORGANISATIONS ▪ CORPORATIONS AND CULTURE: REINVENTING ORGANISATION MAN?

7

and objectives flow from them, inputs in the form of activities are created, which, in turn produce outputs that allow for realisation of goals and organisational success.

Though there may be vague reference to 'environmental influences', the starting point tends to be located within, rather than outside, the organisation: 'there is an assumption that the organisation has some capacity to resist environmental constraints and set its own pattern' (Benson, 1977: 5). Obstacles and variations in these processes *are* acknowledged. Members of organisations may have goals that are contradictory to senior management, creating gaps between formal and informal, official and operative, goals and actual policies (Perrow, 1961). For example, scientific and technical workers tend to be much more committed to their job than to their company, and tensions arise between employees' desire to pursue research for its intrinsic value and pressure on employers to monitor and even close down those projects (Randle and Rainnie, 1994). Furthermore, sub-units of the organisation develop a life of their own, a partial devolution of responsibility resulting in goal displacement. It is management's job to ensure the best possible fit between the goals of different 'stakeholders'. This type of thinking is reflected in standard business mission statements, such as the one in Table 1.1.

Despite some progress towards acknowledging goal diversity and uncertainty, there are huge limitations to this way of thinking about organisations and goals. Oppositional goals cannot be confined to the 'personal'. As Clegg and Dunkerley observe, 'There is no notion of rational structural sources of opposition being generated in the normal processes of organisation' (1980: 317). A sense of reification is still present, in which the organisation is treated as a thing, and the only legitimate goal-seeking collective. Problems cannot be wholly avoided by the use of the 'stakeholder' model (Donaldson, 1985: 24). While stakeholding does help us recognise a variety of interests inside organisations, in some variants it postulates a misleading pluralism in which goals are held to be the result of a relatively equal trade-off between the preferences of competing but co-operative groups (employees, managers, owners, customers). Nor is it enough for Donaldson to assert that the higher levels of management simply 'edit and select' from competing claims. Take the Pifco mission statement set out in Table 1.1. It all sounds good: shareholders can have increased profits, consumers get first-class service, employees get secure employment, and communities get a healthy environment. Regardless of whether corporate management really means it, it may find this much harder to deliver. Value for shareholders, dictated by financial institutions, may mean 'downsizing' and job losses. Efficiency drives to increase the quantity of queries dealt with in a call centre may result in poorer-quality service for those on the other end of the phone line.

The notion that formal organisations, made up of different members, are constituted to co-ordinate wider goals as if this is a form of social contract (Albrow, 1973: 408), underestimates the extent to which

Table 1.1 **Extract from Pifco Holdings plc mission statement, August 1994**

The group exists for the benefit of:

- Its shareholders – by giving them annual dividend growth and long term capital appreciation from the consistent achievement of increased profits.
- Its customers and consumers – by providing products which delight them and represent excellent value in terms of quality, design, performance, reliability and price, together with a first class service.
- Its employees – by giving them secure long term employment, a fair and equitable reward system (including performance-related bonuses, share incentives and share options for senior executives), personal career development and safe and pleasant working conditions.
- The community – by acting as a good corporate citizen by giving support to the less fortunate in society and by adopting environmentally sound policies both within the company and outside.

dominant power groupings have set those goals and shaped the appropriate structures. In practice co-ordination or co-operation may reflect pressure, constraint or acquiescence to power as much as shared goals. Let's take an example to illustrate the problem: the Wapping dispute. In the mid-1980s, Rupert Murdoch announced plans to move production of his press titles from Fleet Street to a new site. This was planned in secret and sprung on the workforce. The subsequent strike was used as an excuse to dismiss over 5000 workers, most of whom never got their jobs back. Not much sign of a trade-off among stakeholders here. The power accruing from ownership gave Murdoch and his associates the means to enforce their objectives. Even those – notably journalists – who voted to accept the move, did so in a context of bribes (£2000 and private health insurance) or threats (the sack). But in one sense there is pluralism in work organisations, albeit different from 'stakeholders'. The array of interests and interest groups that exist goes beyond a conventional management and labour dichotomy. One of the reasons that Murdoch won is that he was able to exploit divisions between journalists, mainly male printers and largely female semi-skilled workers, and white-collar employees – all of whom had a history of sectional antagonism over wages, jobs and working conditions. So there is a sense in which we can refer to 'organisations' having policies or goals, but they have to be clearly recognised as frequently being the property of particular individuals or groups.

All this leads to a need to modify the orthodox definition of organisations as means of delivering collective goals. A more realistic definition would see organisations as *consciously created arrangements to achieve goals by collective means*. This recognises the inter-connected character of organisational practices, without any assumptions about harmonious goals and interests. A final broader point on this issue is important. As we saw earlier, to define or classify organisations in terms of goal seeking distorts the difference between them. We need to differentiate between different types of goals and the wider economic and political influences upon them; how they are constructed and in whose benefit they operate. With this in mind, it is better to think in terms of a variety of *organising logics* that arise out of those contexts and preferences. These may not all resemble the conventional bureaucratic way of doing things. For example, direct selling organisations (DSOs) such as Amway or Avon have been among the fastest-growing commercial organisations:

> " Compared with traditional firms, DSOs appear loose and out of control. They represent an apparent management nightmare that only a thick rule book and a platoon of managers could keep together. In fact, DSOs have almost no rules and, compared with most firms, few managers. Home Interiors and Gifts, for example, with 30 000 distributors, has only 35 managers. ... Direct selling has a logic too, but is radically different from the logic of bureaucratic organisations: a conscious alternative to firms as a way to organise economic activity to make a profit, as a technique for managing labour, and as a means of earning income. (Biggart, 1989: 5–7)

Different logic leads to the choice of particular managerial mechanisms. The scientific workers referred to earlier are subject to normative controls that attempt to mobilise commitment to the work, combined with a large degree of operational autonomy. Many other white-collar workers in conventional bureaucratic hierarchies are being managed through much more economistic methods such as performance-related pay.

Rationality, efficiency and choice
The mainstream emphasis on collective goal seeking is also sustained by a vision of organisations as *rational* instruments or tools; indeed this was a prime theme of 'classical management theory' that formed the

CULTURE, COMPANIES AND COUNTRIES IN A GLOBALISING ERA ▪ MANAGEMENT ▪ CONTROL AND RESISTANCE ▪ POWER IN ORGANISATIONS ▪ GENDER, SEXUALITY AND ORGANISATIONS ▪ CORPORATIONS AND CULTURE: REINVENTING ORGANISATION MAN?

9

basis of modern organisational analysis (see Chapter 8). When we talk of rationality, it normally refers to the logical nature of beliefs or actions. This is an aspect of mainstream perspectives, but the basic feature concerns the development of suitable means to reach specific ends. It therefore becomes inseparable from a notion of *efficiency*. The emphasis is on rationally designed structures and practices resting on processes of calculated planning that will maximise organisational effectiveness. Some traditional theorists have described this in terms of the 'one best way' to run organisations. A more acceptable version of the rational model recognises the contingent nature of the process: 'Organisational arrangements are viewed as the outcomes of means–end decisions to bring situational circumstances and structures into alignment in order to enhance efficiency' (Bryman, 1984: 392). Most mainstream texts continue to deny that there is one formula to fit every situation, but any serious examination of popular management writing and the associated business fads shows that the search for blueprints and formulas – whether via corporate culture or business process re-engineering – has not been forgotten (Pascale, 1990; Huczynski, 1993). The formula for success may differ, but the framework of rational action = efficiency remains the same.

Rationality and efficiency are legitimate aspects of organisational analysis. But in mainstream theory they are presented largely in neutral terms, as if rationality was a simple determinant of organisational structures, processes and goals. Processes are reduced to a matter of technique: devising the appropriate kind of structure, or best fit with a particular environment. A cosy picture is developed of a functional relationship between rational organisations and a rational society. This perspective removes issues of politics, power and control from organisational choices, and critical questions concerning means and ends. Donaldson (1985: 101) tries to get round this by separating the latter: 'The concern with rational means rather than values is part of what makes such studies apolitical.' But there are as many contestable choices to be made about how to design jobs or authority structures as there are about the ends to which they are put.

A rational model emphasising features such as calculability is further confused with rationality or reasonableness *as such*. As Fischer and Sirriani put it:

> " For the critical theorist, mainstream writers have confused the rational model of efficient administrative behaviour with organisational rationality itself … organisations must be conceptualised as tools for the pursuit of personal, group or class interests. (Fischer and Sirriani, 1984: 10–11)

Furthermore, traditional notions underestimate the role of rationality and efficiency as ideological constructs that help to legitimise the positions, rewards and activities of dominant groups (Salaman, 1979: 177–82). For example, when changes take place such as mergers or closures, they are often described in terms of *rationalisation*, as if the decision of managers or boards of directors are inevitable and the only way of doing things. It is important to acknowledge the contested nature of rationality, underpinned by the struggle for scarce organisational and social resources; and indeed, this is the direction taken by an increased range of organisational theorists (Bryman, 1984).

Hierarchy and the division of labour

Mainstream theory is strongly influenced by ideas of organisations as co-operative social systems; self-regulating bodies, tending towards a state of equilibrium and order. This, in turn, rests partly on a notion that organisations are, or should be, unitary bodies combining the activities, values and interests of all their participants. Each part of the system plays a positive, functional role in this process, for example by generating binding social values. Thus the organisation is a system of interrelated parts or sub-units – for example departments, groups and individuals – each functioning to mobilise resources towards meeting wider goals. These parts are at the same time differentiated and interdependent, aiding processes of integration and co-ordination (we return to 'systems theory' in Part IV).

The managerial requirement to integrate potentially diverse goals and activities could, of course, take place in a number of ways. But mainstream theory has tended to emphasise the advantages of a particular pattern of roles and responsibilities. Earlier we quoted Schein on the need for co-ordination to achieve goals. The extension of that sentence reads, 'through division of labour and function, and through a hierarchy of authority and responsibility' (quoted in Mullins, 1985: 2). Such an interpretation of the division of labour has always played a leading role in ideas of how to sustain the social solidarity necessary for the survival of the 'organism' of society or enterprise.

As a consequence of this line of thinking, the way that tasks, functions and jobs are divided, with the consequent specialisation and hierarchies, is all-too-often regarded as an unproblematic, technical or functional necessity. The origins and workings of the division of labour are neglected as an issue, influenced by analyses which emphasise differentiation and interdependence. As a consequence many deep-rooted features of organisational life – inequality, conflict, manipulation, domination and subordination – are written out of the script in favour of behavioural questions associated with efficiency or motivation. Some of these features may be seen as pathological or temporary phenomena arising from breakdowns in organisational systems, rather than a fundamental product of the unequal structuring of the division of labour.

While conflict and struggles over scarce resources are still marginal to most writings about organisations, the situation does appear to have changed with respect to hierarchy. Current managerial rhetoric is awash with terms such as 'empowering the workforce' and 'self-managed teams', which suggest a different way of doing things. We will examine the realities of such practices in Chapter 15.

Management and managerialism

Part of management's social engineering role is to maintain the maximum degree of harmony and generate feelings of belonging in the workforce, reflecting literally the definition of organisation as 'form into an orderly whole'. Common to all versions of rational efficiency is that the logical basis of action is held to reside with the manager. In contrast, employees who restrict or oppose such action are frequently held to be acting irrationally, governed by a 'logic of sentiment' rather than one of efficiency. The more overtly managerial writers are understandably full of references to what management *should* do, and in this sense are clearly *prescriptive* in nature. For some, the role of organisational analysis is to 'help managers in organisations understand how far their behaviour can positively influence their subordinate's productivity' (W. Clay Hamner, quoted in Karmel, 1980).

Effectiveness becomes synonymous with management effectiveness, and options in debates are situated within that framework. Donaldson (1985: 86) disputes this by arguing that though both are concerned with systems effectiveness, their viewpoints are distinguishable. After all, if they were the same, there would be no point in supplying prescriptions. This is true, but the parameters are strictly circumscribed, as in the example supplied that an organisational analyst might advise greater or less socialisation into company beliefs. No question surfaces about the legitimacy of the beliefs themselves.

Not all mainstream writing is openly managerialist, but the underlying assumptions seldom stray too far. In the preface to an early version of a popular textbook (Buchanan and Huczynski, 1985), Lupton remarks that social scientists should not attach themselves to any one organisational group or its problems. But he then gives two examples of key 'puzzles'. Why and in what conditions do workgroups restrict output? What are the origins and costs of impeding technical innovation? Similarly Karmel (1980) identifies key questions. Why do people sabotage equipment? Why does the introduction of a computer make many people unhappy? Why don't subordinates obey? Alternative 'puzzles' such as why alienating technologies are designed in the first place are conspicuous by their absence. In addition, the way such problems are defined, and the recurrent use of the term *practitioners* can only refer to management practices.

Many organisational texts remain a curious and confusing mixture of analysis and prescription. Emphasis on a stream of advice and solutions to managers consistently undermines the generation of valid and realistic knowledge of organisational processes. Two qualifying points to this criticism need to be made. First, there is a need to study management as an activity. Second, an openly 'management science' servicing the needs of such groups inevitably reflects existing socio-economic relations. But such an orientation is particularly dangerous to a broader organisational analysis. As Watson (1980) pointed out, management requirements are likely to focus on short-term pragmatic relevance related to task achievement, or on reinforcing unitary and consensual views of organisational life. Theorists can become in Baritz's (1960) words 'servants of power', enmeshed in restrictive client relationships within the business firm. The problem is less that of the corruption arising from lucrative contracts (though it is worrying when yesterday's advocates of participation become today's advisors on union busting) but that of knowledge and problem solving on management terms. Thus OT is helping to constitute a particular reality without critically analysing it, and runs the risk of reducing theory and practice to a technology of social control:

> [T]he critical scholar is often confronted with the challenge, 'But how does this help managers?' This assumption tethers research to a management point of view: the concerns of other stakeholders are therefore only addressed from this narrow vantage point. There is a conflation between research *on* managers with research *for* managers. (Adler, Forbes and Willmott, 2007: 11)

Not only does this limit the ability of analysis to be a resource for a wider range of participants, it has the negative consequence of ignoring lower-level employees except as objects, or in their defined 'roles' (Salaman, 1979: 47). Limitations arise from the service role itself. Reed observes, 'organisation theory has presented management with a stock of "moral fictions" (such as "managerial effectiveness") that disguise the social reality of contemporary management practice' (1986: 95). Despite or perhaps *because* of that role, there are frequent complaints that official theory propagated to business students and managers is out of touch with the 'real world'.

A science of organisations?

In terms of methodology, many mainstream writers take what Benson (1977) refers to as a 'simple positivist view'. That is, they tend to treat the social world as an extension of the natural one. This leads to an over-emphasis on experimental methods and the *measurement* of organisational phenomena (such as structures, technologies and leadership styles). Second, there is an attempt to discover law-like relationships. At a time when there has been considerable fashionable disdain for science and an intellectual retreat from a concern with evidence and careful theory building, this might seem a way of bending the stick back a bit. The problem with the orthodox notion of a science of organisations is that it tends to restrict the space for critical evaluation. Donaldson (1985: 84) refers to the need to 'reaffirm the commitment to valid general causal laws as the goal' and asserts the superiority of science over lay accounts. This is fair enough but is hardly the point. It is a question of the *nature* of the scientific approach, particularly the mistaken emphasis on laws. The fact that no one can actually identify any does not seem to worry Donaldson, as this is no proof that they may yet be discovered in the future!

Under this mantle of science – whether administrative, organisational or behavioural – generalisations are intended to apply to *all* organisations. On this basis, analysis and intervention can be used to predict and control events, and make prescriptive recommendations. Stress on technique rather than values matches the idea of organisations as rational instruments. The attitude towards scientific intervention into the organisation itself tends to be taken for granted, rather than treated as problematic. Organisational analysis needs to combine rigorous application of a variety of methods and an ability to identify trends, patterns and cause-and-effect relationships, with an acceptance of the inherently partial and contested nature of knowledge.

In conclusion to this section, we would argue that mainstream perspectives have often functioned as theories of regulation and are bound up in the purposes and practices of organisational control. This has prevented the development of 'any coherent or consensual theoretical object of the organisation' (Clegg and Dunkerley, 1980: 213). Instead organisational and societal reality has tended to be taken for granted, with emphasis on that which is prescriptive and short-term. The viewing of organisations as natural systems and as largely autonomous bodies has produced a limited capacity to explain historical changes and the political and economic contexts in which organisations operate. The overall objections of critical theory are summed up by Fischer and Sirriani:

> Common to all of the approaches is a concern over the conservative/elitist bias of organisational theory, a general absence of social class analysis, a failure to connect the organisation to the political economy of the larger social and historical context, a general neglect of political and bureaucratic power, and the ideological uses of scientific organisational analysis. (1984: 5)

An alternative and critical agenda

Having outlined some of the weaknesses, limitations and ideological functions of orthodoxy, this section focuses on the positive dimensions of the alternative to it. An outline of a different agenda has already begun to emerge through the previous discussion, with a concern for issues of power, control, conflict, exploitation and legitimation. Like their mainstream counterpart, critical perspectives are based on a variety of ideas and theoretical sources, ranging from Marxian-influenced labour process theory, and radical variants of a Weberian tradition, to postmodernism, interpretative sociology and radical social psychology. These strands will be developed in later chapters and pulled together in Part III. For the moment, the emphasis is on some of the basic ways of seeing and performing organisational analysis that are shared across many critical approaches.

Reflexivity

Critical perspectives must first of all be *reflexive* by examining how accounts are generated. Part of this process is a capacity to reflect upon the social processes of our own knowledge production themselves so that values, practices and knowledge are not taken for granted. Nor can we take our own experiences for granted. A useful example is provided in the novel *Nice Work*. Robyn Penrose, a university lecturer in English, is sent to shadow the Managing Director of a local engineering factory. She finds the noise, dirt and disorder of the foundry hard to comprehend:

> What *had* she expected? Nothing, certainly, so like the satanic mills of the early Industrial Revolution. Robyn's mental image of a modern factory had derived mainly from TV commercials and documentaries; deftly edited footage of brightly coloured machines and smoothly moving assembly lines, manned

> by brisk operators in clean overalls.... The situation was bizarre, so unlike her usual environment, that there was a kind of exhilaration to be found in it, in its very discomfort and danger, such as explorers must feel, she supposed, in a remote and barbarous country. (Lodge, 1990: 121, 130)

Despite, or perhaps because of, the lack of understanding, she blunders into actions which spiral out of control. In fact, our inability to experience large organisations directly in the same way as individuals or small groups, subordinates or power holders, creates special problems for studying organisations; problems which are often resolved through the use of unsatisfactory substitutes such as metaphors – organisations are 'like' machines, garbage cans or prisons (Sandelands and Srivatsan, 1993).

We have referred previously to unproblematic conceptions of phenomena such as goals and productivity. But a key example would be that of gender. Existing analyses have largely treated gender divisions as irrelevant, or in practice invisible, despite 'the persistent fact that women's position in any organisation differs from men in the same organisations' (Woolf, 1977: 7). In this sense, mainstream orthodoxy has been 'malestream' (Mills and Tancred, 1992). We return to gender themes in Chapter 10.

Instead of reflecting the concerns of established power groups, organisational theory should critically reflect on and challenge existing attitudes and practices. It can draw on the distinction between practical and technical rationality identified by Habermas (1971) and subsequently espoused by many other radical writers. Technical rationality is based on the instrumental pursuit of taken-for-granted goals such as 'efficiency'. In contrast, practical rationality emphasises conscious and enlightened reflection that can clarify alternative goals and action based on the widest communication and political dialogue. These concepts are, in themselves, rooted in Weber's differentiation between a formal rationality concerned with calculable techniques and procedures, and substantive rationality which emphasises the values and the desired ends of action.

The embeddedness of organisations

A further guiding principle is the necessity to be *historical* and *contextual*. Organisational theory and practice can be understood only as something in process, otherwise the search for general propositions and instant prescriptions becomes disconnected from reality, as it has done in conventional ahistorical approaches (Littler, 1980: 157). It is also necessary to counter both the tendency to see organisations as free-floating and autonomous, and the concentration on the micro-level of analysis, or single enterprise. This means locating organisational processes within their structural setting, examining the interaction with economic forces, political cultures and communities. To return to the gender example, it is impossible to fully understand the emergence and development of the sexual division of labour in organisations from the inside. We have to go outside, to examine the family and patriarchal structures in society as a whole in order to shed light on internal issues.

This approach means more than diffuse references to *the environment*. In theoretical terms, organisational issues cannot be comprehended outside of the totality constituted by capitalist society and the mode of production in particular (Burrell, 1980). Donaldson objects to this on the grounds that locating explanations within the wider social system denies that organisational phenomena are topics of inquiry in their own right. But no convincing argument is put forward to justify the desirability or possibility of such analytical autonomy, to say nothing of seemingly denying the validity of the work of Weber, Marx and Durkheim. Donaldson raises a more pertinent point when he argues that 'the notion of totality is a reference to everything – nothing is left out' (1985: 124). It is true that that 'totality' can obliterate complexity in the search for the big picture, or reduce phenomena to a meaningless level of generality. For example, we do not always learn very much from general references to the effects of capitalism and patriarchy without identifying particular institutions and groups of people (agents). There may not be a smooth fit between organisations and each part of the 'totality', but it is possible and necessary to show the concrete ways in which organisations are embedded in specific social, political and economic structures.

Multi-dimensionality

Explanations must be not only multi-layered, but also multi-dimensional. Different modes of analysis are needed to deal with the complexities and levels of human behaviour in organisations. As we have seen, mainstream theories separate the behavioural dimension from employees' roles within the division of labour. Clearly people are constituted as individuals at the level of their identities and emotions, but that process is informed by the same 'structural' and collective phenomena that shape management strategies and job design, and the broader social relations of production between capital and labour, and between the sexes.

Radical writers have long been critical of the psychological component used by mainstream theory as part of the explanation of organisational behaviour. Objections have been made to the treatment of people in organisations as 'psychologically determined entities' with abstractly and individually defined needs, for example the need to belong or for self-actualisation. This has led some critical writers to firmly reject any psychological orientation. In 1980, when such views were more propular, Clegg and Dunkerley argued that people should be considered, 'not as subjectivities, as unique individuals or social psyches, but as the bearers of an objective structure or relations of production and reproduction which are conditioned not by psychology but by history' (1980: 400). While sharing this critique of psychological orthodoxy, we reject the view that people can be considered only as bearers of objective structures. The fact that managers and workers find themselves caught up in structural processes does not mean that they are merely passive agencies or operate solely at a group level. Any circumstances are experienced inter-subjectively, reconstructed and modified.

A purely structural analysis, even where it allows for human action and resistance, fails to get sufficiently inside those routine everyday experiences in which people react, adapt, modify, and consent to work relations. While concepts of motivation, perception and the like inadequately address the problem, some account of subjectivity and identity is necessary. Nor is the question of subjectivity significant solely at the level of the individual. A critical psychology should also identify the ways in which organisations act as 'people processors', through either informal cultural practices or formal managerial strategies, to mobilise consent.

That is not to say that it is easy to integrate the different dimensions. Our aim with the book at this stage is to establish complementarity and points of connection rather than synthesis and the solving of underlying theoretical questions. As subjectivity and psychological theories are the province of later chapters, we will say no more at this stage.

Structure, contradiction and agency

Many critical theorists (for example, Benson, 1977; Storey, 1983) utilise the notion of dialectical perspectives as a crucial means of explaining the dynamic of organisational change. In abstract terms, a dialectical process refers to a movement from thesis to antithesis and synthesis, and derives from Hegel and Marx. More frequently it is used to denote a reciprocal interaction, between structure and human agency or between conflicting groups. It is not always usefully employed. Morgan (1986: 266) produces a list that places 'oppositions' as varied as capital and labour, young and old, and even sales and production

CULTURE, COMPANIES AND COUNTRIES IN A GLOBALISING ERA ■ MANAGEMENT ■ CONTROL AND RESISTANCE ■ POWER IN ORGANISATIONS ■ GENDER, SEXUALITY AND ORGANISATIONS ■ CORPORATIONS AND CULTURE: REINVENTING ORGANISATION MAN?

15

on the same level. But a more focused emphasis on the interaction and structured antagonisms between key economic actors is valuable. We refer to 'structured' because group conflicts are shaped by contradictions – forces pulling in opposite directions – for example, between private ownership and collective social needs. These contradictions help reproduce antagonistic relations that are built into work organisation and society, and which in turn generate conflict and change.

The most direct application to work organisations is expressed in the idea of a reciprocal relation between managerial control and worker resistance. Management control strategies are fundamentally a means of dealing with contradictions, uncertainties and crises in their socio-economic environment. New methods of control inevitably provoke and shape forms of employee resistance and sometimes counter 'strategies'. Over a period of time, management responses are likely to develop into alternative control methods, blending with and going beyond the old. For example, piecework was introduced as a means for management to set targets and control through monetary incentives. But workers on the shop floor frequently devised ways of asserting their own controls over output and earnings. In the 1970s, employers in the motor industry responded by establishing new payment systems based on 'measured day rates', but still using control techniques based on work study and measurement. Over a period of time workers developed their own methods of adaptation and resistance, so the cycle continues.

This kind of perspective puts more substance into the traditional idea of an interaction between formal and informal dimensions of organisational life. However it is formulated, we can view organisations as continually having to respond to and counter *disorganisation*: a process that is underpinned by the divergent goals and interests discussed earlier in the chapter. Those who command organisations are required to mobilise a variety of resources to counter disorganisation. While the actors themselves may not see it in these terms, we can pull together a variety of practices under the conceptual umbrellas of power, control and persuasion or consent. The factors underlying such choices regarding the different forms managerial and employee action takes will be a key and recurrent theme of the book.

Social transformation and change

The fact that we have argued against prescription does not mean a lack of interest in the 'practical' or the applied. One of the problems of the split between organisational sociologists and OB/OT is that it led some of the former to believe that they were studying different objects in distinct ways. For example, Albrow argues that 'the organisation theorist is concerned to help managers and administrators. By contrast, the sociologist is "impractical". His search is for understanding untrammelled by the needs of men of affairs' (1973: 412). While such a view may be in part descriptively accurate, it has dangerous consequences. It tends to legitimise the separation between a narrow perspective that is only interdisciplinary to meet the needs of management problem solving, and a broader analysis that neglects the dynamics of day-to-day practices in organisations.

We have tried to approach the 'practical' in a number of ways. First, we give an account and evaluation of up-to-date empirical research into work organisations, rather than the make-believe simulations that accompany some conventional texts. This involves critically examining the interventions made by social scientists as researchers or consultants as an issue in its own right. Second, we always analyse theories and practices together and as part of specific economic and political contexts. Showing how theories are used by managerial and other groups may sound unexceptional, but the dominant tradition has been to treat the major theories of organisation and management primarily as ideas systems and historically sequenced. The result is that most students do not get a realistic and informed view of the practicality of theory. In addition the impression is often given that theories developed in the past are outdated and 'wrong' compared to the latest favoured perspective. When these are inevitably replaced, cynicism about theory and organisational analysis is the likely result.

But alternative 'practicalities' have to go further than this and provide resources for social transformation. In this context, Benson adds a further dialectical perspective: that of praxis, drawing on the previously discussed notion of practical rationality. Praxis involves developing analytical resources that go beyond reflexivity and can help members of organisations, constrained by existing relations of ownership and power, to critically reflect on and reconstruct their circumstances. Though some critical theorists advocate the prioritisation of 'philosophically informed armchair theorising' (Burrell, 1980: 102), we would agree with Benson's emphasis on theory as an emancipatory guide and as a means for *empowering* a wider range of organisational participants. This needs to be distinguished from recent managerial usage. When empowerment is used to describe 'enabling' employees to chase more customers or do three more jobs, the term joins a long list whose rhetoric is not matched by reality.

A critical use of the term implies no particular form of politics or intervention, but rather empowering employees and citizens to make more choices and to act more effectively to transform workplace relations. It may be argued that this reproduces a one-sided partiality that is the reverse of the management orientation of mainstream theories. There is always that danger. But the existing realities and power relations in organisations will, for the foreseeable future, enable critical theory to maintain a certain distance and intellectual independence. Furthermore, any critical theory not testing its ideas through empirical investigation or practical intervention is ultimately arid. These issues are discussed further in the final chapter of the book.

Summary and key points

Studying organisations has become more important as modern societies have come to be dominated by large-scale private corporations and public bureaucracies. Classifying all of them under some heading such as organisation society doesn't tell us much about the content and context of different types of organisation. It is better to seek out the distinctive characteristics of work organisations and the ways they are socially embedded in wider social systems. The chapter examined some of the common assumptions found in standard textbooks on organisations and OT, and found them wanting. Work organisations are complex arenas where different groups pursue their own interests rather than unitary bodies bound together by common purposes. What passes for rationality, efficiency, natural; hierarchy and universal laws or organisational life frequently mask the power and purposes of dominant elites. There are always conditions and choices that shape the character and direction of organisation. Management is important in the study of organisations, but OT is partial and distorted if its concerns become the focal point. If we want OT to dig deeper and explain more it needs to operate in more critical, reflexive ways. In particular, it needs to attend to historical and comparative processes, and be equally capable of explaining the structures of domination and inequality that constrain our behaviour and the actions we take as employees and citizens to change them.

We should make clear that our project does not involve a rejection of the idea of organisation theory, merely particular conceptions of it. The view taken in this book is that there is a basis for a reformulated OS which has a specific competence in the sphere of work organisations, retains the capacity to cross discipline boundaries, and which combines theoretical and practical emphases. Nor does it involve a dismissal of the whole of 'orthodoxy'. Mainstream perspectives are not homogeneous and there are tensions, as will be explained in Part IV, between concepts derived from Weber, Durkheim and other key figures.

There is also much of value in the body of ideas, in terms of both the issues raised and empirical work generated. Radical and orthodox traditions are not different on every point, and there are partly overlapping objectives for some of the strands of thought, including humanisation of work processes and non-bureaucratic forms of organisation.

We should also keep in mind the observation made in the Preface that what is counted as orthodox or mainstream changes over time and place. Boundaries between perspectives can blur and it is necessary to treat mainstream theory as a series of overlapping perspectives sharing certain ideas and methods, while differing on others. Some concepts and research are useful and compatible with a critical approach; others are not. None can be considered simply as 'tools of management', or embodying the values and interests of the dominant class. Such a view wrongly assumes that there is such a clear set of interests that can be reflected at a theoretical level. The tortuous history of organisational theory and practice in fact reveals a consistent tension between different approaches to regulation, which in turn reflects the conflicting pressures to control *and* engage the workforce. All but the most unreflexive perspectives require some distancing from existing practices in order to act upon them in a way that will be a resource for management. We return to the idea of theories as a resource in Part IV. Meanwhile, subsequent chapters in Part I aim to examine critically the complexities of those relations between organisational theories and practices, beginning with the historical development of large-scale organisations.

Further reading

As this chapter is an introduction and preliminary mapping of organisation analysis, the natural territory of further reading is other textbooks! Grey's wittily titled effort (2005) is not as interesting as promised, but it is a shortish introduction to many of the themes in Part I of this book. An influential and thoughtful version of organisation analysis can be found in Perrow's (1979) *Complex Organizations*. There is even a condensed version in a journal article, 'The Short and Glorious History of Organizational Theory', reprinted in various collections of readings. Talking of such efforts, we particularly like Fischer and Sirriani's collection (the introduction and opening chapter can be found at: http://www.temple.edu/ tempress/titles/324_reg.html) and the more recent collection edited by Handel (2003). Both mix classic and contemporary readings.

Fischer, F. and Sirriani, C. (eds) (1994) *Critical Studies in Organisation and Bureaucracy* (2nd edn), Philadelphia: Temple University Press.

Grey, C. (2005) *A Very Short, Fairly Interesting and Reasonably Cheap Book about Studying Organizations*, London: Sage.

Handel, M. J. (2003) *The Sociology of Organizations: Class, Contemporary and Critical Readings*, Thousand Oaks: Sage.

Perrow, C. (1973) 'The Short and Glorious History of Organisational Theory', *Organisational Dynamics*, Summer, 2–15.

Perrow, C. (1979) *Complex Organizations: A Critical Essay* (2nd edn), Glenview, Ill.: Scott Foreman.

2 the emergence of large-scale organisations

As a character in the recent film *The History Boys* noted, the problem with history is that it appears to be 'just one damned thing after another'. But, as usual, appearance can be at odds with reality. Some periods are crucial because they are formative in the development of ideas and institutions. Our time frame in this chapter focuses on the period at the end of the nineteenth and start of the twentieth century, but moves backwards and forwards in order to understand the process of emergence of large scale as the foundation of business development.

The aims of this chapter are to:

- locate and explain the formation of the large-scale industrial bureaucracies that have been the primary object of analysis for organisation studies.
- show how organisational factors, such as the establishment of managerial authority, were at the heart of early factories.
- demonstrate and illuminate early ways that control was exercised in the mature factory system, including contracting and craft arrangements.
- explain how and why those arrangements decayed, laying the ground for the emergence of the modern business and enterprise and management.

Organising the new work forms

By the start of the twentieth century, business organisations were beginning to be 'transformed from chaotic and ad-hoc factories to rationalised, well-ordered manufacturing settings' (Goldman and Van Houten, 1980: 108). This was not just a product of growth, merger and technological innovation. It was also a question of management. The New York Public Library did not have a single title on management in 1881, but by 1910 carried more than 200 (Shenhav, 1999: 17). Though the trend was in its infancy, firms were beginning to move away from particularist and uneven practices, towards the beginnings of an industrial bureaucracy. Indeed the two were intimately connected given that the increasing scale of work organisation meant that it was no longer possible to rely on personal or unspecified forms of direction. Changes involved systematising and stabilising both the practices of management and the organisation of the labour process. Job hierarchies, new patterns of work supervision, measurement and reward, as well as greater specialisation and detailed division of labour, became more characteristic of organisational life. It is important to trace the genesis and development of this industrial bureaucracy, reflecting on the theoretical issues through the work of Weber, Taylor and others. As we argued in Chapter 1, mainstream writings largely lack this kind of historical and comparative character. Moreover, they tend to treat managerial and organisational theories as ideologies with universal effects in all times and places.

Theories of management are not 'invented' and applied. Rather they form a resource through which both academics and practitioners try to understand and act. How this happens depends on different social contexts and the histories that have shaped them. Of course, we have not the space to provide a detailed business history that captures all events, variations and issues across societies. The aim is to give a broad picture that locates ideas in context and that focuses particularly on employment and labour process questions. In this and the following chapter that picture is predominantly of American and British circumstances. Nevertheless, we are aware of how specific that experience is, and compare it to the formation of management and large-scale organisation in other national contexts as part of Chapter 6.

The rise of the factory system

Work processes prior to the factory system were not characterised by an extensive division of labour, nor by directly imposed coercive authority. In handicraft and domestic production, small producers were typically involved in independent commodity production, often based on the family structure. They owned their own means of production, worked according to their own patterns, and sold the goods at markets. Some trades or crafts were organised through the guild system. This combined employer and employee, normally within the framework and traditional authority of apprentice, journeyman and master. Neither system was flexible enough to be an adequate basis for responding to the needs of an emergent market economy. Industrialisation and the new capitalist production relations developed from a variety of organisational structures, including artisan production, co-operatives, centralised manufacture and the putting-out system (Berg, 1985). We want to focus mainly on the latter.

Mainstream theory commonly asserts that the new and more complex forms of organisation, with the associated detailed division of labour and hierarchies, developed largely because they were technically required by the scale of production, technology and related factors. A number of writers, notably Marglin (1974) and Clawson (1980) have used specific historical evidence on the factory system to challenge this general explanation. Their work focuses on helping to explain why workers were deprived of control of process and product through the centralised organisation of the factory system. A common response is to argue that the impetus was the necessity to shift from hand production to power-driven machinery located in a central source. In addition, there were the benefits of division of labour, pointed to in Adam Smith's famous pin factory example.

Both Marglin and Clawson show that bringing workers together in workshops and later in the factory – for example, in the weaving and spinning trades – did not necessarily involve power-driven machinery or any other technical innovation. In fact, contrary to technological determinist arguments, 'organisational change precedes, both historically and analytically, the technological revolution which is the foundation of modern industry' (Clawson, 1980: 57). The issue of the division of labour is more complicated. Marglin does not argue that it, or hierarchy, was brought into being by capitalist organisation of work. But a distinction is made between the specialisation of occupation and function that is present in any social division of labour, and the particular forms of specialisation involved in the putting-out system and then in the factory. The minute division of work was not necessarily more efficient; rather it provided a role for the capitalist to play in organising production, and enabled the capitalist to take a greater portion of the rewards: 'The social function of hierarchical work organisation is not technical efficiency, but accumulation' (Marglin, 1974: 62).

Counterposing hierarchy and efficiency in this manner may not be very helpful and, given the time lapse, the evidence on this question is inevitably patchy. In a useful critique of Marglin from a Marxist viewpoint, Rowlinson notes that the idea that any significant movement away from hierarchy is inherently a threat to the role and power of employers is somewhat naïve, particularly when historical and contemporary evidence shows that management can live with degrees of work group autonomy (Rowlinson, 1997: 141–4). What, however, is beyond doubt is that though the new framework provided an impetus for technical innovation, efficiency and technical superiority were not the only, or even primary, reasons for the rise of factory organisation. The putting-out system allowed workers a great deal of control over their hours, rhythm, intensity and quality of work. Furthermore, there was a high level of embezzlement of raw materials, as workers sought to secure a fairer return for their labour. Historians have provided a large body of evidence showing that the workshop and the factory were utilised as a means of discipline and control in order to facilitate capital accumulation (Pollard, 1965; E. P. Thompson, 1967; Landes, 1969).

Coercive authority could also be more easily applied, including systems of fines, supervision (for instance, the overlooker system in textiles), the paraphernalia of bells and clocks, and incentive payments. The employer could dictate the *general* terms of work, time and space; including the division of labour, overall organisational layout and design, and rules governing movement, shouting, singing and other forms of disobedience (G. Brown, 1977). Doray gives numerous examples of French factory regulations, including fines for faulty work, writing on walls or entering the factory through the wrong door. He does, however, point out that when applied to the labour process, regulations were not particularly detailed: 'They asserted, in repetitive fashion, the principle of the employer's authority over an unspecified range of activities' (1988: 27–8). It is not surprising that many workers bitterly resisted entry to the factory and the associated forms of discipline. In those early periods, employers were frequently forced to resort to groups such as convicts, paupers and child labour.

To break such resistance, new work habits had to be created appropriate to the discipline of labour time and cash nexus at the heart of the wage relation. Employers' concern with the moral issues of sexuality, drink, bad language and theft was directed less by fidelity to religious doctrine than to the *behavioural* characteristics – obedience, punctuality, responsibility and performance – linked to capitalist rationality and its new forms of organisational culture. As Clegg and Dunkerley observe, the triumph of the formal factory organisation was strongly determined by its 'moral machinery' (1980: 62). This term was used by the economist Andrew Ure, who was noted for his pertinent advice to employers. He and other such advisors, were clear, however, that neither the division of labour nor work values was sufficient for the purpose of achieving the goal of creating 'factory hands'. *Mechanisation* was necessary to destroy old work habits and to tie the worker to the 'unvarying regularity of the machine'.

Marx showed how workers were able to use the employer's continuing dependence on their handicraft skills and knowledge as a weapon of resistance. In turn, Ure recognised that the unity of capital and science was necessary to try to reduce skills to dexterities, create a technical framework independent of the producers, and reduce labour costs by *intensifying* work rather than the limited option of raising hours. Marglin's notion of the factory as a social control device independent of technology is therefore incomplete (Clawson, 1980: 54). Without these kinds of developments, the formal control developed in the factory could not have been adequately realised. It is always necessary to resist the temptation to describe these processes of organisational change in finished rather than relative terms. Employer control remained at a very general level and still had to be accommodated to high levels of worker skill, knowledge and self-organisation. Management as a specialist category was still underdeveloped and work was often labour intensive, with little or no bureaucratic structure. To explain the further development of large-scale organisation we need to focus more closely on the evolution of forms of control.

Modes of control in the transition to bureaucratic organisation

There were a number of obstacles to the development of a more bureaucratic work organisation during the nineteenth century. Even a more mature factory system rested on control structures that were inimical to moves in that direction. As Littler (1982: 69) argues, British industry presented a spectrum of modes of control that, despite differences, were fundamentally non-bureaucratic in nature. Using a range of evidence, three basic modes can be distinguished.

Entrepreneurial or simple control

Factories at the beginning of the nineteenth century could exercise a large degree of power and control personally. Referring to a famous foundry owner, Bendix observes: 'Boulton maintained a personal relationship with his workers, knew their names and their families, and relied upon this relationship to ensure the discipline and work performance needed in his enterprise' (1956: 57). Exercise of authority under entrepreneurial control was therefore simple and direct, and sustained frequently by legal coercion and harsh market conditions. Even at this stage, however, it was not always possible to exert control personally. Foremen could be utilised but, as Rueschemeyer points out, 'an important preliminary solution to the control dilemmas of divided authority was to rely on family ties' (1986: 57). At the required minimal level of co-ordination, the family or close friends of the entrepreneur proved sufficient. Middle managers were virtually absent; in fact, many employers were hostile and suspicious about the idea of a separate 'class' of managers.

Of course this situation could not survive a growth in the size and complexity of operations. Littler (1982) notes that the familial framework was rapidly discarded under such conditions, particularly in the US. Nevertheless, some writers argue that direct and often despotic entrepreneurial authority remained at the centre of what Edwards (1979) describes as simple control. There are important qualifications to be made to the model of entrepreneurial or simple control, particularly Edward's version. It is extremely doubtful whether it was representative of the economy until the end of the nineteenth century as he claims, rather than confined to a minority of firms (Littler, 1982: 64). In addition, though despotic authority was certainly a pervasive influence, it often had to accommodate to the power of other figures in the enterprise, such as craft workers. Hence the image of the all-seeing, all-knowing employer underestimates the struggles at the frontier of control in the workplace. There is also considerable evidence that a more significant mode of control involved contracting arrangements.

Contracting

Outsourcing functions and work to contractors is now a growth area in many companies (see Chapter 11). In the nineteenth century, one of the main reasons why management was so slow to develop was the tendency of employers to delegate responsibility for work organisation to sub-contractors, around whom the employment relationship was constructed. We are concerned here with the internal contractor rather than the independent sub-contractor who was involved, for example, in outwork trades such as clothing and boots and shoes. Evidence from historians, such as Pollard (1965) on the UK, and more recently Clawson (1980) on the US, shows that internal contracting was in extensive use in a range of industries including textiles, iron and steel, mining and transport. What did the organisation of work consist of?

> The inside contractor made an agreement with the general superintendent or owners of a company to make a part of their product and receive a certain price for each completed unit. ... Inside contractors had complete charge of production in their area, hiring their own employees and supervising the work

> process ... were employees of the company, and in most cases they received a day wage from the company as well. (Clawson, 1982: 71)

They accumulated considerable status and power, in both the community through patronage, and the workplace through their high income. In some cases this meant a social position and standard of living higher than company officials, and a capacity actually to pass on much of the detailed work delegated to them by the employer to assistants!

Nevertheless the intended advantages to employers were clear. Responsibility, risks and costs could be partly shifted on to contractors, thus creating greater flexibility in circumstances where managerial skills and knowledge of work operations were limited. In effect, contracting functioned as means of transition through a period of growing enterprise complexity and scale. It was certainly hierarchical, but not bureaucratic in the sense of centralised authority, rules and record-keeping. Yet it proved capable of handling expanded output and technical innovation (Clawson, 1980). It did not encompass all industries or all labour within the firm. Newer industries such as service, process and railways were based on direct employment relations (Littler, 1982: 68).

Craft control

Contracting is often seen as overlapping with the 'helper system', in which skilled workers were assisted by a small number of less-skilled operatives. In some cases craft workers hired and paid them, thus reproducing contractual relations. However, the scale of operations was small, with often just one helper; the practices were exercised by craft workers normally within a trade union framework; and operated often in conjunction with foremen. In fact the helper system is the basis for a model of craft control utilised by writers such as Stone (1973) and Montgomery (1976), in which skilled workers had the power to plan and direct immediate work processes. It is important not to exaggerate this 'partnership in production', for we are talking about a system of worker-directed job controls. But though not the equivalent of employer systems, such controls had a significant capacity to resist and constrain employer authority. Craft control meant that, 'employers, in effect, gave up the right to manage' (Owen, 1994: 2). This was put succinctly by F. W. Taylor in 1911 about his experience in the steel industry:

> As was usual then, and in fact is still usual in most shops in this country, the shop was really run by the workmen, and not the bosses. The workmen together had carefully planned just how fast each job should be done, and they had set a pace for each machine throughout the shop, which was limited to about one-third of a good day's work [that is, the maximum possible]. Every new workman who came into the shop was told at once by the other men exactly how much of each kind of work he was to do, and unless he obeyed these instructions he was sure before long to be driven out of the place by the men. (Taylor, 1947: 128)

This was somewhat exaggerated in order to prove the need for Taylor's scientific management system, and particularly neglected the role and powers of the foremen. Though this varied from industry to industry, there was a far more extensive range of powers and functions than contemporaries have today. The foreman's empire included substantial influence over the manner and timing of production, the cost and quality of work, and responsibility for employees – often including hiring and firing. They operated under similar delegated authority to inside contractors, and enjoyed parallel status within and outside work. But that role must be seen within the framework of craft controls. The foreman would sometimes be a master of his trade or chief skilled worker, and would have to share or at least accommodate to the powers of craft workers and contractors.

Decay and decline of traditional controls

Despite the variety of control relationships, each in its own way functioned as a constraint to management and bureaucracy. The shift further in this direction in the last quarter of the nineteenth century must again be seen not merely in terms of gradual evolution and advance of technique. There were social contradictions as well as inefficiencies in traditional methods. Simple control is a clear case. During the period in question, the size and complexity of industrial firms increased considerably. During the last third of the century the average plant in the US more than doubled in size, and by 1900 there were 443 with more than 1000 wage earners (Nelson, 1975: 4). The impetus for change included mergers, concentration of resources, technical innovation and shifts away from local and regional markets. This leap was particularly marked in the US, given its late entry onto the industrial stage, and the relative freedom of business from social reform traditions and strong union organisation.

Such processes inevitably affected existing social relations and were characterised by an increasing separation of entrepreneurs and top managers from the daily activities of the workforce. Organisationally the crucial issue was a growing gap between the structures and expertise of management, and a more extensive division of labour, with its requirements for new forms of control and co-ordination. For capital, the solution had to go beyond the employment of more managers, towards transforming the structures of managerial activity itself.

Problems associated with internal contracts had more to do with contradictions than straightforward inefficiencies. According to Clawson, these were in two major areas. The very fact that the company had entered into sub-contract arrangements meant that it was difficult to evaluate such activities. Contractors therefore used that power to keep employers as much in the dark as possible, aided by the fact that companies seldom kept many formal records. In addition, the high income and consequent social position of contractors was also a problem in that it was difficult for employers to motivate their own officials, who often felt inferior in power, status and rewards to the larger contractors. As a result of these factors, 'many of the younger generation of employers sought to replace the contractor by a system which offered the company greater predictability and control of the workforce and the manufacturing process' (Shenhav, 1999: 22).

Craft job controls were also a serious obstacle to employers taking full advantage of mechanisation and expanded but more competitive markets. As Stone notes of the steel industry:

> At the same time that their labour costs as a percentage were rising, the labour system also prevented employers from increasing their productivity through reorganising or mechanising their operations. The workers controlled the plants and decided how the work was to be done. Employers had no way to speed up the workers, nor could they introduce new machinery that eliminated or redefined jobs. (Stone, 1973: 26)

This again may be a somewhat exaggerated description, but it helps to explain why both contracting and craft arrangements came under increasing attack. Employers began to abolish internal contracting in order to shift income to the company and to create a hierarchy under their own control and acceptable to their own officials (Clawson, 1980: 119). Companies often tried to convert some of the contractors into foremen, but many preferred to quit. The power of craft workers was also increasingly challenged in the 1880s. A minority of firms tried to formulate a system of co-partnership, in the UK and France based largely on profit-sharing schemes geared explicitly to ensuring loyalty to the company (Brannen, 1983; Doray, 1988). There were other head-on clashes in the 1890s, including those between the Amalgamated

Society of Engineers and their employers in the UK, and major conflicts in the US steel industry, such as the Homestead strike of 1892 (Stone, 1973).

Employers began to assert their general right to run production as they saw fit. This took a particularly virulent form in the US with its weaker unions, as manifested in the 'open shop' campaign run by some employers. The predominant measures used by capital there and elsewhere to challenge and change existing modes of control were, however, less dramatic. An important area was to modify the role of *supervisory labour*. This often involved breaking up the foremen's empire, with a shift away from traditional functions such as hiring and firing and work organisation, towards the narrower but vital sphere of task supervision and discipline. As Littler (1982) shows, this was accompanied by considerable subdivision of the foreman's role. Examples include supervisory labour carrying out quality control, rate fixers, and 'feed and speed' functions. A further interrelated change was in *payment systems*, which became more centrally determined through the office, undermining the bargaining role played by foremen and contractors. In addition, piecework and bonus arrangements spread rapidly.

Significantly, the new arrangements required some formal standards of effort and management record-keeping, which were later consolidated in 'drive systems' geared towards the standardisation of labour through production controls and accounting procedures (Shenhav, 1999: 177). Payment through the office indicated a move towards a more direct employment relationship. It should, however, be noted that, at this early stage in the battle for control of output, management techniques were generally not sophisticated enough to include time study or job analysis, and were constrained by workers' initiative and knowledge. Companies frequently had to rely on the cruder measures of rate cutting and employment of 'rate busters' to prove to the workforce that quotas could be increased.

We have already noted that such changes required an increase in record-keeping, given the need to specify objectives and keep track of results. The administrative aspects of a management system thus began to be set in place, including that of simple cost accounting. In some companies simple organisation manuals began to appear, complete with management principles and charts (Edwards, 1979: 30). Technological changes also accompanied administrative ones; further increases in the detailed division of labour and mechanisation were facilitated by the greater knowledge of productive processes that capital was gaining. Not only was greater output achieved, but the capacity of employers to dispense with skilled workers and exert greater controls over labour generally through standardised procedures was enhanced. As one employer remarked, 'I want machines so simple that any fool could run them' (quoted in Goldman and Van Houten, 1980: 116). Engineering principles oriented towards treating workers as simple costs of production were therefore becoming more important than personal and direct controls.

Of course these developments were part of a broader process of the creation of the modern business enterprise. Chandler (1962, 1977) stresses that viability was only achieved when the 'visible hand of management' rivalled or replaced the market as a means of co-ordinating the flow of materials through enterprise and economy. In other words, a managerial hierarchy was able to supervise a large number of operating units and to co-ordinate, monitor and plan their activities. The path to the new forms of enterprise began in the US with the railroads and the need to manage their vast regional operations, but gradually spread to other sectors, as modern big business in the decades before 1917 was able to integrate mass distribution and mass production. In this context, some firms developed from the internal growth of small single-unit firms which developed national and global networks, others from mergers. The new consolidated, multi-departmental enterprises centralised the administration of production and research facilities, and established vertical integration, attempting to control supplies and markets. Though the convergence between the growth strategies of firms and their new structures was not to reach its climax until after the First World War with the development of multidivisional, multinational enterprises, a salaried managerial class was fast rising in numbers and power (Supple, 1991: 501–2).

However, this emergent managerial revolution did not proceed in a linear fashion or purely as a result of the need to rationalise production. As Shenhav (1999) argues, management as a conscious, specialist and professional activity was given shape and force by the self-interested efforts of particular groups, notably engineers – a process we will examine in greater depth in the next chapter. They were central to enhancing the development of the new ideas through the increase of associations and journals dealing with management methods (Chandler, 1977: 464; Clawson, 1980: 167–8). Entrepreneurial ideologies were complemented or challenged by more professional concerns with the 'labour problem'; and direct recruitment from colleges grew, though specialist technical training was still relatively limited. In addition a growing army of clerical, technical and administrative employees was necessitated by new payment systems, record-keeping and mechanisation, as well as the other growth functions of purchasing, sales and finance: 'at the turn of the century, the USA had the largest proportion of administrative staff to industrial workers' (Shenhav, 1999: 5). It was not just a case of management hierarchy; by the turn of the century the workforce was subject to structures of what Richard Edwards (1979) refers to as hierarchical control. As other writers put it, 'differential job statuses and wages for workers were an integral component of the hierarchical nature of the industrial pyramid' (Goldman and Van Houten, 1980: 122). Job ladders and individuated reward systems were also a means of compensating for the growing homogenisation of labour by artificially dividing the workforce (Stone, 1973).

Summary and key points

The origins and development of the factory system tells us a great deal about the nature of organisations. Though technology and efficiency played their parts, so did the needs of employers to find ways to exercise their authority over work and workers. Control is thus central to organisation, but at this stage existed without extensive bureaucratic structures and rules. Organisations can exist without Management, but they still need to be *managed*. The Management gap was filled by a variety of modes of co-ordination and control, through the direct authority of the employer (simple control), outsourcing the functions to others (contracting) or coexisting with the power of skilled workers (craft control). None of them could survive a variety of external and internal changes and contradictions. Employers began to seek means of asserting more extensive regulation and turned to more formal methods of organisation whether through foremen, record-keeping or technology. As the new century approached the new business enterprise was being born.

It must be stressed that these measures were experimental and varied in nature (Brown, 1977: 82–3). Different countries and even sectors had their own unique characteristics and influences that added to the incoherence of transition processes (Littler, 1982). Finally, though there was a great advance in managerial organisation compared to the earlier period, even in the US it was still very much in its infancy. There was still little systematic and long-term planning, and as for work organisation, management 'was unable to make the qualitative leap to a different system because it had no alternative conception of how production should be organised' (Clawson, 1980: 168). That situation was soon to change, as we shall see in the next chapter.

Further reading

There are some excellent historical studies, most of book length, notably Clawson and Shenhav (extracts at http://www.questia.com/PM.qst?a=o&docId=54849921). Influential shorter accounts of particular periods and issues can be found in Marglin on the early factory system (http://www.economics.harvard.edu/faculty/marglin/papers.html) and Stone on craft control. A good alternative to Stone, chapter two of Haydu's (1991) book on skilled workers in Britain and USA, is available on the web (http://content.cdlib.org/xtf/view?docId=ft9t1nb603&brand=eschol).

Clawson, D. (1980) *Bureaucracy and the Labor Process: The Transformation of US Industry, 1860–1920*, New York: Monthly Review Press.

Haydu, J. (1991) *Between Craft and Class: Skilled Workers and Factory Politics in the United States and Britain, 1890–1922*, Berkeley: University of California Press.

Littler, C. R. (1982) *The Development of the Labour Process in Capitalist Societies*, London: Heinemann.

Marglin, S. A. (1974) 'What do Bosses Do? The Origins and Functions of Hierarchy in Capitalist Production', *Review of Radical Political Economics*, 6: 60–102.

Shenhav, Y. (1999) *Manufacturing Rationality: The Engineering Foundations of the Managerial Revolution*, Oxford: Oxford University Press.

Stone, K. (1973) 'The Origins of Job Structures in the Steel Industry', *Radical America*, 7. 6.

3 Taylor, Weber and the bureaucratisation of the workplace

Approaching the turn of the century, work organisations were beginning to edge towards more formal management systems and primitive forms of bureaucracy. This chapter examines how that situation was qualitatively transformed, focusing on the contributions of the two major bodies of theory and practice associated with Taylorism, Weber and bureaucracy. Both were are and are hugely controversial and this chapter reflects on those arguments in their historical context.

The aims of this chapter are to:

- Show how Taylorism represented the focal point of broader moves towards systematic management of work at the beginning of the new century.
- Demonstrate the embeddedness of the ideas and practices by examining their varied pattern of diffusion across countries and companies.
- Explore the links between Taylorism, Weber and the bureaucratisation of work.
- Set out the principles of Weber's ideal type of bureaucracy and show how they were relevant to the employment relationship.
- Demonstrate how the application of such principles took place through the consolidation of bureaucratic control systems in large private and public organisations after the second world war.
- Address and anticipate debates about the historical and contemporary relevance of Scientifc Management and bureaucracy, particularly through an exploration of the balance of ideological and practical elements.

Taylorism and systematic management

> Taylor bequeathed a clockwork world of tasks timed to the hundredth of a minute, of standardized factories, machines, women, and men. (Kanigel, 1997: 7)

The major means of change was through the work of Frederick Taylor and his 'scientific management' system. Not that Taylorism was unique or totally new; only time and motion study could genuinely be put in that category. A trend towards *systematic management* was already identifiable, as we have seen with instances of more formal management methods, cost accounting, standardisation of work, and use of less skilled workers. Nyland (1987: 56) comments that 'The "systematisers" were a diverse group of engineers, accountants and works managers who argued that US firms had grown to a size where the internal functioning of the enterprise was becoming increasingly chaotic and wasteful.'

Taylor acknowledged the influences of other innovations in management and work organisation, such as inspection systems and employment departments (Urwick and Brech, 1949: 33). However, others felt that the work of systematisers was being overshadowed, while in Britain, when Taylor proclaimed his new system as a 'science', some engineers described it as common sense masquerading under a high-sounding title (Geoff Brown, 1977: 158). Understandable though the reaction was, it missed the point. Taylor was not just in the right place at the right time; he played a crucial role in *theorising* and *popularising* the new ideas. Furthermore, his work was intimately connected to a body of practice, with Taylor 'Napoleon of the war against craft production' (Clawson, 1980: 202). Taylorism was therefore the most conscious part of the systematisation of management, and of the regulation and control of production.

Such developments met the needs of capital in that period (M. Rose, 1975: 58). This was particularly the case in the US, where larger corporations were developing higher levels of product and labour specialisation to cope with rising demand (Littler, 1982). A shift away from skilled labour towards unskilled immigrant workers was taking place, but still within the context of a relatively high-wage economy. This required new forms of co-ordination, integration and control, and methods of keeping down labour costs. The orientation of larger firms towards professional managers, engineers and consultants additionally provided a supportive framework for the rise of Taylorism. Engineers were central figures and carried out wide-ranging activities, including extensive refinements in accounting procedure (Nelson, 1975: 50). In the 1890s Taylor began to publicise his ideas about time study and piece rates, mainly through the American Society of Mechanical Engineers, and gathered round him a group of enthusiastic adherents. As Shenhav observes, engineers 'pursued an industry-wide project of standardisation and systematisation' (1999: 18). They were the key industrial group, two-thirds going on to become managers after graduating. Shenhav explains how they moved their attention from the technical to the social, quoting from a leading engineering journal, *American Machinist*: 'It is beginning to be recognised that the human as well as the non-human machine must be standardised' (quoted in Shenhav, 1999: 72).

Taylor's own work was first carried out at the Midvale Steel Works (owned by a friend of the family), in a variety of 'detective' roles ranging from unskilled labourer to machinist, clerk, gang boss, foreman, master mechanic, chief draughtsman and chief engineer. Experiments were also carried out in a small number of other firms in old and new industries. These were not confined to the US; by the First World War, 1 per cent of French firms had introduced schemes, often in new sectors such as electrical manufacturing and automobiles (Fridenson, 1978). There were similar initiatives on a smaller scale in other European countries. In Britain, a minority of firms experienced the arrival of works engineers, rate fixers, progress men, operations inspectors, work hustlers and other representatives of the growing army of non-producers (G. Brown, 1977: 149–52).

Principles

Many discussions of Taylorism in organisational texts discuss its defining principles around the idea of the employee as 'economic man' and are thus able to treat it as a failed theory of motivation. This is a far cry from the real basis of Taylor's ideas, which were concerned with the control of the labour process. Taylor was adamant that his system was a total package – one best way of organising work. Though affecting the activities of management and workers, the ideas were developed directly out of his obsession with combating the kind of workers' control of output – labelled 'soldiering' – observed at the steel works. He distinguished between natural and systematic soldiering: the former referring to the tendency of wanting to take it easy, the latter to practices deliberately geared to maximising rewards and job security. To solve the 'labour problem' a number of basic management principles were advanced:

1 Developing a science for each element of work.
2 Scientific selection and training of workers.
3 Co-operation between management and workers to ensure that the work is done according to the science.
4 Equal division of work and responsibility between management and workers, each side doing what it is best fitted for.

These sound rather bland, but their significance can be understood only when set against Taylor's description of inefficient practices. Included under this were 'rule of thumb' methods of deciding on the nature of work tasks; workers choosing their own methods of work and training; and workers' knowledge being the basis of productive technique. He was particularly critical of management by initiative and incentive, where workers were given inducements to use their skills and know-how in the most economical way, without strict managerial determination of tasks.

Scientific management started from the belief that management had to reverse existing power relations in production: 'The management assume, for instance, the burden of gathering together all of the traditional knowledge which in the past has been possessed by the workmen and then of classifying, tabulating, and reducing this knowledge to rules, laws and formulae' (Taylor, 1947: 36). The continual concern with rules and laws in Taylor's writings shows why it can be located firmly within a process of bureaucratisation of production. As Braverman (1974: 119) makes clear, it can also be seen as a control system based on the monopolisation of knowledge by management and its use to specify each step of the labour process. This 'separation of conception and execution' is clearly echoed in Taylor's comments such as: 'all possible brain work should be removed from the shop floor and centred in the planning and lay-out department' (quoted in Braverman, 1974: 113).

Other aspects of the above principles are not so prominent. Take selection: Taylor's search for workers who would follow his instructions to the letter is legendary. His tutelage of Schmidt, picked for his strength and stupidity, was repeated elsewhere, as in the selection of Pinnell – 'the hardest working man' in a railway factory – by time and motion men on behalf of British management (G. Brown, 1977: 156–7). When even his time in the lavatory was recorded, and his output measured only after breakfast when his energy was greatest, it was little wonder that Pinnell came to wish he was dead. But despite the interest of some of Taylor's followers, explicit techniques to place the right worker in the right job remained an underdeveloped part of scientific management.

What about the previously-mentioned emphasis placed by OB on Taylorism as the model of 'economic man'? This is largely misleading. Like most of his contemporaries interested in management reform, Taylor did believe that workers were motivated by the pursuit of rational self-interest and that incentive wages – in the form of a differential piece-rate system – were the solution to most labour problems. The tendency to restrict output, however, was seen as an unnecessary product of the absence of any scientific authority for work standards. Management could ensure co-operation on the basis of a consensus established by objective work measurement. Economic incentives could be used to overcome the hostility of workers to giving up traditional job controls. This exchange proved to be a limited and fragile basis for co-operation and certainly did not ever eliminate restriction of output. But an instrumental view of human labour was a far cry from a complex theory of motivation. Taylor was far more concerned with breaking the power of the workgroup and removing the basis for collective bargaining through individualistic payment systems (Littler, 1982: 55).

Ideology and practice

The consequences of the operation of such principles were explicitly recognised by Taylor. There would be a need for: extensive work measurement to predetermine tasks; the employment of cheaper, deskilled and substitutable labour in more fragmented jobs; a large increase in the number of non-productive employees to enforce, monitor and record new work arrangements; and functional foremanship that subdivided traditional responsibilities and involved reporting to the all-powerful planning department. It would, of course, be foolish to believe that all of this smoothly came to pass. In fact there are a number of writers who believe that Taylorism was a 'practical failure' and was not widely implemented, due largely to worker resistance and employer suspicions (Palmer, 1975; Edwards, 1979; Goldman and Van Houten, 1980). This view is often complemented by arguments that its significance is as a management *ideology* which was itself later discredited (Rose, 1978; Burawoy, 1979).

What is the balance of these two processes? We should certainly not underestimate the ideological purposes. Taylor himself emphasised the pressing need for a 'complete mental revolution' in the attitudes of the two parties. Whatever success was achieved can largely be attributed to the stress on the *scientific* character of the system, which traded on the predominantly uncritical attitudes to knowledge under such a mantle. Its technical orientation was of particular appeal and use to engineers in their struggle to establish themselves as the core management group in US industry (Armstrong, 1984). But there was a potential appeal to workers and unions from the same source; 'Under scientific management arbitrary power, arbitrary dictation, ceases; and every single subject, large and small, becomes the question for scientific investigation, for reduction to law' (Taylor, 1947: 211). The theoretical separation of authority from hierarchy was an attempt to construct some level of consent in the employment relation and, with the increased productivity and wages from the system, was to be the basis for the co-operation promised in Taylor's principles.

In practice it never quite worked like this. As an ideology of science it strengthened management by providing, 'the technocratic rationale for authority in formal organisations' (Kouzmin, 1980: 68). It was also flawed and contradictory in nature. It is strange that a science of management had to be based on knowledge and skills appropriated from workers. Of course it never was a science, but rather a control system, and has tended to be seen as a set of techniques to be countered and contested by generations of shop stewards. In one of his weaker moments, Taylor even admitted the stopwatch had an element of 'guesswork'.

Most of the misunderstandings concerning the practical success of Taylorism stem from confusion of what *criteria* to employ. Many of those who see it as a failure are viewing Taylorism as a coherent and total package. This is understandable given that it coincides with Taylor's own views and his tendency to withdraw co-operation when companies refused to follow all the complexities of the schemes. But it is wrong. We need to redefine the criteria in two ways. First, as already indicated, we must consider it as part of broader movement of systematic management that was implemented in a variety of forms. Second, it was also implemented in a selective manner: 'employers looked upon scientific management exactly as Taylor insisted that they should not: as an arsenal of devices designed to simplify and improve the management of labour' (Bendix, 1956: 286). All the elements were juggled about by companies according to their needs and prejudices. A close analysis of the early literature on 'Taylor firms' by Nelson (1975: 68–78) showed that none fully represented the principles set out in *Shop Management*. References to time study can be found in every firm, and planning departments were widespread. But incentive payment schemes were patchy and employers found that functional foremanship embodied too many layers of responsibility.

It is certainly true that resistance to scientific management from key economic actors was considerable (see Shenhav, 1999: 102–31). However, even taking this and other factors into account, we can recognise a widespread, if uneven, diffusion of key aspects of Taylorist practices in industrial societies in the 1920s and 1930s (Brown, 1977; Clawson, 1980; Littler, 1982; Nyland, 1988). Taylor's death in 1915 opened the door to a variety of consultants to introduce further versions of scientific management. As Kanigel (1997: 488) notes, 'During the late teens and early twenties, scientific management split off into pieces and parts, new disciplines, nascent social movements'. Some were short-cut emulators, other were Taylor's disciples such as Gantt, and the Gilbreths with their extension of Taylor's early emphasis on the study of fatigue and their advances in the use of cameras to record and time movements. This factor and changes in the external environment guaranteed that scientific management did not spread in pure form. Additionally, if Taylorism is seen as part of a wider efficiency movement, we can see that it and related principles increasingly colonised 'progressive' thinking, with even feminists trying to develop notions of domestic engineering (Shenhav, 1999: 96).

In current managerial and sociological literature Taylorism always appears as a dynamic duo with *Fordism*. Links there certainly were. Henry Ford's innovations in technical control through the flow assembly line extended Taylorist principles such as job fragmentation and allowed for a greater level of intensity of labour through speed-up of the line and other measures (Littler, 1982: 56–7). In addition, the scale of Ford's operations and his willingness to introduce the 'five dollar day' as a means of combating labour turnover enabled another of Taylor's principles – high wages for high productivity – to be realised. Ford's plants did not use the apparatus of Taylorite time and motion study, but the management nevertheless collected a considerable amount of information on tasks, so that, for example, it had enough information to produce 7800 individual job-profile sheets (Doray, 1988: 96). This reinforces a crucial point, that we must not fetishise Taylorism at the expense of the broader trend towards 'scientific' management. The managerial regime at Ford had its own innovations in labour utilisation, stretching the semi-skilled labour by a permanent process of de-manning and flexibility: a mode of operation that challenges the stereotype of rigid machinery, products and labour under mass production (Williams *et al.*, 1992b).

Meanwhile in Europe the most extensive implementation of neo-Taylorite schemes came through the *Bedeaux system*. Charles Bedeaux was a French full-time management consultant whose schemes were based on his 'discovery' of a universal measure for all work, given the name 'B unit'. He aggressively sold them as cheap and quick methods which did not need to have major consequences for existing management structures. Like the Gilbreths, he entered the unexplored territory of fatigue through basing the measurement on the proportions of work and rest required for completing a task. Though he had considerable international success, Bedeaux had his greatest impact in Britain where employers used the circumstances of the 1930s depression to install the system and utilise it for the purposes of rate cutting and speed-up (G. Brown, 1977; Littler, 1982). This example illustrates the way in which scientific management varied in both form and timing between and within countries. Whereas Britain's late adoption differed from the US and French models, other economies such as Germany and Sweden followed distinctive paths; for example, combining rationalisation measures with greater use of psychological testing (Fridenson, 1978). Contrary to some recent studies, Taylorism did influence the organisation of work in Japan, but 'was used as a vehicle for job analysis and standardised procedures rather than as a comprehensive control system' (Littler, 1982: 156–7). Aspects of the latter, notably the separation of thinking and doing, as well as individual output norms, did not fit into pre-existing patterns of fluid job boundaries, work teams and the power of foremen over production planning.

32 [3]

STUDYING ORGANISATIONS: AN INTRODUCTION ▪ THE EMERGENCE OF LARGE-SCALE ORGANISATIONS ▪ **TAYLOR, WEBER AND THE BUREAUCRATISATION OF THE WORKPLACE** ▪ MANAGING THE HUMAN FACTOR ▪ ORGANISATIONS AND ENVIRONMENTS ▪

Lack of uniformity was undoubtedly influenced by the pattern of resistance from a variety of groups. There has been well-documented resistance from craft and non-craft workers, using every method from strikes to informal disruption (Nadworny, 1955; Montgomery, 1976; G. Brown, 1977). Workers were particularly opposed to effects such as deskilling and speed-up, because, as one put it, he 'never knew a rate to be raised after a time study' (quoted in Baritz, 1960: 98). But the plain fact is that resistance did not succeed in stopping the long-term diffusion of scientific management, though it certainly delayed and mediated it. This is often put down to the gradual shift in union attitudes from opposition to reluctant accommodation and occasional enthusiastic co-operation. There is a great deal of truth in this assessment, though some unions had always had a conciliatory attitude, and the behaviour of official structures should not be confused with that of rank-and-file members who continued resistance. Indeed, the very institutionalisation of scientific management guarantees that it is accompanied by a low-intensity war at shop-floor level.

Changes of this kind were influenced by later progressive Taylorites who lacked his hostility to trade unions and were prepared to give them an institutionalised role in work study and bonus schemes. Scientific management could also be given a progressive aura by its association with planning, Nyland (1988) showing that some of its adherents advocated the extension of the system to the whole society constraining the role of markets. He also correctly points to the neglect of Taylorism's wider capacity to improve work efficiency in the spheres of scheduling, stores management and purchasing and plant layout. Though whether this is enough to commend Taylorism despite the control dimension, is more arguable.

Supervisory and managerial resistance also continued to be a considerable constraint in both the US and Britain (Nelson, 1975: 75–6; Littler, 1982: 181–2). New schemes tended not only to change traditional roles, but to erode decision-making powers. Employers and managers often found it hard wholly to embrace Taylorism. Taylor was often bitterly critical of their competence. It challenged their traditional judgement, discretion and powers, to say nothing of Taylor's straining their patience through contract stipulations that the company must do exactly as he told them. The high costs, disrupted routines and social antagonisms meant that failure was more often linked to managerial opposition than that of workers.

The practices also spread not just across geographic, but social boundaries. Taylor was firmly of the opinion that:

> The same principles can be applied with equal force to all social activities: to the management of our homes; the management of our farms; the management of the business of our tradesmen, large and small; of our churches, our philanthropic institutions, our universities) and our governmental departments. (Quoted in Kanigel, 1997: 438–9)

This overestimated its scope and rate of travel, but Scientific Management was increasingly implemented in a variety of work contexts, especially office. Given the evidence, the problem of Taylorism is not *whether* it was introduced, but *how*, and its *limits* as a control system. We shall return to the former later, but with respect to the latter, right from the start many employers realised that Taylor's neglect of 'the human factor' and of what Friedman (1977) calls 'the positive aspects of labour', such as know-how and goodwill, made it impossible to use on its own. We shall return to the combination with psychological methods later, but even as a means of bureaucratisation of production, Taylorism was insufficient.

Weber and administrative theories of management

For some writers, the concept of bureaucratisation of production is a problematic one. Braverman (1974: 120) objects that it endorses the mistaken view that such work arrangements are endemic to large-scale organisation rather than a product of capitalist social relations. Our argument in this book is that bureau-cratisation is a universal tendency, but can be understood only through the specific forms it takes in different modes of production or specific business systems. But there is a different point at stake. Braverman's influential theory of the labour process is constructed on the implicit assumption that what we have been describing as bureaucratisation could be fully represented by Taylorism. However, what Taylorism provided was a system of detailed control over work, aided by a set of bureaucratic rules, and Clawson (1980: 248) argues that this is in contrast to Weber's stress on the remote and impersonal qualities of bureaucracy.

We will return to this question later. For now it is sufficient to observe that Taylorism had far less to say about the *employment relationship*: 'those structural conditions which surround the appointment, promotion and dismissal of individuals' (Littler, 1982: 37). Athough scientific management was meant to be able to be applied at any given level of task or technology, it 'left management in the position of having a set of principles laying down how to make its workforce more productive, while possessing no body of knowledge that specifically applied from supervisory levels upward in the organisational hierarchy' (Clegg and Dunkerley, 1980: 99). This was particularly important in the context of the previously observed growth of middle management; middle managers were monitoring the performance of the operating units under their command, but were not subject to systematic evaluation themselves. It is Weber and other theorists of formal management and administration who can give us a greater understanding of developments of this nature. The emphasis here is on understanding; Weber was not a theorist-practitioner like Taylor and the ideas discussed below were not immediately implemented in organisations.

In common with most other writers, we do not intend to list all the complex features of bureaucracy that Weber includes as defining characteristics, but instead to group them under two headings.

The employment relationship

The office is a vocation and a full-time undertaking. Officials are selected on a basis of technical qualification, education and expertise. There is separation of office and office holder: it is not his or her property and the employee does not possess the means of administration. Thorough and expert training is part of the conditions of employment.

A career structure is provided based on the organisational hierarchy. Tenure is for life, with fixed salary, pension rights and appropriate social status. Officials are appointed by higher authority, not externally elected, and promotions similarly regulated, for example through seniority.

Work structures and relations

There is a hierarchy of offices, with continuous and regulated activity within a fully ordered system of super- and subordination. Within the chain of command is a division of labour based on defined responsibilities, rights and duties. Calculable rules and regulations, impersonal modes of conduct and a common control system govern the conduct of work. Written documentation functions as a basis of management of the office.

From these characteristics it is understandable that some may question their links to the *bureaucratisation of production*. After all, the impetus for Weber's analysis came primarily from the organisation of the state and the regulation of administrative employees. The historical context is also important for an understanding of the significance of measures such as full-time work as a vocation. In the period under consideration, it was still important to break away from patrimonial, charismatic and other relations, whereby people could be placed in position through inheritance and similar 'private' attributes. Efficiency movements among engineers and other groups in the US at the turn of the century similarly stressed the need to eliminate favouritism, nepotism and unethical practices through standardised systems (Shenhav, 1999: 92).

The emphasis on calculable rules and regulations may seem a bit abstract. But both examples highlight that the ideal type of bureaucracy is linked to Weber's wider theory of *rationalisation*. We discussed the problematic character of the idea of rationality in Chapter 1, but rationalisation is held to be the key modernising characteristic for the development of industrial societies. Authority in industrial societies was rational because it was formal and based on precise and predictable rules, calculation and accounting. For these reasons the bureaucratic organisation and administration best permitted the development of appropriate attitudes, structures and practices in public and private sectors. In this context, bureaucracies are a specific type of rational–legal authority: officials work within a framework in which command and task are based on authority derived from impersonal rules. But Weber's theories are not as separate from production as they may appear. He made it clear that they referred to bureaucratic *management* as well as administration. The Weberian 'causal chain' (R. Collins, 1986: 21–9) links the concept of rationality explicitly to the emergence of capitalist enterprise and markets. These were held to be rational because of their capacity for calculability, predictability and routinisation – through production, distribution, accounting and market pricing mechanisms. Preconditions for this 'rationalised' capitalism started from the complete private appropriation of the means of production which, Weber said, must be unhampered by 'irrational obstacles' such as workers' rights to participate in management. In addition, there was the need for common management, free labour under the compulsion of the 'whip of hunger', mass markets, minimal trade restrictions and institutional, legal support from the bureaucratic state.

Weber also argued that large capitalist enterprises were becoming 'unequalled modes of strict bureaucratic organisation' (Weber, 1984: 32). He was aware and approving of the role played by scientific management in this process. It was 'completely' the ideal vehicle for the necessary imposition of military discipline in the factory, given its capacity for dehumanisation and conditioning of work performance. Techniques such as Taylor's 'shop cards', which specified the daily routines of employees, were ideal vehicles of bureaucratisation. What is more, Taylor saw management by 'scientific' methods as a move away from traditional authority where owners and managers attempted to control by inefficient personal means. On reflection, it is therefore possible to see that Weber's schema is not only compatible with Taylorism, but also that the practices he describes can reinforce systems of work control. Formal structures of management enhance centralisation of power, and hierarchical organisation aids functional specialisation, task fragmentation and labour discipline, while emphasis on predictable performance minimises the discretion of employees.

But, as Littler (1982) argues, it is in the sphere of the employment relationship that Weber adds something new. The career structure linked to the bureaucratic hierarchy strengthened a commitment to the organisation absent from Taylorism. A specific form of bureaucratic motivation is also sustained by the identification of job security, status, rewards and performance with organisational structure. Employees may react against the bureaucratisation of control embodied in rules prescribing the way a task is performed, but welcome rules governing selection, training and promotion within the employment relationship. Nor is this necessarily confined to office administration.

Insights derived from Weberian theory have been applied in Britain and the US from the late 1940s. But companies were able to draw on parallel developments in classical management theory in the interwar period. Other theorists of formal organisation were, like Weber, concerned to tackle the administration of the whole enterprise. By far the most significant was Fayol, a Frenchman who shared the engineering and management background of Taylor. 'Fayolism' inspired, among other developments, the reorganisation of railway and engineering companies, and department stores in France (Fridenson, 1978); and translation of his short text enabled him to gain wider influence. His main concern was to establish the validity of studying and training management itself, not just the management of others. Emphasis was put on formulating general features of management, first in the form of five elements – planning, organising, commanding, co-ordination and control – then through 14 principles. The themes contained in the latter echo and extend Taylor and Weber; they include division of work, stability of tenure, authority of command and subordination of the individual interest to the general. One principle, that of unity of command, differed sharply from Taylor's belief in functional authority.

The basis of the approach in Fayol and other similar theorists such as Gullick and Urwick was oriented to rationalising management structures, often through centralisation and specified spans of control; emphasis on the managerial role in setting and securing goals; and planning for the optimal use of resources. Modern management came to take many of these things for granted, which led some to invest Fayol's theorising with a high status and lasting effect. In fact his work was more of a practical guide with simple 'plan-ahead proverbs' (Perrow, 1979: 70) akin to today's numerous management handbooks. Later writers are more likely to prefer the judgement of Clegg and Dunkerley that 'the "principles" are neither universally empirically applicable, nor theoretically coherent' (1980: 103).

What matters more than flawed hand-me-down principles is that classical theories were engaging with real changes in economy and enterprise. When Chandler began to use the railroad as his blueprint for large-scale organisation, his emphasis was on the emergence of organisational charts, hierarchies of office and functional authority. This can be linked to a wider and related argument from Williamson (1975, 1981) that organisations emerge in the form of hierarchies when markets fail. Or to be more precise, when it is more efficient to internalise transactions – for labour, components, services and so on – within multidivisional or vertically-integrated firms, than to have them mediated by and through the market. Because markets become increasingly complex, prices and other indicators cannot give complete information which allows individuals to cost transactions accurately. This uncertainty and complexity can often be better handled through organisations constituted as bureaucratic hierarchies, because they can monitor behaviour, establish rules and procedures and provide better information and control. Rowlinson (1997) notes that Chandler (1977) is unusual in defending bureaucracy on efficiency grounds, and is borrowing in part from Weber. The end result, however, is that managerial hierarchy necessarily supplements market power.

By 1918, the 'visible hand' that had brought the vertically integrated bureaucracies into existence was extended to defining the role and specific tasks of top management within general offices. The context was a further centralisation of administration, often within new multidivisional structures such as those at General Motors. This process included uniform accounting and statistical controls that allowed senior administrators to evaluate managerial performance and exercise long-range planning. In Chandler's later work (1990), he emphasises that investment in production and distribution that facilitated economies of scale is combined with further investment in managerial skills that lead to economies of scope and enhanced organisational capabilities. Supple comments:

> From these viewpoints, the modern industrial firm is crucially characterised by expansion overseas, by product diversification, and (most significantly) by administrative complexity – that is, by the growth in the number of its operating units, each carrying out a different economic function and all co-ordinated by a management hierarchy. (Supple, 1991: 504–5)

36 [3]

STUDYING ORGANISATIONS: AN INTRODUCTION ▪ THE EMERGENCE OF LARGE-SCALE ORGANISATIONS ▪ **TAYLOR, WEBER AND THE BUREAUCRATISATION OF THE WORKPLACE** ▪ MANAGING THE HUMAN FACTOR ▪ ORGANISATIONS AND ENVIRONMENTS ▪

This focus on organisational design at the broader level is valuable, but partial. Chandler neglected the management of labour, while Williamson fails to make connections between multidivisional structures and employment relationships in his analysis of transaction costs (Rowlinson, 1997: 210).

The rise of bureaucratic control and its contradictions

Bureaucratisation also developed at the level of work and employment relationships. A number of modern radical theorists argue that in the post-war period employers increasingly turned to strategies of bureaucratic control for the shop floor. Techniques centred on stability and predictability of workforce behaviour, based in turn on enhancing rules, hierarchy and detailed division of labour are, 'recognisable to Weberian students of bureaucracy' (Goldman and Van Houten, 1977: 117). Richard Edward's research on companies such as Polaroid, IBM and General Electric points to two crucial features of the strategy: a finely-graded stratification and division of the workforce; and hierarchical structures devised to divide and conquer, which tend to 'break up the homogeneity of the firm's workforce, creating many seemingly separate strata, lines of work, and focuses for job identity' (1979: 133). In addition, impersonal rules form the basis of company policy, and detailed and specified criteria for job descriptions and performance are monitored by supervisors, rather than work tasks being directly enforced. The stress is on positive incentives in performance, not negative sanctions. When taken together with the system of job security and 'career' structure through job hierarchies, long-term identification with the company can be built.

Hence, contrary to Clawson's view, impersonality and 'remoteness' can be an effective control mechanism. It is worth remembering the point established by Edwards: that bureaucratic controls are not necessarily synonymous with close, direct or coercive authority. They rely more on *standardisation* of work processes, outputs and skills. By reducing the amount of stimuli, information and premises for decisions, behaviour can be formalised and regulated (March and Simon, 1958). The resultant indirect or unobtrusive controls are effective enough to enable the workforce to be trusted to make more decisions within established parameters, without necessarily having to change their attitudes. Popular and expert opinion points to the costs of wasteful bureaucracy. But as Richard Edwards observes: 'The core corporations survive and prosper on their ability to organise the routine, normal efforts of workers, not on their ability to elicit peak performances' (1979: 146).

We have been talking as if such bureaucratic work organisation only favours management. This is to miss part of the point. Many of its features benefit workers, or at least those who are long-term core employees. Such benefits include mobility through internal labour markets, seniority rules governing pay and lay-offs, grievance procedures, job protection and demarcation. In well-organised union workplaces, these are enforced through plant-wide collective bargaining or informal shop floor power. As part of this process there is a limited movement towards positive benefits for co-operation rather than negative sanctions: 'a system of mutually binding rules, material and symbolic incentives, and eventually the emergence of an ethos that is impersonally oriented towards performance' (Rueschemeyer, 1986: 94).

This use of Weberian categories as explanatory tools indicates their continuing relevance, but also their limitations. Clearly, bureaucratic structures have no universal rationality. Rather, they are in part consciously constructed by employers for specific purposes that cannot be reduced to 'efficiency'. A further qualification needs to be made in relation to the *legitimacy* arising from bureaucratic systems: undoubtedly they can generate loyalty and commitment, but the position of shop-floor workers is not comparable to that of higher officials of a public organisation such as the civil service, which provides long-term security and stable career structures with a minimum conflict of interests. Private companies are seldom able to match those kinds of conditions, and the centrality of the effort bargain (the implicit 'contract' between employee input and reward) will always tend to introduce uncertainty and conflict into the employment relationship.

The consolidation of bureaucracy in the private and public sectors also led to a lively debate among neo-Weberian writers in the 1950s and 1960s about the variations in, and limits to, the bureaucratic ideal-type. These case study critiques have been reworked many times in texts, but it is worth highlighting some key features and issues, in part to demonstrate that many current debates on new organisations are drawing on an established track record. A central feature has been the unintended consequences of bureaucratic modes of operation, for instance in relation to *efficiency*. Writers such as Merton (1949) have pointed to the dangers of rule-following becoming an end in itself, leading to the excesses of 'red tape'. Standardisation and predictability could easily degenerate into rigidity and defensive behaviour – a kind of 'trained incapacity' resistant to innovation. This was therefore proof of the dysfunctional effects of some bureaucratic practices. *Rationality* does not escape. There is a whole sub-literature stressing the rational propensity for employees to break, bend or modify rules in order to get things done more effectively. Hence the oft-quoted adage that a 'work to rule' is an extremely damaging form of industrial action. Blau (1955) exemplifies this kind of argument through his studies of a state employment agency and a federal law enforcement agency in the US. At the law enforcement agency it was more functional to ignore rules such as those related to reporting attempted bribery, in order to be in a position of power over the perpetrators at a later date.

The case studies also indicate the existence of alternatives within bureaucratisation. The most famous derives from Gouldner's (1954) examination of gypsum mines in a closed, rural community. This showed how a form of bureaucracy based on shared knowledge and consent to rules – characterised as a 'mock bureaucracy' based on an 'indulgency pattern' reflecting the nature of the community – was challenged by a new manager acting on behalf of a cost-conscious parent company. Control was reasserted in a 'punishment-centred bureaucracy' through highly centralised authority, formalisation of rules and new technology. A theme of the above debates was the 'costs' of control, predictability and purely calculative exchange. In part this echoed themes from the then influential human relations movement (see next chapter), notably the tension between formal rules and informal practices, as well as the need for a human dimension in design.

Other well-known post-war studies have developed typologies of organisational structure, with an emphasis on different types of bureaucracy. For example, the Aston Studies (see Chapter 5 and Pugh *et al.*, 1963; 1969) tried to identify causal relations between size, other variables and bureaucratisation, which led them to develop a structural taxonomy, focusing on three main types. *Full bureaucracies* – closest to Weber's ideal type – were based on a high level of standardisation of activities, concentration of authority and impersonal control; but were held not to exist in pure form outside central government. In contrast to this, *workflow bureaucracies* had highly structured activities such as production schedules, but more decentralised authority within the command framework. This type was found to be characteristic of large manufacturing concerns. Finally, smaller branch plants or parts of local government manifested bureaucratised employment relationships, but a low structuring of activities and control exercised in a more personal way; these were dubbed *personnel bureaucracies*.

In a later study Mintzberg (1983) identified five basic configurations:

- *Simple structure* direct supervision based on the strategic apex.
- *Machine bureaucracy* standardisation of work based on the technostructure.

- *Professional bureaucracy* standardisation of skills based on the operating core.
- *Divisional form* standardisation of outputs based on the middle line.
- *Adhocracy* rests on mutual adjustment/informal communication, with support staff playing the key role.

These configurations embody forms that pull organisations in different directions. Naturally hybrid forms can result, or different structures in different parts of the firm; but 'the organisation is often drawn toward one of the configurations in its search for harmony of structure' (Mintzberg, 1983: 288). If the five configurations are examined, we can see that all but the adhocracy are indeed variations on bureaucracy. Borrowed from Toffler's *Future Shock* (1970), the latter's design parameters are based on organic structures, low levels of standardisation and formalisation of behaviour, decentralisation and matrix-like use of specialists. This concept anticipates the arguments, examined in Chapters 11 and 12, that we are seeing a trend towards post-bureaucratic organisation.

Scientific management and bureaucratic work rules: modern legacies

The legacy of Taylorism and bureaucracy has long been sharply disputed. The former has been reviled for its apparent barbarity and economism, while the latter, as Jacques (1990) observes, has been pronounced dead and buried many times for the sins of killing initiative and crushing creativity.

There is little doubt that any burials have been premature. Scientific management was brought out of the broom cupboard by the radical theorist Braverman (1974). The argument that Taylorism constituted *the* means of managerial control in the twentieth century (see Chapter 8 for details) has been shown to be exaggerated, but there is plenty of evidence that key elements of the system have been updated and extended. Ossie Jone's (1994) entertaining account of life as a work study engineer in the 1970s and 1980s shows how the traditional techniques of method and time study were superseded by a system known as Simplified Pre-Determined Motion Time Study (SPMTS). This is merely one of a long line of innovations throughout the century. SPMTS was favoured by the engineers and would have delighted Taylor in that it promised the illusion of the removal of the 'subjective' element of rating from work measurement. Such developments may not convince all the sceptics given that they admittedly focus on a narrow, if well-known, feature of scientific management. 'Engineered standards' via a form of computerised Taylorism are also central to innovations in growth sectors such as warehousing and distribution (Wright and Lund, 1996). Also convincing is the rise of the influential management fix known as business re-engineering or core process redesign, whose tools – activity value analysis, time compression management ,and so on – and ethos are clearly rooted in Taylorism and classical theories (Thackray, 1993). With respect to the latter, as will be seen in Chapter 7, the emphasis in classical perspectives on universal principles and practices in management is also alive and well, particularly in the burgeoning genre of popular business literature.

The intimate and reciprocal interaction between the legacies of Taylor and Weber has been the subject of deservedly influential writings. In *Business Week*, Adler described the system in operation in Japanese-influenced lean production at NUMMI and other advanced manufacturing plants as a learning bureaucracy. Rules remains at the heart of the process: '[NUMMI] is obsessive about standardised work procedures. It sees what one NUMMI manager has called "the intelligent interpretation of Taylor's time and motion studies" as the principal key to success' (P. S. Adler, 1993: 103). Even the benchmarking systems underpinning total quality management (TQM) require a concern for standardised procedures and uniform, dependable practices (Wilkinson and Willmott, 1994; Tuckman, 1994). If anything, bureaucratic rules and standardisation have been spreading more rapidly in the service sector. Evidence for the *bureaucratisation of service* is most recently associated with Ritzer's (1993) 'McDonaldization of society' thesis, introduced earlier. He marshals a considerable array of evidence to argue persuasively that fast food chains are the tip of an iceberg that has extended Weber's principles of rationalisation in the form of calculable, predictable, quantified processes to an increased range of retail, leisure and media services. We should also not forget one of the central arguments of this chapter, that the distinctive contribution of Weber lay particularly in understanding the employment relationship. If current developments are examined, we can observe a number of factors that have combined to increase significantly the use of bureaucratic employment measures. These include fear of litigation in the fields of gender and race, adaptation to legislation on employment rights, and conformity to collectively bargained procedures on equitable recruitment, promotion and dismissal.

Summary and key points

The main lesson of this chapter is that Taylorism and other management theories are not packages and, given the separable nature of their elements, any practical legacy will be diverse and uneven. Furthermore, the history of large-scale organisation shows that managers combine elements of different approaches according to perceived need and fashion. Such combinations happen in part because theories derive from and devise outcomes for different territories. Taylorism was primarily a work design tool for management, Weberian notions of bureaucracy shared an interest in work rules and hierarchy, but widened the scope to considerations of employment relations and formal management structures. Both sets of theory and practices have to be located with broader changes towards Fordist production systems and the growth of large scale multidivisional organisations that shifted the balance of co-ordination of economic activity within capitalism from markets to hierarchies. Content, therefore, depends on context. When that context changes, ideas may become outdated, That is clearly the belief of many modern organisation theorists with respect to the ideas discussed in this chapter. Any definitive answers on contemporary relevance have to wait until later in the book. However, we have made a preliminary assessment that emphasises the continuing relevance of Taylorism and bureaucracy.

The character, pattern and prominence of management ideas depend to a considerable degree on agency – who initiates and benefits from them. In the case of Taylorism, engineers played the key role. But diffusion and consolidation doesn't take place unless practices meet the needs of key actors in the employment relationship and that normally means one or more of capital, labour and the state. Taylorism and bureaucratic measures clearly met some of the control needs of capital, but no managerial system is really sustainable unless it generates some level of mutual gains. We have illustrated, particularly, with respect to bureaucratic employment rules, that workers and their organisations derived benefits, albeit fragile and uneven. Taylorism and bureaucracy clearly left some issues and needs unaddressed. It is widely accepted that the neglect of the informal dimensions of organisational life by classical theories left gaps that had to be filled. How this was done will be considered in the next chapter.

There is a substantial overlap with the readings from the last section, notably Shenhav's and Clawson's historical studies on the origins and nature of Scientific Management and workplace bureaucracy. Robert

Kanigel's fascinating biography of Taylor is a good read and fills a lot of gaps in our knowledge. There remains no better introduction to the contemporary impact of Taylorism than Braverman's *Labor and Monopoly Capital*. There are some fascinating archive films of early scientific management that you can access, for example: http://www.youtube.com/watch?v=PvbG9Sjp970 and http://www.archive.org/details/EasierWa1946. Taylor's book *Shop Management* is also on line: http://melbecon.unimelb.edu.au/het/taylor/sciman.htm.

As for Weber, Littler's is the best explanation of what Weber added to Taylor (and on the diffusion of the latter). There are a lot of accounts of Weber's ideas in which the workplace and economy are a sub-plot – though dated now, Mouzelis on *Organisation and Bureaucracy* is still the most relevant for our purposes. Chapter Eight of Richard Edwards' influential study of the twentieth-century workplace is an indispensable guide to the significance of bureaucratic control. P. S. Adler's much reproduced short piece on learning bureaucracies in modern US car plants is a useful addition. Chandler's detailed studies of the emergence of the modern firm show how hierarchy displaced markets, but neglects the management of labour: Rowlinson (chs 7 and 8) is a useful commentary and correction.

Adler, P. S. (1993) 'Time-and-Motion Regained', *Harvard Business Review*, Jan.–Feb.: 97–107.

Chandler, A. (1977) *The Visible Hand*, Cambridge, Mass.: Harvard University Press.

Clawson, D. (1980) *Bureaucracy and the Labor Process: The Transformation of US Industry, 1860–1920*, New York: Monthly Review Press.

Clegg, S. and Dunkerley, D. (1980) *Organisation, Class and Control*, London: Routledge and Kegan Paul.

Collins, R. (1986) *Weberian Sociological Theory*, Cambridge: Cambridge University Press.

Edwards, R. (1979) *Contested Terrain: The Transformation of the Workplace in the Twentieth Century*, London: Heinemann.

Kanigel, R. (1999) *The One Best Way: Frederick Winslow Taylor and the Enigma of Efficiency*, Harmondsworth, Penguin.

Littler, C. R. (1982) *The Development of the Labour Process in Capitalist Societies*, London: Heinemann.

Mouzelis, N. (1967) *Organization and Bureaucracy*, London: Routledge and Kegan Paul.

Rowlinson, M. (1997) *Organisations and Institutions*, London: Macmillan.

Shenhav, Y. (1999) *Manufacturing Rationality: The Engineering Foundations of the Managerial Revolution*, Oxford: Oxford University Press.

4   managing the human factor

> Before 1912–13, engineering, accounting, and economics were the only bodies of knowledge relevant to systematic management. If consolidations of the 'human factor' were at all involved, they were based on philosophy, ethics and religion. (Shenhav, 1999: 181)

Managers had, by the early part of the twentieth century, already drawn on the expertise of people such as Taylor and other consultants in order to develop systems of controlling the labour process. It was not enough. As Baritz observes in his brilliant account of the historical uses of social science in American industry, 'Increasingly the men who manage and direct industry, find themselves incapable of effectively controlling their organisations' (1960: 3). After the First World War, some major corporations began financing industrial psychology and endowing business schools as part of a process of research and experimentation. That interaction was eventually to result in the emergence of the *human relations* approach to management. The two approaches have traditionally been seen as opposites. Perrow's somewhat tongue-in-cheek description sums it up: 'From the beginning, the forces of light and darkness have polarised the field of organisational analysis, and the struggle has been protracted and inconclusive' (1973: 2). However, the forces of darkness and light may not be as far apart as they seem. As we shall show, corporate co-operation with social scientists arose from the same source as links with Taylorism: the vulnerability of management to the appeal of planning and science.

The aims of this chapter are to:

- Explore the historical development of human relations ideas and practices, their links to Scientific Management and early corporate life.
- Set out the distinctive characteristics of human relations and the extent to which they derive from the Hawthorne Studies and Mayo's perspectives.
- Examine the (often limited) legacies left for modern management, from work design to corporate culture.
- Demonstrate how human resource management (HRM) emerged from the personnel function and corporate welfare to claim the territory of management of the human factor.

Social science and industry: a courtship

The courtship between social science and industry began with the promise of a dowry in the form of a battery of tests and measurements offered to fit people to jobs. While this does represent a shift from measurement of work to measurement of people, it was not wholly new. This kind of intervention represented a version of Taylor's 'scientific selection of the worker' by other means. In fact the *Bulletin of the*

Taylor Society carried articles discussing issues of human personality and arguing that newly recruited workers should be tested for personality, character and temperament. In 1915, an article about one factory noted that:

> A system of cards was used, one side of each card contained information about the worker's identity, parents, ethnic origins and previous employment; the other contained a certain amount of medico-psychological information ('anaemic', 'nonchalant') and notes on the individual's degree of motivation and way of life ('father out of work', 'mother agreed to take care of child', etc.). This was followed by his medical record (doctor, optician, dentist) and by basic health advice on the need for rest and fresh air. (Doray, 1988: 188)

This was part of a growing interest shown by engineers in the human factor and employment issues. Professional journals began to run articles such as 'Personality in the Shop Psychology of the Female Employee' (see Shenhav, 1999: 182).

This primitive psychology was openly geared towards manipulation of the 'uncertainties of human nature' (Shenhav, 1999: 174). In this sense, far from being a different academic species, it is arguable that the human relations current was partly prefigured in engineering discourses and derived from a form of Taylorist revisionism. Nor did it challenge Taylorism on its traditional territory of organisation of work. Nevertheless the battle cry of 'neglect of the human factor' did represent a partial critique that was directed against the costs of scientific management in terms of resistance and disenchantment. The simple appeal and apparent applicability of the variety of tests convinced a growing minority of employers. Problems arose when naïve enthusiasm and unrealistic expectations quickly ran up against the crude nature and limited results arising from the techniques. By the mid-1920s, and in changed economic circumstances, the tests had been abandoned by most companies (Baritz, 1960: 71).

Though a similar overlap in topics with scientific management can be observed (see Table 4.1), accounts of the development of British industrial psychology (M. Rose, 1975: 65–87; G. Brown, 1977: 213–28) show it to be more sober, centralised, less consultancy-based and affecting even fewer firms. It

Table 4.1 **Contents page of Industrial Psychology, ed. Charles Myers**

Chapter

1 Introduction – Charles S. Myers, MD, ScD, FRS
2 The Human Factor in Industrial Relations – J. Drever, MA, BSc, DPhil
3 Work and Environment – A. M. Hudson Davies, MA
4 Work and Rest – Rex Knight, MA
5 Ease and Speed of Work – G. H. Miles, DSc, and A. B. B. Eyre
6 Unproductive Working Time – A. Angles, BCom
7 Industrial Accidents – A. Stephenson, BSc
8 The Measurement of Intelligence and Aptitudes – F. M. Earle, MEd, BSc
9 Choosing a Career – Angus Macrae, MA, MB, ChB
10 Square Pegs and Square Holes – Winifred Spielman, BSc
11 Industrial Psychology and Welfare Work – Sheila Bevington, BSc
12 The Economic Aspects of Industrial Psychology – F. W. Lawe, MA, FSS
13 Industrial Psychology and Agriculture – W. R. Dunlop

Source: Myers (1929).

took a particular interest – derived from experiences of the Industrial Fatigue Research Board during the war – in monotony. Fatigue was, as we have seen, an issue that also concerned the scientific management movement, linked as it was to the need for the successful measurement of work. Common interests and client relations again meant, as in the US, 'a large proportion of their problems had to be taken over from the scientific managers' (M. Rose, 1975: 86). But despite sharing some common assumptions about efficiency, productivity and work organisation, British researchers established a distance, criticising, for instance, the anti-social and abnormal assumptions underlying notions of work rate under Taylorism (Myers, 1926: 81). Myers perceptively noted the hostility generated among workers by scientific management through its attack on skills, and the effects of speed-up and time and motion study. He made attacks on the notion of 'one best way', rightly pointing to the greater complexity of behaviour and industrial conditions. This critique was linked to a more sympathetic consideration of the need to convince the trade unions of the validity of social science interventions, and to win more generally the consent of the workforce. The relatively progressive stance of British industrial psychologists is further illustrated by their alliance with a small group of employers centred on the Quaker families such as Rowntree, who shared their enthusiasm for 'scientific planning' and dislike for the harsher aspects of Taylorism. When those companies began to utilise psychologists, however, there was still considerable suspicion and resistance from employees, particularly when it was introduced at the same time as scientific management methods (G. Brown, 1977: 216). The Quaker tapestry firm, Lee's, divided the managerial responsibility for 'psychology' and Taylorist 'mechanics' between the owner's two sons (Johnson and Moore, 1986). Most British employers, however, still preferred to cut costs simply by squeezing wages and exploiting favourable market circumstances.

But industrial psychology was not as isolated a phenomenon as it appeared. In the US particularly it was part of a wider period of experimentation involving human relations and Taylorist management, as employers chose within and between the new techniques. Richard Edwards (1979: 102) gives an interesting example of the Bancroft textile company employing a consultant to introduce welfare work in 1902, and Taylor's follower Gantt to reorganise production in 1905! Welfarism was a significant part of that context. A paternalistic concern for the well-being of employees in return for loyalty and hard work, had a long pedigree in some companies. Company towns were one manifestation, as employers provided houses, schools, stores, sanitation and lighting in order to attract an adequate labour force. But the rhetoric had shifted from older themes of community and improving the workingman to ones of entitlements and better working conditions (Barley and Kunda, 1992: 372).

Welfare work was also present in conventional circumstances. An increasing number of firms began to employ welfare secretaries whose role ranged from encouraging a 'proper moral atmosphere' to the provision of social and medical facilities. This interest was not philanthropic – 'Capital will not invest in sentiment', as one leading employer put it (quoted in Nelson, 1975: 104). It arose from attempts to grapple with the recruitment and motivation problems deriving from the increasing size of the labour force and a new industrial relations situation shaped by declining loyalty and rising unrest. There was a parallel development in the growth of employment or personnel departments as a means of dealing 'scientifically' with such issues – again showing an overlap with Taylorism. In the US and Britain, professional personnel bodies grew from the seeds of welfare work. But in the latter country, welfarism was strongly connected to the study of fatigue in the laboratory of wartime factories. As in the US, British welfarism was described by one of its leading members as combining 'pity and profit' (quoted in G. Brown, 1977: 185). Lee's issued 'partnership certificates' to employees who had shown a genuine interest in the company. Many workers, particularly the women who were its prime object, saw its motivation as directed primarily towards profit, given the emphasis on improving conditions for the sole purpose of maximising output. After the war, changing economic circumstances saw the decline of welfare initiatives. But in the US, to a greater extent than Britain, there was a broader framework of 'welfare capitalism'. Companies such as General Electric, International Harvester and US Steel continued policies of off-the-job benefits in the form of insurance, healthcare, pensions, social clubs, profit-sharing schemes and other measures (R. Edwards, 1979: 91–7).

The process took many different forms. Take Ford, for example. The company had only limited social provision, but it had social control potential. The 'Sociological Department' had investigators who were empowered to visit homes to check on absentees and monitor an employee's family, values and habits. But this social control mechanism did not exist in the abstract. To act as a counterweight to the assembly line and associated problems of labour turnover and unionisation, Ford had profit-sharing schemes and the famed five-dollar day. The Department could therefore ascertain the 'fitness' of workers for these generous rewards!

In a period in which space was opened up for employers by defeated industrial militancy and repression of socialist organising, welfarism in the US also had close ties to the development of company unions. This was different from the kind of enterprise unions initiated more recently by Japanese employers. The former arose primarily from wartime attempts to institute limited forms of worker representation such as works councils. After the war many large companies, often utilising their new personnel departments, were quick to consolidate this trend by initiating company unions as a focus for formal grievance procedures, thus alleviating the need for independent union representation (Edwards, 1979: 106). There was some success in delaying or undermining unionism, and employers learnt some important lessons on the importance of controlled employee involvement and formal procedures. But, as in Britain, little survived the economic changes associated with the growing depression and sharpening social polarisation. Company unionism and welfarism did not provide an adequate means of pursuing collective interests of workers, while at the same time they became a financial burden for employers without solving any of their fundamental control problems inside the factory.

Hawthorne and beyond

The Hawthorne studies occupy a pivotal place in organisational theory. Begun in the mid-1920s, the research was carried out in the large Hawthorne plant employing 29,000 workers making electrical appliances for Bell as a subsidiary of American Telegraph and Telephone (AT&T). Management regarded themselves as progressive, but this was with regard to a willingness to experiment rather than their general attitudes, for they were strongly anti-union. The significance of Hawthorne does not lie in the results of the research as such, for both its findings and methods are widely regarded as highly questionable (Carey, 1967; Silver, 1987). Rather it reflects two factors. First is the sustained nature of the intervention itself, combining psychologists, sociologists and anthropologists. In this way the courtship between social science and industry became something of a formal engagement. Second, the interpretation of the results became the core of human relations theory and subsequent managerial practices. This was partly due to the propagandising work of Elton Mayo (1946), despite the fact that he did not join the team properly until 1928 and was much more peripheral than those who actually wrote up the detailed research such as Roethlisberger and Dickson (1939/1964) and, to a lesser extent, Whitehead (1938).

Let us retrace these steps briefly. Early experiments centred on varying the lighting for two small test groups of women workers. The purpose was to identify conditions affecting worker performance. Unfortunately no firm conclusions could be drawn, as productivity increased under every level of

CULTURE, COMPANIES AND COUNTRIES IN A GLOBALISING ERA ▪ MANAGEMENT ▪ CONTROL AND RESISTANCE ▪ POWER IN ORGANISATIONS ▪ GENDER, SEXUALITY AND ORGANISATIONS ▪ CORPORATIONS AND CULTURE: REINVENTING ORGANISATION MAN?

4   45

illumination and even for the control group that was not being subjected to any changes at all! At the time this caused great puzzlement, but it was later theorised that the real change had been the segregation of a small group, which blossomed under special attention and treatment. Thus the 'Hawthorne effect' was born, through which it was recognised that the research intervention itself is an independent variable in its effects on human behaviour. Initially the puzzlement led to a further stage of experiments on groups of women selected for their degree of friendship with one another. Again the emphasis was on manipulation of environmental variables, this time of a greater variety: rest pauses, length of working day, group bonus schemes and so on. Observers, initially placed in a test room, were gradually encouraged to act like supervisors and become more friendly with the group. Until 1929, in almost all cases output rose, with the only consistent factor again the effects of creating a special group with its identity strengthened by the replacement of two 'unco-operative' members. However, worker interest in experiments declined and output fell with the onset of the depression. Furthermore, additional experiments with two other groups to further test the effects of incentives and rest pauses had inconclusive results, both experiments being discontinued amidst some discord.

All this confusion might appear to be grounds for giving up. But a more positive line was taken that a constant factor was the significance of employee attitudes and the influence of supervisory techniques upon them. The successful experiments were those that allowed the individuals to coalesce into a group, though it is difficult to imagine how the special conditions could be transferred.

> Right now I couldn't ask for anything better than I have. I just can't explain what it is but I sure like it in the test room. ... I think we work for the most wonderful man in the Western Electric Company. We have no boss. Mr. _____simply waits on us. ... We have privileges that a lot of the other girls don't have. We are allowed to go down and lie on the couch when we are tired or don't feel good, and the matron was told not to say anything to us. Of course, none of us have done that yet because we always feel pretty good and we have rest periods and can do anything we want to in those ten minutes.
>
> (Roethlisberger and Dickson, 1964: 144)

Attitudes are not simply created by interaction with management. Employee preoccupations arise from a variety of sources, so further means were found of identifying them. Even while the above experiments were going on, the company and researchers had initiated an interviewing programme to explore the relations between employee morale and supervision. 'Counsellors' were trained by researchers to play the role of the observers in the illumination phase. Over a long period of time, a variety of formal and more open-ended techniques of interviewing were utilised as a means of gaining information and of detecting, diverting and redirecting dissatisfactions. The counsellor was told by the company, 'to watch constantly for signs of unrest and to try to assuage the tension of the worker by discussion before the unrest became active' (quoted in Fischer and Sirriani, 1984: 182). Employee complaints were treated as unreliable due to their vagueness (hot, cold, damp, smoky or dusty were apparently inferior to 'the temperature in the room was 67°F'); or because they really revealed some personal, external disturbance. Even when told of grievances, management did not act on them. Aside from letting off steam, the process could also be used to adjust employees to the work situation and screen out effective counsellors as management material.

A final phase of research linked together the concern with employee attitudes and the earlier focus on the group. The famed 'bank wiring room' experiments were based on an existing workgroup carrying out wiring, soldering and inspecting tasks with a supposedly unobtrusive observer present. What was 'discovered' on the face of it was no different from Taylor's observations in the steel industry: the work-group systematically controlled and restricted output on the basis of their own conception of a fair day's work and enforced group norms on any fellow workers who deviated by overproducing (rate busters) or under-working (chisellers).

> One day an interviewer entered a department unobserved. There was a buzz of conversation and the men seemed to be working at great speed. Suddenly there was a sharp hissing sound. The conversation died away, and there was a noticeable slowing up in the work pace. The interviewer later discovered from an acquaintance in the department that he had been mistaken for a rate setter. One of the workmen, who acted as a lookout, had stepped on a valve releasing compressed air, a prearranged signal for slowing down.
>
> (Roethlisberger and Dickson, 1964: 386)

The interpretation and reaction were, however, sharply different. Despite the restrictions, cliques and hostilities, a more accommodating picture was endorsed of group identities. Instead of suppressing the group and attempting to individualise its members, human relations is concerned to cultivate its sentiments and switch its loyalties to management. Roethlisberger and Dickson note: 'It is as well to recognise that informal organisation is not "bad", as they are sometimes assumed to be' (1964: 559). As it is fruitless to try and destroy it, management's task is to achieve a greater harmony between the informal and formal organisation. This can be done through controlled participation, effective communication and socially skilled, humane supervision. Referring to the experience of one of the Hawthorne experimental groups, Mayo commented that, 'Before every change of program, the group is consulted. Their comments are listened to and discussed; sometimes their objections are allowed to negative a suggestion. The group undoubtedly develops a sense of participation in the critical determination and becomes something of a social unit' (quoted in Baritz, 1960: 88–9). Here we can see the seeds of every superficial consultation exercise in the managerial toolkit!

As an alternative managerial *tactic* this new way of managing the small group made a lot of sense; indeed a minority of British employers were reaching similar conclusions (G. Brown, 1977: 243). Today, as we shall see later, it is applied in new and more sophisticated ways in current teamwork practices. The problem, however, arises from how Mayo and the human relations tradition theorised their understanding of Hawthorne. They were determined to fashion a general theory of behaviour in organisations. Later management theorists have dubbed a key element of this approach 'social man' (Schein, 1965). For Mayo, this started from a critique of the so-called 'rabble hypothesis' he attributed to economists and management theorists such as Taylor, in which individuals act solely according to rational self-interest. In contrast, 'social man' proceeds from the assumption that the major human need is for social solidarity that can be satisfied through group association. Naturally, this downplays the role of economic incentives. Such associations are seen to create social routines that substitute for logical and individual self-interest. Mayo preferred the term 'non-logical' to 'irrational', but the essential message is clear: workers act according to sentiments and emotions.

Contrary to some accounts, he did not believe that management was by definition and contrast rational, for all individuals were held to be governed by the same abstract instincts and needs. Rather managers and administrators could *become* rational, precisely because they can free themselves from social routines and the accompanying emotional involvement. This is an extremely curious notion, as any analysis of management shows that it has *its own* routines and 'illogicalities'. But it indicates the uncritical attitude of human relations writers towards the economic élites. Interestingly the new theorists of corporate culture (see later and Chapter 11) manage to maintain the emphasis on emotions, symbolism and 'irrationality' without separating management and workforce in the same way.

It must also be said that the empirical basis for Mayo's assertions in the Hawthorne experience is very shaky. Group solidarity was carefully engineered through the selection and treatment of those workers involved, even to the point of replacing 'unco-operative' workers. Even this did not sustain co-operative activity. Mayo interpreted restriction of output as a combination of group sentiments and lack of trust in management. But there are alternative and simpler explanations: 'Restriction of output by voluntary norms was a rational response by primarily economically-oriented agents to the increasingly likely prospect of unemployment' (Clegg and Dunkerley, 1980: 131). Environmental influences on employee attitudes were recognised, but it was held that the consequences could be dealt with and 'adjusted' inside the enterprise.

The denial of economic factors led to some absurd psychologisms. Mayo used the curious term 'pessimistic reveries' to account for industrial unrest of any kind. Put another way, strikes and other actions that restrict output are obsessive preoccupations and signs of maladjustment, even to the point of identifying industrial unrest with mental breakdown and casting trade union leaders as psychological deviants! Not surprisingly, unions very rarely get mentioned in Mayo's writings. That did not stop later followers. The psychologist McMurry argued that not only were unions unnecessary when management acted fairly, but workers joined unions not to protect their jobs and improve pay but because of unconscious cravings to improve the emotional situation at work (Baritz, 1960: 175). Seemingly, social science had not improved much on the primitive psychology of engineering discourses, which two decades earlier had been describing striking employees as 'explosive workers' with strike-prone personalities and backgrounds of juvenile delinquency (see Shenhav, 1999: 189)!

It would, however, be misleading to view human relations through its excesses. To add to 'social man', a second highly influential level of theorisation emphasised the essentially co-operative nature of the enterprise. In fact the two were linked, as Mayo continually referred to the supposed eager desire of workers for co-operative activity. It is easy to dismiss this kind of analysis, particularly given the capacity of human relations researchers to systematically ignore or reinterpret conflictual processes. But they *had* identified significant changes in the socio-economic sphere that brought the issue of co-operation to the fore. They pointed to the disparity between the attention paid to technical efficiency and economic functions, and the absence of 'the development of skills and techniques for securing co-operation' (Roethlisberger and Dickson, 1964: 552). The need to improve the latter was especially important because, as Mayo recognised, the balance between technical and social skills had been disrupted as workers' traditional forms of craft socialisation and identity had been undermined by mechanisation and the assembly line.

Emphasis is therefore put on the role of management to use the formal organisation to intervene in the *informal*, so as to create and sustain consent. Only in this context can we understand what appear to be the superficial solutions of human relations practices, with their prescriptions of 'democratic' supervision, good communications, teamwork and socially skilled leadership. Mayo's 'lifelong obsession with social harmony' (M. Rose, 1975: 115) was not based merely on his distorted empirical observations; it was underwritten by an organic model of society in which equilibrium and stability are the natural order of things, while structural divisions and conflicts are pathological. Mayo was worried about the 'extensive maladjustment of our times' as a period of rapid change undermined values and atomised individuals. The task was to recreate a sense of community inside the workplace.

During the same period Chester Barnard, the President of New Jersey Bell Telephone Company, was developing an even heavier emphasis on the basis for human co-operation, which was to have a major impact on later mainstream theorists (Perrow, 1979). Co-operation necessary to the survival of society could be most clearly observed in organisations. Unequal power and resources were irrelevant against the 'fact' that individuals voluntarily entered and submitted themselves to a common goal unachievable without collective effort. Organisations were rational and individuals were not. But this virtual deification of the formal organisation, like Mayo, still reserved the key role for management. The rationality of the 'non-personal' organisation was in practice again located with the executive élite who, as decision-makers, had responsibility for what Peters and Waterman, in praising Barnard, describe as 'managing the values of the organisation' (1982: 26). For co-ordination was still required to make a system, particularly as a sense of common purpose was not always present among the 'lower participants'. Barnard therefore reinforced the emphasis, not just on co-operation, but on the balance of formal and informal. As Perrow points out, this is the most extreme identification with the formal organisation, devoid of any concern about the negative effects of power and domination, or even the stress in human relations on sympathetic supervision and controlled participation.

Consolidating human relations

 Many managers would agree that the effectiveness of their organisations would be at least doubled if they discover how to tap the unrealised potential present in their organisations. (Douglas McGregor, 1960: 4)

Recognising the significance of co-operative activity was an advance, but it was wrong to transfer the analysis from the workgroup to the organisation as a whole. The fundamental contradiction at the heart of human relations and of Barnard is that co-operation, even of the 'spontaneous' kind, has to be created. Reed refers to an intellectual schizophrenia whereby, 'a theoretical framework is forced to reconcile the contradictions generated by a metaphysic that assumes collective moral consensus as a social given and at the same time advocates the adoption of techniques whereby this may be engineered' (1985: 6). There is a therefore a wide consensus among the critics we have discussed that the significance of the tradition is to be located in its *ideological appeal*. Michael Rose (1975: 124) puts this most succinctly in his memorable comment that Mayoism was the twentieth century's most seductive managerial ideology, in which social scientists and managers fashioned each other in their own image.

There is a great deal of accuracy in the view that one of its major functions was to legitimate the power and authority of both emergent professional 'classes' of managers and industrial consultants. The problem is that such an analysis can slip into giving the impression that human relations was a gigantic, if dangerous, con-trick with no purchase on reality. In part the reverse is true, for it makes sense only as a reaction to and means of shaping new realities. The depth of economic and political crisis meant that 'by the 1930s corporate America felt under siege' (Neimark and Tinker, 1986: 25). Congress had passed corporatist legislation allowing companies greater control over markets and pricing in return for acceptance of codes governing minimum wages and maximum hours, plus guarantees of union membership and collective bargaining rights. In addition, the country was experiencing a huge strike wave of sit-down strikes and factory occupations. Large corporations bitterly resisted the 'New Deal' institutions and the union organising drive. But the more perceptive of them also realised that 'the crisis generated critical problems of social control and legitimation for management' (Boreham, 1980: 25). A second front was opened, drawing extensively on the human relations package of better communication, democratic leadership, co-operation and social integration. This went hand-in-hand with early versions of the managerial revolution thesis, General Motors claiming that the organisation was a community of stakeholders for which management was a trustee.

The success of strikes and union organising drives only consolidated a recognition of the importance of consent and attention to employee attitudes in the more general writings of human relations theorists such as T. N. Whitehead in his *Leadership in a Free Society* (1936). Despite the weakness of the tradition in Britain, Whitehead's book was well received in progressive management circles worried about the changing position of business in a more democratic community. Human relations was able to provide greater legitimation of management authority than Taylor, because it went beyond the narrow confines of 'science' and formal organisation to address issues more in tune with the times. But it would not have made the same impact merely as a body of ideas. It had to help generate new practices.

Though it was still confined to a minority of even the largest employers throughout the 1930s, Bendix, Baritz and other researchers show that an increasing number of firms such as General Electric, General Motors and Proctor and Gamble developed programmes influenced by human relations. The Hawthorne researchers had put considerable emphasis on 'personnel work' in its broadest sense of 'adequate diagnosis and understanding of the actual human situations – both individual and group – within the factory' (Roethlisberger and Dickson, 1964: 591). With this background, greater consideration in many large companies was given to the training of managers and supervisors in the arts of intensive communication, social skills and non-authoritarian leadership that would motivate as well as command. Personnel departments grew further, alongside more use of attitude surveys. General Motors managed to neatly combine them with spying on union activists by employing Pinkerton detectives to carry out the tests! As previously, the war acted as a spur, large companies and the state finding the use of tests an invaluable means of dealing with the problems associated with the sudden employment of thousands of new workers. Despite a sustained attack by more critical academics, the diverse applications and effects of human relations theories had established a bridgehead for the social sciences in industry and, by the 1940s, the movement had gained substantial institutional support (Barley and Kunda, 1992: 374).

The 1950s saw the relationship between social science and industry blossom still further. This was facilitated both by the development of OB and related disciplines in business schools that specialised in the human side of the enterprise, and by the training of middle and senior executives in leadership and management development (Barley and Kunda, 1992: 375). The practices or solutions were not necessarily any less superficial than Hawthorne's. Bendix (1956: 326–7) remarks that the National Association of Manufacturer's newfound attachment to 'two-way communication' was based on the assumption that employers relayed *facts* to the workforce to promote co-operation, whereas what workers say is *information* which management can use to 'eliminate misunderstandings'.

Despite the over-emphasis on solving problems through issues of poor interpersonal relations, and the re-rise of harder managerial 'sciences' such as operations research and systems analysis with their associated quantitative and financial techniques, human relations did not disappear. The body of research and to a lesser extent practical intervention moved on to new topics. Some researchers continued to examine leadership styles or search for the qualities of good leadership (see Chapter 22). Others focused on group processes and dynamics, including the well-known socio-technical studies of the Tavistock Institute in Britain (see Chapter 5). Rhetorical claims, however, foundered on a failure to demonstrate an exact and direct relationship between theory and practice. Perrow, for example, has written sceptically of the 'thirty year history of the effort to link morale and leadership to productivity' (1979: 97). In the piece quoted at the beginning of the chapter, Perrow was dismissive of the contributions from 'the forces of light'. From the vantage point of that decade it looked as if studies of the influence of technology and organisational environments, associated with systems theory, had triumphed: 'management should be advised that the attempt to produce change in an organisation through managerial grids, sensitivity training, and even job enrichment and job enlargement is likely to be fairly ineffective for all but a few organisations' (1973: 14).

Competitors and continuities: the rise of human resource management

There were competitors to the new influences. The human relations school gradually became less visible, giving way, even within the territory of managing the human factor, to behavioural psychology. Mayo and others had always provided, in Bendix's words, a vocabulary of motivation. What developed in its wake was a fully-fledged theory of motivation, promoted by figures such as Maslow, McGregor and Herzberg, which had the additional advantage of challenging Taylorism on questions of job design (see Chapter 19). But Perrow was wrong to believe that a hard structure and systems approach had achieved a durable dominance. The earlier human relations tradition that had lain dormant and often abused for its naïveté suddenly became influential again in the 1980s. Nor was it a question of a particular soft style simply becoming fashionable again. Human relations thinking contained genuine insights within a flawed general framework. The idea that the internal dynamics of the small group could be turned around so that a degree of self-governance could favour management resurfaced in the substantial wave of interest in teamworking from the 1980s onwards (see Buchanan, 2000 and Chapters 15 and 24). At broadly the same time, management theorists and practitioners were also rediscovering the benefits of creating social cohesion and value consensus through organisational 'communities'. The advocates of corporate cultures such as Peters and Waterman (1982) explicitly acknowledged the influence of earlier human relations writers (see Chapter 11).

Despite such influences, human relations theory as such is still largely regarded as a ghost from a past banquet. When people talk now of managing the human factor, human resource management (HRM) is what comes to mind. We can tell this, in part, as a story about changes in functional structures and practices, though this requires us to retrace a few steps. This chapter has already demonstrated that the origins of personnel work lie in the human relations tradition. As a more specific function was consolidated, the humanistic rhetoric was complemented by practices that reflected the forms of adaptation to 'local' environments. Notable in this were the dominant rule-based and hierarchical systems of bureaucratic control developed in large organisations (see Chapter 3), and the expanded legal regulation of the employment relationship established as part of the post-war settlement between capital, labour and the state. The outcome expanded the domain and expertise of the personnel function, but created practices that were largely procedural, reactive and low trust.

As part of the general shift in workplace practices and organisational restructuring in the 1980s, these orientations were put into question. The personnel function was recast as HRM, though in this incarnation it was not to be the exclusive property of a narrow functional department (Tichy *et al.*, 1982; Beer *et al.*, 1985). This was a matter not just of territory but of content. HRM always had a dual usage, signifying a new way of describing the field of people management, and a distinctive approach to managing the employment relationship (Mabey, Salaman and Storey, 1998: 1). The emphasis is on the integration of 'personnel' issues within the overall business strategy; with employees becoming a 'resource' equivalent to something like finance, with ownership of HR issues diffused down to other actors, notably line managers. 'Strategic management' is a term continually invoked to refer to the management of employees

CULTURE, COMPANIES AND COUNTRIES IN A GLOBALISING ERA ■ MANAGEMENT ■ CONTROL AND RESISTANCE ■ POWER IN ORGANISATIONS ■ GENDER, SEXUALITY AND ORGANISATIONS ■ CORPORATIONS AND CULTURE: REINVENTING ORGANISATION MAN?

51

at all levels, directed towards the creating and sustaining of competitive advantage (P. M. Miller, 1989; Kamoche, 1994).

From the beginning, the various usages have been open to dispute. Some have questioned whether the approach genuinely reflects substantial shifts of policy from the old personnel departments, or is simply 'old wine in new bottles' (M. Armstrong, 1987). Many more have queried whether something radically different was actually being delivered in the practice of managing of the employment relationship (see Chapter 11). The latter is important, but need not detain us here – our emphasis is on the continuities and changes from human relations to human resource management.

To project itself as something that was not 'simply a new sign tacked on the personnel manager's door' (Thomas, 1988: 3), HRM had to sell itself as a theoretical and normative narrative as well. As one of us has explained in more detail elsewhere (Thompson, 2007), this has centred on the concept of human capital. Though borrowed from the debates about educational performance, the idea of human capital has helped HRM make a business case for the role of the quality and skills of the workforce in competitive advantage. Individual employees had a responsibility invest in the attitudes and expertise that could enhance their usefulness to the firm. Meanwhile, a strategic approach to HRM is said to be marked by investment in the workforce and this would be associated with enhanced skills, training, career structures and skill and knowledge – based reward systems. In turn, this forms the basis for mutual gains and shared interests through the employment relationship. The management of people is thus given a potential seat at the top table. Typical of this approach was Pfeffer's (1994) 'profits through people' message. He examined seven practices that successful organisations needed to have in order to make a difference, including employment security, selective hiring, self-managed teams and decentralized decision – making, high compensation linked to organizational performance, training, minimal status differences and extensive openness in sharing information. Though HRM retains a link with the 'treat people nicely and they will behave better' traditions of human relations, its newfound legitimacy lies in its capacity to escape the association of managing people purely with soft, developmental approaches. The argument is not free-floating. From the middle of the 1980s HRM theorists began to make a more contingent argument that changes in the external environment were making the internal assets of the firm more significant and strategic. More specialised, dynamic markets and technologies required more flexible, better trained labour. The HRM model was cast explicitly in terms of human capital and high involvement (Kaufman, 2003).

The unifying and often derided slogan, was 'people are our most important asset', but beneath the surface lurked two widely observed variants. First, there is a 'hard' version in which HRM is a much more systematic, rational instrument that can support organisational change through effective mobilisation and measurement of human capabilities and performance (Devanna, Fombrun and Tichy, 1984; Huselid, 1995). There is obvious continuity here with more traditional functional practices, but it is the extent to which reward and other forms of performance management are tied in to overall strategy and bottom-line outcomes that is considered to be decisive.

A softer, normative variant can be identified (Kochan, Katz and McKersie, 1986; Guest, 1987), which links HRM primarily to a transformation of employment relationships based on higher levels of employee commitment and involvement. This orientation received a considerable boost with the development of the excellence literature genre, which promoted culture change as a primary managerial resource. In many firms this enabled the HR department to take a leading role in change programmes, as the definer and measurer of value change (Marks *et al.*, 1997). The variants could and should come together through the pathway of high-performance work systems (HPWS). While this can be interpreted as covering all HRM territories (Huselid, 1995), it is more common for it to be associated with a workplace level and issues such as teamwork, quality and continuous improvement (Kochan and Osterman, 1994). This impacts upon the practices of employee relations. As Guest notes, the underlying goal is to get employees to go 'beyond contract' and away from old-style adversarial collectivism, 'thereby reducing the potential for the effort bargain to operate as a potential focus for conflict and grievance' (1998: 239).

While the intent to restructure the employment relationship away from low-trust industrial relations systems is widely approved, the association with an attack on collectivism and trade unions is more controversial. The rise of HRM, with its unitarist philosophy, more individualistic relations between employer and employee, and direct communication between company and workforce, has undoubtedly coincided with some diminution of the significance of collective bargaining and union power (Blyton and Turnbull, 1998: 9). That is not the only controversy. It is certainly possible to produce *models* that integrate different types of practices, of which the 'mutual gains enterprise', which combines strategic, functional and workplace dimensions, is attractive and coherent (Kochan and Osterman, 1994). However, practices on different territories and through hard and soft mechanisms are easier to reconcile rhetorically than in practice (Legge, 1995). While debates focus on conceptual tensions, they are dwarfed by the problem of holding the different facets of the HRM model together in the context of contemporary organisational restructuring. In particular, performance goals such as greater productivity and flexibility in work organisation are proving difficult to reconcile with changes in employment that undermine loyalty, career and stability. In this context, critical commentators argue that hard, cost-driven approaches are predominating over softer, commitment and trust based policies (Blyton and Turnbull, 1992; Storey, 1992, 1995). We will pick up the human capital narrative and examine the debate on the outcomes of HRM policy and practices in Part II.

Summary and key points

It is conventional wisdom that Taylorism and human relations are at best opposite ends of a spectrum and worst, deadly enemies. This chapter has shown that they shared many of the same origins and concerns in attempting to apply 'science' to the understanding and control human behaviour, or the 'labour problem' as it was known at the beginning of the twentieth century. There, was, admittedly a difference of territory. Taylorism focused largely on the design of work, human relations on employee adjustment to it. While this is frequently described in mainstream writing as technical and human organisation and the need to integrate the two, it may be more accurately thought of in terms of overlapping or sometimes competing control systems. Whatever its record of patchy practices and inflated theoretical claims about social harmony and the power of leadership and communication, human relations would not exist if it did not bring something distinctive to the table. That distinctiveness is a focus on the informal dimension of organisational life – represented in practices such as teamworking and culture change – which Scientific Management wrongly thought could be excluded or marginalised. This recognition is, in part, retrospective and by the time it came, the human factor franchise had been largely taken up by HRM. We began that discussion with a quote from McGregor, of Theory X and Theory Y fame. Despite being written at the end of the 1950s, its language is identical to that of contemporary HRM. Though he goes on to argue that the major thing holding back the efficient and scientific management of the human factor is the adolescence of the social sciences (1960: 5), we would draw a different conclusion. Influenced by conceptions of human capital, HRM is a more coherent set of ideas and better embedded in managerial practices, but its sustainability is as much about social *life* as the social sciences. While the franchise may have changed hands, it is still proving difficult to produce a durable formula that can transform the conflicting, albeit complex, interests that lie at the heart of the labour process and employment relationship.

Further reading

Once again, Shenhav is good on the links between Taylorism and human relations. Baritz's classic *Servants of Power* is an indispensable account of the way that social science began to be used by management. If you can get hold of it, Browns' *Sabotage* is a British variant that also shows how workers resisted the new trends. When examining human relations and the Hawthorne studies it's good to access the original writings, notably Roesthlisberger and Dickson, but the various editions of Rose are a decent substitute. Perrow sets out the conventional scepticism of the more scientific end of organisation theory. On the move from personnel/industrial relations to HRM, Legge and the articles of Guest are a useful start.

Baritz, L. (1960) *The Servants of Power*, Middletown: Wesleyan University Press.

Brown, G. (1977) *Sabotage*, Nottingham: Spokesman.

Guest, D. E. (1987) 'Human Resource Management and Industrial Relations', *Journal of Management Studies*, 24. 5: 503–21.

Guest, D. E. (1989) 'Personnel and HRM: Can You Tell the Difference?' *Personnel Management*, January: 48–51.

Legge, K. (1995, 2nd edn 2005) *Human Resource Management: The Rhetorics, the Realities*, London: Macmillan.

Perrow, C. (1973) 'The Short and Glorious History of Organisational Theory', *Organisational Dynamics*, Summer, 2–15.

Roethlisberger, F. G. and Dickson, W. J. (1964) *Management and the Worker*, New York: Wiley.

Rose, M. (1975, 1986) *Industrial Behaviour*, Harmondsworth: Penguin.

Shenhav, Y. (1999) *Manufacturing Rationality: The Engineering Foundations of the Managerial Revolution*, Oxford: Oxford University Press.

5 organisations and environments

> The society in which these organisations occur, and its relation with these organisations, has been very little studied. To the extent that the outside world does impinge on the structure and functioning of organisations, it is conceptualised not in terms of interests, values, class loyalties, ideologies, market developments etc., but as the organisation's 'environment'. (Salaman, 1979: 32)

The previous chapters provide plenty of evidence that the contexts in which organisations operate, whether they be the rise of monopoly capitalism, the ups and downs of the trade cycle, or political circumstances such as the American New Deal in the 1930s, profoundly shape their nature and development. All the great social scientists who set the agenda for organisational theory examined the workplace in a systemic context. As that theory became a specialist enterprise in its own right, such a focus was lost. Salaman argues that:

The aims of this chapter are to:

- Set out alternative readings of the organisational environment and discuss the issues they raise.
- Contrast and critique closed and open systems perspectives, including the research associated with contingency theory.
- Critically evaluate selection theories, notably the population ecology approach.
- Explore the extent to which managers and other organizational actors can make strategic choices in product and labour markets.
- Indicate and illustrate the ways in which powerful corporations shape rather than adapt to their environments.

Defining the nature and scope of environments

The idea of organisations adapting to the environment is not in itself problematic. It is a question of how it is conceptualised. Mullins (1985: 12) claims that organisations are viewed in their total environment. Unfortunately this does not mean that they are situated within a bigger picture, but rather that lists of multiple influences are provided. Child (1969), in examining a variety of classification schemes, notes that some utilise a narrow conception of task environment based largely on economic factors such as customers, suppliers, competitors and self-regulating groups. Child prefers a broader categorisation taking in product markets, factor markets, technical knowledge, political, and socio-cultural elements (for example, communities, social memberships and values). An even wider and more influential set of factors is employed by R. Hall (1977): technological, legal, economic, political, demographic, cultural and ecological. However, in practice, as we shall see later, most research has tended to focus on the narrower frame, particularly on markets and technology. The criticism being made by Salaman and others is that the dominant readings of 'environment' lack substance, whether broad list or immediate context, and fail to specify the local, national and systemic contexts in which organisations are located.

This is all a long way from early organisational theory. It is conventional wisdom to argue that classical and other perspectives took no account of the environment. Instead they were concerned with manipulating the internal variables of an organisation in the service of goal attainment. Specific emphasis tended to be put on the development of rules or principles maximising the rational and efficient application of resources embodied in work design and other aspects of formal structure. Because this treats organisations as self-sufficient entities, or systems in and of themselves, it has been retrospectively dubbed *closed systems theory* (see Clegg and Dunkerley, 1980: 191–6). Human relations theory too has been criticised for suspending the firm in a social vacuum and ignoring the degree to which its problems were results of outside pressures (Albrow, 1973: 406). This is somewhat unfair. Researchers such as Mayo and Roethlisberger and Dickson did recognise the effects on employees from membership of wider collectivities, such as communities. The problem was more that they and their less discriminating followers tended to believe that the *solutions* could be found through internal adjustment.

If anything, the supposedly more sophisticated neo-human relations perspectives of Maslow, Herzberg and others were more guilty of closed system thinking. Their emphasis on a model of universal psychological needs that, once identified by the intelligent manager, could be harnessed through new forms of organisational design, completely isolated the individual and the firm from social structure (see Chapter 19 for further discussion). Since the 1960s, closed system approaches have largely been frowned upon. However, that does not mean that they have gone away, for two reasons. First, the focus remains overwhelmingly on the *individual* organisation and there is a tendency for theorists to highlight internal and predictable goals–means relationships that can operate as a 'buffer' to the environment (R. Hall, 1977). Second, the popular management search for the magical ingredient to organisational success which can be internally controlled also increases the likelihood of a constant reworking or accommodation to a closed system approach.

Now this is admittedly not the whole picture. The environment *is* recognised through the notion that successful companies emerge through purposeful, though unpredictable, evolution. Though the Darwinian imagery of experiment and evolution is invoked, the message is simple. Companies survive and stay fit and well by adapting to their environment. It appears that the essence of that environment is the customer. The logic is that successful companies are those that have a large market share, long-term growth and high profits. They have adapted to the (customer) environment. Success is therefore simply read off from a diffuse concept of the environment. But we are still returned to internal organisational processes, for what made them successful in the first place 'was usually a culture that encouraged action, experiments, repeated tries' (Peters and Waterman, 1982: 114). This is what Peters and Waterman mean by 'intentionally seeded evolution within companies'.

One final point needs to be made about closed systems. The use of the term 'systems' is not accidental. Mainstream writing has been dominated by varieties of *systems theory*, though greatly extending and modifying early conceptions. This perspective is examined in more detail in Part IV of the book, but we can observe for now that Organisations are systems of interrelated parts or sub-units – for example, departments, groups and individuals – each functioning to mobilise resources towards meeting wider goals. These parts are at the same time differentiated and interdependent, aiding processes of integration and co-ordination. Systems theory is therefore an explanation of the pattern of functioning of organisations in terms of inputs, outputs and transformations, encompassing the variety of social, psychological and technical variables.

A crucial development, however, has been the acceptance of the importance of interaction with the environment; for the survival of an organisation depends on its capacity to adapt to markets, technologies and other situations. Even the description 'closed system' is partly a label of convenience; true only to the extent that the organisation as a whole and the relation between its parts (technical and social, different departments and functions) could be seen as itself analogous to system–environment relations. True systems theory is open and adaptive in character and we need to spell this out in more detail.

Adaptation to the environment: open system approaches

There are a number of different approaches and types of research that treat organisations in terms of adaptation and as open systems, an approach pioneered by Thompson (1967) and Katz and Kahn (1970). But who is adapting and what are they adapting to? The starting point is the need for the organisation to transact with the environment, more specifically to take inputs from the environment and convert them into outputs. As Hannan and Freeman note: 'In the adaptation perspective, subunits of the organisation, usually managers or dominant coalitions, scan the relevant environment for opportunities and threats, formulate strategic responses, and adjust organisational structure appropriately' (1977: 929–30). The operation of the system in markets, and among other organisations, gives essential feedback about its performance measured by realisation of corporate goals.

Systems theory is multi-layered. At its simplest, this can be expressed as society – organisation – subunit (for example, department). As Elliot notes:

> This boundary can be drawn anywhere for the purpose of analysis. If the system one is studying is the whole organisation then the boundary is between the organisation and its environment; if the system being studied is the work group, then the boundary is between this group and the rest of the organisation, which in this case is its environment. (Elliot, 1980: 96)

An example of the latter is the concept of *socio-technical systems*, particularly associated with the work of Trist and the Tavistock Institute (Trist *et al.*, 1963). Primarily it is a way of identifying the key subsystems and the relations between them in the 'conversion' process. Three sub-systems are identified: technical, formal role structure and sentient (individual feelings or sentiments). Working broadly within the human relations problematic of integrating the formal/technical and informal/social dimensions of organisation, an additional twist is given by putting greater emphasis on the technological environment. This environment of the workgroup, in the form of equipment and layout, is seen as a basic constraint on the shape of work organisation. However it does not simply reflect the technology, as the organisation has independent social and psychological properties. Management's task is to create a socio-technical system in which the two dimensions are jointly optimised and mutually supportive. There is some choice at the organisational level, but there are defined limits established by the need for 'economic validity'.

Research support has been particularly associated with Trist and Bamforth's (1951) study of the mining industry. Traditional methods of 'hand-getting' the coal had involved limited technology, short coalfaces, high workgroup autonomy over the pace and distribution of work, and an egalitarian ethos. New 'long-wall' methods bore similarity to mass production, with work fragmentation and more specific job roles. Not surprisingly this led to lower work commitments, higher absenteeism and a host of other standard problems. The researchers' solution was to accept the technology and layout, but to vary the methods of work to a 'composite' approach, in which groups performed whole tasks, were paid collective bonuses and had a degree of self-regulation over job allocation. The results convinced them that management choice could be exercised in favour of methods that took greater care of socio-psychological needs, while accepting economic and technical constraints.

Interestingly, the mining study hardly utilised the wider environment in the analysis at all. Where the environment is mentioned, it is that of the 'seam society' immediately surrounding the workgroup. Most writers within the general approach treat the organisation itself as the system, and although the wider environment determines the general goals such as economic survival in a stimulus–response manner, the environment still tends to be defined in terms of the single unit of organisation. Attention is particularly given to achieving a proper balance of system parts. This would involve integration, co-ordination and differentiation of structures and processes, not just functions such as production or research, but activities of leadership, innovation and the like. It would be wrong to give the impression that these 'boundary exchanges' are characterised by smoothness. While the organisation generally adapts and finds equilibrium by responding to opportunities and risks in the environment, a central concept of open systems is that of uncertainty and related terms: stability, turbulence or indeterminacy. This uncertainty can arise in relations with the environment itself, through clashes with surrounding cultures, or rapidity of technological change, or internally in the organisation's members or sub-units. The interdependence of the system parts includes a measure of specialisation specifically to deal with this problem: 'we suggest that organisations cope with uncertainty by creating certain parts specifically to deal with it, specialising other parts in operating under conditions of certainty, or near certainty' (Thompson, 1967: 13).

Child (1984) identifies *variability* and *complexity* as key processes. 'Variability' refers to the difficulty of predicting changes and departures from previous conditions that will induce uncertainty. 'Complexity' is linked to the degree of diversity in organisational activities and the environments it is operating in. This may mean difficulty in gathering and monitoring information necessary for effective performance. Each organisation needs to design the structures or processes in a manner that reduces uncertainty or adapts to the degree of environmental stability. Aside from uncertainty, the other major factor shaping boundary exchanges is held to be *dependency*. Indeed these factors may be linked, for example when dependency takes an intra-organisational form, whereby the ability of sub-units to cope with uncertainty is shaped by the degree to which a sub-unit activities are central, substitutable, or when it relies on others (Hickson *et al.*, 1973). Outside the organisation, dependency is conditioned by the fact that the environment is a source of scarce resources that have to be competed for. Dependency is the reverse of power, 'As the resources increase or expand the organisation increases in power ... since other organisations become more dependent on the resources' (Clegg and Dunkerley, 1980: 381). These issues have stimulated the development of the *resource dependency* model (Aldrich and Pfeffer, 1976; Pfeffer, 1987), which in turn draws on broader *exchange theory* (Blau, 1964). In this model, emphasis is on the reduction of uncertainty by managing the network of interdependencies among organisations. Organisations exchange with each other and negotiate the environment, seeking to exert power over the nature and rate of exchange. The goal of each actor in the exchange is to reduce their dependency on the other and to force the 'partner' to become more dependent on them: 'Organisations tend to comply with the demands of those interests in their environment which have relatively more power' (Pfeffer, 1997: 63).

The concept of resource dependency becomes a way of understanding power relationships more generally, which we discuss in Chapter 9. But in terms of the environment, a classic case is the 'Just-in-Time' system pioneered in Japan. This is used to control the flow of stocks and materials between large corporations and suppliers in Japan. It works on the basis that small sub-contractors are flexible on the terms of their larger 'partners'. Toyota, for example, has traditionally relied on up to 35,000 small business, most of whom exist in a totally dependent relationship. Alternatively, firms may minimise dependency by seeking alternative sources. This can be seen in the 'world car' strategy pursued by Ford and GM. By co-ordinating design, production and marketing across national boundaries, companies can ensure that components can be acquired from a considerably larger number of locations.

There is a danger of constantly talking as if organisations were 'things' adapting to the environment. However, in practice, open systems theory gives a central role to *management* to maximise a bounded rationality – in other words, to predict and design appropriate structures and responses and to manipulate resources and sub-units effectively. This highlights the connection of environmental uncertainty and dependency to issues of *decision-making*, which has long been a significant aspect of research literature (March and Simon, 1958; Cyert and March, 1963). Because of unevenness in the informational, technological and other environmental conditions, and in internal power relations between sub-units, decision-makers frequently have to cope by forming *dominant coalitions* (Thompson, 1967). As a result, 'Organisational decision-making becomes much less a matter of unquestioned command or rational appraisal and much more a process of political bargaining and negotiation in which the exercise of power plays a key role' (Reed, 1986: 41–2). The positive aspect of this type of thinking is that it begins to see the organisation in a more pluralistic light, with some, albeit limited, recognition of power, bargaining and change processes. Given that dominant coalitions have to exert choice about alternative actions, it also qualifies the emphasis in systems theory to structures as a functional imperative arising from given environmental conditions (Child, 1972).

Contingency theory

The most noted application and extension of the open systems approach is grouped under the heading of 'contingency theory'. As Reed puts it:

> Eventually the theoretical developments taking place within the systems tradition culminated in a 'contingency theory' of organisation which attempted to specify the appropriate 'functional fit' between environmental settings and the internal organisational structures which they required. (Reed, 1986: 100)

In terms of the ideas discussed so far in the chapter, this does not sound very remarkable. Its appeal, however, is in part because of a powerful *normative* dimension in which the emphasis is on practical applications (Legge, 1978). A situational approach requires a 'reading' of the firm's environment by managers and their academic helpers. Furthermore it appealed because the 'if–then' formula constituted an explicit break with the 'one best way' orientation of existing theories, while retaining powerful guidelines for what power holders should actually do to sustain effective organisation. By the mid-1970s contingency theory was the dominant approach and had been applied to specifics such as payment systems as well as to general structures (Lupton and Gowler, 1969).

Curiously, as a theory, it rested primarily on research that took place largely prior to its own development. The most noted such work was that of Burns and Stalker (1961), who studied twenty firms in Scotland and England drawn mainly from the textile, engineering and electronics industries. Management systems and structures were classified according to a range of environments differentiated by degree of predictability and stability. They found that firms operating in an environment with relatively stable and predictable markets, and to a lesser extent technologies, such as those in textiles, tended to have what they called *mechanistic* systems. This broadly resembled bureaucratic models where there is centralised knowledge, clear hierarchy, task specialisation, vertical communication, and a general emphasis on formal structures, decision-making, values and rules. By contrast, in environments where there is more rapid change, uncertain markets, and complex technologies with a requirement for constant innovation, such as in electronics, a more *organic* system predominated which was less bound by traditional structures and roles. Instead, though structures remained within a general hierarchy, they utilised dispersed information centres, lateral communication, meritocratic and expert positioning, ethos and practices, and more flexible tasks and rules.

Rather than getting embroiled in arguments for and against bureaucracy or any structural arrangements, Burns and Stalker were able to argue that both systems were suitable and rational for specific market-led situations. Successful companies were precisely ones that had adapted their strengths to environmental requirements. They did recognise that they were discussing ideal types and that relationships were not rigid. Organisations facing changes in the environment may have to move along the spectrum or mix particular characteristics. Though normally noted less, Burns and Stalker also recognised constraints to changing structures away from mechanistic models, even where it was environmentally desirable. These arose particularly from entrenched interests and routines, consolidated through the operation of internal political systems (Wood, 1979: 353).

The American writers Lawrence and Lorsch (1967) extended this type of analysis by showing that it is wrong to treat firms as homogeneous structures. Sub-units are likely to have different environments and therefore require specific structures and management in order to be successful. As a result, a crucial problem for organisation is finding a balance of differentiation and integration. Their research was based on a smaller number of firms in plastics, food and containers. So, for example, whereas the research departments of the plastics companies operated in dynamic, innovative environments that were reflected in long-term orientations and the least bureaucratic arrangements, production had a stable, technical environment and was dominated by short-term concerns and more bureaucracy. Sales departments were somewhere in between. High-performing firms were those that not only manifested a high degree of differentiation of structures and goals, but had coped by developing adequate means of integration such as specialist teams with such responsibilities. Of course, those organisations where the sub-units do not have to vary significantly can be co-ordinated through conventional command structures. As with Burns and Stalker, the emphasis is not on which theoretical model is 'out of date' but on a continuum of models suited to alternative environments.

The final piece of notable contingency research by Woodward (1958; 1965) shifts the emphasis away from market environments to technology. She started the research as a means of testing traditional propositions popular in administrative theory such as relation between formal structures or size and performance. But in studies of around 100 firms in south-east Essex in the mid-1950s, no consistent correlations were found. Instead a relationship between 'technological complexity' and organisational structure was claimed. Technologies were grouped developmentally according to supposed complexity under a variety of broad categories; eventually reduced to unit and small batch production, large batch and mass production, and process production. Woodward commented: 'While at first sight there seemed to be no link between organisation and success, and no one best way of organising a factory, it subsequently became apparent that there was a particular form of organisation most appropriate to each technical situation' (quoted in M. Rose, 1975: 203).

Among the aspects of formal organisation found to have a direct association with the technical production system were length of line of command, the extent of the span of control of Chief Executives and of supervisors, and the ratio of managers and clerical workers to production personnel. Problems of running organisations with different technologies varied. Unit and process technologies were both found to have little bureaucracy and simple organisational structures based on line specialisation of basic task functions.

This is linked to the predominant problems of product development and marketing for such technologies, which put the emphasis on innovation. Woodward can be situated within a range of technological determinist writings popular in this period (Walker and Guest, 1952; Sayles, 1958; Blauner, 1964). As Michael Rose notes (1975: 202), such studies utilised fairly unsophisticated conceptions of technology as hardware and as the taken-for-granted physical aspect of production, with little or no recognition of social shaping or choice. In fact, there has been some disagreement over whether technology can be seen as part of an organisation's environment. As the dominant approaches have treated it as a factor 'out-there' determining the features of companies, it is perhaps justified to accept that it has to be discussed in that framework without accepting its theoretical rationale.

One of the attractions of the theory generally is that any contingency can be posited as the key to structural variation and business performance. Hence size is seen by some researchers such as the Aston Group (Pugh and Hickson, 1976) and Blau (1970) as the major factor. For the Aston researchers size was one of three primary contextual variables along with external dependency and technology. In turn, each predicts a series of structural variables: specialisation and standardisation, extent of concentration of authority, types of control over workflow. The Aston Group accepted the significance of technology in circumstances such as smaller companies or directly for production, but argued that increased size produced structural patterns based on impersonal control mechanisms, formal procedures, and higher numbers of administrative staff. Though there are associated problems, increased size also confers benefits through capacity to take advantage of specialisation. But the movement towards greater bureaucratisation is present in all three dimensions and it is a heavily deterministic logic where organisations 'have to adapt to adapt in particular ways to the contextual or environmental constraints which face them' (Reed, 1992: 137).

By the beginning of the 1970s, open systems theory had become dominant in organisational analysis. It had certainly displaced the 'romantic rationality' of human relations thinking with its emphasis on natural co-operation with a more hard-headed view that technology, structure and other system variables shaped human behaviour (Perrow, 1979). Despite its one-time dominance, 'contingency theory has since virtually faded from the research and managerial literature scene' (Pfeffer, 1997: 158). Pfeffer attributes this to deficiencies such as its overly complex explanatory structure, which is too disconnected from decision variables available for control in organisations. In contrast, Donaldson (1995) argues that there is a bias in current American organisation theory against seeing managers as positive and controlling agents. In an earlier work he mounted a strong defence of the research programme of which he was a part, while at the same time seeking to extend it. Design strategies are focused on the familiar territory of functional, divisional, area or mixed matrix structures. Strategy might appear to imply choice, but, 'The structure which is most appropriate for an organisation depends on the situational contingencies' (1985: 172). New formulas are developed such as the adoption of functional or divisional arrangements, which depend on the extent to which product or area diversity establishes degrees of interdependency. How much this kind of thinking involves real managerial choices is open to question, as we shall see later in the chapter. What is undoubtedly the case is that organisation–environment theories have moved towards non-contingent explanations based on 'purer' economic logic. Population ecology is a case in point.

Selection theories: the population ecology approach

The population ecology approach is a mainstream theory of organisation–environment relations that shifts the emphasis from adaptation to selection (Hannan and Freeman, 1977; Aldrich, 1979). In their seminal contribution, Hannan and Freeman do not deny that adaptation takes place, but argue that it is not primary and that there is limited evidence that 'the major features of the world of organisations arise through learning or adaptation' (1977: 957). In this sense the perspective is more pessimistic about managerial capacity to respond rationally to external shifts, or exercise control over events. Change comes about largely through new organisations rather than internal transformation.

There are substantial constraints to organisations changing in order to adapt to the environment. For example, failing churches do not become retail stores and vice versa. Such constraints are based mainly on structural inertia: this includes non-transferable investments in resources and people; information blockages; the type of internal political systems identified by Burns and Stalker; conservative organisational ideologies and normative systems; plus external constraints such as legal, fiscal and political barriers. The stronger the process, the more the logic of environmental selection is likely to predominate over adaptation. A further criticism is of the emphasis on the single organisation as a focus of analysis. Instead the appropriate unit of analysis is taken to be populations of organisations; theoretical abstractions relating to classes of organisation that share some common features in terms of their relations with the environment, such as being part of a particular product market.

What is this logic of environmental selection? Over a period of time, environments are held to select some organisations or classes of organisation for survival and others for extinction. Those that have survived are proof of a successful 'fit', or at least of outperforming rivals in given environmental conditions (Pfeffer, 1997: 163–9). As can be seen, the emphasis on natural selection involves borrowing, like systems theory, extensively from biology – transferring a Darwinian survival of the fittest to organisational life, with survival paths within each sector of competing firms. There is even a species analogue for organisations; blueprints which consist of rules and procedures inferred from formal structures, patterns of activity and normative orders, for transforming inputs into outputs (Hannan and Freeman, 1977: 934–5). One 'law' is that of requisite variety; organisations need to be as complex as their environment. If they are less complex they are not likely to be adaptable enough. But over-complexity would probably mean that too much slack is being carried: 'populations of organisational forms will be selected for or against depending on the amount of excess capacity they maintain and how they allocate it' (Hannan and Freeman, 1977: 949). Furthermore the environment is an ecological system populated by sufficient organisations to allow for selection. The full process involves three stages: first are planned or unplanned *variations,* from which appropriate structures or behaviours are drawn; second, natural *selection* eliminates undesirable variations; and third is a *retention* mechanism that ensures the reproduction of those variations that have been positively selected.

The borrowings do not stop at biology, but draw from neo-classical or free-market economics. Perfect market competition tends to underlie the 'rationality' of natural selection: 'Organisational rationality and environmental rationality may coincide in the instance of firms in competitive markets. In this case, the optimal behaviour of each firm is to maximise profit, and the rule used by the environment (market in this case) is to select out profit maximisers' (Hannan and Freeman, 1977: 940). These 'natural laws' are shaped by the kind of competitive struggle over limited resources identified by the resource dependency school. Competition also produces a crucial process for population ecology theory, that of *isomorphism*. When equilibrium conditions obtain, the structural features of organisations – for example, the appropriate degree of specialism or generalism – will correspond to the relevant features of the resource environment. Those organisations that fail will be selected against, though organisations can also purposefully adapt. Of course equilibrium models can be too simplistic. To help deal with this the concept of *niche* width is used. A niche consists of the combinations of resource levels at which the population of organisations can survive and reproduce themselves. It is difficult for new organisations to enter already-filled niches where they cannot compete with existing social and economic resources. In fact there is a curvilinear effect whereby competition increases as densities get higher, with mortality rates eventually rising as founding rates fall (Hannan and Carroll, 1992; Hannan *et al.*, 1995).

Despite the use of some sophisticated historical models to handle data, population ecology analysis frequently remains at a highly abstract level. Hannan and Freeman admit to a frustration with the level of empirical information (1977: 959), a problem that arises partly from the choice not to focus on particular organisations, but on populations over long periods (Clegg and Dunkerley, 1977: 376). But the problems also derive from the theory as well as the method. As Perrow (1979) argues, ecological perspectives are attractive to some theorists because behaviour and events can be interpreted as natural. Evolution through natural selection gives the impression that patterns of activity that serve society are maintained, while those that are dysfunctional fortuitously disappear. Though contingency theories generally allow more scope for individual actors to learn rationally from processes of adaptation, the remarkable thing is not the distinctiveness of population ecology but how much it has in common with adaptation approaches. Hannan and Freeman (1977: 929) admit that processes involving selection can usually be recast at a higher level of analysis as adaptation processes. We are still in the world of 'best fits', with organisations responding to environments. As a theory of organisations, population ecology has had its own density problems, largely failing to be selected as the dominant theory against competing paradigms, at least outside its North American niches. Advocates have turned to combining it with institutional theory (Carroll and Hannan, 2000) or co-opting insights and findings from a variety of approaches in search of a unified, broader evolutionary perspective (Aldrich and Ruef, 2006).

Critique 1: the role of strategic choice

It would be foolish not to recognise that mainstream research on organisation–environment relations has generated some useful knowledge of structural differentiation within and between organisations. The best of it, drawing on perspectives such as resource dependency, has introduced issues of bargaining and power partially on to the agenda. The appeal to 'practitioners', particularly of contingency theory, can be located in the more realistic clarification and yet expansion of managerial role and of organisational success. Indeed at one level the general argument is correct. Clearly organisations do face environmental constraints and often need to adapt to new markets or technologies to survive. For some people, the 'if-then' formula became difficult if not impossible to criticise precisely because it was based on a 'horses for courses' argument. Wood notes: 'Thus ironically an approach which began by dismissing previous work as "panaceas" became itself the new panacea, the "situational approach to management"' (1979: 336).

Contingency theory and wider adaptation and selection perspectives have, however, rightly been criticised for their *environmental determinism*. Environments are not only given determinate power, as in all systems theory, but they are literally reified through the language of environments acting on passive organisations. Somehow managerial actions to change work rules, create dual internal labour markets or hire temporary workers instead of full-timers can be elevated to a principle of natural selection which rewards flexible organisational forms (Aldrich and Stabler, 1987). Perrow notes that such reification makes it difficult to for workers to say 'I was fired by the environment', adding that:

> the new model of organisation–environment relations tends to be a mystifying one, removing much of the power, conflict, disruption, and social class variables from the analysis of social processes. It neglects the fact that our world is in large part made by particular men and women with particular

CULTURE, COMPANIES AND COUNTRIES IN A GLOBALISING ERA ▪ MANAGEMENT ▪ CONTROL AND RESISTANCE ▪ POWER IN ORGANISATIONS ▪ GENDER, SEXUALITY AND ORGANISATIONS ▪ CORPORATIONS AND CULTURE: REINVENTING ORGANISATION MAN?

5   63

As Pfeffer (1997: 163) observes, even organisational mortality may not reflect poor performance, but instead, a choice by successful businesses to sell while the going is good. This neglect of choice is at the heart of the general critique that can be made of the approaches discussed so far. The starting point of such critiques has often been John Child's (1972; 1997) influential concept of *strategic choice*. Strategic choice can operate with reference to the context of the enterprise, performance standards or organisational design. Most emphasis is, however, given to restoring the significance of the internal environment and particularly the degree of discretion available to power holders and decision-makers within the dominant coalitions identified earlier. Contingency and other mainstream perspectives neglect the role of policy formulation and intervention, or see it only in terms of adaptation to the environment. One of the crucial factors this ignores is the existence of multiple contingencies that affect the capacity to achieve internally consistent responses and any potential correlation between structure and performance. There is sufficient 'slack' in most organisation's position and resources to allow different strategies to be considered and pursued, without incurring performance penalties or diseconomies.

The conceptual schema used by John Child allows for important breaks with determinism compatible with a radical analysis. He explicitly distances himself (1972: 6) from technological determinism by stressing the role of decisions relating to control of work. The empirical evidence in this area has been provided in studies from a labour process perspective, including path-breaking contributions from Noble (1979) and Wilkinson (1983a). We will examine this perspective in more detail in Chapter 8 and in Part III. This research allows us to focus on the neglected issue of choice of technology itself, in this case the development of numerical control in engineering that allowed management to replace the direct input of craft workers by tapes and later computers that were externally programmed. Both case studies show that alternative technologies for automating machine tools existed which allowed manual data input that retained operator skills. This was passed over in part because management preferred a system that enabled it to transfer skill from shop floor to programming office and shift authority and control. A more recent example that illustrates the same point is the development of teamwork in manufacturing environments. Used primarily to facilitate labour flexibility and continuous improvement (see Chapters 12, 13 and 20), as a form of social organisation teams have often been introduced without altering the assembly or continuous process technology. In addition, the degree of self-governance given to or taken by teams means that different ways of working can coexist side by side across different lines, as research from the whisky bottling halls demonstrates (Findlay *et al.*, 2000b).

At a wider level, Child's analysis moves beyond the dominance of technical criteria in organisational practices, 'recognising the operation of an essentially political process in which constraints and opportunities are functions of the power exercised by decision-makers in the light of ideological values' (1972: 22). Systems theory utilises an organicist perspective that assumes equilibrium and interdependence. For example, like their human relations predecessors, the Tavistock writers adopt a unitary and socially harmonious view of the enterprise, taking for granted that the primary task is shared by all. It is also consistent with that tradition in taking technical and formal structures for granted, the difference lying in the language of management choice rather than worker adjustment. As Rose notes, once the above constraints have been accepted, even that choice is within strictly determined managerial limits, and 'the socio-technical systems concept may be seen as a device for helping production engineers to discover better "best ways"' (M. Rose, 1975: 216). For Trist and his associates, workers' choices are seen as non-existent in the face of a determinate environment. Resistance to management plans run up against 'uncontrollable forces in the external environment' (quoted in Rose, 1975: 216).

In this light, Child's early work is valuable, but how far does it take us? Certainly too far for Donaldson, who criticises his work for accommodating to the 'critical camp' by emphasising the politics of organisational action. Strategic choice theory is thus counter-productive because 'Study of effective structure requires concern for functional imperatives or systems needs' (1985: 147). Ambiguity is the enemy of design knowledge. For example, if contingencies are variables that specify appropriate structure for high performance, talk of multiple contingencies that can affect a variable makes it impossible to unambiguously specify the right structure for high performance (1985: 144).

Yet there is a good deal of ambiguity as to whether Child's work has sought to modify or supplement contingency and systems theory, or significantly depart from it. Wood notes: 'Put simply, he is arguing theoretically for the inclusion of managerial ideology as an intervening variable between the environment and organisational design' (1979: 350). At this stage, Child tended to consider strategic choice only as a variable and within management terms. Options that involve contesting existing power relations are made largely redundant. As Whittington (1988: 532–3) argues, property rights and structures of class, gender and ethnicity endow a limited circle of actors with command over resources to make strategic choices. Furthermore we need to break from the idea that environments produce situational imperatives, or from the population ecology equivalent that environments can only select out a specifically appropriate form. Child's later work (Child and Smith, 1987) from a 'firm-in-sector' perspective recognises that changes are primarily triggered by markets, but choices still remain and new strategies require an intellectual or cognitive reframing among management.

Conceptions of strategic choice have been deepened, modified and qualified within further research. Purcell (1991) has usefully distinguished between choices at different levels of decision-making. First- and second-order decisions about purpose and form respectively are 'upstream', while 'downstream' decisions are third-order and refer mainly to functional activities, including employment relations. The latter are likely to be constrained by the former, as is shown in subsequent research. Kessler, Purcell and Shapiro (2000) examine the expanded discretion in the sphere of personnel practices available to public sector organisations in the UK. While some new third-order variations were found, discretion continues to be constrained by powerful external pressures from state policies and first-order, upstream decisions on mission, purpose and structure.

Research influenced by labour process theory has also extended our understanding, primarily by situating choice within the constraints and characteristics of the capital–labour relationship. Early contributions on managerial control strategy (Friedman, 1977; Burawoy, 1979; R. Edwards, 1979) established an analytical framework. Child in his later work (1984: 231) refers in detail to Friedman's ideas of strategies of direct control and responsible autonomy. Direct control corresponds broadly to the scientific management tradition of close supervision, minimal responsibility and treating workers as machines. In contrast, responsible autonomy is mindful of the negative effects of worker resistance and the potentially positive gains from worker co-operation and involvement. Hence the stress on enlarged responsibilities and status, lighter controls, greater security and sometimes enriched jobs. These are not abstract choices. Responsible autonomy is more applicable to well-organised workers with controls over external or internal labour markets, who therefore need to be treated as central or core. Workers who are poorly organised, less skilled, and working for companies in highly competitive product markets are more likely to be directly controlled and treated as peripheral. This distinction, however, is too crude and does not fit all sectors.

For Child, Friedman's analysis appears to confirm the relevance of managerial choices within market environments. But this neglects the wider nature of radical explanations. No matter how strategies are described, and Friedman is only one variant, they are shaped not just by markets, but by the capital–labour relation itself. Management is caught in the contradiction of needing to exert control and authority over labour to secure profitability in competitive conditions, while requiring workers to be motivated and co-operative. These contradictions are also conditioned by the general dynamics of capitalist production, either in a particular sector or in the economy as a whole. The development of monopolies within capitalism can enable large firms with power over markets and access to 'scientific' planning and management to experiment without being under undue pressure for short-term profits. We explore this further in the next section.

Critique 2: enacted environments and the power of large corporations

Many corporate 'strategies' put adaptation to the environment in reverse. Take the example of the choices open to management over the nature and sources of labour. Labour markets are clearly part of the organisational environment and decisions about who to recruit are important ones. Employers may not always have much discretion, but the basic criteria of controlled costs, stability and minimisation of risk has been well documented (R. Jenkins, 1982). Hence employers may look for workers with characteristics such as family men with commitments, as at Ford (Beynon, 1975), or draw on informal Protestant family networks in Northern Ireland telecommunications plants (Maguire, 1986). In the former case the company hopes that mortgage and other responsibilities will mean financial dependence and unwillingness to strike, while in the latter employment of people from the same family can increase a sense of social obligation and act as a social control over behaviour such as absenteeism. But a more significant choice is over the *location* of a workplace. Radical labour market theorists (Garnsey, Rubery, Wilkinson, 1985) rightly regard the firm as a social organisation acting collectively. In locating a plant to utilise a specific form of labour, it is segmenting the market, though such effects can also occur when employees seek to build 'shelters' round their own jobs (Freedman, 1984).

There is plenty of evidence to show that large companies have often made their location decisions with specific cheap or controllable labour sources or stable industrial relations in mind (Whitaker, 1986). When GM finally chose Spring Hill, a small town outside Nashville, Tennessee, for its Saturn plant, it was the end of a process that began with a public specification of decision criteria. The subsequent beauty contest had 38 out of 50 states offering a total of 1000 sites that would be created to the requirements (Meyer, 1986: 78). Tennessee has laws outlawing union closed shops. Locating new plants in small towns has been an increasing policy of GM, with the effect that the company *becomes* the environment. The recent huge growth of outsourcing of clerical and service jobs to countries such as India shows that the process is not confined to manufacturing (Taylor and Bain, 2006).

Recruitment and location policies are examples of the power of organisations to *enact* environments. Perrow makes a related criticism of population ecology theory. He argues that to begin with the question, 'why are there so many kinds of organisation?' is to ignore reality. When we are dealing with the big corporations such as the motor giants, it is simply not the case that there is evidence of significant differences. Furthermore, the large firms very seldom die and they dominate the environment of the host of small organisations around them, as we see in the example of the Japanese 'just-in-time' system (see Chapter 15). Perrow (1979: 243) concludes, 'If there is little variation, and little negative selection, then, what is the value of the theory?'

This capacity to set limits to environments was a sub-theme of Child, who drew on Galbraith's (1967) analysis of the 'new industrial state' to argue that any significant countervailing powers to big business had broken down (1969: 54). This stands in sharp contrast to the complacency of conventional open systems theory (Thompson, J. D. and McEwan, 1973: 158), which only conceives of organisations dominating their environment in extreme circumstances, which in turn will generate the countervailing powers dismissed by Galbraith.

Child also sees his own insights as indebted to the work of the business historian Chandler (1962; 1977) on strategy, previously discussed in Chapter 3. Chandler showed how a new multidivisional structure was created as a strategic response to short- and long-term market trends, and technological innovations. The refashioned structures allowed for an improved internal division of labour and resource allocation based mainly on the separation of longer-term strategic planning from operational decisions and practices. A decentralist strategy established market-type conditions within firms. There are parallels between these strategies and more contemporary attempts to extend markets within firms by creating quasi-independent profit centres which have to compete with one another and treat everyone else as customers. In addition, Williamson's related transaction-cost analysis also shows that the thrust of emergent giant corporations was to intervene in and shape economic environments in circumstances where the growth of managerial power in large corporations coincided with the declining influence of the market.

However, there are limitations to how far these frameworks substantially rework conceptions of organisation–environment relations. For Chandler, though the focus is on strategy and the 'visible hand' of management, the extent to which it can incorporate real choice is open to question. The emphasis on the superiority of the multidivisional firm as a form of adaptation to new market and technological imperatives strongly resembles contingency theories. Nor does Williamson's 'transaction costs' theory allow for much diversity. The problem arises from treating the growth of firms through internalisation of the costs of transactions in an unproblematic way. As Granovetter observes, there is an implicit functionalism in the argument that 'whatever organisational form is most efficient will be the one observed' (1985: 503). It is true that firms do seek to internalise costs and for some of the reasons mentioned – environmental uncertainty and bounded rationality. But efficiency may not be the driving force or outcome. For example, if we take research on mergers and acquisitions (see Thompson, Wallace and Flecker, 1992), it would be foolish to believe that every organisation taken out of the market is less efficient or that the newly created combination is more so. Firms take over others often because their control over resources gives them the capacity to dominate their environment, including other firms. This may literally be 'the environment' in the case of biotechnology companies. For example, in the 1990s Monsanto acquired Holden's Foundation Seeds for $1.2 billion, gaining them a 35 per cent share of the corn acreage in the US. It also holds a 40 per cent share in a second major seed company, DeKalb, and then acquired Asgrow, a leading soybean company, plus Agracteus and Calgene, two high-profile agricultural biotech firms (Rifkin, 1999). Such vertical integration allows a high degree of control over the production and consumption of scientific knowledge.

This inability to analyse the power resources available to the various parties in transactions is something we will return to in the next chapter. More realistic analyses do have that orientation. Teulings notes that 'large corporations do not comply with the laws of every market, but rather the other way round' (1986: 146). An organisation with a monopoly or semi-monopoly position can, for instance, create a product market through its own sales policies; or displace parts of its costs on to the environment, as with unchecked industrial pollution. The 2000 US court judgment against Microsoft confirmed exactly the former point. Equally, it would be wrong to believe that each member of a 'population' contributes equally to competition within an ecological niche (Baum, 1995). To return to the example of mergers; such processes increasingly create environments to which other organisations and sections of the community have to adapt. For example there has been a tremendous concentration of media resources through mergers and takeovers such as those initiated in many countries by Rupert Murdoch or Bill Gates. As Schiller comments with respect to the Internet, 'Smaller companies that specialised in what were initially niche markets at the frontier of the liberalisation process worked the new territory. When they succeeded, major traditional suppliers either snapped them up or rushed to develop similar applications of their own' (1999: 28). A pertinent instance is the merger of the world's biggest online service provider, AOL, and one of the biggest media conglomerates, Time Warner to produce Time Warner Inc. As with other media vertical integrations, such a deal linked a content provider with a new form of outlet. AOL's more than 23 million subscribers are a captive market for Time Warner's products. The outcomes not only create a new business conglomerate – whose subsidiaries also include CNN, HBO and Turner Broadcasting System – but give enhanced power to shape cultural and political environments, and the ideological climate of a whole society. Staying on the media terrain, a highly relevant example is the concentration of purchasing power in a tiny number of booksellers. In the UK, since various acquisitions Waterstones has been able to use discounting, product placement and other mass marketing techniques to heavily influence who publishers publish and at what price. Similar trends are present in the USA (Miller, 2006).

A major theme to come out of this discussion is the need to take large firms seriously as economic actors in their own right (Whitley, 1987; Ackroyd, 2002). Though there are a variety of competing options or rationalities within organisations, the subsequent actions frequently constitute market environments more than they are constituted by them. Indeed, as Bakan (2004) shows in his book and film, *The Corporation*, companies are not only required under Anglo-American law to pursue whatever is in the interests of its shareholders without regard to any wider obligations, they are also 'externalising machines'. In other words, it is 'more profitable to the extent that it can make other people pay the bills for its impact on society' (Charles Kernaghan quoted in Bakan, 2004: 70). The trend over the last couple of decades to deregulate business activities and to allow more of what was traditionally the public sphere (prisons, hospitals, schools, airports) to be privatised has only accelerated the remaking of society in the image of the market.

The most obvious case of the capacity to control and change environments is that of the *transnational company* (TNC). The scale of their activities usually leads to considerable impact on national economies (Dicken, 2007). The issue is less whether the TNCs are willing to adapt to the environment in the form of national conditions, than how they contribute to changes in those societal institutions. Increasingly TNCs can call on resources and structures that are superior to many nation states. For example, with sales of $245bn in 2002 (and over four thousand supplier plants in China alone), Walmart is bigger than all but thirty of the world's largest economies (Lawrence, 2004). Such power is further enhanced by changing corporate forms, with a gradual shift from structures based on centre–periphery relations, to global firms that have 'foreign-based units with group-wide functions in management, manufacturing, marketing and/or research and development' (Forsgren, 1990: 9). One of the crucial powers is mobility of capital across national and international boundaries, enabling an evasion of laws on taxes and profits in a particular country. Markets can be shaped and their ebbs and flows ridden by cross-subsidisation and transfer pricing of goods, services, technology and loans between related activities in a TNC's global structure. To return to the example of the Murdoch media empire, cross-subsidisation allowed the price of *The Times* to be drastically cut to drive competitors out of the market, to the extent that News International was taking a loss of 80p on each copy sold of the Saturday paper. Domination of a product market can reduce dependence on external sources of finance. Clairmonte and Cavanagh (1981) illustrate the process with reference to textile transnationals, adding the point that those in oligopolistic positions can act as price makers, thus subordinating markets through cartels and other mechanisms. This has led many countries, such as Sri Lanka and Malaysia, to create a 'friendly' environment in the form of Export Processing Zones in order to attract foreign capital. They offered virtual freedom of operations, cheap labour, bans on unions, and maximum repatriation of profits (Mitter, 1986).

Such dependency has gathered momentum in more recent times, but is not inevitable. In 1998 representatives of the world's 29 richest nations gathered in Paris to put the finishing touches to an accord devised by the OECD (Organisation for Economic Cooperation and Development) to create a level playing field for international investors.

> It amounts to a new set of investment rules that would grant corporations the right to buy, sell and move their operations wherever they wish around the world, without government regulation. It will acknowledge for the first time that corporate capital now has more authority and freedom to act than mere national and local governments. (D. Rowan, 'Meet the New World Government', *Guardian*, 13 February 1998)

However, such was the adverse reaction from civil society organisations and some governments that negotiations were eventually scrapped. The hidden factor constraining business from enacting environments is *legitimacy*. Consumers, citizens and employees have, to an extent, to be persuaded that corporate actions are acceptable. With growing concern about the environment and the costs of globalisation, the sudden rise of anxiety about corporate social responsibility in boardrooms is a sure indication that this is one battle that business knows it has not yet won.

Summary and key points

That businesses are more likely to survive and prosper if they adapt to their environments seems to be common sense. And at one level, it is. Certainly there are few defenders of the old closed systems view. However, we have argued in this chapter for a richer, more complex and more reciprocal view of organisation–environment relations than represented in mainstream open systems and contingency literatures. Such writings focus too much on the narrower frame of technology and product markets, at the expense both of political economy and broader cultural contexts. Neither adaptation nor natural selection perspectives capture the ways in which organisations are constantly making and being made by the economic, social and political institutions around them. How many choices, at what level, and who is making them, are empirical questions influenced by factors such as the different sectors firms are embedded within contexts and the power resources available to key economic actors. The chapter focused on two key concepts – strategic choice and enacted environments – to counter the environmental determinism of mainstream perspectives. While these two critiques proceed from quite different starting points (the former a micro-frame, that latter a macro-focus), they share an emphasis on corporations as powerful economic actors. Yet power is not an inherent property of size and structure. Corporations are powerful, in part, because the political, legal and economic systems they are part of enable them to be. The trend, sometimes captured in the term neo-liberal governance oriented towards free markets, has been to empower corporations. But ideologies and interests change and after all, it's a big planet and there are variations in the nature or environments and the organisations that populate them. These questions can be re-addressed and further illuminated in the global arena. It is to this that we turn in the next chapter.

Further reading

This chapter covers a lot of standard literature and research on which there is little fresh to say. Perrow and Pfeffer's books provide lively and informative commentaries. Child has a useful look back at strategic choice in a 1997 journal article. Donaldson presents his trenchant defences of systems/contingency approaches in a variety of formats. Finally, Barkan's best-selling book on *The Corporation* is not only a good read, but scholarly too.

Barkan, J. (2004) *The Corporation*, London: Constable. (and see http://reclaimdemocracy.org/media_resources.html for more critical resources on corporations).

Child, J. (1997) 'Strategic Choice in the Analysis of Action, Structure, Organizations and Environment: Retrospect and Prospect', *Organization Studies*, 18. 1: 43–76.

Donaldson, L. (2001) *The Contingency Theory of Organizations*, Thousand Oaks, California: Sage.

Donaldson, L. (2003) 'Organizational Theory as a Positive Science', in H. Tsoukas and C. Knudsen (eds), *The Oxford Handbook of Organization Theory: Meta-theoretical Perspectives*, Oxford: Oxford University Press.

Perrow, C. (1986) *Complex Organizations: A Critical Essay* (3rd edn), Glenview, Ill.: Scott Foresman.

Pfeffer, J. (1997) *New Directions for Organisational Theory: Problems and Practices*, Oxford: Oxford University Press.

6 culture, companies and countries in a globalising era

Given that much popular business writing treats managers as free agents able to act in ways constrained only by their own imaginations, it is useful to be reminded of external boundaries and constraints (Morishima, 1995). However, we have argued that even when taking account of the outside world, much orthodox theory does so in an economically and technologically deterministic way. That is, it tends towards single-track notions of efficiency that can be embodied only in specific design configurations between environmental variables (product markets, technologies) and organisational structures. The environment either rules or has rules for successful adaptation and selection. Strategic choice and notions of enacted environments bend the stick back in the other direction, but we need to take the discussion further, particularly in a context of debates about the extended reach of globalisation.

The aims of this chapter are to:

- Expand the scope of discussions of organisation–environment relations by considering how companies and countries are being shaped by and are shaping the new global political economy;
- Set out the nature and limitations of both universal, 'one best way' models of organisation and management and those based on the primacy of national cultures, such as Hofstede's influential writings;
- Explore how organisational analysis is responding to more complex environments through an examination of institutional theories and variety of capitalism models that see the firm as embedded in networks of relationships that have different configurations across societies;
- Give a sympathetic exposition to the systems, society and dominance model as the most effective way of understanding the complex interplay of capitalist political economy, international 'best practices' and the continuing role of national states and employment systems.

Comparative analysis: beyond the American model

It is important for organisational analysis to be comparative, to have the tools to explain patterns of difference and similarity, convergence and divergence. We have already, in previous chapters, pointed to a number of sources of variation in the way in which management theories and organisational forms developed across and within various units – sectors, countries, companies – shaped by the requirements of cultural and other forms of adaptation and pressures from key actors. However, this framework still tends to assume models that arise and are adapted to at given stages along a single line of development. Chandler's account of the rise of the 'modern' integrated business enterprise can be used to illustrate the general argument. He does give a historically-informed explanation of the emergence of the phenomenon. In general terms the US was a seedbed for managerial capitalism primarily because of the size and the nature of the domestic market (Chandler, 1977: 498–500). It was not only faster growing than other nations, but also more open and less class-divided. This encouraged the techniques and technologies of mass production and distribution.

In contrast, domestic markets in Western Europe were smaller and had slower growth. This limited the same kind of developments and kept greater reliance on middlemen to handle goods. Even where integrated enterprises did appear, they often remained small enough to be dominated by owner-managers. This kind of reasoning allows Chandler to evaluate other national experiences against this standard. British entrepreneurs are said to have failed to invest in manufacturing, marketing and management in key capital-intensive industries. As a consequence this 'personal capitalism', dependent on atomistic economic organisation such as the single-plant family firms in industries such as cotton and steel, was a pale version of its US counterpart: 'neglecting investment in administrative capabilities and research, dogged by short-termism, preoccupied with family and personal management, prejudiced against salaried managers, determined to ensure a steady income stream rather than to maximise growth and profits in the long run' (Supple, 1991: 511).

This account of stunted organisational capabilities makes an attractive link to *institutionalist* explanations for Britain's declining economic performance. Such a framework points to factors that shaped industrial development: entrenched employee job controls; the separation of the banking system from finance of industry; and educational provision that failed to produce adequately trained managerial and technical staff. As a result, managerial structures and expertise were underdeveloped and 'the British only adapted patchwork improvements to their existing organisational and productive structure' (Elbaum and Lazonick, 1986: 7). Echoes of such explanations can be found more recently in critics of short-termism and institutional failure in Britain's political economy, such as Will Hutton's (1992) influential work. But the remit is much broader than Chandler's 'internal history' of business enterprise. In emphasising the role of educational, state, legal and other institutions, such writers can demonstrate variations in industrial development.

It can also be argued that given the similarities between Britain and America's financial and industrial systems, Chandler's model of management and enterprise is even less likely to apply to other European countries. Modern American, or perhaps Anglo-Saxon, conceptions of management are built on assumptions of the superiority of a *general science* of co-ordination and control, a profession of management above particular specialisms and functions (Fores, Glover and Lawrence, 1992). In comparison, the Franco-German tradition draws on quite different sources. For example, Rueschemeyer (1986) notes the significance of public administration as a bureaucratic model for private enterprise in Germany, while the French state has developed vocationally-oriented higher education to produce generations of technocrats for the private and public sector. Germany and a number of other countries also have a tradition of engineering-based technical competence as the base for industrial progress. On the HRM terrain, there are different approaches to HRM in the US and Europe, shaped by different intellectual influences and by the fact that in the latter many aspects of the employment contract are decided outside corporate boundaries.

If the form and content of organisational structures and practices are socially constructed, Supple's comments on Chandler have more general application: 'What his assumptions make it difficult to do, however, is to generalise his results to a rounded and substantial exploration of the interrelationships and evolution of economic systems generally' (1991: 510). Our view is that socially constructed organisational diversities are the proper object of analysis for organisational theory. This is not a minor point. Measuring organisations and change against a single, linear standard rears its misleading head again later, this time with Japanese management replacing the American model. But this is leaping ahead of the story. One of the most influential challenges to the standard Anglo-Saxon textbook view of management and organisation has come from Hofstede and other cultural relativists.

The rise (and fall) of cultural explanations

Contingency theory, discussed in the previous chapter, was one critical response to the idea of universal principles of management. Hofstede's promotion of the cultural relativity of organisational practices and theories has perhaps been the other most prominent response. Whereas contingency research emphasised factors such as product markets and technologies, he argued that universal principles could not exist regardless of *national* environments. The accumulation of evidence about different cultures and trajectories of socio-economic development meant that by the 1970s:

> " It slowly became clear that national and even regional cultures do matter for management. The national and regional differences are not disappearing. They are here to stay. In fact these differences may become one of the most crucial problems for management – in particular for the management of multicultural, multinational organisations, whether public or private. (Hofstede, 1990: 392)

Despite the reference to regional factors, in Hofstede's work culture is firmly equated with *nationality*. Nationality has central symbolic value to citizens, creating shared ideas, values and meanings transmitted through family and community. Such social conditioning becomes embedded in, 'an invisible set of mental programmes which belongs to these countries' national cultures' (Hofstede, 1990: 393). In turn, this programming predisposes individuals to act in particular ways and is reinforced by becoming crystallised in institutions such as legal systems, industrial relations and religious organisations. National character and national culture are treated as indivisible. To operationalise these assumptions, Hofstede had to identify a common conceptual currency that could map national cultures and then find a way of collecting data about them. The latter was done on the back of his work as a psychologist for IBM between 1967 and 1971. He was able to collect data through questionnaires to employees in IBM's many multinational units. The findings appeared to demonstrate 'remarkable and stable' differences between countries. There were differences in the mental programming of individuals, but an 'average' pattern of beliefs and values was identified. This and related studies have had a huge impact on scholars and practitioners (see Søndergaard, 1994).

The conceptual framework utilises a four-dimensional model for national cultures:

- *Power distance* This combines societal attitudes based on the extent to which inequalities of various kinds are tolerated, and an intra-organisational dimension related to the degrees of centralisation of authority and autocratic leadership.
- *Individualism–collectivism* Societies will vary according to how loosely or tightly social norms bind individuals into group membership. Collectivist nations are ones that require individuals to subordinate self-interest.
- *Uncertainty avoidance* There is a certain amount of ambiguity and risk in any complex society. Some societies encourage individuals to tolerate high levels of uncertainty, others create institutions to maximise security and avoid risk. Technology, laws and religion can all play a role in defining the extent and character of risk toleration.
- *Masculinity–femininity* This corresponds to the well-known distinction between tough- and tender-minded. This is said to be the outcome of the degree to which a society seeks to maximise or minimise

the 'natural' division of sex roles between men and women. Masculine societies promote performance, achievement, 'big is beautiful'; feminine ones encourage quality of life, relationships and protection of the environment.

These dimensions are also held to intersect. For example, collectivist countries 'always' have large power distances. On the basis of responses to his questionnaires, Hofstede then plots where countries fall on large/strong, small/weak indexes and sometimes relates this to other factors such as gross national product. In this sense, he is doing more than description. There is an implicit normative dimension. When discussing individualism–collectivism, it is stated that wealthy countries are more individualist and poor countries collectivist. Amongst the former are the US, Britain and Sweden; the latter include Taiwan, Pakistan and Korea, with Japan, Austria and Spain in the middle. Other results show that all Latin countries are in a strong uncertainty avoidance/large power distance cluster, along with Japan and Korea. In contrast a small power distance/weak avoidance cluster includes the Netherlands, US, Britain and Sweden. Meanwhile the most masculine are Japan and the German-speaking, the most feminine the Nordic and the Netherlands.

On the basis of these results, Hofstede draws some lessons for management theory and practice. In their own terms they are fairly logical. Leadership in a collectivist society will tend towards the group rather than the individual. If there is low power distance, schemes for employee participation will flourish. Self-actualisation will be more of a motivator in highly individualistic societies such as the US than in those where keeping 'face' within group relationships is a prime social requirement. However, a range of methodological problems has been identified, notably drawing strong generalisations from small samples, taken at a particular time in a specific context that may have changed. Indeed these and other criticisms focusing on the validity of the IBM sample and reliability of results taken solely from attitude surveys have been frequently aired (Kieser, 1993; Søndergaard, 1994; McSweeney, 2003).

While the study was undoubtedly methodologically flawed, it is unhelpful to base a critique too much on those factors. For it is perfectly possible to use a different methodology and come up with the same kind of arguments. The best-known example is the work of Hampden-Turner and Trompenaars (1993). Their best-selling management books use a more sensitive device: scenarios containing ethical and practical dilemmas that have been put to over 15,000 managers at their own multinational seminars. On this basis they identify patterns of responses that reflect different systems of values concerning wealth creation. Seven cultures of capitalism are discussed based on national cultures, including the US, Britain, Japan and Germany. As in Hofstede, there is an underlying critique of an 'American model', in this case because it is failing to respond to new forms of competition from rival cultures. Some of the value dimensions are different, such as universalism versus particularism and analysing versus integrating, while others – including individualism versus communitarianism, equality versus hierarchy – are much the same. The underlying argument also remains similar to Hofstede. Every culture is held to have a tacit dimension rooted in a subconscious set of beliefs that form the bedrock of national identity. These beliefs are the 'invisible hand that regulates economic activity' (Hampden-Turner and Trompenaars, 1993: 4).

Examples of the relationships between such beliefs and practices include the outcomes of American and British preference for universalism, analysing and individualism; in other words for generalisable rules and laws, and for breaking down phenomena into calculable parts. This is then linked to the development of scientific management and bureaucracy, the dominance of the finance function and conglomerate forms of ownership, obsession with short-term performance, high levels of bankruptcies and astronomical salaries. As for the underlying normative message, the two perspectives partly diverge.

Hofstede's 'different is best' outlook is replicated by Hampden-Turner and Trompenaars' view that future economic success depends on understanding trading partners. At the same time success also involves managing these value tensions: 'economic success will accrue to the cultures which do the best job balancing the scale' (Hampden-Turner and Trompenaars, 1993: 10).

It is not difficult to see the basis of the appeal of cultural relativism. It trades on recognisable, if somewhat stereotypical, national characteristics. Normatively the approach has obvious and useful applications in terms of training to make managers more sensitive to trading partners and to local cultural conditions. Other studies have provided valuable cultural commentaries, such as Lockett (1988) on understanding the characteristics of Chinese management. Limits to theories that promote some form of universal human essence, such as Maslow's hierarchy of needs, are helpfully exposed. The progressive intent, notably to question the transferability of textbook (read US) models to circumstances, such as former Communist countries, is admirable: 'what counts is only that a country is managed according to the value systems of its people' (Hofstede and Søndergaard, 1993: 3).

Unfortunately such benefits come at a price, for there remains a massive credibility gap. By locating attitudes within a largely unvarying national character, cultural relativists tend to produce static descriptions that overestimate durability of values and practices. Many of Hofstede's pronouncements look particularly dated. Confidently asserting that the degree of individualism in a culture is statistically related to a country's wealth, the 1970 listing places Japan in the middle, and a number of the East Asian 'tiger economies' with the fastest subsequent rates of growth in GNP firmly anchored at the bottom. In a later contribution (Hofstede, 1991), he has to borrow the idea of 'Confucian dynamism' to fill the gap.

Let us also take the example of the former Communist countries. Most of them manifested high power distance, collectivism and uncertainty avoidance (Hofstede and Søndergaard, 1993). This is hardly surprising given the nature of their shared command economy and centralised party–state apparatus. In contrast, Russia is now experiencing rampant individualism and uncertainty following the collapse of the old solidaristic social norms. While the situation is not as dramatic in other ex-Eastern bloc countries, there is no evidence in either case that this reflects or is driven by changes in national mindsets.

The fact that the descriptions are often no longer accurate raises questions about the feasibility of the analysis. Such perspectives pick up on cultural differences and then believe they have explained them. For example, Hampden-Turner and Trompenaars refer to the 'psychology of short and long-term mind-sets' (1993: 139). But it is not at all clear that finance-driven short-termism derives either from mental models in general, or Anglo-Saxon ones in particular. It is equally possible to argue that the kind of 'greed is good' individualism, with associated high levels of bankruptcy and takeovers, is an outcome, not of a mental model, but specific historical and contemporary institutional arrangements in Anglo-American political economies.

Culturalist perspectives treat as universal what are the outcomes of historical struggle – such as the dominance of the finance function or conglomerate ownership. They treat as culturally specific what are universal trends, notably scientific management and bureaucracy, which were present in France and Germany in parallel with the Anglo-Saxon countries (Weber, 1968; Doray, 1988). Japan is at the top of the list for firms that take a long-term view. This is attributed to Japanese views of time, which in turn are attributed to Buddhist influences. This sounds plausible, but look at the next two countries in: Sweden and West Germany. Each no doubt could be discussed in terms of cultural history. However, what the countries have in common is also significant – institutional configurations within particular market arrangements that promote close relations between the state and major economic actors and a flow of finance between banks and business.

These debates can often get stuck in a 'chicken and egg' rut. After all, institutions can be presented as the outcome of deeply-rooted values. This ignores one very important point. As we have seen, the patterns attributed to national mindsets can and do change. Take, for example, the issue of centralisation and autocratic leadership. Hofstede says that high power distance stems from 'the psychological need for dependence of those people without power' (1990: 397). What that dubious assertion ignores is that societies or sectors within them can become more centralised and autocratic as the result of political changes, management fashions or power struggles. Not only has this got little or nothing to do with any cravings for domination, there is evidence that employees respond badly to such changes. For example, a study by the Carnegie Foundation found extensive and rising dissatisfaction among academics with how autocratic their organisations had become in countries such as Britain and Australia with supposedly low power distance cultures.

Beyond a failure to explain changes in particular places, cultural relativists are unable adequately to understand more general social shifts that happen across societies, albeit unevenly. Notable in this respect has been the increase in risk highlighted by the German sociologist Ulrich Beck (1992). Contemporary political, economic and cultural processes embody greater degrees of instability and change, with consequent impacts on job and social insecurity. This would seem to imply an increase in uncertainty partly independent of any specific national mindset. Defective explanation is a poor basis for policy. Even if we knew what they were, it might not be feasible to 'manage according to the value systems of a particular people' in the contemporary political economy. One of the reasons is that other sources of cultural influence, notably of a corporate nature, may constrain or override traditional national values.

There are two ways in which corporate cultures are playing an enhanced role, with the result that multinational companies are becoming carriers of convergent practices across national boundaries. First, firms are needing to integrate an increasingly diverse number of activities and units. Many management theorists portray culture as the glue that binds those diverse units into cohesive and co-ordinated 'families' (Handy, 1984; Barham and Rassam, 1989; Rhinesmith, 1991). Second, the increasingly global nature of competition creates pressures for them to adapt to the more rapid diffusion of perceived 'best practice'. While the latter may not be primarily cultural in nature, both set limits to Hofstede's argument that 'The convergence of management will never come' (1990: 405). As Kieser (1993) notes, it is remarkable that Hofstede never considers the highly distinctive culture of IBM as a factor and how it interacts with national culture.

Modern business thus creates complex cultural environments for international managers and management. Neither the relativist 'when in Rome' view of adapting to local culture nor the newly fashionable concept of the free-floating global manager who owes no allegiance to any country (Reich, 1991) may be adequate in this context. Knowledge and cultural competencies are forged in the interface between the corporate, functional and national, and managers face pressures to pick up the appropriate cues that signal what kind of cultural difference is operative (Schneider and Barsoux, 1997: 169; Jones, Thompson and Nickson, 1998: 1060). For example, Jones, Thompson and Nickson (1998) examined the meanings attached to terms such as the need for 'Swedish behaviour' in the constituent parts of multinationals from that country. Managers feel comfortable with talk of Swedishness, perhaps because it gives additional meaning and legitimacy. From this perspective, the prominence of Swedish managers in top positions in foreign subsidiaries is less to do with the superiority or distinctiveness of Swedishness, than the advantage such staff give in facilitating the smooth running of the 'global' management structure, with its attendant and often standardised knowledge system. For example, service transnationals need to transfer highly standardised knowledge and practice that supports a corporate brand (Child and Rodrigues, 1993: 11).

However, such systems are always subject to adaptation. International firms necessarily make 'compromises' with local situations and, implicitly, with competing values and ideas of competence.

Overall the message of this discussion is that we need different, more historically sensitive and contextually bounded explanations of culture. Put simply, locating culture in ways of doing rather than thinking allows us to explain how cultures develop and change more adequately.

Culture and institutions: business systems and varieties of capitalism

A focus on culture is a traditional antidote to explanations that over-emphasise economic and technical convergence, given that the former has more scope for grasping 'local' variation and organisatonal distinctiveness. However, as we have seen, culture is a slippery concept that can be applied with misleading results. Institutional theories, which have been around in organisational analysis since the 1970s (Meyer and Rowan, 1977), have been the means for correcting some of the problems associated with Hofstede and associated ideas. Organisations still adapt to the environment, but to different features of it. The emphasis is on normative adaptation and the cultural rules to which organisations conform. This arises not from the requirements for efficiency, but from the need for legitimacy and resource support that is the reward for conforming. Indeed, in some cases rules may be ceremonial and transmitted through myths rather than technical. Not only do organisations conform to the environment, but also to each other. This process whereby organisations increasingly come to resemble each other is described using the strange term 'institutional isomorphism' (Di Maggio and Powell, 1983). The main factors promoting convergence across companies are key agents who adhere to universalistic standards of best practice, notably professionals such as accountants, engineers and personnel officers, as well as the state itself.

We should not be misled by the term 'culture'. This is used to mean social rules embodied in institutional processes more than mental constructs carried about in people's heads. These institutional frameworks are essentially national: as Clegg puts it, 'A stress on culture as institutionally framed and nationally diverse' (1990: 151). An important feature of this approach is to affirm the possibility of successful organisational designs to promote industrialisation in different institutional environments. The emphasis on diverse organisational rationalities is usefully strengthened through the concept of *business systems*, associated particularly with the work of J. Henderson (1992: 4) who describes them as, 'distinctive ways of co-ordinating economic activity that give rise to particular configurations of market–firm relations'. The advantage of this concept is that it attempts to tie together in a coherent way the historical, cultural and institutional processes that shape national or regional economies. It enables a focus on the way in which state, financial, industrial relations and other systems combine together to influence organisational practices. Whitley (1992b) makes a useful distinction between background institutions (for example, family, education) that structure general social patterns and norms, and proximate institutions (for example, labour market systems) that constitute the more immediate business environment.

The role of factors such as state direction and family ownership in East Asian economies figures prominently in institutionalist accounts (Hamilton and Biggart, 1988; Whitley, 1992a; G. Henderson, 1993). Japan has received considerable academic attention for its distinctive forms of ownership and management. For example, in the influential corporate form of *keiretsu*, units are part of vertically organised enterprise groups clustered around a dominant company or companies. Interlinked shareholdings involving subcontractors and banks establish stability and mutual interest in the long-term success of the group; the joint risk-taking and access to capital avoids the short-termism associated with the Anglo-Saxon model (G. Henderson, 1993: 38–9). Crucially, this risk-taking is also shared with the state, as in the well-known example of orchestration of economic development through the Japanese Ministry of International Trade and Industry (MITI).

Japan and other Asian economies have undergone financial crises and lower growth more recently, leading some commentators to question the extent of any 'economic miracle' (Krugman, 1999). Whatever judgements may be made about current events, there is much less doubt that the particular configuration of practices discussed above was frequently a characteristic feature of late industrialisation. In Japan the commercial class was marginal to early industrialisation and the state was the primary agent in mobilising capital and mediating market forces (Littler, 1982). But the primary example of state-sponsored development is found in Korea. Conglomerate enterprise groups, known as *chaebol*, are both directed and disciplined by the state through financial controls, subsidies and incentives. For example, following the bankruptcy of the leading cement producer in the 1970s, the South Korean government transferred its production facilities to another chaebol (Amsden, 1992: 15). This pattern has been repeated continually in the immensely successful restructuring process that made the country into one of the fastest growing in the world.

The state is not the only manager of the industrialisation process. As Amsden (1992: 9) shows, 'Salaried engineers are a key figure in late industrialisation because they are the gatekeepers of foreign technology transfers'. With Korean firms choosing specialised engineers over administrators, we have a further example of different forms of enterprise management within managerial capitalism. Family ownership is a key dimension of South Korea's corporate structures and familialism has been a further characteristic of some East Asian economies, particularly Taiwan and Hong Kong. Family business, particularly among overseas Chinese, operates according to particular lineage and inheritance rules, which, in turn, shape how businesses grow given that a wider sharing of trust is constrained by the familial form. More importantly for our purposes, the forms of co-ordination and direction of the enterprise are necessarily distinctive: 'there is strong patrimonial and personalistic direct control, rather than on the more impersonalised, formalised and standardised control of the rational-bureaucratic model which we are familiar with from the West' (Clegg, 1990: 164). Whatever the source of influence or configuration factors, what is being argued is that dominant social institutions generate distinctive business recipes that are relatively similar within nation states.

It is also worth remembering that there are substantial differences between those economies, as well as common contrasts to 'Western' models, further highlighting the importance of a comparative analysis of management structures and practices (Whitley, 1999). In this respect it is possible to learn from a close cousin of the above perspectives. Such *organisational* theories have a great deal in common with broader institutional perspectives in sociology, particularly the *societal effects* approach (Maurice, Sorge and Warner, 1980). Their research showed that work organisation patterns differ markedly due to nationally specific institutional logics that produce stable organisational and employment patterns. In particular, the national ownership of firms facilitates the absorption of the practices, ideas, and culture from those institutions.

Such logics are particularly located in education, training, labour market and industrial relations structures. This helps to explain why salary structures, career patterns, management and authority relations vary among closely matched French, German and British firms. Within a similar framework Lane (1991) has looked at relations between large, medium and small firms in Germany, France and Britain. She demonstrates that the distinctiveness of 'populations' of organisations arises from their transaction with specific industrial orders. As a consequence national patterns continue to reproduce divergence rather than the homogeneity predicted by old-style convergence theory (Kerr *et al.*, 1960).

Societal effect approaches have stressed the principle of functional equivalence, thus appearing to avoid determinist or 'one best way' fallacies. However, comparison is accompanied, implicitly or explicitly, by evaluation. For example, the comparisons of France, Britain and Germany in the work of Lane consistently favour the latter, particularly with reference to the organisational and technical competencies of firms and their underpinnings in educational training systems. Strong arguments promoting the positive lessons of East Asian business systems can also be seen in the work of G. Henderson (1993).

There are, however, problems within institutionalist frameworks. The earlier versions reproduce a view of 'the organisation as a passive reactor to the environment' (Bryman, 1993: 87) that is equally deterministic as population ecology or contingency, though shifting the focus to normative pressures. Even the more complex accounts run the risk of producing a mirror image of the convergence argument, focusing solely on difference. It is, of course, true that work organisation and other features of the industrial order will always differ from others on a local and national basis. Whether such explanations were ever wholly viable in the past, it is very doubtful that they are now. Societal institutions are increasingly subject to 'external' pressures for change. As Smith and Meiksins observe: 'Institutional analysis tended to focus on and reinforce national differences. The immediate problem with this perspective is to account for change and the dynamic nature of economies that are global, not nationally bounded systems' (1995: 3). Traditional industrial relations also tended to focus primarily on national systems or comparisons between them. This fails to engage with economic internationalisation and is inadequate in a period when those industrial relations regimes are increasingly forged at regional and supra-national levels (Howarth and Hughes, 2000).

It is inaccurate and unrealistic to go on treating organisations as 'societies in miniature' in the manner of Sorge *et al.* (1983: 54), who say that 'the differences between societies are so pervasive as to be immediately and consistently noticeable in every unit'. In reality, as we shall see later, large business organisations such as IBM are themselves carriers of distinctive financial, employment or technical practices. Sparrow and Hiltrop make a similar point with respect to the internationalisation of HRM practices: 'The "culture-bound" perspective runs the gauntlet between generalisations and stereotyping and fails to consider the equally pervasive impact of both individual differences and organisational choice over resource development' (1998: 83).

However, such perspectives are not necessarily conceptually tied to the state as an object of analysis. Neo-institutional approaches are becoming more sophisticated in their understanding of environments. As Warhurst (1997) observes, there is a growing recognition that the institutional environment does not mechanically determine organisational forms. As with conceptions of strategic choice in the previous chapter, there are still choices within constraints, and embeddedness still has to be enacted. Neo-institutionalism is also being extended to cover sectors, regions, and systems. With a small number of giant transnational firms increasingly dominating sectors and 'best practices' spreading rapidly within them, industry recipes consisting of conventions governing marketing, pricing, production methods and industrial relations can become influential (Whitley, 1987). Sectors can be conceived of as an 'organisational field' linking firms and the broader society (Di Maggio and Powell, 1983). Arias has demonstrated the value of this orientation in her analysis of the pharmaceutical industry in Ecuador. Multinationals operating in the area spread modern HRM practices from their headquarters to their subsidiaries. But local firms do not mimic the multinationals and 'seem to constitute a world of their own organised along family business lines' (1993: 24). Organisations in the two fields are responding to different normative environments and relational constraints such as rules set by government favourable to the largest players. So, when discussing how managerial and organisational knowledge is diffused, Arias (1993: 30) argues that, 'Cross national research on transfers should be done within a neo-institutional framework that allows a shifting of levels of analysis from the organisation, to the field, to the national, to the world-system level'. J. Henderson (1992) also fleshes out an institutional analysis by outlining *modes of articulation* between national and global economies. For example, most of the manufacturing economies of the EC articulate to the world economy as independent exporters, with firms distributing and marketing under their own name. In contrast some sectors of the East Asian economies and those of Central and Eastern Europe are more likely to be involved in commercial sub-contracting, where production is structured in commodity chains driven by the demands of distributors and retailers rather than manufacturers.

Despite the persuasiveness of the analysis, Arias goes on to argue that the relevance of national boundaries remains paramount. But too much focus on institutions can neglect the broader trends in capitalist political economy. It is not enough to take the firm and the market as units of analysis, without appreciating the broader dynamics (Warhurst, 1997). A related literature – on varieties of capitalism – should be able to handle a bigger picture (Coates, 2000; Soskice and Hall, 2001). By focusing on distinctive institutions developed to regulate economic life- labour markets, education and training, corporate governance – such theorists identify the presence of a number of ideal types of capitalist organisation. The standard distinction is between liberal (such as USA, Britain, Australia, Canada, New Zealand, Ireland) and co-ordinated (including Germany, Japan, the Netherlands, Sweden, Finland, and Austria) market economies, Coates, however, describes three models. In market-led capitalisms (USA/UK) accumulation decisions are largely left to private companies in open financial markets. State-led capitalisms (Japan, South Korea) combine the market and political dominance of private capital with state direction of growth decisions through administrative and banking structures. Finally, negotiated or consensual capitalisms (Sweden, Germany) may have less direct state regulation of capital accumulation, but management of the economy and enterprise is filtered through co-ordination arrangements in which labour as well as capital has influence and rights. In general, the contention is that differences in these institutional frameworks generate systematic differences in strategy across these 'varieties'.

While such ideal types enable the focus of analysis to move beyond the institutions and cultures of particular countries, with more of an emphasis on the behaviour of firms across borders, regulatory regimes still tend to be identified with the preserve of the nation state. The issue is whether this is still the case in a contemporary political economy. As Hall and Soskice recognise, 'the principal issue raised by globalization concerns the stability of regulatory regimes and national institutions in the face of heightened competitive pressure' (2001: 55).

Globalisation: reality or myth?

The most potent challenge to the idea that national cultures and institutions still shape work organisations comes from the idea of globalisation. Since the term became fashionable, few best-selling contemporary management books are complete without 'global' in their titles. Such hyper-globalisers proclaim a borderless world where international products and services, facilitated by high-speed information and communication technologies (ICT) can transcend traditional spatial and temporal constraints (Omhae, 1990; Rifkin, 2000). Beyond the ranks of popular business writers, influential social theorists talk of a new de-territorialised global order – Empire – whose sovereignty renders the nation state redundant (Hardt and Negri, 2000); an informational capitalism where companies can co-ordinate complex and decentralised activities within electronic networks (Castells, 1996); or less grandly a globalised economy in which corporations have been 'denationalised' from their local origins (Sklair, 2001).

Within some of these frameworks, it is argued that transnational companies can or must create global best practices that operate without respect to local barriers and peculiarities. A good example of such arguments is *The Machine that Changed the World* (Womack *et al.*, 1990), which has had a substantial influence on governments and companies. Drawing on the experience of Japanese production systems and extensive research into the motor industry, the authors promote the principles of 'lean production', which they claim produces efficiently with half the human effort, with considerable zeal. Such principles 'can be applied equally in every industry across the globe' (Womack *et al.*, 1990: 8), as long as motor companies adopt the necessary structures and practices to promote diffusion. An example of the latter would be 'an integrated, global personnel system that promotes personnel from any country in the company as if nationality did not exist' (Womack *et al.*, 1990: 4).

Such perspectives have not gone unchallenged. At a macro-level, some economists, notably Alan Rugman (2000; 2005) have convincingly demonstrated that most economic flows are 'regional'. While the main focus of his analysis is sales, which might underestimate the extent of international integration, it remains the case that few multinational enterprises are global and that most trade, investment and networks take place within the three main triadic blocks (Europe, North America, Asia Pacific). Some sectors (e.g. consumer electronics) are clearly more globalised than others. Services, which now employ 70 per cent of the global labour force, is particularly characterised by local or regional activity. He also notes the success of regional and bilateral trade agreements, compared to global, multilateral initiatives. The latter efforts, as anyone who follows contemporary events would know, frequently fail to take off, as national interests, protectionist trade wars and subsidies prevent progress. At a micro-level, notions of global best practice, there is a danger of simply reverting to the earlier determinism and unproblematic notions of efficiency. *The Machine that Changed the World* has been heavily criticised for getting the statistics wrong and exaggerating Japanese advantage (Williams *et al.*, 1992a). For example, it does not explain how Toyota and other firms take labour out of production, ignoring the specific features of postwar Japanese labour relations, where defeated unions and malleable workforces allow high levels of work intensification. Taking a different direction, Berggren (1993) questions whether the record of Japanese manufacturers at home and in the US transplants on high work speed and employee surveillance, low health and safety standards and exclusion of union involvement in regulating prodction would be acceptable in the very different European context.

Though there is some evidence that aspects of production practices can be uncoupled from culture and transferred across national boundaries (Florida and Kenney, 1991), the claim of superior ways of organising production separates it from the supportive institutional context – the industrial relations system, the subordinate networks of suppliers, state and financial sector support. In other words, we are back to the social embeddedness of economic action discussed earlier. *The Machine that Changed the World* is an extreme case of ideas of globalisation or convergence following single paths. Just like the older convergence theory, discredited for its technological and other determinisms (Kerr *et al.*, 1960), all linear models, including the popular notions of moves from Fordism to post-Fordism or mass production to flexible specialisation (Aglietta, 1979; Lipietz, 1982; Piore and Sabel, 1984) need to be treated with suspicion. This is because they work on stereotypical ideas of homogeneous, static systems and underestimate the pattern of adaptation and varied diffusion that 'best practices' go through. As we will discuss in more detail later, the patterns are still strongly shaped by the residual powers of nation states to create distinctive contexts for economic activity to which firms have positive reasons to adapt (Hirst and Thompson, 1992; Whitley, 1994).

With these factors in mind, globalisation is neither myth nor reality, but rather an uneven, unfinished and overlapping set of processes:

The internationalisation of production and services Foreign direct investment (FDI) and industrial location have obviously been long-term developments. This is now much more prominent. For example, FDI by companies outstripped world output by four times and trade by three from 1983 to 1990 (Beneria, 1995). What is also newer is the organisation and co-ordination of activities by transnational companies at a global level: 'Rivals compete against each other on a truly worldwide basis, drawing on competitive advantages that grow out of their entire network of worldwide activities' (Porter, 1990: 35). Global commodity chains play an increasingly central role in this process (Gereffi, 1996; Gereffi, Humphrey and Sturgeon, 2005).

The de-coupling of states and corporations It has been common ground for some time that international firms are moving beyond their traditional multi-domestic or polycentric forms in which relatively autonomous policies and practices could be geared towards differentiated local markets (Perlmutter, 1969; Porter, 1990). Transnationals that utilise foreign direct investment to establish 'globally' integrated production or service chains are increasingly the key players. Internationalisation is driven, in part, by waves of cross-border merger and acquisition, particularly in more 'open' economies (Morgan, 2005). Though genuinely 'stateless' corporations are rare, their headquarters and operations (assets, employment and sales) are increasingly located outside country of origin. Contemporary corporate structures articulate a complex network of parent–subsidiary relations, as well as direction and co-ordination of economic activities across national boundaries. Know-how which is gained centrally or in one particular subsidiary operating unit is capable of being transferred to the various sub-units of the corporation. Finally, more advanced information technology such as computer networks for co-ordination and control are facilitating standardisation and integration of corporate activities (Marginson *et al.*, 1995).

World markets This tendency refers not merely to the growth, but to the integration of world trade. Included within this framework are the development of relatively standardised, albeit regionally adapted, global products such as the 'world car' announced by Ford in 1994, the erosion of protected national industries (for example, European telecommunications industries or previous state firms), and the acceleration of movement out of mainly domestic markets by particular national capitals.

Increased integration into the international division of labour Within the ideal type of globalisation, 'distinct national economies are subsumed and rearticulated into the system by essentially international processes and transactions' (Hirst and Thompson, 1992: 360). This may include the development of international state apparatuses that interact with and shape the international division of labour (Pitelis, 1993). Supra-national state systems such as the EC, the North American Free Trade Agreement (NAFTA) and Asia Pacific Economic Co-operation (APEC) are not new, but 'What is significant today is the sheer increase in their number, the growth in their territorial scope, and their acquisition of important new functions' (Jessop, 1992: 10). New countries, regions or social formations (for example, the post-Communist economies of Eastern Europe, are gradually brought into the financial and corporate workings of the global economy and pressured to specialise in the provision of certain goods or services such as cheap labour. In some cases, notably China, the size and significance of those economies fundamentally re-shapes the terms of competition.

The internationalisation of financial markets Deregulation due to neo-liberal state policies and the role of new communication technologies in facilitating accelerated round-the-clock trading are the key factors promoting the growth of truly global markets for finance. Crises in one financial market now quickly spread to others. In addition, there has been a shift in the locus of power from product and labour to capital markets. Financial markets and institutions are now the main driver of firm behaviour as they are pressurised into delivering enhanced 'shareholder value' (Thompson, 2003a). There has also been closer integration with production. Transnational banks offer new services to multinationals, such as the financing of acquisitions, management of liquid assets and leasing arrangements. At the same time, increasing numbers of banks are subsidiaries of multinationals. It is therefore possible to speak of transnational finance capital in which the two actors, 'are organically linked in their internationalisation' (Andreff, 1984: 66).

Sweden is not unique. The available evidence shows that while national institutions still matter, the scope of national systems and is diminishing under these pressures. In Germany traditional corporate

---

The Swedish Model – sink or swim?

Such trends are undoubtedly influential ones, with the result that some of the space for the national and local is squeezed as organisational forms and practices demonstrate convergent tendencies. This can be seen in Sweden, a country traditionally associated with a distinctive post-war national model of society and employment system. Like a number of co-ordinated market economies, that model is based on regulation through collaboration between powerful employer and union organisations and the state (governed for 44 years until 1976 by the Social Democratic Party). But it was distinctive in its 'solidaristic wages policy' that sought to promote greater equality and efficiency through centralised and consolidated wage bargaining, as well as active labour market measures that promoted full employment. These policies were particularly beneficial to the large internationally-oriented firms and their workers.

These arrangements, of course, eventually generated their own internal strains with emergent crises first surfacing in the mid-1970s. Such strains were exacerbated by the rapid internationalisation of the Swedish economy, which has had to cope with the dual pressures of an accelerated drift of capital abroad and competition at home from Japanese models and other variants on lean production. Unions and employers asserted their own ways of dealing with crisis, the former emphasising the need for more high quality jobs, the latter, for more flexibility in work and wages (Thompson and Sederblad, 1994). However, the closure of Volvo's Udevalla and Kalmar plants dealt a blow to attempts to create a new 'Swedish model' based on innovative work organisation. One of the reasons was that the company found it hard to resist the pressure of comparisons and the possibilities of moving the production between units, that international competition and an alliance with Renault brought (Sandberg, 1993: 8).

In general, the crisis in the model did not lead to significant changes or new structural reforms (Anxo and Niklasson, 2006). But in the 1990s the model was put into question again with rising inflation and falling employment. A globalising political economy again played a significant role. Governments could no longer simply respond by devaluing the currency or creating more public sector jobs given that de-regulated international finance markets had to be reassured about budget deficits. The large Swedish firms, meanwhile, had become even more internationalised in their markets and operations, and therefore more sensitive to comparative costs. One response was a new wage norm agreed in 1997 between the social partners in the sectors most exposed to international markets based on the average increase in wages of Sweden's main European competitors (Anxo and Niklasson, 2006). This is part of a wider trend towards wage dispersion. Such developments and other labour market initiatives indicate continuity and change in the Swedish model. Whilst still tripartite, collaborative and (relatively) egalitarian (Taylor, 2006), the new global and domestic context has resulted in more differentiated practices in a more open economy.

---

governance based on a balance of stakeholder interests and 'patient capital' has been challenged by the rising power of domestic financial interests and demands for greater attention to shareholder value (O'Sullivan, 2000: 9). In the workplace, intensified global or regional competition is leading to decreased worker autonomy and skill, with greater rationalisation and standardisation of the labour process (Springer, 1999; Schumann, 2000). Such a pessimistic account is disputed by others (Jürgens *et al.*, 2000; Vitols, 2001). They argue that there is still a predominance of large shareholders that take a long-term strategic view, and co-determination of workplace and economy between capital and labour limits the move towards shareholder value. Whatever the judgement, Germany and Sweden represent one end of an international governance spectrum. There are still varieties of capitalism, but within a different set of circumstances and constraints. It is certainly true that the national state's activities are constrained by having to operate within the existing market framework. Particularly in a world system of interlocking manufacture, trade and finance, no nation state can ignore the requirements of capital accumulation and reproduction. Capital can utilise its resource power to place unique pressure on the state's economic management processes. Within these 'new rules of the game', corporate rather than state governance has tended to become dominant. Some commentators argue that national governance has been re-cast as a series of 'competition states' that have to frame growth strategies in the light of new global market disciplines (Elger and Burnham, 2001: 4).

However, the above discussion should not be taken to say that transnational and other large firms have total power over national and local environments. In part, this is, as we have argued because globalisation is far from a complete process. In addition, it is still filtered through national and regional governance and trading blocs. For example, government policies still often support 'their' transnationals in the race of globalisation, in particular where political and military hegemony is at stake. As indicated earlier, though states can no longer act as if national economies were insulated from international competition, there are still distinctive national trajectories within globalisation (Boyer and Drache, 1996; Hirst and Thompson, 1996). The relevance and diverse nature of state action is also a product of the continuing requirement for economic restructuring to be legitimated through involvement of a range of social actors and co-ordinated for enhanced effectiveness. In this context modified and enlarged forms of tripartism still constitute part of domestic repertoires in a number of European countries (Katz, 2005).

Additionally, states can still play key roles in promoting technological competence, subsidising capital accumulation or bargaining over production and investment decisions (Jenkins, 1984; Gordon, 1988; Jessop, 1992). As Whitley notes (1987: 140), the capacity of large firms to determine their own market 'niches' requires a level of analysis of the political economy of international and state agencies, yet this is seldom recognised in organisational analysis. The state also continues to act as a 'collective capitalist': attending to long-term interests even against particular business demands; providing facilities such as a national transport network or housing that single capitals cannot; and regulating and incorporating demands from subordinate classes through concessions and institutional channels which do not threaten existing class power. These transactions are complex and may bring particular states, or supra-national formations such as the EC, into conflict with capital. The state does not function unambiguously in the interests of a single class; it is a state in capitalist society rather than the capitalist state, and it is an arena of struggle constituted and divided by opposing interests rather than a centralised and unified political actor (Pearson, 1986). In sum, the state still matters, but within a significantly changed global political economy. We need a framework that can distinguish not just between, but within countries.

Beyond convergence and divergence? Understanding comparative influences on work and organisation

Given our emphasis on the changing relations of capital, labour and the state in the current context, to take the discussion further we need to pull together what we know of the forces that shape organisational forms and practices. A model developed by Smith and Meiksins (1995) and further elaborated by Smith (2005) is useful, in which they distinguish between three kinds of effects on work and organisation. (See Figure 6.1.)

System effects are commonalities generated by social formations such as capitalism as a mode of production or patriarchy. All societies and the organisations within them have to operate within the parameters set by systems, for example competitive relations between enterprises, the conflicting interests of capital and labour. These processes create rules of the game that shape social relations in the workplace and constrain organisational choices. Tsoukas (1994a) demonstrates how this operated with respect to firms in state socialist systems, utilising the previously discussed concepts of institutional theory. He argues that socio-economic systems have a macro-logic that conditions and provides continuities in the organisational characteristics of firms irrespective of particular histories and societies. In the case of state socialism, collective ownership, command planning and a heavy emphasis on ideology leave little space for autonomous economic agents. Firms therefore increase their chances of survival by displaying conformity, often of a 'ceremonial' nature, to the party–state apparatus. The macro-rules and institutions are isomorphically reproduced at micro-level, overseen by the party structures in the workplace and a hierarchical and rule-bound style of management: 'The organisation becomes a political-cum-ideological miniature of the state' (Tsoukas, 1994a: 34). It is perfectly possible to explain the dependent relations between state and enterprise in such societies without the baggage of institutionalism and allowing for more variations (see Smith and Thompson, 1992). But the general point about system effects still stands and indicates why naïve attempts to transfer managerial techniques from West to East may fail. It is worth noting that the fact that the transition from command to market economy is still in its relatively early stages may be a more substantial barrier to such transfer than Hofstede's emphasis on national mindsets.

Under capitalism, the relations between system and organisation are more loosely coupled and there is greater diversity of institutional configurations at both levels. This is where societal effects are most pertinent. As we have already discussed this point extensively we need not dwell on it here, except for one observation: some nation states provide stronger and more distinctive institutional environments than

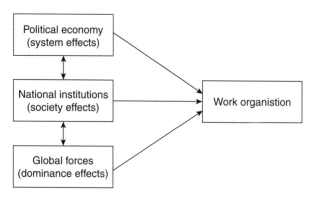

Figure 6.1   **A model by Smith and Meiksins**

others. Japan is always the example, but Sweden, Germany, or Austria would equally fit the bill. What they have in common is more densely structured institutional frameworks influenced by a strong social settlement between key actors – capital, labour, and the state – which shapes the relations between them and enhances the connections between social, economic and political institutions. In some circumstances societies with strong social settlements can generate dominance effects. This is because particular societies come to represent conceptions of success and progress, with models of 'best practice' concerning labour markets, labour processes and other factors exported from one society to another. Smith goes on to show how new entrants to the international division of labour may create different ways of organizing the firm, employment relations or work organization, and supplier relations and reinvent themselves and influence others in the system.

While Japan played this role in the 1980s, the US, Sweden, Germany and Japan have all played such a role at some time in the post-war period. You may have noticed that this term is always placed in inverted commas signalling that it is not intended to be taken literally. Best practices are socially constructed and not necessarily simply read off from actual success. They are read through ideological spectacles and mediated by a country's position and power in the international division of labour. Dominance does not indicate automatic or uncontested adaptation. There is always competition between such practices, aiding the process whereby key actors in and across societies 'search' for viable and legitimate models. The original framework was useful, though it tended to treat work organisations as the recipient of influences, embedded in contexts rather than an independent force. The immense power of contemporary transnational corporations is given more recognition in the reworked version. Firms such as IBM, Toyota or McDonald's are also creators and purveyors of 'best practice'. Such effects are a form of cross-organisational learning in that firms are more receptive to change than states (Smith, 2005). More rapid learning processes are also allied to factors such as the internationalisation of consultancy, business schools, and the market for management literature (Mueller, 1996). The internationalised workplace acts to condense the effects of globalising capitalist forces and national institutional rules on particular work and employment standards within local and unique work situations. Greater convergence can result from the fact that such comparisons can be coercive in a context of competitive benchmarking (Ferner and Edwards, 1995; Berggren, 1996).

How the various influences of system, society, 'best practice' and organisation align themselves is not predictable or in a fixed hierarchy. This is because there are a number of complex transactions between capital, labour and the nation state within the international division of labour (Thompson and Smith, 1998: 196–8). Social scientists need to show how these transactions work and levels are linked in concrete instances. Global capitalism remains a dynamic system in which different strategies are available to establishing competitive advantage for companies and countries. In that competitive struggle, forces of divergence and convergence are in continual tension. Within the new structural constraints, firms have some room to make strategic choices, selecting policies and solutions that can shape their environment. For transnational companies a key tension is reflected in the contradictory pressures to standardise their operations, products and services so as to maximise the scale and cost benefits of global integration, while at the same time attempting to serve the needs of specific markets.

A favourite formula for solving this problem is the prescription for such organisations to be glocal (Bartlett and Ghoshal, 1990a). But this is little more than the kind of slogan beloved of popular business texts. One of the reasons for complexity is that different facets of societal or corporate organisation will be subject to differential pressures. For example, while there are now more discretionary powers for firms to adopt common human resource policies (Schienstock, 1991), industrial relations systems are the least likely to be internationally standardised because they are most embedded in national institutional frameworks. This may be one of the reasons why N. Adler and Bartholomew (1992) found that many firms did not seek to benchmark 'excellence' in global HRM practice. Production and management systems, however, are subject much more directly to dominance effects from perceived best practices and the need of transnationals to integrate their diverse activities and structures (Thompson, Flecker and Wallace, 1995). In other words, contrary to a number of writers, it is not just the existence of a 'global mind-set' that determines the likely extent of integration, but the very real pressures to standardise that impinge more on some corporate activities and in some sectors than others.

Summary and key points

In this chapter we have broadened the discussion of organisation-environment relations from the local to the global. Much classic organisational theorising was undertaken when firms operated mainly in national contexts. A focus on the 'local' has been a useful antidote to 'one best way' notions. For a long time Hofstede and other explanations focused on the primacy of national culture has been the most widely used corrective to universal principles of management. However, not only are these perspectives methodologically and conceptually flawed, they are increasingly outdated. Culture is less a case of permanent national mindset than shifting sets of institutions. While national institutions still shape and constrain organisations, the complex mix of influences have broadened their scope. The most useful concept to emerge from these debates has been varieties of capitalism, which narrows the range of difference without obliterating it. However, in turn, this has been put into question by the trend towards globalisation. In the resultant debates, as with discussion of models of organisation–environment relations in the previous chapter, it has proven difficult to escape the dichotomies of determinism and choice, convergence and divergence. Part of the answer may lie in different units of analysis. A focus on countries and states will inevitably highlight differences. But as product, capital and labour markets internationalise, it makes sense also to focus on companies, particularly as carriers of common techniques and organisational learning. When allied to perceived notions of global best practice, this creates what Smith (2005) calls 'dominance effects'. In his model, which we find persuasive, such effects compete with system and society effects to influence the workplace in complex and contested ways. Overall, the 'environment' therefore has to be conceived not as a given force within which dependent organisations adapt and transact, but as a global political economy whose levels provide a shifting dynamic within which organisations reciprocally interact.

Further reading

Given the centrality of Hofstede's analysis it is certainly worth reading some of his many contributions (see his website http://www.geert-hofstede.com/). Hofstede actively responds to his critics, so it's useful to look at some of the debates. A recent critique from McSweeney (2003) is reproduced and discussed extensively on the site. Despite the column inches devoted to Hofstede, readers looking for a credible culturalist perspective would be advised to explore the Hampden-Turner and Trompenaars (1993) variant. Institutionalist accounts of culture and business are best represented by Whitley (1999), while Coates (2000) provides a good account of the varieties of capitalism perspective. Our chapter draws on Smith's society, system and dominance analysis (Smith and Meiskens, 1995; Smith, 2005).

Coates, D. (2000) *Models of Capitalism*, Oxford: Oxford University Press.

Hampden-Turner, C. and Trompenaars, F. (1993) *The Seven Cultures of Capitalism*, New York: Doubleday.

Hofstede, G. (1980, 2nd edn 2003) *Culture's Consequences: International Differences in Work Related Values*, Beverley Hills, Calif.: Sage.

McSweeney, B. (2003) 'Hofstede's Model of National Cultural Differences and their Consequences: A Triumph of Faith – A Failure of Analysis', *Human Relations*, 55. 1: 89–118.

Smith, C. and Meiskens, P. (1995) 'System, Society and Dominance in Cross-National Organisational Analysis', *Work, Employment and Society*, 9. 2: 241–67.

Smith, C. (2005) 'Beyond Convergence and Divergence: Explaining Variations in Organizational Practices and Forms', in S. Ackroyd, R. Batt, P. Thompson and P. Tolbert (eds.), *The Oxford Handbook of Work and Organization*, Oxford: Oxford University Press.

Whitley, R. (1999) *Divergent Capitalism: The Social Structuring and Change of Business Systems*, Oxford: Oxford University Press.

We saw in earlier chapters that the first quarter of the twentieth century marked the emergence of professional management as social force, specialist occupational category and set of distinct work practices. This development was integral to changes in the organisation of capitalist production, with the modern bureaucratic enterprise increasingly based on the joint stock company, often in the new multi-divisional form, with its separation of ownership and management. In this type of structure, middle managers headed autonomous divisions that integrated production and distribution by co-ordinating flows from suppliers to consumers in the more clearly defined markets (Chandler, 1977). Such divisions administered their functional activities through specialist departments. All this encouraged the professionalisation of management and the rapid spread of administrative techniques. However, as Tsoukas (1994b: 289) argues, despite the emergence of managerial hierarchies and increased visibility of their tasks and functions, 'it has not been easy to answer the question, what is management?'

The aims of this chapter are to:

- Give an exposition and critique of mainstream perspectives on management and its functions, presenting classical theories in their practical context, notably the project to create a profession and the rise of managerial capitalism.
- Examine contrasting literatures on managerial work and consider whether post-Second World War research that paints a more realistic picture of what managers do is an overreaction to classical views.
- Explore ideas of management as a labour process, emphasising managers as controllers and controlled.
- Break down the idea of a unified management category by examining the variety of functions and groups, as well as the impact of competing groups such as engineers, accountants and human resource specialists.

The nature of management: classical theories and beyond

Problems of analysis have not been helped by the fact that management has often been treated as a singular, unproblematic process. Shenhav (1999: 102–5) criticises Chandler and others for treating the rise of managerial capitalism merely as a functional response to changing technologies and markets. This 'edits out' the contested rationality underlying the emergence of management systems. Particular groups, notably engineers, promoted such thinking and their own role as neutral arbiters within the systems, while some employers and many labour organisations were suspicious or hostile. Engineers worked to extend the boundaries of their profession by trading on the general rise of interest in management and planning that was characteristic of the early part of the century. However, as P. Armstrong (1984) shows, they were to find it difficult to sustain the privileged role as the focal point of management. The knowledge base of the 'profession' was to become increasingly disconnected from their productive expertise.

Management thought became intimately linked to the appearance of a distinct occupational grouping, organisational theory being used as a resource to understand the complexities of the large-scale organisation and management's role within it. A key theme underlying the contradictory and partial organisational prescriptions, strategies and tactics was the belief in principles and even 'laws' concerning the nature of managerial activities and functions. As Child observes:

> Management's claim to professionalism, for instance, was only plausible if it could be shown to possess some uniform and generalised body of knowledge upon which its practitioners could draw. The so-called 'principles of management' could be presented as a theoretical base upon which the subject of 'management' rested. (Child, 1969: 225)

This belief in the power of professionalism has been a recurring feature of management thought, but has been sometimes difficult to sustain in the face of unethical practices and quick-fix fads. Responding sceptically to the growth of the latter, Hilmer and Donaldson (1996: 172) argue that 'good managers are more likely to emerge and gain respect if management is viewed as a profession that develops and applies an evolving body of knowledge'. Furthermore, that knowledge should be seen as 'impartial and expert'. Interestingly, one of the more perceptive popular management writers, Pascale (1990) attributes the startling explosion of fads to the idea of professional management, notably that there is a set of transferable generic management principles.

Such views have their roots in the inter-war period of 'classical management' theorists such as Fayol, Taylor and Barnard, discussed briefly in Chapter 3. As we saw, Fayol was the most concerned to elaborate common characteristics of management. These consisted of *planning* general lines of action and forecasting; organising human and material resources within appropriate structures; *commanding* the *activities* of personnel for optimum return; *co-ordination* of varied activities and *control* to ensure consistency with rules and command. These were situated within a detailed set of principles reflecting the division of labour and hierarchy of the bureaucratic enterprise, tempered by equitable treatment and personal responsibility. One of the effects of this way of thinking was to define managerial functions by a process of abstraction from specific activities into a conception of general management (P. Armstrong, 1987a). Managerial work would differ not in kind but only in the proportion that is actually 'managerial'. This would have a profound influence on management thought, spreading the idea that knowledge, skills and experience are common and transferable.

Meanwhile in Britain, Mary Parker Follet was producing prescriptions for a science of behaviour informed by the concerns of the human relations tradition. Emphasis shifted to the 'art' of getting things done through people. Management could learn this science because it was derived from situational laws governed by the needs of the system. As such, management could represent and integrate all interests through its capacity to apply optimal solutions through depersonalised authority. In the post-war period, classical writings have been challenged by a body of more detailed studies of managerial work.

The post-war literature (such as Drucker, 1955; Stewart, 1967; Mintzberg, 1973; Kotter, 1982) shared the central concern of the classical writers to identify common functions and criteria for effectiveness. There has been an even greater emphasis on the individual as a unit of analysis, a problematic of 'what do managers do?' (Hales, 1986). The answer given is a positive one. Drucker starts his well-known text by saying that, 'The manager is the dynamic, life-giving element in every business...the only effective advantage an enterprise has in a competitive economy' (1955: 13). Texts continually invoke as examples captains of industry such as Bill Gates of Microsoft. In this elevated role, the manager is presented almost as a free-floating centre of power. Organisations are still frequently treated as closed systems with the assumption that 'it was largely within management's own powers to fashion behaviour and relationships as might best suit their own purposes' (Child, 1969: 168). Paradoxically, by focusing on the individual, management can be analysed as if it was homogeneous, leading to the conception of the 'universal manager' carrying out a generalised set of functions standing above any specific context (Mintzberg, 1973).

Theorists could agonise about whether management was science, art, magic or politics (Watson, 1986: 29), but all options rest on the analytical and practical skills of 'successful managers'. The constant struggle for competency is further linked to the assumption that management *effectiveness* is tangible and identifiable (Hales, 1986: 88). To this end anything can be quantified and learned. The focus of course changes. It may be, for instance, the fashionable qualities of managerial excellence (see Hitt *et al.*, 1986: 1011).

These various assumptions underwrite the more fundamental view of management practices as a neutral resource, the central task of which is deciding what should be done and getting other people to do it. In this view, which we describe as technicist, managers can embody and carry out the central mission of the organisation and secure its desired objectives. Such thinking, as Shenhav (1999: 1) observes, reifies management and purges its history of the conflicts that have given it distinctive shape. It also links back to the idea discussed in Chapter 1 of management as the guardian of the organisation, being a rational tool to secure goals. By conceiving of the ends as unitary and the means as objectively rational, the socially-constructed, political character of organisational arrangements is removed (Berkeley Thomas, 1993: 37). If rationality is assumed to be unambiguously represented through formal decision-making and structures, deeper questions about ends and means in organisations are lost. So, for example, who occupies positions of authority and whose purposes managerial work serves cannot be determined by an 'impartial appeal to the requirements of an impersonal, technical logic' (Alvesson and Willmott, 1992: 6).

In mainstream writings, managers are also seen as functionally necessary in a deeper sense. The functions are 'indispensable' and are ones which '[no one] but the manager can perform' (Drucker, 1977: 39). As Willmott observes (1984: 350), this view confuses the general process of *management* of resources with the role of manag*ers* empowered to command others within specific institutional frameworks. Put another way, it wrongly assumes that 'the management function must, of necessity, reside with a particular category of agents who manage or administer other agents' (Hales, 1988: 5). In particular circumstances, work teams or worker co-operatives can equally be said to be carrying out managerial functions.

Organisational theories seldom acknowledge the wider context in which managerial work is undertaken. Whitley argues that it is better to attempt to 'specify general features of managerial tasks in terms of their functions in the organisation and change of economic enterprises as interdependent units of resource co-ordination and control, rather than identifying the characteristics of all jobs by "managers"' (1984: 343). Elsewhere, the wider theory of a 'managerial revolution' was being articulated. Part of the idea of an 'organisation society', as discussed in Chapter 1, this theory rested on a particular interpretation of changes in the nature of the large corporation. As the dominant form, joint stock companies were held to be characterised by a separation of ownership and control, share dispersal and a corresponding rise in the importance of a professional managerial élite who run the new corporations. While the growing significance of management is indisputable, many adherents of the theory (Berle and Means, 1935) took the new corporate system to be a 'purely neutral technocracy', with managers of a different background and experience exercising social responsibilities. Tougher versions (Burnham, 1945) envisaged a managerially planned and controlled society beyond the workplace, with management becoming the dominant class of all industrial societies.

The managerial revolution thesis had a wider significance for social theory, often influenced by systems thinking (Reed, 1984: 278). At its core was the view that capitalism as a system based on individual private ownership was being supplanted by a post-capitalist society in which old political disputes about ownership were irrelevant (Dahrendorf, 1959). But these theoretical developments enabled management writers such as Drucker to assert that 'we no longer talk of "capital" and "labour", we talk of "management" and "labour"' (1955: 13). Some scepticism was expressed by senior managers who referred to 'claptrap' about social responsibilities, reminding their colleagues that they remained the servants of their employers (J. Child, 1969: 152–3). Managerial capitalism had extended its tentacles. But we should keep in mind, following the discussion in Chapter 6, that such assumptions about theory and practice may be culturally-loaded. What is presented by Fayol and others as logical necessity, may be the outcome of historical development and social context (Hales, 1993: 3). Organisational life in Germany and other countries was not dominated by the search for a profession of management: 'Continentals appreciate the specialist nature of most executive jobs: they do not see why specialists should be described as "managers", nor are they notable for having occupational groups which call themselves "professionals". European business does not seem to have suffered through the lack of either idea' (Fores and Glover, 1976: 104). As Grint (1995: 5) observes, what management is 'really like' is in part a function of how we historically and cultural construct the category. *British* management and its 'rationality' is strongly linked to particular conceptions of national identity.

Researchers in this area add further objections to mainstream concepts of rationality that were raised earlier. The emphasis shifts from the political character of managerial practices to the limits of their knowledge. March and Simon (1958) introduce the concept of 'intended rationality', recognising that there are considerable constraints to the capacity to access and evaluate a full range of options. The existing structures of specialisation and hierarchy in organisations, as well as the routine practices identified in a Weberian analysis, will limit the content and flow of information and set agendas for decision-making. As a result, organisational participants are boundedly rational, having to work with simplified models of reality, and there is 'limited search' and 'satisficing' rather than optimal choices. Cyert and March (1963) point to similar processes such as 'uncertainty absorption', whereby in order to maintain stability of operations, rules and processes are geared to short-run decisions and frequent reviews. What emerges are policies and decisions by 'incremental comparison'; not a rational science, but a 'science' of muddling through (Lindblom, 1959). We discuss the question of the rationality of management at greater length in the next chapter.

Management practices: a new realism?

Demarcating the boundaries of rationality helped to extend the study of management. But discussion of the core issue of defining and classifying activities moved on to a more detailed 'realism'. Fores and Glover argue that, 'observation shows that [this] classical view is largely a convenient fiction. ... In reality, executive work is complex, confusing to the outsider, and rarely predictable (1976: 194). What 'observations' are they talking about? By getting a large and varied group of managers to fill in diaries, Stewart (1967) drew up classifications based on how they spent their *time*. This produced emissaries, writers, discussers, troubleshooters and committee men. A later study (1976) focused on patterns of contact; this time identifying hub, peer-dependent, man-management and solo. In contrast, Mintzberg (1973) confined himself to five chief executives and classified ten roles with three headings. Under *interpersonal* come figurehead, leader and liaison; under *informational* are monitor, disseminator and spokesman; and under *decisional* come entrepreneurial, disturbance-handler, resource allocator and negotiator. Many of the categories used in these and other studies are largely interchangeable, for example leader/figurehead/spokesman (Hales, 1986). New terms such as 'network building' and 'setting agendas' correspond in substance to old favourites such as 'planning'. Hales (1993: 3) is surely right that Fayol's basic formulation endures, despite subsequent claims that it is outdated or superseded. He produces a composite list (see Table 7.1) from six of the best-known studies, which 'exhibit striking parallels with the supposedly outdated "classical principles of management"' (1986: 95). In addition, some of the variations merely reflect managerial *ideologies*, with modern writers in a more democratic era preferring to describe command as motivation (Mullins, 1985: 121).

Nevertheless, it remains the case that the new empirical studies do partly break with traditional approaches and those found in popular management books. Once the complication of producing labels and lists is set aside, more realistic insights are available. We have already referred to Cyert and March's findings on the short-term incrementalism in the sphere of decision-making. But the significant breakthroughs are aided by a willingness to use a greater variety of research methods than those used in broadbrush analyses of managerial functions. Structured or unstructured observation methods, time-budget studies and self-report questionnaires can capture a greater sense of fluidity and processual factors (Horne and Lupton, 1965; Stewart, 1967, 1976; Mintzberg, 1973; Kotter, 1982; Burns, 1982).

Such studies purport to reveal that the image of the reflective strategist, thinker and planner is a myth. An alternative picture is indicated through the language of realism. Though there are variations between the studies, management practices are said to be opportunistic, habitual, tactical, reactive, frenetic, ad hoc, brief, fragmented and concerned with fixing. This arises primarily because the manager has to adapt to continued uncertainties, limited information and contradictory pressures, not least on time and energy. As a result, routines are shaped by short time spans, the domination of face-to-face interaction and lateral communication in gathering and using information. For Mintzberg, this actually corresponds to managerial preferences for use of informal structures, gossip and speculation.

Nor are such activities necessarily bad for effectiveness and efficiency. Though energy can be dissipated in conflict and power struggles between cliques, Kotter (1982) points out that patterns do emerge based on establishing and maintaining networks vital for co-operation and a flow of information. The 'realist' challenge to the scientific and rational character of management is useful and widely accepted. It has not, however, established unchallenged intellectual domination. Not only do textbooks remain influenced

Table 7.1 **Managerial functions**

1 Acting as a figurehead and leader of an organisational unit
2 Liason: the formation and maintenance of contacts
3 Monitoring, filtering and disseminating information
4 Allocating resources
5 Handling disturbances and maintaining workflows
6 Negotiating
7 Innovating
8 Planning
9 Controlling and directing subordinates.

Source: Colin P. Hales (1986) 'What Do Managers Do? A Critical Review of the Evidence', *Journal of Management Studies*, 23. 1: 95.

by prescriptions from Fayol, but preoccupations with new lists of functions can still be described as variations on a classical theme. Indeed the actual choice of new lists is extensive. Many popular management writers recycle a limited number of activities under new and more exotic titles, including that of jungle fighter and gamesman (Maccoby, 1977). Much more influential has been Peters and Waterman's (1982) list of eight characteristics associated with 'excellent' companies, itself influenced by the classic writings of Barnard. Lists of any kind continue to be the outward form of a belief in a universal, transferable and common essence of management, a disposition that has been relatively constant in the development of organisational theory (Huczynski, 1993: 98). Partly in response to the excesses of claims about new forms of organisation and management, influential voices are calling for a return to that 'essence', though it may be redefined in different ways, for example as the pursuit of rhetoric, identity and robust action (Eccles and Nohria, 1992).

Watson (1994: 37) suggests that new empirical studies have produced an overreaction to classical perspectives. Drawing on his own research among managers he argues that there is a need to get back to basic principles, while recognising the inherent complexity of practice. Put more analytically, he is suggesting that we can distinguish between the real functions (such as planning and co-ordinating) that management has, and the activities through which effectiveness is sought. Nor is this impetus to return to some of classical themes purely theoretical. The past decade has seen the rise of a competence movement in a number of countries that aims to specify a common currency of occupational standards and develop managers with the aid of behavioural and task measurements (Burgoyne, 1993).

There are also inherent limits to the realist research. It is, as Hales (1988) notes, an internal critique, and at the heart of the problem is the fact that it is at the empirical level only. Realism can show us that management is not what it is made out to be. Instead it portrays the activities of managers 'as a quite arbitrary set of roles with little suggestion as to why they are as they are' (P. Armstrong, 1986: 19). The pervasive image of ad-hocery and muddling through seems to deny both purpose and coherence. Hales (1986) rightly observes that by focusing on individual jobs, rather than management as a process, behaviour is unsituated and neglects the institutional context and functions. This is worsened by the tendency of behavioural analysis to concentrate on observable activities in a non-problematical way. For all its limitations, responsibilities and functions were the focus of classical theory and many of the criticisms levelled have been attacks on a straw man (Berkeley Thomas, 1993: 51). In this sense 'realism' marks a retreat from a broader framework of analysis.

Understanding managerial work requires questions to be asked not just about what managers do, but what they have to ensure others do: in other words, an emphasis on the control of particular organisational units in the labour process, albeit as one phase of the management process rather than the whole story (Hales, 1988: 5). As one manager commented to Watson in response to the question, what is the essential difference between a managerial and non-managerial job, 'Gut feel says to me: in a managerial job you have some aspect of controlling other people – directing things. I don't like the words I am using here but if I'm actually honest, it's about directing other people' (1994: 49).

Analysing management in terms of its control functions on behalf of capital is associated with labour process or neo-Marxist perspectives. These criticise the previously discussed approaches for focusing on individual activities, marginalising the neglect of the broader structural context. Or, as Tsoukas puts it, 'By reducing the study of managers to the study of individual actors on the stage, the script and the setting which enables actors to perform in the first place are neglected' (1994a: 294). However, to leap from the individual to structure runs the risk of producing over-generalised, over-deterministic accounts. Indeed, many commentators have objected precisely on these grounds, arguing that the managerial activity of making the organisation work is multifaceted, and that managers cannot be treated as 'ciphers' who simply serve other, higher interests (Alvesson and Willmott, 1992: 7). Managers may pursue their own interests and identities (Watson, 1994); act in a genuinely altruistic way on behalf of the organisation (Grint, 1995); or promote sectional interests, for example engineering, that are distinct from those of capitalists (Shenhav, 1999).

We explore some of the relations between management, strategy and control in more detail in the next chapter. However, as Grint (1995: 51) admits, labour process accounts have become subtler in their explanations of why managers do what they do. In particular, as Tsoukas (1994a: 294) notes, neo-Marxist research has tried to overcome the problem of the leap from individual to structure by introducing more complexity into the picture through a focus on management divisions of labour. The next section considers these contributions.

Bringing the threads together: the managerial labour process

What is required is a structural analysis that can account for both the constraints on and complexities of managerial behaviour: a perspective that is neither deterministic nor voluntaristic. *One* way forward begins from a remark made by Braverman that 'Management has become administration, which is a labour process conducted for the purpose of control within the corporation, and conducted moreover as a labour process exactly analogous to the process of production' (1974: 267). An offshoot is that the alienating conditions attached to the purchase and sale of labour become part of the managerial apparatus itself. Though little more than an aside, it has been utilised by a number of writers, notably Teulings (1986), to produce an analysis of management's role in the administrative apparatus of industrial organisations. The very fact that management is a 'global agent' carrying out the delegated functions of capital means that it is part of a collective labour process at corporate level. As we have previously indicated, this delegation in part reflects the transfer of functions such as co-ordination from the market to management and administration.

Traditional analyses of middle management have tended to focus on the contradictory pressures from above and below, but that underestimates the consequences of greater differentiation of levels and roles. So, for example, large administrative divisions are, in the case of accounting, 'producing nothing but elaborate mechanisms of control associated with the realisation of capital and its enlargement' (Johnson, 1980: 355). But it is not only a case of the emergence of specialised functions and departments. Differentiation also takes place in terms of *levels*. Teulings puts forward a model based on the existence of four distinct management functions: ownership, administration, innovation, and production (see Table 7.2). Two major consequences of the new division of labour follow. First, though the power of the administrative machinery of which management is a part has increased, the power of *individual* managers tends to diminish due to the rationalisation and routinisation of their activities. With the development of more complex managerial structures, new techniques have been introduced to integrate, monitor and control middle and lower management (Carter, 1985: 98):

> " Years ago there might be five hundred fellas but you would only have one boss. Now everyone has a chief. ... You can't discuss the job with them, everything is ticked in little boxes now. The boss is scared because if they don't treat everyone in a standard way they are afraid the other bosses will report them.
> (Plessey engineer quoted in Thompson and Bannon, 1985: 170)

Hale's analysis of management divisions of labour qualifies Teulings by showing that some management functions – those that the latter designates as operational – have their origins in the labour process rather

Table 7.2 **Institutionalisation of distinctive management functions at separate levels of management**

Function	Levels
I the ownership function – accumulation of capital	institutional management – creation and preservation of legitimations
II the administrative function – allocation of investments	strategic management – development of objectives
III the innovation function – product market development	structuring management – new combinations of production factors
IV the production function – control of the direct labour process	operational management – direction and co-ordination of direct labour

Source: W. M. Teulings, 'Managerial Labour Processes in Organised Capitalism', in D. Knights and H. Willmott (eds) (1986) *Managing the Labour Process*, Aldershot: Gower.

than the market, and that there is not an exact correspondence between functions and levels. Those divisions are vertically fractionalised so that 'there is a differentiation within the performance of management work in terms of the extent to which agents are involved in the decision-making process' (Hales, 1988: 10; and see Hales, 1993, chap. 8). As Watson (1994) shows in his account of a major UK telecommunications firm, even senior plant-level managers will frequently find themselves frustrated by centralised control in companies that takes place at cost to their strategic inputs oriented towards long-term viability. Many will be subordinated to senior management through merely providing information from which decisions are made.

The activity of managers managing other managers takes place in different forms in the modern corporation, whether it be multidivisional structures, holding companies or conglomerates, where varying forms of decentralisation go hand-in-hand with increased accountability, monitoring and performance review. Such controls are not wholly new. Even the detailed studies of management functions discussed earlier in the chapter had the purpose of restructuring and rationalisation. Both Mintzberg (1973) and Drucker (1979) favoured using techniques to split off routine activities from senior layers, introducing separation of conception and execution within management itself. At a micro-level, techniques such as management by objectives became significant. These reproduced an aspect of the relationship workers have with 'scientific management', though presented as a form of control and motivation arising from the objective demands of the task (Drucker, 1955). There is also a history of managers becoming more literally victims of their own control devices (Storey, 1983: 93), as shown in studies such as Nichols and Beynon (1977) on the chemical industry.

But a strong case can be made that the conditions of managerial work have deteriorated as the labour process has tightened around their activities. There are two main dimensions to this trend. First, there is work intensification, flattening-out of career structures and exposure to redundancy, associated primarily with de-layering. The latter is geared towards reduction of co-ordination costs by reducing the number of levels in the managerial hierarchy. While, there is room for debate about the extent of de-layering (see Chapter 13), an increasing number of studies have highlighted its negative consequences. Middle managers in particular are becoming prime victims of organisational restructuring, affecting power and status, as well as security and opportunity (Littler, Bramble and McDonald, 1994; Newell and Dopson,

1996; Scarbrough and Burrell, 1996; Sennett 1998; McCann, Morris and Hassard, 2008). As the latter study notes, the intensification of the middle management labour process has become normalised in circumstances of intensive competition and perpetual restructuring: 'In return for greater financial rewards (at least in the private sector), managers were resigned to increased surveillance, greater work intensification, levels of responsibility, reduced security, and fewer opportunities for promotion' (McCann, Morris and Hassard, 2008: 365).

Second, there is the technological capacity to track the activities and measure the performance of managers (Boreham, Parker, Thompson and Hall, 2008). This refers both to the transparency of contemporary ICT, that can decompose and reorder managerial tasks and its ability to gather information on that work (Scarbrough and Burrell, 1996). We traditionally associate technological surveillance with routine work, but the systems created to measure and control those activities have a dual function – they can also be used to monitor the performance of factory managers (Zuboff, 1988), call centre team leaders (Houlihan, 2002) or air traffic controllers (Hallier, 2004). Practices such as balanced scorecard add verifiable and often web-based data to the traditional domain of setting and measuring managerial performance. While tales of managers and professionals being available round-the-clock by email and mobile phone may be exaggerated, there is solid evidence from general (Fraser, 2001) and case studies (Collinson and Collinson, 1997) that electronic surveillance can create new expectations of managerial time and effort. In one sense these findings are reassuring for, if popular management texts are to be believed, ICT and new organisational forms are making middle management redundant. While we examine the evidence on such matters in Part II, it is worth making the point that managers are not mere information relays in an organisational hierarchy (Mutch, 2002). Information systems cannot wholly displace the tacit knowledge, personal skills and political manipulation that keep the show on the road. Managerial fashion may dictate the endorsement of post-bureaucratic nostrums, but as some surveys show, new layers of management are almost as likely to (re)emerge as tiers disappear (Storey, Mabey and Thompson, 1997).

A further consequence of changes in the managerial labour process is the growth of structural conflicts and imbalances between the different levels and functions. Teulings argues that each level of management tends to follow a rational logic of its own, enhancing the potential for defence of specific group interests, for example between production-oriented operational management and the strata concerned with innovation in product markets. Such tendencies are worsened by the absence of, or limits to, formal mechanisms to resolve or bargain conflicts. Instead they are likely to be dealt with at the operational level, leading to a disproportionate emphasis on changing the practices of shop floor workers. As managerial structures and functions become more complex, there tends to be an increase in competing claims to 'ownership' of particular ideas and practices. Such competition cannot be wholly understood within the kind of framework that talks of levels. It neglects the role of what P. Armstrong calls inter-professional competition (1984; 1986; 1987b). It has long been recognised that professional groups pursue market strategies based on claims to exclusivity of knowledge and monopolies over a set of practices (Johnson, 1972; H. Brown, 1980). But the examples and models have mostly come from the older and 'social' professions such as law and medicine, with professions active in business seldom figuring as prominently. One of the reasons for the neglect is that the sociology of the professions has emphasised the traditional 'role conflict' between professional autonomy and the bureaucratic principles of work organisation (Child, 1984; Rueschemeyer, 1986). Radical writers interpret these trends in terms of the conflict between acting for capital, while increasingly taking on the characteristics of employees. Some refer to the growth of a new professional-managerial class (Ehrenreich and Ehrenreich, 1979), with others prefer to talk of the proletarianisation of the 'middle layers' (Braverman: 1974). While some insights can be gained from such perspectives, a primary focus on issues of class location is limited. Armstrong's model allows us to focus on the specific role of the professions in the managerial labour process.

Professions, managers and HRM within a business context

For Armstrong (1989), employers and senior managers are inescapably dependent on other groups to secure corporate goals and policies – an *agency* relationship. So in practice, management functions for capital are mediated by competition between occupational groups. Each profession has a core of specialist knowledge and activities that can form the basis of advancement through a 'collective mobility project'. But the core can only be used effectively if it is sufficiently indeterminate to prevent parts being detached, or routinised. While the general point might apply to all professions, those active in business have to face rival claims over the carrying out of control functions. For example, drawing on the work of Layton (1969), Armstrong (1986: 26) argues that scientific management's techniques and justification for the control of labour through the 'planning department' was an expression of an ideology of engineering. Industrial engineering rests on the design of operating procedures which monitor and control labour costs (Storey, 1983: 275). But the attempt to place engineers at the apex of the firm through the diffusion of such techniques has clearly not been fully achieved, given that engineers do not predominate in the higher levels of management. At the heart of this 'failure' lies the difficulty of maintaining a monopoly over control practices that could be carried out by others.

To make matters worse, British development has taken place based on a definition of management hostile to engineering. This is because of a combination of finance and marketing as favoured specialisms, and the tendency to define management as a set of general functions and skills divorced from productive expertise (see earlier in this chapter). One commentator noted that a result has been 'a whole generation of MBA students who will not go near a manufacturing strategy. ... They want to be in at the gin-and-tonic end with the financial strategy' (quoted in Armstrong, 1987b: 428). Other professions have gained because of the popular belief that the education of engineers does not equip them for dealing with people and money. As a potential agency they therefore experience difficulty in establishing the vital commodity of 'trust' with those in positions of power. It is therefore not surprising that many engineers seek a route out of production into senior management through courses such as MBAs. The consequent low status of engineering identified in the Finneston Report and by Child and colleagues (1983) is, however, as we have seen, a peculiarly Anglo-American phenomenon. In contrast, German management is dominated by professional engineers, due in part to the historical relevance of engineering techniques and technical education to competition with British and other manufacturing goods, and to access to training in financial techniques.

In the case of accounting and other financial specialisms, there has been a dramatic rise from the days of poorly paid clerks and bookkeeping tasks. Some of the factors involved include the development of management accounting as cost-control techniques in the industrial restructuring during and after the depression of the mid-1920s. In the United States, the control function of management accounting can be clearly identified in the following definition from the National Association of Accountants:

> the process of identification, measurement, accumulation, analysis, preparation, interpretation, and communication of financial information used by management to plan, evaluate and control within an organisation and to ensure appropriate use and accountability for its resources. (Quoted in Wardell, 1986: 28)

Other factors include once again the need for co-ordination and control over middle managers in multidivisional companies and the legal requirements for control through auditing. The cohesiveness of an accounting élite in business has been facilitated by the acceptance of an inevitable 'horizontal fissure' in the profession. This has allowed a range of routine tasks to be delegated to 'accounting technicians' (Johnson, 1980; Glover *et al.*, 1986), thus maintaining indeterminacy and monopoly over core practices. Accountants have also undertaken an aggressive campaign to encroach on the spheres of other professions through such measures as manpower audits and human resource accounting (Armstrong, 1986: 32). Though only a minority are closer to real power, the spread of a 'financial rationality' means that British boardrooms are increasingly dominated by those with a background in banking or accountancy, within a 'managerial culture which is often preoccupied with accounting measures and procedures' (Armstrong, 1988).

Such developments began to threaten the power of the personnel function, a segment of management that has also enjoyed a major long-term growth. From the days of its origins in company welfare workers, the Institute of Personnel Managers grew to more than 20,000 members before becoming the Chartered Institute for Personnel and Development (CIPD) that now claims an expanded membership of 130,000. Throughout that development, personnel professionals have had a continual struggle to convince business power holders that they could move from welfare to general management functions. They consolidated a hold over administrative functions such as interviewing and record-keeping, as well as expanding into the newer areas of staff development and determination of wage rates and incentives (Carter, 1985: 102). In a partnership of mutual convenience, the behavioural sciences have helped develop a mystique that 'the personnel manager is probably the only specialist in the organisation whose role can be distinguished by the virtually exclusive concern with the management of human assets' (Mullins, 1985: 129). As Kelly and Gennard observe, 'the authority and power of the HR director is based on the function's possession of expertise in people management knowledge and skills' (2001: 89). However, the problematic of 'dealing with people' has inherent limits in establishing a monopoly of knowledge or practice, particularly when its 'behavioural nostrums' are routinely taught to the full range of business students (Fowler, 1985). It is therefore unsurprising that surveys (Daniel and Millward, 1983) have traditionally reported a lack of qualified and trained personnel staff in many companies. While the use of specialist HR managers may have spread, large numbers of small and medium-sized companies appear to survive without such them.

Fortunately for the profession other factors began to work in their favour, notably increased legal regulation of the employment relationship, such as the spate of employee legislation and codes of practice in the UK in the 1960s and 1970s, and the recommendations of the Donovan Report (1968) that firms should centralise and formalise their bargaining procedures. Both measures allowed personnel to extend and monopolise spheres of expertise, as well as exercise greater authority over lower line managers (Armstrong, 1986: 37). But deregulation of labour markets, decentralisation of bargaining and scrapping of aspects of employment law have given a further twist to the ratchet of inter-professional competition by eroding or redistributing established personnel functions. This is complicated by the rise of human resource management (HRM). On the surface it seems positive; after all personnel managers have long trumpeted the importance of treating human resources as an organisation's greatest asset rather than a cost to be minimised. HRM can then be seen as an upmarket version of personnel with a tactical name change (Torrington, 1989). This is perhaps the 'soft' version of HRM, with the harder versions stressing the integration of the management of human resources into core business strategy and practice (Guest, 1989; Storey, 1989). The significance of the latter is that it enables, perhaps obliges, other managerial groups, particularly line managers, to take HRM 'on-board'.

Whether it was in fact becoming more strategic or more effective was always open to dispute (Guest, 1990), but the perception of greater centrality has sparked off a struggle by managers across a variety of functions to absorb the rhetoric and responsibilities of HRM (Poole and Mansfield, 1992). The efforts of traditional practitioners to defend and carve out new territories is not helped by periodic and widely-reported stories such as the one from a team at the London School of Economics that produced the headline: 'Personnel officers are a waste of time says new study' (*Independent on Sunday*, 15 May 1994). In the USA, considerable heat was generated by an article 'Why We Hate HR' (Hammond, 2005) featured on the front cover of *Fast Company* magazine. Noting that the function still doesn't appear to occupy a seat at the top of the corporate table, Hammond repeats the familiar gripes about focusing on administrative trivia and rule monitoring. However, how central the HR function is, like most things, is not universal. Studies such as Jacoby's (2005) account comparing corporate governance in the US and Japan, continue to find a more significant role in employment systems with higher trust relations. Compared to countries such as Japan, HR managers in the USA have been experiencing tougher times. Even in the low-trust UK, there are studies that seek to correct the pervasive pessimism about the central role of HR. Focusing on the role of senior HR managers on a variety of boardroom bodies, the case studies of Gennard and Kelly (2001) report a persistent degree of informal and formal influence. This is facilitated by a variety of career routes, with some combining functional expertise with experience of general management, thus adding to boardroom credibility. Focusing on the skills and trajectories of individual HR directors may not always give us an adequate picture of the function and its competitive position. Arguably it is not so much their skills, but their role in skill formation in the wider workforce that has greater salience. From the mid-1980s onwards, the raised profile and status of HR has largely depended on the crucial role attributed to employee skills, knowledge and commitment in organisational performance (Pfeffer, 1994; 1998). This 'profits through people' message leads to a focus on clusters of HR practices that successful organisations require in making a difference, including employment security, intensive and selective recruitment, and investment in training. This approach was the underlying basis of the 'bargain' for employees to buy into high-performance work systems or new psychological contracts.

But, as one of us has remarked elsewhere, 'what if in contemporary capitalism people are not "our most important asset"' (Thompson, 2007: 88)? It is widely observed, even in mainstream business research, that with the pursuit of shareholder value dictating more short-termism, downsizing and perpetual restructuring, the burden of risk is increasingly transferred to employees, who are exhorted to take over responsibility for skill and career development and/or abandon any hope of stable, long-term employment (Deal and Kennedy, 1999). Such trends, discussed in more detail in Chapters 12 and 15, diminish the credibility of the power and pervasiveness of its primary agency – the HR function (Rubery *et al.* 2005). Drawing on the experiences of the fracturing of the social contract between employers and employees, Kochan (2006), a leading advocate of HRM, has argued that the function is undergoing a crisis of trust and a loss of legitimacy in the eyes of its major stakeholders. He calls for a major re-evaluation of the values and professional identities that inform specialist HR roles, and a broader alliance than the close relationship with high-flying senior executives. That won't be easy given the economic climate shaping the actions of firms in liberal market economies. Harder, economic models of HRM that enable firms to monitor and measure people as assets measure may appear to be more sellable (Elias and Scarbrough, 2004; Royal and O'Donnell, 2005). Of course, HR managers are not a single, homogeneous group with same functions and interests. Perhaps, like other professional groups, HR is heading for a split: 'a polarised profession consisting of a mass of "clerks of works", performing routine administrative work for a newly self-confident line management, while a few élite "architects" of strategic human resources policy continue to operate at the corporate headquarters level' (Armstrong, 1988: 25).

Whatever the direction, the work of Armstrong highlights that managerial groups have constantly to fight to establish their usefulness through the agency relationship. Given successive waves of organisational restructuring driven by the latest managerial fads or new environmental pressures, the territory for that battle is constantly shifting. Many large organisations have undergone major change programmes, often culture-led, in recent years. Companies are increasingly seeking to recruit managers who have experience of such programmes, irrespective of their function of origin. The HR function is in a difficult position, given that senior executives often aim to decentralise responsibilities to line mangers, and may be reluctant to let HR, or indeed any functional group, be seen to 'own' the change process. Research from Marks and colleagues (1997) on the spirits industry suggests that HR personnel can seek influence through their expertise as 'managers of culture'. Culture is often seen as the glue that holds change initiatives together, and culture is ultimately seen to be 'about people'. This creates opportunities for HR to influence change agendas and measure the success or otherwise of measures geared towards transforming attitudes and performance. Other avenues for restoring potential lost legitimacy draw on knowledge economy rhetorics such as the 'war for talent' and the reputational advantages conferred by being seen as an 'employer of choice' or 'best company to work for' (Boxall and Purcell, 2003: 12).

Change processes are not just associated with HR, but may set off sharp inter-professional conflicts. In a valuable study of newly privatised utilities in the UK that explicitly uses Armstrong's framework, Mulholland (1998) identifies a struggle between 'public sector survivors' and 'movers and shakers'. The former are older managers primarily from engineering and technical backgrounds within the water and electricity industries, while the latter are younger, with a graduate background, and reputations built through efficiency drives in the private sector. Mulholland demonstrates that because they are 'tainted' with public sector values, engineers have become non-preferred managers, their competencies marginalised and status diminished. In contrast the private sector experience and entrepreneurial attitudes of the newly-recruited group mean that they have become the trusted and preferred agency of senior management. As one corporate manager put it: 'Obviously the people who came into the industry aren't carrying the baggage of forty years of nationalised industry culture.... They are knocking aside the tribal custom for us' (Mulholland, 1998: 191).

The kind of analysis in this section usefully adds to an understanding of the complex levels and functions within managerial work. Some of these ways of seeing could be equally applied to other managerial functions and practices. For example, some of the newer groups such as business consultants, research and development engineers and IT analysts have found it necessary to assert their knowledge to challenge the existing expert division of labour (Reed, 1992a). As we shall discuss in more detail in Chapter 16, IT specialists have been particularly active and successful in laying claim to the more recent territory of knowledge-management systems (Scarbrough and Swan, 2001). This discussion of competing expertise draws attention to a wider point about management. As Whitley (1984) argues, there is limited standardisation across managerial tasks and this helps to explain the lack of progress in establishing management as such as a profession. The growth of MBAs and other qualifications suggests attempts to develop certification of skills and knowledges, as well as a career route. But they can best be seen as a form of individual credentialism and filter into higher-paid jobs, and not necessarily a convincing one, with some employers showing considerable scepticism (Oliver, 1993).

Summary and key points

We began this chapter by arguing that though traditional and more recent mainstream research offers important insights, the perspectives are partial and flawed, presenting management as if it is neutral and de-politicised, neglecting the divisions and contradictions embedded in the managerial labour process itself. While 'realist' studies that note the messy and sometimes muddled realities of managerial life are a useful corrective to classical perspectives, the focus of analysis on the individual manager leads to a neglect of broader processes, functions and levels. In the second half of the chapter, we argued that the actions of different groups within the managerial labour process was a useful way forward. Drawing on the work of Armstrong and others, a focus on competing agencies and professions emphasises the specific historical bases and differences in the development of management theories and practices. This is particularly the case between different national traditions, though we have had little space to elaborate on them here. The discussion embodies the general purpose of the chapter: that of developing a structural analysis of management that recognises the contradictory sources of influence over activity. It should be clear that managers need not be treated as over-determined 'ciphers' in order to explain their work in a structural way. A conception of agency can be utilised that accepts considerable variation in management practices, as well as enabling us to understand the rise of new groups competing for influence. We have also been able to illustrate the competing rationalities of contending groups, without accepting the mainstream notion of a single, neutral rationality underpinning managerial theory and practice. Some of these issues resurface again in different form in the following two chapters. Power and control are central dimensions underpinning the activities of managers as well as central to an understanding of organisations in their own right.

Further reading

There are two very good bodies of theoretically informed empirical work on managers from British writers. Hales (1986; 2000; 2002) writes about changes and continuities in general managerial work, while Armstrong (1984; 1987a; 1988; 1989) discusses different groups of professionals and managers. A newer research project from McCann and colleagues promises similar insights. Mintzberg's (1973) study of managerial work was a landmark in the US and he continues to produce interesting analyses around this and other business topics (see http://www.henrymintzberg.com/).

Armstrong, P. (1984) 'Competition between the Organisational Professions and the Evolution of Management Control Strategies', in K. Thompson (ed.), *Work, Employment and Unemployment*, Milton Keynes: Open University Press.

Armstrong, P. (1987b) 'Engineers, Management and Trust', *Work, Employment and Society*, 1. 4: 421–40.

Armstrong, P. (1988) 'The Personnel Profession in the Age of Management Accountancy', *Personnel Review*, 17. 1: 25–31.

Armstrong, P. (1989) 'Management, Labour Process and Agency', *Work, Employment and Society*, 3. 3: 307–22.

Child, J. (1969) *British Management Thought*: A Critical Analysis, London: George Allen & Unwin.

Hales, C. (1993, 2nd edn 2000) *Managing through Organisation*, London: Routledge.

Hales, C. (2002) '"Bureaucracy-lite" and continuities in managerial work', *British Journal of Management*, 13. 2: 51–66.

Hales, C. P. (1986) 'What do Managers Do? A Critical Review of the Evidence', *Journal of Management Studies*, 23. 1: 88–115.

McCann, L., Morris, J. and Hassard, J. (2008) 'Normalized Intensity: The New Labour Process of Middle Management', *Journal of Management Studies*, 45. 2: 343–71.

Mintzberg, H. (1973) *The Nature of Managerial Work*, New York: Harper & Row.

8 control and resistance

> Asked what the secret of successful automotive management was, a senior General Motors executive replied, 'Control. Deal control. Product control. Labour control.' (Quoted in Huczynski, 1993: 185)

The aims of this chapter are to:

- Assert the significance of control against a tendency of mainstream analyses to present it as marginal or of diminishing relevance.
- To elaborate critical perspectives on control, particularly those that derive from labour process theory and its emphasis on a variety of managerial strategies within the contested terrain of the workplace.
- To examine various objections to labour process concepts and to make a qualified defence of them.
- To discuss and evaluate more recent research on control, particularly those that argue for a decisive shift towards surveillance and self-discipline, ultimately pointing to patterns of continuity as well as change.

We can see from the discussion in the previous chapter that practically and theoretically management is intertwined with control. Yet why and how is strongly contested between mainstream and critical approaches. This chapter examines contrasting perspectives on understanding control. It is primarily about conceptualisation rather than current evidence of the *outcomes* of control strategies and techniques. These will be dealt with mainly in Chapter 15.

Mainstream mis/understandings

The treatment of control in mainstream writing is ambiguous at best, marginal at worst. Frameworks that assume goal consensus can often simply ignore or trivialise the issue. When it is discussed explicitly in standard textbooks, the chapters devoted to it are sometimes of a rather bizarre nature in almost omitting any reference to conflicts between groups. The talk is of technical inputs and outputs in a self-adjusting system, performance standards and feedback mechanisms. It is also seen in a unitary way: 'controlled performance' with an assumption of goal-consensus. Control is reduced to a *monitoring* device, with management's role to check progress, ensure that actions occur as planned, correct any deviation, or reassure us that what we are doing is appropriate (O'Reilly and Chatman, 1996). Some writers (Lawlor, 1976) put an emphasis on people desiring control, for example getting enjoyment from dependence on higher authority. This is the other side of the coin from attributing control to the pathological desires of particular individuals – those that are described as 'control freaks'. Resistance is smuggled in occasionally when discussing the *behavioural* implications as people 'react' to control processes, requiring management to adjust strategies accordingly.

This apparent absence of control from the mainstream is, however, somewhat misleading. The issues are there but they are articulated in different language and concepts. As the influential mainstream writer

Pfeffer notes, 'control is at once the essential problem of management and organisation and the implicit focus of much of organisation studies' (1997: 100). The key term here is *implicit*. When control is discussed it is often alongside co-ordination. Any complex division of labour requires mechanisms to set goals, allocate responsibilities and evaluate the effectiveness of performance. Co-ordination is a more neutral term than control and more compatible with an assumption that management is a largely neutral set of techniques and competencies.

Even when texts do have chapters with control in the title, they often pass over quickly into other issues such as job design, organisational structure or leadership. In the first instance, debate is focused on designing structures which facilitate levels of control and co-ordination appropriate to types of work that require different levels of discretion and standardisation. In the second, discussion of leadership styles such as the classic polarity of authoritarian versus democratic is a way of discussing control, but through the language of influence and motivation. So what is described in mainstream writing as technical and human organisation and the need to integrate the two could be alternatively thought of in terms of competing control systems. For example, in their historical survey of American managerial discourse, Barley and Kunda (1992) distinguish between rational (for example, scientific management, systems theories) and normative (for example, human relations, organisational culture) ideologies of control. Rather than one simply displacing another, there are successive and alternate waves paralleling broad cycles of economic expansion and contraction.

We do accept that not all control processes arise from, or are structured by, antagonistic interests. Stock inventories and financial budgeting are necessary and not always conflictual features of any system of work organisation. A written job description may under certain conditions actually allow employees to assert power or control. But most control processes remain difficult to separate from the social relations of work, even when they appear to be neutral. This was the important conclusion of Blau and Schoenherr (1971), who used the concept of *insidious* controls to highlight the way in which management can utilise impersonal and unobtrusive means. Examples include selective recruitment of staff whose sense of professionalism or expertise enables them to work without direct controls; use of resource allocation as a financial discipline; and controls embodied in technology. Thus even those staff who exercise considerable work autonomy, such as those in higher education, have a series of indirect constraints over their actions.

In practice mainstream theory is more uncomfortable with its own marginalisation of control than the above discussion might suggest. The simple indication of that can be seen in the frequency with which the death of Taylorism or bureaucracy is announced. Implicit in these pronouncements is the recognition that control does exist, but the preference that it *shouldn't*. From the human relations writers of the 1950s, with their distinctions between (bad) theory X and (good) theory Y, to the advocates of 1970s-style job enrichment, control has been presented as unnecessary and outdated. Democratic leadership styles and autonomous workgroups have been seen as the basic precondition for job satisfaction and high productivity. Recent formulations have moved the debate further on. It is said that we now live in a world where change is so frequent and expertise so fundamental to the work process that 'command and control' is not merely undesirable, it is actually bad for business. Picking up on themes from the academic literature (Walton, 1985), the editor of a Scottish business journal asserts that:

> The pyramidal, hierarchical school of management is, at long last, being dragged to its knees and kicked to death. Command and control is not an option in what is rapidly becoming an economy founded on knowledge and the skills of those who have it. In such an economy it seems employees will have to be involved in strategic decision-making if organisational goals are to be achieved. (B. Millar, *Scottish Business Insider*, October 1998)

The language of contemporary management theory and practice has therefore been based around two axes: empowerment and commitment. The former suggests that organisations are delegating control to project groups and work teams, so that they become *self*-managing; the latter implies that values rather than rules have become the prime means of co-ordination. As indicated earlier, it is not our intention to examine these claims at this point. We will merely observe that they represent a continued evasion of the relevant issues. Control is either rhetorically abolished or presented in softer, more neutral terms. One of the problems with such approaches is their aspirational nature and the subsequent tendency to conflate prescription and description. Take, for example, the empowerment literature. In an incisive review, Hales (2000: 503) comments that, 'the burgeoning prescriptive or celebratory literature is replete with conceptions of empowerment which display equivocation, tautology and contradiction in equal measure'. He suggests that it is not clear whether power is to be achieved or received, what kind of powers are being enhanced (voice in decisions or choice over actions?), or the extent to which individuals or teams are expected to exercise delegated responsibilities. Such ambiguities tend to be terms – such as 'directed autonomy' – that paper over in words what is likely to be contradictory in practice (Waterman, 1988). Mainstream theory lacks conceptual frameworks that are robust enough to deal with the nature, types and levels of control. For this we have to turn elsewhere.

Critical perspectives: labour process theories of control and resistance

Pfeffer rightly observes that 'the ambivalence about the effects (if not the effectiveness) of social control is in part responsible for the development of a critical perspective on organisations and their control practices' (1997: 135). In contrast to mainstream theorists, radical writers on organisation and management frequently *begin* from an analysis of control relations. Whereas mainstream perspectives treat control and co-ordination together, radical theorists argue that management performs a *dual* function in the enterprise (Carchedi, 1977; R. Edwards, 1979). Managerial practices are a necessary means of *co-ordinating* diverse activities, but they also bear the imprint of conflicting interests in the labour process, a conflict that reflects the unique nature of labour as a commodity. This orientation was reflected in the first radical text to make a major impact as organisation theory, which began by defining the theoretical rationale of organisational analysis: 'For this volume we have proposed as such an object the concept of organisation as control of the labour process' (Clegg and Dunkerley, 1980: 1). This framework derived from Marx's analysis of the capitalist labour process, which was updated and revitalised by Braverman (1974) and a range of other 'labour process' theorists discussed below.

All societies have labour processes, but under capitalism they have specific characteristics. The most significant is what Marx referred to as the transformation of labour power into labour. In other words, when capital purchases labour it has only a potential or capacity to work. To ensure profitable production, capital must organise the conditions under which labour operates to its own advantage. But workers pursue their own interests for job security, higher rewards and satisfying work, developing their own counter-organisation through informal job controls, restriction of output, and the like.

To resolve this problem, and because they are under competitive pressure from other firms to cut costs and raise productivity, employers seek to control the conditions under which work takes place. This argument is often misunderstood. Pfeffer says that Marxist analysis 'asserts that control, not efficiency, is the object of organising arrangements' (1997: 180). While radical approaches would challenge particular conceptions of efficiency, control is not an end in itself, but a means to transform the capacity to work, established by the wage relation, into profitable production. It is a term summarising a set of mechanisms and practices that regulates the labour process (P. K. Edwards, 1990). Richard Edwards (1979: 18) distinguishes three elements in any system of control:

1   direction and specification of work tasks
2   evaluation, monitoring and assessment of performance
3   the apparatus of discipline and reward to elicit co-operation and compliance.

Such elements may, however, be best described as detailed control, in that they are normally connected to immediate work processes, whereas general control refers to management's capacity to subordinate labour to their direction of the production process as a whole. This distinction made by P. K. Edwards (1990) and other writers is of significance in that it allows for recognition of tremendous variations in how detailed control is exercised. Such a model can even allow for employers giving workers significant discretion over tasks, as in semi-autonomous work groups, if it maintains their overall control. Control is also not absolute, but, at least at the immediate level, a contested relationship. Conflict is built into the wage–effort bargain, with even mainstream writers recognising that an employment contract outlining required performance runs up against employees with their own goals and wants. As each 'party' seeks to exert its influence over the formal and informal aspects of the employment relationship, the outcome is a constantly changing 'frontier of control' (Goodrich, 1975) or 'contested terrain' (R. Edwards, 1979).

    This latter point illustrates the centrality of resistance to labour process analysis. Richard Edward's research shows how control and resistance exist in dialectical relation. In other words, forms of worker self-organisation and action stimulate management to develop control practices, out of which a systematic pattern might emerge (such 'strategies' are discussed in the next section). Over a period of time, workers learn new ways of resisting those practices, and so on. Labour process accounts became known as a 'control and resistance' model. One of the best illustrations came from the British researchers Edwards and Scullion (1982). Detailed case studies show how workers adapt their behaviour, through actions such as diverse as absence, labour turnover and sabotage to particular modes of control over work organisation or rewards. Equally, they are able to demonstrate how management develop policies and practices on issues such as the provision of overtime as a means of trying to counter powerful shop-floor controls. In another important contribution, Hodson (1995; 2001) examines a range of ethnographic studies to illustrate how forms of resistance, ranging from sabotage to pilferage, develop through openings created by managerial control systems.

    What about the role of management? Claims of independent actors carrying out a neutral role are disputed by evidence concerning the top strata of management (Zeitlin, 1974). By their motivation, social background and connections, rewards and shareholdings in corporations, most managers are part of the capitalist class. While a useful corrective, this 'sociological' analysis is not the crucial point. For example, a number of entrepreneurs are from a traditional working-class background. But what matter are the structural location and functions in the organisation. If anything, entrepreneurs from this background tend to identify even more closely with their new role. These roles require management to carry out functions of control and surveillance, exercising hierarchical authority over workers separated from the means of production. While it is not always clear that it is possible to distinguish between a 'neutral' co-ordination and an 'antagonistic' control, managers do act as agents carrying out the 'global functions' of capital, functions which, as we observed in Chapter 3, were delegated as part of the bureaucratisation of production. The idea of agency conjures up rather crude images of conspiracies and empty vessels: 'In the capitalist system, the principal function of management is to exploit labour power to the maximum in order to secure profits for the owners of capital' (Berkeley Thomas, 1993: 61). But the generality 'to the maximum' is meaningless. There are only specific and diverse means through which the requirements of capital are brought about, in which management takes an active rather than predetermined role.

Critical analyses sometimes get tangled up in attempts to designate managers to precise class positions. This theme does not concern us here (though see Johnston, 1986 for a critical account). What is important is that we have available a framework for understanding management practices which provides an alternative to the dominant combination of behavioural and managerial revolution theories. The fact, for example, that executives of a large corporation have the formal status of employees is, as Braverman observes, merely the form given to the domination of capital in modern society:

> Their formal attribute of being part of the same payroll as the production workers, clerks and porters of the corporation no more robs them of the powers of decision and command over the others in the enterprise than does the fact that the general, like the private, wears the military uniform, or the pope and the cardinal pronounce the same liturgy as the parish priest. (Braverman, 1974: 405)

Instead of the separation of ownership and control, radical writers distinguish between real or economic ownership and agents holding actual possession (De Vroey, 1975; Carchedi, 1977). Managerial agents are governed by the external constraints imposed by the dynamics of competition and capital accumulation, with profitability remaining the crucial criteria through which the successful management work is judged. If anything, this is enhanced by property ownership and related forms of control becoming increasingly depersonalised with the rise of finance, pension funds and other institutional shareholders. Individual enterprises become 'simply units in a structure of intercorporate relations' (J. Scott, 1985: 142), the division of ownership and possession resulting in greater vulnerability for managers who know they may be removed from office (Holland, 1975). A structural analysis does not imply that the growth of new forms of managerial labour is irrelevant. As we saw in the previous chapter, the heterogeneity of management has increased with the sheer extent and diversity of delegated functions and the competing groups, such as accountants and engineers, who lay claim to them.

Management strategies

Critical perspectives have been conditioned by Braverman's (1974) argument that the twentieth century saw the tightening of managerial control, primarily through the application of Taylorist and scientific management strategies. Detailed evidence is provided of the extension of such methods from simple to complex production and its use in the transformation of clerical labour. When allied to managerial shaping of science and technology through mechanisation and automation, work design and organisation continue to embody key Taylorist principles such as task fragmentation and the separation of conception and execution. Braverman provided an important corrective to the widespread view that Taylorism was a failed system, superseded by more sophisticated behavioural theories to be used for motivational and job design tools (see M. Rose, 1975).

But it is widely recognised that Braverman overestimated the dominance of Taylorist strategies and practices, and underestimated the varied and uneven implementation, influenced by worker hostility, management suspicion and appropriateness to given environments. In Chapter 3, we tried to reach a balanced assessment. If Taylorism is taken to be part of a broader movement towards 'scientific' management focused on fragmentation of tasks and their subjection to increasing job measurement and evaluation, as well as the structuring of work processes so that skills and planning activities are located off the factory and office floors, then particular elements remain a highly significant component of control strategies, though seldom on their own.

Precisely because Braverman confused a particular system of control with management control in general, the question of *strategy* was put firmly on the agenda because of the resulting debate on alternatives. This is not to say that issues of strategy had no place in the existing organisational literature. We have already seen in previous chapters how Chandler (1962) regarded strategy, defined as long-term planning and resource allocation to carry out goals, as the characteristic feature of the modern multidivisional firm. But control over employees was not systematically dealt with. Strategy has also been increasingly part of the agenda of the business policy and corporate management literature (Steiner and Miner, 1978). Radical perspectives differ from both in avoiding the prescriptive search for the 'best way'; remaining free to analyse what management does, rather than what it should do.

What of the alternative strategies raised in the labour process debate? Some of the best-known contributions have already been discussed in previous chapters. As we noted earlier, Richard Edward's (1979) model is based on historically successive dominant modes of control, which reflect worker resistance and changing socio-economic conditions. A nineteenth-century system of *simple* or *personal* control by employers exercising direct authority gave way to more complex *structural* forms with the transition from small business, competitive capitalism to corporate monopolies. The first of these forms was *technical* control typified by the use of the assembly line that can pace and direct the labour process. The contradiction for management is that it created a common work experience and basis for unified shop-floor opposition. In contrast, a system of *bureaucratic* control (see Chapter 3), embedded in the social and organisational structure of the firm rather than in personal authority, offers management a means of re-dividing the workforce and tying it to impersonal rules and regulations. With his co-thinkers among radical economists (R. Edwards, Reich and Gordon, 1975; Gordon, Edwards and Reich, 1982), Edwards has also argued that employers consciously create *segmented* labour markets as a response to economic crises and as a divide-and-rule strategy, particularly using gender and race.

In contrast, Friedman (1977) rightly eschews the notion of stages, preferring to set out ideal types or strategic poles of responsible autonomy and direct control which run parallel throughout the history of capitalism (for a description see Chapter 8). Each strategy generates its own inflexibilities in areas such as hiring and firing and task specification. The choice of strategy is governed by variations in the stability of labour and product markets, mediated by the interplay of worker resistance and managerial pressure. There is, however, an element of common ground in the belief that there has been a gradual historical tendency towards more consensual, integrative strategies; utilising internal markets, institutionalised rules and in some cases, work humanisation schemes. This is also the view of the other major control theorist, Burawoy (1979). He periodises the development of capitalist work organisation in terms of the transition from *despotic* to *hegemonic* regimes. The former involved relations of dependence and coercion that did not prove viable for capital or labour. Workers sought collective representation and social protection from the state. Capital also had an interest in state regulation of conflict and a minimal social wage that would boost purchasing power. The shift to hegemonic regimes was also based on an internal state in the workplace that provided an 'industrial citizenship', utilising grievance machinery and regulated bargaining which minimised likely resistance and class solidarity.

Subsequent events have not been kind to such models. The 1980s and 1990s have seen organisational restructuring based on downsizing and de-layering, the search for flexibility in work and employment, a move away from collective and joint regulation of the workplace and a growth in job insecurity. It is always possible, of course, to adjust the model, which Burawoy does by defining the new dominant factory regime as one of *hegemonic despotism*. This is not a return to arbitrary tyranny, but the apparently 'rational' power of a capital that is mobile across the globe, over the workforce (1985: 150). However, the problem is not just with specific projections, but linear thinking more generally. New conceptual categories of this nature merely illustrate the fundamental problem of the control theories we have been examining. Alternative strategies have been put on the map, but too often within what has been described as the 'panacea fallacy' (Littler and Salaman, 1982) or 'monism' (Storey, 1985), that is, the idea that capital always seeks and finds definitive and comprehensive modes of control as the solution to its problems. Admittedly, this is somewhat less true of Friedman, who in his own defence argues that responsible autonomy and direct control have in-built contradictions and are 'two directions towards which managers can move, rather than two predefined states between which managers choose' (1987: 3). But there is still a sense of a search for all-embracing categories, which have their parallels in behavioural theory, such as Etzioni's (1961) structures of compliance, or Schein's (1965) linear models of economic, social and complex man.

Nevertheless, the control debate sparked an extensive and useful amount of empirical work influenced by labour process theory. Early case studies tended to focus on reaffirmation of theses of deskilling and tighter controls (Zimbalist, 1979), or critiques of them highlighting mediating factors such as markets and worker resistance (Wood, 1982). Subsequent efforts were concerned to establish trends in their own right. Studies dealing with the introduction of new technology have stressed that deskilling and direct control represents only one of a range of management strategies (Wilkinson, 1986). Child's (1985) research shows even more clearly how ideas of strategy can be used, while recognising variations in goals and environments. He identified a variety of strategies including elimination of direct labour, sub-contracting, polyvalence or multi-tasking and job degradation. These were connected to an even wider set of influences, including those of national economic cycles, government policy and the culture of organisations.

Other research applied models to specific industries, but without any claims for universality. A good example is the use by researchers of Richard Edwards' control concepts. Murray and Wickham (1985) studied two Irish electronics factories employing mainly female semi-skilled workers, showing that direction, discipline and evaluation are all carried out according to explicit rules rather than direct controls. Supervisors do not monitor production performance and enforce discipline. This is left to inspectors on the basis of statistical records that can identify the operators responsible. Supervisors, however, are central to processes of evaluating the social character of the 'good worker' in order to facilitate promotion through the internal labour market. The elaborate and artificial hierarchy created at the plants meant that one third of workers had been promoted from the basic assembly grade, thus confirming Edwards's view that employees are given positive material reasons for complying with bureaucratic rules. More recently Callaghan and Thompson (2001) used the growth of call centres to revisit Edwards, observing the similarities between automated call distribution systems and previous descriptions of technical control in which managerial authority is embedded within supposed objective mechanisms of work distribution and measurement. We return to this issue and study in the final section of the chapter.

A further direction was to focus on specific strategies and processes of control such as recruitment policies (Fevre, 1986; Maguire, 1986; Winstanley, 1986; Callaghan and Thompson, 2002) that were neglected in an exclusive focus on the labour process. The most extensive research was initially carried out on *gender*. Socially-defined notions of femininity as a form of control have been observed in multinationals operating in the third world (Pearson, 1986). Plant management consciously exploits cultures of passivity and subordination by combining an image of the company as a patriarchal family system with the manager as father figure, Western-style beauty competitions and classes (Grossman, 1979). In the West, Grieco and

Whipp's overview argues that 'managerial strategies of control make use of and enhance the sexual divisions in society' (1985: 136). Studies of office and factory workers (Glenn and Feldberg, 1979; Pollert, 1981; Westwood, 1984; Bradley, 1986) show that management uses women's marginality to work, arising from the family, to frame its labour control policies.

In reflecting on the above debates, a degree of common ground emerged. Product and labour markets, worker resistance and a range of other external and internal factors are recognised as mediating control strategies and shaping power relations in the frontier of control between capital and labour. The variations in strategy that result are not random, but reflect the fundamental tension we have talked of between management's need to control and discipline, while engaging workers' commitment and co-operation. Strategies therefore contain inherent contradictions (Storey, 1985; Hyman, 1987). These are enhanced by the difficulty of harmonising the different managerial functions, sites of intervention and decision-making, which includes technology, social organisation of labour and relations with the representative bodies of employees. Hyman notes that 'there is no "one best way" of managing these contradictions, only different routes to partial failure' (1987: 30). Management of large organisations is therefore likely to try combinations of control strategies and practices, appropriate to particular environments or sections of the workforce. As one of us has remarked elsewhere:

> The most consistent weakness of existing theory has been to counterpoise one form of control to another. ... No one has convincingly demonstrated that a particular form of control is necessary or inevitable for capitalism to function successfully. (Thompson, 1989: 151)

Whatever the limitations of the ideas, as Pfeffer notes, 'labour process theorists have been enormously influential in stimulating a discussion of work place control, not from the point of view of organisational efficiency or management but from the point of view of its determinants and its effects on workers' (1997: 184). The above 'consensus' fails to satisfy those within and outside the radical perspective, who are critical of the explanatory power of concepts concerned with management control strategy. For some, the problem with a Marxist-influenced agenda is that, like more orthodox accounts, it wrongly assumes high levels of rationality, this time applied to top management (Bryman, 1984: 401; Grint, 1995: 51). Others go beyond the previously noted criticism of 'panacea fallacies' to object to the treatment of management as omniscient, omnipotent and monolithic. Based on her study of chemical plants, Harris mocks the image of managers who have the attributes of deity and 'papal inerrancy' when dealing with workers, commenting that radical writers assume that senior management 'always know what is in capital's interests and unfailingly order things so that they work together for its greater good' (1987: 70). There are conflicts within management reflecting contending interest groups and the difficulty of carrying out integrative functions. Nor is it always possible to draw a neat dividing line from workers given that managers are also wage labourers subject to controls. The distortions in such analyses are held to derive from a wider determinism and functionalism in which 'managers are regarded as unproblematic agents of capital who dispatch their "global functions" in a rationalistic manner' (Storey, 1985: 195).

Capital's interests are not given and management practices cannot be 'read-off' from them. Assumptions of a 'tight-coupling' underestimate the diversity and complexity of such practices, and the significance for decision-making processes within the enterprise. It is also the case that in addition to the responsibilities that managers have to the control apparatus of the enterprise, they need to control their own personal identities and make sense of their own work in the employing organisation. Managerial work therefore has a 'double control' aspect in which there is a strategic exchange between individuals and organisations

110   **8**

STUDYING ORGANISATIONS: AN INTRODUCTION ▪ THE EMERGENCE OF LARGE-SCALE ORGANISATIONS ▪ TAYLOR, WEBER AND THE BUREAUCRATISATION OF THE WORKPLACE ▪ MANAGING THE HUMAN FACTOR ▪ ORGANISATIONS AND ENVIRONMENTS ▪

(Watson, 1994). The consequence of the above critiques is the belief that too few insights are generated into what 'flesh and blood' managers actually do.

At a general level many of these criticisms would be accepted across a wide spectrum. But some carry it much further: 'current uses of the terms "strategy" and "control" are somewhat misleading guides both to actual management conduct and to the causes of particular outcomes in work organisation and industrial relations' (Rose and Jones, 1985: 82). We can break this down into two issues: do identifiable management strategies exist and are practices centred on controlling workers?

Questioning strategy

Those who argue against the idea of coherent strategies with a fixity of purpose believe that management activities are more likely to be piecemeal, unco-ordinated and fragmented, with at best a striving for logical incrementalism. Management is concerned primarily with 'keeping the show on the road' (Tomlinson, 1982: 128), corresponding with the 'realist' views discussed earlier.

Supportive research was outlined in areas such as work reorganisation schemes (Rose and Jones, 1985) and new technology and skills in engineering (Campbell and Currie, 1987). Any strategic capacity is held to be inevitably undermined by a plethora of sites of decision-making, varied objectives among different management specialists and interest groups, the need to smooth over diverse and contradictory practices, and the requirement of sustaining a consensual accommodation with employee organisations. The result is an unpredictable variety of managerial intentions characterised by a 'plant particularism' (Rose and Jones, 1985: 96), and control structures as merely 'temporary outcomes' (Storey, 1985). Campbell and Currie plump for the idea of 'negotiated preferences' and there is a general orientation towards explanations based on *practices* rather than strategy.

Some of these differences may reflect the sector being researched. For example, engineering is well known for its 'seat-of-the-pants' approach to management, whereas other sectors such as food or chemicals are noted for more strategic methods. Nevertheless, this kind of approach is confirmed by some writers on industrial relations (Purcell and Sissons, 1983), who note the problems created by the absence of management strategies towards their own employees, particularly ones that are integrated into overall business objectives. Instead there is a continued dominance of reactive and opportunistic practices directed towards immediate problem solving (Thurley and Wood, 1983: 209). What *kind* of strategy is said to be absent is not always made explicit. But the basic model used is similar to that popularised by Chandler, which, like many other adaptations to the business sphere, is strongly influenced by military experience and terminology (Shaw, 1990). That is, it posits detailed and co-ordinated plans of campaign in which conscious, long-term planning based on corporate goals is supported by appropriate courses of action and allocation of resources. This can be seen in the business policy debate (Steiner and Miner, 1978; Porter, 1980) in which generations of students are warned of the negative consequences of the absence of corporate strategy, and scholars debate different models of structure, strategy and competitiveness. Similarly, standard models of strategic HRM emphasise the need for coherence and integration both within its component parts and with wider business strategy (Tichy *et al.*, 1982). Indeed, HRM is sometimes seen only to offer something new if it has strategic value (Kamoche, 1994).

The problem with mainstream notions of strategy is that it is all too easy to counter textbook ideal types of coherence and integration with the messy reality of real companies and sectors. As with the more 'realist' views of management discussed in the last chapter, the insights of social science have been applied to demonstrate how organisations muddle through rather than plan rationally. The promise of complete knowledge and controllable environments is seen as neither desirable nor feasible in fragmented, turbulent, postmodern times. As a result, in the last decade strategy has gone from buzzword to boo-word. It has been 'problematised' to the point that the concept is no longer fashionable even in strategic management circles (for a useful overview, see Whipp, 1996). Complaining that discourses of strategy are primarily about shoring up the power of senior managers and consultants, Knights and Morgan reject the concept altogether: 'Nothing new is really added by talking the discourse of strategy; on the contrary, a limit is put on our understanding of the special phenomenon because we are forcing action into a particular rationalistic and individualistic framework' (1990: 480).

But conceptions of management strategy in the above frameworks are in themselves problematic. A stereotyped polarity is set up between a conception of objective rationality that implies perfect foresight, choice and follow-through; and a bounded rationality of constrained choice in complex realities. Too often the critics collude in forcing action into a conceptual straitjacket. By adopting a straw man of 'strong' strategy, they have set criteria for strategy so stringently that it becomes impossible to meet them (Child, 1985). While it is wrong to attribute coherent, rational intent to management, it is equally mistaken to assume that strategy has to be seen as always consistent, systematic and without contradiction. Strategies may not always be effectively followed through at the implementation stage, as with the introduction of new technology. They may not constitute a coherent package for the whole operations of a company, perhaps manifesting a disjuncture between job design plans and employee relations. Coherence is an important variable, but it has to be set against the knowledge of inevitable contradictions and the likelihood of 'loose-coupling' between planning and practices. Strategies are likely to be accompanied by bargaining within management and with the workforce, so making the end result uncertain. As Friedman rightly notes, 'Irrationality, inconsistency, lack of system certainly exist and must be allowed for; however, a more useful concept to introduce is failure' (1987: 294). Even where changes are introduced without clear intent, they can establish the preconditions for subsequent strategy (Hyman, 1987: 47).

While managers frequently act on the world with poor information, they can and do act strategically. It is only necessary for researchers to show a degree of intent or planning, and to infer a logic over a period of time from the frequency and pattern of action, or from 'emergent outcomes' (Hales, 1988: 12). Boxall and Purcell make a similar point in a different way: 'It is possible to find strategy in every business because it is embedded in the important choices the managers and staff of the firm make about what to do and how to do it' (2003: 28). The same criteria apply to the activities of workers. Groups such as printers or doctors do not always behave in a fully conscious or coherent manner. But observation reveals a clear pattern of occupational and job controls, and strategies of closure aimed at excluding competitors, often women (Cockburn, 1983; Witz, 1986). The latter point reinforces research on households that shows that strategies emerge from 'bottom-up', day-to-day activities – a weaker, but still legitimate sense of strategy that relies on social scientists observing and analysing predictable patterns (Wallace, 1993).

Of course, the capacity for strategy is not random. Certain external conditions are likely to push management in that direction. Streek (1987) puts forward a persuasive case that economic crisis and rapidly changing market environments have created a 'general strategic problem' whose core element is the need for *flexibility*. However, the very nature of uncertainty and varied conditions in sectors and countries produces different strategic responses. For example, countries such as Germany and Austria with traditions of tripartite state, union and employer bargaining have seen moves towards economic liberalisation and labour flexibility that retain a strong union role and corporatist regulation of wages, labour and product markets. The hostility of all economic actors in Germany to the prospective takeover of telecommunications giant Mannesman by a UK competitor in 1999 was a case in point. Streek's analysis not only builds in an explanation of such variations, but it also provides a framework for understanding the general conditions under which strategies develop. At times of crisis and readjustment, 'the variety of strategies and structures within the collectivity of firms is bound to increase at least until a new standard of "best practice" has been established' (1987: 284). In other words, there is always ebb and flow in intensity and direction of organisational practices, but strategic patterns do emerge and can be observed, particularly in the cauldron of highly internationalised sectors where a small number of giants compete for dominance.

Questioning control over labour

The second strand of critique questions whether the centrality given to control of labour is actually reflective of managerial behaviour. It is argued that we cannot view management strategies and tactics from the vantage point of the labour process, but must consider the role of product and labour markets, and technologies. Control proceeds in a complex cycle from planning to implementation, involving groups such as accountants and industrial engineers. It is also true that labour costs may be only a relatively small proportion of the total, particularly in capital-intensive industries, so the emphasis of managerial controls may be elsewhere. With such factors in mind, some argue that analysis should focus on the 'multiple constituents' of management expertise beyond the confrontation of capital and labour in the control of the workplace (Miller and O'Leary, 1987: 10). Such a critique can be presented in a Marxist form. Accumulation and costs of production are what matter to capital and its agents, not control. If anything, managers are dominated by problems of the *outcomes* of the labour process, including sales, marketing, supply and cash flow. Kelly uses the concept of the full circuit of capital to argue that we must be concerned not only with the *extraction* of surplus value through controlling the labour process, but its *realisation* through the sale of commodities, as well as the prior *purchase* of labour. On these grounds, 'there is no sound reason for privileging any moment in the circuit' (1985: 32).

Morgan and Hooper used a similar framework in their research into the Imperial Tobacco Group in the 1970s to distinguish between three circuits of capital. *Industrial* capital refers to that used in the management and design of the production process itself; *commercial* to the sphere of buying and selling and therefore functions such as marketing and advertising; and *banking* to the process of capital used in lending and borrowing, governed by accountancy and financial controls.

These distinctions are used to argue that critical theories of the labour process have often lost sight of the role of capital and ownership because of the emphasis on management control. The case study shows a series of strategies pursued in tandem, representing the particular circuits. To break out of a static tobacco market, top management prioritised commercial and banking strategies, rather than developing existing labour processes. In particular, companies such as Imperial were drawn into investments in the share and gilts markets. These proved successful, but when the resultant money was invested in production this had disastrous results. Firms are thus conceptualised as 'sites of a complex integration of circuits of capital' (Morgan and Hooper, 1987: 623), which management must integrate and control. This takes us back to the opening quote of the chapter in which the General Motors executive was seeking control in a number of spheres.

During this period of debate, other writers questioned whether control can be regarded as the factor that distinguishes between a dominant management and a subordinate labour. Management has non-control functions and characteristics of employees, while workers exercise job controls and may be involved in the regulation of others (Melling, 1982: 249). At a more theoretical level, Cressey and MacInnes (1980) observe that workers have an interest in the viability of their own units of capital as well as resisting subordination, matching capital's dual relationship with labour as a commodity and as a source of co-operation necessary for profitable production. Some mainstream writers use their own research into the chemical industry (Harris, 1987) and those of chemicals, engineering and biscuits (Buchanan, 1986) to argue that workers basically accept managerial authority, give commitment and effort willingly, and have convergent interests with management, thus negating any preoccupation with control. This is likely to be linked to a rejection of 'zero-sum' conceptions of power in which one side necessarily gains at the expense of the other (Harris, 1987: 77). Even some radical writers believe that capital and management are not necessarily dominant, with unions having considerably more power, even in a recession, than usually acknowledged (Kelly, 1985: 49; Rose and Jones, 1985: 101).

It is certainly true that, as Hyman observes; 'If most orthodox literature on business strategy ignores or marginalises the conflict between capital and labour, most Marxist literature perceives nothing else' (1987: 34). This has a curious parallel with the virtual total emphasis in organisation behaviour on 'man-management'. So the full circuit of capital is a very useful and necessary concept for understanding the capitalist enterprise. Furthermore, change and crisis often arise from disarticulation of the moments of the circuit (Kelly, 1985), as we saw in the Imperial example. Such concepts can be combined with more orthodox accounts of the changing pattern of *corporate control* which plot how large firms seek to solve their competitive problems by reshaping structures and forms of intervention in the market (Fligstein, 1990). Such 'modes of control' have included vertical and horizontal integration, the multidivisional form and, more recently, financial means of integrating diverse portfolios built up through acquisition.

However, these perspectives do not invalidate a specific emphasis on relations of control between capital and labour. This is not just another process equivalent to marketing or financial accounting. The management of workers and work remains at the heart of the enterprise and indeed of economic reproduction as a whole. But such an orientation need have no marginalising effect on the analysis of other social relations. As P. K. Edwards (1990) observes, the problem of 'privileging' one part of the circuit arises only if the analysis assumes that this one part determines what happens in the others.

As we made clear at the start of the chapter, we are not saying that control is normally the *goal* of management, but rather a *means* embodied in strategies and techniques. It is true that management strategies are not always developed with labour's role in mind. But it is ultimately difficult to separate a concern with 'outcomes' such as product quality of financial targets from acting on labour in some way. Strategies towards markets or technologies will often be constrained or mediated by labour policies and the practices of workers (Friedman, 1987). In addition, as Child notes, 'strategies which are unspecific towards the labour process may still have relevance for it' (1985: 110). An example is the introduction of new technology which, much research shows, is frequently used as a means of more general work reorganisation. Finally, irrespective of the detail of arguments about the outcomes of high-performance work systems, it is widely accepted that labour productivity is the most appropriate measure of human resource management of the firm (Boxall and Purcell, 2003: 8). Given the inherently incomplete nature of employment contracts, a strong focus on labour controls – of various types – is an inevitable corollary, particularly in a mainly labour-intensive service economy.

On the issue of the existence of co-operation and common interests, we would wholly concur. In fact we would go further. As one of us has observed: 'Workers do not always need to be overtly controlled. They may effectively "control" themselves' (Thompson, 1989: 153). Participation in routine practices to create interest or increase rewards can generate *consent* to existing structures of control and power, as Burawoy's (1979) famous studies of production 'games' indicate. What is puzzling is why some writers insist on co-operative and consensual processes being counterposed to those of control and conflict. It is increasingly recognised that all have to be theorised as different products of the contradictory relations within the enterprise. Not only do consent and control coexist; 'the mobilisation of consent' through culture strategies forms an increasingly central part of management–employee relations strategies in many sectors. This will be examined in detail in Chapter 11.

We also accept that workers exercise controls, but it would be a serious mistake to regard them as *equivalent* to those of management. This would fail to distinguish between *types* of control, particularly between the general and detailed dimensions referred to earlier in the chapter. At the general level of direction of production, managerial dominance is guaranteed by their stewardship of the crucial organisational resources. This is not 'zero-sum' because it cannot be 'added up'. Clearly, however, control of immediate work processes is largely zero-sum, in that if workers control a given item, then management cannot also do so (P. K. Edwards, 1990).

New directions – surveillance and shifting the locus of control

Having gone through successive forms of criticism concerning ideas of control strategy, the more recent period has seen the emphasis move back to new accounts of control. Some of these arise from empirical shifts in work and employment. For example, the growth of front-line service work means that the *customer* may mediate the standard management–worker dyad, providing information on employees, and directing their behaviour or values (Frenkel *et al.*, 1999; Sturdy *et al.*, 2001). The most significant challenge to established labour process frameworks, however, comes from the argument that the locus of control has shifted from external to internal. We have already identified one version of this earlier in the chapter. A move to seeking employee commitment can be seen as a form of *internalised control* that does not rely on external rewards and sanctions, or rule-following. Cultural controls rely primarily on acceptance of values and peer enforcement. In one of the earliest contributions, Ray (1986) argued that control by corporate culture was the last frontier, in that it had enabled organisations to generate sentiment and emotion, simultaneously internalising control and linking personal with corporate identity. It is argued that the expansion of work that has a higher discretionary content and more ambiguity leads management to give less direction and elicit more reciprocated trust through 'info-normative control' (Frenkel *et al.*, 1995).

Issues of culture and control will be examined fully in Chapter 11. At this stage we want to concentrate on a parallel argument about a shifting locus, this time with the emphasis on surveillance replacing, or becoming the dominant mechanism of, control. On the surface this does not appear to be consistent with an internalised direction. After all, surveillance is normally associated with collecting and storing information, using it to monitor behaviour and establish discipline (Dandeker, 1990). However, the argument is less about mechanisms than their *effects*. Case studies (Zuboff, 1988; Sewell and Wilkinson, 1992; Sewell, 1998) of high-tech manufacturing make much of the enhanced capacity of management to collect, display and attribute performance data through electronic surveillance. Because stockpiles of labour and parts are eliminated through quality (TQM) and just-in-time (JIT) systems, production arrangements are highly visible. The information is generated from and fed back through teams of employees that appear to have autonomy, but in practice internalise production norms and discipline themselves through systems such as Nissan's 'Neighbour Watch' (Garrahan and Stewart, 1992). Such information is unobtrusive and perceived to be objective, therefore accentuating its legitimacy. Teams may produce self-surveillance independently of an information-driven process. Delegated responsibilities, whether for routine production decisions or, more exceptionally, induction and evaluation of team members, mean that employees have to develop their own disciplinary 'rules', thus collaborating with management to identify and reward the 'good worker' (Barker, 1993; McKinlay and P. Taylor, 1996). Such studies argue that as a consequence of such discipline and the removal of any 'slack' from the production system, 'worker counter-control (in the sense described by Roy and many others) is effectively eliminated ... the ultimate goal of management under a TQM/JIT regime must be recognised to be Total Management Control' (Delbridge, Turnbull and Wilkinson, 1992: 105).

The growth of call centres has also boosted new theories of control. Surveillance undoubtedly plays a pivotal role in the way that integrated telephone and computer technologies facilitate the access and retrieval of data in the service interaction between desk-bound employee and external customer. Of particular importance is a sophisticated capacity remotely to record and assess the speed and 'quality' of the work. Not only are performance data made public, but also a proportion of the calls will be monitored remotely and used to reward and discipline employees. As a result, the previously identified 'objectivity' of the statistics is combined with constant, but unseen surveillance. Not only do employees internalise controls, but also the controllers are redundant: 'In call centres the agents are constantly visible and supervisor's power has indeed been "rendered perfect" – via the computer monitoring screen – and therefore its actual use unnecessary' (Fernie and Metcalf, 1997: 29).

In the most developed theorisation of such trends, Sewell (1998) argues that the interaction of 'vertical' electronic surveillance and 'horizontal' peer-group scrutiny has produced a new model of control, countering the optimistic gloss of the empowerment and team literatures, while moving beyond the limits of traditional labour process theory. The implication of Sewell's argument is that such a combination solves the direct control/responsible autonomy dilemma that has historically troubled generations of managers, to say nothing of management theorists.

Surveillance is not a new phenomenon. As we saw in Chapter 2, many writers have described the early factory in terms of the attempted subordination and surveillance of recalcitrant workers, using the work of historians to illustrate how employers used new systems of rules and control techniques to induce 'appropriate' morals and work habits. In the most detailed examination of the issues, Dandeker (1990) links surveillance primarily to processes of bureaucratic rationalisation that have developed throughout this century. By 1990, 10 million workers in the US, including many professional and managerial employees, had become subject to electronic performance monitoring (Pfeffer, 1997: 114). Given these trends and recent socio-technical systems, it is difficult to deny that *some* shift towards electronic and self-surveillance has taken place in *some* industries.

Whether this constitutes an overarching development requiring an entirely new conceptualisation is a different matter. Many practices highlighted in the manufacturing case studies were identified by earlier writers making a critique of lean production (Parker and Slaughter, 1988b). Yet they were described as a form of work intensification – 'management by stress' – in other words, more a shift in the effort bargain than the frontier of control. The idea that electronic surveillance is unobtrusive is a strange one. Performance display is characterised by its visibility to management and employees. It can therefore only be unobtrusive if the information it relays is accepted as objective. Yet there is considerable evidence that employees challenge the accuracy of the data, or use them for their own purposes against management (Zuboff, 1988; Bain and P. Taylor, 2000).

Call centres are clearly a new development, but do we need new concepts to explain them? Callaghan and Thompson (2001) argue that Richard Edwards' control framework provides better insights than recent 'electronic sweatshop' perspectives. His three dimensions of a system of control and distinction between stages of direct, technical and bureaucratic control strategies have been fully outlined earlier in the chapter. Call centres predominantly use a system of technical control. In terms of Edwards' first dimension, automated call distribution systems (ACD) enable management to direct the speed, direction and character of the work tasks. Technical control in call centres goes further than assembly lines in assisting companies to operationalise the second dimension – monitoring and evaluating performance. The performance of individuals and teams can be compared within or across sites. In turn that information can be linked to the apparatus of reward and discipline through the formal assessment and review process. One of the weaknesses of Edwards' framework is its linear nature. If this is dispensed with, we can see that his 'next' system – bureaucratic control – is used in call centres to define skills and tasks, and specify behavioural and performance standards. In the Callaghan and Thompson case study, Telebank has 19 core standards of behaviour and a 7-point scale to measure the skills of operators during appraisal, which is used to generate high and low scores. This indicates that many controls in the modern workplace remain external. To take another example, normative rules in strong culture companies may be different from traditional task-based control, but they are still rules. There is still the question of whether such rules are internalised. Management's sources and use of information may have increased, but there is little evidence that they are unobtrusive or regarded by employees as objective and unconnected to visible authority relations. Far from supervisory power being 'rendered perfect', there is evidence that customer service representatives (CSR) strongly dislike the emphasis put on 'the stats' and the disciplinary uses made of them (Bain and P. Taylor, 2000; Callaghan and Thompson, 2001). Employees distinguish between the 'friendly' supervision of coaching to improve skills and the disciplinary use of performance data. As with manufacturing, CSRs challenge the objectivity of the data and turn it against them: 'I check everything, I take it away and check it, I don't just sign it. I go back into the system, you can actually remember a lot of things when you go back in and see the name. I know that people have had arguments with the research section' (CSR quoted in Callaghan and Thompson, 2001: 32). Though individual, technology-paced working and remote surveillance makes resistance difficult, CSRs learn informally to manipulate the codes used to claim relief from work tasks, and become skilled in setting their own pace and variation from the company scripts when talking to customers (P. Taylor and Bain, 1998; S. Taylor, 1998; Callaghan and Thompson, 2001).

None of the above observations seeking to qualify 'shifts of locus' arguments are intended to deny that changes in the nature and frontier of controls have taken place. These have been recently summarised by Thompson and Harley (2007). Many of the conceptual confusions in analysis of workplace controls would be solved if it was recognised that new forms seldom wholly displace old ones. This is what Thompson and Harley refer to as continuity, in combination. Labour process and other perspectives accept that the normative sphere has been an expanding area of managerial practice, without endorsing the view that these have replaced or even marginalised the more traditional mechanisms of bureaucratic rationalisation, work intensification, or some features of scientific management. This can be seen in both the manufacturing and service sectors. With respect to the former, Japanese-style lean production has combined work intensification and multi-tasking under modified traditional methods, described by Adler (Chapter 3) as 'democratic Taylorism'. At the same time, management focuses more on the normative sphere in order to by-pass trade union representation and secure worker identification with broader organisational norms (Danford, 1998; Delbridge et al., 2000). As for services, to return to the call centre example, surveillance and monitoring is intended to create an 'assembly line in the head' (P. Taylor and Bain, 1998). Through the work is organised in many ways around very traditional methods, to gain competitive advantage from service interactions, companies frequently seek to generate high commitment and shared identity through corporate cultures or teamworking (Thompson, van den Broek and Callaghan, 2004). The outcome is a distinctive form of high-commitment, low-discretion work system (Houlihan, 2002).

More generally, the outcome in modern work settings is increased hybridity of control structures as environments and organisational structures become more complex (Alvesson and Thompson, 2005). Even in knowledge-intensive industries large companies reply on combined and integrated control structures. A good example is provided in Alvesson and Kärreman's case study of a global consulting firm. The company directs much of its control practices towards 'cultural engineering' in order to shape employee identities and identifications. However, to close any gaps and minimise uncertainties, it also creates 'a vast bureaucratic and output measuring apparatus' (2004: 441), including extensive financial controls, standardised work procedures and formal HRM systems for recruitment, promotion and evaluating performance. The lesson drawn is that:

> Socio-ideological control is thus intimately tied to bureaucracy and output control. It is not, as claimed by most of the literature on control … an alternative to the latter two, useful in situations where complexity and uncertainty make rules for prescribing behaviour and the precise measurement of results impossible. (Alvesson and Kärreman, 2004: 441)

Interestingly, the authors note that the combined and reinforcing nature of these controls does not guarantee their effectiveness. For example, there was 'overwhelming evidence' that time reports from employees were faked. This brings us back to an earlier theme of the chapter: the linkages between managerial controls and worker resistance.

A further reflection on resistance

In this chapter we have shown numerous examples of the persistence of worker resistance, especially to new normative forms of control that focus on worker attitudes and emotions. Though different judgements are, in part, an outcome of how case study and survey evidence about the extent of worker buy-in to managerial norms is interpreted, it is also a dispute about concepts. Categories used to describe and explain resistance have been strongly influenced by the language and experience of industrial relations with its organised collective actors – trade unions, employers and the state. As Thompson and Ackroyd (1995) and Kelly (2005) have argued, the decline of formal organised conflicts such as strikes, alongside falling trade union membership, has too often been treated as synonymous with the decline and disappearance of conflict as such.

While the concept of worker resistance was an attempt to broaden the categories of description, much of the discussion focused on organised non-compliance in large manufacturing workplaces. Something even broader was needed and eventually supplied through Ackroyd and Thompson's (1999) analysis of 'organisation misbehaviour' (see also Ackroyd and Collinson, 2005; Ackroyd, 2008). Originally directed towards a critique of mainstream and radical views that emphasised the dominance of new forms of cultural control and electronic surveillance, it also acts as an integrated 'map' of worker action and agency focused on four resource territories that both management and employees try to 'appropriate': working time, working effort, the product of work and work identities. The term misbehaviour is used ironically to draw attention to what is missed and misunderstood by orthodox accounts that assume conformity of behaviour as the norm, and to signify counter-productive behaviour – anything you do at work that you are not supposed to do.

These traditions largely focus on conflicts around the effort bargain. The mapping of organisation misbehaviour reflects changes in workplace and academic politics by including identity in the multi-dimensional framework, thus rendering 'a whole new realm of workplace practice … visible' (Fleming,

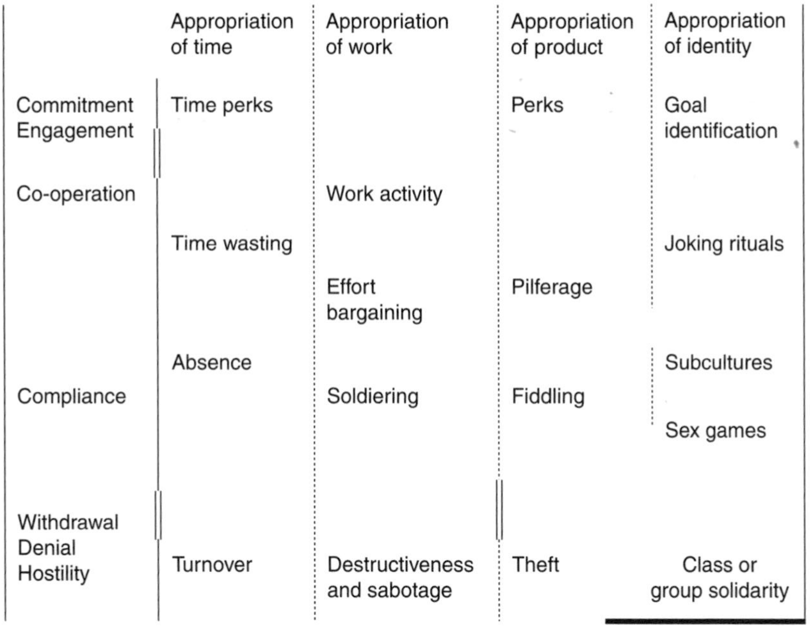

	Appropriation of time	Appropriation of work	Appropriation of product	Appropriation of identity
Commitment Engagement	Time perks		Perks	Goal identification
Co-operation		Work activity		
	Time wasting			Joking rituals
		Effort bargaining	Pilferage	
	Absence			Subcultures
Compliance		Soldiering	Fiddling	
				Sex games
Withdrawal Denial Hostility	Turnover	Destructiveness and sabotage	Theft	Class or group solidarity

Figure 8.1 **Mapping misbehaviour**

Source: Reproduced with permission from S. Ackroyd and P. Thompson (1999) *Organizational Misbehaviour*, London: Sage.

2001: 191). Put another way, the expanded categories helped us to see a new contested terrain where managerial efforts to mobilise employee emotions, commitment and personality through cultural and socio-technical practices potentially clashes with worker identities and interests. The very ambition of some companies to mould employee identity through culture change programmes and mission statements often patently at odds with day-to-day workplace experience renders them vulnerable to employee cynicism that becomes a resource for resistance (Fleming and Spicer, 2002; Fleming, 2005). A good example is provided by Taylor and Bain's (2003) graphic account of how call centre workers use humour, not only as informal dissent, but in one case as part of a campaign for union recognition.

Despite the continuity with the traditions of industrial sociology and opening up of new territories for dissent, some researchers in a labour process tradition (Martinez and Stewart, 1997) have argued that the misbehaviour categories are too individualistic and accept at face value too much from the arguments about the decline of trade unions and collectivism. But Ackroyd and Thompson's intent was to expand the scope of concepts to understand dissenting and non-compliant activities at work, rather than to argue that the conditions for broader forms of collective action and organisation have diminished. We shall return to issues of resistance in the next chapter, when influential Foucauldian arguments about panoptic power are examined.

Summary and key points

In mainstream accounts, neither control nor resistance is treated as a substantial feature of organisational life, but largely as a failure of systems that are otherwise based on creativity, consensus and commitment. By analysing managerial control as a structural imperative of the capitalist labour process given that markets and formal contracts alone cannot deal with the gap between the potential of purchased labour and the desired profitable outcomes of that labour, LPT pushes the issue to centre stage. That perspective is not top down, but is a reciprocal model of control and resistance. Given both the general nature of divergent interests between capital and labour, plus the way that any control system builds up internal contradictions, the conditions for resistance are always present and tend to develop further over time. Nor is it a story solely about constraints on managers. LPT frames its accounts in terms of rival and/or changing strategies of control, with echoes of Child's concept of strategic choice discussed in the previous chapter. Such strategies are seldom coherent in conception or content. But we can observe patterns of labour-control practices that form a significant, though far from sole, feature of the managerial repertoire. Because conditions change and employees learn to evade and exploit existing ways of doing things, control practices are inherently dynamic. In recent debates, considerable emphasis has been put on new forms based on surveillance, cultural engineering and self-discipline. The position taken in this chapter is that, though there has been some shift in the direction of policy, their intended effects – to encourage employees to internalise controls – is far from certain or complete. It is always wise not to confuse the formal capacities of technological and managerial systems with their actual usage and effectiveness. Control systems were never one-dimensional and now, given the diversity of challenges and conditions, their forms are more likely to be combined and hybrid in character. Like control, resistance also sometimes changes its form and content. In the final part of the chapter, we outlined some new ways of understanding such trends, drawing on Ackroyd and Thompson's mapping of organisational misbehaviour. This framework, though only part of the total picture, helps broaden our accounts of resistant and dissenting behaviours, while helping to explain their persistence in a context where others have proclaimed their demise. This is, however, not the end of some of these discussions. We shall return by a different route, to issues of culture, control and resistance in the following chapter on power and the later one on culture itself.

Further reading

The two Edwards, Richard and Paul, are a good starting point. *Contested Terrain* (R. Edwards, 1979) is probably the most influential book on control and resistance and is a very good read, while the UK-based contribution of P. K. Edwards and Scullion (1982) deserves to be better known. Hyman's (1987) journal article is still the best overview of labour process perspectives on control, an interpretation supported by the fact that it remains one of the most downloaded papers from *Work, Employment and Society* after 20+ years. Of the new Foucauldian-influenced accounts of control and surveillance, Sewell (1998) is deservedly the most influential, though you might also look at the critique by Thompson (2003b). On current debates on resistance, Ackroyd and Thompson's (and associated) various discussions of misbehaviour are a good starting point, and Taylor and Bain (2003) an excellent application to call centres. Hodson (2001) does a similar job, drawing on many of the same ethnographic labour process studies, but ties the discussion into wider issues of dignity at work. Alvesson and Kärreman's (2004) paper is a good example of a contemporary treatment of control that combines a range of concpets and theories discussed in this chapter.

Ackroyd, S. and Thompson, P. (1999) *Organizational Misbehaviour*, London: Sage.
Alvesson, M. and Kärreman, D. (2004) 'Interfaces of Control: Technocratic and Socio-ideological Control in a Global Management Consultancy Firm', *Accounting, Organizations and Society*, 29: 423–44.

Collinson, D. and Ackroyd, P. (2005) 'Resistance, Misbehaviour, Dissent', in S. Ackroyd, R. Batt, P. Thompson and P. Tolbert (eds.), *A Handbook of Work and Organization*, Oxford: Oxford University Press.

Edwards, P. K. (1986) *Conflict at Work: A Materialist Analysis of Workplace Relations*, Oxford: Blackwell.

Edwards, P. K. and Scullion, H. (1982) *The Social Organization of Industrial Conflict: Control and Resistance in the Workplace*, Oxford: Blackwell.

Hodson, R. (2001) *Dignity at Work*, Cambridge: Cambridge University Press.

Hyman, R. (1987) 'Strategy or Structure: Capital, Labour and Control', *Work, Employment and Society*, 1. 1: 25–55.

Sewell, G. (1998) 'The Discipline of Teams: The Control of Team-based Industrial Work through Electronic and Peer Surveillance', *Administrative Science Quarterly*, 43: 406–69.

Taylor, P. and Bain, P. (2003) 'Subterranean Worksick Blues: Humour as Subversion in Two Call Centres', *Organization Studies*, 24. 9: 1487–509.

Thompson, P. (2003) 'Fantasy Island: A Labour Process Critique of the "Age of Surveillance"', *Surveillance and Society*, 1. 2: 138–51.

Thompson, P. and Ackroyd, S. (1995) 'All Quiet on the Workplace Front? A Critique of Recent Trends in British Industrial Sociology', *Sociology*, 29. 4: 1–19.

CULTURE, COMPANIES AND COUNTRIES IN A GLOBALISING ERA ▪ MANAGEMENT ▪ **CONTROL AND RESISTANCE** ▪ POWER IN ORGANISATIONS ▪ GENDER, SEXUALITY AND ORGANISATIONS ▪ CORPORATIONS AND CULTURE: REINVENTING ORGANISATION MAN?

8   121

9

power in organisations

Power is a much used and little understood term. Take em*power*ment, which you might think is something to do with power. Apparently not: 'senior managers need to realise that empowerment is not about increasing the power of employees' (Randolph, 1995: 30). In business practice, empowerment is about increasing *responsibilities*, and employees need to be disabused of the understandable confusion that they are going to have more input into decision-making. Such confusion is unfortunate because power has become a 'hot' topic in current popular management literature. Successful managers are those who learn to use power, not just to get their own way, but to get things done. As Tom Peters puts it, 'Anyone who loves accomplishing things must learn to love (yes, love) politics' (*Independent on Sunday*, 15 May 1994).

The aims of this chapter are to:

- Explain why power and politics has been neglected in the study of organisations and examine ways of putting it back in the picture.
- Set out traditional accounts of the bases of power available to individual managers and other actors when viewing organisations as political systems.
- Use Stephen Luke's three-dimensional model of power as a means of critiquing and moving beyond traditional accounts.
- Explore and evaluate new theories and research on power, particularly influential accounts derived from Foucault and other post-structuralists.

Power in mainstream theory

'The natural place to look for an understanding of power in organizations is that extensive body of work known as "organization theory"' (Cockburn, 1990: 76). In the more favourable recent context there has been a rash of books seeking to legitimate power for managerial use. These include self-help manuals promising tips on how to fight the guerrilla war in the boardroom (Drummond, 1996) and more substantial contributions which wisely warn practitioners that while organisational politics can be managed, it cannot be 'managed away' (Buchanan and Badham, 1999: 21). It did, however, take a long time to get to this point. For many years Pfeffer (1981; 1992) was something of a lone voice among organisation theorists in attempting to develop accounts of power. In contrast to control, most traditional organisational behaviour textbooks simply do not have chapters on power or, if they do, admit that it has been largely ignored or subsumed within other issues such as leadership (Luthans, 1981: 387). Cockburn's explanation is that such theory has been devised from the viewpoint of the owners and managers who control organisations. This may be less a case of reflecting the viewpoint of managers, than the conventional ways of viewing

> Getting things done requires power. The problem is that we would prefer to see the world as a kind of grand morality play with the good guys and the bad ones easily identified ... In corporations, public agencies, universities and government, the problem is how to move forward, how to solve the many problems facing organisations of all sizes and types. Developing and exercising power requires both will and skill. It is the will that often seems to be missing. To manage with power means recognising that in almost every organisation there are varying interests. It means figuring out what point of view those various individuals and subunits have on issues of concern to you ... and thus it is imperative to understand where power comes from and how sources of power can be developed. Finally managing with power means understanding the strategies and tactics through which power is developed and used in organisations.
>
> (Jeffrey Pfeffer, interviewed in *Business Magazine*, November 1993)

their activities that we examined in the previous chapter. Willmott (1984: 350) sums this up succinctly: 'the common sense, technical, images developed by managers to account for their activities get returned to them in the form of apolitical descriptions of the reality of their work'.

Power relations can simply be simply written out of the picture, for example by redefining 'subordinates' as 'non-managers' (Mullins, 1985: 238). They then have a shadowy existence, hidden within discussions of why management finds it 'difficult to delegate', and focusing on personal disposition rather than the structures of power that shape them. Debates on management style will contain occasional advice on when to use authoritarian methods – Hitt *et al.* writing that in today's large corporations 'fear must be used cautiously' (1986: 43). Furthermore, power is the hidden agenda when managerial prerogatives are stressed, though the ideological needs of management may blunt the directness of language. But what else is meant when the phrase 'management must manage' is used? Some of the roots of the neglect can be traced to the historical association in organisation theory between rational, formal organisation and legitimate authority (Clegg and Dunkerley, 1980: 433–4). Rational decision-makers and efficiency maximisers should have no need for power. Reflecting a wider functionalist perspective that sees power as 'a legitimate regulation in a society based on common values' (Barker and Roberts, 1993: 195), theorists such as Parsons see authority as granting a consensual 'power to' structure the behaviour of others (Storey, 1983: 54–5). 'Zero-sum' notions of power, in which there are clear and incompatible differences of resources and interests, are explicitly ruled out. Alternatively, power is linked to the breakdown of authority and the growth of informal practices. This can be seen in a standard definition of organisational power quoted in Luthans: 'the management of influence to obtain ends not sanctioned by the organisation' (1981: 389). Power therefore is seen as inhabiting the shadow side of organisations, arising when rationality fails (Egan, 1994). In the real world, as Jackall observes in his study of corporate managers, 'political struggles are a constant and recurring feature in business, shaping managers' experience and outlooks in fundamental ways. Of course, such conflicts are usually cloaked by typically elaborate organisational rhetorics of harmony and teamwork (1988: 24).

In this context, it has been possible to raise the profile of analyses of power only by demonstrating its instrumental character, showing that it can act as an aid to rationality and efficiency. One of the most sophisticated accounts does exactly that. Enrolling Machiavelli as a guide, Buchanan and Badham (1999) argue that the change agent's effectiveness is considerably enhanced if she or he can indulge in some 'power-assisted steering' to complement the traditional humanistic roles of social engineer and therapist facilitator. To persuade practitioners, a contingent explanation is a useful addition to an instrumental one. In more recent writings on power, Pfeffer has filled this gap. Power as a resource is not just generally useful, it has become more necessary because informal channels of influence have been growing as hierarchy diminishes. Flatter organisation means that 'the exercise of formal, hierarchical control is less consistent with organisational values and ways or organising' (1997: 136). A disassociation of power from formal structure is both bizarre and at odds with Pfeffer's standard model of competitive struggle for resources among sub-units. The 'less hierarchy' argument is also heavily disputed, as we shall see in Chapter 13. But Pfeffer's contingent explanation is attractive to organisation theory, because it is absolutely consistent with the existing conceptualisations of power as a primarily backstage, informal phenomenon.

Mainstream models

Given the relative absence of a focus on power, organisation studies has had to rely on a small but influential number of studies. The dominant orientation is towards an analysis of the micro- or internal politics of organisations that Pfeffer defines as: 'Those activities within organisations to acquire, develop and use power and other resources to obtain one's preferred outcomes in a situation where there is dissension or uncertainty about choices' (1992: 10). To sustain this approach, organisation theory draws on a definition of power developed by Dahl (1957), which itself is based on Weber (1968). Analogous to the impact of one billiard ball upon another, power is seen as the ability of A to get B to do something they would not otherwise do, despite any resistance.

A narrow focus on power in a solely organisational setting was itself indicative of what Hinings (1988: 4) refers to as the continuing divorce of organisation theory from sociology. Within this framework one of the best-known contributions is from French and Raven (1959), who start from the concept of 'bases of power' located in organisational resources. They are available for use singly or jointly by the manager, but depend on the perceptions and responses of those 'targeted'.

- *Reward* The use of resources as rewards, where -the target values the chosen method and believes it can be delivered. Can include not just money, but promotions, increased job satisfaction and social recognition.
- *Coercive* The capacity to enforce discipline. Rests ultimately on the fear of the likelihood of psychological or material punishment, whether loss of overtime bonuses or humiliation in front of the peer group for poor sales figures.
- *Referent* The personal characteristics of the manager are perceived as attractive by employees, generating feelings of identification. Similar to Weber's concept of charismatic power.
- *Legitimate* Power is made acceptable by subordinates acquiescing in the right of power holders to influence them. Linked strongly to the idea of authority.
- *Expert* The existence of power as knowledge or other forms of expertise attributed to individuals or groups, which others feel obliged to accept. It is in itself a type of legitimacy.

There is some evidence concerning the application and effectiveness of these sources of power (see Luthans, 1981: 395–401). Not surprisingly it shows that non-formal sources such as expert power impact most favourably on organisational effectiveness. But given the questionnaire methods used, this may tell us more about cultural expectations than actual work practices. This reflects genuine and broader problems in measuring power, particularly when trying to separate capacity from actual use. Researchers have had to rely on survey methods that in turn rely on respondents' assessment of factors such as the reputation of individuals or departments.

In practice, this may be measuring perceived influence, or at best the relation between influence, tactics and outcomes (Kipnis and Schmidt, 1988). That is not the only problem. The French and Raven categories are widely regarded as too individualistic, though the basic argument about individual bases of power is developed in more depth by Pfeffer (1992). Power is seen as a structural process linked to task specialisation. Given that some tasks are more central than others, the individuals involved have more chance to exert influence. However, in reality the relational structures of power are more likely to involve *networks* (Knoke, 1990) or *coalitions* (Cyert and March, 1963) which compete for resources and influence within organisations. Individuals seeking sources of power normally have to work within sectional interest groups, such as departments or specialist occupations. Pettigrew's (1973) research showed computer programmers locked into a power struggle with systems analysts. Their weapons were ideologies of expertise, exclusivity of technique by avoiding written records, and control of recruitment policies. Political *skills* are vital in these processes and, as we have seen, are increasingly viewed in a positive light in the popular managerial literature. Skills such as advocacy may be useful to the company in a competitive environment, and the management of creative contention is central to the building of alliances and informal networks that are sometimes dubbed 'dominant coalitions' (Kotter, 1982).

This political view clearly starts from the kind of 'realist' assumptions, discussed in the last chapter, that 'see the manager not as a servant of the owners nor as a technocrat serving the system, but as a manipulator trying to compete and co-operate with others in order to pursue his own ends' (Lee, 1985: 206). Such a vision of sectional interests and firms as sites of struggles between different groups and coalitions is also of necessity *pluralist* in that it begins from a recognition of multiple and competing goals, as well as internal bargaining processes. Indeed, organisations can be conceptualised as politically-negotiated orders that are neither the harmonious entities beloved of managerial theory, nor the arenas for class conflict associated with radical critics (Bacarach and Lawlor, 1980). A practical spin-off can be seen in present business practice which is currently awash with references to stakeholders. Admittedly this is a 'soft' version, where companies take an inclusive approach that treats shareholders as just another group alongside employers, customers, suppliers and the wider community (RSA, 1994; Handy, 1994). Tougher varieties recognise owners as a more powerful set of players among the multiplicity of interests (Watson, 1994).

In sum what this material adds up to is a view of organisations as political systems. As we indicated earlier, aspiring managers are now guided towards a positive view of power as influence and appropriate tactics – tweak your antennae, network like mad, confront the troublemakers (Clare Dight, Career section of *The Times*, 27 October 2005) – that can ensure survival and career development. Whereas Dight attributes 'politicking' to human nature, academic versions emphasise the systemic aspects. Politics in organisations, like the wider society, is shaped by the scarcity of resources. In the best account of such processes, Buchanan and Badham define it as a game 'in which individuals and groups seek to defend and to extend their turf' (1999: 15). The scarce resources include power itself, influence, status, reputation, space and money. They too tend to describe political behaviours in terms of tactics such as image building, selective information, scapegoating others and making alliances. So, for example, in bureaucratic hierarchies, credit flows upwards and is usually appropriated the highest ranking officer: 'The person who appropriates credit redistributes it as he chooses, bound essentially and only by a sensitivity to public perceptions of his fairness' (Jackall, 1988: 21).

If all this is going on, how does the organisation function? The resultant internal political systems tend to stabilise themselves through the stake in the survival of the whole system held by the competing parties, and the extra power wielded by top management. While the political conflicts are mostly experienced by individual managers as the outcome of personal biography and relationships with immediate bosses up and down the hierarchy (Jackall, 1988), the dynamics of internal power are predominantly structural and collective. A coherent explanation synthesising a range of other studies is provided through the *strategic contingencies* model of Hickson *et al.* (1973). This starts from the observation that it is necessary to treat power as being about the allocation of scarce resources and as the property of a social relationship – particularly the departmental division of labour between purchasing, marketing and so on – rather than individual action. These social relations are shaped by external and internal factors. Internally 'heavy-weight' interest groups are able to influence not just matters within their own spheres, 'but beyond that in matters that would be thought to be the primary concern of other specialist units' (Hickson, 1990: 176).

At the external level, we return to the open systems model discussed in Chapter 5. Coping with uncertainty is a crucial feature in transactions between organisations and the environment. The internal institutions charged with this responsibility are the *sub-units* such as departments. Power enters the picture through the familiar frame of resource-dependency, because those sub-units that can cope with uncertainty will be able to exercise power in their competitive struggle for resources with their rivals. Hickson and McCullough (1980) use the example of purchasing agents who were trying to expand their limited power base by attempting to move, from merely placing orders and ensuring delivery, to the provision of information to management and planning new products. The tactics used involved building alliances with contacts in other departments and manipulation of rules. But power could only really be gained when the customer environment contained a variety of suppliers, thus increasing the dependency of other sections on purchasing.

Such examples indicate that structural contingencies constitute a number of variables that shape power. Ability to deal with uncertainty is complemented by the degree of *dependency* on other units, the extent to which activities are *substitutable*, and on the overall level of *centrality* to the organisation. Therefore power is gained through the process of exchange and control of strategic contingencies. Though the point is not often made, this kind of analysis can be extended to shop-floor employees. 'Lower participants', as Mechanic (1962) describes them, can also utilise power derived from control over uncertainty. Among his examples were hospital orderlies who exploited their skills and access to information in order to control waiting lists for operations against more senior medical staff who were not interested in administration.

A critical evaluation: three-dimensional analyses

The literature on internal politics and power is very useful, particularly when set against the traditional conceptions of rational, apolitical management. But there are costs, some of which arise from the limitations of pluralism. Talk of stakeholders and a multiplicity of interests competing for scarce resources is again an advance on images of consensus and fairness, but is too often a comfortable rhetoric that is fundamentally unrealistic about the distribution of power inside (let alone outside) organisations. Owners hold the key stakes in corporate resources and even employees' countervailing powers have diminished sharply in recent economic, political and legal climates. There is also an illusion about management. Of course, managers represent a sectional interest, or more precisely a series of sectional interests. But they are also an agency of ownership interests: not passive prisoners, but certainly constrained actors. Even Watson's (1994) informative and determinedly pluralistic account of managers trying to assert their desires to maintain manufacturing interests at ZTC has to recognise that they are working within short-termist, cost-cutting rules set by the dominant corporate coalition.

There is also the issue of the relation between internal and external power relations. Limitations flow from the analysis being confined to a particular level of power relations. As we have acknowledged, there are problems in measuring power. Reputational methods tend to reaffirm the obvious, for example that level in the hierarchy is significantly related to a respondent's perceptions of an individual's power (Pfeffer,

1997: 146). Alternatively, power is analysed through its symptoms, by what is observable through behavioural exchange and by identifying who the players are. As a result, any research that does exist on power concentrates mainly on its exercise, taking, as we shall show later, the formal organisation and deeper power relations for granted.

While the better frameworks, such as Buchanan and Badham's (1999) 'turf rules', can illustrate what underlies the power game in different contexts, a predominantly interpersonal focus tends to trivialise power by treating it as 'politicking' or 'office politics'. Though the 'pitch' that serves as the context for the turf game can be contextualised as comparative corporate or national contexts, it tends to be treated as particular structures and cultures within organisations (Buchanan and Badham, 1999: 32). Even when dealt with in a more substantial way, as in strategic contingency theory, the focus is primarily on *horizontal* power: 'Conventional organisation theory seldom considers the power within organisations, the power exemplified by top management, as an expression of power relations external to the organisation' (Cockburn, 1990: 77).

Vertical power hierarchies are set aside by the interpretation of the division of labour as consisting of relations between sub-units. Such neglect is reinforced by the tendency to see managerial authority and goals as always accepted by workers, or at least subject to joint regulation and negotiated outcome through the interplay of power. Substantial power differences and sources of dissension are therefore underestimated. We need to deal with 'power over' as well as 'power to', and treat managerial authority as a form of organisational power. Though power is multifaceted, zero-sum circumstances can and do exist, whether they are manifested in distribution of profits in dividends or wages, or the right to bargain collectively or not.

Clegg's (1977) early critique is pertinent to this debate. French and Raven and strategic contingency theory can show how managers use resources to exercise power. Neither explains the prior distribution of power – how some people come to have access to these resources while others do not. The exercise of power is premised on institutional frameworks and rules; 'the "power" of the sub-unit has to be grounded in the prior *capacity* to exercise power which managers possess' (Clegg, 1977: 27). Furthermore, managerial power has to be located within deeper structures of economic domination that underpin its use and legitimacy. A prime example is the concentration of ownership and control in the transnational company. The power to switch resources and relocate operations simply cannot be explained at the level of the single enterprise and its sub-units. Without such a structural framework, we are left with a micro-level analysis capable only of explaining the skills of 'politicking' rather than political power. We are also left with a view of managers solely as self-interested manipulators and power-seekers with little understanding of the broader dynamics and constraints which dispose management to use power in the first place.

These differences in perspective can be clarified by reference to the wider debate on power, taking the three-dimensional model of Lukes (1974; 2005) as a framework. The behavioural literature is primarily *one-dimensional* in that it focuses on the observable activities of particular 'subjects', seeking proof of power in processes such as decision-making. This formulation, which draws on Weber's definition outlined earlier, is specifically linked to *intended effects* and imposition of will: 'Power is only relevant to our understanding of behaviour and organisation, when there is conflict' (Dawson, 1986: 148). On this basis rests the behavioural assumption that power can always be observed and measured.

In the broader debate the one-dimensional view has been criticised by writers such as Bachrach and Baratz (1962), utilising the concept of 'non-decision making'. This may sound odd, but refers to the capacity of power holders to limit those issues that are contested or even discussed. The approach usefully distinguishes between the sources and bases of power. By controlling agendas and mobilising the bias inherent in greater access to institutional resources, values and even the language of legitimacy, they can keep to safe issues and exclude others that threaten their interests. Though the research deals with political actors, there is no doubt that management actions can be seen in this light. Crucial decisions regarding investment or the introduction of new technology very seldom reach normal bargaining, except perhaps to deal with the consequences. In industrial relations terminology they are 'non-negotiable', particularly when market trends favour employers. Even with worker-director schemes such as those at British Steel in the 1970s, management could manipulate the rules of the game and socialise workforce representatives to the extent that their interests were not seriously contested (Brannen, 1983).

Lukes (1974: 21) pays tribute to this 'two-dimensional' analysis, but argues that it remains too much on the terrain of observable behaviour. Elite power can prevent grievances, and therefore conflict, from ever arising by shaping the very wants and preferences of subordinate groups. This is not a question of brainwashing, but of the hidden structures of power. Market mechanisms and the distribution of wealth and property constitute power relations – such as ownership rights – which frequently come to be taken for granted. Nor should the formation of consent be conceptualised as a process distinct from the operation of power. Though there are concrete practices that arise from such relations, they are not always observable in the traditional sense. Power does not necessarily need a subject. As Clegg and Dunkerley observe, 'Much of the time the power of capital does not have to be exercised to be present ... because this exercise is grounded in a structural "capacity" which frequently obviates the need for its exercise' (1980: 495). Put another way, power is what Lukes calls a *dispositional* concept, incorporating both the production of effects and the *capacity* to produce them. Take the previously discussed example of the diffusion of 'best practice' in large companies. What is perceived to be 'best' is largely taken for granted within existing structure of property and power. Ownership of resources thus sets the actual grounds through which agendas are set.

Though the processes cannot always be measured, the outcomes can, in terms of structural inequalities between groups. For Lukes, this indicates that a latent conflict exists, 'which consists of a contradiction between the interests of those exercising power and the *real* interests of those they exclude' (1974: 284). His three-dimensional explanation of power in general therefore coincides with radical perspectives on organisational power, which would draw on Weber and Marx's analysis of the deeper economic roots of domination. This involves a different understanding of 'dependency' in which there is a 'fundamental asymmetry of power between employers and workers' (Rueschemeyer, 1986: 76), based on workers' lack of control of the means of production. The propertyless have to 'seek access to resources owned or controlled by the few' (Fox, 1974: 284). When Nissan opened their factory in the North East of England, they had 30,000 applications for 300 jobs. Not surprisingly this enabled them to pick workers and a union wholly on their own terms. This 'structural' account of power differs sharply from the use of that term in mainstream theory, reflecting a one-dimensional focus that signifies position in the formal structure or division of labour (Pfeffer, 1997: 144).

Nevertheless Lukes' work has been subject to considerable criticism, even from other radical theorists (see Clegg, 1989). He wants to retain an emphasis on power that presupposes human agencies that make choices, but on the other hand recognises that those choices are not equally available in circumstances of differentially constraining structures. At the level of individuals it is fairly easy to attribute intentions, but much more difficult when the individual is imputed an 'interest' because of membership of a group, whether that be capital and labour, men and women, or professionals and skilled workers (Barker and Roberts, 1993: 210). When Lukes argues that A may shape B's preferences in a manner inimical to B, how do we know what the latter's 'real' interests are without attributing preferences to them or arguing that what they actually think or act is 'false'? How do we recognise the power to persuade without reproducing totalitarian images of agencies that control all our thoughts and desires?

In the second edition of his book, Lukes mounts a powerful defence which is even more critical of the limits of one- and two-dimensional processes that focus on the exercise of power, given that power is at its most effective when least observable. The reason for this emphasis is the insidious nature of hidden power and its outcomes in imposing 'internal constraints'. The existence of such power constrains the choices people have, thus helping to secure their compliance. These formulations 'address the ways in which domination can work against people's interests by stunting, diminishing and undermining their powers of judgment and by falsifying, distorting and reducing their self-perceptions and self-understanding' (2005: 124). Lukes' discussions range extensively and intelligently over a range of literatures concerning power, but ultimately come back to his own internal constraint – how do we research things that are hidden, how do we know that power suppresses or hurts peoples' interests when the outcome is compliance or consent? Lukes defends the idea of 'real interests' and even 'false consciousness' by arguing that hidden forms of power as domination restrict or preclude the formation of potential preferences pertaining to our capabilities as purposeful agents with a capacity to shape our own futures. It is, in other words, a clash of capacities. As a philosophical argument, this may be persuasive, but it is limited without an empirical content and research agenda, particularly one that is directed at work and organisations.

The debate on dimensions of power demonstrates that there have been intractable problems in defining what power is and where it is located. A particularly intractable problem has been how to conceptualise deeper, hidden forms of power, 'Since it advantages or disadvantages individuals without being consciously mobilised' (Hardy, 1996: S8). An increasing number of radical theorists, as Lukes himself notes in the new edition, have sought refuge in the work of the French writer, Foucault, to escape those limitations.

Foucault, post-structuralism and disciplinary power

On the face of it an analysis based on surveillance techniques and forms of knowledge originating in monastic and military orders in the sixteenth and seventeenth centuries (Foucault, 1972; 1977; 1984) might seem to have limited relevance to contemporary organisation theory. But the attraction is based on the approach to power and how it can be applied to modern (or postmodern) organisations: 'deeply embedded within his detailed analyses of concrete historical situations and events there is a rich and complex model of the mechanism of power which is of direct relevance to organisational analysis' (Marsden, 1993: 108).

That appeal derives partly from restoring an idea of power as productive rather than prohibitive or solely repressive, creative and constitutive as well as limiting and constraining. This is characteristic of broader *post-structuralist* thinking. Indeed one can have post-structuralist theories of power without reliance on Foucault (see Leflaive, 1996). Such perspectives are not mere echoes of Parsons' emphasis on positive-sum rather than zero-sum relations. For power is held to be the central feature of social life from which there is no escape. Foucault uses the term 'capillary' to explain that power does not come from above, from a central source. Rather, it 'circulates through the entire social body' (Fraser, 1989: 24), into the furthest reaches and localities. Power is embodied in heterogeneous micro-practices, in everyday life rather than in a special sphere. But as particular forms become generalised in a network of relations, Foucault allows himself to use the term 'strategy' to describe the results. Resistance may break out at different points in the chain, and while that resistance recreates power, it promotes a ceaseless process of shifting alliances and tensions. Power, therefore, is discontinuous rather than stable.

Nor is power something that is possessed by an individual or group. This can be considered to commit the sin of belief in a *sovereign* power held by agents making rational decisions or attached to and formally administered by states, corporations or other groupings. From a Foucauldian perspective, power is understood without reference to agency, its mechanisms impersonal and independent of conscious subjects. In one sense this seems to extend Lukes' third, structural dimension of power in which the agency (such as capital) and its effects remain hidden. But Foucault's disciplinary power removes entirely a deliberately controlling relationship between subject and object, the imposition of A's will over B (Barker and Roberts, 1993: 216), even when conceived of as thought control and ideological hegemony (Clegg, 1989: 182). A similar argument is developed by Leflaive: if organisations or any of their members are defined as power holders, that is merely a *status* bestowed upon them; 'sovereignty, defined as the embodiment of power in the exercise of will, is not a characteristic of our contemporary environment' (1996: 43). Power lies outside its possessor, in routines and narratives that confer fluid, temporary capacities to act effectively.

This is part of a post-structuralist emphasis on decentring the subject. Power operates not through agencies with specific interests, but through *discourses*: practices of talk, text and argument that continuously form that which they speak. Disciplinary practices produce knowledge that is inseparable from power. Language thus becomes a central feature in the discursive production of power, and power/knowledge discourses constitute norms of acceptable conduct, constructing social identities. All this sounds very abstract, but Foucault underpins his concepts by an historical account of the emergence of a distinctively *modern* power. Pre-modern sovereign power had depended on personalised bonds of obligation. In contrast, the techniques of disciplinary power were developed and refined in religious institutions, prisons, asylums, hospitals and workhouses at a local level, rather than overseen by the state. Such microtechniques were concerned with evaluating, recording and observing individuals in an exhaustive and detailed way. During the early nineteenth century, surveillance spread from the institutions that were first faced with the mass management of large groups of people, especially to the factory:

> The dark satanic mills of Yorkshire and Lancashire simply latched on the disciplinary apparatus already let loose from the monastery into the poor house, the work house, the orphanage, the barracks and so on. (Clegg, 1989: 173)

In the range of modern institutions, power also becomes increasingly focused on the body as an object, distinguishing Foucault's analysis from a more conventional emphasis on ideology and moulding of the mind (see Hassard, Halliday and Willmott, 2000; Wolkowitz, 2006). Developing originally in the eighteenth century, *bio-power* was aimed at the control of wider populations, their movements, gestures and routines, such as the posture of pupils and marching steps of soldiers. These processes were also facilitated by the partitioning and regulation of time and space (Dandeker, 1990: 25). Penology, medicine and psychiatry become the focal points for the development of new power/knowledge discourses that punish deviation from normative standards.

But the prison remained the purest exemplar and microcosm of disciplinary techniques and knowledge: power is fundamentally *carceral* in character. The most potent imagery of Foucauldian theory is the *panopticon* – Bentham's design principle based on a circular building with central observation tower – which, from prisons to the new model housing estates, facilitated a unidirectional disciplinary gaze. In other words the observed can be seen but cannot see, while the observers see everything but cannot be seen. So effective are such practices that individuals begin to discipline themselves to be, in Foucault's words, docile and useful bodies. The overall effect of disciplinary practices is summed up by O'Neill: 'in the bourgeois social order the prison, the factory and the school, like the army, are places where the system can project its conception of the disciplinary society in the reformed criminal, the good worker, student, loyal soldier and committed citizen' (1986: 51–2). Bentham's panopticon was never built and there are issues about how extensive similar projects were (McKinlay, 2006), but any doubts have not stopped it becoming one of the most pervasive images in social science. This is, in part, because the emphasis is less on a physical manifestation, than on panoptic power expressed through electronic and self-surveillance, as discussed in the previous chapter. Surveillance constitutes organisations and their members as subjects of power (Leflaive, 1996: 25).

Applications to contemporary organisations

These perspectives have given theorists the language to interrogate past, present and future. O'Neill is one of those theorists who have used Foucault to help *reconstruct the past*. The process of the emergence of the factory and large-scale organisation is overlaid with the conceptual apparatus of the disciplinary society. Indeed much of the material discussed in Chapters 2 and 3 is represented in precisely this way. Industrial discipline was a central theme of the later rise of scientific management, which Weber praised for its military character. Equally such systems also involved an immense expansion of managerial knowledge and calculation of workers' time and motion. Theorists working in the tradition of Marx and Weber see these developments as the necessary preconditions for sustaining the appropriation of profit and the removal of the obstacle of worker control over aspects of the labour process. But for followers of Foucault, 'The causality is all wrong. New forms of disciplinary power preceded the establishment of the factory by at least two centuries' (Clegg, 1989: 188).

Foucauldian perspectives are also proving a means of *reframing the present*. The work of Townley (1990; 1993), Burchell *et al.* (1985) and Marsden (1993) focuses on identifying the social technologies of contemporary specialists in human and organisational behaviour as power/knowledge discourses. These latter-day 'soft cops' in HRM, accounting and consultancy, are concerned to 'observe, examine and normalise performance and behaviour' (Marsden, 1993: 118–19), carrying on a tradition established by human relations and its efforts to habituate the employee to the changing conditions of work in the large corporation. At a more micro level, Townley (1990) repackages the personnel function as a power/knowledge discourse with the Foucauldian terminology of dividing practices (enclosure, partitioning and ranking). All the elaborate emphasis in organisational theory on power expressed through the politics of decision-making, inter-group conflicts over resources, regulations and rights is held to be a sideshow diverting attention from the substance of power. At the heart of that process is the monopoly of knowledge by management and its agents, a form of discursive closure that marginalises other representations and identities (Deetz, 1992).

It is in Deetz's analysis of disciplinary power in the modern corporation that we see the most complete application of Foucault. Organisational processes act to produce corporate obedience, where 'The disciplined member of the corporation wants on his or her own what the corporation wants' (Deetz, 1992: 42). Similarly for N. Rose (1990), the culture and discourses of the modern corporation have become a crucial means through which human feelings, emotions and thoughts have become increasingly managed and governed. In either case, how this is actually achieved is vague, given the need of such theory to avoid mentioning deliberate operations of directive power. But attention is drawn to an accumulation of local power/knowledge discourses that disperses into norms and standard practices of moral, medical, sexual and psychological regulation. Elsewhere in the same book of readings, reference is made to the capacity of knowledge products of personnel and organisation psychology (such as performance appraisal) to 'gaze at, scrutinize, classify and count individual characteristics and behaviours. Collected data are analysed and stored, ensuring that an individual's legacy, good and bad, is not forgotten' (Steffy and Grimes, 1992: 192). In the previous chapter we discussed new forms of surveillance that draw on illustrative examples from the power of information systems and the behavioural technology arising from the expansion of culture change programmes. Willmott (1994) supports Deetz's critique of the colonising tendencies of the modern corporation, arguing that the creation of monocultures displays nascent totalitarianism. Employees are not only coercively socialised, but also positively attracted to such cultures because they learn to tie their own identities to the associated norms and knowledge. Their subjectivity becomes 'self-disciplining' as individuals begin to feel secure within the corporate identities (Knights and Willmott, 1990: 550). Such analyses draw on Foucault's use of the term 'subject': meaning where an individual is made subject and makes themselves *subject* to a form of power through the association between identity and self-knowledge.

We will look in more detail at issues of corporate culture in Chapter 11 and identity in Chapter 25. Nevertheless, whatever the source of new processes, Deetz argues that the effects are greater than the prison exemplar, because the modern corporation goes home with its members and colonises competing institutions such as the media (1992: 38). Similarly, in supporting and explaining Foucault's view that all organisations resemble prisons, Burrell (1988: 232) argues that, 'Whilst we may not live in total institutions, the institutional organization of our lives is total'. Opposition is largely self-defeating since those who play the game become addicts to the rules, and the pursuit of sovereign rights through bodies such as trade unions hides the disciplinary processes that produce the struggle in the first place (Deetz, 1992: 42). In addition, resistance does not threaten power, because 'It means that discipline can grow stronger knowing where its next efforts must be directed' (Burrell, 1988: 228). Clegg is similarly pessimistic in noting the organisational outflanking of resistance, due to subordinated agencies, '[l]acking the organizational resources to outmanoeuvre existing networks and alliances' (1989: 19). As Collinson (1994) observes, this analysis draws on Foucault in arguing that knowledge and information structure access to power. Subordinates either have too little of both, or their knowledge of the likely outcome of action is so predictable that it is similarly inhibitive.

Again, as we saw in the previous chapter, this imagery of all-powerful total institutions is reproduced in another Foucauldian-inspired literature, whose object of inquiry is new production techniques such as JIT and TQM (Sewell and Wilkinson, 1992; Delbridge, Turnbull and Wilkinson, 1992; Webster and Robins, 1993; Sewell, 1998). Marrying Foucault and Braverman, they argue that more effective surveillance techniques enhance managerial control of the labour process. Webster and Robin's alternative history of the information revolution traces a line of descent from Bentham's original conception of the panopticon, through Taylorism as a means of monopolising knowledge in management, to the contemporary flexible firm which has the capacity of IT to centralise information from an increased range of geographically dispersed units. Shop-floor techniques utilise more extensive information systems that can collect data on worker performance and behaviour. This is described as an electronic panopticon that brings the disciplinary gaze to every aspect of worker activity. This orientation has been reinforced by the growth of call centres, whose sophisticated surveillance capacities have led to the label 'electronic sweatshop' (Fernie and Metcalf, 1997), which has stuck even in the popular media. The outcomes of 'perfect supervisory power' without direct supervision (Fernie and Metcalf, 1997), and new factory regimes that combine electronic surveillance and self-discipline, is the removal or marginalisation of worker resistance. Chapter 15 explores further current trends in the reorganisation of the labour process, but we cannot take the above description for granted, regardless of its widespread usage.

Critique

We have already critiqued conceptions of the novelty and effectiveness of surveillance. Here we want to examine in more detail some of the accompanying theorising of power. Whether Foucault's history is accurate or methodology competent is beyond our scope (but see Giddens, 1982; Walzer, 1985; Habermas, 1987) and, we suspect, not pertinent to his appeal in and out of organisational analysis. New languages to describe old realities are always attractive to academics, in this case despite, or perhaps because of, the obscure and opaque terminology. Dandeker (1990) recaps the history of the growth of the modern business enterprise, rounding up all the usual suspects – Chandler, Edwards, Clawson, Williamson, Littler – without ever demonstrating that his overarching concept of *surveillance* depicts anything substantially new or distinctive.

Townley's work, referred to earlier, has helped stimulate some useful studies of particular HRM practices, such as appraisal (Newton and Findlay, 1996), but it also illustrates the dangers of over-privileging language and discourse. She argues that personnel can be understood as the provision of language or knowledge to reduce the space between what the formal contract of employment promises and what the employee's practice delivers. Aside from the fact that all managerial agencies operate in this gap, such conceptions distort the power resources available to and drawn on by those involved in managing the employment relationship. Language is part of that resource, but it is not, of necessity, the defining feature. Employment laws and labour markets may be more significant in empowering personnel, and may have only peripheral connection to any new power/knowledge discourse. In the context of accounting controls, Armstrong (1991) argues that Foucauldian analyses present disciplinary powers without reference to material sanctions and rewards. For example, the new accounting regime at the American company ITT was adhered to, not because those involved had internalised its disciplinary discourse, but because they were paid 25 per cent over the going rate to do so:

> [W]hen confronted by resistance, the systematic surveillance and behavioural norms of disciplinary power can only work within a matrix of physical coercion, economic power, negotiated order, or some combination of these. In other words, Foucauldian representation of the manner in which accounting controls operate are incomplete because Foucault's 'microphysics' of power is itself incomplete. (Armstrong, 1991: 31)

In Chapter 1 we used the example of the Wapping dispute involving News International and print unions. A combination of bribes, threats, sackings and the use of new anti-union employment legislation was among the 'non-discursive strategies' that proved highly effective in Rupert Murdoch's victory.

Power is a *dispositional* concept – a capacity that may not need to be exercised. But dispositions do not float freely above real social relations. When we examine capital and its managerial agencies it is clear that power is *somewhere* and its use may, in some circumstances, be rationally intended. Power is both a relationship *and* administered by individuals or collectivities. It therefore remains legitimate to refer to 'power holders', though never in an exclusive and uncontested sense. As Lukes (2005: 72) notes, the attribution of specific powers to particular agents, individual or collective, can be relatively straightforward when we can identify the means and motive of a particular agent to bring about a particular outcome. Jackal's observation of the operation of corporate hierarchies illustrates this complex nature of power very effectively:

> Because he stands at the apex of the corporation's bureaucratic and patrimonial structures and locks the intricate system of commitments between bosses and subordinates into place, it is the CEO who ultimately decides whether those commitments have been satisfactorily met. The CEO becomes the

> actual and the symbolic keystone of the hierarchy that constitutes the defining point of the managerial experience. Moreover, the CEO and his trusted associates determine the fate of whole business areas of a corporation. (1988: 21)

The key term here is actual and symbolic. A CEO can and does use specific power resources to influence events, but, as Jackall notes, the existence of those powers generates a continual discursive conversation up and down the hierarchy about his/her intentions, actions, style, image and ideology. The latter acts as a form of indirect 'discipline'.

Removing 'power holders', particularly in support of the view that power is productive for all, tends to gloss over substantive differences in sources and effectiveness of power. As we illustrated in the previous chapter, there are some circumstances in which workplace decisions may be zero-sum – they cannot be 'possessed' by both management and workers. By setting aside such distinctions, Foucauldian analyses run the risk of softening its substantive origins and effects. For example, Hardy seeks to move beyond negative 'power over' connotations to consider how more sophisticated multi-dimensional frameworks can help managers develop a broader array of mechanisms that facilitate successful strategic change. In particular, they can help 'those seeking to orchestrate collaborative action by preventing conflict over strategic options from emerging' (1996: S4). Negative consequences are limited to the recognition that such help may leave employees to the 'abuse' of this more sophisticated and less visible power (1996: S14).

One of the reasons why post-structuralist views are persuasive is that they trade on polarised conceptions of power. Their target is stereotypical: power as top-down, fixed and stable. Reality is considerably messier than this. Take the conflicts around the World Trade Organization (WTO) in 1999. There is no doubt that we can identify the discursive constitution of power, through, for example, ideologies of progress and globalisation. We can also see how unstable power is, and the extent to which it can be disrupted by a variety of 'local' voices and interests. However, it remains the case that the WTO has both sovereign power holders, particularly in the agenda-setting leading nations, and the power to set rules for economic exchange that fundamentally structure social relationships across the globe. The WTO conflict is an illustration of the fact that power is not necessarily unobtrusive, invisible, 'low-profile' (Fraser, 1989: 23), or used unilaterally only as a last resort (Deetz, 1992: 40). It may be said that the example is not organisational, but high-profile disputes are not the only source. As we have seen, employment relationships in this century have become progressively more bureaucratised. Yet Deetz (1992: 37) criticises Richard Edwards' (1979) theory of bureaucratic control because it refers to identifiable rule and routine instead of a complex set of practices which become internalised as common sense and personal identity. This judgement is hopelessly inaccurate. Far from taking rules of payment, measurement and task allocation as given and natural, workers and their representatives have engaged in a persistent low-intensity war to use and manipulate them to their own advantage. Not only that, but there have been highly visible artefacts, such as Ford's 200-page 'Blue Book', for each side to draw on as a resource in the power struggle.

Such examples confirm other evidence from shop-floor life that specific forms of knowledge are a key resource through which resistance can be mobilised (Collinson, 1994), a process illustrated with respect to call centres in Chapter 8. A further problem is that the contested rationality between capital and labour is reduced to a local site of struggle. It is claimed that having decentred the loci of power, Foucault may be 'the last pluralist' (Clegg, 1989: 7). It is true that there is an emphasis on the dispersed and local character of power, with associated micro-technologies of discipline investigated in their own right. However, the label of pluralism does not sit well with the theoretical substance of disciplinary power, which has prison and panopticon at its centre and determining force, and all organisations conceived of as total institutions, going way beyond Goffman's (1961) intentions. By treating the workplace as an extension of disciplinary practices and the factory, hospital and other organisations as paler versions of carceral institutions (Burrell, 1988), the specific character of employment relations in a capitalist society is lost. For example, control is treated merely as another version of discipline, and functionally oriented towards the creation of obedient bodies rather than sustaining exploitation (Clegg, 1989: 176). Vague and extravagant references to control over body and soul can be justified by only extreme examples such as AIDS testing in the workplace (Deetz, 1992: 140–1).

Resistance, again

Just as the pairing control and resistance is central to labour process theory, resistance is often bracketed with power in Foucauldian analyses. This, as many commentators have pointed out, is a very problematic pairing. The main problem is that because power is everywhere and nowhere, the impression can be given that it is omnipresent, a force that there can never be any escape from. Lukes argues that this one-sidedness in Foucault derives from being more interested in the design than the actual impact of disciplinary practices: (Foucault) 'had no interest in analysing such mechanisms by examining variation, outcomes and effects: he just asserted that there were such effects' (2005: 98). Resistance is part of the formal picture, but is under-theorised (Smart, 1985) and the dice loaded against it, because, 'only power is positive and productive, while resistance is simply a reaction to its production' (Dews, 1987: 99). One of the sources of this 'bleak fatalism' is that power and resistance are seen to simply to feed off one another, thus ratcheting up disciplinary practices without space for break points, transitions and reversals (McKinlay, 2006). Fragmented, insubstantial and counter-productive, resistance largely disappears from view, to be replaced by the language of docility and obedience (J. O'Neill, 1986: 55). In fact, the whole conceptual framework is saturated with the language of colonisation and conquest – images more appropriate to *Invasion of the Body Snatchers* than the complexities of organisational life. The problem is not so much with the Foucauldian description of new managerial techniques of power, but the assumption that they actually *work*.

As Lukes (2005) observes, in his later writings Foucault distanced himself from this 'ultra radical' view that had rendered (politically desired) resistance to domination unintelligible. Subject to criticisms from those hostile (Thompson and Ackroyd, 1995) and more sympathetic (Newton, 1998; May, 1999) to their perspective, a number of post-structuralist writers, noting this problem, have drawn back from some of the consequences of this 'over-disciplined' view of organisational life (Leflaive, 1996; Sewell, 1998), some claiming that this mistaken belief in totalising power is not to be attributed to Foucault anyway (Knights and McCabe, 2000). Whatever the cause, one of the effects was that a number of such writers began to develop new ways of developing more plausible accounts of the interrelationships between power and resistance. The emphasis is on the discursive dynamics around the construction of meaning and subjectivity. Resistance is conceptualised primarily as informal 'micro-politics' where individuals adapt to and subvert dominant discourses (Spicer and Bohm, 2007: 1670). One of the most influential of these more recent accounts is Thomas and Davies (2005) on public sector restructuring under the aegis of New Public Management (NPM). They argue that we should not see individuals as passive recipients of these discourses of change. Instead, they seek to understand the differing ways in which individuals struggle to create, appropriate and transform the discourses of NPM. Resistance is stimulated by the contradictions, weaknesses and gaps between what Foucauldians call 'alternative subject positions' – the identities offered within the dominant discourses that may clash with the meanings being sought by identity-seeking employees. The effect is a 'chipping away at the micro-politics of power', disturbing and weakening the grip of dominant discourses (Thomas and Davies, 2005: 701).

Foucualdian perspectives have become more sensitive to the limits of the corporate colonisation of subjectivity and to the practical and symbolic distance that employees maintain from such attempts. This is welcome, but there are still problems, many of which derive from the removal of the agent and the focus on discourse as both the cause and medium of power-resistance relations. Emphasis on talk and text tends to remove the gap between intent and outcome. Despite their formal distancing from the excesses of power determinism, there is little sign of dissent and resistance in the case studies of writers such as Sewell and Wilkinson (1992) and and Sewell (1998). What management or managerial discourse says it is doing is too often taken as synonymous with effects and effectiveness. Yet, where studies of companies with a strong normative and surveillance agenda let us hear the voice of employees, we get a much more complex and balanced picture of power and resistance (Zuboff, 1988; Kunda, 1992; McKinlay and Taylor, 1996). This issue is returned to in Chapter 13.

In the more recent studies such as Thomas and Davies (2005), we do get some sense that employees and managers are not just passive recipients of power/knowledge discourses. However, showing how individuals position themselves within the range of discourses is in danger of trivialising the idea of resistance, reducing it, despite the grand label of micro-politics of power, to the everyday things we all do to adapt and survive at work. As Newton (1998) had noted of earlier arguments, it remains difficult to see how through these discursive language games, agents are actually making a difference. This reduction of resistance to discursive practices derives, in part, from the refusal of post-structuralist writers to accept that resistance is conditioned by potentially divergent interests of capital and labour. Indeed, Thomas and Davies describe labour process theories as constructed from an oppositional, negative paradigm, with a 'worker corps kicking back against management control' (Thomas and Davies, 2005: 685). While we accept that resistance and other forms of dissenting behaviour cannot be confined to economic actors engaged in formal, collective struggles at work, such bending the Foucauldian stick back towards resistance runs the risk of focusing on a narrow and often not very significant range of practices. This defect is certainly avoided in Spicer and Böhm's (2007) ambitious mapping of both individual and collective resistance to the 'discourses of management' across multiple movements in both the workplace and civil society. But even leaving aside the issue of whether such varied practices and domains can be conceptualised within the same framework, the restrictive focus on discourse remains. The key and largely unanswered question is why would anyone want to resist a (management) discourse? There would seem to be two potential answers to that question. First, the discourse in question actually makes a difference (for the worse) to an employee's conditions. Second, the discourse is perceived to pose a threat to the employee's (individual or group) sense of identity. Such a possibility is considered in Ackroyd and Thompson's (1999) typology of misbehaviour discussed in the previous chapter. Here, identity is one of four domains of contestation (with time, work, product) in which economic actors attempt to appropriate various material and symbolic resources. No doubt this framework requires further development, but it does at least potentially address the issue of discourse and resistance without reducing one to the other.

Summary and key points

This chapter has set out an argument for taking power more seriously than in mainstream organisational theory, where it has traditionally remained in the shadows, perceived as unofficial and unusual. We have discussed all the major contributions to an understanding of power within and beyond organisations. When it has discussed the issues, mainstream accounts have tended to focus on the surface of power, that which we can observe through the behaviours and outcomes of relations between managers and subordinates. Such considerations of organisations as political arenas have generated important lessons and insights, but they are limited in scope and explanatory power. More recent contributions take a broader and deeper look at the phenomenon. The chapter utilises Luke's three-dimensional model, with its emphases on agenda setting and power as a capacity that doesn't always have to be exercised in order to constrain preferences and actions. Lukes engages with Foucault and his followers, who have become ever more influential. Such analyses are, in essence, another version of ideas of hidden power, but they raise the question of whether it is possible to take power *too* seriously?

Power gets everywhere, but it is not everything. As Fraser observes, 'Foucault calls too many different sorts of things power and simply leaves it at that' (1989: 32). It is important, for example, to demarcate a boundary with control. For radical theorists in a labour process tradition, 'Power is expressed in organisations through the control of the means and methods of production' (Clegg and Dunkerley, 1980: 476). Though power will be exercised in order to reassert control by management, this should not mean that power is marginal or subsumed under control. The ability of employers to exert controls over labour is conditioned by a variety of different power relations. In particular companies or sectors, crucial factors will include those arising from product and labour markets, the state of employer and worker organisation, and factors identified by strategic contingency theorists such as management dependence on specific occupational and workgroups. As we have seen, control structures are also shaped by broader non-industrial power relations, such as those embodied in employment laws that sustain the power of capital, or relations of social dependence in the community that are transferred into the workplace. Processes of control and power are both independent and interrelated inside and outside the workplace. More concrete discussion should reveal those complexities, not treat them as synonyms or analogues. Similarly, while broader analyses are welcome, power may not be the same everywhere. Much of the discussion ably set out by Lukes derives from studies of the American political process, while Foucault's analyses of power were derived mainly from settings such as prisons and asylums, where the factory was totally absent from his work (McKinlay, 2006). Work organisations and employment relations are arenas with distinctive structures, practices and actors.

In the light of the evidence discussed in this chapter, power should also be accepted as inherently multi-dimensional. As with Lukes, Foucault's motives in trying to transcend the limitations of sovereign or one-dimensional power are admirable. But the result has sometimes been a conceptual and practical prison rather than a genuinely complex picture of power. Though some power decisions may be zero-sum, conceptualisations need not be. The advantage of Lukes' framework is that whatever its limits, the recognition of different levels or dimensions of power remains valuable. It is perfectly possible to focus analysis primarily on one dimension, without denying the significance or influences of others. In advocating an ethnography of micro-politics in organisations, Badham notes that 'There is no presumption here that the absence of explicit or tacit attention to "deeper" structural influences on politics means that they do not exist. These factors may be manifested in or combined with an ethnography of politics focusing on political strategies and tactics' (1997: 3). Alternatively it may be possible to apply all three dimensions of Lukes' schema to explain different aspects of the same phenomenon, as Wilson and Thompson (2001) do with respect to sexual harassment. Gender and sexuality are, in fact, good illustrations of how we need to allow for the possibility that power may be a highly distinctive phenomenon inside different social relations. This will be one of the themes of the next chapter.

Further reading

Buchanan and Badham's lively account of organisational politics as turf wars nicely straddles theory and practice, mainstream and critical (and there's a new, second edition too). On the mainstream side, Pfeffer's book arguing for managing with power is still important, though now a little dated. In contrast, Luke's new edition should really be the starting point of any reading on the subject. Stewart Clegg has a long interest in theorising the issues and his *Frameworks of Power* has been influential, but it is very hard going. Given the pervasiveness of Foucault and his followers' complaints that everyone misinterprets him, it would be churlish not to recommend *Discipline and Punish*. Of the modern Foucauldians, Deetz's chapter gives a succinct exposition of the perspective. On power and resistance, Spicer and Böhm provide a fair assessment of both pro- and anti-Foucauldian views. Away from purely academic debates, Jackall's deservedly praised account of corporate managers and power structures combines insight and readability.

Buchanan, D. and Badham, R. (2008, 2nd edn) *Power, Politics and Organizational Change: Winning the Turf Game*, London: Sage.

Clegg, S. (1989) *Frameworks of Power*, London: Sage.

Deetz, S. (1992) 'Disciplinary Power in the Modern Corporation', in M. Alvesson and H. Willmott (eds), *Critical Management Studies*, London: Sage.

Foucault, M. (1977) *Discipline and Punish: The Birth of the Prison*, Harmondsworth: Penguin.

Jackall, R. (1988) *Moral Mazes: The World of Corporate Managers*, Oxford: Oxford University Press.

Lukes, S. (2005, 2nd edn) *Power: A Radical View*, London: Palgrave.

Pfeffer, J. (1992) *Managing with Power: Politics and Influence in Organizations*, Boston, MA: Harvard Business School Press.

Spicer, A. and Bohm, S. (2007) 'Moving Management: Theorizing Struggles against the Hegemony of Management', *Organization Studies*, 28. 11: 1667–98.

10 gender, sexuality and organisations

> No company can afford to waste valuable brainpower simply because it's wearing a skirt. (Anne Fisher, *Fortune*, 21 September 1992)

In the past decade businesses and business academics have discovered gender. Compared to other areas this has been somewhat late. There is a massive and important body of research and theory on gender, work and family (see Dex, 1985; Walby, 1986; Thompson, 1989; Bradley, 1996; Crompton, 1997; Rubery *et al.*, 1999). However, that debate on the sexual division of labour focuses on occupational divisions, differential control in the labour process, female labour-force participation, segmented labour markets, or more broadly on patriarchy and capitalism. Organisations tend to be treated as passive recipients of wider social forces, with power appearing only indirectly, for example through access to employment. It is essential to 'see how organisational form+s structure and are themselves structured by gender' (Witz and Savage, 1992: 8). That gap has been progressively filled with a variety of explanations and policy prescriptions. The aims of this chapter are:

- To set out the theoretical and practical underpinnings to the concept of the glass ceiling.
- To examine how organisational analysis and practice has become gendered, the rival perspectives that seek to account for such outcomes and the research that may support contrasting claims.
- To explain and explore the shift in organisational analysis from gender to sexuality.
- To examine explanations and evidence concerning the interrelations between sexuality, power and organisations.
- To re-visit and assess gender equity policy issues in the light of considerations of recent theory and evidence.

The glass ceiling: policy parameters and intellectual frameworks

As indicated above, this chapter takes its cue from the way that gender issues have been refracted through the lens of organisational processes and perspectives, but how? While mainstream theory has been slow to recognise the issues, its critical equivalent has found various ways of occupying the territory. In the contemporary economy, an increasing number of types of work have become 'feminised' as women have supplemented or displaced men in the labour market (Bradley, 1997). But a quantitative change has also been accompanied by qualitative shifts in content of jobs and employment. To address such shifts organisation theory has 'borrowed' the idea of 'gendered jobs' – ones that associate task requirements with the perceived qualities of a particular sex – and has begun to debate the extent to which organisations and their structures, bureaucracy in particular, can be considered as gendered.

Reflecting the migration of women into the higher levels of a number of occupations and professions, the women in management literature (Ledwith and Colgan, 1996) also emerged as a significant presence. Though the associated policy discussion was on issues of equal opportunity and managing diversity (discussed at the end of the chapter), empirically and conceptually the focus continued to be the 'glass ceiling', a term originally coined by the *Wall Street Journal* to describe the invisible, informal barriers to progress through organisational hierarchies. This narrower frame – the potentially gendered opportunity structure of organisations – which forms the main subject matter of this chapter, has costs. Female managers are not the majority of women workers and the bigger, sociological picture can sometimes be obscured. As UK government figures show, the prime cause of the gender income gap is the concentration of women in lower-paid sectors of the labour market (*The Guardian*, 21 February 2000). Nevertheless, there are advantages in a narrower focus, drawing on what has been largely a 'dialogue between feminist theory and organisation theory' (Wajcman, 1996b: 262). Something new and specific has been added to an existing, powerful body of knowledge. At the same time the basic theoretical frameworks are reproduced and re-examined (see the parallels, for example, in the gender and technology debate: Grint and Gill, 1996; Webster, 1996).

That a new body of theory has had to address absences and disconnections is not surprising, as the visibility of gender in organisational analysis itself has been low. Recent surveys (Acker and Van Houten, 1992; Hearn and Parkin, 1992; Collinson and Hearn, 1994; Calás and Smircich, 1992; Alvesson and Billing, 1997) have trawled the major landmarks of theory and research from Taylorism to human relations and contingency theory, and have noted that though organisational processes are clearly influenced by gendered power relations, employees and managers appear to have no gender, and men and management are synonymous:

> Organisational scholarship has been, primarily, a literature written by men, for men and about men: how to gain the cooperation of men to achieve organisational ends through rationality: how to *man/age*. (Calás and Smircich, 1996: 222–3)

This early phase that challenged 'malestream' organisational analysis can be described as making women visible or hearing women's voice (Gherardi, 2003: 224). Weber is placed firmly in the centre of this malestream. For him, the rise of bureaucracy brings with it an instrumental rationality in which impersonal rules, procedures and hierarchies are operated with technical efficiency. This is contrasted with traditional forms of authority reliant on individual privilege and personal allegiance. Issues of gender and sexuality are thus despatched to a private realm along with patrimonial and patriarchal relations, no longer to endanger rational–legal authority in the public sphere.

Banishing gender from the theory is far from the actual practice of organisational life, as many critics have subsequently argued (Pringle, 1989; Cockburn, 1991; F. Wilson, 1995). But by the time this conceptual invisibility was being challenged, a particular form of absence – from the management of organisations – had become the focal point of argument. The 1980s were in fact characterised by a degree of optimism that this was about to change. After all, women had been entering into the lower reaches of management and the professions, after having come to dominate the white-collar ranks in previous decades in many countries. According to 'trickle-up' assumptions, it was a question of watch and wait. To move the process along, equal opportunity initiatives were being taken by or forced upon many large companies, such as those involved in Opportunity 2000 in the UK. Progress, was, however, not wholly dependent on corporate beneficence. Optimism was fuelled by a combination of demographic, cultural and economic changes, such as the shift from manufacturing to private and public services, and from domestic to transnational companies. Taken together, they should have created a competitive imperative for companies to make room at the top (N. Adler and Izraeli, 1988; Adler, 1994). In other words it was not merely a matter of women getting *into* management, management was getting seriously into women.

That was the theory – the practice has been different. By the mid-1990s the realisation was dawning that progress had been limited. There was movement in some specialisms (for example, human resources and marketing) and some sectors (for example, banking and finance), but by and large the glass ceiling was proving very durable. In the US a government-financed Glass Ceiling Commission estimated that women held only about 5 per cent of senior executive positions (*The Economist*, 10 August 1996). Institute of Management (1995; 1996) surveys painted a depressing picture in the UK: in 1995 the number of female managers was 10.7 per cent and that increased only fractionally during the later 1990s. Those in the senior category constituted only 5 per cent and at all levels there were differences in pay and perks, even for those similarly qualified and experienced. These trends largely held true in sectoral studies, such as those in the health service (IHSM Consultants, 1994), and more detailed qualitative assessments of the position in large companies at the forefront of equal opportunity initiatives (Wajcman, 1996a; 1998). Higher up the ladder the position is worse, with less than 3 per cent of executive directors women (Caulkin, 1999). Even in Sweden with its family-friendly social policies and high rates of female labour-force participation, only 3 per cent of senior executives were female, and an earnings gap of between 10 per cent and 30 per cent existed (Kimmel, 1993). Australia too has a figure of 3 per cent in an economy where women make up 43 per cent of the workforce (*Guardian*, 17 January 2000).

Has anything significant changed in the new century? It depends on what level of the organisational hierarchy we look at. Right at the top, *The Guardian's* annual boardroom survey shows that the number of women holding executive director roles has been static or falling – in 2007 it was 16 out of 527 posts in FTSE companies compared to 20 in 2003. The trend is confirmed by the 2008 Equality and Human Rights Commission Report Sex and Power that examined 25 different fields of work and in 17 the number of women holding top posts was falling or static. A Natwest Bank survey of Managing Directors showed that though more women were rising to the top, the 'success is often fuelled by working longer hours and sacrificing more of their personal time and happiness' (*The Herald*, 20 July 2004). Lower down, the picture is more promising. Returning to the Institute of Management (now Chartered Management Institute) surveys, they report that the number of women in management positions has trebled in 10 years so that in 2005 women constituted 31.1 per cent of Britain's 4.5 million managers, though that category reaches right down to team-leader positions. Women are also being promoted faster and at a younger age, and their pay is increasing faster, though still falls significantly short of men's. A spokesman for the Institute claimed that, 'Talk of the glass ceiling has given way to a skylight effect. Increasing numbers of women are clambering through to get to the next stage. But many still feel that they are clocked by the old boys' network and have to work twice as hard as the men to get round this obstacle' (quoted in *The Guardian*, 19 September 2005). In the same survey in the following year, the figure for the proportion of women managers fell for the first time in 2006. That is, of course, just a snapshot of the UK position, though it is broadly consistent with international and comparative data (Wirth, 2001). In sum, there is no single ceiling across sectors and countries and there are signs of progress, albeit uneven. Nevertheless, we cannot simply treat unequal outcomes as solely the result of different age cohorts of male and female managers as if time alone will prove the healer. Most commentators continue to believe that there is something different about the 'careers' of female managers that requires explanation.

Gendering organisational analysis

As Acker (S. Acker, 1992: 248–9) observes, to document difficulties and differences is one thing, to explain them is another. She contributed one of the most influential concepts in this task – the gendered substructure of organisations: the frequently implicit rules and arrangements that underlie practices taken for granted as rational. Elsewhere this has been described in terms of masculinist structures of order and control (Lewis and Simpson, 2007). But if the structures and practices are gendered, how are they so? The explanations we examine in this section have contrasting answers, though they all move beyond any account that rests on individual differences, whether these are biological (G. Wilson, 1997; Browne, 1998), psychologically based (Davidson and Cooper, 1992), or derived from economic models such as human capital theory (Becker, 1985). Here, the cause of unequal access to opportunity and power is located in socialisation, sexuality, psychology or natural disposition. But gender inequality in organisations is simply too persistent and deep-rooted to be accounted for by any variant on 'you get out what you put in', to say nothing of the fact that women's qualifications tend to be superior to their male counterparts.

Kanter and organisational context

The disparity between ideal type and reality was picked up earliest by one of the few feminists working within conventional management theory. Kanter's (1993) *Men and Women of the Corporation* was a landmark work, setting out a serious critique of the male bias within internal power structures and an explanation for the widely-observed 'glass ceiling' restricting progress up the hierarchy (Davidson and Cooper, 1992; Rees, 1992). The emphasis on internal is important, because Kanter does not treat the corporation simply as a reflection of the outside world: 'to a very large degree, organizations make their workers into who they are' (1993: 263). She adopts what is described as a structural model, in the same manner discussed in the previous chapter with respect to writers such as Pfeffer. In other words, 'structural' refers to organisational rather than societal context. Kanter identifies three central determinants of behaviour: the structure of opportunity, the structure of power and the proportional distribution of people or social composition of jobs. Where the distribution is strongly skewed against women they will be marginalised, excluded and treated as 'token'. Tokens suffer from increased visibility and their performance tends to be judged by group rather than individual criteria.

Kanter demonstrates that no research exists that proves any sex differences in power as manifested through leadership or management styles: 'a preference for men is a preference for power' (Kanter, 1993: 199). In contrast, locked into the lower reaches of the hierarchy and sex-segregated jobs, women internalise relative notions of worth. Or, because they are playing to man-made rules, women have to resort to watchful strategies to avoid any role traps that would reinforce one of the many gender stereotypes (mother, seductress, iron maiden) that lie in wait. Cycles of powerlessness are further reproduced through the perceptions and actions of men, who use power resources to reproduce structures in their own image. This is also an informal process. Men prefer their own company and share certain language and understandings. This 'homosociability' reproduces the existing gender order. Dominant organisational cultures and ideas of rational decision-making and effective management are overlaid with notions of masculinity, and the space for difference is closed down (Ramsay and Parker, 1992). Men are seen as making better managers because they are tough-minded, unemotional and authoritative. The 'other gender' comes to be defined as temperamentally unfit for power; Cockburn characterises this view as: 'Women are not capable of authority. And they turn into nasty people when in authority' (1991: 89).

Subsequent feminist commentators, while acknowledging its path-breaking character, have often been harsh on Kanter. Her work has been located as part of a naïve liberal feminism that was trying to demonstrate that women are people too (Calás and Smircich, 1996), and as a contingent approach that treats bureaucracy as only 'accidentally gendered' (Halford, Savage and Witz, 1997: 7 and see Simpson, 2004). This is a little unfair. Gender is coincidental rather than accidental – it coincides with male power in organisations. Kanter does not believe that bureaucracy is neutral, but she does think that it can be *made* rational. She works within a neo-Weberian tradition that reveals the informal and varied nature of bureaucracy. But that particular form is not fate. If women are not 'different', the acquisition of power by women could or should 'wipe out' sex, and it is organisations that have to be remade, not individuals. The boss–secretary relationship and other evidence of organisational sexuality are seen as patrimonial, pre-bureaucratic relics (Pringle, 1989). Relics can be rectified by a gender-neutral rationality.

Despite the critiques, there is contemporary evidence around that supports her core empirical arguments, rather than the broader theoretical spin given to them. In her studies of gender and culture in eight Italian firms, Poggio observes that relationships tend to be more egalitarian where women cease to be in the minority: 'The different sizes of the female component ... seemingly bear out the interpretations based on the concept of "token" ' (2000: 398). Simpson's (1997; 1998) studies of career barriers demonstrate that gender mix continues to be the most significant determinant of women's experience in organisations. Many women working in mixed or female-dominated environments found them supportive and enabling. Due Billing (1994: 187) sums up the argument: '(when) significant groups of well educated women enter bureaucracies the gender-based aspects of bureaucratic life may very well be reduced considerably'. In contrast, 'token' women continue to encounter men's networks and 'clubs' that maintain asymmetric power relations through informal mechanisms, including sexual innuendo and harassment. For example, in more evenly mixed circumstances, the demands of increased workload were often acknowledged and some balance between home and work catered for. In many organisations, however, men used their additional capacity or willingness to stay late – 'presenteeism' – as a competitive weapon, recolonising management for themselves and criticising women who left 'early'. There has also been sympathetic research on the nature and impact of male networks in organisations (see Pfeffer, 1997: 93–8).

Kanter's desire to emphasise the social construction of gender rather than the burdens of sexuality is understandable, but her analysis does lead to conceptual problems. First, that the process of social construction is conceived far too narrowly. While it is useful to locate specifically organisational dimensions, 'Curiously absent is any sense that men and women are locked, indeed formed, in an unequal gender order that spans not only work, but childhood, sexual intercourse, domesticity, street culture, and public life. There is no sense of how the organization came to take the damaging form it did' (Cockburn, 1990: 86). As a consequence neither individual nor systemic male power is adequately confronted. Kanter underestimated male resistance, in part because homosociability was treated only as a by-product of vertical occupational segregation. Second, in arguing that powerlessness, not sex, is the problem for women, Kanter fails to see the way that the two processes are interwoven, or how new forms of power and control appear around the construction of sexuality (Pringle, 1989: 88).

Part of the problem is that Kanter utilises the narrow Weberian conception of power as freedom of action and ability to get things done. As we observed earlier, though, it is 'structural' rather than individualistic and, as with French and Raven, her whole discussion covers the well-trodden territory of the first dimension of power as a relatively fixed resource, operating through the panoply of peer alliances, sponsors and the like. While insightful in its own terms, such a framework inevitably neglects the broader dimensions and relational character of corporate patriarchy (Witz and Savage, 1992: 16).

Kanter's work represents the best of her tradition, but the limitations of orthodox organisation theory, particularly the tendency to separate the workplace from broader social and historical processes, are frequently reproduced. Though she opened the gate, other perspectives had to be present to establish gender as a fundamental structuring principle of power and organisations (Mills and Tancred, 1992; Witz and Savage, 1992).

Theorising difference

Most theories attempting a gendered analysis emphasise durable difference rather than potential sameness. One of the most interesting developments in this respect has been a shift in mainstream behavioural and managerial literature that has turned previously 'negative' female qualities into positive assets. In an influential *Harvard Business Review* article, Rosener claimed that a second generation of managerial women were making their way to the top, not by aping men, but by being themselves: 'They are succeeding because of, not in spite of, certain characteristics generally considered to be "feminine" and inappropriate in leaders' (1990: 120). In this, the claims of evolutionary psychology are stood on its head. Those that believe that natural selection can explain workplace behaviour argue that the 'sparse representation' of women among senior executives arises from their genetic predisposition not to be aggressive, competitive and willing to take risks (Browne, 1998). In contrast, men's testosterone predisposes them to strive for status and dominance, and only women exposed to an unusual amount of these hormones will be aggressive enough to compete in the workplace (G. Wilson, 1997).

In contrast, like Rosener, many management writers, organisations and consultants now claim to find a 'natural selection' in reverse. There is a strong similarity between how women see their leadership qualities (participative, collaborative, interactive, consensual, focused on soft skills such as teambuilding) and the new structures and styles required in the modern decentralised, post-bureaucratic organisation (Martin, 1993; Institute of Management, 1994; Change Partnership, 1999). The editor of *Management Today* (quoted in *Guardian*, 7 March 1999) having surveyed 1000 British managers, recently pronounced that 'If men want to be successful managers, they must behave like women'. On an international stage, it is claimed that in transnationals characterised by networks of equals women are well suited to move organisations from hierarchies to horizontal webs of relationships (N. Adler, 1994). Some of these arguments overlap with claims made in the more general management literature of a move towards post-bureaucratic structures (see Chapter 13). As Linstead and Catlow (2004: 96) state: 'With flatter, and perhaps more fluid, organisational structures upward mobility is seen to enable womens' career progression with structural barriers dispersed'.

There is also a surprising continuity with some of these arguments among radical feminists, though shorn of the optimism about working within the male system. Ferguson (1984) regards the structures and discourses of bureaucracy as inherently male. She locates the problem in women's exclusion from the public realm. When they do emerge, not only are their jobs marginalised, but so are the more expressive values and modes of action developed in the private sphere. Such an alternative rationality can provide a means for women and other people in subordinate positions to challenge bureaucratic, male power. Such thinking draws upon a view that has always been present within feminism, expressed by the novelist Fay Weldon, that 'women had special virtues that men had not' (*New Statesman*, 27 September 1999). Those virtues are corrupted by the system and male power and would be better directed towards building women-led or women-only structures which would be participative and non-hierarchical. There are also parallels here to eco-feminism, where science and nature are seen as in themselves masculine (Griffin, 1984). As Calás and

Smircich note, 'Radical feminists have taken the traditional association of women with nature (in contrast to man with culture) and found it a source of strength and power' (1996: 226). Thus it is held that there is a different way of knowing the world that is less verbal, more emotional and spiritual.

Many other commentators, feminist and otherwise, have found the above conceptions of difference to be *essentialist*: in other words that we can read-off behaviour from some inherent essence that is, in this case, male or female (Due Billing, 1994). Sometimes this is biological, reducing women to their sexual and reproductive capacities, albeit as a source of strength rather than weakness. Even when not *biologically* essentialist, such arguments tend to treat men and women as fixed categories, and are unable to deal with change and variation in roles and practices: 'Cross-cultural research has shown that there is no behaviour or meaning which is universally associated with masculinity or femininity: they are socially constructed and changing categories' (Grint and Gill, 1996: 5).

An emphasis on social construction of identity has become increasingly promoted through Foucauldian and post-structuralist perspectives. Preferring to talk of discursive rather than material resources, such writers emphasise the existence of a bureaucratic *discourse* that relies upon a male rationality which shatters the apparent neutrality of rules and goals (Pringle, 1989). Through case studies such as the boss–secretary relationship, Pringle stresses the requirements of masculine rationality and its associated identities in the workplace to do battle with the feminine 'other'. Other contributors to the debate treat gender as a form of power/knowledge (Fineman, 1993; Putnam and Mumby 1993). It is argued that instrumental rationality within bureaucracy is defined by its opposition to emotionality. Feelings expressed by employees are either denied, suppressed or appropriated by the company for its own, instrumental ends. These observations overlap into discussion of emotional labour (see Chapters 15 and 23). Indeed, Simpson and Lewis (2007) argue that the introduction of emotion into organisations has been largely 'added-on' to the prevailing rationalist paradigm, thus re-writing emotions as masculine. This, they say, can be seen in the development of metrics for measuring emotions and their performance (for example, among front-line service workers) and in the emergence of 'emotional intelligence' as a potential corporate asset.

The potentialities of discursive construction of gender identity are highly varied. Class, age or ethnicity can cut across gender, producing different types of masculinity and femininity. Indeed, having separated sex and gender, it is then possible to argue that 'Masculinity is and can be performed by women. Women who are successful managers perform *hegemonic masculinity*' (Cheng, 1996: xii, original emphasis). While an emphasis on *performing* gender is useful, it is difficult to avoid concluding from this type of argument that women cannot 'win'. If they rise to the top, they have then 'joined the other side'. Post-structuralist writing (which we return to in the next section) is at the same time highly relativist in identifying different discourses of masculinity and femininity, but can also seek, and talks of, single, durable gender differences. For example, in the collection of articles by Cheng (1996), hegemonic masculinity is used as an overarching concept to explain dominant patterns in different work contexts such as those of trial lawyers, manufacturing management teams and military colleges. An over-emphasis on gender can subsume other influences on attitudes and behaviour that may impact on men and women, notably occupational and professional identities. So, for example, nursing has traditionally promoted a preference for control over emotions in the name of professional values (Bolton, 2000). It does not take us very far to use hegemonic or any other form of masculinity to explain this. Theorising gender in organisations has to avoid assuming or over-emphasising difference, and carefully explain the origins and impact of gender relations. As Wajcman notes, 'management incorporates a male standard that positions women as out of place. Indeed, the construction of women as different from men is one of the mechanisms whereby male power in the workplace is maintained' (1998: 2). One of the problems is too much emphasis on the discursive element and not enough on what men and women actually do in their work. In her critique of Ferguson's account of gender and bureaucracy, Due Billing argues that:

> Ferguson talks about discourses but does not deal with how gender is constructed and reconstructed or how specific elements of bureaucracy enter into it. Although great care is taken to state a distance from biological determinism there seems to be an unstated presumption that most men benefit from the status quo or carry such 'traits' that they cannot be included in a feminist discourse about bureaucracy. (1994: 183).

To return to an earlier discussion, any evidence that new nurturing, soft skills are practised in organisations by women or anyone else is thin to non-existent. 'Feminine' values may be self-attributed, and tell us more about how managers like to see themselves than what they actually do. It is also notable, in Rosener's case, that her sample was drawn overwhelmingly from small and non-traditional organisations where the space to behave differently may be greater.

Of equal importance, more empirically rigorous studies show that attitudinal differences between men and women at work are exaggerated. Studies of commitment show little or no difference between the sexes (Ramsay and Scholarios, 2005). Based on her research into large multinationals with ostensibly progressive HR policies, Wajcman observes that 'there is no such thing as a "female" management style and that the similarities between women and men far outweigh the differences between men and women as groups' (1996b: 333). Surveying a range of other studies, Izraeli and Adler (1994: 9) also note that 'negligible differences' were found. Both sexes are increasingly constrained by the lean and mean character of contemporary organisational life, with growing performance pressures on managers (Simpson, 1998). When the example is given of subjecting emotion to measurement, it may be less a case of its masculinisation, but an indication that gender is not the only thing being mobilised. In other words, the boundaries are not only between gender and organisation, but also those of the capitalist labour process in which the drive for profitability draws all human skills and attributes into its commodifying web.

Such outcomes are not a reason to displace gender as a key factor. Women continue to *experience* considerable constraint to career progression, while men retain greater opportunities to use formal and informal networks to advance their interests. What Wajcman, Simpson and others highlight is the difference between gender styles and gendered treatment. Much of the current literature is getting the significance of this the wrong way round. By over-emphasising the former, too much optimism is being generated about possibilities for women managers in a harsher, more directive corporate climate. As a senior female manager reported to Wajcman, 'The word that is being used is discipline ... and these changes in management style favour a male style ... management say the right things on diversity issues, but the tangible results are getting worse' (1996b: 275). If we want to be able to understand the messy and complex picture of how men and women think and act, 'we should see gender relations within organisations as complex, dynamic and potentially at least, unpredictable' (Halford, Savage and Witz, 1997: 13). This is best explored with reference to culture and career.

Culture, careers and networks: embedding gender

The gendering of organisational analysis has brought fresh insights to existing issues, for example to conventional accounts of bureaucracies as male career structures. Public and private bureaucracies developed along gendered lines, introducing large numbers of women into routine clerical jobs. The existence of practices such as marriage bars, where a female employee would be compelled to retire on marriage,

146 10

STUDYING ORGANISATIONS: AN INTRODUCTION ▪ THE EMERGENCE OF LARGE-SCALE ORGANISATIONS ▪ TAYLOR, WEBER AND THE BUREAUCRATISATION OF THE WORKPLACE ▪ MANAGING THE HUMAN FACTOR ▪ ORGANISATIONS AND ENVIRONMENTS ▪

facilitated the retention and promotion of male clerks. In this sense the growth of large-scale organisations has seen the creation of mini-patriarchies where the expansion of the public sphere is shown to be 'premised on men's power and dominance in the private domains' (Hearn, 1992: 81). Even when those practices finished, evidence (Crompton and Jones, 1984) shows that internal labour markets in sectors such as banking provided alternative career routes for male clerical employees.

However, Hakim's (1995; 2004) controversial work has challenged feminist orthodoxies. Using UK data sets, she argues that women's location in lower-status, lower-paid jobs is primarily an outcome of voluntary strategy rather than involuntary imposition. Many women choose to value benefits such as flexible hours, friendly workmates and good relations with the boss rather than career advancement. While it is important to recognise differentiated motives and circumstances among women, critics have argued that Hakim pays insufficient attention to the social and historical contexts that shape preferences and may lead some women to make pragmatic adjustments and accommodations (Anker, 1997; Ramsay and Scholarios, 1998). It also remains the case that a substantial number of 'career women' face real constraints inside and outside the organisation. Paradoxically, it is the existence of such constraints that helps to explain why it is overwhelmingly women who take up options of flexible work provisions, thus entrenching gender inequities in career paths. (Everingham, Stevenson and Warner-Smith, 2007)

Taking a more inside view, our understanding of organisational culture has also benefited from a gender 'twist'. It functions as a useful gateway to gender analyses because culture focuses on the way that individuals construct the understandings and subjectivities that underpin behaviour and structure (S. Acker 1992). Culturally-defined norms and values therefore crucially contribute to maintaining and reproducing the dominant patriarchal ideologies and practices (Alvesson and Billing, 1992; Green and Cassell, 1994). The argument, as we have seen, is that in bureaucracies, women are frequently strangers in a male-defined world. Culturally competent behaviour reflects largely masculine monocultures (Gerhardi, 1996; Alvesson and Billing, 1997). This goes beyond the more explicit cases of defence of male identity or resistance to women attempting to establish a presence in largely all-male preserves such as the police, the fire service and mining (Salaman, 1986; Keith and Collinson, 1994; Abrahamsson, 2006). There is evidence of women managers being perceived as threats to male self-image (Sargent, 1983; Cockburn, 1991). The latter study quotes one female senior manager: 'They certainly saw me as a huge threat when I first came. They made me feel very, very uncomfortable for six months. The woman bit. Men don't like it. They don't feel comfortable with women as superiors' (Cockburn, 1991: 141–2). Such women, as Sheppard's (1989) study found, often feel compelled to devise strategies of how to 'blend in'. The collection of essays in Colgan and Ledwith (1996) also provide numerous examples of the ways in which women in different occupational contexts devise adaptation strategies to survive and progress in male-dominated environments. In their study of how senior women in the UK NHS managed and understood their careers, Linstead and Catlow argue that the key process is about reconciling the tensions between the male norms of the profession and the differences of being a female in such contexts. The women had to demonstrate that they could be tough and impersonal, while drawing on more 'feminine' styles to respond to their own and other women's preferences. Referring to an incident in a meeting in which she assertively faced down an attempt by the Chief Executive to label her behaviour as emotional, one interviewee commented that, 'I don't like my wants to be labelled as irrational or emotional ... That moment validated me as a woman on the Board' (2004: 107). What about the reverse scenario – 'token' men in predominantly female occupations? Drawing on her interviews with male librarians, cabin crew, primary teachers and nurses, Simpson (2004) demonstrates that men have to engage in considerable gender work in order to compensate for threats to their masculinity. Different 'strategies' are identified that can be seen as equivalents of the kind of choices facing women on whether or how to 'blend in'. However, 'hegemonic masculinity' confers upon 'token men' the resources to emphasise their leadership and other competencies, thus moving up the career ladder more rapidly, while at the same time often being able to operate within a 'comfort zone' of enjoying the company of women and 'female' activities.

Increasingly, the analysis of culture has been complemented by that of networks. Access to networks has long been seen in conventional organisational theory to be a crucial factor in gaining structural advantage. Recent studies have demonstrated that women and ethnic minorities have less access to informal networks, and have different opportunities to convert their own organisational resources to network advantage (Ibarra, 1993; 1995). Whereas women feel comfortable in formal settings such as meetings, men create cultures in which in- and after-hours socialising can play a crucial role in sharing information, playing 'office politics' and securing privileges (Tierney, 1996; Simpson, 1997; 1998). Not surprisingly, women tend to use formal processes to seek promotion, while men prefer informal ones (*The Economist*, 10 August 1996). Surveys reveal that though women identify a variety of barriers to career advancement, the club or clique-like character of senior management is perceived to be crucial (Wajcman, 1996b). Interestingly a much smaller proportion of men identify informal networks as a problem, which suggests that the taken-for-granted masculinity of organisational cultures renders them invisible to the 'dominant sex'.

Cultures are, however, not homogenous. Poggio (2000) identifies a continuum of 'women-friendliness' in her culture case studies. Different types of masculinity may produce a range of managerial styles, from authoritarianism, paternalism, entrepreneurialism, careerism to informal relations where men form an in-group that simultaneously differentiates them from other groups of both sexes. The last group corresponds to the 'locker room culture' identified in a typology developed by Maddock and Parkin (1993); other gender cultures include the traditional 'gentleman's club', the 'barrack yard', and the more contemporary 'gender blind' and 'feminist pretender' arrangements, where new men affirm equal opportunities while nothing has really changed. This can be broadened further by referring to cross-cultural factors. In some national or regional cultures, such as those in East Asia where family businesses remain influential, membership of social networks outweighs credentials as a form of access. This can work for women in some circumstances, but militates against progression in the broader corporate economy (Izraeli and Adler, 1994: 8).

Halford, Savage and Witz (1997) draw useful and broader theoretical conclusions compatible with these kinds of findings. Organisations are neutral and depersonalised, but their gendered substructures are embedded within different cultural and historical contexts. Furthermore, organisations are populated by agents who reinterpret and contest existing practices and procedures. Gender, therefore, is inherently variable and continually enacted. Webster makes a similar anti-essentialist point about women's relation to technology, which she describes as 'one of exclusion through embedded historical practice, reinforced and reproduced in contemporary work settings' (1997: 25). Many of the examples and arguments drawn from such perspectives increasingly depend on analysis of sexuality instead of, or in addition to, gender. It is to this that we now turn.

Enter sexuality

Sexuality had begun to creep out of the shadows of gender in the sociology of the workplace through well-known studies of the characteristics of female (Pollert, 1981; Westwood, 1984) and male (Willis, 1977) wage labour, and the use of sexuality and gender as a method of control (see Thompson, 1989: 196–7). What such studies facilitated was a move beyond issues of sexual division of labour to those of sexuality in the division of labour. This rested largely on the fact that work behaviour was overlaid with masculine and feminine identities. In this light, homosociability is not only a rational economic action to secure collective interests, but it is also a way of defining and defending sexual identities. This is as true of pranks and practices of the female factory workers studied by Pollert and Westwood as of the male workers in truck plants (Collinson, 1992), or abattoirs (Ackroyd and Crowdy, 1990). While some of this might seem to be at the marginal, social end of work activity, defence of sexual identity can be connected with protection of access to employment. This is most tellingly revealed in Cockburn's (1991) examination of the attitudes and practices of printworkers, who clearly felt female employment to be a threat not only to their livelihood, but to their sense of (masculine) self that had become inextricably bound to the nature of their craft.

The entry of sexuality into organisational theory, while drawing on the above studies, has also been contingent on a number of other developments. The first route has been the critique of the previously-discussed Weberian model of *de-sexualised bureaucracies*. From this absence, sexuality suddenly began to be found everywhere – in language, practices, relationships, displays, design, hierarchies and managerial strategies. In some instances it is seen primarily as a tension between a partially-submerged underlife of sexuality and the dominant calculative rationality that would seek to repress it in the name of efficiency (Burrell, 1992); in others it appears as a substantially-embedded set of practices much nearer the surface of everyday organisational life (Hearn and Parkin, 1987; Hearn *et al.*, 1989). To return to a previous example – that of Shepherd's (1989) account of 'blending in' strategies of female managers – it is clear that this frequently involved changes in appearance and body language so that female assertiveness would not threaten male sexual authority (we return to issues concerning the body later in the chapter). Whether focusing on underlife or surface practice, what was being revealed was the public nature of what had been previously consigned to the private realm. In their detailed examination of sexual misbehaviour in the workplace, Ackroyd and Thompson (1999) argue that this is not merely a theoretical shift, but a practical one. The decline in gender-segregated workplaces and the increase in female employees has combined with workplace cultures that allow more elements of sociability and informality to create greater opportunities for sexual interactions. Both employers and employees have blurred the boundaries between the public and private, and between organisational and social selves.

Such trends help to explain the growing litigation and politicisation surrounding both convivial and coercive sexuality at work. In other words, companies are finding it increasingly necessary to regulate sexual interactions. While there is a growth of codes governing romantic relations, most of the emphasis has been on sexual harassment. Indeed, this has been a second route to visibility in management and organisation theory (Gutek, 1985; Stanko, 1988; Di Tomaso, 1989; Collinson and Collinson, 1989; 1994; Thomas and Kitzinger, 1997). There is no single and precise definition of harassment, in part because it is overlaid with particular legal contexts and treatments (Wilson and Thompson, 2001). Nevertheless, there are common themes focusing on the unwanted, intrusive or persistent nature of the behaviour. Such practices can 'pollute' the work environment, according to a European Commission code of practice. Again while there are contrasting explanations, there are also common themes. Whether at the office party or in promotion processes, sexual harassment can be seen as a means through which individual men exert their power over women. The varieties of forms of harassment can be seen as power plays or controlling gestures arising mainly as responses to the threat to identity and material interests when women enter male occupational territories, or from the abuse of power in supervisory and other authority relationships. Unlike Kanter's analysis of gender, sexuality cannot be confined to the organisation. Barbara Gutek's detailed and authoritative study utilises the concept of sex-role overspill to emphasise the broader social connections: 'the carryover into the workplace of gender-based roles that are usually irrelevant or inappropriate to work'. These may include conceptions of women's nurturing capacity or being a sex object, to the stereotype of men's natural leadership ability.

The third route is filtered through the discussions of sexuality and power. As Halford, Savage and Witz note, 'What has emerged from the radical feminist and radical organisation literature is a clear view that women's subordination at work is "eroticised" or "sexualised"' (1997: 21). These complex relations require a separate discussion in their own right, though themes also overlap with those already discussed in the first two routes.

Contrasting perspectives on sex, power and organisations

At one level, associations between sexuality and power in the workplace are uncontentious. Pringle's (1989) work on the boss–secretary relationship successfully established this territory, demonstrating the historical roots and contemporary features of the 'office wife' phenomenon in which women are used to enhance masculinity and authority. Analyses of service sector work have extended the argument. Adkin's case studies are used to argue that 'women employees had as a condition of their employment, the requirement to provide sexual services for male customers and employees' (1992: 214). This is not meant literally, but refers to controls over forms of dress, appearance, and engagement in being chatted-up and other verbal sexual interactions. Women's work is therefore eroticised subordination. In some ways this has built on previous discussion of emotional labour. Hochschild's (1983) study of flight attendants, as well as the later British account by Tyler and Taylor (1997), show how companies require the largely female employees to manage their own feelings to improve the 'quality' of the service encounter. Part of this process of 'acting' involves a projection of sexuality through visual and verbal display; the female flight attendant is 'part mother, part servant and part tart', as one of Tyler and Taylor's respondents put it (1997: 13). A perceptive and revealing recent account of the history of flight attendants (Barry, 2007) illustrates that the price of 'the wages of glamour' were an employer requirement to perform femininity through physical attractions and charm. Barry also shows, however, that unionisation drives were based on the desire to be valued as safety professionals. Similar patterns of mobilisation of emotions and sexuality were identified by Filby (1992) in his account of the uses of female labour at the quality end of betting shops. These and other studies highlight the growing significance of interactive service work in the economy and its vulnerability to sexualisation.

Emphasis has also been put especially on the process of embodiment (J. Acker, 1990; Halford, Witz and Savage, 1997: 25–8; Wolkowitz, 2006). Beyond the obvious examples of dress and display, consideration has been given to the routine degree of sexualised body work through interactions of doctors, nurses and other medical staff (Witz, Halford and Savage, 1994), and the associations between skill and physicality in police work (Keith and Collinson, 1994). In the latter, bodily discourses provide not only a means of keeping women officers in their proper, feminine place, but are used to make further, regional distinctions: 'In the South the people are like the landed gentry, so the police are just big girls' blouses' (female police sergeant, quoted in Keith and Collinson, 1994: 17). Wolkowitz makes the point that as workers are increasingly concentrated in jobs in the service sector, particularly carrying out tasks that rely on interaction with a customer, client or patient, the body becomes 'a focus of diverse labour processes' (2006: 2). Here, the body is treated as a site for emotions, appearance and physical effort, all of which are increasingly commodified by employers in search of greater output from the whole person. The most obvious of such processes is that of aesthetic labour – managerial interventions in how employees look as part of the sales and service encounter (Witz, Warhurst and Nickson, 2003). As recent surveys have shown, many employers in sectors such as retail in the UK not only make this a key factor in recruitment and selection, but also provide training in behaviours such as body language and personal grooming (Nickson, Warhurst and Dutton, 2005). As with emotions (Bolton, 2005), while potential employees already have such capacities and attributes, the employer seeks to script corporeal as well as verbal interactions.

While these and related issues pull academic and practical attention to the triangle of gender, sexuality and power, understandings of power are precisely the factors that divide many contributors to the debate. Take the question of sexual harassment. Though this is clearly *about* power, it does not necessarily involve a particular *theory* of power. Whereas Gutek does not see sexual coercion as the norm of male–female relations inside or outside work, the increasing number of radical feminists writing in this area are only too happy to do so. Admittedly much of this has nothing to do with the workplace as such. Sexuality is seen as the primary source of male power (MacKinnon, 1979), and heterosexual desire as the eroticisation of conquest and subordination (Jeffreys, 1990). Harassment is the conduit to the organisation in studies focusing on academia (Ramazanogulu, 1987), social work (Wise and Stanley, 1990) or professional education (Carter and Jeffs, 1992). What these and other writers have in common is the view that harassment is not aberrant, unusual or different in kind from flirtation, banter or affairs: 'it is instructive to note that "sexual harassment" and "ordinary sexual encounters" follow more or less exactly the same levels of expression' (Wise and Stanley, 1990: 20). All this is a version of MacKinnon's argument that organisations are the site of compulsory heterosexuality. As a theorisation of power, this takes us back to zero-sum notions where, in this case, men and women are erotically joined solely through mutual threat and share no common interest. Or as Carter and Jeffs (1992: 240–1) put it, 'Sexuality is always about power and is always about "us" as well as "them".'

Others, particularly those influenced by post-structuralist and Foucauldian perspectives, would agree that sexuality and power are intimately linked, but strongly question its characterisation. Foucault's writing sees sexuality and the body as central to power and its reproduction and has influenced much, though not all, of the above discussions. Such studies 'explore how power disciplines and shapes women's bodies, movements and expressions' (Cooper, 1994: 437), though it works through internalisation and self-monitoring rather than coercion from the top or as the result of ideology. As we discussed earlier in relation to gender, seeing organisational sexuality in terms of discursive production necessarily requires an emphasis on social construction and fluidity rather than fixed and essential power relations:

> Subjectivity is constituted through the exercise of power within which conceptions of personal identity, gender and sexuality come to be generated. Thus, men and women actively exercise power in positioning themselves within, or finding their own location among, competing discourses, rather than merely being 'positioned by' them. (Brewis and Kerfoot, 1994: 8)

Research shows that some of these positioning processes are based on discourses of *difference*, which promote negative representations of women or men who do not play the masculinity game (Collinson and Collinson, 1989; Cockburn, 1991). Post-structuralist research has been particularly concerned to make the performance of masculinity more visible. Its reproduction is strongly linked to sexuality in that mobilisation of masculinities draws on 'discourses, jokes, behaviours and styles' that bolster sexual identities (Gherardi, 2003: 228). Simpson and Lewis (2007) draw on the work of Brannan (2005) and others to argue that within sexualised customer service work (such as that of call centres) male employees are encouraged to enact a masculine identity through flirting with female customers and the performance of 'suitor roles' that display dominance, authority and control. Returning to Simpson's studies of minority men in traditional female occupations, she argues that her own and other studies indicate a particular anxiety derived from the threat to masculine identities from stigmatisation associated with femininity and homosexuality: 'men need to prove to other men, rather than other women, that, they are sufficiently "male"' (2004: 364). But this will vary according to work situations and the available knowledge resources. Studies of local government and banking by Witz, Halford and Savage identified the deployment of discourses of gender *complementarity*. Mixed-sex workgroups were endorsed by management as a means of countering the undesirable effects of all-male or all-female sociability. But employees positioned themselves too, finding fun in flirtation and romance. Contrary to the radical feminist argument, 'All the women drew an extremely clear boundary between "flirtation" and "sexual harassment"' (1994: 20).

Greater space to see the interrelationships between power and pleasure arises, in part, from Foucault's theorisation of the former as productive, relational and capillary (see previous chapter for a wider discussion). Viewing events from the 'bottom-up' and through micro-practices is much less likely to result in behaviour being read-off from universal conceptions of position and behaviour. In Pringle's work, secretaries were far from passive objects of the boss's banter, deriving pleasure from imitating, exaggerating or ridiculing existing stereotypes (1989: 103). This can be supported by other studies which are not necessarily from a Foucauldian perspective. Discursive practices in which women use sexuality and 'sexy chat' as a means of acting as subjects is best exemplified in Filby's (1992) previously mentioned study of daily life in betting shops. Though management tried and partly succeeded in using women's bodies and personalities to promote the product, female employees turned the tables by developing their own aggressive 'scolding' and 'joking' routines to keep customers and managers in their place.

Evaluation: under- and overpowered explanations

Foucauldian theory and research on power and sexuality has proven a useful antidote to essentialist conceptions of men as automatic power holders and women as eternal victims. It reinforces existing research that shows the workplace as a site for a variety of forms of sexual and romantic relationship (Ackroyd and Thompson, 1999). Sexuality is the most complex of social relations, and 'we need a model of power relations which can also deal with power as it is exercised in friendly or intimate encounters' (Davis, 1991: 81). Of course, all sexual relations cannot be described in this way. But even in the case of the most instrumental of sexual exchanges – prostitution – the dynamics of power and control cannot necessarily be described as men securing direct power, nor as motivated solely by the desire to affirm a masterful manhood (O'Connell Davidson, 1994a: 2).

But it is the very specificity of sexuality as a site of power that creates a problem. In different ways, both the radical feminist and Foucauldian perspectives fail to recognise this. For each theory sees sexuality as the standard template of how power works, and this has a number of negative consequences. Radical feminists cannot see sexuality without seeing power: 'both its intention and its end, its product, is power' (Wise and Stanley, 1990: 15); hence they fail to grasp its varied construction and practice. Foucauldians, at least those writing in this area, cannot see power without seeing sexuality, and therefore tend to extend the latter's reach beyond its usefulness. Glucksman observes that:

> it is important to retain a means of analytically distinguishing between different articulations of emotional/sexual and economic relations in the different spheres of work. The temptation, however, having discovered the sexuality and emotionality of organization, may be to so privilege this aspect that it is treated as the prime characteristic of organization or the workplace. ... The inevitable effect would be to collapse economic into emotional/sexual relationships, so conflating the two. (Glucksman, 1995: 66)

Much of the rhetoric about the body falls into this kind of trap. For example, Witz, Halford and Savage comment on a woman manager who had worn a red suit in order to get noticed at a dinner:

> " It really does serve to illustrate how embodied organizational participants can call up their embodiment through ways of presenting the body. The choice of a red dress is evoking a number of associations between red and the womanly body – the most obvious is the association with red and sexuality, the least obvious is that between red and bleeding. (Witz, Halford and Savage, 1994: 23–4)

This exaggerated emphasis is rooted in the Foucauldian and post-structuralist legacy on such research. As Wolkowitz (2006: 16) notes, this pulls in two directions, between the construction of 'docile bodies' on the one hand and, on the other, the disruptive potential of bodily pleasures and play as a form of resistance. She argues, rightly in our view, that part of the problem is the neglect of the employment relationship and paid work in the study of the body. Taking the cue from Foucault, studies theorise the management of all social life operating through power targeting the individual through their body. But organisations are not simply 'containers of different bodies and sexualities' (Gherardi, 2003: 223), bodies in the bedroom, prison or workplace may be subject to different pressures and respond in distinct ways. Body work is much wider than a focus on sexuality implies and while sexualized labour has rightly become a more important topic, it is a very small minority, even of service interactions. Furthermore, the very fluidity and complexity recognised in post-structuralist perspectives may not be as applicable in other sites of power, particularly when we remember that the object of analysis is organisational sexuality. Whereas power is zero-sum in only the most coercive sexual encounters, in many workplace situations it is, as we argued earlier, often not as negotiable and is possessed and exercised by agents with a radically unequal access to power resources. Organisational sexuality is therefore influenced by the potential characteristics of both sites of power, with varied consequences for choice and constraint. Resistance too, may take on distinct forms. Again, as Wolkowitz (2006: 26) argues, employees frequently locate a sense of self outside of and in contrast to their roles as worker, in part as a means of providing a barrier to 'greedy corporate demands for "body and soul"'. She and other recent contributors to the debate (Pettinger, 2004; 2006; Warhurst and Nickson, 2007) call for a broader focus on body work that emphasises the continuing materiality of workplace activity located within the broader political economy. We will return to these issues in Chapter 15.

Fascinating as these discussions are, do they have any significance for organisational practices? We believe that they do, though not always in a direct way. Take the post-structuralist view that, 'Power here is not the oppressive power implicit within liberal feminism as a zero-sum analysis where power is a possession. Rather, power for Foucault is productive, it allows us to think ourselves and our individuality as we find/fit ourselves in(to) various discourses' (Brewis and Kerfoot, 1994: 8). One might answer that the problem is that organisational processes, gendered and otherwise, are not just discourses in relation to which we can position ourselves. Gender regimes are constituted through symbolic order and material practices (Wajcman, 1998: 3). The constraints to the success of equal opportunities policies, for example, are also linked to material sources of power, particularly those expressed through internal and external labour markets. Without this recognition of relatively durable structures and constraint, gender risks 'being swallowed up in the bottomless swamp of permanently shifting meanings and ambivalent discursive constructions' (Komter, 1991: 47). We explore this and related issues in the section below where we want to link the theoretical discussions to more practical issues about dealing with gender inequality, not merely to add a policy dimension, but because the discussion raises key theoretical questions.

From equal opportunity to managing diversity?

Equal opportunity (EO) policies advocate formal, collective responses to gender inequalities in the workplace, marking an end to an individual differences approach that promoted the idea that women had to 'fit in' in order to succeed. In contrast, under EO the onus was on organisations to change. This ranged from targets to improve the number of women at various levels of the organisation; formalisation of procedures and specification of equitable conduct dealing with access to and treatment in jobs; family-friendly career support systems, including career breaks, job sharing and flexible hours; and additional training such as assertiveness and personal development. Overall, it can be seen as the prime policy response to the heightened visibility of gender issues outlined in this chapter, as well as a somewhat more reluctant compliance with legal regulation of sexual and other forms of discrimination.

EO was always controversial. Business critics resented 'bureaucratic' regulation of labour markets and processes. Meanwhile, radical critics (Symons, 1992; Simpson, 1997) often saw it as a form of liberal feminism which encourages a superficial view that organisations could be gender-neutral if appropriate procedures and policies were followed, and inequalities could be dealt with if opportunities were made available and women took them. Given the evidence examined in this chapter, it has not been difficult for critics to find problems to feed on. Even flagship progressive companies, such as those involved in Opportunity 2000 in the UK, have been shown to make limited progress (Wajcman, 1996b) and the adoption of formal policies in both small and large companies can often disguise something of an 'empty shell' in terms of actual practices (Hoque and Noon, 2004). An emphasis on formal procedures tends to neglect underlying structural and attitudinal factors. As a consequence, external or internal legislation may be ignored or marginalised in practice, particularly where senior managerial support is weak or operational managers are hostile (Jewson and Mason, 1986; Collinson *et al.*, 1990).

Managerial writers began to use such evidence to mount a critique of the 'ineffectiveness' of EO and US-based affirmative action policies (Blakemore and Black, 1996). An alternative was advocated under the heading of *managing diversity*. That has proven very influential in practitioner communities (see Kandola and Fullerton, 1994). The content of diversity differs, as management and policy makers struggle to come to terms with the growing heterogeneity of the labour force in terms of gender, ethnicity, age and disability (de los Reyes, 2000). In some contexts such as Sweden, as de los Reyes observes, issues of ethnicity and migrant labour predominate, though in general, 'few studies deal with the impact of ethnicity in work organisations' (2000: 260). Nevertheless, there are commonalities in the approach. As the employment policy director of Grand Metropolitan put it, 'Managing or valuing diversity differs from the conventional approach to equal opportunities in that it seeks to create a climate whereby those involved want to move beyond the achievement of mere statistical goals' (Greenslade, 1994: 28). Like many companies and some academics (Robinson and Dechant, 1997) they prioritise the business case for any measures, notably that diversity reflects demographic change and therefore the available talent pool, enhances competitiveness by adding value to the capacity for innovation, and matches the profile of clients and customers.

The policy terrain shifts to an emphasis on personal development, support for individuals through coaching and mentoring, education to change the culture of the organisation, and broadening managerial responsibilities beyond the human resource function. This is obviously linked to and extends the scope of HRM – competitive advantage is not just through people, but their diversity (Herriot and Pemberton, 1994). Multiculturalism can be achieved without the divisiveness of EO, with its associations with preferential treatment, conflict, exclusion and special interests (Blakemore and Black, 1996). The different perceptions, language and ways of solving problems of men and women are complementary and both can add value (Masreliez-Steen, 1989). The outcome is a stated belief in the inherent value in diversity, a shift from a problem to be solved to a positive attribute of and for the organisation.

As Kirton and Greene (2000) note, there is a shift away from norms of assimilation and towards 'positive messages' about recognising talent through and despite social differences. Some feminists working in the management field support this. N. Adler argues that an equity approach assumes similarity, while MD is based on assumed difference: 'The first focuses on increasing the representation of women managers; the second, on increasing their utilisation at all levels of the organisation' (1994: 24). Such arguments clearly reflect the broader shifts in approach towards a 'soft' essentialism in feminist thought: that women can be themselves and be of value without having to assimilate. Indeed, as Liff (1999) observes, diversity depends on such notions of difference. This kind of approach is superficially attractive. It draws its main explanatory power from an understanding of the significance of the kind of informal cultures and networks discussed earlier, and some of its policy mechanisms, such as mentoring, may be a useful addition. Even when not reduced to individuals, diversity can be tied into attempts to 'deconstruct' the unity of categories such as race and gender, emphasising the plurality of groupings within each.

However, MD remains limited in theoretical and practical terms. It attempts to combine what would appear to be contradictory: a focus on individuals rather than groups, yet recognition of collective categories and changed goals. The shift of emphasis towards individuals disconnects those goals from any collective force of disadvantaged groups, and regards all difference as equally salient (Kirton and Greene, 2000: 113). Measuring progress qualitatively rather than quantitatively uses the language of complementarity and depth, yet allows organisations to evade the constraints of targets and facilitate male appropriation of 'feminine styles' without substantive change in representation or progression (Wajcman, 1996a: 347). Complementarity, according to Adler, means that 'firms expect women managers, to think, dress, and act like women' (N. Adler, 1994: 26). Aside from the fact that this is at odds with previously-discussed evidence about the much exaggerated differences between the attitudes and behaviour of male and female managers, there is 'the danger that any argument based on women's attributed differences from men will be used to reassert their essential inferiority and justifiable exclusion from certain public roles' (Webb, 1997: 163). On a wider point, as Noon argues, given that it is associated with a management rhetoric that focuses upon individuals and identifies personal traits as being more important than social group characteristics, 'Diversity discourses are not constructed to confront power relations, dominant ideologies or organizational goals' (2007: 775). Focusing on the unique contribution of each (diverse) employee dilutes diversity and dissolves difference of circumstance and experience between groups (Liff, 1997; Linehan and Konrad, 1999).

For all its weaknesses, EO offers a minimum defence in terms of policing procedures and behaviour, and a focus on social justice rather than the inherent fragility of a contingent 'business case' (Noon, 2007). Yet procedures and rules are also seen as part of the problem by some feminists. Put more theoretically, bureaucracy is presented as a discourse of male rationality and a distinction is made between male and female types of social action; the former embodied in authoritarian methods of control or hierarchical ways of decision-making, the latter in ways of organising dependent on emotional connection, nurturance, intimacy and co-operation (Ferguson, 1984; Grimshaw, 1986; Bologh, 1990). The glass ceiling is left intact in favour of constructing an entirely different kind of building – a 'womanspace' (Calás and Smircich, 1996: 227). As Due Billing (1994) argues, in utilising essentialist notions of male and female rationality, Ferguson and others are in danger of throwing the practical and theoretical baby out with the bathwater. Rules are a potential asset for employees and though male-dominated cultures can lead to processes and outcomes that advantage men; this is not inherent to bureaucracy, which is not static, particularly, when (in a parallel argument to Kanter), large numbers of women enter and seek to change structures. This judgement appears to be consistent with the evidence we have examined that it is the formal domains of organisational life where women feel more comfortable and protected (Simpson, 1997: 126). Where female professionals and managers align their identity and cultural support mechanisms with career opportunities, the glass ceiling can be porous and permeable (Linstead and Catlow, 2004). It is true that changing informal cultures is a more difficult and long-term task, but the issue is whether it is more effective when combined with formal mechanisms. Achieving substantive equal opportunity will be a struggle, it will require more extensive legislation to encourage family-friendly policies, it will be lengthy and there will be losers. None of this fits easily into the way that many proponents of HRM view the world.

Summary and key points

Few issues have risen in prominence and generated so much new writing than gender and sexuality in organisations. This is welcome, both for making relevant practices visible and challenging the concepts (new reflections on traditional ones such as power and culture, emphasis on new ones, notably the body) and boundaries (public/private, work/life) of organisational analysis itself. Such challenges may also feed into discussion and action on policy. As we showed in the previous section, recent and more sympathetic thinking on gender differences has helped facilitate a shift from equity models to those of managing diversity (a shift about which we share a degree of scepticism with other commentators). Despite the sometimes close links between perspectives and practices in these areas, new theorising doesn't always produce changed practices, at least not directly or immediately. Though women continue to take more professional and managerial position at the lower and middle levels, a glass ceiling continues to be part of organisational life. Despite the continued practical obstacles to career progression, *some* things have changed in gender relations at work. Our review of the evidence clearly shows shifts away from the earlier stereotypical associations of 'ideal' management with masculinity. However, while these views have virtually disappeared among women, they are still present in the perceptions of many male managers (Brenner *et al.*, 1989). Even where women are still struggling as 'tokens' in difficult environments, there is little evidence that they are falling into the restrictive role traps identified by Kanter (Simpson, 1997). In contrast, while male managers may endorse general statements about equal treatment, their views are often 'soft' and more deeply-held beliefs sometimes remain unchanged. For example, Wajcman (1996b) found that while there was no difference between the sexes when they were asked which sex made better managers, a sizeable minority of men (21 per cent) said they would prefer to work for a male manager.

We have also mapped a number of theoretical shifts. It is highly unlikely that organisation theory will ever return to gender-neutral models of bureaucracy or anything else. Indeed, as we have shown in this chapter, debates on the glass ceiling and other issues have added fresh insights that complement existing knowledge of gender and work, such as on labour markets (Rubery *et al.*, 1999) and professions (Witz, 1992). The distinctiveness of that debate and its focus on organisational factors should not let us lose sight of the bigger picture. A capacity to enter the labour market and rise up the career ladder remains strongly affected by unequal domestic responsibilities, so studies of work–family boundaries need to inform organisational analysis (Crompton with N. Feuvre, 1996; Burke, 1997; Wajcman, 1998; Applebaum *et al.*, 2005). Conflicts between job and family are particularly acute where mobility is a prerequisite for career advancement and social norms strongly reinforce the primacy of female domestic roles, as illustrated by Ng and Fosh's (2000) study of international airlines in East Asia.

In this chapter we have focused on two key debates and literatures, but it is worth noting that there may be tensions between them. We need to be careful about treating the issues of gender and sexuality as somehow always linked or equivalent. Indeed some commentators believe that the avalanche of writing on sexuality is beginning to squeeze out attention to those many aspects of the 'gender paradigm' that are distinguishable from issues of sexuality (Witz and Savage, 1992). In relation to this, some conventional economic issues have tended to be marginalised in the emphasis on culture, discourse and identity. More controversially it can be argued that re/discovering gender has sometimes led to diminishing the importance of other interests and identities – for instance, class, occupational and professional – which may, in given circumstances, have more influence on employee behaviour. It is also worth remembering the need to differentiate within gender categories given that they will cross-cut with those other social divisions. Organisational analysis now has the conceptual resources to study the 'gender substructure' of organisations. It remains an empirical question as to the significance and character of those structures and practices.

Further reading

You would be unlikely ever to go short of reading on these topics, but whether much new is being added is another matter. On the general territory of gender, management and organisations a new edition of Alvesson and Due Billing's (2008) useful textbook promises to bring debates up-to-date. Wajcman's (1998) assessment of whether feminine and masculine styles of management really do exist is an important corrective to populist assertions. On equal opportunity, diversity and its management, Cockburn's early work was path-breaking and Kirton and Greene's (2000) text, though now a little dated, was the first critical take on the subject. Noon's (2007) lively recent commentary fills some of the gaps. Moving to sexuality, Pringle's book on secretaries and Cockburn's on printers are highly readable classics whose insights remain indispensible, as is Filby's (1992) journal piece on the same subject. The emerging body of work on the body has not generally distinguished itself on the clarity and readability front. Thankfully, we now have Wolkowitz to guide us perceptively through this contentious territory. Witz, Warhurst and Nickson's (2003) paper broke new ground on aesthetic labour.

Alvesson, M. and Billing, Y. (2008) *Understanding Gender and Organisations* (2nd edn), London: Sage.

Cockburn, C. (1983) *Brothers: Male Dominance and Technological Change*, London: Pluto.

Cockburn, C. (1991) *In the Way of Women: Men's Resistance to Sex Equality in Organizations*, London: Macmillan.

Filby, M. (1992) 'The Figures, the Personality and the Bums: Service Work and Sexuality', *Work Employment and Society*, 6. 1: 23–42.

Kirton, G. and Greene, A.-M. (2000) *The Dynamics of Managing Diversity: A Critical Approach*, Oxford: Butterworth Heinemann.

Noon, M. (2007) 'The Fatal Flaws of Diversity and the Business Case for Ethnic Minorities', *Work Employment and Society*, 21. 4: 773–84.

Pringle, R. (1989) *Secretaries Talk: Sexuality, Power and Work*, London: Verso.

Wajcman, J. (1998) *Managing Like a Man: Women and Men in Corporate Management*, Oxford: Polity and Blackwell.

Witz, A., Warhurst, C. and Nickson, D. (2003) 'The Labour of Aesthetics and the Aesthetics of Organization', *Organization*, 10. 1: 33–54.

Wolkowitz, C. (2006) *Bodies at Work*, London: Sage.

11 corporations and culture: reinventing organisation man?

In the past couple of decades, social science has seen what some commentators refer to a 'cultural turn' away from concerns with the economy and structure towards values, language and the symbolic sphere (Sayer and Ray, 1999). Organisational analysis has had its own 'turn' as the management of culture came to be of central interest to corporations and those who study them. This was associated initially with a wave of literature in the early 1980s that sought to bring the 'lessons' of Japanese corporate success to Western audiences and was followed by culture becoming a central piece in the emergent perspectives of human resource management (HRM) and organisational change more generally. Culture, however, was not always such a high-profile issue in managerial thought and practice, at least not outside the realms of Hofstede and persuading managers to be more sensitive to the values of other nations (as discussed in Chapter 6). Arguably, it is an issue that is currently of less significance to managerial theory and practice.

The aims of this chapter are to:

- Explain how culture became a core issue for management and HRM in theory and practice.
- Describe and interpret the selling of corporate culture as a product.
- Critically evaluate the available evidence for the distinctiveness of culture as a concept and the impact of culture change on practices and attitudes.
- Examine conceptualisations of culture as a form of normative control.
- Explore the constraints on culture as category and practice and to assess whether it is of diminishing utility in contemporary organisational and economic climates.

The fall and rise of organisation man

In 1956, William H. Whyte – an editor at *Fortune* magazine – wrote the influential *The Organization Man*, a vituperative attack on the 'social ethic' shaping the values of those in the middle ranks of private and public corporations:

> If the term Organization Man is vague, it is because I can think of no other way to describe the people I am talking about. They are not the workers, nor are they the white-collar people in the usual, clerk sense of the word. These people only work for the Organization. The ones I am talking about belong to it as well. They are the ones of our middle class who have left home, spiritually as well as physically to take the vows of organization life, and it is they who are the mind and soul of our great self-perpetuating institutions. (Whyte, 1956: 1; 2002)

This ethic – be loyal to the company and the company will be loyal to you – was deemed by Whyte and his supporters to to be a collectivist nightmare that morally legitimated the powers of society against the individual. Among those blamed were Mayo and his obsessive concern for belongingness and group adjustment. Whyte's solution was for the individual – the endangered self – to fight a rearguard battle against the organisation, with the aid of some useful advice such as 'how to cheat at personality tests'. As Peters and Waterman note (1982: 105), the association with grey conformity made corporate culture a taboo topic.

But by the end of the 1980s, organisation man was back in fashion. Though some continue to doubt the idea of people 'belonging' to the company (Lessem, 1985), IBM's 'corporate fascists' with their historic emphasis on conformity and commitment could get their overdue kudos as well as smile politely on the way to the bank (Pascale and Athos, 1982: 186). Despite all the hymns of praise to corporations, the credit for reviving the issue largely goes to American academics and management consultants, notably the two mentioned above, plus Ouchi (1981) and Deal and Kennedy (1988) – all except Ouchi connected to the McKinsey consultancy company. However, it was filtered through a reading of the Japanese experience that located their success in the existence of strong cultures and 'turned-on workforces'. In other words, cross-national competitive advantage was seen to be linked to cultural factors (Dahler-Larsen, 1994).

Corporate culture was put on the agenda. This can be defined as the way in which management mobilise combinations of values, language, rituals and myths, and is seen as the key factor in unlocking the commitment and enthusiasm of employees. To the extent that it can make people feel that they are working for something worthwhile, it is projected as part of the solution to the historic search for meaning or the holy grail of commitment in the study of organisations. For work humanisation theorists such as Herzberg and Maslow, that search was connected to the provision of intrinsically satisfying tasks through job redesign. The ground shifted to the psychosocial benefits from identification with the company and its superordinate goals. There may be characteristics that make companies successful, as in the famous lists of Peters and Waterman or Goldsmith and Clutterbuck – autonomy, zero-basing, productivity through people – but corporate culture is the core and the glue that binds the increasingly diverse activities together. When the project is defined as developing a non-deified, non-religious 'spiritualism', it is to be expected that advocacy often takes on a distinctly evangelical tone, with managers and workers exhorted to love the company. Such acts of will can break the 'attitudinal barriers' that hold firms back (Goldsmith and Clutterbuck, 1985: 5).

More conventionally, there was an emphasis on culture *strategies*, with senior management taking the process of value-shaping seriously. But perhaps strategy is the wrong word. Corporate culture is part of a proclaimed shift from the hard S of strategy, systems and their quantifiable objectives, to the soft S of style and shared values. We should not underestimate the shift in management theory, and to a lesser extent practices, that this would require. Changing people's emotions or what they think had mostly been off-limits to the dominant strands in OB. It is summed up in Herzberg's answer to a question about the problems of employees at a seminar: 'Don't worry about their attitudes or personality, you can't change them' (Carr Mill Consultants, 1973: 7). Similarly, when commenting on March and Simon's views, Perrow argued that, 'to change individual behaviour, you do not have to change individuals' (1973: 147). Under systems of bureaucratic or unobtrusive control, what had to be changed was the structure of communication, rules or selection, along with provision of the appropriate rewards and sanctions. As Perrow said, somewhat tongue in cheek, 'after manipulating these [structural] variables, sit back and wait for two or three months for them to take hold' (1973: 27).

Managerial and professional employees – such as Whyte's organisation men – were subject to moulding and socialisation processes, though how seriously or effectively is open to question. But for all the unitarist rhetoric about goals, routine manual and clerical workers were not really expected to identify with the company. It was more a case of 'if you've got them by the balls, their hearts and minds will follow'. *Normative regulation* changes this: 'It is only with the advent of the "excellence" literature that management is urged to become directly involved in determining what employees should think, believe or value' (Willmott, 1992: 72). How this is supposed to work can be seen in the statement from a manager at a famous high-tech US company: 'Power plays don't work. You can't make 'em do anything. They have to want to. So you have to work through the culture. The idea is to educate people without knowing it. Have the religion and not know how they got it' (quoted in Kunda, 1992: 5).

Product and perspective: the corporate culture merchants

'In culture there is strength' is the ominous-sounding new law of business life proclaimed by Deal and Kennedy (1988: 19). What such writers are actually talking about is a specific product: 'a culture devised by management and transmitted, marketed, sold or imposed on the rest of the organisation' (Linstead and Grafton Small, 1992: 332). But what is it that gives such strength? One of the most recurrent themes is *attention to employees*: ownership in a shared vision rather than changes in work or working conditions. The notion of 'pillars' occurs again, this time in creating a committed workforce. The British personnel writers Martin and Nichols (1986) name three: a sense of belonging to the organisation, a sense of excitement in the job, and confidence in management. In general terms 'the notion of employee commitment is built on the internalisation of the norms and values of the organisation' (Kelly and Brannick, 1987: 19).

Interestingly there is explicit recognition of the benefits of *emotional* engagement: affectiveness more than effectiveness. As 'man is quite strikingly irrational' (Peters and Waterman, 1982: 86), employees can be appealed to through symbolism and the ceremonies and awards of 'hoopla'. In the new corporations it is the role of those at the top to act as symbolic rather than rational managers; scriptwriters and directors of the daily drama of company life (Deal and Kennedy, 1988: 142). By symbolising the organisation internally and externally, heroes become a crucial component of the leadership process. For Deal and Kennedy, John Wayne in pinstripes is an appropriate role model. Leadership is invested with a large burden in cultural management, reflecting in part research that has identified the *founder's* influence in shaping values (Schein, 1985). Indeed, for Schein, culture and leadership are simply two sides of the same coin: cultures are created by leaders, and a key function of leadership is the creation and occasionally destruction of cultures. A notable example is the late Anita Roddick's pivotal role in the Body Shop organisation. The underlying message of the publicity is 'Work for the Body Shop and you're on a permanent high', and that high has been sustained by training schools, roadshows and videos with the founder to the forefront. According to one trainer during Roddick's lifetime, 'Staff get desperate for the fix of Anita' (*The Times*, 28 September 1991).

In addition, the focus of such organisations is on disseminating values through stories, myths and legends about the company, its products and heroes, backed up by rites and rituals which reinforce cultural identification. The latter also helpfully facilitates the goal of a large dose of Skinnerian positive reinforcement, where *everyone* is made to feel a winner. Management in general is expected to use non-authoritarian styles to create a climate of trust. Some writers make a nod in the direction of feminism by referring to nurturing qualities and androgynous managers (Naisbitt and Aburdene, 1985: 207).

Though the package of corporate culture is new, some of the ideas were not. Popular management writers seldom discuss theoretical sources, but Peters and Waterman acknowledge that 'The stream that today's researchers are tapping is an old one started in the late 1930s by Elton Mayo and Chester Barnard' (1982: 5). Human relations influences can most clearly be seen in the focus on managing the informal organisation, workers as irrational creatures of sentiment, and social needs to belong, whereas the shadow of Barnard looms over conceptions of the organisation as a co-operative social system and on the role of the executive in articulating and disseminating values and superordinate goals. This is, however, given a harder edge. The predisposition to consensus and identity sharing gives way to a more conscious harnessing of needs and promotion of cultural mechanisms to secure common values.

But there may also be deeper, less direct roots: 'it is in the various writings of Durkheim that a conceptual framework for discussions of corporate culture may be found' (Ray, 1986: 290). We will examine these writings in Part IV, but most corporate culture books draw on assumptions that modern life and work organisation involve a loss of moral community and common values. Deal and Kennedy do so explicitly: 'corporations may be the last institutions in America that can effectively take on the role of shaping values' (1988: 16). In this sense it is not entirely true that for the first wave of managerial writers, it was as if the idea of organisational culture had 'sprung from nowhere' (Martin Parker, 1999). But Parker is right in his broader point that writings on *corporate* culture had conveniently 'forgotten' the rich history of work on the informal side of organisations in Weber and Taylor, let alone human relations; as well as other contributions such as industrial psychologists on 'organisational climate'.

Such complexities got in the way of the dumbed-down version of culture presented in that first wave. The *evidence* for the dual claim that strong cultures exist, and that they constitute the primary reason for better or even excellent performance, is also somewhat dubious. Though more companies sought to join the 'culture club' (Thompson and Findlay, 1999: 163), many of the same names tended to appear across the range of US books: IBM, Proctor and Gamble, Hewlett-Packard, McDonald's, Delta Airlines. So do some of the 'baddies', notably Harold Geneen and ITT who seemed to get it in the neck consistently. In the UK the roll-call has included Marks and Spencer, Plessey, Sainsbury, Burton and Schweppes. As for the information about the companies, the opening sentence of Deal and Kennedy begins, 'S. C. Allyn, a retired chairman of the board, likes to tell a story' (1988: 3). With the partial exception of Ouchi, stories, vignettes and anecdotes about the dedication and commitment of corporate heroes and managers, or the devotion of ordinary employees, constitute a large proportion of the evidence presented.

Of course they are not the only sources. Across the books, it is possible to find interviews with top management; testing the culture by conversing with the receptionist; profiles based on company documents; use of formal statements of objectives and philosophy and of biographies and speeches; and questionnaires filled in by chairmen asked to rank their firm according to 'excellence' criteria. Occasionally, as in Goldsmith and Clutterbuck (1985), there is reference to interviewing people on the shop floor, but there is no sign of the results.

There was considerable positive reference to slogans such as Delta Airline's 'the Delta family feeling', IBM's 'IBM means service' and 'respect for the individual', or GE's 'Progress is our most important product'. Apparently *everyone* knows and believes in Tandem Computer's slogans such as: 'It's so nice, it's so nice, we do it twice' (Deal and Kennedy, 1988: 9). McDonald's has an extraordinary quality assurance and level of care for its people (Peters and Waterman, 1982, xix–xx). The slogans of privatised utilities in the UK, such as BT's 'We answer to you', and the numerous statements of supermarkets and other companies about customer care could be put in a similar category (Legge, 1995). These kinds of statement about 'qualitative beliefs' are then linked to a second set of quantitative information detailing the superior financial and economic performance of the given companies over 10 or 20 years. Strong cultures are the assumed link, but there is no direct evidence, or real discussion of other market or environmental variables. A rare statement of this kind comes from Deal and Kennedy: 'we estimate that a company can gain as much as one or two hours of productive work per employee per day' (1988: 15). No criterion or proof is ever given.

Mini 'cases' are also developed in the popular literature, for example of Hewlett Packard's 'HP Way'. Open-plan offices, open managerial styles, extensive formal and informal communication, and team and workforce meetings are just some of the mechanisms to generate the high commitment that is the key to quality and innovation. Something like the 'HP Way' is a classic rhetorical device: a communicative symbol whose goal is primarily to mobilise organisational commitment and project community of interest. Stories about the heroic exploits of founders Bill and Dave reinforce a collective identity and organisational goals. Peters and Waterman found it impossible not to become fans. A more serious academic account of a similar organisation is given in Kunda's (1992) *Engineering Culture*. The mostly male engineers at 'Tech' operate in what appears to be an informal, egalitarian, work and play hard environment, sustained by a commitment to job security and technical innovation. Slogans and metaphors permeate working life – 'do what's right', 'he who proposes does', 'having fun', 'tech is a bottom-up company', 'we are like a football team' – and there is a mini-industry of meetings, rituals and workshops that reproduce company culture. Unlike managerialist accounts, Kunda actually demonstrates how culture permeates the everyday language and perceptions of employees, though, as we shall see later, the range and impact is uneven.

Focusing on this first wave of popular management books, however influential, risks associated the issue with (what was then) the latest fad and doomed attempts to transplant culture-specific Japanese systems. The corporate culture literature did indeed become less prominent as other panaceas such as business-process re-engineering took centre stage. But it was by no means been entirely displaced. Culture became the main ingredient of broader change programmes, as well as providing normative and behavioural scripts for more specific initiatives in areas such as customer care and TQM (du Gay, 1996; Reed, 1996a; Thompson and Findlay, 1999). Similarly, the battle to introduce private sector styles and methods into the public sector and the widespread adoption of mission statements indicate that the identification and transmission of values remains on the organisational agenda. As we saw in Chapter 6, corporate culture is also advocated as the solution to the problem of integrating global companies that are too diverse and complex to be run by rules from the centre. Finally, the management of culture is recognised as one of the central features of HRM, given that employment relationships are seen as moving away from bureaucratic hierarchy and low-trust industrial relations towards securing real *commitment* (Guest, 1987; Legge, 1989; 1995). It is to this link that we now turn.

HRM and the management of culture

In Chapter 4 we discussed the move from personnel to HRM practices. There are two key connections to culture. If the managerial role is seen as shifting towards the symbolic sphere, HR managers are the central resource and functional gatekeeper of these processes. As Michael Peretz of Apple Computers in Europe put it:

> The role of the Human Resource Manager, the 'priest' in whose hands the company's 'Ten Commandments' lie, is to ensure the survival of its soul. Far from merely providing a functional service determining salary rises and fringe benefits, the human resource management function forms the very heart of a company, and its manager exists to confirm the company's particular values and try and apply them in practice. (Schneider and Barsoux, 1997: 128)

Second, if employees are the key strategic resource, then commitment is the key to unlocking the untapped human capital. In turn, that requires conscious development of the value base of companies, such as mission statements, and new and expanded means of communicating them; as well as the battery of participative measures such as teamworking and team briefing to generate a high-trust culture associated with 'soft' versions of HRM (Storey, 1989; Guest, 1989). The imputed strategic character of HRM thus facilitates the development of strong cultures by integrating policies of recruitment, reward and retention. Across how much territory this integration can take place is debatable. For example, those advocating culturalist perspectives influenced by the work of Hofstede and others (see Chapter 6) argue that HRM must be made meaningful across cultures. Multinational companies 'must discover and pick their way through these national differences' in norms associated with recruitment, training, performance, and so on (Schneider and Barsoux, 1997: 135).

Notwithstanding this qualification, in many national contexts, culture has become a shorthand for a new ideology and rules of the game accompanying a shift from collectivism to individualism in the management of the employment relationship (Sisson, 1990). Collective bargaining and unions are bad words in the new world of *unmediated* relations between the organisation and the individual. An example of such practices is that of direct communication with the workforce. Winning companies have a culture that enables 'a passion for disclosure of information' (Goldsmith and Clutterbuck, 1985: 73). Hence the rash of briefings, videos, house magazines, open days and consultative forums. Trade unions are not given much of a part in strong-culture companies. At best they are considered a recalcitrant junior member, and at worst an unnecessary obstacle. The HRM advocates Kelly and Brannick deliver a blunt warning: 'The ability to organise will be curtailed, if not openly challenged by management, and the role of the trade union as an element of the communication network will lose its significance' (1987: 20). In fact such employment practices already constitute a significant part of strategies by a growing number of companies to make themselves union-free by removing or substituting for any employee desire for collective representation (Basset, 1989). Any independent, 'sub-cultural' source of alternative values, trade unions, profession or occupational groups is therefore an obstacle to the development of a unitary, cohesive culture.

Certainly there have been prominent companies that fitted this picture, notably the major US computer firms such as IBM (Dickson *et al.*, 1988) and Hewlett Packard. They carefully constructed their employment practices to individualise employees' relations with the company. Prominent features of this approach have been personal wage 'negotiation' and performance evaluation, immediate grievance accessibility to management, and an internal labour market that provides for mobility and job security. Though individual practices such as direct communication continue to grow (Kersley *et al.*, 2005) the broader typicality of culture-led ER practices in foreign transplants or greenfield sites is in doubt. Interestingly, evidence from case studies (for example, Martinez-Lucio and Weston, 1992; Marks *et al.*, 1997) and wider survey evidence such as the Workplace Employment Relations Survey (Millward *et al.*, 1992; 2000) that HRM practices, in the UK at least, exist more extensively in unionised workplaces. A recent authoritative review of HRM theory and practice (Legge, 2005) barely mentions culture and focuses overwhelmingly on the growth of 'hard' HR practices. Raising such questions about the character and extent of HRM and strong cultures is part of a much wider critical evaluation, to which we now turn.

Critics and questions

Questioning the novelty

The extent of strong-culture companies has been exaggerated. These were trends within some, but not all organisations. Many companies, small and large, have and will carry on with 'weak cultures' and would not recognise a culture strategy if it landed on the MD's desk. However, it does happen, though how new or novel current initiatives are is open to question. As Jacques (1996) has demonstrated, corporate capital has always been concerned to 'manufacture the employee', for example in the 1920s through welfare programmes, company unions and workplace social communities (see also R. Edwards, 1979). Companies such as Cadbury and Marks and Spencer in the UK do have corporate cultures of a highly distinctive nature, but there have always been strong-culture companies. Such organisations have often used management styles based on 'sophisticated paternalism' which combine high levels of employment security and social benefits with careful screening of recruits, direct communication and in-house training, wrapped up in a 'philosophy' of respect for the individual (Miller, 1989). And all this before any thought of corporate cultures and HRM!

Accounts by historians and sociologists show that we can trace paternalism back to older patterns. Joyce (1980) shows that from the mid-nineteenth century many Victorian firms, particularly those influenced by religious non-conformism, developed a social paternalism embedded in the interwoven fabric of work and community life. Though often associated with small firms, paternalism survived and changed form as size and scale increased, though family ownership still played a key role. At Lee's Tapestry Works on Merseyside between the wars, considerable efforts were made to develop 'a sense of belonging and a feeling of loyalty to the firm' (Johnson and Moore, 1986). There was an 'exceptional' family atmosphere, company saving schemes, a holiday camp and partnership certificates issued to employees or 'members' as they were called from 1931. Glucksman's study of factories in the inter-war period gives an account of the Peak Frean biscuit factory in South London. Though Peak Frean was not characteristic of the majority of firms, it prided itself on its welfare provision, had 'a large sports ground and games room, dances and social events were organised, and the house journal, *The Biscuit Box*, was distributed to all workers' (1990: 96). Both the companies were non-union. But this is not an inherent characteristic of such firms. Ackers and Black's (1991) overview and case studies in the development of paternalist capitalism demonstrate that major players – Pilkington, Rowntree, Cadbury – came to accept a form of unionism and collective bargaining in their own paternalistic image.

Even after the war many large workplaces generated employee identification based partly on stable employment, as well as being a focal point in and for local communities. A typical example is English Electric in Liverpool (Thompson, 1994). Worker identification with the firm was enhanced by almost all promotions coming from the shop floor, thus creating a strong internal labour market, though top management tended to be imported. The company owned houses and had its own hospital and dentist on site. There was an extensive company social life, including an annual sports day which catered for 10,000–12,000 children and a flower show, a variety of clubs, dances and shows. These were all organised on a voluntary basis by a combination of management, staff and workers. The firm, though paternalistic, was not anti-union and officially recognised a number of appropriate trade unions. Though managers did not always like it, they worked within an industrial settlement in which a system of bureaucratic controls over work and employment relationships empowered shop-floor union organisation.

In the late 1960s, the company was taken over by GEC, their main competitor. They began to run down production and transfer products out of the place almost immediately. A new layer of senior management was brought in with very different attitudes. Within a short time the whole social side of the factory apparatus was wound down. What happened at English Electric was indicative of the breakdown of the old culture paradigm under the impact of the first major wave of post-war restructuring of capital in the mid to late 1960s. Under the impact of this concentration of capital, firm mobility, mergers and acquisitions and the decline of company towns and occupational communities, old forms of identification tended to break down. British management responded in a variety of ways. There were many measures designed to tighten controls on the wage–effort bargain, for example the replacement of piecework by measured day work. Others changed the pattern of accommodation and attempted to further institutionalise the factory-level union organisation. A smaller minority tried progressive work redesign schemes such as work humanisation, but 'Anyone who talked about employee "loyalty" and "all pulling together for the good of the firm" was regarded as a nostalgic crank who did not understand modern industry' (Ackers and Black, 1991: 30).

Paternalistic cultures became a minority phenomenon, though they continued to exist in different forms, often in smaller firms. One such traditional paternalist company of 300 workers is described in a case study by Wray (1994). 'Ourfirm' built on local traditions of company welfare provision and a dependent, quiescent labour supply. Its management articulated a paternalist philosophy, high pay and profit-sharing, and links with the local community. Even here, steady growth led to difficulties in maintaining 'the personal touch' that underpinned paternalist relations. Middle management and demands for a union on the shop floor have grown in tandem. Despite the breakdown of old patterns, both case studies project continuities between paternalism and the rise of a new unitarism in the form of corporate culture and HRM, so that 'the future may look more like the past than the present' (Ackers and Black, 1991: 55). But how reliable are the contemporary claims in the wider literature?

Questioning the evidence

Given the reliance of the product on stories, myths and other forms of 'organisation talk', what executives and managers say in words or on paper tends to be taken as proof for the existence of string and distinctive cultures. There was little critical reflection on this. Martin and Nichols are at least honest in admitting that:

> we cannot be sure of the extent to which the companies we studied were *actually* successful in creating that commitment or whether that commitment contributed to their success. All we can say is that the managers in question reported that their efforts to create commitment met with a positive response and produced a significant improvement. (Martin and Nichols, 1987: ix, our emphasis)

In addition, they present some useful, if brief and largely propagandising, cases. As for most of the literature, much of the time even corporate slogans are taken as virtually incontrovertible evidence of culture and effects, because they are taken to be synonymous with superordinate goals.

With this kind of evidence, so much of it resting on bland management statements, unattributed quotes and plain assertion, it is tempting to dismiss the whole enterprise as a fairy tale. Drucker, the best-known management writer, pulled no punches in describing *In Search of Excellence* as 'a book for juveniles' and a fad that would not last a year (quoted in Silver, 1987: 106). The lack of rigour in research methodology has been a persistent theme of critics (Hammond and Barham, 1987: 8–14; Guest, 1992). Samples of companies, for example those used by Peters and Waterman, were selected and treated in a cavalier and uncontrolled manner, dropping some from the original list and using evidence from others not in the sample at all (Silver, 1987: 113). The tenuous link between cultures, excellence and performance turned out to be highly fragile. Companies were included whose performance was far from excellent, and a significant number subsequently ran into difficulties, as *Business Week* (1983) reported under a headline of 'oops!' An important book on IBM (Delamarter, 1988) – by a senior economist who had worked in the US Justice Department on the anti-trust case against IBM – pointed out that the company built up its dominance by undercutting its competitors in vulnerable market sectors and paying for it through excess profits from customers who had little choice. Commenting on *In Search of Excellence*, the author argues that:

> According to the authors, IBM has benefited from a strong central philosophy that was originally laid down by its charismatic leaders, the Watsons. They present a simple, appealing model for IBM's success – excellence in management. But this view is dead wrong. IBM's success comes from the power of monopoly. (Delamarter, 1988: xvii)

Follow-ups such as Peters and Austin's *A Passion for Excellence* (1986) failed to quell the doubts, particularly as the same author has apparently decided (Peters, 1989) that there are now no excellent companies in the US. The treatment of theory and evidence is similarly suspect, with eclectic and uncritical use of parts that suit particular arguments, even if they are not compatible with the general perspective. The use of Skinner in *In Search of Excellence* is a case in point. A further remarkable aspect is the failure to learn from their main inspiration, the human relations tradition. There is no sign of recognition of the central flaw that arose from the Hawthorne Studies, that intervention based on 'attention to employees' produces independent effects on performance. At least some of the hoopla and contrived events could produce a stream of Hawthorne effects of a short-lived and superficial nature.

Of course, expectations of high-quality evidence from popular management texts would be somewhat naïve. What is more disappointing is that a number of academic theorists appear to be making similar mistakes in confusing what managers and companies say they are doing with the more complex and messy reality on the ground. This is largely a by-product of the influence of post-structuralism in organisation theory (see Part IV). While accounts of corporate discourses are often fascinating for what they reveal about managerial values and intentions, a theoretical approach that makes no distinction between these 'representations' and reality runs the risk of exaggerating their coherence and influence. In reviewing these accounts (for example, Rose, 1990), Thompson and Findlay (1999: 172–4) found that there was a large gap between strong claims and weak evidence. The stated goals of senior management and other power holders, whether in documents or through interviews, is frequently the only evidence. Evidence of how discourses are operationalised outside the text, or how intent is turned into concrete influence over behaviour and attitudes, is hard to find, particularly as detailed primary data on employees are largely absent.

Finally, is there anything more conclusive from the more varied studies of culture change programmes, particularly those associated with HRM? Legge (1995) attempts to evaluate that research and finds it inconclusive, owing to a range of methodological and conceptual problems. There has been little research on the explicit links between culture and commitment, particularly of an in-depth and longitudinal kind. Even more importantly, both culture and HRM tend to have been treated as generic headings for a variety of interrelated changes, from which it is impossible to disentangle the key variables. While it is not surprising that managers may have absorbed the message, given their centrality as focal points for the articulation and dissemination of values, there is less evidence that this has worked its way fully through to the shop and office floor. Or, if it has, the effects are on manifested behaviour rather than internalised values. This is a crucial distinction to which we will be returning later in a more extended discussion of the evidence on effectiveness of value transformation.

Questioning the concepts
The previous discussion illustrates the need for a complex understanding of culture. Too often the corporate culture debate has been working with impoverished conceptions of culture which mistake style for

substance. A complex and realistic analysis would avoid treating culture as a catch-all for the soft aspects of management (Hammond and Barham, 1987: 10), or as a reified and monolithic phenomena. There is some recognition of *sub-cultures* on functional or gender lines, but not enough, and anyway these can be *managed* to produce a healthy tension within the corporate framework (Deal and Kennedy, 1988: 152–3). Martin (1992) identifies this perspective as an *integrationist* one, viewing organisations as monocultural and bound by homogeneity of purpose. In contrast, a proper recognition of sub-cultural cleavages and conflicts of interests would reflect a *differentiation* perspective.

It is precisely the assumption that culture can be managed that is called into question by a range of critics that Willmott dubs 'culture purists'. Such critics take their cue from the influential paper by Smirich (1983), which argued that it is better to regard culture as something an organisation is, rather than something an organisation *has*. It is a process not a checklist, and something continually being creatively remade by all participants, rather than fixed (Wright, 1994). As a result, in the context of a variety of often contradictory influences, cultural development is just not as amenable to direction or use as an integrative device as is believed (Martin and Siehl, 1983: 53). Nor can it be simply fitted into overall strategic goals. As Ackroyd and Crowdy (1990) illustrate in their study of the highly-distinctive informal interactions of slaughtermen, many of the meanings attached to work behaviour are embedded in a particular class or regional culture. Their very externality adds to the lack of feasibility of managerial influence. Such instances emphasise the variety of identities that employees bring to or affirm in the workplace. Martin (1992) dubs this a *fragmentation* perspective, drawing on postmodern ideas of shifting contexts and meanings.

Whether it can be managed or not, it remains the case that the complexity of organisational cultures has been neglected and employees treated as an 'empty space' within which values can be inserted. There is, 'a tendency in the organisational culture literature to treat workplace culture as independent of the labour process' (Alvesson, 1988: 3). Without recognition that the labour process is fractured by a variety of social cleavages, organisational analysis will continue to neglect the dimensions of conflict, power and even consent. As well as the case studies referred to in this chapter such as Kunda, there have always been rich sources to draw on such as Salaman's (1986) study of the occupational culture of the London Fire Brigade; accounts of making-out on the shop floor (Nichols and Beynon, 1977; Burawoy, 1979; Delbridge, Lowe and Oliver, 2000); and gender at work (Willis, 1977; Pollert, 1981; Westwood, 1984; Kondo, 1990). Using such insights, we can avoid nonsensical ideas that strong cultures produce conflict-free organisations (Kelly and Brannick, 1987: 1). After all, despite IBM's worldwide strategy for a union-free environment and sophisticated industrial relations system, it still had to contend with an international organisation of IBM workers opposed to its policies (Howard, 1985). Even where IBM has been successful in securing employee identification with its individualistic culture, as in the West of Scotland, those same workers had collectivist attitudes towards general social issues and supported trade unionism, even if they felt a union was unnecessary in their particular circumstances (Dickson *et al.*, 1988). This illustrates a further important point, that any analysis should show what is unique about organisational as opposed to national, regional, family or other cultures; something that is largely absent from the management literature (Hofstede, 1986). On that basis it would be possible to examine how the societal and organisational cultures interact.

Given the numerous flaws and the benefit of hindsight it is tempting to dismiss most writing on corporate cultures as simply the emperor's new clothes. In *Management Today*, Thackray (1986) argued that the American manager needs a language that goes beyond particular functions. Buzzwords therefore come and go and culture has entered on the scene as Western pride has been shaken by Japan and old certainties have been eroded by economic and occupational shifts. New ideas are required to motivate the troops and a 'gaggle of culture consultants', as well as human resource and personnel teams and others whose empires expand with the literature, are feeding at the honey pot. It appeals to managers because it proclaims that their activity and skills can produce the results, as Mayo once did in relation to early human relations. Silver (1987: 123) also argued that corporate culture was the latest attempt by management consultants to 'wrap each new technique in packaging slightly different from that of its predecessors'. If it is a fad and one that vastly overestimates its capacity as a change mechanism, then the whole trend is destined to go the same way as others: 'Culture appears to have been reduced to the status of yet another concept, which, like many before it, has reached the decline stage of its "life cycle"' (Ogbonna, 1992a: 6).

But all this is bending the stick back too far. Willmott (1993a) criticises the 'purist' position for moving from a judgement that the corporate culture literature is so deficient that it is unworthy of serious attention. Meek is an example, when she argues that if culture is embedded in social interaction, 'it can *only* be described and interpreted' (1988: 293, our emphasis). This may be underselling its potential as a control mechanism. There may not be a definitive authentic culture in organisations, but there clearly are 'official' ones which power holders can at least attempt to impose on others. Having questioned the largely managerial evidence about companies and culture, the rest of the chapter looks at alternative and more critical explanations of what has been happening inside organisations.

Re-conceptualising culture: commitment or control?

Corporate culture writers tended to present their prescriptions as an *alternative* to control (Naisbitt and Aburdene, 1985: 53; Kelly and Brannick, 1987: 8). But the perspective is riddled with glaring contradictions. We are told that 'in institutions in which culture is so dominant, the highest levels of autonomy occur' (Peters and Waterman, 1982: 105); while Deal and Kennedy assure us that companies with strong cultures can tolerate differences (1982: 153) and that outlaws and heretics are encouraged in companies such as IBM (1982: 50–1). At the same time the latter authors tell us that managers do not tolerate deviance from company values and standards (1982: 14), and that middle managers as well as blue-collar workers should be told exactly what to do (1982: 78). The books are so anxious to convince us that these are anti-authoritarian, 'no-boss' set-ups, that we are expected to accept that calling workers cast members (Disney) or crew members (McDonald's) in itself banishes hierarchy and class divisions. In Silver's (1987) brilliant demolition of the excellence genre, he reminds us of the reality of McDonald's 'people-orientation': 'Behind the hoopla and razzle-dazzle of competitive games and prizes lies the dull monotony of speed-up, deskilled Taylorised work – at McFactory. And McFactory's fuel is cheap labour – part-time, teenage, minimum wage, non-union workers' (1987: 110).

Reconceptualising the process in terms of new forms of management control is not entirely foreign to the more academic of the culture literature, which openly describes the process as a form of organisational control (Ouchi and Johnson, 1978; Martin and Siehl, 1983). Nor is it inconsistent with many of the statements from the more popular works, such as, 'Strong culture companies go into the trouble of spelling out, often in copious detail, the routine behavioural rituals they expect from their employees' (Deal and Kennedy, 1988: 15). Cultural or *normative* control is essentially concerned with the development of an appropriate social order that provides the basis for desired behaviour (Kelly and Brannick, 1987: 8). Unless they are professional or knowledge workers with strong prior occupational norms, in order to let people loose to be 'autonomous' they have to be programmed centrally first, with a central role played by more intensive selection and training (Weick, 1987). Tandem Corporation's exhaustive selection process is likened to an 'inquisition' by Deal and Kennedy (1988: 12). One of the offshoots is that those who are chosen are likely to have a much more positive image of themselves and the company. It is not surprising, given such developments, that some management writers have begun to worry that corporate culture produces conformist thinking inimical to creative organisational development (Weick, 1987; Coopey and Hartley, 1991).

Cultural controls also operate through expanding the sphere of social activities in the organisation. Communicating company goals can take place outside the workplace. Part of GM's Hydra-matic Division's Quality of Working Life (QWL) programme includes week-long 'Family Awareness Training' sessions at education centres (Martin Parker, 1985: 17–19). This does not refer to the employee's nearest and dearest, but to the notion of company as family. Once outside the normal environment and in circumstances where everyone is individualised, psychological exercises and techniques are used to break down old identities. GM questionnaires rate those with limited scores on loyalty to the company as having a low quality of work life. Breaking down the boundaries between economic and social activities is something that is often characteristic of Japanese corporations' methods of using the peer group as a means of integrating both shop-floor and managerial employees. Broad (1987: 11) notes that 'Social gatherings organised by team leaders and foremen are regularly held among all male employees'. Many of the other books are similarly full of accounts of cultural extravaganzas that function to develop a sense of community through a form of *compulsory sociability*. The existence of teams in call centres when there are no conditions for team *working* is another illustration of the intended role of social bonding and group identity (Thompson *et al.*, 2004).

How should we understand the significance of this trend? Some radical theorists go further than simply analysing culture in terms of control by arguing that corporate culture represents an alternative and dominant mode. The key theoretical influence is the work of Ray (1986) discussed earlier. She points out that bureaucratic control, though an attempt to integrate employees positively through internal labour markets and the reward system, is still control by incentive. This may generate contradictions around the struggles of the workforce to establish work rules and job guarantees. In addition, 'while bureaucratic control may prompt individuals to act as if the company is a source of meaning and commitment, that is an entirely different matter from seriously believing it. In other words control remains externalised rather than internalised' (1986: 292–3). Even humanistic controls deriving from the various branches of the human relations tradition do not possess the real tools to generate sentiment or emotion. The difference is that *normative* control works less through formal structures and mechanisms than through informal processes, value systems and management of the emotions.

Ray's analysis was complemented by like-minded empirical studies such as Alvesson's well-known accounts (1988; Alvesson and Kärreman, 2004) of consultancy firms in Sweden. Typically, the founders would establish an open and charismatic managerial style capable of generating strong emotional ties among the consultants employed. A particular problem for the management was that the work was by its very nature variable and flexible, and therefore could not be controlled by conventional means. It was also largely carried out at the client's workplace, potentially undermining the consultant's sense of identity with his or her own firm. This is compensated for by a large number of social and leisure-time activities with the emphasis on fun, body contact, informality and personnel support; which in turn build social and emotional ties and a sense of company as community. Some of these are consciously linked to presentations of corporate performance to enhance favourable perceptions.

Further support comes from research on the retailing sector. Employees have to be subjected to engineering the soul so that they can automatically deliver the quality service required by the new, more enterprising customer (du Gay, 1991a). Ogbonna and Wilkinson (1988) and Ogbonna (1992b) detail such engineering in a supermarket where management have initiated a substantially expanded staff training and development programme that ranges from the recruitment of 'like-minded' people to a 'smile campaign'. Supervisors claim that 'We are able to detect when a check-out operator is not smiling or even when she is putting on a false smile ... we call her into a room and have a chat with her' (Ogbonna, 1992b: 85).

While it is entirely possible to understand such practices as a form of feelings rules (see Chapter 8). However, the above perspective counterpoises control through conventional rules and regulations to changing the way that employees think and feel. The latter is seen as 'considerably extending' the scope and penetration of managerial domination (Willmott, 1993a: 522). Willmott makes a forceful case that in combining normative rules with the erosion of alternative sources of identity:

> Corporate culturism extends the terrain of instrumentally rational action by developing monocultures in which conditions for the development of value-rational action, where individuals struggle to assess the meaning and worth of a range of competing value-standpoints, are systematically eroded. (Willmott, 1993a: 3)

Monocultures are designed to avoid contamination by rival ends or values and, to the extent that they succeed, become the vehicle of nascent totalitarianism, accompanied by classic 1984-style doublethink of 'respect for the individual' in organisations where employees are seduced into giving up any autonomy. This analysis is wrapped up in the kind of Foucauldian terminology discussed in Chapter 9, where corporate culture programmes exert self-disciplining powers that trap people within the promise of secure identities and personal development. Similar Foucauldian themes of cultural 'seduction' and discursive colonisation of self are pursued in Casey's (1996) US case study of the Hephaestus corporation. Put more simply, through team practices and family rhetoric, the company produces 'designer employees', who buy into the secure identity offered by the simulated community.

The limits to cultural influence in theory and practice

In criticising culture purists, Willmott persuasively argued that we should take corporate culture seriously. But perhaps he has taken its significance and effectiveness *too* seriously. In arguing that the 'governance of the employee's soul' (1993a: 517) is a key ideological element of a new global regime of flexible accumulation, he is in danger of over-extending the concept and maintaining a separation from traditional forms of control associated with Fordism, Taylorism and bureaucracy. Corporate culture should not be isolated as *the* defining feature of contemporary forms of control. While Willmott rightly says that management is trying to extend the sphere of instrumental action to rules governing emotions and the affective sphere, traditional controls, as we have seen in recent chapters, remain important in a number of ways.

Even within those organisations that do implement cultural controls, they are intended to complement not eliminate the need for bureaucratic, technical or other systems. In the supermarkets described earlier, employees are subject to the surveillance of TV cameras in the manager's office looking for deviations from the desired behaviour, as well as controls through new technology that can record productivity such as the EPOS (electronic point of sale) system. In Kunda's excellent ethnography of 'Tech' we are given examples of both normative and technical controls. With reference to the former, managers evaluate subordinates on personality criteria: 'Jim has a people problem. He is gruff and angry with people and says exactly what is on his mind. ... I want him to control himself. Next year he is going to be evaluated on that. I'm watching him. He knows it' (manager quoted in Kunda, 1992: 187). But employees are also aware that managers check up commitment by looking at who is logged onto the computer after hours. Though he sees a shift in focus from bureaucratic to normative controls at Tech, Kunda rightly acknowledges that systems of cultural control, 'build on, rather than replace one another' (1992: 220). This is consistent with the evidence on the growing hybridity of controls discussed extensively in Chapter 8.

This continuity and combination can be ignored or misunderstood by making culture into an overarching concept. For example, Wright talks of the 'culture' of Fordism, which 'is converted from a mission statement into detailed practices, dividing each task into tiny details and specifying how each should be done' (1994: 2). In contrast, the culture of flexible organisations relies on empowered, self-disciplined workers. Culture in this sense, however, should not be seen as *everything*, but rather as managerial attempts to mobilise values and emotions to support corporate goals. An expanded array of often-traditional rules and sanctions is then used to enforce the new moral order and extend levels of identification between employee and organisation. Academic confusion about how far to extend the use of culture reflects similar trends among managers. In their studies of the Scottish spirits industry, Marks and colleagues (1997) noted the deployment of two rhetorics: the first signified culture as a vision or set of shared values intended to guide the change process; the latter as a much more diffuse way of describing 'the way that we do things round here'. The problem with the latter usage is that almost any change in practices can then be subsumed under the 'culture' label. The other thing worth noting is that the practice-led usage can exist independently of any explicit attempt to change values. Additionally, we only have to return to previous examples of IBM and Hewlett Packard to see that their respective 'Ways' are sustained by careful structuring of the employment relationship around individualistic means and ends. Like the studies referred to earlier, Harrison and Marchington (1992) also examine the growth of customer care programmes in retailing, but argue that 'The preoccupation with culture may blind us to the enduring importance of promotion structures, remuneration incentives, and working hours in shaping employees' acceptance of managerial initiatives' (1992: 18).

The key thing about this observation is that such polices and practices can change and that, in turn, is one of the factors that affects the second element – the effectiveness of corporate culture as social engineering. We should keep in mind that Ray (1986), the inspiration for many extravagant claims about culture as the ultimate control, distinguished between intent and outcome, and was very circumspect about the extent to which it would work outside the US and independently of other managerial techniques. Beyond the ranks of post-structuralism, there is a large degree of scepticism in case studies, surveys and literature reviews on the limits to culture, or at least to the extent to which commitment has been internalised (Guest, 1992; Ogbonna, 1992b; A. Scott, 1994; O'Donnell, 1996; McKinlay and Taylor, 1996; Wilkinson, Godfrey and Marchington, 1997; B. Jones, 1997; Leidner, 2006). Take the British Airways manager quoted in Höpfl (1992: 10): 'We know it's hype – they know its hype. It's okay. It's reassuring. It makes you feel good. But do I believe in it – well that's a totally different question.' Employees may be conceptualised as empty vessels in which to locate corporate values, but that is not how it works in practice. As Leidner (2006:146) observes, '[the] argument concerning workers' vulnerability to the cultural control of organizations seems to take for granted that the identities held out by employers are attractive to workers and would uphold their sense of themselves as autonomous individuals'.

Employees may comply with demands for adherence to the language of mission statements, appearance and demeanour in the sales process, or participation in quality circles *without* internalising the values and therefore generating the 'real' commitment. Though studies record a diversity and unevenness of responses, the prominent themes are distancing behaviour, cynicism, deep acting, and resigned behavioural compliance rather than value internalisation. Employees may go through the motions of cultural conformity while remaining sceptical that, for example, supposedly distinctive 'Ways' are any different from the methods used by rival international hotel chains (Thompson *et al.*, 1998). The dramaturgical theme is continued through employees developing a variety of means of disengagement or distancing from corporate values through cynicism, parody and irony (Fleming and Spicer, 2002). Advocates such as trainers for Body Shop may claim that cynicism cannot survive the participative culture, but that is belied by interviews with staff: 'They want you to feel part of a team, but you're not. They want you to feel important when you're just a shop assistant. If you want to stay there, you do better as a Roddick clone' (quoted in *The Times*, 28 September 1991). Considerable evidence of cynicism and distancing was also observed by Kunda. Many employees used an alternative language to describe the culture – 'the song and dance', 'pissing contests', 'Tech strokes', 'burnout', 'doing rah-rah-stuff' – or rival slogans – 'I'd rather be dead than excellent', 'There is unlimited opportunity at Tech, for inflicting and receiving pain'.

All this is not to imply that attempts at culture change have no effect or are viewed in an unambiguously hostile manner. As Rosenthal and colleagues' (1997) supermarket case study shows, systematic exposure to change discourses may impact on attitudes, particularly when employees identify with some of the aims of quality, or customer care programmes. However, the authors make clear that this is a long way from total acceptance or control. What comes over in this and many other studies is that, far from seduction, employees are highly aware of the complex aims and outcomes of managerial action. They may be aware that they are acting as a form of coping strategy (Ogbonna and Wilkinson, 1988; S. Taylor, 1998), or staff may use the rhetoric to try and bring management into line with what they have been told about the way that customers and employees should be treated (Rosenthal *et al.*, 1997; Callaghan and Thompson, 2002). These examples take us back to the idea that culture cannot be treated as the property of management. If it is embedded in social interaction, employees produce as well as absorb meanings, transforming culture in the process (Meek, 1988).

As these studies and earlier ones such as Kunda (1992) illustrate, much of this ambivalence is directed towards maintaining a private self, or showing that they understood the real politics and status processes underneath the official surface; a process that Collinson (1994) refers to as 'resistance through distance'. Employee awareness of the nature of the dominant culture will vary, for example, by position in the organisational hierarchy. As our discussions of gender demonstrated in Chapter 10, women managers could 'see' the informal masculinity of values and practices, whereas men largely took them for granted.

Even more controversially, we can ask whether the predominance of behavioural compliance without commitment actually matters. Supporters may point to a time lag whereby behavioural precedes attitudinal change (Schein, 1985). But in the light of serious research, this seems optimistic. Are we back full circle to Perrow's view that to change individual behaviour, you do not have to change individuals? Some critics would appear to agree. Drawing on their research customer care programmes, Harrison and Marchington argue that, 'management does not actually have to achieve value change among the workforce to successfully implement customer care' (1992: 18). The conventional armoury of management control and remuneration measures, or indeed the coercive effects of fear of job loss, may be sufficient. While there is evidence that initiatives focusing on changing behaviour have been far more successful than those on transforming values (Hope and Hendry, 1995; Marks *et al.*, 1997), there is no need to question the distinctiveness of 'hearts and minds' programmes. Our disagreement with theorists such as Willmott is not about whether some firms try to develop monocultures, but with the extent to which they can ever be successful. Willmott (1993a: 538–40) argues that the very process of role-playing and cynical disengagement entraps employees in the insidious controls of the culture and confirms the appearance of tolerance and openness.

Such interpretations risk underestimating the fragility of corporate culture and the creative appropriation, modification and resistance to such programmes. Corporate culture cannot eliminate the powerful informal group norms that are the bedrock of organisational life. Workgroups are just one of a number of sources of competing claims on commitment and loyalty. Attempts to prioritise an aggressive corporate identity may disrupt the delicate balance between these specific and superordinate allegiances. This is particularly the case in the public sector where traditions of professional autonomy and an ethic of service are increasingly at odds with a new managerialism bent on central direction and enforcement of the bottom line (Anthony, 1990; Harrison and Marchington, 1992). Increasingly bitter conflict between general managers and staff in the NHS, universities and the BBC is indicative of the tensions arising from attempts by senior managers to impose a 'strong culture' and a web of rules to enforce it. In any organisational context, but particularly where competing professional, commercial and personal goals are present, employees will face difficult value conflicts and behavioural choices.

Resistance may also be generated by the selective or partial nature of participation in the culture and its attendant reward systems. Such programmes are aimed often only at the 'core' workforce, as Kunda's case study demonstrates. Class 2 workers, mainly clerical and temporary, received inferior benefits and were treated as non-persons, 'just not techies' as one manager put it (1992: 209). Unsurprisingly they only gave a minimal self back. This example reinforces the point that culture is sustained by material, institutional supports. Senior management may be taking greater risks with such initiatives because employees are being asked to invest more of their public and private selves, thereby raising the possibility of enhanced resentment when the promises of large-scale culture-change programmes prove difficult to deliver, as at British Airways (Höpfl, Smith and Spencer, 1992). This is but one of the trends in corporate development which are working against the stability of cultures of company loyalty and commitment. As the 1990s progressed, it became a decade largely inimical to the culture message and 'corporations retreated from the human resource practices that had made them alternatives to governments' (Starbuck, 2003: 443). Contradictions are raised by the clash between concerns for individual development in organisations and the continuous pressure for rationalisation of resources and for more effort. In addition, what the management pundits call 'downsizing' – the cutting out of middle layers of the company discussed in more detail in Chapter 13 – is hurting most the 'organisation men, conditioned to look to large corporations as the fountainhead of security' (Thackray, 1988: 80). Hope and Hendry (1995) argue that in this context research into imposed culture-change programmes does not demonstrate they have been effective as change mechanisms or control devices.

Loyalty, obedience and goal identification are not easy to sustain when companies are scrutinising their policy manuals to remove implied promises of job security or even termination benefits:

> How the hell can you preach this flexibility, this personal and business development at the same time as you are getting rid? As someone said to me yesterday, an operator, 'Why am I in here now doing the best I can getting this product out when tomorrow morning you are going to give me a brown envelope?' I had no answer. (Manager quoted in Watson, 1994: 209)

In essence this is little different to the tensions identified between 'hard' and 'soft' versions of HRM, where workers are expected to be both dependable and disposable (Legge, 1989). Ackers and Black raise the question of whether it is possible that new forms of corporate paternalism can ever reproduce the depth of social relationships fostered by firms embedded in local communities and stable markets: 'The impersonal, footloose multinational, with its mobile, diffuse, high-turnover workforce, and even more transient management team, appears ill-equipped to fashion an emotional nexus with its workforce'

(1991: 56). This may be exaggerating the difficulty, but current trends at the very least expose the highly contingent nature of any culture–commitment link.

A leading commentator, who has done a number of well-known studies of managerial rhetorics and practices, describes the new trend as one of market rationalism:

> Unlike the proponents of strong cultures who called for a reform of bureaucracy by infusing its denizens with values, norms, belief systems, and emotions that would change their behaviors to the firm's advantage, Market Rationalists seem to have little patience for culture, no matter how strong. Instead, they call for a radical restructuring that generally involves reducing rather than transforming the workforce, eliminating hierarchical layers and functional departments, and 'outsourcing' – subcontracting away most anything apart from what came to be called 'core competencies' (Kunda and Ailon-Souday, 2005: 203)

In the new, harsher climate, employees are asked to behave like an organisation, be agile and open to change, rather than be committed to or feel for the organisation. In return, they will become more market*able* and employable, taking responsibility for shaping their *own* identity for new, flexible times. Leidner (2006) observes that such changes are making sociologists focus less on how workers' subjectivity is dominated by the corporation and more on the loss of the structures that enabled a stable identification in the first place. And it's not just sociologists who are changing their tune. There has been a flurry of books and articles commenting on the rise of new individualism at work in a 'new economy' (Leinberger and Tucker, 1991; Munk, 1998; Pink, 2001). Many refer to the death or generation after 'the organization man', Munk observing that young workers know that loyalty is 'for suckers' when their employer can dispense with their services at any time. As with Whyte's original book, it may be that these are comments about a specific and smaller segment of the working population that their proponents acknowledge, but it is difficult to imagine a dominant 'normative rhetoric' based on culture re-emerging for some time to come. So, what's left?

Reflections and new directions

So, is the issue of culture at work, to quote Monty Python, a 'dead parrot'? There is certainly less interest in and less being written about corporate culture and culture change, as well as recognition by some of its advocates that conditions are not conducive to their old ideas (Deal and Kennedy, 1999). Some of that interest has, however, been transferred onto parallel territories, notably managing the identity of the corporation. This is deemed necessary because in an 'age of identity', firms are locked into identity-based competition (Bouchikhi and Kimberly, 2007). Some of the rhetoric is familiar. The firm is assumed to be a privileged carrier of values – 'no longer just a workplace, but a socially and emotionally loaded entity', that 'stakeholders, draw much of self from belonging to or buying from' (xxv). Dig deeper, however, and you find that the key symbolic resource for this competition is not the corporate culture, but the brand and reputation (Olins, 1996). This is not only the unique signifier to the outside world, but it is also what survives the turbulent environment of 'boundaryless' organisations where who your employer is and how long your employment will last is not clear. In other words, corporations need organisational identities for economies where conditions for commitment to an organisation are weak. Nor are arguments for identity as the key resource to be managed by organisations confined to popular business texts. Clegg and colleagues (2007) have recently reported on the way in which, through their leaders, 'organisational identity work' takes place and a legitimate identity is constructed. Though the focus is on rather than in organisations, such writing is more typical of the extensive attention paid in organisation analysis, to the processes of shaping identities. Others, similarly influenced by postmodernism and the 'cultural turn', have shifted their attention to the cultural *industries*: 'symbolic-intensive organisations – that successfully produce cultural products, such as fashion houses, movie companies, architectural firms' (Lawrence and Philips, 2002: 438). As we devote a whole chapter (23) to identity and identity work later in the book, we will say no more at this stage, other than this is where much of the emphasis on culture has been transferred.

The presence of culture in management theory was never the same thing as its presence in practice, so its marginalisation in the former is not identical to its significance in the latter. While the days of large-scale culture-led change programmes seem, for the time being anyway, to be over; there are a myriad of other ways in which culture and change may remain connected. Managerial goals and actions have to be legitimated and that can't be done only by reference to the requirements of the market. If a normative dimension is necessary, 'culture will remain as a primary language of change, both general and specific, central to the management of meaning' (Thompson and Findlay, 1999: 183). Culture provides key elements of a 'vocabulary of motive' that seeks to justify managerial action to itself and others (Webb, 1996). Culture strategies remain embedded in corporate consciousness and its survival is made more likely precisely because of the dual usage referred to earlier as values and practices. In other words, even when the mission statement or other artefact has been discarded, the very 'catch-all' character of culture means that it can absorb the loss of vision and values in an emphasis on 'the way we do things round here'.

Management-initiated culture change will continue, but in more specific and localised territories. When employers want or need to confront and change particular behaviours, the vocabulary of changing the culture is likely to come to the fore. An example would be knowledge management initiatives. Large science-based companies that want to encourage innovation and knowledge sharing in new and more collaborative 'communities of practice' cannot just introduce new procedures or techniques, but have to frame the change in terms of cultural norms (McKinlay, 2005). Similarly, there will still be room for discussion of managing through culture, in those circumstances where specialised products and services and high autonomy for professional/expert labour leads firms to rely mainly on normative controls (see Chapter 8). A more widespread example of localised culture change programmes would be public sector 'reform'.

Summary and key points

In this chapter we have tried to set out both the significance and the limits to attempts to reinvent 'organisation man'. We have shown that the initial selling of corporate culture in popular management books was based more on wishful thinking and overblown rhetoric than hard evidence. Yet an examination of the wider social science literature on culture and change also produces considerable scepticism about the scope of concepts and practices, as well as whether employees actually internalise the new values. Given the theoretical faults and practical constraints, it is sometimes difficult to see why the product became so influential. Part of the explanation undoubtedly is that it fitted the mood of a certain period. Silver (1987) adds a wider ideological and political dimension to the explanation. It is certainly true that a clear subtext of Peters and Waterman and Deal and Kennedy is that the discovery of excellent companies in the West means that all good things do not come from Japan and that with a rediscovery of corporate-led vales and entrepreneurialism, America could stand tall again (Silver, 1987). In Britain, similar links existed between the rise of corporate culture and a broader ideology celebrating the market and the spirit of enterprise (du Gay, 1991b). But it is not simply a sign of a particular time. Cultural differences between and within organisations do matter. The problem lay in the over-investment by managers and academics in the belief that corporate cultures could be fashioned into coherent and core strategies, and once rolled out could obliterate rival sources of values, thus engendering buy-in from employees. The cultural content and conditions have become more fragile. Without the perception of employment security, career paths and internal labour markets, what makes a culture 'strong'? It is difficult, for organisations cannot be 'value-led', if the values are not effectively supported and sustained in practice (Thompson and Findlay, 1999).

However, for all the limitations of content and presentation, the corporate-culture literature has touched on genuine issues that, as we argued at the start of this chapter, were partly neglected in the past. Organisation theory was too dependent on a rationalist outlook where employee behaviour could be changed by altering the mix of carrots and sticks, with insufficient attention paid to symbolic resources and hearts and minds. Such issues became important for HRM and its attempts to address issues of employee commitment. Culture needs to be looked at in a context free from the merchandising process and its simplified assumptions. The tragedy is that we have a lot to learn from studying organisational cultures (Frost *et al.*, 1985; Pheysey, 1993), particularly as culture mediates all change processes. Creating a culture resonant with overall goals is relevant to *any* organisation, whether it be a trade union, voluntary group, producer co-operative or direct selling operation. Indeed it is more important in such consensual groupings. Co-operatives, for example, can degenerate organisationally because they fail to develop adequate mechanisms for transmitting the original ideals from founders to new members and sustaining them through shared experiences. Such an emphasis by no means rules out studying specifically corporate cultures as management strategies. But this has to be within the plurality of cultures and interest groups in the workplace. The decline of corporate culture directed to employees may enable organisation analysis to return to broader considerations of culture – the way we do things round here – except that 'we' is not just management. Organisation 'man' may be back on the agenda, but the cultural agenda cannot only be set in the boardroom.

Further reading

As one of the themes of this chapter has been the diminishing prominence of writings about corporate culture, there isn't a great to add to the influential contributions from the 1980s and 1990s. It's difficult to recommend actually reading any of the popular management classics, but Guest's (1992) review is a useful short cut. The best study of real corporate and other cultures remains Kunda's ethnographic case study *Engineering Culture*, which came out in a revised edition in 2006. We have drawn extensively from Kunda and Ailon-Souday's (2005) equally sceptical account of contemporary developments in updating the chapter. From the academic debate about the significance and success of corporate attempts to mould employee values and identity, Ray (1986) provided the template for may of the arguments and Willmott's (1993a) influential and much reprinted journal article critiqued the purposes, but accepted the impacts. The original of the latter can be found at http://www.management-aims.com/PapersMgmt/63WillmottJMS.pdf and an interesting reflection by the author at http://www.management-aims.com/PapersMgmt/63Willmott.pdf. There are a number of case studies that critically examine the evidence of culture change programmes, including Ogbonna (1992) and Rosenthal and colleagues (1997). Thompson and Findlay (1999) provide a sceptical overview of the quality of the much of the managerial and academic evidence. As we started with

Whyte's *The Organization Man*, it is worth mentioning that there is a new edition (2002) of this classic with an afterword by his daughter. You can also access a number of the chapters at http://www.writing.upenn.edu/~afilreis/50s/whyte-main.html.

Guest, D. E. (1992) 'Right Enough to be Dangerously Wrong: An Analysis of the In Search of Excellence Phenomenon', in G. Salaman (ed.), *Human Resource Strategies*, London: Sage.

Kunda, G. (1992; 2006) *Engineering Culture: Control and Commitment in a High Tech Corporation*, Philadelphia: Temple University Press.

Kunda, G. and Ailon-Souday, G. (2005) 'Management, Markets and Ideologies: Design and Devotion Revisited', in Ackroyd, S., Batt, R., Ogbonna, E. (1992) 'Managing Organisational Culture: Fantasy or Reality?', *Human Resource Management*, 3. 2: 42–54.

Ray, C. A. (1986) 'Corporate Culture: the Last Frontier of Control?', *Journal of Management Studies*, 23. 3: 287–97.

Rosenthal, P., Hill, S. and Peccei, R. (1997) 'Checking Out Service: Evaluating Excellence, HRM and TQM in Retailing', *Work, Employment and Society*, 11. 3: 481–503.

Thompson, P. and Findlay, T. (1999) 'Changing the People: Social Engineering in the Contemporary Workplace', in A. Sayer and L. Ray (eds), *Culture and Economy after the Cultural Turn*, London: Sage.

Thompson, P. and Tolbert, P. (eds), *The Oxford Handbook of Work and Organization*, Oxford: Oxford University Press.

Whyte, W. (2002) *The Organization Man* (2nd edn), University of Penn, Sylvania Press.

Willmott, H. (1993a) 'Strength is Ignorance; Slavery is Freedom: Managing Culture in Modern Organisation', *Journal of Management Studies*, 30. 5: 515–52.

part II

contemporary changes in working life

Introduction

In the past quarter century popular and scientific writing has been awash with claims of fundamental changes in work and organisation. The world of management theory and practice, in particular, always appears to be changing fast, but new buzzwords and themes continue to surface with bewildering rapidity. Academia is not that different, with new labels for change – most pre-fixed with post – competing for attention. Across the many territories of change and twists and turns of argument has been a widely-held belief that the days of bureaucracy are over. New 'post-bureaucratic' forms of organisation move from the 'holding' to the 'enabling' company, to collaborative joint ventures, management buy-outs, contracting out parts of the organisations, personal networking, virtual organisation facilitated by the Internet, mini-factories and industrial boutiques. This is not, however, predominantly a micro-level story. Conceptualisations of new forms of work and organisation only make sense when placed in a broader context and that is normally some kind of new economy narrative.

As we shall see in Chapter 12, the idea of a different kind of economy that displaces industrialism, capitalism or latterly a form of both – Fordism – has been around a long time. Here we focus on those change arguments that began in the 1980s when paradigm break theories peaked. To describe and analyse contemporary changes in work and employment, as this Part of the book seeks to do, is not straightforward. This is essentially because of the scale, scope and complexity of those perceived changes. On the one hand the changes are often packaged as a general new economy narrative such as post-Fordism, or the Knowledge Economy. But examine any of the stories closely and you find that they contain a variety of sub-plots about particular changes in work or employment relations, organisational structures or market regimes. Social scientists and other commentators often line up to produce optimistic or pessimistic versions of these stories, sometimes overlapping with an 'all change' versus 'no change' division. While we address such interpretations, we do not organise the material around them for the simple reason that there is simply too much evidence to assess and it is too complex to be contained within overarching frameworks. Instead, Part II organises the discussion by territory. We begin with big picture accounts that provide contrasting narratives of change, focusing on the evolution of Fordism/post-Fordism debates into new accounts such as the knowledge economy. Having looked at some of the overarching themes of organisational transformation and their connections to work and employment relations, subsequent chapters move on to a more specific look at the theory and research in the main substantive areas said to be characterising and shaping change: from labour markets, to modern corporations, labour processes and knowledge management. Only after a close examination of the arguments and evidence in each territory can we then conclude on an interpretation of trends and patterns.

The objectives of Part II are to:

- Give expositions of the arguments and evidence used by those advocating new economy models before subjecting them to evaluation and critique.
- To outline key concepts and evidence concerning distinctive trends in corporate structures, labour markets, work relations and managing knowledge and to identify connections and disconnections between them.
- To evaluate the evidence of change in each sphere through the following criteria:
  - ○ Continuity – how different?
  - ○ Content – what depth and character?
  - ○ Context – how widespread and in what circumstances?
  - ○ Connections – how interlocking, systemic and strategic?
  - ○ Consequences – what are the effects of changes on employment relationship and employee attitudes and actions?

the bigger picture: society, economy and organisations

In previous chapters we have considered theories of organisations in their environment, but in a general way. Here, we focus on contemporary conceptualisations of the bigger picture within which work and organisational change are located.

Introduction: paradigm shift or shifting paradigms?

The idea of a new economy is one of the oldest stories in the book. Conceptualisations of new economy and organisations (NEO for short), have been around for quite a long time, certainly from the beginning of the 1980s, and, arguably a lot longer in the writings of Drucker on post-capitalism (1959; 1968), or Bell (1973). There appears to be something of a paradox here. If we had a 'new economy' in the 1950s or 1960s, can it be new again in the 1980s and again in the 1990s? What this alerts us to is that we may have experienced less a case of a paradigm shift in the real economy than shifting paradigms about the economy. There is a long history of claims that industrialism or capitalism have been transcended or superseded and therefore that organisations can and must behave in very different ways. Drucker's concept of post-capitalism and post-capitalist organisations was an early variant of what is now called a knowledge economy thesis whose central claim is that the traditional factors of production – land, labour and capital – are becoming obsolete and that the only critical source of competitiveness and innovation is knowledge. Meanwhile, Daniel Bell presented technocrats as the custodians of a post-industrial society and their institutions (universities, research labs) as superseding the business firm as its axial structures.

Amongst the assumptions contained in these and related paradigm break theses was the idea of the economy overcoming scarcity and the profit motive, or the projection of what is expected to be the main principle and driving force of the future society – knowledge, personal services, the electronic technology of computers and telecommunications. The themes remain familiar today, but the labels change – post-industrial became postmodern, post-economic, post-scarcity, or the knowledge economy, personal service or service class society (F. Webster, 2002). Whatever the label or periodisation of 'new', each variant identifies some kind of qualitative or systemic break – a decisive period of transformation, and the first since Taylor, Fayol and Ford.

Across the conceptualisations there are also continuities in what is attributed as the cause or driver of such transformations. The primary culprit is our old friend, 'the environment'. For example, commentators frequently talk of new 'strategic contingencies' in a global economy marked increasingly by turbulence and volatility which produce environmental shocks arising from slower economic growth, intensification of competition, and a rising rate of product innovation in new forms of knowledge and information technology. The bureaucratic structures and decision-making processes of traditionally-designed organisations cannot handle the consequent forms of uncertainty and discontinuous change adequately (Heydebrand, 1989; Pascale, 1990). The perceived need to respond to new market conditions has not been the only 'learning experience' motivating Western business organisations and management commentators. The 'Japanese threat' was particularly important in changing perceptions of the nature of competitive advantage in the 1980s, and in doing so set in motion a major process of emulating or modifying the ingredients believed to be the basis of superior performance. We shall return to some of the ripple effects of these debates on ideas of flexibility and corporate culture in Chapters 13, 14 and 15. Globalisation (discussed extensively in Chapter 6) performs much of the same function as focal point for attributions of causes of change.

Other than market environments, the most commonly identified driver of change is information technology (IT), or more recently information and communication technology (ICT). Whether in the form of PCs, networks and email systems, or the Internet, technology can be seen as a key factor of organisational decentralisation and power-sharing, even to the point of creating 'something close to an information democracy' (Hamel and Prahalad, 1996: 238), or a labour market dominated by a variety of freelancers, e-lancers and teleworkers. The trend can also be conceptualised as the focal point of a broader socio-economic formation. Indeed the same authors refer to change from a machine age to an information age.

An obvious objection to the above arguments is that inflated fantasies and prescriptions often arise from the evidence-free zones of popular business texts. But messages about a paradigm also reflect changing theoretical paradigms among academics. Returning to our example of ICT, one the world's leading social theorists, Manuel Castells, also posits a new mode of development: *informationalism*. Though shaped by capitalist restructuring, it is fundamentally oriented towards the accumulation of knowledge: 'the informational indicates the attribute of a specific form of social organisation in which information generation, gathering, processing and transmission become the fundamental sources of productivity and power' (1996: 21).

More broadly, organisational theorists such as Clegg (1990) are also convinced that Weber's iron cage of bureaucracy – rule-driven, hierarchical and centralised organisation – is no longer a requirement for efficiency. The particular influence on such writers (see Hassard and Parker, 1993) is a theorisation of paradigm shift based on a move from modernity to postmodernity. Indeed for Clegg (1990: 2), 'organisation theory is a creation of modernity'. The latter is linked to an increasing division of labour, in which jobs, tasks and roles are highly differentiated. In contrast, 'Postmodernism points to a more organic, less differentiated enclave of organisation than those dominated by the bureaucratic designs of modernity' (1990: 181). Flexibility is once again the watchword, with organisations changing their external boundaries through chains, clusters, networks and strategic alliances, and internal arrangements such as teams and profit centres (Clegg and Hardy, 1996). Nor, it is argued, must we be bound to the constraints of rationality itself, with its emphasis on calculation, direction and design. With environments that are ever-changing and unpredictable, organisations are more likely to succeed by being reactive. Managers will spend their time on promoting the core corporate values and symbols rather than strategic planning.

This emphasis on living with chaos and managing culture echoes themes in popular management. Though the language of environmental turbulence is replaced by more academic and radical sounding 'post' labels and phases of capitalism, the message that major changes 'out there' are producing an organisational response is common, as is an emphasis on key influences such as new forms of information technology. In current debates it is more likely that the term 'knowledge economy' will be used, but regardless of the label, we see familiar themes of networks replacing hierarchies, flatter organisations, with collaboration and collegiality displacing command and control (Despres and Hiltrop, 1995). We have certainly not exhausted previous or contemporary paradigm change labels. For example, as Warhurst and colleagues note (2008, 91):

> Manufacturing-associated paradigms used to both describe and explain the structure and operation of the capitalist economy have been jettisoned in favour of those associated with services, and a number jostle each other for attention, most obviously 'McDonaldization' (Ritzer 1993) and, more recently, Disneyization (Bryman 2004).

What this quote illustrates, however, is that the big pictures differ both in the themes they draw on and the claims they make. For every benign perspective of a service society, there is a McDonaldisation; for every post-Fordism, there is a neo-Fordism. The rest of the chapter retraces some of the key steps in argument and evidence.

From Fordism to post-Fordism?

The early to mid-1980s saw significant changes in the political and economic terrain. Big companies began to reposition and restructure their activities as a means of responding to new forms of Japanese and other competitive threats. Meanwhile states had their own versions of financial crisis as they struggled with the Keynesian legacies of welfare expenditure and expanded social intervention. Neo-liberal regimes such as those administered by the Thatcher and Reagan governments in the UK and US were one manifestation. The overall pattern of crisis and change began to be interpreted as a move from Fordism to post-Fordism. Such models had a macro- and micro-dimension. So, for example, Mulgan (1989) refers to the replacement of 'strong power' under the Fordist corporations characterised by pyramidal structures, formal rules and close controls, by a post-Fordist order based on weak power controls and decentralised leadership, horizontal communication and self-regulating units. We can see here some of the classic themes of post-industrial, post-bureaucratic narratives.

Fordism is more than assembly lines. Typically associated with large firms, mass production and standardised work, we should see it in the context of the development of managerial capitalism, discussed in earlier chapters. Both are attempts to regulate the market, reduce uncertainty and create the conditions for a stable business and societal model. Such stability can come about only through productivity gains and economic growth that underpins a social settlement between the major economic actors (capital, labour and the state). Above all, Fordism, in its various national guises, was characterised by a virtuous circle of mass production and mass consumption, overseen by an interventionist, welfare-Keynesian state and sustained by the long post-war boom (Jessop, 1990). Corporate management oversaw a business model based on retaining and reinvesting the resources of the firm that underpinned mutual gains at workplace level (O'Sullivan, 2000). Of course there were conflicts between those actors and varying degrees of success across companies and countries, but Fordism had a degree of fit or cohesiveness – a systemic character.

The fact that a system works for a number of decades does not mean it will go on working. During the 1970s, Fordism

> broke down through a combination of internal rigidities (e.g. exhaustion of productivity gains and workplace conflict) and external shocks (e.g. new competitive pressures). This disrupted the willingness and capacity of employers and states to sustain the virtuous circles underpinning social settlements at societal and workplace levels. (Thompson, 2003a: 362)

Those who sought to develop various alternative models argued that the Fordist system of mass production was inflexible and incapable of permanent innovation. One of the most sophisticated accounts has been provided by theorists of flexible specialisation (Piore and Sabel, 1984). This is the term given to efforts, 'to convert the traditional highly integrated, corporate structure into a more supple organisational form capable of responding quickly to shifting market conditions and product demand' (Piore, 1986: 146). Flexible specialisation works on a kind of *design chain* that works downwards from changes in markets and technologies, through firm structures, to work organisation and employment relations (see Figure 12.1). Though rival purveyors of the big picture may contest the detail, we discuss it in some detail because it is characteristic of much contemporary theorising.

It starts with increasingly specialised demand for customised quality goods, which renders the old economies of scale redundant. The shift to new market conditions is facilitated by production and information technology such as flexible manufacturing systems (FMS) and manufacturing automation protocol (MAP) which are general purpose and programmable, allowing switches within and between families of products on more of a small-batch basis (Williams *et al.*, 1987: 409). Once such choices are made,

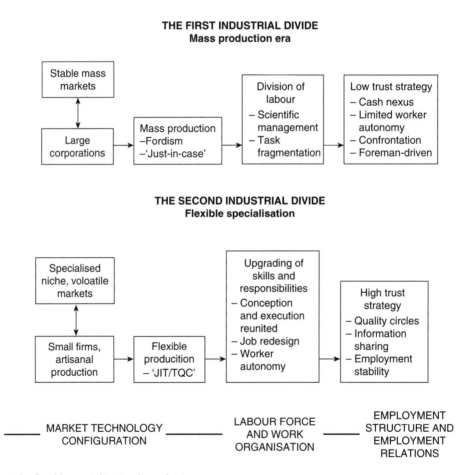

Figure 12.1 *The flexible specialisation hypothesis*

Source: Thomas Bramble (1988) 'Industrial Relations and New Management Production Practices', *Labour and Society*, 112, June.

manufacturing economies are seen as being locked into a technological trajectory. Large corporations cannot adequately handle the flexible markets and technologies, therefore networks of small firms grow in significance. As Harrison observes:

> " a multitude of writers continue to preach the virtues of small firms as engines of contemporary economic growth. We are told that…consumers increasingly seek more customised fashion-oriented goods and services. Mass markets become saturated, the demand for such commodities as clothing and furniture becomes increasingly fragmented.…These developments are said to conjoin to favour technically adroit, well-informed small enterprises. (B. Harrison, 1994: 6–7)

Further down the chain, fragmented and repetitive work organisation characteristic of Taylorism is no longer appropriate. Collaboration between designers, producers and managers is both feasible and necessary, while craft skills and 'the production worker's intellectual participation is enhanced' (Piore and Sabel, 1984: 278). In turn, that creates the need for high-trust work relations in which there is an exchange between participation and greater job security.

This kind of analysis of the logical fit between flexible forms of technology and flexibility in skills and work structures is paralleled in Kern and Schumman's *The End of the Division of Labour* (1984). This talks of the reprofessionalisation of production work and new production concepts; and also finds support from some other writers on advanced technology. (Gill, 1985; Francis, 1986). There are also parallels with accounts of post-Fordism and related concepts such as disorganised capitalism (Lash and Urry, 1987); but advocates of flexible specialisation see differences and problems (Hirst and Zeitlin, 1991).

Flexible specialisation is said to allow transnationals in some instances to begin to reverse the international division of labour, in which assembly processes are located in low-wage areas of the Developing World, while maintaining research and design at home. Technical innovation, capital-intensive manufacturing and far higher levels of productivity from smaller workforces enable redomestication of activities; though the developing countries are likely to still utilise the low-skill, mass production methods. In the advanced economies, decentralised production will be the order of the day, as smaller plants can operate efficiently within the same range of products and be close to the customer to save transport and other costs.

Piore and Sabel admitted that working economic models of flexible specialisation based on networks of small firms are limited to regions such as Veneto and Emilia Romanga in Italy. But it was certainly possible to identify firms or sectors that appear to qualify. General Motor's Saturn Plant utilises flexible equipment to produce specifically tailored products, without retooling and with a high level of worker participation (P. B. Meyer, 1986: 74). Technology such as computer-aided design systems have enabled clothing firms to both create and then speedily respond to customer demands for a greater range of design and colour. Standardisation and long runs are said to become uneconomical. Computerisation also helps large firms such as Benetton to centralise marketing and skilled processes such as design and dyeing among its small core workforce of fewer than 2000 people, while decentralising its other production work to small sub-contractors, and franchising its sales outlets (Fergus Murray, 1983; Mitter, 1986). Small IT firms have been found to be geographically and structurally mobile, utilising their lack of hierarchy and pervious boundaries to adapt successfully to new competitive challenges (Ackroyd, 1995).

Critique

There are a number of complex and interrelated claims made in post-Fordist models. Some are concerned with organisational structures, work and employment relations, which are the subject of subsequent chapters. Here, we want to focus mainly on the bigger picture and particularly on macro- and market processes. Though flexible specialisation is less fashionable these days, its account of changes in firms and markets remains typical of NEO arguments. The theory rapidly became a new work organisation paradigm and therefore a target for extensive critique (Smith, 1987). A number of studies, notably Williams and colleagues (1987), convincingly argued that the conceptual polarity between mass production and flexible specialisation is misleading. Traditional mass production is still widespread, particularly where semi-skilled women workers doing labour-intensive assembly and packing jobs remain a cheaper or more reliable option (Pollert, 1988a). In addition mass production does not always use dedicated equipment to make standardised products, but can handle diversification within flow lines. Wood (1989b) has shown that the world car – the archetypal example of mass production within the international division of labour – remains prominent, albeit in modified form. Economies of scale have fallen, but the break-even point is still high. Japanese and other companies have established variety within mass production with the use of JIT and not always with advanced technology (A. Sayer, 1986).

The obsession with the Fordist stereotype also ignores inconvenient facts about the past. On the one hand the operations of Ford's key plants, such as those as Highland Park, never corresponded to the description of inflexible Ford*ism* (Williams *et al.*, 1992b). On the other, the spread of Fordism has been exaggerated. Most plants in modern economies have never contained assembly lines, and Fordism never travelled far outside mass manufacturing (Williams *et al.*, 1987; B. Jones, 1997). As Bryn Jones has noted, there is a persistent tension in production paradigms between Taylorist bureaucracy and Fordist integration, and pressures for product versatility (1998: 11). This tension has been reproduced in different ways within and across national economies. Japanese flexible manufacturing systems tackle capital and skill utilisation in ways distinct from European and American practices. But none resemble anything that resembles a flexible specialisation or post-Fordist model: 'on the key measures of product-range, system-versatility and worker polyvalence, most FMSs operate within Fordist and Taylorist pre-conceptions' (1998: 21).

Even the identification of flexibility with manufacturing itself neglects the service sector as the major growth area of such practices (Hyman, 1988). The flexible specialisation thesis and post-Fordists also made exaggerated claims for the use of programmable technology (Jones, 1997). Advanced technology such as FMS is very expensive, particularly for the small firms that should be in the forefront of customised production. Furthermore, not all new technology is either inherently flexible, or being used in a flexible way. The emphasis is more likely to be on control and co-ordination of the labour process, quality and routing rather than product flexibility (Wood, 1989b: 9).

Nor are mass markets necessarily saturated. There are a huge range of industries still based on mass and large batch production, and the pattern with goods such as colour TVs and DVDs is for production to be based on families of interrelated models. This is particularly the case in Britain, where large manufacturing firms have tended to 'eschew the production of complex products' in search of diversified production activities and standard products for mature markets (Ackroyd and Proctor, 1998: 166, 170). Fragmentation of demand, or what companies call 'positioning strategies', is more often an attempt to create a market rather than reflect new consumer tastes. Big firms can produce for mass and niche markets, as the ugly phrase 'mass customisation' indicates. Notwithstanding this hybrid capability, key industries, such as food, are actually destroying regional, craft production in the march towards global standardised products and marketing (Levitt, 1991; C. Smith, 1991). Indeed, it is ironic that the most explosive global growth is in fast food, which is 'dominated by homogeneous products. The Big Mac, the Egg McMuffin, and Chicken McNuggets are identical from one time and place to another' (Ritzer, 1993: 155). Ritzer may sometimes overdo the extent to which production and service has been McDonaldised, but the uniformity of high streets and shopping malls is testimony to the continued dominance of standardised commodities, mass markets and large firms. Supermarkets are particularly associated with the growth of cheap, mass produced and packaged food products, whose economies of scale and buying power gradually drive their small retailer competitors out of business. The share of groceries sold by the biggest retailers in the UK has grown from 20 per cent in 1950 to 85 per cent in 2007. But as successive UK Competition Commission Reports (2000; 2008) and academic research (Newsome *et al.*, 2007) have shown, the big supermarkets are also at the apex of a supply chain that routinely passes on risks and costs to its (smaller) suppliers, even to the point of making them pay for product promotion and 'excessive' amounts of shoplifting!

Similarly critical observations, Jones (1998) notes, can also be applied to Italy, where flexible specialisation theory draws much of its inspiration. Even on their 'home-ground' in Emilia-Romagna, the majority of production is still Fordist in nature, while quality craft work is the preserve of the majority of middle-aged men: 'Semi-skilled assembly work, plastic-moulding, and wiring work is carried out by women, while heavy foundry and forging work is done by Southern Italian and North African workers' (F. Murray, 1987: 88). Overall, as the work of the Williams team (1987) demonstrates, the statistical and case study evidence used by Sabel and Piore was frequently poor or non-existent.

There is a wider message about small firms here. While there are sectors where innovative networks of such firms are playing a significant role in economic development. As usual, however, discontinuity perspectives have oversold the message. Across the globe, manufacturing and services remain dominated by large, indeed increasingly larger, firms. Counting the numbers of firms is misleading. It is true, for example, that in the US, 85 per cent of all individual enterprises in the computer industry employ fewer than 100 people. But the 5 per cent that employ 500 or more account for 91 per cent of employment and sales (Harrison, 1994: 5). Such trends are repeated sector by sector. In the UK, more than half of all employees work for organisations with more than 500 employees (Teasdale, 2000: 7). Even a persuasive advocate such as Perrow has to admit that the output of small firm networks on a global scale is 'probably trivial' (1992: 445). Moreover, small firms have been less technologically innovative than large ones, and their profitability often rests primarily on long hours and low wages (Amin, 1991; Harrison, 1994).

Meanwhile, big firms keep on getting bigger. The concentration of capital in mega-corporations is present in every sector and its characteristic effect is to reduce choice and competition. In *The Last Days of the Giants*, Baldock (1999) asserts that the current merger wave is the 'last throw' of the big corporations as they try to fight off the threat from e-commerce. A decade earlier, Tom Peters (1992) had described mergers as 'madness'. The fact remains that the global boom in mergers and acquisitions continues unabated. Despite relatively poor returns for shareholders, United Nations figures show that cross-border mergers and acquisitions drove foreign investment volumes to a new record of $856 billion in 1999 (Mark Atkinson, *Guardian*, 10 October 2000). With market expectations of double-digit growth per year, such activity is the quickest way into mature industries. In addition, economies of scale and scope are more important than ever, particularly for knowledge-intensive firms with huge research and development costs. Responses vary from strategic alliances to link-ups such as the £110 billion merger of Glaxo Wellcome and Smith Kline, but the message remains the same – big is still beautiful. Academics who proclaim the onward march of diversified and fragmented markets don't seem to notice that it doesn't even apply to one of their own products – books. As Miller (2006) shows, there has been a long-term erosion of independent bookstores by discounting chains and superstores (such as Barnes and Noble and Waterstones). At the same time, independent publishers have been eaten up or squeezed out of business by massive media conglomerates such as Verlagsgruppe, Reed Elsevier or Bertelsmann. Such independents now account for just 5 per cent of book sales in the US (Schiffrin, 2001; Epstein, 2002). Amongst the consequences are a decline in shelf-life, variety of products and risk-taking. If academics talked to their own commissioning editors they would hear a story of the big bookshops and even university outlets unwilling to stock anything but textbooks.

There is one possible fly in the ointment of this diagnosis – the rise of the Internet. Its power to change the rules of commodities and competition is regularly proclaimed. The next section outlines and assesses such claims, but treats them as a sub-plot of a wider narrative about the 'new economy'.

The new 'new economy'

Though many of the claims made by post-Fordism and flexible specialisation perspectives remain prominent in the business and social science literatures, the package does not. The 'big picture' franchise has passed to theories of the 'new' or knowledge economy (Nonaka and Takeuchi, 1995), and some of the leading lights of post-Fordist theories such as Leadbetter (1999) are now prominent advocates of new models. There are a number of parallel narratives that draw on similar and overlapping themes concerning the Internet, knowledge and services.

Typical of those who combine these themes is the populist commentator Jeremy Rifkin (2000). He argues that we have entered an 'age of access' in which a hyper-speed network economy supplants market capitalism, rendering the ownership of physical capital redundant and making intellectual capital – concepts, brands, derivatives, copyright, values – the primary resource. Informational products and services can float free of physical space, and the traditional business cycle of boom and bust and even of scarcity can become a thing of the past. As Henwood (2003) documents, such arguments were clearly underpinned by the bull markets, dramatic rises in valuations and profits associated with 'dotcom' and other 'new economy' firms in the mid to late 1990s.

The focus on intangibility or immateriality draws on accounts of a service society where outputs are inherently more difficult to prescribe or measure, and where production activities have been largely displaced by a consumption economy. As Warhurst and colleagues (2008) note, while the term 'consumer society' has been around since the early post-war period, postmodernists have promoted the idea that the meaning and identity which individuals once derived from production have been displaced by those derived from consumption (Pakulski and Waters, 1996; Bauman 1998). Even Ritzer (2001), who previously wrote about the industrialisation of services, now seems to be convinced that e-tail and the e-net are ushering in an era of de-materialised consumption sites.

It is more often described as a 'knowledge' economy as this embodies the soft, intangible, weightless, immaterial or numerous other terms that are used to contrast to the old economy and its hard, measurable things (Coyle, 1997; Leadbetter, 1999; Kelly, 1999). Knowledge, then, is seen as having caring and sharing qualities. It cannot be developed or managed within relations of command and control. Its ephemeral quality is held to facilitate all the distinctive and benign features of the 'new' economy – for example, the move towards networks and creativity and the break from control and hierarchy. The web is seen as a gigantic mechanism for sharing knowledge. A recent book from two prominent business consultants dubbed as *'wikinomics'* the supposed trend towards 'mass collaboration by consumers and producers in the creation of new goods and services such as open source software' (Tapscott and Williams, 2007). As we noted earlier, a more academic and highly influential version of such developments is put forward by Manuel Castells (1996; 2001), who refers to informational capitalism. This is a specific form of social organisation in which the generation, gathering, processing and transmission of information becomes the fundamental sources of productivity and power.

The combination of info-technology and intangible assets is then held to change fundamentally the rules of the economic game. For these observers, rather than the accumulation of capital, socio-economic life is characterised by the flow or circulation of ideas and information. Liberated from real-world borders and their geographic anchor in material production, the products of knowledge can thus float free of physical space and traditional economic burdens. A variety of business analysts, journalists and the occasional economist argued that a combination of the falling cost of information and the huge market for knowledge-based products could move beyond the traditional business cycle:

> On this view, the economics of scarcity were being superseded by those of abundance in an economy of increasing returns and extensible digital products which cost next to nothing to reproduce and could be used by more than one person at the same time. (Feng *et al.*, 2001: 473).

In another critique of new economy hype, Thomas Frank (2000) quotes the business magazine *Forbes* as claiming that the infinite speed and zero cost of software and e-commerce has re-written the physics of the information age. While Castells does recognise this is still capitalism, indeed a variant with increased powers, he does see the ICT-enabled arrangements as enabling the 'capitalist mode of production to overcome the limits of time and space and become truly global' (2003: 5)

Critique

The central flaw in new economy theories is their use, indeed misuse, of the idea of immateriality, intangibility and the like. The 'weightless' character of knowledge, services or software products and their location in the minds and communities of the knowers is said to make the economy fundamentally different from the old, profit-driven hierarchical predecessor. The new categories are said to change the economics, management and even physics of production and distribution. However, this formulation is factually inaccurate and conceptually confused. What gives weight to an object or idea in a market economy is its status as a commodity and its capacity to be assigned a value in the market. Its physicality or otherwise is wholly irrelevant. A similar point can be made about the growth of new kinds of services and consumption. As Warhurst and colleagues (2008) note, e-tail might appear to be a tale of de-materialisation, but in a capitalist economy, materiality is based on the commodification process and should not be confused with bricks and mortar. Amazon may sell things in different ways but the fundamental business requirements remain the same. Moreover, firms competing in the electronic marketplace are serviced by an army of conventional employees and labour processes in warehouses and offices. Similarly, advanced ICT may bring us emails, texts and other electronic message as if part of a wholly virtual universe, but that requires an extensive physical infrastructure of cables and the like that, again, are produced by workers in factories and installed by their equivalents in the streets. As Doogan (2008: 7) observes, 'the production and consumption of knowledge and information remains materialist even if its circulation is immaterial'.

Returning to the nature of knowledge, this too can be calculated, rationalised and ultimately commodified (see Yakhlef and Salzer-Morling, 2000):

> [T]he big challenge for corporate capital is to locate, enclose and exploit new forms of intellectual property. ICTs open up greater possibilities within this search, but do not prescribe the form or content. Ownership and control of productive assets is still the central question, no matter what the array of new economy theorists say. (Boreham *et al.*, 2008: 7)

A simple example is the emergent intellectual property regime in biotechnology. Global corporate players have been rushing to establish patents on genetic material, so that they can 'own traditional knowledge and take advantage of the privatisation of life forms' (J. Vidal, *Guardian*, 13 April 2000). Value can and is being assigned to these so-called intangible assets. Furthermore, though companies are dependent on scientific, knowledge workers to 'mine' this gene pool, the transformation into saleable commodities relies precisely on separating that knowledge from the knower. Though a new drug or piece of software can create value without a transaction taking place, such valuation only anticipates future transactions – 'immaterial' products are ultimately valuable if successful commodities are created (Henwood, 2003: 20). Corporate power places constraints on the process of independent, collegial knowledge production, as universities become ever more dependent on private sources to finance scientific research. Nor in market terms do knowledge-intensive industries behave any differently from more traditional sectors. Rifkin (1999) details how, contrary to the network myth, the concentration of capital (and vertical integration) is unabated. Global pharmaceutical companies have recently spent $3.5 billion buying up biotech firms. When they are not buying them up they are tying them to licensing agreements (at the cost of $1.6 billion expenditure).

This can be a temporal confusion. While the early stages of the creation of new products and markets can sometimes result in less hierarchical organisation and more open forms of competition, the standard pattern of consolidation and concentration of capital tends to follow. Autonomy and creativity are maximised during periods of pursuing knowledge and creating systems. Yet the commercialisation of the products of knowledge takes the form of standardised, highly-structured systems in areas such as software design or surveying. We can see similar trends with respect to the Internet. It is true that many new e-commerce companies have come into being, backed by venture capitalists and making a lot of money for their founders. However, the trends in what Schiller calls 'digital capitalism' are also towards concentrated ownership and vertical integration:

> Smaller companies that specialised in what were initially niche markets at the frontier of the liberalisation process worked the new territory. When they succeeded, major traditional suppliers either snapped them up or rushed to develop similar applications of their own. (Schiller, 1999: 28)

Huge mergers such as that between Time-Warner and AOL in 2000 or the global computer games business of French media conglomerate Vivendi and US-based Activision in 2007 merely confirm that the direction of change is towards concentration of capital and the erection of quasi-monopolies over knowledge and information. With this in mind, the association of knowledge production and acquisition with new forms of ownership is a mixture of wishful thinking and confusing the early stages of market formation in an emergent sector with its mature, normally oligopolistic characteristics. As their predecessors before them, knowledge economy theorists are unwilling or unable to explain such trends.

With respect to macro-economic issues, the most startling claims were connected to projections of some fundamental change to the business cycle. Writing this chapter at the time of a major global crisis in financial and housing markets associated with the credit crunch, such claims don't look too robust. But actually, the new economy bubble had well and truly bust by the start of the new millennium. As Henwood (2003: chap. 5) demonstrates, what the hype attributed to some change in the nature of economic relations was in fact a contingent combination of a profit boom, plenty of money looking for investment and a range of stockmarket intermediaries with a vested interest in hyping the new stocks. Layers of claims that immaterial products and services are somehow beyond measurement can generate trading activity, but ultimately reality has a tendency to bite back. Over-valued internet and high-tech companies perished or were taken over, often by old economy rivals such as Condé Nast's absorption of new economy cheerleader, *Wired*.

In one sense the opposite was happening of that postulated by new economy theorists. For all the talk of 'wikinomics' and a digital age of co-production, free goods and labour, the long-term trend is towards an extension of the commodity form. Braverman (1974) long ago pointed out that the distinction between whether labour produces a good or a service is less relevant than whether it produces a vendible commodity. More recent studies from prominent social scientists (Huws, 2003; Hochschild, 2003) illustrate how activities once regarded as belonging largely to the private sphere – cooking, cleaning, child-care – are being relentlessly commercialised. If you have money, you can purchase pretty much any service, including people who will plan and organise your time, as well as pick up your laundry. It is true that digital products have made it harder for some industries, such as the record business, to sell their traditional products such as CDs. But this is the nature of technical and organisational innovation under capitalism. Specialist record companies are or will be part of broader media conglomerates that are shifting their focus of money making to new synergies between content, platforms and outputs (licensing, merchandising, touring, legal downloading).

Concluding comments and contrasting narratives

> [T]he fact that a model goes into crisis does not mean that it is replaced by a clear alternative. Despite the search...for coherent prototypes in Sweden, Italy, Germany and Japan; as Clarke [1990] notes, 'Post-Fordism is not a reality, nor even a coherent vision of the future, but mainly an expression of hope.' (Thompson, 2003a: 362)

We have seen in the previous sections that there are a number of overlapping themes from the 'models' established through new economy narratives, each version tends to see the end of the dominance of large firms, mass production, bureaucratic organisation and competition based on cost. In its place are decentralised, consumer- and worker-friendly business models based on some intangible or dematerialised source of competitive advantage. Unfortunately, something else is repeated – excessive optimism, stereotypical polarisation of old and new, limited evidence, hyping of unrepresentative examples and neglect of diversity, As a number of writers have noted (Eccles and Nohria, 1992; Webster, 2002; Williams, 2006), for all the claims of novelty and the imperatives of new technologies and new market conditions associated with managerial and social science commentators, they share considerable continuities with previous waves with post-industrial, post-capitalist discourse from Drucker (1959; 1992) to Daniel Bell (1973).

What then, if anything, has taken the place of Fordism? One of the purveyors of flexible specialisation, Charles Sabel (1982) had previously preferred to talk of neo-Fordism. This term rested on reference to corporate attempts to maintain continuity with mass production, deskilling and labour controls, while moving away from standardisation. Neo-Fordism was seen as coexisting alongside a new high-tech cottage industry that combines craft forms of production with computerised technology (see also C. Smith, 1987: 1). There is a great deal of accuracy in such a picture, but despite continuities more significant changes have taken place, particularly in the 1990s. This difference in decades is significant. The 1980s were a decade of optimistic predictions about paradigm breaks, with the emphasis being on culture inside the organisation and various forms of soft/er capitalism outside. Move on a decade and the real-world picture looked different and bleaker. A second, more pessimistic narrative of contemporary political economy developed under such labels as casino, turbo- or financialised capitalism (Littwak, 1999). Particularly in Anglo-Saxon varieties of capitalism, more aggressive, volatile and unstable market regimes came into being spurred by the retreat of state regulation and the rise of free-market, neo-liberal political projects with their emphasis on financial deregulation and privatisation.

Hostile takeovers and buy-outs in the latter part of the 1980s had been an early sign of a corporate search for ways of restoring profit levels. By the early 1990s shareholder activism, backed by pension funds and other institutional investors, was in full swing. In the previous decade competitive advantage had been located in product markets, notably through lean production. Under shareholder value-growth regimes, institutional investors, utilising new and more sophisticated metrics of measurement, sought ever increasing rates of dividend payments and appreciation in share price as markers of financial performance (Froud *et al.*, 2006). At a macro-level, one consequence was 'the financialization of everything' (Henwood, 2003: 191) – an economy in which everything is under constant auction and where companies such as Enron made money by betting on the outcomes of transactions rather than actually making and selling things (hence casino capitalism). The new economy bubble briefly fed that financial frenzy. At a micro-level, O'Sullivan (2000) describes the business model as a shift from retain and reinvest to downsize and distribute. Managers and employees increasingly found themselves on the receiving end of de-layering, divestment and other forms of perpetual restructuring, Meanwhile, the loyalty of corporate management had been bought by tying their rewards to stock options. The 2008 credit crunch is the first sign of a systemic crisis in financialised capitalism.

Such instability clearly makes it harder for companies to invest in firms-specific assets, notably the jobs and skills of their employees, but this is a story that we will have to pick up in later chapters, particularly the Conclusion to Part II. At this stage, we have only outlined (aspects of the macro-) part of the story about contemporary change in economy, work and organisation. A full account of what kind of alternative has emerged after but not post Fordism has to wait on chapters examining more specific changes. The really difficult task for organisational analysis is to grasp the patterns, dynamics and characteristics of continuity and change. To begin this journey we start with an examination of changes in corporate structure and organisation.

doing the business: hierarchies, networks and the governance of the firm

A central feature of new economy, new organisation perspectives is a projection of the changing structure or what is now often referred to as the governance of the firm. We saw in the last chapter that the large, bureaucratised corporation is often associated with industrial, Fordist societies. Not surprisingly this is now seen as a casualty of change. Hierarchies are out and networks or 'heterarchies' are in. We were sceptical in the previous chapter about the extent to which mass production and the core features of capitalism had changed. It is, however, feasible that the firm itself could be changing in distinctive ways and this issue will be the focus of this chapter. There are two dimensions of possible change: transformations in the internal structure of units of organisation and structures of co-ordination across those units. The traditional issues addressed by organisation theory such as decision-making hierarchies and centre–periphery relations are central to such considerations. In this chapter we will consider the key concepts and evidence rather than underlying theories, which will be considered in the final part of the book.

Narratives of changing organisation: post-bureaucracy and networks

Two overlapping narratives lie at the heart of new economy, new organisation perspectives in this sphere. The first and most long-standing is an argument about moves towards post-bureaucratic organisation and the functional decentralisation of managerial structures. The second takes a similar line on organisational outcomes, but within a slightly broader frame, focusing on a shift in modes of co-ordination from hierarchy and markets to networks and trust relations. As they draw on much the same argument and evidence, we shall consider them together, though sequentially, before subjecting them to evaluation and critique.

For mainstream organisation theory, challenging bureaucratic designs ultimately rests on change in the sphere of *structure*. During earlier periods, organic structures or ad-hoceries were *one* way of adapting to (turbulent) environments. Now it is frequently presented as the norm, a permanent condition of organisational life and, as McSweeney (2006) observes, an 'epochal' change. In other words, (globalised) market, (innovative) technological and (complex) cultural environments are too unstable, unpredictable and fragmented to be served adequately by large, hierarchically structured organisations.

To explain these arguments, it is useful to return to four categories with which post-bureaucratic change is associated: decentralisation, disaggregation, de-layering and disorganisation. Big is no longer merely not beautiful, it is seen as positively dangerous and anachronistic. As part of a process of *decentralisation*, companies are said to be breaking up their bureaucracies and setting up smaller or independent units, or developing new corporate structures where divisions operate as autonomous profit centres with delegated decision-making powers. Heydebrand (1989: 330–1) argues that profit centres overcome the market–hierarchy dichotomy and reduce the need for CEO control, while encouraging direct negotiation among sub-units. Integration will be provided by overall strategy, information technology and corporate

Old	New
stability	disorganisation/chaos
rationality	charisma, values
planning	spontaneity
control	empowerment
command	participation
centralisation	decentralisation/disaggregation
hierarchy	network
formal	informal/flexible
large	downsized/delayered

Figure 13.1 **A post-bureaucratic organisation?**

cultures. After this organisational revolution, the more autonomous units will be 'guided by a coherent vision rather than by memorandum and managers-as-cops' (Peters, 1989: 31). Units will therefore be more loosely coupled and decision-making more dispersed, as in matrix systems with multiple accountabilities. 'External' surveillance and control will be increasingly replaced by new forms of market disciplines between the autonomous units, or even work teams, who are each other's customers (Clegg, 1990: 180).

The break-up is linked to *disaggregation* or *de-integration*, which goes beyond the internal redistribution of power by reducing the corporation to a relatively small core as central functions are dispersed to small firms, are outsourced to specialist units and franchises, sub-contracted to telecommuters in electronic cottages or other forms of virtual organisation (Jackson, 1999). Handy (1989) refers to such trends as a move towards federalism, or beyond to the 'donut' organisation that has nothing in the middle. The centre has only to keep a broad watching brief on finance and longer-term policy. This deconcentration of capital (Perrow, 1992) puts into reverse the historic trend towards vertical integration: 'If the old model of organisation was the large hierarchical firm, the model of organisation that is considered characteristic of the New Competition is a network, of lateral and horizontal interlinkages within and among firms' (Nohria, 1992: 2). Such a characterisation of current trends connects to the vision promoted by flexible specialisation theorists, of industrial districts populated by small entrepreneurial firms coexisting happily in a new division of labour with their scaled-down, larger sisters. The growth in franchising is also sometimes linked to such development trends (Labour Research Department, 1986b; O'Connell Davidson, 1994), though the motive is primarily to transfer risk in uncertain markets while retaining control of supplies, prices and business style.

The combined effects of these two trends are that 'new organisations are small or small sub-units in [a] larger organisation' (Heydebrand, 1989: 337). Peters (1992) makes the most sustained assault on previous orthodoxies about organisation scale. Technology and brainware are taking the scale out of everything, while networks can create the efficiencies that vertical integration once did. As proof, he cites data showing that the average size of firms is getting smaller. Even when they stay large, big firms are trying to act small, because the latter are winning the innovation game.

Networks appear in another form, an alternative to internal hierarchy, as organisations go through a *de-layering* process. 'Downsizing' may sound like another term for the same process, but its normal meaning is slightly different. While downsizing is often a cynical euphemism for sacking people, claims are made for a trend towards flatter, less hierarchical forms where whole layers of middle management have been removed on the back of new, horizontal communication channels and devolution of responsibility to self-managing and project teams, a trend enhanced by single status deals that remove barriers between categories of employees. Quinn Mills (1993: 8) even invents a new label: the post-hierarchical firm.

Finally we have *disorganisation*. Peters, for example, has travelled from 'thriving on chaos' to 'necessary disorganisation' in the ephemeral world of the 1990s. Bureaucratic structures and rationality are based on planning. In contemporary unpredictable environments, attempting to plan, predict or control the future is pointless when there is no way of knowing what it will be. As a result, 'The era of strategic planning (control) may be over; we are entering an era of tactical planning (response)' (Moss Kanter, 1993). It is not just scientific management, but science *in* management that is held to be out-of-date and 'positively counterproductive' in a 'world of perpetual novelty and change' (Freedman, 1992: 26, 37). As we saw in Chapter 7, even in more mainstream academic spheres doubts are being cast about the utility of concepts of business planning and strategy.

Indeed, this is only one way in which popular management writing is reinforced by post-modern perspectives that emphasise the reactive nature of organisational behaviour in circumstances where there is inherent uncertainty and disorder in a multiplicity of local situations (Cooper and Burrell, 1988), and also lay stress on new chaos theories of science in which nature appears as random as a throw of the dice (D. Freedman, 1992). Organisations are 'out of control' (Kelly, 1994) but that's fine because that is part of the continual cycle of creation and destruction undertaken by 'mobius strip' organisations that have no identifiable top or bottom, beginning or end (Sabel, 1991). Alternatively some commentators describe the consequences of change in terms of the growth of boundaryless organisations as internal flattening of layers between management and external drift towards subsidiaries, sub-contracting and supply chains blur the legal and economic relationships within networks (Ashkenas *et al.*, 1995).

As Ray and Reed (1994a) observe, there are a number of prominent social scientists associated with paradigm break perspectives who dispute the underlying dynamic of Weberian bureaucratic rationalisation, including Lash and Urry (1994), Harvey (1989), Beck (1992) and Castells (1996). Instead they point to more decentralised and dispersed corporate forms emerging from globalisation and informational modes of development. The latter is associated with the influential work of Castells, which we began to discuss in the previous chapter. In his recent work Castells (2001) sees the Internet as the organisational form of the information age, facilitating new forms of co-ordination that combine flexibility in task performance, decentralised decision-making and decentralised horizontal communication. He is also typical of many recent writers in attributing to new forms of information technology a determinant role in facilitating many of the above changes. As the 'new economy' has a 'techno-logic' transforming it (W. Taylor, 1994: 66), the design chain has a different driver, though with broadly the same outcomes. 'It's a voyage that begins with technology and leads inexorably to trust' (Webber, 1993: 24). As we saw earlier, anything from fax machines to new computer link-ups is a key and benign driving force of new ways of working: 'Today, technology is following its own dynamic direction toward distributed computing of greater and greater power and diffused, not centralised information' (Quinn Mills, 1993: 15). ICT is therefore seen as central to a number of trends outlined in this section, including reducing co-ordination costs and reducing the number of levels of hierarchy and facilitating the development of sub-contracting, outsourcing and other means of disaggregation (Boreham *et al.*, 2008).

Markets, hierarchy and trust

This kind of argument is made not merely at the level of the individual workplace or organisation, but across organisations. The most common term applied to new, flexible inter-organisational forms is a network. For many, they are seen as fundamentally different from the traditional large firm. As with the single organisation, the imagery is of co-operative alliances held together by trust and reciprocity rather than rules, authority and hierarchy (G. Thompson, 2005. Indeed some observers have dubbed such decentred or decentralised structures as 'heterarchy' (Solvell and Zander, 1995). Networks are presented not merely as a hybrid, but as a distinctive organisational form with unique characteristics and logic of operation. Such forms are seen to arise, in part, from more permeable organisational boundaries ranging from alliances between firms, franchises and supply chains. The emphasis is on strategic relationships, partnerships and collaboration between a variety of structures created out of the collapse of the vertically integrated firm (Womack *et al.*, 1990; Quarrie and Hobbs, 1997). Under such arrangements what is left of the main firm appears as a co-ordinating hub for the extended networks of suppliers, subcontractors and profit centres – a 'systems integrator, organizing the specialist consortia of sub-units over which it has no direct control' (G. Thompson, 2005: 512). Such relationships tend to be long-term and facilitate the continual exchange of ideas and personnel. Once again, the Internet is seen as creating important preconditions for network forms of organisation that allow companies and individuals to co-ordinate complex and decentralised activities across the globe, overcoming many of the conventional limits of time and space.

To fully explain the argument underpinning the rise of networks, we have to take a step back and consider the economy as a system comprising different modes of co-ordination: markets, hierarchies and networks (or community). Organisation theory has long held the view that how organisations and individual economic actors behave will be shaped by dominant forms and patterns of interaction between these modes of co-ordination, but has traditionally seen the outcomes as a balance between hierarchy and market. Market forms co-ordinate on a basis of price and competition, simplifying transactions and offering simple choice, flexibility and transparency. Hierarchies, meanwhile, internalise transactions within integrated authority hierarchies, reducing costs and establishing chains of command and reliable rules and norms. Neither, however, are seen to be good at collaboration, pooling resources, sharing knowledge and developing strong bonds of altruistic attachments (Powell, 1990). Networks co-ordinate on the basis of trust between actors, manifested in informal relationships, value systems and codes of ethics. As a result, it is claimed, they can be both more efficient (because they cope better with uncertainty and complexity) and more legitimate (because they generate more commitment and normative identification) than markets or bureaucracies (Courpasson, 2000; Heckscher and Donnellan, 1994).

Perhaps the most sophisticated recent argument put forward about a shift from markets and hierarchies to trust has come from P. Adler (2001). It is an advance on similar contributions because it is more complex and more cautious. Adler recognises that the death of the large firm and its power has been exaggerated and sees the issue as the growth of network relations within them; also recognising the networks themselves can be co-ordinated in a variety of ways. In addition, he accepts that contemporary modes of co-ordination typically deploy a complementary mix of price, authority, and trust mechanisms. Indeed Adler pursues a somewhat strange argument that all three modes may be increasing as firms sharpen market-like and hierarchical processes, but develop trust mechanisms to an even degree. Organisations are presented as increasingly resembling collaborative communities, an argument pursued through a more recent case study of a US hospital. Though central direction and quasi-market mechanisms have been growing, the dominant trend is for professional hierarchy to mutate into various manifestations of the 'community principle' (teamworking, project groups, communities of practice), with the beneficial outcome of greater capacity for innovation and knowledge sharing (P. Adler, Kwon and Heckscher, 2008). There is some support for such trends in studies of knowledge-intensive firms where professional or expert labour requires high levels of autonomy and flexibility; and where cultural norms may be more effective glue than central dictation (Kärreman, Sveningsson and Alvesson, 2002).

Speaking of community, trust and informality within the organisation is one thing, a transfer to collaborative multidivisional corporations another. Yet Adler is willing to go down that route, referring to firms as increasingly infusing trust into their relations with other firms, developing alliances and other forms of interfirm networks. In essence this is because trust particularly corresponds with the needs for coordination of knowledge-intensive activities:

> In outline, the argument is, first, that alongside the market ideal-typical form of organization which relies on the price mechanism and the hierarchy form which relies on authority, the third form, the community form ... relies on trust. Empirically I argue that trust has uniquely effective properties for the coordination of knowledge-intensive activities within and between organization ... modern economies are becoming increasingly knowledge-intensive, trust is likely to become increasingly important in the mechanism mix ... specifically in the employment relationship, in interdivisional relations, and in interfirm relations. (P. Adler, 2001: 215–16)

In an increasingly knowledge-intensive economy, trust can significantly reduce risks and transaction costs, replacing contracts with handshakes and the like. Such perspectives repeat the optimistic claims about knowledge discussed in the previous section. Whereas under hierarchy/the old economy, knowledge is treated as a scarce resource and concentrated in specialised, centralised functional units, in the new scenario it is more available and can be shared and accessed without the same competitive disadvantages. A similar argument is advanced by Graeme Thompson, who asserts that 'Cooperative networks between firms thrive on communication and information flows between their members' (2006: 510).

Both Adler and Graeme Thompson admit that there is limited evidence for a qualitative shift in modes of co-ordination. The former says that the evidence is evidence is suggestive rather than compelling; while the latter observes that 'data limitations prevent any clear confirmation that there are business networks operating in any depth' (2006: 526). Such scepticism is shared and extended by a range of critics.

Critique: reconfiguring the large firm

The rhetoric of replacing centralised bureaucracy by decentralised, 'disorganised' networks does not rely solely on the balance of large and small firms, but on the nature of modern corporate structure. Hierarchical structures are more durable than the business literature would have us believe. In fact a consistent theme of previous studies has been the gap between the potential for decentralisation and the reality of subordination to traditional functional structures, narrowly defined cost efficiency and conservative cultures (Cummings and Blumberg, 1987; Child, 1987; R. Williams, 1988). Reviewing the post-bureaucratic literatures, McSweeney (2006) refers to the 'paucity of evidence' and observes that the sparse number of actual studies of empirical developments suffer from a combination of imprecision and unwarranted generalisation on the basis of localised and uncommon practices.

However, there is little doubt that there have been considerable changes in organisational structure and inter-organisational relations are a key level of analysis (Marchington and Vincent, 2004: 1029). Traditional bureaucracies are, in one sense, being broken up with the creation of a myriad of smaller units such as profit centres and internal markets within large firms. Business periodically adjusts the balance and mechanisms of central control as it seeks to adapt to new economic and political conditions, though these vary considerably by sector and country. In the UK, current changes are part of a longer-term shift away from 'Americanised' strategies and structures which were relatively unresponsive to market flexibility and product and process innovation (McKinlay, 1999). However, both the intent and the outcome of such changes are in danger of being misunderstood and misrepresented.

It is certainly true that we need to move away from the assumptions of the earlier generation of organisation research (discussed in Chapter 5) that firms were largely stand-alone entities. Today, large organisations have more complex, fragmented structures, but their power and reach is actually more extensive (Ackroyd, 2002). In a further wide-ranging review of the literatures, Alvesson and Thompson (2005: 495) reported that 'With respect to interorganizational relations, neither surveys nor case studies give any significant support to the idea that "pyramidal hierarchies are replaced by looser networks" (Sennett, 1998: 85).' One of the key concepts for moving the debate on is to distinguish between the delegation of operational autonomy and strengthened financial and other controls by the central structures. Just as studies of the labour process such as Shaiken and colleagues (1986) show that the primary managerial concern remains that of centralising control and reducing unpredictability, so analysis of new corporate structures demonstrates that decentralisation of the form is accompanied by centralisation of the substance of power. At companies such as British Telecom, the system of profit centres relies on accounting structures, marketing forecasts and limits on the discretion of plant managers to control and monitor costs (Hallet, 1988; McKinlay, 1999). As Hallet observes, 'District managers, supposedly freer than ever in the age of devolution, complain of now being more tightly restricted by budgets imposed from above over which they have less influence' (1988: 35). Research into privatised utilities in the UK reports a large gap between the rhetoric of autonomous units transacting with each other and the reality that profit centres are mostly monopoly suppliers to each other. In addition they are closely controlled through corporate business plans, capital expenditure, employment and revenue allocations and targets (O'Connell Davidson, 1993). 'Empowered' managers are often equally as sceptical as their shop-floor equivalents:

> I'm going to be constrained by my management. My management is going to be constrained by their management. And so on up the ladder. The chairman of the board is going to be constrained by the board and the financial market. (Product manager quoted in Potterfield, 1999: 84)

The sheer spatial and functional diversity of units at national and international level, particularly following complex patterns of merger and acquisition, has led to a more flexible, project-based initiatives and intensive use of IT and other communication channels. However, at the same time there has been a considerable strengthening of financial control systems, resource allocation models and target setting that give corporate headquarters much more sophisticated means of monitoring and regulating the management of subsidiaries (Thompson, Wallace and Flecker, 1992; Ackroyd and Proctor, 1998; Ruigrok *et al.*, 1999; Hill, Martin and Harris, 2000). A survey of the largest companies operating in the UK revealed that in a substantial majority, 'headquarters exerts tight controls over business unit operations and profitability targets are not devolved' (Armstrong *et al.*, 1994: 13). This may vary by function, with more autonomy devolved in areas such as human resource policy, though constrained by strict budget allocations (Sisson and Marginson, 1995; McKinlay, 1999). In such areas the route to centralisation is likely to be indirect. As we saw in Chapter 6, the capacity of transnational companies to establish standardised management systems and production organisation is facilitated by their ability to transfer know-how and 'best practice' within the organisation. The real networks are increasingly globally integrated production or service chains, with standardisation rather than local autonomy the main feature (Gereffi, 1994; Gereffi *et al.*, 2005; Thompson *et al.*, 1998).

Disaggregation, deconcentration and outsourcing of functions and operations is another real trend, though, as we have seen, the evidence for some of its supposed forms such as flexible specialisation and industrial districts is vastly exaggerated (Amin, 1989). Contracting out functions and services does, admittedly, lead to what Grimshaw and colleagues describe as 'disordered employment hierarchies', as a complex pattern of relations and responsibilities between different groups of workers ensues. But as their case studies demonstrate, it is not 'all change':

> Such changes frequently involve the development of hybrid elements within established organizational forms, rather than their transformation into 'new' forms or 'networks'. Similarly, our evidence points to complex and contradictory arrangements that decompose bureaucracy without being, in any meaningful sense, 'post bureaucratic'. (Marchington *et al.*, 2005: 3)

A further characteristic and bureaucratic mechanism of disaggregation has been franchising. Case studies (Felstead, 1994) demonstrate that business formats imposed by the central company dictate precise procedures and criteria governing operations, finance, and transfer of 'know-how'. In the case of the shift from direct employment to franchised operations in milk delivery, managers contradicted the new philosophy of partnership between company and franchisee. They admitted that the system of supervising roundsmen was exactly the same as before, and that their work was closely prescribed by the franchise contract, with the added 'bonus' that the franchisees had lost all previous employment rights and benefits. Like the self-employed workers studied by Rainbird (1991), any autonomy was largely lost in longer days, intensified labour and other signs of self-exploitation. Even where groups such as freelance media workers have a reasonable degree of telework autonomy, research shows that almost half are dependent on a single client for business, often their former employer (Baines, 1999). UK Labour Force Survey data reveals that 12 per cent of the self-employed had only one customer and that 7 per cent were previously an employee of their main customer (Teasdale, 2000: 9).

The reality of dependency was pointed out some time ago in Rainnie's (1988) authoritative study of small–large firm relationships. In industries such as clothing, the large firm is able to dictate methods and profit margins, transfer costs and uncertainties to the smaller unit. This is similar to supplier networks in JIT systems. Nissan established the first British and possibly European example of a spatially concentrated production process (Crowther and Garrahan, 1987). A large site enabled the company to maximise influence over the industrial environment and the supply of components. Car manufacturers have been able to put a similar squeeze on component suppliers. The Fiat Melfi plant in Southern Italy includes 22 component makers who simply run their products onto the production line. We discussed in the previous chapter the growing power of buyer-driven supply chains, such as those dominated by large supermarkets, that can dictate price, performance and even patterns of labour organisation and usage (Newsome *et al.*, 2009). All this is hardly surprising. Networks are inevitably constituted by units with differential access to resources and therefore amounts of power, as even relatively mainstream organisation theory such as the resource dependency perspective has shown (see Chapter 5).

Benetton has been held up as the archetypal post-bureaucratic firm. In fact, such companies indicate the existence of a new type of *extended hierarchy* that takes in decentralised and desegregated units, but still has the powerful large firm at the centre. As Wood (1989a: 24) observes, 'the Benetton case does not match up to the image of a nexus of firms all flexibly specialised and employing highly committed, skilled workforces. It appears if anything more like a network dominated by the large firm along the lines of Atkinson's flexible firm'. Harrison (1994: 25), too, refers to Benetton's complicated layering of high-end design in the core, with external sub-contractors and homeworkers as part of a wider hierarchical production system. For him, this is just one example of 'concentration without centralisation'. Instead of dwindling, concentrated economic power is changing shape through downsizing and disaggregation, networks and alliances. But at the centre remain big players: 'production may be decentralised, while power finance, distribution, and control remain concentrated among the big firms' (1994: 20). Further evidence for the hierarchical nature of networks is provided in Mackenzie's (2008) case study of sub-contracting regimes in the Irish telecommunications sector. Noting that the outcomes of changes in the sector resulted in hybrids of market, hierarchy and network, Mackenzie nevertheless shows that new arrangements enabled the strengthening of mechanisms of contract enforcement and a variety of opportunity and incentive controls as a means of coordination between purchaser and suppliers. In contradiction to the standard projections in the literature there was actually a trend from looser network to 'progessively centralised relations' (2008: 882).

What about the other sense of hierarchy – removing the middle layers? Again, this is undoubtedly a significant trend. But de-layering is not synonymous with the destruction of hierarchy, at least not if it means any diminution of centralised power. Paradoxically, the thinning-out of middle levels of command can, as we saw in more detail in Chapter 4, actually lead to more power to strategic decision-makers and more workload for middle managers (McCann, Hassard and Morris, 2008). Hales (2002) undertook a series of cross-sector and national case studies to explore the de-layering and internal network thesis. His findings were that any operational autonomy was, within a clear system of performance management, accountable to the centre and hierarchical control. In an organisational world constituted through line management, direct reporting and accountability, the removal of intermediate levels, with their attendant committees and other structures, also removes the potential for removing obstacles to central control and coalitions of countervailing power. For example, in some firms, 'radical delegation of decision-making also had the explicit objective of reducing the power of divisional "barons" and sharpening executive responsibilities' (McKinlay, 1999: 155).

McKinlay also details the growth of qualitative measures, such as rates of new product and process innovation and customer satisfaction that complement budgetary controls. This is particularly the case in the public sector, where forms of control and co-ordination based on professional autonomy and self-regulation have been under attack from expanded corporate and state influence. In higher education, universities have had to respond to research and course evaluation exercises through external funding agencies by greatly increasing the monitoring and control of performance at departmental and individual level: 'increased bureaucracy becomes necessary to cope with the proliferation of control, audit, monitoring, reporting and accounting functions that carry out the tasks previously undertaken by academics themselves' (Parker and Jary, 1994: 7). In schools, a survey showed 91 per cent of teachers and 95 per cent of lecturers identified a growth of bureaucracy as being one of the main factors shaping their recent experience of work (*Guardian*, 7 and 14 March 2000).

IT does indeed have a powerful role in all these processes, for example when automated purchasing cuts out the need for specialised functions. But the idea that technology automatically redistributes power and democratises information flows is both naïve and deterministic. Though IT is flexible enough to allow for varied uses, the vast increase in information available on work activities can in itself reproduce managerial power to monitor, control and predict performance. Giordano accurately observes that this means 'the development of an industrial organisation whose planning and financial decisions are centralised and whose operations are frequently decentralised and highly interdependent' (1985: 11). The chairman of the international conglomerate ABB, whose global information system helps control the 400 companies and 240,000 employees gives an example of this:

> We also have the glue of transparent, centralised reporting through a management information system called Abacus. Every month Abacus collects performance data on our 4500 profit centres and compares performance with budgets and forecasts. You can aggregate and disaggregate results by business segments, countries and companies within countries. (W. Taylor, 1991: 100)

This kind of potential of ICT is a core feature of Ackroyd's study of UK firms. He argues that, 'The extensive use of IT also explains how large organizations can be more radically dispersed and made up of large numbers of small elements whose activities are monitored coordinated, and overseen by a small headquarters staff' (2002: 174).

Where does this leave the broader conceptualisation of markets, hierarchy and trust? As noted earlier, much of the evidence on the properties and perceived advantages of networks are speculative and problematic (Jessop, 2002; Reed, 2005a). P. Adler (2001) escapes the problem by claiming that all three modes of co-ordination are increasing, but given that some decisions on resource allocation can only be taken in a particular way, it is difficult to see how far such a formulation can be stretched. The problem may be not so much the idea of the growth of networks, but the argument that their mechanism of co-ordination is trust. Ackroyd argues that, 'It is questionable whether there are any actual examples of interorganizational relationships based purely, or even mainly, on trust. Most also seem to involve authority and other forms of coercion' (2005: 453). Elsewhere Ackroyd (2002) draws on extensive evidence about the structure and activities of large UK firms to make a case that what he calls the decentred or capital extensive firm is actually a particular kind of network in which significant power and strategic capacity is retained at the centre or 'hub'. This new, directed network, analogous to a conglomerate of business units, allows corporations to maintain or extend their spheres of interest, control information flows, as well as an ability to purchase and dispose of the portfolio of assets without bearing all the costs of traditional ownership. In acting in such ways, networks combine elements of hierarchy and market rather than constituting a separate means of co-ordination. He is also careful to remind us that it is dangerous for organisation theory to seek out one organisational type as exemplifying current trends.

Much of Adler's arguments about the beneficent properties of trust rely on dubious claims about the benign and widespread characteristics of knowledge in the economy (see previous chapter). However, even in knowledge-intensive firms, studies show that there is selective bureaucratisation (Kärreman, Sveningsson, and Alvesson, 2002). Alongside cultural co-ordination are more traditional modes of hierarchical control such as formalised systems, monitoring of behaviour and standardised rewards. As noted elsewhere:

> In general terms, we can identify a common search across manufacturing, private, and public services for more flexible, responsive ways of organizing, while maintaining a capacity for formalization and central control. Rather than the classic contingency argument of a fit between an organizational structure and its environment, it is better to see contemporary organizational forms as a series of hybrids, within which bureaucratic mechanisms normally remain dominant. (Alvesson and Thompson, 2005: 501)

This hybridity, confirmed in the previously-referred to case studies of Marchington and colleagues (2005), refer to co-ordination both within and across organisations and illustrates the capacity of bureaucratic forms to migrate, differentiate and combine with other mechanisms (see also Reed, 2005a). The discussion in this chapter by no means exhausts consideration of issues of bureaucracy and post-bureaucracy, particularly because, as Marchington and colleagues note (2005: 13), literatures on the projected rise of a networked society have been largely abstracted from employment issues. While we have focused here on questions of overall decision-making structures, in the following two chapters we shift to issues that include the prevalence and character of employment and work rules.

14 labour in the market: flexible futures?

Perspectives and practices on new forms of organisation necessarily move beyond issues of structure to the content of employment and work. The focus of this chapter is on the former and in particular on trends in labour markets and occupations. When examining such issues it is immediately apparent that flexibility has been the dominant language of organisational and economic change. During periods of significant change in work organisation, attention is often directed towards a particular phenomenon that is seen as an obstacle to efficiency. In the past it has been 'overmanning' or unofficial strikes. Since the 1980s, within the general reference to the defects of Taylorism and Fordism, it has been work and employment rules: regulatory mechanisms established by workers and managers to govern the workplace. The growth of non-standard forms of employment has been linked with the post-bureaucratic agenda of eroding formal and rule-bound modes of recruiting, mobilising and regulating labour (Felstead and Jewson, 1999a: 9).

As Rubery (2005: 31) notes, the Fordist model focused on male workers employed under standard employment contracts within a single organisation. Changes in the economy, occupational structure and sources of labour, notably the entry of large numbers of women into the job market, have brought that traditional model into question. The Fordist model inside the labour process also began to be regarded as problematic. At the start of the 1980s, *Business Week* (1983) celebrated a revolution against rules that place constraints on management's right to allocate and organise labour. As we have seen in previous chapters, under systems of bureaucratic organisation and control, employers had gained from rules by being able closely to specify job assignments and operate internal labour markets. Unions could restrict arbitrary power and enforce adherence to rules that benefited workers. In addition to such areas as task demarcation, seniority rules governing job protection, lay-offs and promotions were established. Because work rules were embodied in contractual relations, rights and grievance procedures, they gave unions bargaining power. Employment protection in law also enhanced status rights that limited what employers could gain from contractual exchange (Streek, 1987: 241–2). The flexibility offensive was directed against not just the 'rigidities' of work rules but also their high, often fixed, costs in terms of compensation and movement (Mangum and Mangum, 1986). Flexibility therefore required that the firm's internal and external boundaries be redrawn, bringing into question employment contracts and the location of work, as well as the previously-mentioned work rules (Guest, 1987). In this chapter we will, therefore, look at the discourses and practices of flexibility at the levels of the firm and the broader labour market. Some of these flow from the broader theories discussed in the previous chapter. As Fevre (2007) notes, many social theorists associated 'flexibilisation' with an 'age of insecurity'. Sharing Fevre's scepticism, this chapter will focus on empirical trends, both in the labour market and encompassing an examination of occupational shifts and particular arguments around the growth of new kinds of flexible employees who 'own' their own knowledge and skills – free or portfolio workers. It is worth mentioning what we won't be covering. Issues concerning flexibility of work relations will be covered primarily in the following chapter.

A central issue in studying employment systems and labour market institutions is that of cross-national comparison and variation. While we will try and note major variations, it is simply beyond our scope to outline and evaluate the variety of national systems and the welfare, labour supply and other arrangements that underpin them. We will focus primarily on the experience of the UK and on key national differences. With the latter in mind, a useful guideline is the delineation of two broadly different routes to post-Fordism by Koch (2004). *Capital-oriented flexibility* is geared towards the needs of employers and compels labour to adapt in largely involuntary ways. Employment for part-time and other categories is insecure, non-standard work such as self-employment increases, and the role of the state is either minimal or confined largely to providing legislation conducive to the powers of employers to hire and fire as they see fit. In contrast, *negotiated flexibility* is a subject of co-ordinated or central bargaining between the major economic actors. While non-standard forms of employment may increase, flexibility has defined limits and allows for better work-life balance. Legislation protects the rights of labour and welfare measures cushion the effects of insecurity, with active labour market policy facilitating re-training and relocation of workers.

The flexible firm model and beyond

> In the post-Fordist period, there has been a seemingly relentless move towards more diverse employment relationships, based on non-permanent contracts, agency work, self-employment, short, long, and indeed variable working hours. These tendencies, although widespread (Standing, 1999), have been greater in some societies than others, depending upon the form and strength of the regulatory system. (Rubery, 2005: 43)

The earliest and most widely used analytical framework for understanding the moves by employers to vary their workers and work was provided by the *flexible firm* model developed by Atkinson (1984) and the Institute for Manpower Studies (IMS). It is based on a break with existing unitary and hierarchical labour markets, relying on organisation of internal means of allocating labour, in order to create a core workforce and a cluster of peripheral employment relations. Put slightly differently, whereas previous labour market segmentation was largely outside the firm, the new arrangements redraw the boundaries to give employers more flexibility and less risk. Though not in itself a macro-, big-picture model, the flexible firm has been associated with post-Fordist perspectives; and, while derived from British experience, it has had a much wider influence, in part because the growth of flexible and non-standard labour has been global, though of course varied in character (see Felstead and Jewson, 1999b). We shall now look at some of the major types of flexibility considered in the model.

Functional flexibility refers to requirements that employees undertake a greater variety of tasks or roles. Core workers gain greater job security in return for managers' right to redeploy them between activities and tasks as products and production requires. Often referred to as multi-skilling or multi-tasking this issue belongs in the sphere of work relations and will be considered in the next chapter. At the level of the firm, *numerical* flexibility is the capacity to vary the headcount according to changes in the level of demand so that there is an exact match between the numbers needed and employment; or as one senior manager bluntly put it, 'A workforce that can be picked up and put down whenever I need them' (quoted in Burchell *et al.*, 1999: 8). At a broader societal level governments and other state-level economic actors can also seek to implement polices that create more flexible labour markets, either from the employer interest (e.g. making it easier to dismiss), or in favour of the employee (e.g. the right to be given flexible hours to fit in with outside responsibilities).

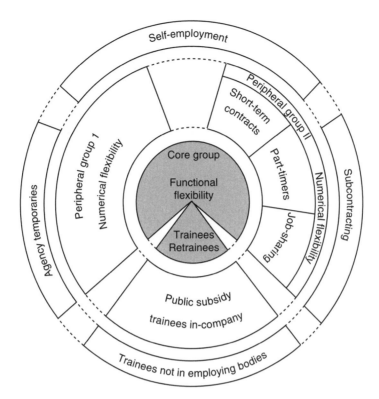

Figure 14.1 **Model of the flexible firm**

Source: C. G. Magnum (1986) 'Temporary Work: The Flipside of Job Security', *International Journal of Manpower*, 17. 1: 14.

Early UK surveys for the IMS showed that most larger firms claimed to have increased numerical flexibility, though sectoral variations indicated a predominance in service work (Atkinson and Gregory, 1986). Substantial, if uneven, growth across Europe was confirmed by a range of bodies, including the International Labour Organization (Standing, 1986. However, it is also widely recognised that accurate comparative mapping of changes is difficult, given different methods of data collection, varying legal and academic definitions and overlapping of categories. Even within national contexts, it is important to disaggregate the categories and look at long-term trends. For the UK, P. Robinson (1999) produced some important correctives to early and over-generalised images of numerical flexibility. Using Labour Force Survey data from 1979–97, he shows that full-time permanent employment has indeed declined from around 75 per cent to 62 per cent. The share of part-time employment rose correspondingly by 8 per cent, self-employment by 5 per cent and temporary work by 2 per cent. However, the small print indicates that the decline of full-time work occurred most sharply during the 1980s recession and now slowed considerably, while the non-standard categories all show different patterns. Part-time employment has not only been growing throughout the period, it has been doing so steadily from 1945. Self-employment grew rapidly in the 1980s, but has now come to a halt, while the growth of temporary employment was largely a 1990s phenomenon.

So what happened? With respect to part-time employment, the proportion for women remained largely stable, but doubled among men. However, much of this can be accounted for by the emergence of students onto the labour market as higher education has expanded in the 1990s. The rise in self-employment to

13 per cent of the UK labour force affected most sectors, rather than those that have traditionally used such arrangements, suggesting that contracting out functions and services was a general, though limited, trend (Clutterbuck, 1985). There has been a big growth of temporary help service agencies in a number of countries, notably the US and that growth is no longer confined to marginal or manual workers in manufacturing, or to seasonal work. The sharpest increases are among professionals in financial services and the public sector, such as lecturers on renewable or rolling contracts.

Robinson's interpretation of the data, like other recent work, challenged a number of the received wisdoms in the flexibility debate. First, 'the more dramatic assertions about the arrival of a "core–periphery" model in employment relationships find relatively little backing in the data' (1999: 90). Robinson's judgements coincided with other academic critiques. Teasdale's analysis of UK Labour Force Survey data sums the picture up succinctly: 'there is little sign of irrevocable long term trends or of recent dramatic shifts ... [People] will continue to spend most of their working lives in "conventional" jobs as full time permanent employees. Indeed with women spending more of their life in the labour market, the conventional job will be the experience of a greater proportion of the population' (2000: 26). An earlier, influential and highly critical examination of the evidence in relation to the peripheral category was made by Pollert (1988a; 1988b). She pointed out that evidence has tended to conflate long-term changes and standard practices to vary production with genuinely new employment patterns, an argument supported by Marginson's (1991) distinction between high level of use and change in use of non-standard employment. Pollert went on to use a variety of sources to show that most of the figures for temporary, part-time, homeworking, self-employment and sub-contracted work were greatly exaggerated. Again, where there has been an increase it is often on the basis of already-established practices, and on the basis of state sponsorship in the public sector rather than management strategy in the private. Finally, the use of 'peripheral' itself does not really do justice to the centrality of such forms of work, particularly that done by women, to a modern capitalist economy.

What about more recent trends? There is, at least with respect to the UK, something of a paradox. As White and colleagues (2004: 25) observe, 'Virtually all employers have this kind of flexibility in their kit-bag ready for use.' The results of a Department of Trade and Industry survey in 2005 was written up as 'the demise of the traditional nine-to-five job' (*The Guardian*, 5 July 2005). Amongst other things, the proportion of workplaces where 'some staff' have switched from full to part-time hours has risen from 46 per cent to two-thirds. White and colleagues were drawing on their own survey – Change in Employer Practices (CEP) – one of a number done in the recent period that also include Working in Britain 2000 (WIB) and the 1999 Labour Force Survey (LFS) by the government Office of National Statistics. Nolan and Woods (2003) give an overview of the findings. Four in five workplaces have some part-time employees; four in five workplaces use at least one of temporary staff supplied by agencies; their own temporary employees; people employed on a casual basis; freelance (self-employed) workers, homeworkers or outworkers. Outsourcing has been adopted in every part of industry, with at least 50 per cent of workplaces outsourcing four or more services. A number of types of flexible labour appear to be at least complementary, if not strategic. Workplaces that are using three or more of the five main types of flexible labour amount to over a quarter (28 per cent) of the total.

Nevertheless, full-time work remains dominant, with the WIB survey estimating the ratio to be 9 out of every 10 employees, compared with 8 out of 10 in 1992. 'Some staff' can mean quite small numbers. Fixed-term and temporary contracts account for a smaller proportion of employees than in the late 1990s. More importantly and paradoxically, the surveys reveal that the use of flexible labour is hitting a ceiling, with the number of employers with increases offset by nearly as many others who are cutting back their usage.

As Figure 14.2 demonstrates, in the UK at least, there is little evidence of substantial casualisation and the figures cast doubt on the more speculative social theorists (e.g. Beck, 1992; 2000) who have talked about the ' "Brazilianization" of labour markets and the end of the work society'. Of course, Britain is only one country. Category by category, the uses of flexible labour differ markedly across Europe, as Figure 14.3 below charts with respect to temporary labour.

Some of the explanation of differences can be located in welfare state and legal policy that gives employers differential incentives to employ labour in particular contractual categories, but other business and sectoral factors help explain the patterns. The key point, however, as Fevre's (2007) review of the evidence across the OECD shows, is that there is no long-term secular increase in temporary work, though there have been short-term increases and more durable higher incidences in countries such as Spain, Portugal and Poland. As he says, if there is an age of insecurity, it isn't in the citadels of advanced capitalism that the social theorists claim to have discovered it.

Despite these wise words of caution, the flexibility picture is broader than the proportions of categories of non-standard labour. Job security has been a central and highly contested issue in academic and policy circles. The early debates on the impact of flexibility were populated by negative accounts of the re-hiring of redundant steel and other workers under sub-contractors with significant loss of pay, benefits and health and safety protection (Fevre, 1986; Mather, 1987); as well as the most dramatic example of the Burton Group in the UK, who announced in 1993 that they were turning most of their retail employees into part-timers who had to wait each day for a phone call to indicate whether they would be needed! The replacement of some permanent with casualised contracts seemed to be a worldwide trend, even in Japan, the home of 'lifetime employment' (at least for core workers). Studies indicated that deliberate measures to erode employment security and increase the number of workers on non-standard contracts were characteristic of a growing number of large Japanese corporations (Kyotani, 1999). Yet if we measure

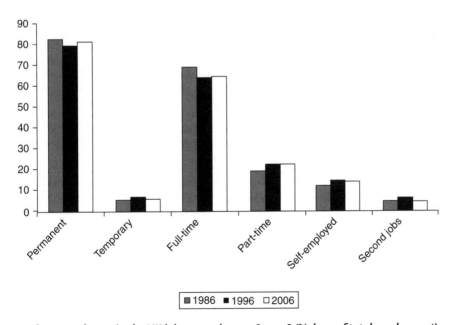

Figure 14.2 **Employment change in the UK labour market 1996–2006 (%share of total employment)**
Source: from Coats (2009) with permission.

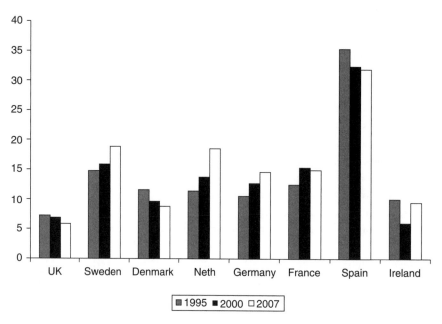

Figure 14.3 **Temporary work as a percentage of total employment**
Source: from Coats (2009) with permission.

labour market insecurity by job tenure, the picture does not look so gloomy. Evidence from the UK and other countries (Doogan, 2001; Nolan and Wood, 2003; Green, 2006; Auer, 2006) is that the length of job tenure is relatively stable or increasing (in the UK on average from six years and two months to seven years and four months), though that disguises a small decline for men and significant improvement for women. There is admittedly large country variation, but 'the long term employment relationship is still the dominating form of employment in many European countries and is a long way from disappearing' (Auer, 2006: 25).

There are also alterations in the use of time, as employers seek to vary attendance in order to meet fluctuations in workload and gain general control over time scheduling. Some high-profile cases of zero-hours contracts, such as those in the Burton Group and Burger King, have received considerable publicity. But instances where employees are required to be available for work solely at their employer's discretion are the exception (Cave, 1997). More frequent practices have included buying-out overtime and breaks or ending them as rights, and introducing round-the-clock, round-the-shift systems, with the use of part-time and temporary labour to cover peak demand (Yates, 1986; CAITS, 1986; Wainwright, 1987). It is also worth noting that time flexibility may not always be captured in contractual arrangements. There is also evidence of workers being asked to significantly change their hours and availability as a result of supply chain pressures exerted by large retailers (Newsome *et al.*, 2009).

Home and teleworking

Images of this kind of work have ranged from manufacturing homeworkers, for example women domestic outworkers in sectors such as textiles, electrical components and toys (Mitter, 1986; Allen and Workowtiz, 1987), to glamorous networkers from Rank Xerox, F International and ICL linked by computer in 'electronic cottages' (Control Data Corporation, 1985). While the former pattern has involved up to one in twenty firms (ACAS, 1988), it has been easy to dismiss the latter as exotic exceptions. However, advances in communication technology and the Internet have put virtual working more firmly on the agenda, with commentators highlighting the benefits for the co-ordination of teleworkers (Mirchandani, 1999) and professionals in 'virtual', cross-functional teams in and across work units (Nandhakumar, 1999). If we examine evidence from recent UK surveys, it seems to point to a growth in the high-tech rather than low-tech. At 7 per cent, WIB 2000 survey indicates that there has not been a significant increase in the number of employees working from home. Taking a narrower definition of those whose main work is in the home, Teasdale argues that 'homeworking proper' constitutes just 600,000 people. Noting that these numbers have not changed, he notes that, 'It would appear that teleworking has changed how homeworkers do their job rather than making more homeworking possible and moving jobs from larger workplaces' (2000: 24). Nevertheless, drawing on their CEP survey, White and colleagues (2004) argue that homeworking is the exception to the current plateau, with one in three managers forecasting an increased usage in workplaces that do not currently use homeworkers.

As with other categories of non-standard labour, we have to be extremely careful about the nature and adequacy of the data collection. As Boreham and colleagues (2008) note, definitions are inconsistent across studies and official national statistics. The key issue is whether people are counted if they work at home for any length of time or some more restrictive category is used. So, European data from the ECaTT project found striking levels of homeworking, with growth rates between 20 per cent and 30 per cent in countries such as France and the UK. EC figures in 2002 indicated that counting all forms, 13 per cent of employed people were teleworkers. Impressive as these data are, they need to be disaggregated with some care. However, that figure falls to 2.1 per cent if the criterion is regular (at least one day a week) work of this kind. Clearly there is a difference between the categories of home- and teleworker.

Episodic telework is much more feasible for professional workers who are subject to output rather than process controls. This is reinforced by the fact that workplaces with high levels of ICT are at the forefront of the trend (White *et al.*, 2004), suggesting that employers of high-tech workers feel able (because of the surveillance technology) and compelled (for cost-cutting reasons) to shift more activities to teleworking: 'teleworkers are overwhelmingly likely to be male, predominantly in the 30–49 age category, and to come from significantly higher educational backgrounds. They are disproportionately drawn from the Financial and Business Services sector and are much more likely to work for large organizations' (Boreham *et al.*, 2008: 104). This move of the debate from margin to mainstream is a reflection of its strong link to the wider theme of knowledge work and employment, which we will discuss later. We also discuss some of the psychological conditions and consequences of homeworking in Chapter 23.

Reflections on flexibility

To return to the earlier paradox, the evidence shows that flexibility is widespread, but that we need to be cautious about the extent and spread of the various forms. Felstead and Jewson noted of the above trends, 'A common feature of all these types of employment is that they diverge from the pattern which became regarded in mid-twentieth century advanced capitalist economies as the "norm" ' (1999: 1). Yet, if flexible labour, albeit uneven is a normal feature of contemporary labour markets, it is not viable any longer to go on talking about 'standard' employment, particularly as the increasing amount of part-time work is driven by female preferences and that much of that work becomes either permanent or full-time (Bach, 2003). As flexibility spreads across categories and sectors it also make it harder to sustain a clear differentiation between core and periphery. For example, fast food chains have been one of the fastest growing parts of the economy. But this 'core' sector, employing mainly the young, black people and women on part-time and unsocial hours, has workers with decidedly peripheral employment conditions. Alternatively, one can have regular, continuous employment such as that experienced by contract cleaners, but still be insecure due to the particularistic choices available to clients and incoming management (Allen and Henry, 1994: 9); or be performing core functions such as research and development, but gradually be losing privileged status due to competitive, external contracting (Whittington, 1991a).

Nevertheless, some commentators see an additional reason for scepticism – hyping flexibility and over-emphasising job insecurity tells us more about the social-theoretic enterprises of some well-known writers than it does about the evidence, with the additional risk of serving a neo-liberal agenda that places the juggernauts of the market, competition and globalisation ahead of political choices and regulation (Doogan, 2005; Fevre, 2007). In a rejoinder to Fevre, Conley (2008), however, highlights a common concern with the secondary analysis of large-scale survey data, that it aggregates what in practice may be quite diverse trends and experiences. She provides evidence that temporary work in the UK is mostly in certain public services (e.g. education, health) and in distribution hotels and restaurants – sectors where you find a disproportionately large number of women. This reinforces a long-standing critique that flexibility analyses tend to set aside the issues of gender and ethnicity by recasting dual labour markets as benign, progressive or inevitable (Pollert, 1988a).

However, whilst, part of the strategic rationale for numerical flexibility was to externalise some of the uncertainty, costs and risks to a variety of holders of labour service, we should not assume that potential employees do not see benefit in some of these arrangements. Earlier UK Labour Force data showed that only 12 per cent of part-timers would prefer full-time work. In contrast, 39 per cent of those in temporary employment were 'involuntary' and current data continue to show that many people on temporary contracts would like full-time work. The example of part-time work shows that increased flexibility may be positive for the choices of some potential employees and this appears to support the argument of Hakim (1990; 1996; 2004) that many women choose employment which social scientists have often labelled as peripheral or belonging to secondary labour markets (though see critique in Chapter 10). The example of temporary work, meanwhile, indicates a degree of constrained choice. Both bring into focus an important general lesson. The goals, impacts and experiences of flexible labour markets are extremely heterogeneous – hardly surprising given the range of practices, actors and institutions involved. This diversity has led some commentators to attach considerable scepticism to any claims of coherent model, strategy and novelty surrounding flexibility and the flexible firm (Legge, 1995). Such points are well taken, though, as Proctor and colleagues (1994) point out, it is too easy to adopt stringent criteria for strategic intent by employers that prevent a recognition of emergent strategy demonstrated through consistent patterns and decisions. This judgement reflects the broader argument about strategy and control made in Chapter 8.

Even if the numbers covered by particular types of flexibility and their coherence as a package have been exaggerated, there is clearly a 'dark side' that affects a considerable minority of labour market participants. For example, Conley (2008) also notes that 52 per cent of migrant labour from Poland and other accession states are employed in temporary work. The current figures also reveal that 5 per cent of employees – mainly in cleaning, catering and personal services – hold more than one job (Nolan and Wood, 2003). Whilst this figure is unchanged, it does remind us that there is a minority of workers, mostly at the sharp end of the service sector, who have to juggle stressful, low-status and poorly paid jobs, often with no employment rights or trade union protection (Philpot, 2000; Pollert, 2009; Bok and Simmons, 2009). These conditions have been brought to academic and public attention in well-crafted journalistic accounts such as those by Toynbee (2003) and Ehrenreich (2001) in the UK and USA respectively, but can also be found in recent case study research on care, hospitality and other workers (Bolton and Houlihan, 2009). Such examples follow long-established trends. Most of the worst aspects have always been at the 'periphery'. Trends towards decentralisation in industries such as clothing resulted in a modern 'burgeoning sweatshop economy' based on women and ethnic minority workers (Mitter, 1986). Super-exploited workers at the end of clothing supply chains certainly counter images of the happy, autonomous employee in the electronic cottage (Allen and Wolkowtiz, 1987; Phizacklea, 1987), but we have to acknowledge that non-standard does not necessarily mean casual or low-skill. Rosenberg and Lapidus (1999) demonstrate that for the US, while contingent workers often lose out comparatively in terms of pay and benefits, there is huge diversity, including independent contractors who have relatively beneficial work and employment conditions. This echoes a wider theme that we will pick up and evaluate in the next section.

Occupational change: knowledge work and portfolio people

We can ask the question of what the contemporary labour market actually look like from a different angle, that of occupational change. There is a clear clash of conceptions in this area between knowledge-economy perspectives and the hourglass economy thesis. The former has certainly been the dominant orthodoxy for some time now and we can identify two claims about the shape of the labour market. First, that increasing knowledge intensity in the economy – the extent to which complex knowledge forms the core source of value – leads to the spread of jobs and occupations based on knowledge work. Knowledge work generalises across increasing territories the kind of employment relationships and task structures that allow for creative application and development of that knowledge. It provides the main engine of growth in the modern economy, spreading high-skill, high-expertise employment outside the traditional professional high-tech heartlands. In particular, the search for more creativity and participation from routine employees through devices such as teamworking compels employers to devolve responsibilities and increase trust (Frenkel *et al.*, 1995). The second claim is more specific and perhaps more modest, that a fast-growing and central part of the labour market are portfolio workers. Part of the logic of this argument derives from the notion that one of the characteristics of knowledge is that it belongs to the knower and moves with the individual rather than being specified and controlled by the organisation. This interpretation tends to treat this kind of numerical flexibility (outsourcing and homeworking) less as a management strategy and more as a choice of individual 'employees' cashing in on their knowledge, and the dependency of organisations upon it. Hamel and Prahalad (1996: 238) refer to 'a world of independent labour contractors'. While this may be something of an exaggeration, plenty of other commentators would regard it as a trend. Handy (1995), Leadbetter (1999) and Pink (2001) link the emergence of a knowledge economy to the growth of portfolio of free agent workers, who will work either simultaneously or sequentially for a number of employers. In this context, short-term contracts no longer have a negative connotation, as they reflect the rapidly-changing business environment, with its emphasis on projects and teams.

Let's take the latter claim first. The new scenario is said to be creating opportunities for a bargain to be struck between organisations wanting expertise and commitment, and highly mobile professionals who can use their knowledge to increase employability and build portfolio careers within occupational communities (Heckscher, 1997). There are certainly some glowing reports of the work conditions and employment packages of highly mobile net workers in the US, of whom 15 per cent are apparently offered free massages and 31 per cent free dry cleaning (Guardian, 21 September 2000). We have already examined evidence to show that in the UK and Europe both temporary work and home or teleworkers are relatively small and heterogeneous categories. However, we know from recent UK surveys that high-ICT workplaces are more likely to have people on temporary contracts, to use agency temps and self-employed freelancers (White *et al.*, 2004: 28). We also know that in most OECD countries and in the US in particular temporary-help employment work and the labour-market intermediation agencies that supply it surged dramatically in the 1990s (OECD, 2002). Of all the jobs produced in the US in this period, the temporary-help industry was responsible for 10 per cent of them. There is also evidence for the growth of highly skilled portfolio workers from Barley and Kunda's (2004) study of itinerant contractors in California's Silicon Valley. Many ICT workers were increasingly turning to organising their working life through staffing agencies and horizontal, peer-based networks. Supportive evidence on the positive effects of temporary-help agencies on occupational mobility and job upgrading also comes from a recent Spanish study (García-Pérez and Muñoz-Bullón, 2005).

The issue remains, however, of how to interpret these trends. They certainly show that the association between labour market flexibility and low-skilled, low-wage lobs can no longer be sustained, given that scientists, engineers, teachers, ICT specialists nurses are among the ranks of temporary employees (White *et al.*, 2004). However, as the same authors point out, the use of temporary and outsourced labour in some categories may also indicate that 'the belief that ICT is a gateway to the promised land of high skilled knowledge work may well be plain wrong' (2003: 38). Other studies also show that a prime motive of using agency temps (in high- and low-skilled occupations) was to reduced the pressure on companies to raise the wages of their own workers and avoid the costs of firing new ones (Houseman, Kalleberg and Erickcek, 2003). Finally and perhaps of most importance, the figures generally do not tell us whether those involved are reluctant conscripts or enthusiastic adherents. What we can say is that there is a huge difference in significance between the casualties or survivors of corporate restructuring, and the smaller number of people with scarce skills who can set themselves up as independent contractors. In the above examples, the employer-led argument concerning numerical flexibility can be seen to still have some purchase, reinforcing earlier evidence that the growth in many forms of contingent work is primarily driven by changing employer preferences (Goldin and Applebaum, 1992; Burchell *et al.*, 1999).

In sum, there are more self-managing portfolio workers, but they are relatively few in number. Those whose knowledge is scarce and independent enough to make free agents are insufficient to make a generalisable argument across the contemporary economy.

Finally, what about claims that knowledge work is the engine of growth in the new economy? As Warhurst and Thompson (1998; 2006) demonstrate, at the heart of NEO arguments are a host of conceptual and empirical confusions, many of which derive from the use of proxies such as qualifications, occupations and use of ICT to calculate (and consequently exaggerate) the exent of knowledge work. For example, there is a consistent conflation of knowledge and information. Lists of 'knowledge workers' (for example, Handy, 1995: 4) consist of heterogeneous occupations who have little in common other than handling information. Financial services, for example, frequently require little more of workers than information transfer – the inputting of customer details onto pre-programmed screens and software. As even an exponent of the knowledge economy, Robert Reich, observes, 'The foot soldiers of the information economy are the hordes of data processors stationed in back offices with computer terminals linked to worldwide information banks' (1993: 23). It is also easy to conflate the production of high-tech goods with the need for a workforce of highly skilled workers (Keep and Mayhew, 1999). Even knowledge-intensive firms 'actually require quite small numbers of highly skilled employees once the major information transfer technologies have been put in place. A very small élite of system designers and strategic managers is required, whilst the globally dispersed plants and offices can be serviced by workers with very much less training and knowledge' (Ackroyd and Lawrenson, 1996: 157).

Occupations requiring 'thinking' skills will expand, but that expansion will be limited in scope and potential for employment growth (Brown and Hesketh, 2004). Even if we take occupations as the measure, 'the proportion of the (UK) workforce engaged in the professions, scientific and technical occupations has increased over the 1990s from 34 to 37 per cent' (Nolan and Wood, 2003: 170). While some of these are new economy jobs, two in five of this increase is accounted for by expansion of the established professions. Similar estimates for Canada (Livingstone and Scholtz, 2006) and the USA (Henwood, 2003: 72) put the figures for knowledge work at about 25 per cent of current figures. At the same time, Nolan and Wood (2003) also show that the figures for manual workers has been 'remarkably stable' at around 40 per cent of total employment. This figure expands considerably when routine clerical and secretarial work is added in. In other words, most employment growth, actual and projected, is in service work, and within that predominantly at the low end in serving, guarding, cleaning, waiting and helping in the private health and care services, as well as retail and hospitality industries – both in the US and the UK (Crouch, 1999; Brown and Hesketh 2004; Warhurst and Thompson 2006). Using US figures, Henwood makes a similar observation. Comparing the relatively limited projected growth of 'infotech' employees, he says, 'A selection of mundane old economy jobs – retail salespersons, cashiers, telemarketers, truck drivers and office clerks, who on balance earn a third of what IT workers do – account for the same share of growth' (2003: 73).

Much of this constitutes a growth in no or at least limited knowledge work, if measured in conventional terms. Recent skill surveys reveal that 41 per cent of personal services, 62 per cent of sales and 80 per cent of 'other occupations' require no qualifications for entry (Brown and Keep, 1999). When managers were asked what proportion of their workforce could be described as skilled (such as professional, associate professional, technical or craft), there were some startling results. For example, 40 per cent of managers in wholesaling/retailing and 57 per cent of managers in financial services said that they had no skilled non-managerial employees (Cully *et al.*, 1998, and see Keep, 2000). There is an increasing emphasis from many employers on employee attitudes, character and even their 'aesthetic' qualities rather than formal knowledge and skills (Nickson *et al.*, 2001; Henwood, 2003). Such facts are almost completely unacknowledged by NEO theorists, who fail to recognise the diversity of employment and skill trends. Henwood concludes that the American economy 'produces a fair number of high-end jobs, a lot of low-end jobs, but not much in the middle' (Henwood, 2003: 73). This judgement is consistent with the increasingly influential hourglass economy thesis that updates a traditional skill polarisation argument to describe an occupational structure where expansion takes place at either end, but is weighted towards the bottom (Nolan, 2003; Goos and Manning, 2007). This argument is persuasive, but as a metaphor may over-simplify current trends. As P. Anderson (2009) demonstrates, if the UK standard occupational classification is used, the proportion of jobs in 'intermediate occupations' has remained relatively unchanged, though there has been a downward trend in skilled trades and a rise in associate technical and professional categories. Such a reconfiguration of middle ranks of the occupational hierarchy is, however, consistent with a critique of over-optimistic knowledge economy or other upskilling perspectives.

Conclusions

> The extremely widespread use of flexible labour and outsourcing show that the cost-pressures and uncertainties of a more competitive world have penetrated to virtually every corner of the economy and even affects the kinds of work done by managers and professional staff. (White *et al.*, 2004: 38)

The above comment returns to the earlier paradox – if flexible labour is so widespread, why is it so uneven across categories and contexts? Part of the answer is that in this chapter we have been looking at numerical flexibility, which is only part of the overall package. Perhaps the packaging is part of the problem. Like flexible specialisation, discussed in the previous chapter, the flexible firm has borne too much of a conceptual and empirical burden. Though less sweeping in its range, the latter made claims of sufficient strength and visibility to attract a degree of criticism similar to that of flexible specialisation or post-Fordism. Pollert (1988a; 1988b) argued that both share vital commonalities, including a celebration of the market and consumer sovereignty, legitimation of the view that the solution to organisational and economic problems lies in altering the behaviour of labour, the resurrection of a dual labour-market analysis, and a futurological discourse underwritten by a post-industrial analysis in which flexibility marks the vital break from the past. In a memorable phrase, Pollert observes that both flexibility arguments fuse 'description, prediction and prescription' (1988a: 43). However, because one is a management policy model and the other a grand theory, the flexible firm can be utilised in some instances as an explanatory tool, without all the burden of any wider conceptual and historical baggage (Proctor *et al.*, 1994). We shall return to this point later.

Even if we use more conceptually and empirically specific frameworks to understand labour market flexibility, variations between countries make it difficult to identify clear patterns. As Rubery (2005: 35) notes, 'International comparisons of labour markets have also called into question the ubiquity of the flexible firm approach and demonstrated that there is more than one way of responding to the new market challenges.' Once universalistic claims are scaled down, it is possible to identify more 'local' flexibility strategies. As we observed earlier, the state as well as state or employers can be key actors in shifting the balance of power through flexibility in labour markets. For example, neo-liberal governments such as those of New Zealand in the 1990s and Australia under the recent Howard administrations, embraced labour-market deregulation and legal weakening of employee protection. A reciprocal growth of employment insecurity and some forms of non-standard work were among the outcomes (Ryan, 1992; Burgess and Strachan, 1999). However, there is no consistent relationship between the degree of regulation of labour markets and the extent of non-standard employment. Highly stylised models such as Koch's (2004) distinction between capital-oriented and negotiated flexibility are, at best, ends of a spectrum. Regulated markets such as those in Southern Europe and Scandinavia have had higher rates in many categories of flexible employment than the more deregulated UK and US. This is not as surprising as it appears. We need to focus on employment regimes as the huge variations in patterns of standard and non-standard employment derive from complex 'incentives' given to employers and potential employees alike to engage in different types of labour-market action (Coats, 2009):

> Not surprisingly, the study of de- and re-regulation from a comparative perspective has brought to light deviations from the theoretically constructed post Fordist development paths. Just as their Fordist predecessors, recent Western European growth strategies must be understood as results of negotiations and struggles between different classes and social groups, with concrete outcomes varying from country to country. (Littlewood *et al.*, 2004: 27)

Tight regulation of standard employment may benefit those in work, but therefore encourage firms to take people on a temporary or other flexible basis (Cousins, 1999). A new policy hybrid – flexicurity – has emerged on the back of the success of Denmark and to a lesser extent the Netherlands in combining relative freedoms for employers to hire and fire with generous benefits for employees, plus strong unions (Westergaard-Neilson, 2008; Salverda *et al.*, 2008; Muffels and Luijkx, 2008). This is also confirmed in

Auer's (2006) International Labour Organization research. 'Protected flexibility' has to be conceived as dynamically distributed across the life cycle of individuals, with more flexible jobs for younger workers, more stability once family formation starts, with protected transitions between job changes. Irrespective of the merits of flexicurity, patterns of labour-market flexibility reflect the interaction of three main forces: general trends in capitalist political economy, the negotiation of local social settlements between the key actors (and their available power resources), and the general state of the economy. The latter often provides a simple explanation of why a particular form of non-standard labour increase or declines in usage. These interactions may also apply to other employment trends, whereas patterns of work relations – such as those we label functional flexibility – may be the outcome of a narrower set of capital–labour relations within particular firms and sectors. Researchers who have argued for a scaled-down, less prescriptive version of the flexible firm, are often drawing on analysis of such practices. Indeed, using evidence from a database of large British manufacturing firms, Ackroyd and Proctor (1998) argue that a distinctive pattern of production at plant level can be identified and described as 'the new flexible firm' (see also Proctor, 2005). Such arguments form part of the much wider picture examined in the next chapter.

15 work systems: restructuring the division of labour

The labour process is a vital arena if the promises of organisational and workplace transformation in a 'new economy' are to be fulfilled (Adams and Demaiter, 2008: 351). Advocates of change argue that practices have to shift from narrow, demarcated tasks to fully flexible, interchangeable labour, while employees' attitudes have to be move from grudging compliance to high commitment. In the original 'design chain' of flexible specialisation, discussed in Chapter 12, the last steps in the sequence were a high-trust strategy based on skill upgrading and worker autonomy. Similar themes reappeared in talk of the primacy of horizontal co-ordination in knowledge work, as well as the growth of functional flexibility.

Outside management concerns, broader social science debates in this area have traditionally focused on the trajectory of skills – whether they are being upgraded or degraded – and what the possibilities are for quality of work and working life. Though important, a focus on skills in isolation from the broader division of labour is conceptually and empirically limited. This chapter conceives of the appropriate territory as being a work system in which the main issues are skills and tasks, autonomy and control, work intensity and work-life boundaries.

In more recent times many of these issues have been packaged in a broader guise of 'high road' strategies for workplace transformation and competition based more on quality than cost, with the 'highs' being commitment, involvement, skill, and performance, in addition to trust (Applebaum and Batt, 1994). We begin by considering how general ideas about work design and quality of working life (QWL) have travelled along and towards this 'road'.

Work redesign: from QWL to teams and high-performance work systems

Description or advocacy of reform of work organisation is hardly new. In particular, the language and practices of contemporary practices seem to be continuations of the 1970s quality of working life (QWL) or work-humanisation initiatives. QWL had long been a generic or umbrella term subsuming anything from job enrichment to participation schemes. Yet we know that despite the extensive publicity for high-profile cases such as Volvo Kalmar and some reports of gains in productivity and quality (Daniel and McIntosh, 1972), by the end of that decade most of the work-reform initiatives had diminished or disappeared (Ramsay, 1991). It is therefore tempting to dismiss the new language and practices as a rebranding exercise. Yet the supporters of such approaches would argue that the speedy reappearance of new forms of employee involvement through quality circles, team briefings and other initiatives in the early 1980s showed the persistence of attempts by employers to create new work paradigms that could move beyond the limits of Taylorism and Fordism.

New forms of involvement derived in part from technology such as flexible manufacturing systems and production processes, notably just-in-time (JIT) systems (Sayer, 1986; Tailby and Turnbull, 1987). Under JIT workers are expected to do on-the-spot problem-solving and therefore to use their tacit knowledge.

Indeed they have little choice given that reduced buffer stocks mean subsequent activities would break down without such action. That such systems were largely Japanese in origin indicates where the threat was coming from. The spread of quality circles and mid-1980s initiatives such as GM's QWL and Ford's Employee Involvement programmes in the US indicates the extent to which emulation of a perceived Japanese model was high on the agenda of Western manufacturers. The comparatively short-lived nature of many such initiatives by no means ended the influence. Since that period the spread of Japanese transplants into the US and Europe has been extensive, and their apparent success led to further pressures that combine demonstration effect and emulation. The transferable ingredients of Japanese productive expertise were repackaged as the system of *lean production* pioneered by Toyota, particularly in *The Machine That Changed the World* by Womack, Roos and Jones (1990). We discussed the issue of transferability in Chapter 6, but as a design template, lean production conforms to the anti-bureaucracy menu by stressing that in this brave new world, firms will employ teams of multiskilled workers whose jobs will be more challenging and productive, and carry more responsibilities.

The range of new involvement and communication practices had limited impact and sustainability, not simply because they were often imitative, but because 'these schemes tended to be "bolted-on" rather than integral to the work process' (Marchington and Wilkinson, 1998: 16). TQM programmes promised a broader, more holistic approach than localised quality circle techniques (Hill, 1991). In the pursuit of the goal of continuous improvement in the production of goods and services, TQM differed by starting from the top and cascading through the organisation. Flatter structures and reduced hierarchy develop as workers take increased responsibility. The consultant-driven (Hammer and Champy, 1993) emergence of business process re-engineering (BPR) continued a holistic approach, promising that a focus on processes rather than functions would flatten hierarchies and produce complex jobs for smart people. Though BPR spoke the standard language of HRM and post-bureaucracy, its route to competitive advantage lay in an integration of work and technical system redesign (Greenbaum, 1998: 136). Given the history of organisational change, it is hardly surprising that BPR initiatives squeezed out 'slack' with little consideration of the human dimension or consequences. Subsequent criticism and retreat meant that the management fad had reached burnout in about five years (Buchanan, 2000: 26).

As the acronyms have come and gone, teamworking has emerged as the core of work reform and the 'heart of the lean factory' (Womack, Roos and Jones, 1990: 99). The managerial literature is full of inflated empowerment rhetoric and exhortations to create self-managing teams so that 'no boss is required' (Dumaine, 1990: 40). There is, in fact, a wide consensus that current teamworking is distinguished from its 1970s predecessor by its much more instrumental, pragmatic orientation, with little concern for job enrichment and industrial democracy (A. Jenkins, 1994; Applebaum *et al.*, 2000; Proctor and Mueller, 2000). Mathews argues that contemporary initiatives fundamentally reorganise the process of work: 'In place of command and control structures designed to enforce rigidity and compliance, the new production systems call for management that offers facilitation, guidance and co-ordination between self-managing groups of employees who are capable of looking after the details of production themselves' (1993: 7).

There is certainly considerable evidence for the *spread* of initiatives, as 'teams have progressively replaced the individual as the unit of work organisation' (P. Adler, 1997: 62). Adler notes that the proportion of leading US firms claiming to utilise self-managed work teams has risen from 6 per cent in 1979 to 28 per cent in 1987 and 68 per cent in 1995. In Britain, the WERS survey reported 74 per cent of workplaces had teamworking in 1998 (Cully *et al.*, 1998), and that figure remained stable at 72 per cent in the 2004 equivalent (Kersley *et al.*, 2006). One of the problems in assessing the spread and character of the practices is to know what we are comparing across time and territory (Benders, 2004).

However, there seems little doubt that despite teamwork being continually 'rediscovered' over three decades, the current wave is proving more durable (Buchanan, 2000). That durability is primarily associated with employers becoming convinced of the 'bottom-line' benefits of teamworking, rather than any distinctive job redesign objectives. In an authoritative review of the evidence, Batt and Doellgast (2005) note that studies in a variety of sectors claim better performance through practices such as information sharing and problem-solving. Interestingly there is some agreement across managerial and some radical commentators that management in an increasing number of companies has had some success in devolving responsibilities to the group, getting employees to think and act like managers, and thus generating a genuine sense of shared values (Wickens, 1992; Barker, 1993; Sewell, 1998). In this way the workgroup can be used to redirect collective goals towards the company in a way that fulfils the old human relations dream, though the idea that employees have internalised management values through teams is, perhaps, over-exaggerated (see Chapters 8 and 24).

For all the spread and significance of teamwork, not everyone would consider it *in itself* to be the bedrock of work redesign. The idea of HPWS, developed primarily in the USA (Osterman, 1994; Applebaum and Batt, 1994; Lawler *et al.*, 1995; Huselid, 1995), is based on the *interlocking* character of the management of work, organisation and employment. Work organisation, as already outlined, depends upon 'the decentralisation of the gathering and processing of information to non-managerial employees' (Appelbaum and Berg, 1999: 1), with participation and problem-solving enabling front-line workers to contribute to operational decisions and performance. Work-based teams are supplemented by off-line problem-solving and project groups are needed. Such practices are reinforced by skill-formation strategies based on enhanced training in social and technical skills, plus more rigorous and selective recruitment, and incentives that make rewards contingent upon team or company performance, whether that be merit pay, profit sharing or group incentives. Finally, trust is enhanced by employees being encouraged to become stakeholders in the firm, primarily by the development of a mutual gains approach that, among other things, seeks to replace adversarial industrial relations by partnership and participation (Bluestone and Bluestone, 1992; Kochan and Osterman, 1994).

In these sense, we have seen the argument shift from particularistic claims, such as those about enhanced involvement, to ones based on a general, strategic combination of high performance work practices. At times it can sound as if management has reached the pot of gold at the end of the rainbow, with better soft (for example, trust) and hard (performance) outcomes. However, in their favour, HPWS theorists, unlike popular management writers, are relatively hard-headed about what 'high road' practices consist of and have empirical tests for their presence. There is recognition that new work systems are about not general empowerment, but much more localised involvement and are contingent in their positive and negative effects on workers (Applebaum and Berg, 2000). Because of differences in method, the evidence on the diffusion of HPWS is limited and fragmentary (Harley, 2005: 43). Piecing together what is possible, Harley argues that a number of nationally-based studies have reported a substantial take-up of individual practices, with a smaller number of organisations and sectors manifesting the 'bundles' associated with HPWS models (Applebaum *et al.*, 2000; Millward, 2000). The content and effects of such practices is much harder to identify. A number of the prominent studies have claimed to have found a positive association with company performance (Huselid, 1995; Ichinowski *et al.*, 1996; Applebaum *et al.*, 2000). British research on similar lines has been more circumspect. Wood and de Menzes (1998) found a widespread adoption of high-commitment practices, though of a diverse rather than 'packaged' nature; and also did not identify significant performance differences.

However, while surveys are good at telling us how extensive practices are, they are less useful in demonstrating the substantive content of change. The main drawback is the reliance on mail questionnaires or telephone surveys to managerial informants for data on practices and their impact. Such informants are being asked to report practices in which they have a role or status, and may slip into a normative or intentional mode (Guest, 1999a). Reliability is also problematic because, in many case studies, 'high-road' companies are being identified as 'transformed' if a certain number of practices are present, telling little about the substance of any of the changes, or the extent to which they have really challenged traditional structures or correspond to employee experience (Biewener, 1997). Finally, in assessing performance outcomes, it is hard to disentangle the effects of direct participation from that of other variables and to determine the direction of causality (Marchington and Wilkinson, 1998), or the relative importance of different dimensions of the system – such as teams – to outcomes for firms or workers (Batt and Doellgast, 2005).

None of these factors are reasons for not doing survey work, and there have been attempts to overcome some of these limitations (for example, Guest, 1999b; Applebaum *et al.*, 2000). They do, however, point to the need for caution about interpreting the results. It is helpful for such approaches to be complemented by qualitative, case study methods, and to disaggregate the component features of 'high performance' practice. With this in mind, the rest of the section focuses on three: skills, tasks and rules; autonomy, control and surveillance; and the effort bargain and work intensity.

Skills, tasks and rules

There are only limited insights to be gained from discussing changes in demands for skills or knowledge that rely on proxies. Changes in the numbers of employees in different occupational categories or who achieved particular levels of qualification may be interesting, but they don't tell us very much about what people actually do at work, or with those skills and expertise (Warhurst and Thompson, 2006). In addition, when reviewing survey evidence, Lloyd and Payne argue that, 'Overall, despite the claims about HPWO and skills, they are derived from a very weak evidence base that does not go beyond identifying some limited statistical association' (2006: 158). Even with such methodological constraints, a limited amount is clear. The UK Skills Surveys of 1997 and 2001, based on employee perceptions, show some positive links between new work practices and 'behavioural' competencies such as problem-solving. As the recent UK survey of employers indicates, 'the day of rigidly defined jobs and tasks is already well past' (White *et al.*, 2004: 41). Job structures are more complex, tasks more varied and employees are trained to enable them to cover other jobs.

Such outcomes are consistent with the long-standing concept of functional flexibility, itself part of the flexible firm debate discussed extensively in the previous chapter. Functional flexibility is often assumed to lead to higher levels of skilled labour (Ackroyd and Proctor, 1998: 179), but examination of the evidence shows that new practices were mostly directed towards removing 'barriers' between grades and categories. This may be achieved by merging production grades or ensuring job rotation. The growth of teamworking has also facilitated functional flexibility, as job rotation and additional training has enabled many companies to move towards complete interchangeability of labour (Proctor and Mueller, 2000: 11–13). The capacity to rotate workers across tasks, however, is normally predicated on their prior fragmentation, rather than combining them into something more holistic (Findlay *et al.*, 2000a).

Most research into manufacturing work has been critical of claims surrounding the positive impacts of flexibility on tasks. While skill variety or functional flexibility is often necessary to exploit arrangements such as JIT and modular production, variations or new responsibilities such as self-maintenance may be small and it is more accurate to speak of an enlarged number of interchangeable tasks carried out by substitutable labour (Elger, 1990; Pollert, 1991b; Delbridge, Turnbull and Wilkinson, 1992; Geary, 1985). This emphasis on continuity with the past is given partial endorsement by more realistic management writers, such as Peter Wickens, formerly of Nissan. He admits that 'lean production retains many Taylorist elements' (1992: 84), and notes that the work of line operators is still 95 per cent prescription and 5 per cent discretion. While multiskilling and multi-activity jobs are a significant change, it is much harder to argue that they constitute the end of Taylorism. Putting these together, adding on further deskilled tasks (NEDO, 1986), or extra ancillary duties such as inspection, does not normally make a substantial difference to their content.

A central point has been that the multiskilling at the heart of functional flexibility represents a modest enlargement of the range of tasks required rather than any more fundamental change in the direction of skill enhancement (Elger, 1991). Ackroyd and Proctor (1998) are more sympathetic to the idea of their being a 'new flexible firm' in which labour is a central source of flexibility, but can see no evidence that it is associated with highly skilled polyvalence. Influenced by their diversified activities and finance-based forms of control, such firms have substituted flexible labour and organisation for capital investment. Managers work within a framework of reorganisation and reregulation of existing resources, focusing on elimination of unproductive activities, broadening roles and responsibilities and adjusting external relations, rather than constituting qualitatively new practices.

There has also been confusion in the discussion that increased flexibility means fewer rules and therefore, less bureaucracy (Alvesson and Thompson, 2005). In fact it tends to mean the reduction of one type of rule: demarcation between tasks. Rules still govern organisational life. American surveys show that 'the vast majority of employees work in establishments with extensive formal procedures' (P. Adler and Borys, 1996: 61). Tasks themselves, at least in routine jobs, are still subject to high degrees of standardisation. What is more, the techniques for ensuring this – worksheets, performance codes and job evaluation – are classically Taylorist (Williams *et al.*, 1992a; Thompson *et al.*, 1995). Slaughter (1987) shows that teamworking at NUMMI involved specifying, measuring and timing every move in greater detail. Interviewed by the *Wall Street Journal* (18 May 1999), a plant manager admitted that standardisation poses problems for workers who thrive on developing their own personal style: 'To be true to these ideas, you're really supposed to dictate everything', from which knee to kneel on, to how far an arm should be moved to carry out a task. Nor is this confined to factories. Warehousing increasingly uses computer-based systems to produce 'engineered work standards' that can specify tasks and maintain 'real-time' control over workers (Wright and Lund, 1998). As we have noted earlier, the benchmarking systems underpinning TQM and BPR require a concern for standardised procedures and uniform, dependable practices (Wilkinson and Willmott, 1994; Tuckman, 1994). Such instances do not surprise some supporters of lean production. In an influential *Harvard Business Review* article defending Taylorist time-and-motion discipline and bureaucratic structures as essential for efficiency and quality, Adler notes that '[NUMMI] is obsessive about standardised work procedures. It sees what one NUMMI manager has called "the intelligent interpretation of Taylor's time and motion studies" as the principal key to success' (1993: 103). In a review of evidence on lean teams, Benders (2005) notes that standard operating procedures are often gathered into handbooks, and displayed as posters above work-stations, so that employees could easily see how a particular job had to be done.

What conclusions can we draw from the above evidence? We do not think it would be justified to describe lean production, teamwork and TQM as a form of 'super-Taylorism'? (Slaughter, 1987). Whether Taylorism and bureaucracy are 'necessary' or not, Adler's description of the arrangements at NUMMI and other advanced manufacturing plants as *learning bureaucracies* is useful. Though standardisation and rules are central and workers' knowledge continues to be appropriated by management, the move away from narrow specialisation towards devolved responsibilities, problem-solving and continuous improvement, however limited, marks a significant break from those parts of Taylorism based on a clear separation of conception and execution. More generally, the conception of skill needs rethinking in circumstances where the relation between a person and a machine is being replaced by the relation between a team and an integrated production system. While many of the *individual* tasks continue to be further deskilled under the impact of standardised procedures and uses of new technology, teams and project groups mark form of collectivised effort (Durand, 2007) and the collective labour of the group involves expanded cognitive abilities and extra-functional skills, for example in the form of greater need for problem-solving and decision-making powers, or qualities such as communication and co-operation (Thompson *et al.*, 1995). One consequence is that, 'profitability can depend quite heavily on the performance of workers who are technically unskilled or semi-skilled but behaviourally highly skilled' (Sayer, 1986: 67). This helps explain the paradox that many companies are engaging in detailed and intensive selection and screening processes for relatively routine jobs, often recruiting young 'green' labour. When the NUMMI plant was established, all candidates for employment undertook three days of interviews, job simulations and discussion on the firm's philosophy and objectives (Wood, 1986: 434). However, the situation with respect to 'new production concepts' is never static. Even in Germany, where 'participative rationalisation' was based on some degree of consensus between capital and labour and progressive forms of autonomy and job enlargement, commentators noted a re-emergence of more traditional forms of Taylorism. Planning and optimisation are once gain the property of rationalisation experts inside and outside the plant, with 'forced standardisation' and short job-cycle times (Springer, 1999; Schumann, 2000).

Obviously, manufacturing environments vary considerably in their patterns of skill utilisation and not all practices are based on 'taking complexity out of jobs' (Biewener, 1997: 13). Among higher-level technical employees a detailed division of labour can be an obstacle to creativity and flexible response, and managerial strategies, for example in the computer industry, have ebbed and flowed between various ways of dividing and combining labour, supporting both deskilled and upskilled jobs (Greenbaum, 1998; Beirne *et al.*, 1998). An alternative way of addressing the problem is to fragment the work into new hierarchies of labour, as is shown by studies of computer programmers (Kraft and Dubnoff, 1986) and software developers (Sharpe, 1998). In a more recent assessment of the evidence on technical work, Barley is sceptical of such claims, which he says, 'mistook specialisation for fragmentation of work' (2005: 385). He goes on to argue that skill sets need to be analysed in a more grounded manner, taking into account situated knowledge within varied labour and product markets. Nor can technical skills be 'read-off' from qualifications. A recent study of IT workers (Adams and Demaiter, 2008) showed that self and informal learning, often within peer networks, constituted key sources of skill development. This reflects the largely project-based character of such work and related jobs like those in creative industries, for example new media firms. While such trends exemplify the self-ownership of a body of technical skills and knowledge typically found in a profession or highly organised occupational group, there are problems in how this is recognised and accredited (Christopherson, 2004).

Though much of the research on flexibility and skills was initially focused on manufacturing, we do need to take note of other trends. Given the preponderance of service jobs in a contemporary economy, ranging from the routine sales interactions to professional service firms, it is hard to identify a single trajectory. But in a comprehensive review of the research, Frenkel argues that, 'In general, service work is comparatively low paid and less secure than most other kinds of work ... [and] is not especially complex;

it is located at the lower range of the skills, creativity and knowledge continuum' (Frenkel, 2005: 357) Despite the dubious association in new economy perspectives between the spread of the service sector and the rise of the knowledge economy, it is widely recognised that task fragmentation and rules have been spreading into the service sector. Evidence for the *bureaucratisation of service* is associated primarily with Ritzer's (1993) 'McDonaldization of society' thesis. He marshals a considerable array of evidence to argue persuasively that fast food chains are the tip of an iceberg that has extended Weber's principles of rationalisation in the form of calculable, predictable, quantified processes to an increased range of retail, leisure and media services. Bryman (2006) has more recently repeated the exercise for 'disneyized', fun factory jobs.

Such arguments echo earlier research such as Gabriel's (1988) study of a variety of catering jobs. He demonstrates that the industry has shifted from reliance on the social and technical skills of the workforce to an industrial model that rests on standardised organisation of tasks and a technologically determined work pace. While not all jobs in the sector are as routine as fast food, the standardisation of the service encounter is widespread, including in upmarket hotel chains (Jones, Nickson and Taylor, 1997). A prime reason for this is that many retail and service outlets believe that to maintain a competitive edge, a friendly, high-quality service encounter must be produced over and over again. Consistency of product is ensured by training, monitoring through report cards, and surveys on employee attitudes and behaviour through real and company-employed 'shoppers'. Service can also be bureaucratised by increased monitoring of employees, either through information technology such as the EPOS system in supermarkets or through 'control by customers' (Fuller and Smith, 1991).

However, as with manufacturing, albeit with a different content, tasks have been reconfigured and expanded, reflecting the distinctive role of the customer in much service work (Lediner, 1993; Korczynski 2002). The incorporation of emotions and appearance into work requirements is a case in point. This tendency was identified in labour process research such as that by Fuller and Smith (1991) as approximating to a further and more radical development in the bureaucratisation of service through feeling rules. This term draws on the work of Hochschild on flight attendants and other employees involved in emotional labour (Bolton, 2005), briefly discussed in Chapter 10. From fast food and insurance work (Leidner, 1993), to supermarkets (Ogbonna and Wilkinson, 1988) and call centres (S. Taylor, 1998), service increasingly requires scripted interactions and standardised displays of feelings through smiles, forced niceness and other forms of verbal interplay and body posture. Putnam and Mumby note, 'When emotions are incorporated into organisations, they are treated as commodities' (1993: 43). The growing literature on aesthetic labour in service work (Witz *et al.*, 2003; Pettinger, 2006) emphasises the desire of employers to specify and script bodily interactions in some specialised sales and service interactions (Warhurst *et al.*, 2008).

Though this tendency is not as pronounced in manufacturing, new *normative* controls have been introduced whereby management ask for and reward conformity to behavioural rules, particularly governing attitudes and action inside the team. An increased emphasis on selecting and training 'the appropriate worker' shows that a traditionally neglected part of Taylor's agenda is being renewed (Wood, 1989b: 11). To return to the service sector, it is also worth noting that there is a parallel to the attempt to tap into employees' tacit knowledge to improve competitiveness. However, interactive service work, such as call centres,

> draws on capacities and attributes located (often unconsciously) within each worker. These workers draw on limited technical knowledge during their work, but they do have to develop a consciousness of their social skills and awareness of when and how to deploy these. (Thompson, Warhurst and Callaghan, 2000: 128)

Table 15.1 **Henry's table order of service**

1 Customer greeted at reception.
2 Customer accompanied to table and given menu and special cards.
3 Waitress asks for drinks/wine order.
   Glasses for wine put on to table.
4 Drinks/wine dispensed.
5 Waitress takes food order (and wine) acknowledging specials.
6 Waitress offers:
   – choice of jacket potatoes or chips
   – degree of cooking for steaks.
7 Waitress reads order back to customer.
8 Waitress takes order for pitta bread.
9 Glasses for wine and wine to table.
10 Starter cutlery to table.
11 Starters taken.
12 Appropriate starter accompaniments.
13 All starters cleared.
14 Main course served.
15 Appropriate main course accompaniments.
16 During main course:
   – 'Is everything alright?'
   – 'Would you like more wine/drinks?'
17 Main course cleared.
18 Customer invited to go to sweet display or given details.
19 Sweet and coffee orders taken.
20 Liqueurs offered with coffee.
21 Bill to customer – invite to pay at reception.
22 Customer pays.
23 'Goodnight' – acknowledge.

Call centres have been the focus for an interesting debate on skills and work organisation. Noting the technologically-driven routine nature of much of the work, some commentators (e.g. Poynter, 2000) have argued that such jobs are Taylorised, de-professionalised and have more in common with manual work. It is not difficult to find elements of fragmentation, close technical control and scripted interactions in call centre work, though it is worth remembering that call centres have begun to migrate to semi-professional spheres such as nursing and social work (Smith *et al.*, 2008; van den Broek, 2008). However, while many customer service representatives may be unqualified, it would be misleading to describe them as unskilled. This is because of the variety of social competencies and emotional demands made in the job. It is for this reason that call centres, like many other services, invest so heavily in rigorous selection and training procedures more usually associated with more complex work (Callaghan and Thompson, 2002; Houlihan, 2002). It may resemble aspects of an assembly line, but as Taylor and Bain (1999) put it, it is an assembly line 'in the head'. It is also a question of also what workers do with skills. In response to the managerial requirements of many new service jobs, employees become multiskilled emotion managers

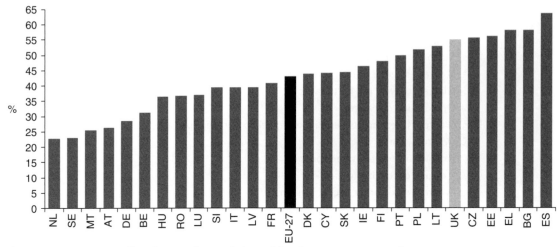

Figure 15.1 **Percentage of employees who say their work involves monotonous tasks**

Source: European Working Conditions Survey 2005; from Coats (2009), with permission.

in their own right – resisting demands, reserving their feelings or conferring their emotions as 'gifts' to clients and customers (Bolton, 2005).

Social competencies are a long way from traditional technical, knowledge and task-centred notions of skill. But social scientists have to find ways of recognising the broader palette of skills and sources of labour power that capital is seeking from the modern worker, while rejecting the optimistic scenario of a generalised upskilling of work in a knowledge economy. If the latter was true, it would be unlikely that Britain would have such a job content problem, as Figure 15.1 reveals. The significant variation in job quality across countries indicates a variety of content and context factors at play (Coats, 2009).

Autonomy, control and surveillance

Empowerment has been the dominant rhetoric of change in work relations and enhanced worker autonomy over tasks and methods, a key premise and promise of HPWS (Applebaum *et al.*, 2000). Evidence with respect to autonomy in general and any connection to high performance practices more specifically is mixed. Autonomy certainly matters to workers and is more important than a particular form of work organisation such as teams, while employees who report high levels of autonomy also generally report positive experiences of other aspects of work (see Harley, 2001; Danford, 2003). Analysis of the WERS 1998 data indicated some link between HPWS and enhancement of autonomy (Ramsay *et al.*, 2000). Yet further analysis of survey data (Harley, 1998) and case studies (Potterfield, 1999; Hales, 2000) shows that little connection exists between managerial mechanisms of empowerment and employee autonomy. In his review of the evidence on HPWS, Harley argues that while there are associations between the presence of HPWS in organisations and positive employee aspects of their experience, 'The evidence specifically concerning the role of employee autonomy is, however, extremely limited and at best equivocal' (2005: 45). Neither employee 'voice' in decisions nor 'choice' in work arrangements show any sign of substantive improvement. With respect to the UK, recent trends are also discouraging, with the recent UK Skills Survey showing a significant decline in discretion among UK workers since the 1980s (Felstead *et al.*,

2001). Nor is this confined to the UK. Green's (2006) review of European trends in the 1990s revealed that six countries registered declining discretion, two rising and seven relatively stable.

How do we explain such data? One route could be a repeat of previous patterns akin to Ramsay's (1991) cycle of controls theory, whereby early effects resulting from pressure on employers diminish or are routinised. Scepticism concerning specific claims in the area of enhanced autonomy is certainly informed by negative experience of previous waves of reform. As we argued earlier in the chapter, however, while usage of individual techniques might rise and fall, the general trend towards some forms of employee involvement is widespread and durable (Marchington, 2005). It may be useful to look more closely at particular practices. With respect to the earlier wave of TQM, evidence shows that while workers did respond positively to attempts to draw on their expertise and reductions in close supervision, existing hierarchies still constrain attempts to delegate power and expand involvement for employees (Dawson and Webb, 1989; McArdle *et al.*, 1994; Kerfoot and Knights, 1994; Wilkinson, Godfrey and Marchington, 1997) and even managers (Munro, 1994). Both TQM and BPR involved substantial continuity with Taylorist and bureaucratic traditions through the use of technology as an instrument of change and the separation of system design from execution (Grey and Mitev, 1995; Blair *et al.,* 1998; Knights and Willmott, 2000), and the accompanying techniques of work process measurement and codification tend to counter any emphasis on enhancing employee discretion (P. Adler and Borys, 1996: 61).

Patterns do not necessarily repeat, and we were sympathetic earlier to the view that current forms of teamworking represent a more fundamental change. For example, using her own case study, Batt (1999) argues that TQM had no discernible effects on performance, whereas self-managed teams significantly increased impact. There are a number of 'textbook' cases of self-managing teams, such as the two US sites investigated by Cutcher-Gershenfeld and colleagues (1994). They are not, however, representative. Critics have from the inception outlined a familiar range of criticisms that stress the relatively limited nature of delegation of authority (Wood, 1989; Boreham, 1992). Other case studies and small-scale surveys of the amount of autonomy across key decision rights in teams shows that the empowerment rhetoric is often empty and managerial prerogative largely intact, with, for example, only a small minority of teams electing their team leader (Fucini and Fucini, 1990; Turner and Auer, 1994; Danford, 1997; Murakami, 1997). Significantly, this judgement is supported by larger studies. A survey of over 5000 European workplaces revealed that only 4 per cent corresponded to standard definitions of strong, high autonomy teams, with Swedish and Dutch establishments having the highest concentration (Benders and Huigen, 1999; Benders, 2005). These limits on team autonomy have been confirmed in other studies. The 1998 WERS survey showed that only 5 per cent of the 65 per cent of workplaces that had teams were self-managing based on appointment of team leader, task responsibility and co-decision over how work was done (Cully *et al.*, 1998); while a cross-national survey in the motor-components industry demonstrated that the role of operators in many decisions was minimal, whether in lean or traditional work environments (Delbridge, Lowe and Oliver, 2000).

It is important, however, that such evidence is about *limits* to, not absence of, change. One of the major sources of dissension between supporters and critics of a lean production model is the extent to which modern work systems can be efficient with extensive team autonomy, as well as more holistic jobs and long task cycles (see Sandberg, 1995; Benders, 2005). The critics prefer a more European socio-technical systems model, such as that practised at Volvo. For the supporters, the closure of the flagship Kalmar and Udevalla plants was proof that such arrangements are inimical to efficiency. Adler admits that at lean production plants such as NUMMI in the US, 'the emphasis on standardised methods meant that workers had no autonomy whatsoever in how they performed their tasks' (1995: 213–14). Lean production teams, inside and outside Japan, are about participation and continuous improvement, not autonomy. However, the research of even the harshest critics (for example, Robertson *et al.*, 1992; Danford, 1997), demonstrates that employees prefer working in teams and welcome the chance to exercise greater discretion, and are disappointed when promises of increased participation and responsibility prove empty (Milkman, 1997; Wilkinson, Godfrey and Marchington, 1997). Put another way, employees in a variety of manufacturing and service settings are reported to experience teamwork as a mixed blessing – welcoming the increased latitude of decision-making, but concerned about work intensification (Benders, 2005).

Other critics of teamwork tend to be those influenced by Foucauldian frameworks, who see the new arrangements as opportunities for management to extend control through electronic surveillance and peer pressure (Sewell and Wilkinson, 1992; Barker, 1993; 1999; Sewell, 1998). The argument rests on the assumption of extensive self-governance, which, in turn becomes self-policing. We have already critically evaluated such views in Chapter 8. While it is the case that both teamworking and other initiatives such as TQM stimulate management to strive for a degree of what Wood (1986: 432) calls 'attitudinal restructuring' to instil greater co-operativeness and self-discipline, there is little evidence they have been successful (Findlay *et al.*, 2000b). There is also an assumed link to autonomy in Foucauldian claims that does not appear to stand up. If we take the overwhelming weight of evidence considered above about constraints on autonomy, it is difficult to see how such claims can be sustained, or at least generalised very far. Second, peer pressure in teams is not necessarily linked to self-governance. Small workplace groups in Japan have long had a strong element of compulsion, yet we know that teams have little or no autonomy. Itoh's (1984) account of Matsushita brings out a common theme that 'voluntary' activity in quality circles is founded on being forced to give suggestions: in this case, three a month ranked on a scale of one to nine. Loyalty is also cemented not only through peer group pressures, but also through cheap loans to buy houses and other financial inducements related to the process of creating company man (Briggs, 1987). Finally, surveillance is not necessarily linked to teamwork, self-governing or otherwise. Ironically, the workplace sites where surveillance does appear to be most strongly entrenched are call centres, yet teams are largely formalistic in character given the individualistic nature of the tasks. (Thompson *et al.*, 2004)

Service work, even at the lower and middle levels, has been regarded as having greater scope for 'empowerment' given its more varied, individualistic nature, the relative absence of machine pacing and the need to exercise personal discretion and responsiveness in customer interactions (Lashley, 1997). Yet the evidence concerning the scripting and monitoring of service interactions considered earlier in the chapter does not encourage a positive assessment. Many employees, such as those in travel agencies or insurance brokers, work within highly circumscribed IT systems that place strong constraints on discretion. That is why, in part, the work is able to be transferred to call centres, which are, of course, machine-paced. In a specific review of the relations between service work and task-based participation (Sturdy and Korczynski, 2005) take a middle position, pointing to a recurrent tension between the personal tailoring that some services require and the Taylorist mechanisms employers utilise to standardise and reduce costs. Satisfying the 'sovereign' consumer can mean both empowering the front-line employee to take extra responsibility and seeking to reduce the extent of uncertainty in service interactions. Controlling *for* these variations can thus lead to control *over* employees.

Yet as Sturdy and Korczynski recognise, service work is highly varied and there is a big difference between front-line workers in luxury hotels (Sherman, 2007) and the daily grind faced by restaurant servers (Gatta, 2007). Frenkel (2005) gives a detailed and fair assessment of the trends with respect to autonomy. Some front-line jobs, even those that are lower paid, such as care workers, do have greater scope for discretion. Mass service models (such as most call centres) are geared towards standardisation and task prescription, but mass customisation (such as specialised shops, health clubs) involves more complex work and therefore to deliver the service to the customer, employees have to be more flexible and self-regulating. Workers providing professional (such as consultancy) services are more likely to have few direct task rules and to be subject to normative and output controls (Alvesson and Thompson, 2005). Service workers in the UK public sector have also seen their work discussed through the lens of empowerment within a more general framework of the 'new public management' (Clarke and Newman, 1997). Nurses are a case in point. As health has been reorganised they have been asked to take on extra responsibilities and to be more functionally flexible, with the carrot of an improved structure of skill progression. Case studies undertaken by Cooke (2006), however, show a perception of increased workload, deteriorating conditions and low morale. An important contributing factor was the myriad of targets and associated paperwork that comes with those new responsibilities.

Knowledge work may not be expanding as fast as its proponents assert, but surely the argument that professional and technical labour is governed increasingly by collegial and horizontal forms of co-ordination, is at least nearer the mark? Given that knowledge work is too complex to be vertically controlled, management has to throw out the rule book and develop horizontal co-ordination, with collegial, collaborative methods (Hamel and Prahalad, 1996; Barley, 1996). In some senses, the answer must be yes. It is true that creative work generally and knowledge-intensive work in particular require much higher levels of autonomy and trust from particular groups of employees. There has been a great deal written about the growth of communities of practice and other informal networks that facilitate learning and self-organisation (Seely Brown and Duigid, 1991). The characteristic form of work organisation for many creative workers, such as those in software production and new media sectors, is the project group and this temporary assemblage of a variety of forms of expertise is likely to operate somewhat outside the shadow of the conventional corporate hierarchy (Christopherson, 2004).

Yet, as with other groups of workers, conditions and contexts change and 'it would be wrong to assume that those who are really doing knowledge-intensive work automatically experience high levels of autonomy' (Boreham et al., 2008: 16). In the previously-referred to 2001 Skills Survey the decline in task autonomy was at its sharpest among technical and professional employees (Felstead et al., 2001). There are a number of potential explanations for this, some, paradoxically focusing on the growth of knowledge management systems themselves. While these are discussed in detail in the next chapter, the language of capturing, converting and codifying knowledge tells its own potential story of the tensions between encouraging creativity and innovation and the growth of mechanisms and metrics to record and measure such activity. The major corporate goal in industries such as pharmaceuticals is to considerably reduce the life cycle of molecule-to-market projects from 14 to 8 years, hence the focus on knowledge manament (McKinlay, 2005). This requires an attempt to facilitate the creative process as a learning resource *and* exerting greater control in development and documentation. In economies with little labour-market regulation, the absence of strong professional and occupational groups that exercise collective discretion over working conditions renders project groups vulnerable to this kind of corporate pressure (Christopherson, 2004: 552).

Where quasi-markets are impacting on groups such as teachers, direct market pressures are increasingly constraining the time for creative experimentation among technical workers in the pharmaceutical industry (Randle, 1995). Whether this is new, increasing, or consistent is another matter. A tension between creativity and control or commodification has always been at the heart of expert labour, a fact often forgotten in recasting discussion through the language of 'knowledge flows' and 'stocks of knowledge' (Hull, 2000). Current market and organisational conditions are, if anything, exacerbating those tensions. With reference to other kinds of creative worker, we have also already noted the negative effects of increased bureaucratic and managerial control in the work of public-sector professionals, such as doctors, social workers and academics as government has stepped up audit, targets and codes of conduct (Alvesson and Thompson, 2005).

Empowerment, or 'constrained involvement' as Durand (2007) calls it, is not merely hollow rhetoric, even for routine workers. But enhanced responsibility and sometimes increased discretion have come with a price in terms of workload and effort bargain. It is to that territory that we now turn.

Work intensity, the new insecurity and work-life boundaries

In this chapter we have, so far, dealt largely with how work is *organised*. There is a further key dimension of experience – how *hard* do we have to work? NEO perspectives, and the lean production variant in particular, have promoted the idea of 'working smarter not harder', and this has received some support from extensive plant studies such as those carried out by Applebaum *et al.* (2000). However, this has to be set against a substantial body of research that identifies a rising tide of labour intensification associated with new forms of work organisation and management. This was certainly the message from a variety of critics of lean production, some associated with trade unions (Turnbull, 1988; Parker and Slaughter, 1988b; Elger, 1991; Garrahan and Stewart, 1993; Fucini and Fucini, 1990). Intensification has been associated particularly with advanced work arrangements such as JIT, which rely on continual and controlled pressure (Turnbull, 1988 13), internalising disciplinary pressure within the group (Sayer, 1986: 66), and conforming to new behavioural rules. In one of the most influential contributions, Slaughter gives a vivid account of 'management by stress' at NUMMI, where the goal is to stretch the system like a rubber band. Breakdowns and stoppages of the line are encouraged as this can indicate where weak points are and how they can be corrected, fine-tuned and further stressed. Workers who fall behind may have video cameras trained on them to 'help' in this process. TQM is also partly geared towards eliminating slack and waste in the system, and workers have reported that 'empowerment' involved considerably harder work (McArdle *et al.*, 1994). Flexibility itself has always involved employees bearing extra burdens. When *Business Week* (1983) discussed job flexibility, most of the examples were simply of enlarging jobs by adding extra duties, cutting the size of work teams, or eliminating breaks. Many employees feel that management 'abuse' the extra flexibility and efficiency gained through teamwork by cutting the size of teams or by applying extraordinary performance pressures (Springer, 1999; Findlay *et al.*, 2000b).

Task restructuring is, however, not the only source of work intensification, nor are manufacturing workers the only recipient of its effects. Customer service representatives suffer intense stress and emotional exhaustion as they try to balance the twin pressures of demands for quality and quantity in high surveillance environments (P. Taylor and Bain, 1998; Batt, 1999; Deery and Kinnie, 2002). The key problem is the management-defined responsibility of the CSR to absorb, depersonalise or manage in other ways the requests and responses from customers who are themselves frequently stressed out by poor service, long delays and computerised voice options. Service workers in the public sector have faced rising pressures of work intensity from outsourcing, sub-contracting market testing, 'best value' and the other quasi-market mechanisms that have often led to lower pay, worse conditions and less security (Toynbee, 2003). Rising stress levels and work intensification as a result of re-engineered jobs, staff cuts, internal markets and greater external assessment have also been reported by public sector professionals (Willmott, 1993b; Dent, 1993; Leverment *et al.*, 1998). A broader study of five UK professions (Konzelmann *et al.*, 2007: 24), reported that, 'increased client expectations, changes in technology and in government policy augmented both the quality and intensity of work'.

The private sector is not exempt from similar pressures on higher-level employees. Institute of Management (1995) surveys and qualitative case studies in the UK (Collinson and Collinson, 1997) provide confirmation of increased time pressures and workloads. Intense work demands may also arise from trying to take advantage of co-ordination of projects across time zones in increasingly globalised industries such as software production. This is one example of the way in which at particular times in the production cycle, highly autonomous teams in more 'virtual' conditions can find themselves under external and self-imposed pressures to meet deadlines. Time is, in fact, at the heart of the management of knowledge work. As recent studies of software developers (Greenbaum, 1979; Beirne *et al.,* 1998; Ó Riain, 1998; Sharpe, 1998; Kraft, 1999; Reid 2007) demonstrate, project teams, experimentation, trust and creativity are essential preconditions of the creative phase. But as projects move beyond the development phase, managerial control is reasserted through targets and deadlines. In addition, control is exercised through performance metrics, project monitoring procedures, packaged software products and automation. If all else fails, software production can be 'exported' to another part of the global production chain. The software technology parks of India provide not only cheaper expert labour, but also a standardised software production pattern (Sharpe, 1998: 370). Taking these elements together, Ó Riain (1998: 289) refers to 'a system of time–space intensification' in the global workplace. Amongst some groups of creative and expert labour, particularly those who work in new media occupations, autonomy and mobility come with a price – amorphous job titles and roles, unregulated working conditions and long hours (O'Connor, 2007; Smith and McKinlay, 2009).

Most of this evidence comes from qualitative case studies where work intensity may not be the main focus. However, there is a new, more specialised set of studies using a combination of objective and self-report indicators to measure physical and mental effort (Reid, 2007). Amongst the most influential, in the UK at least, has been Burchell's (1999; 2002) survey of 20 companies. Using a multi-dimensional model, they go beyond job stability and fear of job loss, to feelings of insecurity related to pace and nature of change in the workplace, as well as the effects on well-being of employees and their families. More than 60 per cent of employees claim that the pace of work (and the effort they have to put into their jobs) has increased over the past five years, linked primarily to reduced staffing levels in response to heightened market pressures. Interestingly, the biggest increases are among professionals, as Table 15.2 makes clear.

Table 15.2 **Percentage change in reported job insecurity 1986 vs 1997**

Occupational category	% change
Professionals	+28
Clerical	+10
Managers	+9
Associate professionals	+9
Craft	−4
Operatives	−7

Source: *Job Insecurity and Work Intensification: Flexibility and the Changing Boundaries of Work*, by the ESRC Centre for Business Research at Cambridge University published by the Joseph Rowntree Foundation.

This study can be seen as part of part of an alternative insecurity thesis (Heery and Salmon, 2000; Green, 2001; Burchell, 2002). As we saw in the previous chapter, job tenure rates, at least as a general trend, do not show much deterioration. Nor are uses of non-standard labour on a consistently upward trajectory. As Nolan observes, given the contrasting evidence, 'It is difficult to account theoretically for the coincidence of employment stability and personal insecurity' (2004: 382). However, while insecurity in the labour market may have been overstated, sources of insecurity in the labour process are a different matter. It is widely acknowledged that there has been a transfer of risk from capital to labour, an increase in responsibilities for employees, subjection to accountability, measurement, appraisal, normative and technical controls.

Whereas in the past, many large companies shielded most of their workers from the insecurities of the marketplace, downsizing and de-layering have become central to successive waves of corporate restructuring, as firms seek ways of cutting costs to improve financial performance and meet competitive pressures. There is a threefold impact on employees, especially in middle management: the removal or diminution of career ladders, greater insecurity, and intensification of work for the survivors of restructuring. This observation holds good across a number of countries, including the US (Cappelli, 1995); Australia (Bramble, Parry and O'Brien, 1996); New Zealand (Inkson, 1993), Britain (Institute of Management, 1995; 1996) and Japan (Japan Labour Bulletin, 1 May 1994). Green (2006) also observes that work intensification took place in 12 of 15 European countries in the 1990s, though his explanation tends towards associations between advanced technology and effort intensity. Irrespective of cause, the impact on employees goes far wider than the ' "casualties" expelled from core to periphery because they cannot add value' (Handy, 1995: 6–7). Contrary to the flexible firm model, a key part of burden of securing extra performance has fallen on the core workforce, who are left to bear the burden of such changes in extra workload, often under the heading of 'empowerment' (Biewener, 1997):

> What recent research has also emphasised is evidence of a contradictory combination of work intensification and new areas of employee responsibility; what in management-speak is 'empowerment' is more accurately described as degradation through stress. (Hyman, 2006: 40)

As we noted earlier, this has also been the trend among public sector workers such as nurses in the UK and Australia, whose workloads have borne the brunt of improved standards of care and delegated responsibilities from managers (Buchanan and Considine, 2002; Cooke, 2006).

The effects of many of the above changes are, argues one leading study, 'strongly associated with tension in the home' (Burchell et al., 1999: 51). Arguing that there has been a severe time squeeze and 'overwork' has become a a basic condition of modern economic life, the US author Juliet Schor (1993) provides evidence that US employees are working an average of additional 163 hours a year. We are not going to deal with the policy dimension of this debate, in part, because there is little evidence that either family-friendly policies or employee-initiated time flexibility is widely available or widely used (Hochschild, 1997; Hogarth et al., 2000). Nor are we going to deal with how employees seek to cope with, manage or 'restore' work-life boundaries (see Hyman et al., 2005; Kylin and Karlsson, 2008; and later, Chapter 23). Instead, we want to focus on what the debate tells us about the impacts of trends in work relations on work-home boundaries.

In the introduction to a recent collection of essays on these boundaries, Warhurst and colleagues (2008) challenge conventional explanations, arguing that the debate is limited both empirically and conceptually. Given the tendency to treat the two as distinct spheres, they might have a point about concepts, but empirically, their view is more contentious. Though they accept that British workers have longer hours than their EU counterparts, they claim that the long working-hours culture is a 'myth', pointing to the steady fall in working hours during the post-war years to below 40 hours per week. This is linked to a wider argument against a 'flight from work': 'most employees do not want to work fewer hours and those who do want or have to work fewer hours, already have options to do so' (2008: 4). As an alternative to the long-hours driver, they attribute the concern with work-life balance to the 'chattering classes', more precisely to the professional workers who are having increasing difficulty managing the boundaries between more intensive and incursive work demands (e.g. 'presenteeism') and their home lives.

While the latter point is consistent with other evidence (Gallie *et al.* 1998; Simpson, 1998), the more general argument seems a rather narrow interpretation, based on a superficial and selective reading. Warhurst and colleagues don't even mention the bedrock Department of Education and Employment study (Hogarth *et al.*, 2000) that does refer to a dominant long-hours culture. It shows that most workplaces have staff working in excess of standard hours and that those who work extra hours do so by an average 9.6 extra hours per week, often in professional or managerial jobs. Two extensive UK surveys (White *et al.*, 2004) go further by demonstrating extensive 'negative job-to-home spillover'. Such spillover increased with additional hours worked similarly for men and women, but goes beyond this: 'We find clear evidence that high performance practices are an important, if previously ignored, source of negative spillover, even after controlling for working hours' (2003: 188). Amongst those identified are appraisal systems and group or team motivational practices. Overall, the results suggest that the further high-performance practices diffuse, the more there will be interrelated effects of work intensification and more severe pressures on home life.

Their claims are also consistent with other evidence (Burchell, 2002; Hyman *et al.*, 2005). In their case studies of employees in software firms and call centres, Hyman and colleagues show that in both there are tangible and intangible extensions of work into the household. Unpaid overtime and taking work home was quite frequently reported, especially among software respondents. Spillover was also reflected in terms of feeling stressed because of the job: 45 per cent of employees in call centres and 33 per cent in software reported feeling exhausted after work quite often or all the time. As the authors (2003: 234) note, 'The findings demonstrate that hours of working are becoming more elastic and that employees frequently take work home and think about work while away from the workplace.'

Conclusion: high road, low road or detour?

> The central message in this literature is that work restructuring is a complex and contradictory process.
> (Batt and Doellegast, 2005: 149)

The evidence and issues discussed in this chapter have indeed been complex. Taken as a whole the evidence does point to real changes in work relations taking place, albeit uneven and quite different from the descriptions and prescriptions found in some managerial and social science literatures. The most recurrent concept – HPWS – used to frame changes in work relations, has come in for a lot of criticism, particularly when applied to its intended locations. Most studies note the persistence of traditional 'low-road' managerial practices. Evaluating a range of British evidence, Marchington and Wilkinson (1998) observe that a raft of direct participation measures have been implemented in a half-hearted, limited and ad hoc manner rather than in a holistic and integrated way. This is confirmed by many of the surveys and case studies discussed in this chapter. Many British firms continue to rely on labour flexibility and reorganisation of existing resources (Ackroyd and Proctor, 1998). Milkman (1998) reaches similar sceptical conclusions from her own and other research on US workplaces that most firms remain wedded to a low-trust, low-skill road.

Despite these types of criticism, HPWS do not necessarily carry the same burden of inflated rhetoric and expectations as some other management models and is compatible with a perspective which recognises that the transformation of the labour process remains at the heart of the search for profitability. A downsized version is compatible with the evidence examined here. At the heart of change is what both Green (2006) and Coats (2009) describe as a paradox concerning job quality. Most jobs, though in different ways, have become more demanding and while that means that, for some, they are more interesting and challenging, the jobs are also harder and subject to greater surveillance and performance targets. As has been argued elsewhere (Thompson, 2003: 362–3), the changes that have taken place in work relations can be summed up as a qualitative intensification of labour. Changes in work contexts and content means that employers are compelled to seek a more intensive utilisation of labour power. This includes ways of appropriating and transmuting workers' knowledge, as well as accessing and mobilising emotional labour and a variety of 'extra-functional' skills. As a consequence, many types of work are characterised by greater work intensity, while contingent conditions in product and labour markets have been ratcheting up work intensification in most sectors. These are high-performance work systems, but not as have been sold to them.

Where HPWS perspectives fall down is in the absence of their projected reciprocal bargain – more investment of discretionary effort by the employee to be matched by greater investment in human capital and firm specific assets by the employer. As we have shown in the various chapters of Part II (and in Chapter 11), this, by and large, hasn't happened. Instead, the changing burden of risk, roles and responsibilities has shifted from capital and the state, to labour. We shall pick this theme up again in the Conclusion to Part III.

knowledge and its management

16

> The knowledge management fraternity is with Alice in the land through the looking glass, talking to Humpty Dumpty, for whom words meant what he wanted them to mean. (T. Wilson, 2001: 2)

The aims of this chapter are to:

- Explain how knowledge management (KM) relates to the issues of the knowledge economy and knowledge work.
- Examine the role of informally created knowledge in attempts to integrate strategy and implementation in change and innovation processes.
- Query the status of tacit knowledge and the ability of knowledge management to achieve its stated aims.
- Explore and evaluate the practice of KM through its links to high-commitment working and social identity.

Knowledge has figured prominently in other chapters of Part II, so why a separate treatment here? The idea of a knowledge economy has emerged as perhaps the most widespread and seductive idea and policy prescription of recent times. In Chapter 12, we were highly critical of that view. Though knowledge-intensive industries such as pharmaceuticals and bio-tech are vital to international competitiveness, they are not typical of a modern service-based economy. Nor does the centrality of knowledge to those industries mean that they operate according to some completely different economic logic than the standard profit-seeking capitalist firm. We showed in Chapter 14 that in contemporary economies, the largest occupational growth was in low- and middle-range service jobs that required a range of social competencies and interpersonal skills; thus casting doubt on the idea that knowledge work is the primary engine of growth.

Having been sceptical of the first two propositions – knowledge economy and knowledge work – where does this leave knowledge management? Well, this of course is the subject matter of the chapter and herein lies a problem. There isn't the extensive body of research on knowledge management that exists for labour processes and markets, so we haven't as much to report on and from as in previous chapters in Part II. Inevitably our discussions are more conceptual and speculative, while still trying to address contemporary developments and practices. Perhaps equally inevitably, definitions are slippery. If we take our lead from the emergent literatures, we could be addressing anything from the field of artificial intelligence to that of medicine (T. Wilson, 2002) and KM does not necessarily mean the same thing in all of the various fields it has colonised. Mullins (2005) defines KM as the promotion and formalisation of learning within the workplace, aimed at linking training with the needs of the business. The interesting thing here is that the definition actually mentions neither knowledge nor management – they are merely inferred as part of the learning process.

However, let us sketch a couple of preliminary arguments about why the management of knowledge matters and what might be its principal dynamics. The first can be found in outline in Chapter 15. More flexible work systems have required a move away from rigid specialisation and towards forms of teamworking and other arrangements that emphasise a limited degree of involvement learning and responsibility for quality. As Warhurst and Thompson (2006) argue, this is not so much knowledge work, as knowledgability *in* work. While technical, scientific and professional workers are already operating in more knowledge-intensive environments, they too are under pressure to speed up learning and innovation. For example, McKinlay's (2005) study of the pharmaceutical industry argues that the major corporate goal in the industry is to reduce the life cycle of molecule-to-market projects from 14 to 8 years. This requires an attempt to facilitate the creative process as a learning resource *and* exerting greater control in development and documentation. Taking these two trends together, Warhurst and Thompson argue that:

> Both routine and expert labour have undergone significant changes, with a central focus on attempts to enhance the conversion of tacit to explicit knowledge, though differing significantly in content and context. (2006: 794).

This doesn't tell us how KM practices operate (see Scarbrough and Swan, 2001; Alvesson and Kärreman, 2001; McKinlay 2005). This brings us to the second theme of the chapter – the tension between information and knowledge. T. Wilson (2002: 19) identifies Karl Sveiby as 'perhaps the founding father' of KM having published (in Sweden) the first book on the topic in 1990 and who in 1996 identified that KM has an 'IT track' and a 'people track':

> It is possible to distinguish two distinct emphases in KM, one focusing on communications and information technology, the other on people. The apparent attraction of technology is that it will enable the storage of vast amounts of knowledge which people can contribute to and access at will. Computerized systems also allow managers to monitor use, and to establish which kind of knowledge is being used by whom, and so facilitate the measurement and valuation of knowledge assets. From this perpective, emphasis is placed on capturing individually held knowledge, thus making it an organizational asset, not simply a personal one. (Gourlay, 2001: 29)

We shall return to this fundamental distinction in KM below. But as Gourlay indicates, where KM really intersects with the sphere of organisation is in turning knowledge into an organisational asset, i.e. in the generation of *intellectual capital* and its use of power, learning, innovation and culture in that process.

Companies as knowledge creators

Whatever its genesis and nature, all instances of KM have at their core some notion of the control of *information-processing* and of the valorisation of intellectual capital. The focus on intellectual capital according to (Nonaka, 1996: 25–31; and see Nonaka and Takeuchi, 1995) is central to the Western information-processing tradition in which:

- Knowledge is formal and systematic, characterised by:
  - hard data
  - codified procedures
  - universal principles

- The value of knowledge is assessed through key metrics such as:
  - increased efficiency
  - lower costs
  - improved return on investment.

This perspective on knowledge/information is clearly representative of the classic Taylorist, Theory X approach to management – what Herzberg (1968) called the classic 'industrial engineering' approach and is, of course, the enduring model for the valorisation of human capital. Nonaka contrasts this Western information-processing tradition with the Japanese approach, which he claims has led to the '*knowledge creating company*' (KCC) where the only reliable source of competitive advantage is knowledge. Thus successful strategy is linked to knowledge creation from the knowledge that lies latent in the organisation's members. Such knowledge creation requires the creation of a sense of identity between the employee and the organisation, again reminiscent of the classic unitarist call of HRM interventions.

Nonaka takes the notion of knowledge creation further with the 'spiral of knowledge' (1996: 20–2), which outlines the conversion process from tacit to explicit knowledge in four stages:

> The first step, *socialization*, transfers tacit knowledge between individuals through observation, imitation and practice. In the next step, *externalization* is triggered by dialogue or collective reflection and relies on analogy or metaphor to translate tacit knowledge into documents and procedures. *Combination* consequently reconfigures bodies of explicit knowledge through sorting, adding, combining and categorising processes and spreads it throughout an organisation. Lastly, *internalisation* translates explicit knowledge into individual tacit knowledge. (Hildreth and Kimble, 2002)

It is evident that knowledge creation has explicit links to learning and commitment through the socialisation and internalisation stages and we could posit these as the basis of the 'people track' in KM, which is in essence the basis of organisational learning and training. Externalisation and combination may not specifically reflect an IT track, but do reflect an information track where experience is systematised and codified, which in essence is the basis of management research within organisations.

The most crucial concept in this formulation is that of externalisation or articulation, the conversion of *tacit knowledge* into *explicit knowledge* (see Nonaka, 1996: 21–2). The notion of tacit knowledge is taken from Polyani (1958) and its use by Nonaka focuses on the fact that it is hard to formalise, difficult to communicate and its generation is personal, subjective and rooted in action and skills. Explicit knowledge exists externally to the individual and can be readily recorded and communicated. The communication of such explicit knowledge to others is, according to Nonaka, the main vehicle for the socialisation of new recruits (Starkey, 1996: 8) and is in turn the foundation of innovation, though in terms of socialisation at least we have previously argued that it is informal processes, rather than the formal content of, for example, induction systems, which are the main vehicle of socialisation. Likewise with innovation, we position informal creativity at the heart of innovation processes (see Thompson and McHugh, 2002), so in this sense KM could simply be another attempt to formalise the informal and the conversion of tacit knowledge into explicit knowledge as another vehicle for the appropriation of expert power.

For Nonaka the conversion of tacit into explicit knowledge requires challenges to accepted and articulated ways of doing things, to standard operating procedures (SOP) and existing forms of language and mental models, or more prosaically we could say it requires both attitudinal and behavioural change. The challenge involved in the conversion process might also paradoxically involve challenge to Nonaka's own spiral of knowledge in that the externalisation stage requires the translation of tacit knowledge into documents and procedures, which are precisely what are to be challenged in the conversion process. So the process of conversion could require challenge to the outputs of the translation process, again a classic Catch-22 situation where managerial actions may work to obviate their own effects.

The knowledge creating company also needs a 'knowledge-rich' environment where information is be freely available to all and employees are 'deluged with information'. This is seen as the antithesis of Western-style top-down management where knowledge is drip-fed in a trickle-down, 'need-to-know' fashion. Nonaka typifies the knowledge-creating company approach as 'management as chaos', where the role of management is to provide employees with a conceptual framework that helps them make sense of information and replenish their information-creation capacities, with senior managers probing the defences of their employees, looking for ways to stimulate new learning, a procedure which would hold undoubted familiarity for lab-rats everywhere. The Japanese influence in the knowledge-creating company is taken further in Nonaka's claims about the relative treatment of what he terms the 'logic of redundancy'. In the West, redundancy is seen as characterised by waste and duplication, what we could call the condition of *being redundant*, a condition familiar to the human 'knowledge assets' of companies when they become surplus to requirements. The Japanese interpretation of redundancy is advanced as the conscious overlapping of information, business activities and managerial responsibilities. This is more akin to the concept of redundancy in engineering where multiply redundant systems are used to provide error checking or failsafe routines in crucial systems such as the computers on a space shuttle. The effects of such redundancy for Nonaka are in that they encourage 'cognitive common ground' through frequent dialogue and communication, transfer of tacit knowledge and the spread and internalisation of new explicit knowledge. So systemic redundancy may work to provide a generalised feedback mechanism for the organisation, a sort of computerised suggestion box or electronic quality circle enacted through the 'spiral of knowledge'. As noted by Scarbrough (2003: 508), 'KM initiatives typically seek to collectivize … different kinds of knowledge which are currently dispersed among groups and individuals within and outside the organization. The aim is to make the knowledge and learning generated in one sub-unit available to others'.

For all that Nonaka's formulation appears to be concerned with the role of managers in shepherding knowledge creation it also seeks to emphasise the bottom-up nature of knowledge management. Answers and solutions are said not to be in the purview of top managers, whose role as 'romantics' is to promote ideals and what 'ought to be', and to clear obstacles and prepare the ground for team self-organisation. In managing knowledge, answers are said to be in the minds of 'front-line' employees, who are 'the experts in realities of work', the 'what is' rather than the 'ought to be'. Being the experts, however, does not protect them from needing to have their defences probed in order to give up their front-line knowledge and enduring loyalty. Such probing in the pursuit of ideals is no different to managerial attempts to *unfreeze* the attitudes of workers (while 'probing' them out of their comfort zones no doubt) in change processes and is completely in line with the traditional calls of HRM, culture initiatives and transformational leadership to mobilise the commitment and learning of employees. And just as with all modern unitarist appeals, it is teams that provide the legitimising context both in theoretical and practical terms. The assumption of group-based effects on behaviour that is inherent in all teamworking is at the heart of KM like all modern change initiatives, the pooling of information and integration into new collective perspectives purportedly giving teams the autonomy and freedom to set their own goals. Whether such autonomy would extend to setting goals contrary to the overall business strategy might, however, amply demonstrate the boundaries of employee freedom and the power of managerial 'ought to be' over the realities of 'what is'.

The classic problem for change initiatives in HRM has long been in mobilising line managers to implement centralised HR strategies when they often have neither the training nor the inclination to take on such an expansion and intensification of their of roles. Unsurprisingly Nonaka's KM does not disappoint in reiterating this dilemma, middle managers being painted as 'the true knowledge engineers'. Their job is to interpret ideals and translate them into practice, to synthesise the tacit knowledge of front-line employees and senior executives, and make it explicit. As if this was not enough they also have to incorporate this explicit knowledge into new technologies and products and to manage conflict when individuals challenge the status quo. In a marvellous piece of irony this latter duty raises the spectre of middle managers rushing in to manage the conflict produced by senior managers when they idealistically sally forth to probe the defences and challenge the status quo of employees in their romantic quest to fashion knowledge out of other people's work. The engaging image of middle managers as the Sancho Panza to senior management's Don Quixote may yet prove to be the greatest legacy that KM as a concept will have to offer, though the likelihood is that the role of knowledge engineer will end up as yet another layer of unlooked for responsibilities and duties.

KM and the KCC could then appear to be yet another response to continued failures to effectively integrate strategy and implementation, one sold on offering the missing managerial link between learning, strategy, innovation, HR and Japanese management, with a smidgen of complexity/chaos science to keep it fashionable. On the other hand we might argue that just like the people management roles foisted onto line managers by strategic HR interventions, KM may possibly just be what managers always did, with an additional layer of systematisation, formalisation and standardisation to make prescriptive panaceas out of conventional wisdom and everyday action. Since employees have consistently managed to socialise themselves within the organisation, pursuing their own agendas and resisting attempts to automatise their behaviour and harmonise their attitudes and values, KM as a strategy speaks of abandoning any attempt to control directly their smelly bodies and irrational minds, seeking to draw from them the raw stuff of their organisational experience and alchemically transform it directly into product. What is not in doubt is that even to be marginally effective in creating competitive advantage, the spiral of knowledge creation requires that the substance of KM, tacit knowledge, has to be synthesised, translated and converted to make it amenable to the organisation: it is knowledge itself that has to be socialised. And yet we might well wonder what is lost or garbled in this organisation-wide game of Chinese whispers, that is, we might question how accurately explicit knowledge actually reflects the tacit knowledge from which it has been cobbled together.

Tacit knowledge vs. explicit information

As Nonaka contrasts KM to the Western information-processing approach we might reasonably expect that some fundamental distinction exists between knowledge and information, and yet the spiral of knowledge creation assumes that one can be transformed into the other. Wilson (2002: 3–5) summarises the distinction between 'information' and 'knowledge' as follows:

- 'Knowledge'
  - consists of what we know
    - i.e. mental processes of comprehension, understanding and learning
  - goes on in the mind and only in the mind
  - cannot be 'managed'
    - 'except by the individual knower and, even then, only imperfectly'

- 'Information'
  - can be manipulated
  - consists of:
    - 'data' – simple facts
    - messages – outside of the mind, which:
      - can be assimilated, understood, comprehended and incorporated into knowledge structures
      - are not identical for the sender and the receiver
      - are embedded in a context of relevance to the recipient
  - collections of messages can compose 'information resources' which
    - can be 'managed'.

If Wilson is correct and knowledge cannot be managed, then can it be created out of information in the way that Nonaka's spiral demands? Knowledge creation assumes that tacit knowledge can be 'known' and either can somehow be transmitted without noise or that the knowledge 'synthesized' by 'knowledge engineers' is of the same quality/value as the tacit knowledge. This seems to revolve around a question of cognitive access to tacit knowledge and Wilson criticises Nonaka for misreading Polyani and confusing tacit knowledge with *implicit* knowledge (2002: 36–40). Implicit knowledge is that which we take for granted in our actions, and which may be shared by others through common experience or culture (39) whereas in Polanyi's concept 'tacit' means 'hidden'. Tacit knowledge is hidden knowledge, hidden even from the consciousness of the knower (37). Implicit knowledge, in other words, is expressible: tacit knowledge is not (40). Wilson then, would seem simply to refute the possibility of KM and is even sceptical about the status of subjective knowledge:

> The fact is that we often do not know what we know: that we know something may only emerge when we need to employ the knowledge to accomplish something. Much of what we have learnt is apparently forgotten, but can emerge unexpectedly when needed, or even when not needed. In other words we seem to have very little control over 'what we know'.

This notion of not being fully cognisant of what we know will become familiar to us in discussions of scripted and 'mindless' behaviour in Part III and raises the issue of 'tacit' or unacknowledged skills. There is no doubt that the tacit skills of workers are commodified in the labour process and there can be no doubt that skills can be captured by technical systems, as demonstrated in the appropriation of craft skills in everything from the Jacquard Loom to modern CNC manufacturing systems. Workers may employ their skills through expert systems and information-sharing networks and share the resulting outcomes to improve processes. But this is still in essence the management of information which can at best be used to build or enhance knowledge by and for the individual worker. It may simply be that the knowledge vs. information or tacit vs. explicit conception of knowledge does not account adequately for the various contexts in which knowledge is produced, transferred and utilised. As with motivation, leadership, etc., the usual OB response here is the development of typologies or classifications of which that can accommodate such contingencies. Blumentritt and Johnson (1999: 6) have reviewed categorisations of knowledge as seen below:

- **codified knowledge** – in our model essentially equivalent to information – knowledge that has been made explicit by a human; the method of making it explicit may involve writing it down or using other means of capturing, or may be in the form of a demonstration; it is in a readily transferable form.

- **common knowledge** – knowledge that is accepted as standard without having been made formally explicit, often in the form of routines or practices; commonly learned through working in a particular context.
- **social knowledge** – knowledge about interpersonal relationships and cultural issues; includes the knowledge of 'who can help me in this situation' to cultural issues in different roles.
- **embodied knowledge** – the experience, background and skill a person has accumulated during their lifetime; for this reason it is strongly connected to the person themselves. It relies on pattern and links a person can make to a given set of information to build and create appropriate knowledge to solve a problem. (Blumentritt and Johnson, 1999: 6, based on the work of Collins, 1993, Musgrave, 1993, Blackler, 1995, Lundvall, 1996, Fleck, 1997, Millar, 1997, and Polyani, 1958)

What this framework does is to confirm the separation between knowledge and information in the forms of *embodied* and *codified* knowledge respectively and then interposes the notions of *common* and *social* knowledge. These latter two categories essentially differentiate the conception of implicit knowledge into knowledge about situational and social contexts. In this sense what exists on information systems is codified knowledge and what is being captured by KM systems is common and social knowledge, that is, implicit knowledge. The utility of converting even implicit knowledge into explicit knowledge would seem to be questioned further by Scarbrough (2003: 513) as, 'Knowledge cannot be readily extracted from its social setting through purely technological means. Attempts to do so only reinforce and refract existing divisions of knowledge'. Blumentritt and Johnson's framework does not exactly reconcile Wilson's and Nonaka's views on the status of tacit knowledge, but can offer an explanation for what KM systems are doing if they cannot manage such knowledge.

Blumentritt and Johnson go on to conclude their review as follows:

- **Knowledge and information are different** – Knowledge requires the context of an intelligent medium. ... Consequently, even the best information management systems are not able to manage knowledge
- **A boundary between knowledge and information can be clearly established** – ... This boundary is obvious in every communication that an intelligent system is involved in (visual, written or spoken) because what is communicated is not knowledge but the result of a knowledge process and can never contain all the parts that have been involved in the process of reaching this result ...
- **Knowledge cannot be managed with the same tools as information** – Software- and electronic network-based information management systems have no capability to manage knowledge. Attempts to capture or store knowledge on a medium without intelligence requires the knowledge to be transformed to information, whereby the essential knowledge ingredients are lost ...
- **The interaction of knowledge and information can be described in a model** – To use information a certain standard of knowledge is necessary because information cannot substitute knowledge ...
- **The management of information is already well developed** – the management of knowledge is still in its infancy – ... Knowledge, because of its complexity and its union with intelligent systems, poses a greater challenge. (1999: 12–13)

On the surface Blumentritt and Johnson appear to agree with Wilson that knowledge cannot be managed, and with Scarbrough that technology cannot easily capture knowledge. Overall that would tend to confirm our earlier argument that explicit knowledge may not be an accurate reflection of tacit knowledge. McKinlay (2005: 243) claims that tacit knowledge can be transferred orally, though it is 'necessarily embedded in the collective experience of a particular work group or occupation', and adds, 'the problem of managing knowledge is not new: all work is and always has been, in an important sense, "knowledge work" and its management has always been contested'. For McKinlay knowledge work, 'is most clearly associated with professional or expert labor who have access to formal bodies of abstract knowledge', though at the same time:

> the labour process perspective has long looked to enclaves of skilled workers encircled by management projects that seek to encroach, if not dislodge, skills and knowledge that provide workers with some alternative moral authority and practical power base. (McKinlay, 2005: 243)

For the purposes of understanding what KM is and does we probably do not need to classify knowledge beyond

- Explicit – codifiable and capable of being managed
- Implicit – negotiated, shareable but only partially manageable
- Tacit – embodied in intelligent systems and unmanageable

Such a formulation shows a remarkable similarity to the classic extrinsic, social and intrinsic model of needs and rewards (see Chapter 21) and the similarity is not incidental, the motivation typology describing the content of motivation in terms of what is external, shared and internal to the person, and the knowledge classification does precisely the same. Motivation theory moved on from examining content because what it produced was universalistic models which could not handle individual motivations and were mainly useful for justifying job design initiatives. Process theories of motivation proved much better at accounting for the subjective aspects of motivation, but at the same time proved too complex to be of any real managerial utility. Also, just as we will see with motivation theory, it is likely that more cognitively-oriented theories of KM may give us more accurate descriptions of how intelligent systems manage knowledge, but prove so complex that they will be of no direct use to managers, at best remaining the province of academics and technical specialists.

KM as strategy and practice

So far we have taken KM and its claims seriously, mounting a critique based on the nature of knowledge. KM though, is essentially a practice and we need to examine what KM systems are and what they do. Regarding the nature of KM, Wilson (2002: 44) argues that it, 'is in large part, a management fad', based on the twin foundations of information management and the 'effective management of work practices'. His review of journal papers, consultancy websites and business school courses suggests that, in many cases, '"knowledge management" is being used simply as a synonym for "information management"' (2002: 33–4). KM has also been used as a synonym for 'organization learning' or 'expert systems' (28–9) and Wilson further asserts that it is possible to do a 'search and replace' operation on IM articles, replacing IM with KM without producing any change in their actual content:

> The software industry has become particularly prone to search and replace marketing, with almost everything from e-mail systems to Lotus Notes groupware being re-branded as 'knowledge management' software. (34)

On this basis the 'IT track' of KM appears to be just that: the management of explicit information masquerading as the management of tacit knowledge. It is the 'effective management practices' embodied in the people track in its role as the basis of learning, training and socialisation that should be the arena for the conversion of implicit and tacit knowledge into explicit knowledge. Wilson, however, dismisses this as, 'Predicated upon a Utopian idea of organizational culture in which the benefits of information exchange are shared by all, where individuals are given autonomy in the development of their expertise and where "communities" within the organization can determine how that expertise will be used' (2002: 45). There are few detailed empirical accounts of how new knowledge management systems work. McKinlay (2002; 2005) shows the tension between creativity and control in his case studies of Worldrug, a large pharmaceutical company. Mechanisms for the former, such as electronic cafes and intranets, sit alongside much more bureaucratic measures, such as data warehouses and other IT-led support tools with little dialogic character, to store and codify tacit knowledge. We will explore two further examples in order to tease out some of the characteristics of KM strategy (KMS) when practically implemented. Wilson cites the example of the 'legend, promulgated by Davenport (1997)…that Microsoft has a "knowledge management" strategy' (2002: 42–3), consisting of the:

- Development of a structure of competency types and levels;
- Defining the competencies required for particular jobs;
- Rating the performance of individual employees in particular jobs based on the competencies;
- Implementing the knowledge competencies in an online system;
- Linkage of the competency model to learning offerings.

To Wilson this strategy is no more than a training programme; it may integrate competencies into online evaluation and learning but if that represents a KMS, then in this instance KM is little more than a rhetorical device, KM's relationship to information management becoming analogous to the relationship between HRM and personnel management elsewhere. Like HRM, KM here is based on rhetorical appeals to strategic integration which in practice delivers no more than the formalisation of procedures and processes. This strategic integration of information management is evident in Sieloff's account of Hewlett-Packard's, 'traditional approach to knowledge management' (1999: 47–8). Sieloff, Knowledge Management Program Manager at Hewlett-Packard, emphasises the role of knowledge-sharing in innovation. This traditional approach consisted of a number of putative strategies:

- Small, autonomous business units
- Management by walking around
- Open office environment
- Sharing, high-trust culture
- Loyal, empowered people
- Permission to experiment and fail
- University towns (placement of business units in).

As a KM strategy the elements of this approach are not so coincidentally typical of those of the HCM strategies employed by high-tech companies worldwide. Sieloff does note that:

> Of course, at the time no one thought of these things as knowledge management strategies. To Bill Hewlett and Dave Packard, this was just good people management. Nevertheless, they laid the foundation of what was, and still is, a corporate culture that encourages both knowledge creation and knowledge sharing. (48)

What we have here is KM written into the story of what has been exemplified at HP as the 'HP way' and being used to reinforce and legitimise the 'Bill & Dave' myth. Sieloff records that this traditional and largely informal culture ran into difficulties, 'when growth and competitive pressures called for more formal or more global knowledge management strategies' (48), but at the same time there was localised resistance to the 'creeping bureaucratisation', for example, 'Why adopt formal methodologies and follow formal procedures, when work could be made more interesting by allowing more individual creativity and initiative to be applied?' (48).

Sieloff recalls that after embracing the 'data driven discipline and formality of total quality control (TQC)' and 'accelerating' local learning to cope with rapid growth in the 1980s, HP met problems in the redundancy (not in Nonaka's terms we assume) of informal knowledge-capture processes in different manufacturing units and instituted matrix structures to 'encourage the flow of knowledge' (49). This flow of knowledge was mainly about quality and relationships with vendors, but by the early 1990s, the need to take advantage of economies of scale and low-cost overseas labour led to larger, vertically integrated and specialised business units. This move away from smaller autonomous business units gave control through vertical integration, but typically also slowed responses and hampered flexibility, the result being that, 'Lean competitors, relying heavily on outsourcing, were able to move more quickly, both in seizing new opportunities and in abandoning old practices' (50).

The KM response to these problems from HP offered, 'consolidation and centralization of processes that had formerly relied heavily on the personal, and often inconsistent, knowledge of local agents' (Sieloff, 1999: 50) and covered:

- online reference databases
- shared document repositories
- automated software distribution and installation procedures
- groupware (Lotus Notes).

These information-oriented developments were said to facilitate *communities of interest and practice* to make their 'collective knowledge more visible and sharable'. The main place where this knowledge was visibly shared was in the, 'voluminous databases of known problems and solutions' in the customer response centres, which replaced, 'the routine troubleshooting activities of individual support engineers' (1999: 51). Herein lies the fruit of KM – a programmed response system for customer enquiries, mainly facilitating the employ of unskilled call-centre labour. This might be at odds with McKinlay's (2005: 251) more optimistic take on the potential of communities of practice (Wenger, 1991) 'to alert managers to the necessary existence and social organization of tacit knowledge in the workplace', where, 'Effective management turns upon the sensitivity of managers to the dynamics of communities of practice, the ability to intervene while going with the grain of the informal organization'. The experience for the core workforce at HP was somewhat simpler, where the KM strategy included the design of 'open office environments' where 'not collaborating becomes impossible' (Sieloff, 1999: 52) and where:

> Technology support for distributed teams needs to go beyond the conventional thinking of groupware environments and video conferencing capabilities, in order to restore some of the 'casual proximity' that is lost in remote interactions. Examples might include passive monitoring of workspaces by network cameras (so one could easily see when a teammate was available and interruptible). (52)

The practice of KM in this circumstance appears to rely mainly on social facilitation effects (see Chapter 20) of a coercive nature, combined with a form of co-surveillance; it would only need to be linked into a 3G video-capable phone system to literally put everyone in each other's pockets. The unanticipated consequence of all of this forcible sharing for HP though was what Sieloff characterises as an, 'asymmetrical impact on the flow of information' (1999: 52), or in other words nearly 6 million emails, phone calls, faxes and webpage views per day, which in themselves represented a huge information management problem (the redundancy problem again) but bring us no closer to a strategic system for managing knowledge. The final development cited by Sieloff is the 'HP Consulting Organization' which was involved in an 'aggressive program to create and nurture dozens of "learning communities"' (53), the major outcome of which was 'an expert yellow pages application', in other words a *telephone directory* categorised by topics specific to HP's business. The future plans for the Consulting Organization were of course redolent with KM rhetoric:

> Knowledge maps are created to help people understand what knowledge is needed and what is available at each step in a particular consulting process...A central knowledge desk will formalize a new intermediary role to accelerate the process of locating and delivering just-in-time knowledge to the consultants...managing both the formal and the informal aspects of their knowledge environment. (1999: 53)

Even if this were no more than simple rhetoric, what would it actually amount to? The entire just-in-time knowledge mapping 'strategy' relies once again on the creation of formalised SOPs and providing an element of bureaucratising the work of consultants where it has not been already replaced by call centres. This is a long way from the original intent Sieloff ascribed to HP's KM strategy, that is, making work 'more interesting by allowing more individual creativity and initiative to be applied...' (48). It is even further removed from Nonaka's KCC which of course paints SOP's, redundancy and the like as exactly what should be challenged in the process of 'knowledge creation'. And finally, HP's KM strategy is light-years away from Wilson's 'utopian culture' in that information is shared forcibly, autonomy exists only as far as which script or SOP to use and communities are a resource to be milked for their know-how. What it is closer to is the view of KM initiatives we noted above from Scarbrough (2003: 13) that KM systems, 'only reinforce and refract existing divisions of knowledge'. The extant divisions of information exchange at HP are not only reinforced by the KM strategy, but they are also reproduced and transformed as a workplace experience both individualised by an HR strategy, and at the same time under pressure to act as a collectivised unit in service of producing value out of intellectual capital. As to the acceptability of KM practices, citing Morris (2005, McKinlay (2005: 249) notes that 'The extent to which a knowledge codification wins the support of professional staff may be determined by their perception of its appropriation of surface information and its irrelevance to the deep knowledge demanded by their practice.' So KM systems are acceptable only up to a point and that point is where the actual interests of those whose knowledge is being managed come into play.

Knowledge management, control and performance

We have argued that there is some evidence to show that KM does not so much manage knowledge as manage the formalisation and standardisation of learning. KM may essentially be similar to HRM in that it can function as a collective mobility project for those in the KM industry (Wilson's 'IT boys' and their ilk). KM can also be seen to have connections to the so-called *high performance workplace* (HPW) characterised by the kind of factors outlined by Bauer (2004: 4):

> The main feature of these High Performance Workplace Organizations (HPWO) is a change from a Tayloristic work organization, characterized by task specialization, a pyramidal hierarchical structure,

and a centralization of responsibilities, to a Holistic organization featuring flat hierarchical structures, job rotation, self-responsible teams, multi-tasking, a greater involvement of lower-level employees in decision-making, and the replacement of vertical by horizontal communication channels. These innovative workplace systems are often accompanied by complementary human resource management practices. In addition, firms relying on innovative workplace systems often give employees the appropriate incentives to participate in decision-making through the use of alternative payment schemes. Furthermore, these firms often implement special training measures and appropriate hiring strategies to ensure a workforce with the necessary skills to work in these innovative organizations through employer provided training and appropriate hiring strategies.

The main premise of HPWOs is that firms can be achieve higher flexibility, higher product quality, and higher performance while remaining cost competitive by inducing workers to work harder and using the skills and information of their employees more effectively through moving decision authorities closer to theose who have the relevant information. It has further been hypothesized that HPWOs are "win-win" systems that do not only benefit employers but also their employees through higher wages and increased job satisfaction.

The HPW is essentially a motivation strategy which takes the basic Theory Y approach (see Chapter 21) and tries to avoid the 'vicious cycle' of giving employees ever greater discretion, responsibility and autonomy by adding behavioural controls based on goal-setting, performance-based reward, competence-based flexibility and a focus on quality through customer service and 'added value' costing.

The major constraint to individual autonomy provided by the HPW lies in ceding control to the group rather than the individual, and the role of KM here is in making individual learning and experience available to teams in a standardised and controlled format. Since tacit knowledge, as we have argued above, is inherently difficult to manage, it may not be amenable to any substantive control, or at least beyond the merely technical systems Sieloff demonstrates. KM, however, tries to treat knowledge as manageable, using the filtering and categorisation mechanisms of information management backed up by HRM systems and procedures to try to exert control over both the information track and the people track in organisations. Of course, though knowledge may be unmanageable in macro-terms, it certainly *is* amenable to social control, There are potential parallels with Alvesson and Kärreman's (2004) case study of control in a modern IT/management consultancy, where they observe that hard, structural controls are complemented by normative or ideological ones that focus on values and behaviour. KM initiatives could act to provide mechanisms that attempt to ensure behavioural fit, selecting and identifying those who are willing to fit with corporate identities and practices.

As with elements of HRM, the people track of KM is another group-based concept applied indiscriminately to 'teams'. Sharing is crucial to KM strategies and is dependent on cohesiveness/openness/trust because it is a factor in the salience of group identity. However, if the sharing involved in KM practices is 'forced sharing', then this is not amenable to engendering trust and will tend to produce less salient group identities and is less likely to promote productivity. (We address these issues in more depth in Chapters 24 and 25). The products of our knowledge can certainly be bought, just like our labour, but sharing knowledge is more likely with those that we have some relationship with, for example the sharing of *experience* in a mentor or master-apprentice relationship. This again leaves KM in the same situation as sophisticated computer-numerically controlled machinery that can capture skilled behaviour but not the socially situated experiential knowledge it is based on. In addition, attempts to formalise social controls over knowledge – for example by restricting access to information or the ability to socialise or communicate – will tend to be subverted by informal association and action. This means that whether as an individual, group or organisational resource knowledge is still controlled only through relationships and by formalising information and knowledge sharing, KM underestimates the value of relationships and thus knowledge to the individual.

At its most basic then, KM is another attempt to translate social control into structural control and, as with the motivational techniques we will discuss in Chapter 21, we would expect it to emphasise short-term rewards and suffer from diminishing returns or habitualised adherence to chores or box-ticking exercises. KM is a hard, single strategy approach to a plurality of soft problems though the only hard problems it actually addresses are information management problems, and in this it is more akin to Japanisation or organisational learning as cover stories for hard-strategy practices. The notion that integrated knowledge-based systems can provide the key to competitive advantage is little different to the notion that structurally integrated manufacturing systems would provide the solutions to problems of productivity. If KM is ever to have any success in doing what it should do well in the area of soft strategies, that is, in forging real communities of practice, then caveats of the sort put forward by McKinlay will need to be addressed:

> " Ironically, KM initiatives are more likely to be sustainable if they begin from the premise that all forms of knowledge are not the sole prerogative of management. Equally, more durable KM projects will accept the inevitability of its limits: that important working knowledge will remain tacit, partly due to its highly contextual and ephemeral nature but also because workers can draw upon this resource to regulate their working lives; to sustain practices that are geared toward equity rather than efficiency; and to erect barriers against managerial incursions into professional, occupational, or individual ethics. KM projects based upon solving widely recognized, practical problems tend to enlist greater workforce support than top-down initiatives triggered by possibilities offered by information and communication technologies. Inevitably, however, this creates tensions between short-term success and long-term viability. (McKinlay, 2005: 259)

The key argument in this chapter is that real knowledge management is in actuality knowledge self-management and that informal communities of practice already manage knowledge for themselves in the workplace. Attempts to formalise and standardise knowledge as in Nonaka's Knowledge Creating Company will always have to struggle with the problem that tacit knowledge is inherently difficult to manage and in practice knowledge management initiatives are often reduced to information management systems overlaid with a gloss of traditional HR. Likewise, mobilising line managers as 'knowledge engineers' is fraught with the same difficulties as devolving responsibility for HR to the line. Examining the putting of KM strategy into practice further highlighted how uneasily the IT and people tracks of KM sit together and how initiatives serve to reproduce and reinforce extant divisions of power and information exchange. The connections between KM, HR and the high-commitment workplace were explored to point to linkages with issues of motivation, teamwork and subjectivity, to be examined further in Part III. We will return to KM again in considering personality and HRM in Chapter 19, but will first look at issues of subjectivity in OB as our introduction to Part III.

Further reading

Though critical of its content it would be churlish not to mention Nonaka and Takeuchi's (1995; 1996) arguments about the knowledge-creating company. Good overviews and insights into the conceptual issues can be found in Blackler (1995), Swan and Scarbrough (2001), Alvesson and Kärreman (2001) and

McKinlay (2005). McKinlay's (2002; 2005) case studies offer some of the few reliable empirical studies. Wilson (2002) and Scarbrough (2003) are sceptical of KM and perceptive about the domination of the information dimension. Wenger (1998) and Brown and Duigud (1991) provided the template for communities of practice that KM initiatives often seek to imitate.

Alvesson, M. and Kärreman, D. (2001) 'Odd couple: Making Sense of the Curious Concept of Knowledge Management', *Journal of Management Studies*, 38. 7: 995–1018.

Blackler, F. (1995) 'Knowledge, Knowledge Work and Organizations: An Overview and Interpretation', *Organization Studies*, 16. 6: 1021–46.

Brown, J. S. and Duguid, S. (1991) 'Organizational Learning and Communities of Practice: Towards a Unified View of Working, Learning and Innovation', *Organization Science*, 2. 1: 40–57.

McKinlay, A. (2002) 'The Limits of Knowledge Management', *New Technology, Work and Employment*, 17. 2: 76–88.

McKinlay, A. (2005) 'Knowledge Management', in S. Ackroyd, R. Batt, P. Thompson and P. Tolbert (eds.), *The Oxford Handbook of Work and Organization*, Oxford: Oxford University Press.

Nonaka, I. (1996) The Knowledge-Creating Company, in Starkey, K. (ed.) (1996), *How Organizations Learn: Strategy, Structure, Process and Leadership*, London: Routledge.

Nonaka, I. and Takeuchi, H. (1995) *The Knowledge-Creating Company*, New York: Oxford University Press.

Swan, J. and Scarbrough, H. (2001) 'Knowledge Management: Concepts and Controversies', *Journal of Management Studies*, 38. 7: 913–21.

Scarbrough, H. (2003) 'The Role of Intermediary Groups in Shaping Management Fashion: The Case of Knowledge Management', *International Studies of Management and Organization*, 32. 4: 87–103.

Wenger, E. (1998) *Communities of Practice: Learning, Meaning and Identity*. Cambridge: Cambridge University Press.

Wilson, T. D. (2002) 'The Nonsense of Knowledge Management', *Information Research*, 8. 1 (http://informationr.net/ir/8-1/paper144.html).

part II: conclusions and key arguments

To summarise these five chapters, given the variety of issues and evidence, would be impossible in a short space. But does a more general pattern emerge as we reflect on all these contemporary changes in work, organisations and employment? The standard framing device in such discussions is to set out optimistic and pessimistic scenarios. In a recent overview of the evidence on trends in job quality, Coats (2009) distinguishes, for example, between 'sunny uplands' and 'bleak house' and finds that Britain is a bit on the gloomy side, but that better outcomes elsewhere indicate that economic actors can and should make choices. Sounds fair enough. Another framing device is 'all change' or 'things don't change much'. The two dimensions are not interchangeable. After all, one can think that everything is changing and for the worse.

It is certainly tempting to adopt a sceptical view of change, if for no other reason than that most of the claims made in big-picture perspectives (mostly discussed in Chapter 12) are so unconvincing. As Nolan (2003: 476) comments and contrasts to the complex and detailed findings from the ESRC Future of Work programme, 'The reality is that both the pessimistic and optimistic scenarios remain weakly grounded in any systematic theory or evidence.' To try and make sense of these complexities, we set out some criteria at the start of Part II. These focused on assessing the continuity, content, context, connections and consequences of change. Content and context speak primarily to detailed developments that have been addressed in the substantive chapters. What about the other criteria?

With respect to basic issues of continuity, we were particularly critical of the two most dominant new economy narratives – post-Fordism and the knowledge economy. The former emerged as a largely optimistic paradigm break account in the mid-1980s. It was never big on evidence and if we look around us it's not blindingly obvious that we have an economy dominated by specialised markets, served by small, decentralised and post-bureaucratic firms whose employment relations are based on job security, high trust and high skill. Almost all markets are increasingly dominated by large firms, albeit with diverse activities and hybridised structures. As for the other and more recent narrative, the growing importance of knowledge to *some* firms does not change the dominant economic logic of capitalism and the labour market is not being flooded by armies of mobile, high-powered knowledge workers whose ownership of their own assets has companies at their mercy. The largest job growth is in personal and mass service sectors.

However, two themes from these narratives more than a grain of truth and resonate with the evidence. From post-Fordism, we can accept that the search for flexibility in product and labour markets, and labour processes has been central to corporate and state strategies and in that pursuit they have been largely successful. Knowledge economy perspectives do trade on one important point. Work organisations, whether through teams, emotional labour or knowledge management, have been trying to access and utilise the tacit knowledge, skills and social competencies of different categories of employees in different ways. Though there are many continuities in current structure and practices with Fordism and

Taylorism, these trends represent significant discontinuities. It is not accurate then, to describe the contemporary situation in terms of fundamental continuity, such as neo-Fordism. It's still capitalism, but a more flexible form, as Sennett notes:

> Today the phrase 'flexible capitalism' describes a system which is more than a permutation on an old theme. Rigid forms of bureaucracy are under attack, as are the evils of blind routine. Workers are asked to behave nimbly, to be open to change on short notice, to take risks continually, to become ever less dependent on regulations and formal procedures. (Sennett, 1998: 27)

As we illustrated in Chapter 15, one of the outcomes of flexible capitalism is that work is more demanding, with mixed results. On the one hand, many workers embrace aspects of those demands by investing their capacities and part of their identities in work, seeking solace or satisfaction. This is particularly true of women, whose levels of satisfaction are higher than men, despite disadvantage and unequal treatment (Bolton and Houlihan, 2009). However, as we have also shown, the price paid by labour has been high. Whether presented in positive (empowerment) or brutal (lean and mean or the Chinese and Indians will get your job) terms, extra effort and responsibility has been combined with increased specification and monitoring of performance in particularly unattractive ways. And as work has become more elastic, its demands have increasingly seeped into the home sphere. The price has been high, in part, because the reciprocity integral to the claims of post-Fordism and high-performance work-system perspectives either did not emerge in any systematic or strategic way, or has decayed and diminished. Whatever the attractions of new forms of work relations, it has not been matched in the sphere of employment relations. We do not have rampant casualisation of the labour market and most workers welcome flexible choices of when and how to work, when they are available. But the 'new insecurity' is based on the transfer of risk from capital to labour.

> These management systems are intended to impose risk on individual employees in order to elicit higher performance and seek to make future earnings contingent while introducing a more exacting scrutiny of employee behaviour. (Heery and Salmon, 2000: 14)

Employees are being asked unconditionally to invest more of themselves and work collaboratively in the job, while any employer promises are purely conditional; the result is a 'collectivisation of effort and decollectivisation of risk' (Burchell *et al.*, 1999: 60). This is increasingly recognised by mainstream management theorists: 'In all the talk about the new responsibilities of employees, there is little talk about the new responsibilities of managers … the fact is that most employees feel that they are the company's most expendable resource' (Hamel and Prahalad, 1996: 239). Furthermore, there is little indication that employers are living up to expectations of return investment. Not only are employees being asked to take over responsibility for career development, studies show that employers are making less investment in training and skill development, in part because of fear that such investment will be lost through redundancy or exit from their firm (see Cappelli, 1995: 2001).

Such mainstream writings tend to frame the issue in terms of the 'psychological contract', the informal, perceived obligations between employer and employee. It is accepted that employment relations may be less secure than in the past and that increased downsizing, de-layering and flexibility for firms has disrupted the old contract. An employee interviewed by Heckscher sums it up with considerable clarity:

> My basic mindset was, there's an implicit contract, I expect that the company will provide me a career, development opportunities, and reasonable pay and benefits: and they, in turn, should expect from me

> that I'm willing to work very hard for them. When either one of us is unhappy with that situation, the contract is broken. And up until the past few years, as a corporation I had faith that that would occur. (Heckscher, 1995: 18)

Heckscher, like some other management commentators, sees the consequences in predominantly benign terms. The new arrangements will have the benefits of being based on open negotiation and the promise of equality between organisation and individual, rather than paternalism and effort–security bargain. The individual will not have to subsume his or her personality in the organisation, and the breakdown of paternalism will allow more women and minorities to enter the ranks of management. On the surface this new social contract and the end of loyalty as a bond between organisation 'man' and the corporation seems somewhat lop-sided. However, it is felt that there is a mutual gain as long as notions of opportunity and advancement are reimagined. Finally, there are new obligations: rather than employment, firms provide opportunities and transferable skills to help people become more *employable*, thus furthering a career across organisations and within occupational communities rather than up a single corporate ladder. The UK body representing the HR profession – the CIPD (2005) – has joined in, claiming that a new generation of 'millennials' are not interested in a job for life, but rather want excitement, a sense of community and a life outside work.

As we acknowledge in Chapter 14, there are highly mobile, knowledge-rich employees who can flourish in the new circumstances, but to present the changes in terms of some kind of universal 'new deal' is either disingenuous or a distortion of the facts. As commentaries by otherwise sympathetic observers in the UK (Coats, 2009) and the USA (Kochan, 2007) show, the HR profession has proved unwilling or unable to explain the failure of its own promises and mantras on the centrality of human capital. No matter how many times it is repeated that 'people are our most important asset', this is 'a plot in search of practice' (Thompson, 2007: 86), at least in the variety of capitalism that prevails in those economies. This brings us to the question of *connections*. Notions of HPWS rest on the idea of effective links between the strategic, functional and workplace levels. Post-Fordism and knowledge-economy narratives assume cohesive relations – a fit – between the requirements of product markets, labour markets, work design and employment systems (see the flexible specialisation diagram in Chapter 12 for an example). But *after* Fordism, that is not how it has worked out. If we take HPWS, we've certainly had the high *performance* from labour, but not the supporting employment *system* from capital.

There are two significant and interrelated sources of disconnection present in contemporary political economy. The first derives from the dominance of capital markets rather than product and labour markets as the drivers of firm behaviour (Lazonick and O'Sullivan, 2000; Thompson, 2003). As we noted and supported in Chapter 12, an increasing number of radical and mainstream economists have been using the term financialised capitalism to describe such shifts in the circuits of capital (Froud *et al.*, 2006; Bellamy Foster, 2007). The credit crunch has brought home the reality of such economies, but the pursuit of shareholder value already had a destabilising effect on the management of work and employment relations. Shareholder value as a growth regime focuses on asset management and anticipated revenue streams. Downsizing, merger and acquisition and perpetual restructuring have become the norm in many sectors, rendering progressive objectives in work and employment spheres – investment in skills, training, employment stability and careers – much harder to prioritise or sustain as the broader pressures work their way down to the workplace level (Jenkins and Delbridge, 2007).

The second source of disconnection and instability is the growth of fragmented employment arrangements, an argument associated with the research of academics at Manchester Business School (Marchington *et al.*, 2005). We discussed their findings in Chapter 12, noting moves away from dominance of a single employer model to complex inter-organisational arrangements where contracting out functions and services leads to multiple employers and clients, with more people working for agencies supplying temporary workers, particularly at the interface between private and public sectors. Their case studies show that such blurring of boundaries might result in more rapid promotion or other better employment prospects, but are more likely to undermine job security and introduce different pay structures and rates. For management, the shift to market-based transactions across more permeable boundaries make stable strategy and policy harder, with a lack of clarity on who is responsible for skill development and other HR practices. Neither, given the trend towards deregulated labour markets in many societies, has the state stepped in to fill such gaps. As Ackroyd and colleagues (2005: 13) observe, 'This institutional lag has left individuals on their own to craft makeshift solutions ... families have absorbed the costs of corporate restructuring and conflicts between work and family or work and personal life have become a salient pattern in the fabric of everyday life'.

Finally, that leaves the question of the consequences of such trends for worker attitudes and behaviour. Marchington and colleagues (2005) note the loss of employee voice, resentment at being 'sold' to another employer and the difficulties of sustaining commitment. The double disconnection between more demanding work and the failure of employment and corporate governance support structures seems highly likely to damage the basic effort bargain as well as the broader psychological contract. That appears to be supported by survey evidence, in the UK at least. We already noted in Chapter 15 that employees reported significant increases in work effort. Some of the same surveys indicated that more than 40 per cent of employees think that management can be trusted 'only a little' or 'not at all' and three-quarters claim that management and employees are not 'on the same side' (Burchell, 2002). The Mercer Human Resource Consulting Group found similar figures and that trust declined with length of service (Caulkin, 2003). Most tellingly, the CIPD's own employee surveys (CIPD, 2007) reveal considerable unhappiness about how they are managed, with only a third trusting senior management.

This wave of dissatisfaction or 'violation of the psychological contract' does not necessarily lead to overt conflict and resistance. Such feelings may be offset by positive satisfactions in the job, which is consistent with some survey evidence (Parent-Thirion *et al.*, 2007). Or it may be that labour- and product-market uncertainties constrain employee ability or willingness to take action, particularly in circumstances of declining union presence in the private sectors of modern economies. There also seems to be some evidence that fragmented workforces can lead to some tensions between different categories of workers (Newsome *et al.*, 2009; Hopkins, 2009). However, the idea that organisations have not incurred any significant 'costs' from this broken bargain would be mistaken. As we have seen, both recent and earlier case studies and surveys show sharp declines in employee commitment and morale, particularly in downsized companies (see Cappelli, 1995: 586). Moreover, demotivation and lack of identification with company goals are directly related to feelings of job insecurity (Burchell *et al.*, 1999: 53–7). Among the consequences of such changes are increased defensive behaviours and attitudes, with emphasis put on securing the positional advantage of individuals and functional groups, and exacerbation of competitive struggles to 'impress' the corporate hierarchy between generational, gender and professional groups among managers (Collinson and Collinson, 1997; Hallier and James, 1997; Mulholland, 1998). In one sense, employees have got the message: individual ambition, not organisational loyalty, is what matters. As Sennett (1998) eloquently argues, whether this is a solid basis for the kind of trust relations that can sustain creativity and commitment in organisational life is another matter.

Further reading

Given the variety and depth of changes discussed in Part II we are somewhat spoilt for or perhaps overwhelmed by the choice of relevant and important books and articles. To keep things simple, we have focused on the larger integrative studies that will give the reader overviews of changes in and across different spheres. Handbooks are increasingly the vehicle for presentation of research and we have drawn extensively on the *Oxford Handbook in Work Organization* edited by Ackroyd and colleagues (2005). Ackroyd's (2002) somewhat neglected book is probably the best guide to the nature of the modern (mainly British) firm and its markets, networks and hierarchies. It takes a different view of similar issues than P. Adler's (2001) well-known journal piece. While we have been sceptical of Castell's (1996; 2000) work, but it remains a comprehensive and in many ways impressive work. His later, smaller work – *The Internet Galaxy* – is a useful short-cut to many of his controversial arguments. The book by the American business journalist Doug Henwood (2003) is a marvellous antidote to new-economy hype. We have also used many of the studies that are part of the Future of Work programme that was funded by the UK Economic and Social Research Council, especially White and colleagues (2004). There is a very useful overview of many of the projects provided in a Special Edition of the *British Journal of Industrial Relations* edited by Nolan and Wood (and see http://www.leeds.ac.uk/esrcfutureofwork/ for a complete view of outputs). Other very good overviews of large-scale research projects and surveys on changing organisations, work and employment are Marchington and colleagues' (2005) *Fragmented Work* and Green's (2006) *Demanding Work*. Harley and colleagues' (2005) collection provides a useful picture of trends in participation and involvement, and two new edited volumes from MacDonald and Korczynski on services and Bolton and Houlihan on contemporary work contain a lot of the recent critical and cutting-edge writings.

Ackroyd, S. (2002) *The Organization of Business*, Oxford: Oxford University Press.

Ackroyd, S., Batt, R., Thompson, P. and Tolbert, P. (eds.) (2005) *A Handbook of Work and Organization*, Oxford: Oxford University Press.

Adler, P. (2001) 'Market, Hierarchy, and Trust: The Knowledge Economy and the Future of Capitalism', *Organization Science*, 12. 2: 215–34.

Bolton, S. and Houlihan, M. (eds) (forthcoming) *Work Matters: Critical Reflections on Contemporary Work*, Basingstoke: Palgrave.

Castells, M. (2001) *The Internet Galaxy: Reflections on the Internet, Business and Society*, Oxford: Oxford University Press.

Castells, M. (1996, 2nd edn, 2000) *The Rise of the Network Society, The Information Age: Economy, Society and Culture Vol. I.*, Cambridge, Mass.; Oxford, UK: Blackwell.

Green, F. (2006) *Demanding Work: The Paradox of Job Quality in the Affluent Economy*, Princeton, N.J.: Princeton University Press.

Harley, B., Hyman, J. and Thompson, P. (eds.) (2005) *Democracy and Participation at Work: Essays in Honour of Harvie Ramsay*, Basingstoke: Palgrave.

Henwood, D. (2003) *After the New Economy*, New York: The New Press.

MacDonald, C. and Korczynski, M. (eds.) (2008) *Critical Perspectives on Service Work*, London: Routledge.

Marchington, M., Grimshaw, D., Rubery, J. and Willmott, H. (eds) (2005) *Fragmenting Work: Blurring Organizational Boundaries and Disordering Hierarchies*, Oxford: Oxford University Press.

Nolan, P. and Wood, S. (eds.) (2003) 'Mapping the Future of Work', *Special Edition of British Journal of Industrial Relations*, 41. 2.

White, M., Hill, S., Mills, C. and Smeaton, D. (2004) *Managing to Change? British Workplaces and the Future of Work*, Basingstoke: Palgrave Macmillan.

part III

understanding organisational behaviour: issues and agendas

introduction: regulating organisational behaviour

> Specifically, I would suggest that the effective organization is garrulous, clumsy, superstitious, hypocritical, monstrous, octopoid, wandering, and grouchy. (Karl Weick)

Our argument here in this chapter previews the overall argument in the whole of Part III that while containing much of value, mainstream OB approaches have tended to offer a fragmented, partial account of the human condition, and moreover, one frequently distorted by a managerial agenda.

The aims of this chapter are to:

- Introduce how psychology approaches issues of organisational behaviour and the regulation of work-place behaviour.
- Briefly survey industrial/organisational psychology using historical and contemporary examples to explore what kind of knowledge organisational psychology produces.
- Explore the topic-based nature of the mainstream agenda in OB along with its inbuilt limitations.
- Revisit the issue of subjectivity and how it is conceptualised in this text as opposed to mainstream OB.

In a review of the 'discipline' of organisational psychology as a professional practice, Blackler described it as follows:

> The subject 'organisational psychology' can legitimately be understood to include all aspects of behaviour in organisations that may be studied from a psychological point of view. By common usage, however, the term is normally used to refer to applied social psychological studies of organisation. Important areas of practical and theoretical concern have included motivation, attitudes and job satisfaction, job and organisation design, interpersonal and group behaviour, leadership studies, approaches to participation and industrial democracy, conflict, decision-making, and the planning of change. (Blackler, 1982: 203)

This is by no means exhaustive of the work undertaken by organisational psychologists. Topics could be added from those more usually associated with occupational psychology, such as selection, placement and counselling, and new issues and areas of study are constantly opening up, such as diversity and emotion at work. Lists of topics are not, however, very helpful in understanding the distinctive character of the discipline. To do this, it is useful to begin with where it actually comes from.

Technologies of regulation?

Historically the subject has manifested a problem-centred approach dealing with the major perceived difficulties of organisational society at the time:

> Industrial Psychology thus covers a wide field. It deals with the human, as contrasted with the mechanical and economic aspects of labour. Its chief aim is to reduce needless effort and irritation and to increase interest and attention throughout the workers in industry. (C. S. Myers, 1926: 11)

In a similar vein, Hollway (1991: 4–5) cites Alec Roger in the 1950s as giving a neat definition of the paradigm for occupational/industrial psychology as 'Fitting the man to the job and the job to the man', (FMJ/FJM). The issue here is one of the quality and integrity of the psychological practice and knowledge applied in the area, and the FMJ/FJM paradigm gives us a client-centred definition which from the start has given a technical orientation to work in the area. Such a definition relies heavily on the notion of a value-neutral, objective science that is independent of the power relations in the organisations and societies within which it is practised. The reality is, of course, that both power and knowledge are not singular, unitary or completely objective. Even a person believing he or she is a value-free carrier of fully objective scientific knowledge has to utilise and exercise that knowledge in the real world, and the one thing we do know is that power relations in organisations are seldom, if ever, completely equitable.

Without such awareness, new practical and theoretical knowledges from the repertoire of organisational behaviour can function as *technologies of regulation*, used to control and discipline employees. Such practices were inherent in the origins and early development of the sub-discipline of *industrial psychology*. In the first two decades of this century, employers drew on the variety of psychological theories on offer (Bendix, 1956: 200–1). For example, *behaviourism*'s orientation towards 'human engineering' was a particularly useful source of advice for managers seeking to manipulate environmental stimuli in the form of penalties and incentives, in order to produce appropriate worker responses. At the same time, rival schools such as *instinct psychology* could suggest means of employers meeting 'innate' needs such as self-expression, which were being distorted by evil Bolsheviks and union organisers. Perhaps most practically, *vocational psychology* could provide a battery of tests and measurements for applications to selection and placement. It was in this latter sphere that industrial psychology really took off in the US, boosted by the extensive use of tests for intelligence and other factors during the war.

Psychology in industry had in fact begun in the area of advertising, but it soon shifted from manipulation of consumers to workers. Most concepts and techniques were extremely primitive, but psychologists such as Munsterberg promoted the idea that they could be applied to the 'labour problem'. The accumulation of knowledge about individual differences provided the basis for a varied apparatus of testing and measurement techniques geared to vocational counselling, placement testing and job analysis, with suggested correlations between factors such as intelligence, personality and potential work performance. Munsterberg summed up the general aim as finding 'those personalities which by their mental qualities are especially fit for a particular kind of economic work' (quoted in Baritz, 1960: 3). There was a widespread tendency to claim bogus relationships between national or racial characteristics and suitability for jobs (Kamin, 1979). In Britain, organisational psychology was relatively isolated from its American cousin. The National Institute of Industrial Psychology, founded under the leadership of Charles Myers in 1921, took a painstaking and broader interest in the related issues of training, rest, monotony and fatigue at work (see quote above and Hollway, 1991 for an analytic account of this venture). But even here consultancy pressures dictated programmes of vocational guidance, selection and testing.

It was these kinds of development that led Baritz (1960) to develop his famous analysis of psychologists and other industrial social scientists as *servants of power*. The science of behaviour was seen as giving management 'a slick new approach to its problems of control' (1960: 209). Included in the 'bag of schemes' were attitude surveys, selection devices, motivation studies, counselling and role-playing. Events in the 1930s Hawthorne studies, discussed in Chapter 4, were a particularly powerful confirmation of the social engineering role that could be played by social scientists, in this case under the framework of human relations theory. Those kinds of superficial and manipulatory practice are still being recycled today. For example, the reaction to objective problems that employees face in their work, recognised in the modern stress research literature, has led to the astonishingly innovative introduction of employee counselling programmes! Baritz's great insight was to recognise that the service provided by social scientists to industry meant that 'control need no longer be imposed. It can be encouraged to come from within.' Workers could be manipulated to internalise the very ideologies and practices that ensured their domination.

A perfect modern example of this is the role played by industrial psychologists in some of the new human resource management techniques. The American writer Grenier (1988) worked as part of a team hired by Johnson and Johnson, the medical products company, to create the required conditions for the setting up of a new plant on a greenfield site in New Mexico. This involved many of the elements discussed in Chapters 12 and 15: quality circles and semi-autonomous work teams, status and symbolic harmonisation of conditions, extensive socialisation into a corporate culture facilitated by psychological testing at the selection and hiring stage. None of this of course is necessarily negative or manipulative, even the secret tape recordings of work team meetings to help identify success in fostering group identity and dynamics. But the hidden agenda of the whole project was a 'union avoidance' campaign, and this came to light when some of the workforce began an organising drive. The social psychologists became active and central participants in the struggle inside the heads of employees. All the supposedly innocent information collected became a means of screening workers and their attitudes. Team meetings in particular played an important role in identifying pro-union workers, and Grenier was asked to develop an index through which to rank workers in their degree of support. Grenier later publicly revealed this process and himself became subject to surveillance and intimidation.

Not all social scientists of course have been concerned with such manipulatory practices, and there has been a considerable amount of useful work done on employee satisfaction. The modern equivalents of Baritz's servants of power are not necessarily 'on the payroll', but still have a tendency to accept managerial norms as the parameters of their activities. In the same way as the newspaper owner does not have to threaten journalists to toe the editorial line, mainstream behavioural scientists generally internalise controls, and largely unacknowledged self-censorship becomes the order of the day. In other words, the institutional relationship between the disciplines and their client groups remains a crucial problem.

Later, in developing out of industrial and human relations psychology in the 1950s and 1960s, organisational psychology brought to the study of work organisations an emphasis on descriptive and experimental research incorporated from social psychology. This was allied to the concern with applied psychology that had given impetus to industrial psychology in the early part of the century, and the human relations tradition discussed in earlier chapters. Later inputs to organisational psychology from areas such as socio-technical systems theory and operations research have further cemented the relationship of the subject with the interests of power groups in organisations.

That the practitioners of organisational psychology and organisation theory have often been located in such institutions as business schools, rather than in industry or psychology departments, also reinforces the conception of the subject as a discipline in its own right, with its own client groups and professional concerns. At the same time this distances them enough from their clients and subject matter to enable them to concentrate more on the theoretical understanding of organisations than was the case with the more strictly application-led industrial psychology. In turn, this enabled retention of much of the humanistic theoretical orientation derived from social psychology. Theoretical ideals of this nature do not, however, often survive exposure to the needs of the main client group. As with industrial psychology before it, this results in the subject becoming chiefly directed towards the practical needs of management.

A humanistic perspective fully cognisant of the effects of organisational work on the interests and identities of employees is unlikely to promote harmonious relations with clients whose major tasks include the deployment and control of an organisation's 'human resources'. Nor would an organisational psychology that grounded its theory and practice in an understanding of the politics of production be likely to be in a position to fully give itself over to the demands of these clients. The upshot of all this is that the explanations, instruments and techniques developed from mainstream theories often function to sustain and implement a culture of domination in the workplace. Organisational psychology, though paradoxically informed by humanistic concerns, has both a role as an agent and a vested interest in mobilising the consent of organisational members.

Topics and texts

Given the above discussion, it is not surprising that the areas from social psychology that have been enlisted into organisational psychology's project of understanding human behaviour are often limited to those having functional utility. Texts tended to be presented under chapters or headings focusing on topics such as learning, perception and motivation, reflecting psychological explanations of individual personality; and topics such as leadership and group processes, which incorporate social-psychological explanations of interpersonal dynamics. However, topics in the sphere of aggression, affiliation and prejudice, which within social psychology were assumed to deal with influential determinants of human behaviour, were not routinely assimilated into organisational psychology.

This is an odd separation, given that such factors may be expected to have at least some bearing on practices within organisations. The difference is largely that the latter set reflects areas of subjective experience which, although of importance to individuals and groups in organisations, are not of direct relevance to the production process, except insofar as they might interfere with it. Rather, the factors are treated as external to what is considered necessary and appropriate behaviour at work. Similarly, issues of discrimination, though a structural feature of organisational life, have long been marginalised and not constituted as significant objects of study. Aggression has been addressed obliquely in OB through the issue of organisational conflict, but the perspective used examined conflict, for example, as a problem to be resolved or avoided rather than to be understood as a possible consequence of inequalities of power and resources.

Since the first edition of this text, researchers have begun to look at issues of anti-social and aggressive behaviour in organisations in more detail (see Giacolone and Greenberg, 1997). They are producing evidence to show that factors such as downsizing, role diversity and increased reliance on part-timers are increasing the levels of emotional disturbance and aggression in the workplace (though the aggression is often indirect, passive and verbal, with the glaring exception of 'going postal'). Likewise there have been moves of late to address issues such as discrimination in general OB texts, but this has generally been under headings such as *managing diversity* (see Chapters 10 and 25 and also Weightman, 1999: 225–6). This, along with the issues of workplace bullying and 'dealing with problem people', is probably being addressed in the context of managing organisational liability to litigation on the basis of equal opportunities and employment legislation.

When concepts are introduced into the mainstream agenda there is also the danger that they will run into difficulties with existing psychological conceptions in those areas. We have already seen this in relation to the very loose usage of 'knowledge' in the knowledge management literature (see Chapter 16) and will see it again in relation to groups, teams, well-being and emotions.

The competing mainstream explanations of psychological and social processes were treated in OB texts almost as if they were discrete accounts of human development and activity. Taking an area such as learning (see Chapter 20) which must be integral to any account of psychological development, the mechanisms and processes of apparently mutually exclusive perspectives such as the cognitive and behaviourist models were categorised through the assumptions about human nature that underlie them. Thus we had the 'models of man' approach to OB, where theories were assessed through the assumptions they make and the implications of those assumptions for social behaviour. There was nothing intrinsically wrong with this as a method of analysis, but it did tend to reinforce the exclusivity of differing approaches, which are in fact no more than varying conceptions of the basic processes by which we all develop and negotiate our changing identities.

Subjects and subjectivities

While there is undoubted value in a topic-based approach, it tends to miss out many issues and experiences, notably for us those of subjectivity and identity. Our approach to the 'subjective factor' in organisations tried to do this by focusing on the experience of people in work organisations through the common themes of subjectivity and identity. Both concepts present problems of interpretation, and there is considerable overlap in their usage. Our usage of 'subjectivity' followed Henriques and colleagues' (1984: 2–3) twofold definition (though see Pritchard, 1998 for a critique of our usage of this). First is the *condition of being subject*: the ways in which the individual is acted upon, and made subject to the structural and interpersonal processes at work in organisational life; second, the *condition of being a subject*: possessing individuality and self-awareness. Thus the term encompasses the fundamentally contradictory experience of work and the subjective development and regulation of people's 'emotions, desires, fantasies, a sense of self' (Banton *et al.*, 1985: 44).

Socially produced identities are a central factor delineating people's experience of work and cannot be dealt with without concepts deriving from the study of structural processes such as organisational design, control strategies or the impact of wider social formations. But they in turn will be incomplete without reference to the factors surrounding the *construction* of the subjectivity and experience of those involved. Organisational psychology should allow us to enter these areas necessary for a fuller account of 'organisational behaviour'. But the relation between organisational psychology and the subjective factor in the study of work organisations was and still is by no means clear. Though organisational psychology and its practitioners might be expected to have a natural concern with the identities and subjective experience of participants, the range of issues and topics traditionally presented in the area did not consistently address these concepts. We will return to the general limitations of the mainstream agenda in Part IV, but in its content, that agenda can be thought of as a journey through the processes by which individuals become social participants who perceive, learn and are motivated beings with individual personalities. Our intention here is to treat the mechanisms and processes identified by competing approaches as inputs to, rather than exclusive accounts of, this developmental process. This is because the fragmented treatment of subjectivity in OB meant that the implied journey through an individual's development into a social being never explicitly takes place.

The concept of identity commonly involved the notion that there was an irreducible core of social and individual being that uniquely identifies each of us. Psychologically, identity variously incorporated concepts of self and self-esteem, structures of values, attitudes and beliefs, personality and associated traits. Sociologically, it included concepts of self and of roles and reference groups. Lasch (1985: 31–2) noted a shift of meaning that did not admit a fixed or continuous identity, but a '*minimal self*' which, because of our need for an 'emotional equilibrium', retreats to a 'defensive core, armed against adversity' (1985: 16). The conception of identity used here, then, is at odds with the conceptions of identity that have come to the fore since the first edition of this text in that though acknowledging the social construction of our identities, we reject the relativism of much modern writing on identity by still granting identity processes some agency (see Chapter 7 Summary) in directing behavior.

Our usage then, incorporates the notion of self-aware and participative subjects, who maintain a valued part of their identity against the unpredictability of the external world, while being acted on and constrained by organisational ideologies and practices. These themes of subjectivity and identity are examined in the context of interrelated arguments, together providing a framework capable of addressing issues of structure, agency, individual action and experience. We will begin in the next chapter, however, with the understanding of perception and its relations to attitude, since both are fundamental psychological processes on which many of the topics and issues to be visited later are dependent. In this way we can both make topics easier to identify and follow for the reader, at the same time as recognising that all of the psychological and relational processes we will discuss are dependent on the development of the perceptual processes which shape our view of the world.

Summary and key points

In an account of individual experience in the workplace, which attempts as we do to place psychological knowledge and technique in the context of behavioural regulation, we need an appropriate starting point. We have taken an historical approach which argues against the separation of topics within OB. However, our problem in emphasising the thoroughgoing interdependence of concepts and issues in understanding behaviour in organisations is that this is not the reality of standard discussion of behavioural issues. We have therefore argued for maintaining many of the traditional topic and conceptual divisions in order to engage with the existing forms of explanation. At the same time we will in Part III try to bring topics together where they are dependent on similar bodies of knowledge, such as perception and attitudes, learning and change and stress and emotions. We have briefly readdressed the issue of the missing subject which gave us much of the impetus for the original versions of this text and will return to this in Chapter 22 to reintegrate our main themes and bring the conceptual threads together.

18 perception and attitudes: seeing what to think

> Gestalt psychologists, such as Samuel Renshaw, have devised methods for widening the range and increasing the acuity of human perceptions. But do our educators apply them? The answer is, No.
> (Aldous Huxley, 1954: 29)

Though not perhaps subscribing to Huxley's views about mescaline as a pedagogic tool (though we can think of a few people it might do some good to), it is easy to understand the frustration felt by being privy to simple lessons that others do not seem to learn, this being especially true of the principles of human perception. We all know what stereotypes are, but we cannot help using them. Many managers today have had some teaching in OB and should know what a *halo effect* is, but few would give thought to how it might affect their appraisal of their subordinates. The problem is that more than with other OB topics, the basic processes of perception seem very abstract compared to the everyday world of work, with its conflicts of interest and shifting allegiances to groups. But to understand how we come to have those interests and allegiances we need to know how we apprehend, organise and utilise the information coming to us from our surroundings. In a sense then this chapter, like Chapter 16, is about knowledge management, except that here the processes are internal to the person and largely unconscious. Our exploration of perception and attitudes will move from a fairly straightforward account of psychological processes, through a consideration of how we know about others, to how techniques and methods developed from theory are utilised to judge and control our behaviour.

The aims of this chapter are to:

- give an account of the processes through which we comprehend the world and the other people with whom we interact and those processes by which others make judgements about us.
- show how the reciprocal assumptions made by others and ourselves produce a social world where we actively transform our perceptions, ourselves and our world according to our context.
- explore the inherent biases produced in our perceptions of ourselves and others by attribution processes.
- locate and explain the importance of attitudes accounting for and changing organisational behaviour.

Perception: learning what to see

We perceive the world, we perceive others and they perceive us. The problem is that those perceptions are not reliable and that lack of reliability has real consequences in the world of work. Perception can be defined in terms of 'the dynamic psychological process responsible for attending to, organizing and interpreting sensory data' (Buchanan and Huczynski, 2000: 212). This is usually explained within a perspective that emphasises information processing and seeks to explain how our perceptions of ourselves, others and our environment shape our attitudes and behaviour. The utility of understanding perceptual processes lies in the fact that people's perceptions of themselves and others can be manipulated to change attitudes and behaviour in the situations and contexts within which work takes place. The practices which were associated with the 'Japanisation' of British industry in the 1980s, such as single-status canteens and clothing, provide an example of this, in that they are intended to alter perceptions of the divisions between management and labour within the employment relationship, in order to create attitudes (see below) more compatible with organisational goals.

Perception, then, is the umbrella heading for the processes through which we organise and interpret the range of visual, aural, tactile and chemical stimuli that impinge on us. As these processes enable us to comprehend and order the world around us, they must also underlie the manner in which we go about constructing identities.

Perceptual processing

The organisation, processing and interpretation of incoming stimuli are the basic subject matter of *cognitive* (knowing through sensation or perception) psychology. Much material in this area deals with the neurophysiology of perceptual systems. But as our focus is on organisational psychology we do not intend to deal with the detailed cognitive processing of information, as the ordering and organisation of these systems are not wholly determined by their structure. In social, interpersonal and self-perception, the determinants we are concerned with are the past and present influences and constraints on us, and our actively directed interests. Perception, then, is not just the process of seeing, but involves our other senses and is intimately connected with the notion of intention. In other words, what we see and hear is transformed according to how our system of values, attitudes and beliefs informs our actions. The formative content of identity could, in this light be viewed as produced by the *filters* through which our perceptions pass in order to select out what is of value to us.

Basically, to perceive something we have to be attending to it. This does not mean that we take in only those stimuli that we notice. Rather, we take in everything our particular range of senses allows us to. What it does mean is that we actively process and act upon only those parts of the incoming data that concern us. A crowded and noisy office, where we cut out much of the background noise in order to concentrate on the people we are listening to, can illustrate this concept of *perceptual selectivity* or *selective attention*. This effect, commonly referred to as the *cocktail party phenomenon* (attributed to Cherry, 1953) means we can still pick out and shift our attention to references to ourselves, or to other things that interest us coming from other parts of the room, temporarily or permanently cutting out the immediate conversation we had been intent on a moment before. Hence we appear to have some mechanism that can shift our attention and select the stimuli to which we attend, according to which appear of the greatest current relevance. Thus having to concentrate for long periods on a single type of stimulus, for example components being inspected on a production line, requires effort in face of the distractions coming from other stimuli in our environment.

Perceptions are often classified as primary or secondary on the basis of whether they come from actual or vicarious experience, though it may be more proper to view these classifications as related to forms of attention. Indeed Titchener (2005) claims there is no real difference between primary and secondary attention. Primary attention is towards what Titchener (94–8) labels the 'biologically powerful' stimuli which 'force' their attention on us due to their intensity, repetition, movement or novelty (see Figure 18.1 below). Secondary attention (95) is more a process of 'giving attention' to the point of forcing our attention away from our ongoing primary perceptions. Keltner (1973) claims that we attend primarily to strong or unique stimuli and secondarily to learned selection patterns, but we may also depend upon derived

primary attention where secondary perceptions become habitual and unconscious. Titchener characterises derived primary attention as 'fast locked against the irrelevant' (2005: 98), in other words it enables us
to concentrate our attention and even to 'surpass yourself' as we might when we operate at the top of our
skills. The downside of this though is that in situations where we enthusiastically adopt 'a belief or theory'
it can 'throw into brilliant relief all the facts that tell in its favour, but blinds you to the considerations
that make against it' (2005: 98).

We may not be consciously aware of directing our attention because, as Titchener notes, we are predis-
posed to notice some things rather than others. Our perceptual systems are structured to pay attention
to things that change and things that stand out from their surroundings, and we might also perceive
information as being more valid when it comes from what we consider to be an 'authoritative' source.
Thus criticism of our work from a respected peer or a superior responsible for evaluating it will be taken
more seriously than that from sources less close to our own interests. These filtering processes are summarised in Figure 18.1 below. The outcomes of these processes in perceptual selectivity thus underlie both
the *intentionality* of attention and its direction towards those things that have *salience* for us. Salience
represents what is most outstanding, relevant or important to us and furnishes the criteria we use to
filter our perceptions in line with our *perceptual set* (see Pashler, 1998, on the perceptual set and attention). Perceptual set represents our individual and unique readiness to perceive what we *expect* to perceive,
dependent on the *context,* our *inferences* and our subjective *interpretation* of sensory data. Like derived
primary attention selection, our perceptual set acts to *bias* our perceptions, focusing on some stimuli and
ignoring others. Our perceptual set further reflects our perceptions of our social position and ourselves
and is, in effect, the outcome of our socialisation processes (see Chapter 20). For instance, we often appear
to be set to perceive people of lower status to ourselves as less competent, inferior and more generally inadequate. This type of set extends to social groups and to wider social divisions – men, for example, generally
perceive women as less competent than themselves, reflecting the social value placed on gender rather

Environmental stimuli →	Sensations →	Attention →	Perception
Sources	*Sensory filters*	*Attention filters*	*Perceptual organisation*
(Things we can sense)	(Limit our perceptions)	(Direct our perceptions)	(Gives meaning to perceptions)
Light	Range of sensitivity and threshold values of senses (e.g. not being able to see UV or IR light)	Primary stimulus characteristics (e.g. size, intensity, frequency, contrast, motion, rate of change, novelty)	Figure-ground Proximity Similarity Continuation Closure Categorisation (see below)
Air pressure			
Heat			
Chemicals			
Gravity			

Figure 18.1 **The perceptual process**

Source: Based on D. J. Cherrington (1989) *Organizational Behaviour: The Management of Individual and Organizational Performance*, Boston:
Allyn & Bacon, pp. 82–6.

than any reliable sex differences. Likewise men tend to attribute competence shown by women to luck rather than skill (Deaux and Emswiller, 1974), showing that their subjective adaptation of their perceptions will tend to reinforce the security of their male identity. Our perceptual set when linked to derived primary attention shows us how we can be driven by ideologies and become susceptible to processes such as *groupthink* (see Chapter 20).

The consequence of all this is that we put actual effort into interpreting the world around us, rather than simply taking it all in as a camera might. But a haphazard interpretation of the myriad stimuli coming to us would be worse than none at all. We need a system of interpretation; our perceptions need to be organised. Wertheimer and the 'Gestalt' School identified the classic principles of *perceptual organisation* up to the 1920s (see McKenna, 2006, for applications and examples).

Perceptual organisation

- figure-ground
- proximity
- similarity
- continuation
- closure

These principles show that we tend to place organisation on stimuli, by focusing on significant or moving rather than background factors (*figure-ground*), by associating stimuli that: are close together or in *proximity*; have *similarity*; are moving in the same direction or that appear to be a *continuation* of other stimuli. According to the principle of *closure* we fill in gaps in perceptual input to give meaning to apparently disorganised information underlining the fact that we actively *transform* our perceptions in order to make sense of our environment. The cocktail party phenomenon mentioned above is essentially an auditory figure-ground effect and the principles of continuation (or continuity) and closure are responsible for the effects seen in the phenomena of *pareidolia* or *apophenia* which explain why people often see meaningful information in random stimuli, for example Jesus' face in a piece of burnt toast.

The importance of the gestalt principles for providing insights into how we go about constructing our personal and social world is not generally given great emphasis in the organisational psychology literature: apart, that is, from the extent to which they can be utilised in the construction of the kind of test instruments used in recruitment and selection procedures. That our perceptions are ordered to extract and construct meaning out of our environment both helps to engender our individuality and makes us vulnerable to those who seek to limit or channel the kind of information we receive. By placing perceptual stimuli, people and events, into categories, we effectively take short-cuts in our comprehension of the world. We enable ourselves to deal with the numerous stimuli that impinge on our senses by reducing the necessity to analyse each new stimulus as a unique object. This does, however, mean that we treat the things and people with which we interact through their relation to the subjectively determined, but apparently objective, categories into which we place them. Thus, to some extent, we *reify* everything and everyone we come across. We produce them as mental representations of our own creation, yet we treat them as if these images were in fact real. The images and slogans associated with corporate cultures and missions are precise examples of attempts to channel our perceptual organisation into acceptance of a dominant reality through supplying a ready-made basis on which to apply closure to contexts and concepts on which we might not have accurate information.

Perceptual categorisation

It is *through the processes of perceptual categorisation* (see Augoustinos and Walker, 1995: 106–9) that the major perceptual factors dealt with in organisational behaviour texts can best be understood (these are summarised in Table 18.1 below). By selectively perceiving we generate a system of categorisation, the level of *cognitive complexity* in which affects our capacity to learn, act and express ourselves; for example, to a non-sailor sails are sails, but to a sailor they are jibs, sheets, mainsail, etc. – the sailor has greater cognitive complexity in this context. Categorisation involves an *accentuation effect* (1995: 106), which acts to increase both perceived similarities within categories and differences between categories, so, for example, we tend to feel we have more in common with an *in-group* than an *out-group*. Categorising people on the basis of limited cues, such as gender, skin colour, bodily characteristics, social, regional and national identity, and then treating an individual as having the generalised traits associated with that category is the pervasive phenomenon known as the *stereotype*, identified by Lippman (1922). Stereotyping is the perceptual equivalent of the *ecological fallacy* in statistics whereby the characteristics of a population are erroneously attributed to an individual member of that population, for example union members may be statistically more likely to also be members of the Labour Party than the general population, but this does not mean that individual union members are more likely to be Labour Party members, as there are many other factors influencing individual membership decisions. Stereotypes have advantages in that they enable us to make quick assessments of others and of situations. You can, for example, have a stereotype of what a particular kind of person or meeting will be like and react accordingly, or you may need quickly to assess the intent of someone who enters your office or wants to come into your house. Although it has psychological uses to the individual, stereotyping can also have negative social consequences: for example, men in secretarial work might be seen as only seeking temporary employment, unambitious or gay (Callan Hunt, 1992). Stereotyping, then, is one of the mechanisms through which racism and sexism are socially enacted and given ideological justification. Thus a branch manager in a case study of the insurance industry comments on his perceptions of why women are unsuitable for sales work: 'Yes, it can be a soul destroying job, and women are either not hard bitten enough to ride off insults or those that can are pretty unpleasant people' (Knights and Collinson, 1987: 155). It would appear that in the face of an established stereotype, you just can't win!

Table 18.1 **Perceptual categorisation**

- **Selective perception** – people selectively interpret what they see on the basis of their interest, background, experience, and attitudes
- **Accentuation effect** – increases perceived similarities and differences within and between categories
- **Stereotyping** – judging someone on the basis of one's perception of the group to which that person belongs (similar to the *ecological fallacy* in statistics)
- **Halo effect** – drawing a general impression about an individual on the basis of a single characteristic
- **First impressions** – initial assessments tend to be carried over to future attitudes (similar to primacy/recency effects)
- **Contrast effect** – evaluating characteristics is affected by comparisons with others ranking higher or lower on the same characteristics
- **Self-fulfilling prophecy** – rating positively or negatively will affect future relations and hence ratings, as well as affecting our assessment of ourselves
- **Projection (assumed similarity)** – attributing one's own characteristics to other people

Another process given force by our categorisation of stimuli is the so-called '*halo effect*' identified by Solomon Asch (Asch *et al.*, 1938), which is essentially another process by which we produce stereotypes. When we come across new persons or situations we can only assess them in terms relevant to our own experience and the limited cues we have about them. This initial assessment, whether positive or negative, tends to be carried over into the attitudes we build up to that person or thing because of the powerful categorisation effects of *first impressions*. Thus if we rate a new workmate in a positive fashion on the basis of our first impression, we would tend to continue to rate them positively in the future, though as Hodges (1974) noted – negative first impressions are more resistant to change than positive ones. The effect of first impressions is linked to the *primacy-recency effect* in learning, in that the first and the most recent information we have on a topic tend to be remembered better than other information. So not only are we a prisoner to the first impressions others get of us, we are also only as good as the last impression we have made as well. The judgments we make of others and vice versa can be distorted by these effects and this distortion can be further enhanced by the *contrast effect* where we tend to make judgements not by absolute standards but by comparison with someone or something similar. Salespeople can take advantage of this by showing us a top-of-the-range product to increase our expectations from the product we want to purchase and they can then reinforce this by also showing us a poorer-quality product to enhance the contrast to the purchase they wish us to make.

An added complication is that if we rate someone positively, then this will probably in itself improve our relations with them. This may in turn produce a *self-fulfilling prophecy* (Merton, 1949), which would act to validate our first impression and at the same time falsely improve our opinion of our ability to judge others (see Attribution below). Perceptual categorisations can act to negate as well to as reinforce each other, for example the halo effect can work against stereotyping, in that meeting a member of a group about whom we hold stereotyped views, who makes a good first impression on us, may weaken a negative stereotype. On the other hand, we may simply view the person as an exception, and perceptual selectivity may bring us to focus on the aspects of their appearance or behaviour that fulfil the prophecies of our stereotypes. Such processes might also have powerful effects on new recruits in organisations, since stereotypical attitudes can be socially communicated. This is backed by evidence such as that of Salancik and Pfeffer (1978), whose *social information-processing model* of job design implies that our reactions to our work are significantly influenced by cues picked up from our co-workers. In an organisation where the prevailing experience of power relations is unitarist and hierarchical, we might expect new managers or workers to hold stereotypes about each other that will heavily reflect categorising processes, in that their experiences will tend to be interpreted through the dominant attitudes of their peers.

We also have a tendency to categorise others in the same light in which we categorise ourselves. Suspicious or aggressive persons, according to this principle of *projection* – or more properly, *assumed* similarity – will view others as being more suspicious or aggressive in nature than will people who tend to be more trusting or placid. We can apply this notion to the kinds of attitudes and values in the 'new realism' identified in industrial relations since the 1980s and expressed in the 'New Labour' rejection of rejection of 'Clause 4 socialism'. To someone who sees themselves as 'looking after number one', those who stand for the values of class solidarity and union loyalty might be seen as stupid, unrealistic or hiding a lust for personal power behind a facade of caring for others. In this fashion the standards of social comparison (Festinger, 1954) by which we judge the world and those in it in form the social identity that we ourselves project to others.

Perceptual categorisation and social identity

To project categorisations onto others, we must also be categorising ourselves. We can produce stereotypes about ourselves, perhaps regarding our probable or favoured responses to certain people or things.

We can also apply the halo effect to ourselves, for example if we perform well at a particular activity the first time we try it, we will tend to rate ourselves better in the future, and vice versa. The major sources of the categorisations we use are the various groups to which we belong, as the membership of these groups provides us with the basis of the social identities which we take up in various situations. Thus the norms and standards of conduct of a group to which we belong will inform both the kinds of stereotypes we use and the identity that recognises our right to make such judgements. If a group can be said to have an identity, then that identity is communicated to its members in their self-perceptions and becomes part of, possibly a major part of, their own identities. Given that the major groups that many of us belong to are related to work and work organisations, our identities tend to be constructed in terms of our perceptions of ourselves within work organisations. Even the identities of the unemployed might be defined to a great extent by their lack of attachment to work groups.

The major theoretical position on identity from social psychology itself, Tajfel and Turner's *social identity theory* (see Tajfel, 1982; Fiske and Taylor, 1991; Haslam, 2004), is essentially a theory of intergroup behaviour as it relates to personal and social identity (see Chapter 24 on groups). Social identity theory, is also known as CIC theory for categorisation – identification – comparison:

- *Categorisation* – we categorise things, people and ourselves to make sense of our environment and to direct appropriate behaviours. In social terms the categories are mainly determined by the groups we and others belong to and behaviours by the norms associated with those groups
- *Identification* – depending on the situation we define our self-concept in terms of our being unique individuals or as group members, giving rise to our personal vs. our social identity
- *Comparison* – we try to maintain a positive self-concept by making favourable comparisons of ourselves with other persons and groups. (See Haslam, 2004: 290–4 for definitions.)

In terms of comparison there are a range of strategies used by individuals and groups to maintain what is termed *positive distinctiveness* whereby we see ourselves as relatively better than other groups on categories that are salient for us. Thus we may maximise the distinctions between ourselves and others of similar or lesser social status, but minimise the distinctions between ourselves and groups of greater status. These strategies include (see Haslam 25–6) *individual mobility*, which is associated with a belief in the possibility of individual social mobility and with low status groups that individual members may wish to dissociate from. 'In the workplace for example, women who perceive there to be no "glass ceiling" may believe that the best strategy for advancement is to progress as an individual…rather than trying to engage in collective action designed to improve the treatment and status of women in general' (Haslam, 2004: 26). As opposed to a belief in social mobility *social creativity* implies adherence to a *social change* belief system where individual mobility is seen as unlikely or impossible and involves redefining group membership as positive for the individual. This leads to groups that perceive themselves to be of high status on particular dimensions using them as their basis of comparison with others, while groups of low status on particular dimensions will tend to minimise differences on relevant categories or choose new categories for comparison. For example, we might recognise the rich as more powerful than us, but consider ourselves morally superior to them. *Social competition* is a more radical expression of a social change belief system involving confrontation or direct action (similar to problem-oriented coping strategies; see Chapter 23) to 'challenge or maintain the status quo' (Haslam, 2004: 27) in order to improve the relative status and power of the group. This latter strategy requires high levels of group solidarity and is likely to lead to conflict with other groups.

We should, however, be careful not to place too much emphasis on group influences, as social identity theory is criticised for not accounting for the individual adequately and group processes may increase our chances of mis-categorising others. The ecological fallacy, for example, specifically refers to misperceiving individuals based on group categories and we appear to have increased tendencies to stereotyping in when involved in intergroup negotiations (Haslam, 2004: 122). Such problems have led to the development by Turner and also Oakes and colleagues (in Augoustinos and Walker, 1995: 127, 213) of *self-categorisation theory*. This deals with how individuals perceive themselves as having shared characteristics with a group, increasing the salience of shared social identity, to the extent that their self-perceptions become *depersonalised*. Depersonalisation in this sense is not the same as the kind of de-individuation found in cults or military training but is more a case of switching attention to salient factors in group identity rather than those associated with self-identity, much in the same way as perceptual selectivity operates in the cocktail party phenomenon discussed earlier. The factors determining the direction of perception to the individual or group are referred to as:

- *Comparative fit* – based on the principle of meta-contrast (Turner, 1985), which is esentially a sort of figure-ground effect (see above) applied to social stimuli. Comparative fit reflects the ease with which stimuli can be divided into categories and where the differences within categories are smaller than the differences between categories. Conditions of high comparative fit tend to be dependant on contexts where specific social categories become more salient and increase the potential identification with a distinct group. For example, supporters of different football clubs can still identify with rival supporters in the context of supporting their national team at the World Cup.
- *Normative fit* – high normative fit is found where the differences between groups can be associated with known categorisations (as reflected in stereotypes we are familiar with), which acts to increase the salience of the differences and identification as distinct groups. For example, normative fit would be high for a group of senior managers discussing company cars, but low if they were discussing bus routes to work.
- *Perceiver readiness* – based on Bruner's (1957) notion of perceptual readiness (or perceptual accessibility), perceiver readiness relates to how well categorisations fit with the perceiver's "knowledge and theories about the social world and their expectations, motives, values, and goals" (Reynolds and Turner, 2001: 169). So the salience of a categorical identification with a group is dependent on our perceptual predispositions, referred to above as our perceptual set, illustrating the influence of our personal history and prior expectations on our identification with particular groups.

Comparative fit is mainly dependent on primary attention and the categorisation of primary stimuli, whereas normative fit is in turn dependent on perceiver readiness and perceptual set and thus more associated with secondary or derived primary attention. Because of the importance of context, self-categorisation theory acknowledges the possibility of more than two levels of identity (referred to as *levels of abstraction*), beyond the division between personal and social identity, which accounts for the levels of necessarily abstract stereotypical categorisation we apply to ourselves within particular contexts as follows:

- superordinate – for example, self as part of humanity
- intermediate – for example, self as part of a group
- subordinate – for example, self in personal terms (see Augoustinos and Walker, 1995; Hogg and Abrams, 1990).

Social identity theory and self-categorisation theory are in agreement that we validate perceptual information in line with the group context that the information is produced in and that the perception of ourselves as unique individuals and as members of groups are equally valid:

> The cognitive system, governed by uncertainty reduction and self-enhancement motives, matches social categories to properties of the social context and brings into active use (i.e. makes salient) that category which renders the social context and one's place within it subjectively most meaningful. (Hogg and Terry, 2001: 7)

Attribution theory

The organisation and categorisation of our perceptions enables us to comprehend and interpret our world in a contextual fashion, and on this basis we are able to make judgements dependent on how we interpret the intentions of others. This is a crucial task for any individual, as it is linked to the fashion in which we identify the links between cause and effect in events. *Attribution theory*, initiated by Heider (1958) and developed by Kelley (1971), shows how we tend to be biased in our judgements of others' intentions. We tend to make attributions:

- when we make excuses or attach blame
- when we try to explain unexpected or negative events
- when explaining success and failure (both our own and of others).

This means that we make attributions in relation to our actions in all of our relationships, be they home, work, friends or even careers. Attribution theory is founded on the notion that we make causal inferences, calculating the level of individual responsibility for our actions assuming that we know right from wrong and have free choice. The parameters on which attributions can be based are identified by Kent and Martinko (1995a: 20–6, 1995b: 56–8; based on Weiner, 1985) as *locus of causality* (internal/ external); *stability* (stable/ unstable); *controllability* (controllable/ uncontrollable); *globality* (situational/ cross-situational) and *intentionality* (intentional/ unintentional). When we identify the responsibility for actions we are mainly attributing them as due to internal (or *dispositional*) factors or to external (or *environmental*) factors, and are essentially attributing the cause to personal characteristics or social/environmental factors. The way we make these judgements according to Kelley (1971) is based on our ability to discriminate between different types of information about what we perceive in our own and other's actions as in Table 18.2 below.

Table 18.2 **Internal vs external attributions (based on Kelley, 1971)**

	Internal	External
Distinctiveness Information: Does the person display different behaviours in different situations?	High	High
Consensus Information: Does everyone behave the same way in this situation?	Low	High
Consistency Information: Does the person respond the same way over time?	Low	High

Low consensus and consistency tend to lead to dispositional attributions and vice versa, but high distinctiveness can lead to both internal and external attributions. However, when estimating dispositions Heider also identified the *discounting principle* whereby behaviours can be discounted or ignored when called for by the situation, which reflects the fact that sometimes in social perception we may pay more attention to strong situational cues and ignore a person's characteristics. For example, we may distrust the overtures of an insurance seller who asks about our health, regardless of what we think of him or her as a person.

Attribution appears to provide a fairly reliable guide to the causes of behaviour, but as with other perceptual processes we are prone to mistakes in attributing intentions. Worse still, we have an inclination, termed the *fundamental attribution error* (Ross, 1977), to judge people's intentions in terms of dispositional rather than environmental factors, thus tending to attribute the causes of their actions to their personality or nature. Knights and Collinson (1987: 151) noted that women office workers were seen to require high levels of supervision and control, which was not attributed to their 'experience of subordination and blocked mobility but to their gender'. The 'discontented and moody' behaviour they were seen to exhibit was thus attributed to their gender-based disposition, and further used to disqualify them from jobs in sales.

Commentators such as Quattrone (1982) have suggested that we always make dispositional attributions in the first place and then adjust our judgement as we become aware of relevant situational factors. These fundamental errors are brought together in the notion of *correspondence bias* (see Gilbert and Malone, 1995 for an extended discussion) which proposes that in general we tend to conclude that people have dispositions that correspond to their behaviour due to a number of factors:

- *Wanting dispositions:* we prefer to make dispositional attibutions as predicting other's behaviour gives us a sense of control and may also increase our sense of security in that people get what they deserve if their actions can be blamed on their personality.
- *Misunderstanding situations:* we tend to underestimate the evidence of situations and overestimate the evidence of behaviour as it is easier to identify.
- *Misperceiving behaviour:* we tend to perceive behaviour according to our expectations, which means that as with normative fit (see above) we will tend to fit behaviour to known stereotypes of dispositions that fit the behaviour.
- *Failure to use information:* we may fail to take situational information into account as it takes effort to overcome initial dispositional attributions (see Quattrone above).

As if this were not bad enough we also tend to exhibit what Miller and Ross (1975) term *self-serving bias*, which is the propensity to attribute our successes (and those of our friends or groups we belong to) to our personality and our failures to external circumstances (and vice versa for those we disapprove of). This bias can be directly linked to the notions of perceiver readiness and comparative and normative fit (see Haslam, 2004: 34–5).

Though attribution theory does imply that the more information we have about other people, the greater our capability of making accurate environmental attributions about their actions, the evidence is not great that we are either better able or even more inclined to see things as not necessarily intentional or inherent in people's natures but due to their social and personal circumstances. For example, the choice to initiate a strike may be attributed by employers or managers whose knowledge of their employees consists mainly of stereotypes, to bloody-mindedness or their militant nature. In Lane and Robert's (1971) account of the long strike at Pilkingtons in St Helens, the tradition of paternalism meant that management could interpret the action only in terms of intruders such as 'scousers', revolutionaries or both. One would hope that attribution theory implies that managers who know something of life at the lower end of an organisational hierarchy might be more likely to attribute workers' decisions to factors relating to the workplace or its environment, making a more realistic assessment of the situation in the process. Of course, attribution processes are just as prevalent in managerial activities themselves, as noted by Leavitt and Bahrami (1988: 65): 'managers are both blessed and cursed by that tendency to ascribe causality, because the causality – either way – is often ascribed to them rather than to other aspects of the situation'.

As an example, judgements on the performance, ability and effort of others, that is, of their behaviour and characteristics, are today routinely subsumed into judgements of a person's commitment. Thus the concern is not just with what we do or who we are, but whether we 'mean' what we are doing and what we present ourselves as in systems of high-commitment working (see Chapter 16). In traditional OB terms, this would be reduced to judgements of whether individual satisfaction, motivation, and so on tend to be derived mainly from intrinsic, social or extrinsic sources. It is possible, however, that the outcomes from judgemental processes are both more dependent on, and more faithfully reflective of, attributional process than they are of any activity or characteristic of the person under judgement. For example Dejoy (1994: 3), in a study of safety work, notes that 'actions to manage safety derive more from attributions than from actual causes'. Likewise Gronhaug and Falkenberg note that:

> Attribution and attributional research serves as a point of departure to capture how managers and organizations make sense of their internal and external environments, enabling them to act purposefully. (Gronhaug and Falkenberg, 1994: 22)

To some extent we are, in making attributions, making assessments of the personality or identity of others. But our ability to make consistently valid attributions is questionable. We constantly have to make judgements on the basis of too little or inaccurate information. On this basis we are assumed to carry around our own *implicit personality theories* (Asch *et al.*, 1938) about how people look and behave. These act as barriers to the kind of new information we will take in about them. Also, according to Langer (1981), we often behave in a more mindless and less rational manner than assumed by attribution theory, using habituated scripts which we act out in appropriate situations (see Chapter 19). In sociological terms this notion of scripting is linked to the 'habitus-project' distinction made by Bordieu in his 'theory of action' (1977; 1994). *Habitus* equates to our dispositions, our 'embodied history' which we bring with us from our past personae and which act as a set of cognitive and motivating structures, without, however, impinging on consciousness or will. This 'internalised second nature, forgotten as history' distinguishes the notion from purely behavioural mechanisms and from the value-free judgements of more rational-cognitive explanations.

According to Martinko (1995: 11) in a survey of OB texts, attribution theory is generally considered in detail only in chapters on perception, and attributional studies are sometimes cited in chapters on leadership and selection. In UK texts, where attribution is covered, the apparent emphasis is on achievement and performance appraisal, though there is also a tendency to relate it to a person's *locus of control* (for example, see Johnson and Gill, 1993: 72–3). Martinko is keen to emphasise the role attribution theories have played in the development of work on areas such as learned helplessness, achievement and expectancies in the study of intrapersonal motivation. At the same time Martinko emphasises the problems involved in the study of attribution in organisations, particularly regarding its measurement and application. (See Martinko, 1995, for extended discussions of these issues.)

These factors, coupled with our tendency to make dispositional attributions, make both our perceptions of others and ourselves highly subjective and prone to fallibility. We can add one last layer to the barriers to accurate perception, one that is receiving increased attention in these days of global markets and information exchange, namely ethnocentrism. This is the tendency to view the world through the values, norms and roles of our own culture or even subculture, and to devalue or show hostility to those of other cultures (see Jackson, 1994). Because our perceptual worldview is learned, we can come to an understanding of other cultures by exposure and, in the case of modern export management and 'international management', by specific training. Our sensitivity to those in other cultures depends on monitoring our reactions to information filtered through our own ethnocentrism. Thus, in constructing identities out of our perceptual world we need to make constant reference to sources of knowledge and comparison that we have built up over time. In social terms, among the major sources of such knowledge are the attitudes that we and others espouse and through which we make the categorisations on which we depend for comparisons.

The attitude problem

All that we see, learn, are and do is not just part of ourselves, but part of the social world around us. Others can judge us on what we do, what we appear to be, and can attribute the reasons for our actions; but to predict how we are likely to react to situations, there are a limited number of possible avenues to be explored. In social and interpersonal terms, we depend a great deal on the verbal statements of others to estimate their likely responses to situations and events. Likewise our own verbal statements communicate our position in regard to issues, objects, events and our social transactions and negotiations. Attitudes, as such statements of belief, evaluation and feeling are termed, are of necessity a major component of sociopsychological study, and this study of attitudes has correspondingly been one of the main sources of data and practice in the development of OB.

When we consider the structured environment of the workplace, performance can be measured, though an employee could be both a hard worker and a 'troublemaker'; personality can be assessed, though this may often produce counter-intuitive results not trusted by the client (see next chapter); and behaviour itself can be regulated in attempts to ensure future compliance. However, such information as can be generated through such techniques does not necessarily provide the requisite depth of information for the planning and systematic control desired by modern organisations. Rothwell and Kazanas (1986: 15) argue that even 'sophisticated quantitative techniques' are 'generally not superior to the kind of structured expert opinion that can be gleaned from survey results'. They see attitude surveys as fundamental to the process of human resource strategic planning in procuring 'a means of tapping employee creativity and knowledge about the organisation and of building genuine commitment to future success'.

In the 1870s Charles Darwin referred to attitude as the facial expression of emotion (Petty and Cacioppo, 1981: 20), though these days attitudes are most commonly regarded as purely psychological constructs consisting of three main components: the *conative* (behaviourally-oriented), *cognitive* (belief-oriented) and the *affective* (emotion-oriented). This is based on Rosenberg and Hovland's (see Ajzen, 1988) model, which more correctly identifies these 'components' as abstractions, based on verbal and non-verbal responses, from which the construct of attitude is inferred. The implication here is that the evaluations implicit in the components can differ while at the same time leading to a unified expression of 'attitude'. For example, an employee may dislike the kind of work undertaken in a new department he or she is being asked to move into (negative affect), but believe that the workers in that department are a cohesive and effective team to work with (positive cognition), and thus agree to make the move (positive conation) (based on Ajzen, 1988: 20). It is important to note that in the example given, the enquirer could infer a wholly 'positive' attitude from the conative component alone, unless the employee actively expressed the negative affect. More commonly it is the cognitive component which is subjected to measure, Taber (1991: 598) claiming that in one major area of attitudinal measurement, 'current job satisfaction assessments may be assessing what workers think about their job satisfaction, rather than how they feel about their jobs'.

Though discriminations between such components have been made in depth in the socio-psychological literature (see Ajzen, 1988: 21–3), these distinctions are rarely carried through into the design or analysis of studies in the wider literature making use of attitudinal measures. In essence, attitudes are often taken as indicative of an undifferentiated consistency of response, which is in turn predictive of behaviour or intention. An implicit assumption of much research involving attitudes is that they are informed by and reflect value systems. The distinction between attitudes and values is generally that attitudes are directed towards specific objects and that values are evaluative standards. In effect this makes them an output of the filtering and ordering processes by which we perceive and learn. As such, attitudes have been considered as embodying psychological functions for individuals:

- **Adjustment:** utility of object in need satisfaction; maximising external rewards and minimising punishment.
- **Ego defence:** protecting against internal conflicts and external dangers.
- **Value expression:** maintaining self-identity; enhancing favourable self-image; self-expression and self-determination.
- **Knowledge:** need for understanding, for meaningful cognitive organisation, for consistency and clarity. (From Katz, 1960, in Kahle, 1984: 18)

There is not a great deal of confirmatory evidence for this model and this may in some part be due to its being merely descriptive rather than prescriptive or diagnostic. It says little about the measurement of attitudes, or the relation of attitudes to behaviour that has generated much of the research in the area. According to Eiser (1986: 13), 'an attitude is a subjective experience involving an evaluation of something or somebody'. This active experience of perceiving, interpreting and evaluating experiences with a public reference to others should be contrasted with the more general usage of attitude as an object to be measured, correlated and tabulated. As subjective experiences, attitudes must have some consistent linkage to social behaviour or, as Eiser notes, 'it would be difficult to know what such verbal expression *meant*' (1986: 13). The problem really arises when it is assumed that attitudes can predictably cause behaviour.

Attitudes and behaviour

The failure of socio-psychological research to find strong correlative links between attitudes and behaviour led to a decline in attitude-based studies in the 1970s. However, work on the specificity of behaviour as related to attitude, notably by Ajzen and Fishbein, brought the subject back into focus. Ajzen and Fishbein argued (1980) that attitudinal measures have to correspond with the particular components of a behaviour in order for prediction to be possible. These component elements of behaviour are the specific *action* itself, the *target* of the action, the *context* in which the action is performed, and the *time* the action is (to be) performed. The assumption is that the more of these components that can be measured accurately, the more likely that the attitudes will predict behaviour. The problem once more is that many attitude surveys measure only the cognitive target component, that is, the attitude to the thing itself – rather than the attitude to the use or doing of the thing or to the when, where and how in which the behaviour would be expected to take place. In other words, they ask, 'what do you think of this?', without asking 'what about doing it under these specific conditions?'

Ajzen and Fishbein in their 'theory of reasoned action' link the prediction of behaviour to what we know of the person's *intention*, which is a function both of the attitude towards the behaviour and of their *subjective norm* regarding the behaviour. Thus we have to take into account not only their positive and negative feelings, but also the social pressures surrounding the particular behaviour. Attitude here has two sub-components: beliefs about the consequences of the behaviour, and affective evaluations of (in other words, feelings about) the consequences (Perloff, 1993: 95). Likewise, subjective norms have two sub-components: normative beliefs about whether significant groups or individuals approve or disapprove of the behaviour, and the person's motivation to comply with such normative beliefs (1993: 97). In addition to such qualifications it should be noted that the Ajzen and Fishbein model has been criticised for being too rational-cognitive in nature and that the effect of more 'mindless' behavioural associations, such as the accessibility of an attitude and the effects of past behaviour, selective perception/direct experience and habit (Triandis, 1980; Bentler and Speckart, 1981; Fazio, 1985) are also important determinations of the attitude–behaviour correlation.

Attitude change

Because of the presumed effects of attitudes on behaviour, there is a concomitant concern with the possibility of changing attitudes (and hence behaviour). The possibilities of changing attitudes are often linked to the persuasive characteristics of persons as *sources* (attractiveness, trustworthiness and expertise); as *targets* (high or low self-esteem); and of *messages* themselves (levels of threat). The routes to attitude change were generally explained in terms of Kelman's (1961) three sources of attitude change, *compliance*, *identification* and *internalisation* (discussed further in Chapter 21).

Kelman's sources of attitude change

- Compliance – from gaining rewards and avoiding costs
- Identification – from social influence and emotional attachment
- Internalisation – from social norms and individual value structures

The mechanisms of attitude change were explained through the reduction of psychological tensions as conceived in *balance theory* (Heider, 1946) and the drive to self-consistency and self-justification in *cognitive dissonance theory* (Festinger, 1957):

Cognitive dissonance theory (Festinger 1957)

- We strive to maintain consonance, or consistency, among our attitudes.
  - It is easier to change our attitudes than to change our behaviour
  - We sometimes change attitudes to make them consistent with our behaviour
  - We have attitudes towards both behaviours and identities
- There are two conditions under which we are likely to change our attitudes:
  - Commitment – attitudes have to be relevant to us
  - Internal attribution – we have to have the impression of being self responsible (free choice).

Perhaps the most important aspect of attitude change in organisations is the gaining of public commitment (Deutsch and Gerard, 1955; Tedeschi, Schlenker and Bonoma, 1971), where 'whenever one takes a stand that is visible to others, there arises a drive to maintain that stand in order to look like a consistent person' (Cialdini, 2001: 72).

The key factor in public commitment is *visibility* in that more visible public commitments are seen to produce more enduring effects in changing attitudes and behaviour than private commitments (see Eiser, 1986). Corbett (1994: 56) gives an example of this need for consistency in what he terms 'Internal Marketing': in competitions where tie-break questions are used to give a reason or slogan for buying a product, 'tens of thousands of people testify in writing to the product's appeal and they experience a powerful psychological pull to believe what they have written'. The reason that public commitment is so powerful in attitude change is perhaps best explained with regard to Bem's *self-perception theory*.

Bem's self-perception theory

- Individuals come to know their own attitudes, emotions, and other internal states partially by inferring them from observations of their own overt behaviour and/or the circumstances in which this behaviour occurs.
- To the extent that internal cues are weak, or ambiguous, the individual is in the same position as an outside observer, who must rely upon external cues to infer the inner states.

The classic example of self-perception is Festinger and Carlsmith's (1959) \$1/\$20 experiment where subjects paid to tell lies to another subject (actually a confederate) for \$1 are more convinced (after observing their compliance to counter-attitudinal behaviour – telling lies) that there must have been some truth to what they were told to say than than subjects who paid \$20, who did not need to believe the lies to tell them.

The discussions below on attitude surveys and personality tests, and those in Chapter 21 on goal-setting and development profiling, all concern attempts by organisations to gain public commitment to corporate objectives. The overall effect of such systems is to reinforce individual responsibility for fitting in to organisational objectives. This can be linked to the currently popular practice of 'project-based working', where individuals are steered towards or allowed to follow their own initiatives in developing and implementing solutions to organisational goal barriers, with appraisal being based on the success with which they carry their projects through. This is a familiar problem in today's NHS where professional managers come into previously medical-led departments and introduce ham-fisted changes which make things more difficult and then use their success in pushing the project through to leverage their CV for a better job (see Chapter 20), leaving the staff to sort out the long-term problems they don't care about.

The paradoxical possibility that if attitudes are consistent and predictive because they reflect predispositions, then it will be very hard to change them, is seldom exercised to any great degree in the management literature which makes so much of attitudinal research. The likelihood is, however, that attitudes are much more variable than is often assumed, and that even if changing core values is difficult, the changing of more operational attitudes and more particularly the generation of new attitudes can be controlled by the use of agenda-setting devices, including attitude, morale and opinion surveys. If this was not the case, then newspapers would only have news in them and global corporations would not spend so much time and money on media marketing.

Hollway (1991: 90–1 and 146–50) cites various examples indicating that the interpretation and use of surveys has, since their inception in the 1930s, often been more of a public relations than a human relations exercise, and that they 'could be used to produce a self-fulfilling prophecy effect' (1991: 91). Rather than surveying and analysing individual and cultural diversity, they are largely tools of cultural conformity. Referring back to the earlier notion that norms and habits affect the translation of attitudes into behaviour, we might suppose that the best strategy for changing attitudes is to embed them in self-enacting scripts which people are forced to internalise as a necessary part of their social and organisational functioning.

The usage of attitudinal measures in the workplace can be more readily understood with reference to the focus that Zimbardo and colleagues (1977) note in looking at attitude change from the perspective of populations rather than individuals:

> Even though we cannot predict the behaviour of single individuals, we should be able to predict that people (in general) will *change* their behaviour if we can *change* their attitudes of greatest relevance to the behaviour in question. We cannot predict which people will change or how much they will change, but a change in the attitudes of the population should be accompanied by a change in the behaviour of the population. (Zimbardo *et al.*, 1977: 52)

In this light, the utility of assessing attitudes as a cultural technology of regulation can be demonstrated by Boddy and Buchanan's advice on managing 'change projects':

> Assess attitudes. What evidence was there about the enthusiasm and commitment of those working on the project? Were there signs or hints of resistance, which might suggest a change of approach? Were staff becoming frustrated by delays, difficulties or changes to plan, which the manager needed to do something about? Or were they enthusiastic and positive about the activity, and going out of their way to make it work? (Boddy and Buchanan, 1992: 150)

This is presented as an element of 'managing the control agenda', a major facet of the 'continuous monitoring process to keep variances acceptably small' (1992: 149). The important notion here is the status of attitudes as evidence: even if not the 'enduring entities' they are so often assumed to be, they reflect the psychic status of persons within evaluative hierarchies and the choices of individuals to show whether they intend to collaborate or not with managerial practices.

Summary and key points

We have journeyed through our perceptual processes, examining how we transform and organise our perceptions and how we categorise events, others and ourselves. We have noted that dominant organisational cultures try to shape and channel our perceptions by controlling access to and the ideological flavour of information. We have made linkages to processes of social identity, highlighting the influence of groups and processes such as comparative fit in constraining our interactions with others. Finally we examined the judgemental processes of attribution to consolidate our theme of perceptual bias and underwrite our concerns with how we develop attitudes and values.

In examining attitudes we have focused on their reliability in predicting our behaviour and the validity of instruments used to measure and change our attitudes and values, taking care to make extensive links to other topics such as motivation. The values we internalise, the attitudes we exhibit, will all reflect the choices, however limited, that we have made and the learned constraints within which we act. Our unique history of learning and socialisation (see Chapter 20) enables us to produce a subjective identity malleable in both our own terms and those of the others and the organisations we encounter. We produce something which others see as our 'personality' but which in effect is simply an actively managed and continually rehearsed manipulation of our identity, fitted to what we have to do and what we want to do.

Further reading

The basics of perception are covered in a myriad of social psychology and OB texts from which the reader can really take their pick. A really in-depth account, if needed, is Kimchi and colleagues (2003), which while heavily neurological makes direct linkages to learning and development. Mark Martinko's work keeps the flag flying for attribution in the organisational arena despite its being largely ignored by many; a good update to the 1995 readings we cite here is his 2004 collection. On social cognition and social identity Hogg and Terry (2001) provides useful readings while Haslam's (2004) text is an excellent scholarly resource. Attitudes too are somewhat overlooked these days and though the (1986) Eiser text is still influential, Zimbardo and colleagues (1977) account is the most readable if you can still find it; check out the text on cults, especially the Moonies.

Eiser, J. R. (1986) *Social Psychology: Attitudes, Cognition and Social Behaviour*, Cambridge: Cambridge University Press.

Haslam, S. A. (2004) *Psychology in Organizations: The Social Identity Approach* (2nd edn), London: Sage.

Hogg, A. and Terry, D. J. (eds.) (2001) *Social Identity Processes in Organizational Contexts*, Sussex: Psychology Press.

Kimchi, R., Behrmann, M. and Olson, C. R. (eds.) (2003) *Perceptual Organization in Vision: Behavior and Neural Perspectives*, Psychology Press.

Martinko, M. J. (ed.) (1995) *Attribution Theory: An Organisational Perspective*, Delray Beach, FL: St Lucie.

Martinko, M. (ed.) (2004) *Attribution Theory in the Organizational Sciences: Theoretical and Empirical Contributions*, Charlotte, NC: Information Age Publishing.

Zimbardo, P. G., Ebbesen, E. B. and Maslach, C. (1977) *Influencing Attitudes and Changing Behavior* (2nd edn), Reading, MA: Addison-Wesley.

19 masks for tasks: personality

> Personality is an unbroken series of successful gestures. (F. Scott Fitzgerald)

As in the previous chapter we move from a fairly straightforward account of psychological processes to examining how personality factors are translated into behavioural regulation in the workplace and how personality itself becomes a facet of how we manifest identities in personal and interpersonal terms.

The aims of this chapter are to:

- show how the focus on personality in OB is on the categorisation of behavioural factors.
- demonstrate and illuminate how the control agenda is exercised in the selection process.
- examine the links between notions of personality, character and identity.

Personality: definitions and models

Personality is defined in terms of 'the physical, mental, moral and social qualities of the individual' (McKenna, 1987: 11), or more prosaically as whatever makes you different from other people. It is understood as a complex of characteristic features or traits that describe the particular types and/or dimensions through which personalities are categorised. This may be the ultimate contradiction in organisational psychology, in that the study of 'unique' personalities is placed almost wholly in the service of the production of standardised measures aimed at the categorisation and selection of individuals so that they can be fitted into their appropriate niches in organisational cultures.

The psychological understanding of how an individual develops a distinctive personality depends, like that of perception, on the notion of categorisation. Categorisation was originally applied to *temperament* in an early theory of balance attributed to Hippocrates (around 400BC) in which a person's health and personality were affected by imbalances in the four *bodily substances* or *humours*; this was later developed by others such as Galen into categorizations of *character* (see Table 19.1).

This was a remarkably resilient characterisation of personality which held sway well into the mid-nineteenth century, and as we shall see below, is even influenced by the modern field of psychometrics. There were many later theories and practices which attempted to link personality to bodily factors, the most notable of which were Phrenology (see Paul, 2004: chap. 1 for a good account) and Sheldon's (1942) notion of somatypes:

> Endomorph – pear-shaped or fat; focused on digestion; friendly, lethargic;
> Ectomorph – slim or thin; focused on nervous activity; shy, cerebral;
> Mesomorph – athletic or muscular; focused on blood circulation; aggressive, active.

As an explanation of personality this is obviously refuted just by the experience of growing older, many ex-ectomorphs and mesomorphs ending up as endomorphs and not any friendlier for the experience,

Table 19.1 **The bodily humours and character**

Bodily substance	Associated character
blood	**Sanguine** – happy, generous, optimistic, irresponsible, courageous, amorous
yellow bile	**Choleric** – short-tempered, angry, violent, vengeful, ambitious
phlegm	**Phlegmatic** – unemotional, calm, sluggish, pallid, cowardly
black bile	**Melancholic** – introspective, irritable, sentimental, despairing, gluttonous

though they may attest to the lethargy. Somatypes are still given credence in body-building circles, which is rather ironic since it was the mesomorph that was most associated with the predispositions to criminal behaviour which were Sheldon's main interest in showing relationships between body type and temperament. Again, as we shall see below, the interest in deviant or pathological personality is probably the main legacy of this type of approach. The failure of these approaches was in their inability to account for the range of observed characteristics and the obvious contradictions from people who did not fit the stereotypes. The major alternative to bodily categorisations was the psychodynamic model mainly known through Freud's (1927) notion's of the three *levels of awareness* and three *components of personality*. Freud distinguished awareness first in terms of our *conscious* mind, consisting of what we are currently paying attention to, essentially similar to what we have previously identified as primary attention; secondly our *preconscious* mind, those things we are aware of but not currently paying attention to, similar to the derived primary attention introduced above to the extent that we can deliberately bring things into the conscious mind (as with the 'cocktail party phenomenon'). Lastly our *unconscious* mind is the origin of much of our behaviour and is largely independent of the conscious mind and more importantly for Freud is the reason we can find it difficult to control aspects of our behaviour, particularly our less socially approved ideas and impulses because we can have *unconscious motivations*. Though not the same as the mindless action or *habitus* (Bordieu, 1994; see also Chapter 18) that leads us to script our behaviour, the unconscious is main player in the arena in which Freud's three components of personality (the *superego*, the *id* and the *ego*) struggle for supremacy, or as one of Freud's critics, the personal construct psychologist Donald Bannister, put it:

> Man is basically a battlefield … a dark cellar in which a well-bred spinster lady and a sex-crazed monkey are for ever engaged in mortal combat, the struggle being refereed by a rather nervous bank clerk. (Bannister, 1966: 22)

The struggle between the moralistic supergo, the impulsive, pleasure-oriented id and the rational ego causes us to experience anxiety, the response to this being the employment by the ego of a range of tactics or defence mechanisms which transform our perceptions to enable us to cope with anxiety-induced tensions. The range of potential tactics were first categorised by Freud's daughter Anna (1937), but more recently have been classified by the American Psychoanalytic Association (1994) into the *Adaptive Functioning Scale* see Table 19.2.

The range of potential defence mechanisms is far greater than indicated above, as even a cursory web-search will show, and though Freudian theory is widely discredited and generally not seen as influential on OB the notion of ego defences still offers insight into how personality processes are operative in

Table 19.2 **The adaptive functioning scale**

High Adaptive Level: dealing with stress by increasing feelings of well-being	Mental Inhibition Level: keeping out threatening ideas, feelings, etc. by diminishing awareness	Disavowal Level: keeping unacceptable, impulses, ideas, etc. out of awareness	Action Level: dealing with stressors through action or withdrawal
Affiliation	Displacement	Denial	Acting Out
Altruism	Dissociation	Projection	Complaining
Anticipation	Intellectualization	Rationalization	Rejecting Help
Humor	Reaction Formation		Passive Aggression
Self-Assertion	Repression		
Self-Observation	Undoing		
Sublimation			
Suppression			

Source: Based on DSM-IV Adaptive Functioning Scale, American Psychiatric Association (1994).

allowing us to adapt to the world around us, even if we sometimes do this by falsifying the world. We have already encountered projection as a distortion of our perceptual processes and seen rationalisation in the process of dissonance reduction in our beliefs (see Chapter 18); other defence mechanisms such as denial, dissociation and intellectualisation will come into focus in our later consideration of stress, coping and identity work (see Chapters 23 and 25).

Essentially the psychodynamic approach shows the limits of what categorisation can achieve as an explanation of personality processes but does not help to explain why categorisation is still the focus of the use of personality theory within OB. Because personality within OB is generally understood through categorisation, its relationship to the construction of identity cannot be separated from the activities of those who produce and use the categories. Hence the explanation of personality in an organisational setting is more directly connected to the use of personality theory by managers than was the case with perception.

Describing personality as that which makes an individual different from others essentially defines it as that which sets the boundaries of what you are and what you are not. However, the way the notion of personality is used in OB highlights this type of definition, developed from the humanistic psychology of Rogers, Maslow, etc., as an idealised, liberal conception that is in direct contradiction to operational concerns with the controlled performance of work. The concern for personality in OB centres around the identification and prediction of *consistent* and/or *distinctive modes of response* in individuals. Some of the more recent approaches, which attempt to account for the interaction of personality with situational factors, would term these modes of response as dispositions, which include emotions, cognitions, attitudes, expectancies and fantasies (Clark and Hoyle, 1988). However, distinctive behaviours in this sense are not the same as uniquely individual behaviours; they would be typical ways of reacting to people or situations which would distinguish an individual as belonging to a category of persons. Thus people who are seen to react in a consistently unco-operative fashion may be placed into a stereotypical category whereby their future behaviour will be assumed to be typical of that sort of person who is 'difficult' or a 'problem person'.

Behaviour, then, is assumed to be inherent in the individual's personality, with the concomitant underlying assumption that it is biologically or genetically fixed. Being fixed, it is possible to predict, and being possible to predict it becomes a useful tool in controlling behaviour. Personality theory becomes an exercise in discovering how these various modes of response vary over time and between situations, in order to refine the levels of categorisation and prediction possible. For example, what kind of observed behaviour in a person is sufficient to label him or her as a troublemaker? Or what type of situation will influence a person to reveal different aspects of or levels of his or her 'undesirable' behaviour? Approaches such as that of Clark and Hoyle (1988) and that of Aronoff and Wilson (1985; see Hosking and Morley, 1991: 9–13), which attempt to contextualise personality in the social process, do acknowledge that dispositions can be modified by situations and experience, but still focus on how these variables can be combined to predict behaviour.

Types, traits and tests

For OB as a 'science', this concern with prediction frequently results more in a battery of methodologies and techniques for selecting the 'right person for the job' than in an account of personality. Methods such as personality 'tests' and inventories are used to select prospective employees or candidates for promotion into categories which show how well they fit into organisational culture, thus making it easier to take decisions about them, effectively performing the same function for an organisation as stereotypes do for an individual or group. They help to sort out the bewildering variety of information available about organisational members into categories which can be easily comprehended and dealt with. The last thing with which a science of personality of this sort is concerned is that which makes us subjectively unique individuals. There may be interest in what makes a particular individual different to others, but only to the extent that it might be a pointer to a characteristic useful or damaging to the organisation.

In delineating categories of personality characteristics, psychologists tend to fall back on two main sets of concept. The first of these, personality *types*, are predetermined categories into which we 'fit', and which represent broad generalisations of character such as 'moody' or 'lively'. The second, personality *traits*, are habitual behaviours or tendencies to behave in particular ways: for example tendencies to react in an anxious, reserved or outgoing fashion. Types or personality factors are generally used to refer to patterns or clusters of traits or personality variables, which can be used to map the profiles of individuals using factor analysis of responses to self-report questionnaires. The Eysenck Personality Inventory (EPI: Eysenck and Wilson, 1975) groups clusters of trait variables – such as reserved, unsociable, quiet, passive, careful – into type factors, in this case introversion. The factors used by Eysenck, introversion–extraversion and stability–neuroticism, are based on Jungian psychodynamic theory, which in turn borrowed its trait descriptions from the classic model provided by the four humours, though changing the names of the types. The traits used by Eysenck are essentially similar to those utilised by two of the most popular inventories, the Myers-Briggs Type Indicator and Cattell's 16PF (Personality Factors). These days types have developed into the 'Big Five' personality dimensions characterised by tendencies to extraversion, emotional stability, agreeableness, will to achieve and openness to experience. So overall, personality inventories still have their philosophic basis in whether or not you have an excess of blood, bile or phlegm.

Personality inventories are still used by organisations on tens of millions of people every year in selection and to determine who will make good managers or will be eligible for promotion. Cattell's 16PF scale, which is based on the same basic types as the EPI, is widely criticised on both its content and generalisability, and yet still is used because it appears to select people who will make good managers. Hollway (1984) notes that it does not really matter whether the 16PF tells us anything realistic about personality, as it actually works by fulfilling the expectations of existing managers about what makes a good manager. That is, it identifies people like themselves, who are in the main 'male, middle-class and middle-aged' and, in the West, most often white. Since it is possible to work out which are the appropriate types of answer to the questions, it does not really matter if the respondent does not actually belong to the same social groupings as the dominant organisational culture he or she is trying to enter. It will help if they do, as it makes 'correct' responses easier to identify, but the ability to lie correctly is just as good a sign that the candidate is capable of becoming, and willing to become, the kind of person who will fit. Some inventories contain *motivational distortion* scales, which supposedly detect lying, though actually indicating that people are presenting an image of themselves which serves their self-interest. Such motivated lying also represents a type of public commitment (see Chapter 18) which may make it more likely that we would shift our attitudes in a direction favourable to the culture we are trying to join. Candidates who are unwilling to frame the right kind of responses, or are incapable of doing so, may automatically select themselves out, regardless of their actual managerial potential. Graduates going through the 'milk-round' of career selection may sit similar tests up to five times in the course of their applications and the conclusion that such tests are used for 'people processing' rather than individual treatment of personal characteristics and differences is hard to escape, and produces the conclusion that they are more effectively 'gatekeeping' mechanisms rather than selection methods. Indeed, such tests were originally used in the UK in the First World War to screen out 'neurotic' soldiers: that is, those who did not want to fight! Current doubts on the use of tests have led to recommendations on using techniques such as structured interviews and role-playing in *assessment centres*, though the expense and effort involved makes it unlikely that these would be used extensively in smaller organisations or where labour is easy to replace.

Steve Blinkhorn (a designer of tests himself) and Charles Johnson claimed in *Nature* (1990) that tests are full of errors, lack statistical validity and are difficult to replicate, and that there is not much evidence that tests predict job success except at the extremes of the range tested. Figure 19.1 below illustrates this in that a trait such as aggressiveness is only predictive at the ends of the range where people tend to be either permanently aggressive or permanently passive, most of the time our level of aggressiveness is contingent on the circumstances we are in and the trait is not predictive. In any case, the scores obtained in testing are often not influential or even used in actual selection decisions, and of course, job seekers being questioned are unlikely to respond dispassionately. Their conclusions were that many different types could actually be successful in any particular job, and that much of personality testing is in fact no more than 'pseudoscience'.

One of the most reliable personality types that has been identified is the Type A vs. Type B behavioural pattern (see Friedman and Rosenman, 1974). The traits associated with Type A behaviour include achievement orientation, status insecurity, time urgency, competitiveness and aggression, traits often erroneously associated with managerial or leadership ability (see Chapters 22 and 23). Type A personalities are also said to suffer from increased levels of stress, heart disease and social isolation through paying less attention to relationships and alienating others. Type B behaviour is characterised by a relaxed manner, patience and friendliness and associated with a less stressful lifestyle – just the kind of person you really want for a manager, even though recruitment testing for managers tends to select for Type A, to all of our everlasting regret. In fact the Type A behaviour pattern is just that, a behaviour pattern, and is probably caused as much by the nature of work as any underlying characteristics in the person.

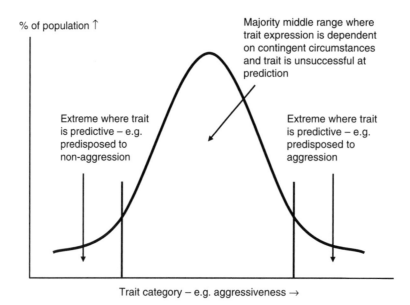

Figure 19.1 *The predictive validity of personality traits*

Personality testing has undergone something of a revival in recent decades, as a new generation of computerised personality profiling systems are coming onto the market. Their ease and speed of use, combined with neat computer printouts detailing managerial potential, reinforce an air of spurious objectivity in their validity as managerial tools. Most of them are still of course based on systems such as the EPI, but do not impose the same levels of cost in terms of licensing and training for their administration and interpretation as the older paper-based systems. Greater use has, however, also led to greater numbers of legal challenges to personality testing (see O'Meara, 1994 for a summary). A good example is the use of the polygraph or 'lie detector' in the US, which was for a long time a staple in the testing of employees due to its claim to be able to detect lying based on changes in the electrical conductivity of the skin. However, the reliability and ethical implications of its use has led to restrictions since 1988. *Voice Stress Analysis* (VSA) has since been touted as a method which can replace the polygraph, though with a fine irony the American Association of Police Polygraphers cite a 1996 US Department of Defense study to the effect that there is 'no credible evidence to validate voice analysis as an effective instrument for determining deception'. This has not stopped Birmingham City Council in the UK from introducing *Voice Risk Analysis* (VRA), a VSA screening technique for detecting 'benefit cheats'. VRA is described by Bruce Burgess, another 'professionally trained' polygraph examiner, as: 'about as reliable as tossing a coin', though, 'telephone tests could work well as a deterrent ... because if people think they're being tested, they're less likely to make false claims' (BBC, 2007). At the same time though, if people are less likely to make false claims when they are being tested as Burgess claims, then why would we need motivational distortion scales? As with personality inventories in recruitment then, the intent is once again to modify or deter specific behaviours, not any reliable indication of the variable (honesty) which it purports to measure.

Employers have in fact made widespread use (mainly in the US) of personality-style tests claimed to measure an employee's *honesty* or *integrity*, though these in turn have been legally challenged, leading

284 19

INTRODUCTION: REGULATING ORGANISATIONAL BEHAVIOUR ▪ PERCEPTION AND ATTITUDES: SEEING WHAT TO THINK ▪ **MASKS FOR TASKS: PERSONALITY** ▪ LEARNING AND CHANGE ▪ MOTIVATION: THE DRIVE FOR SATISFACTION ▪ LEADERSHIP: MIGHT OR MYTH? ▪

some employers to turn to techniques like graphology (popular in Europe) and astrology (popular in the Far East) for selection and *gatekeeping* purposes. Other forms of selection/screening that may be influential in the future include *genetic screening*, used to detect tendencies to congenital disease (and possibly stress through tendencies to heart disease), and *lifestyle screening*, used for detecting hazardous elements of personal lifestyles, for example dangerous hobbies, addictions and so on. These are driven mainly by the possible reduction of insurance costs that could be achieved through their use (as was also the case for the smoke-free workplace), and by the costs of retraining replacements. Overall the value of all of these developments, beyond their actual attitudinal and behavioural effects, is in their capacity to reduce complex factors to simple stereotypical categorisations. Thus, they make the decision-making process for personnel departments simpler, more cost-effective and less dependent on skilled staff – a veritable Taylorism of recruitment.

Personality and selection

In utilising tests, employers are essentially clutching at straws, and on this basis will probably use anything that will help them make some kind of systematic decision. The underlying assumption behind techniques such as the 16PF, that managerial ability is somehow related to personality factors, would almost certainly ignore the kind of managerial ability it takes to, say, hold down a job, run a household and bring up children. But of course the dominant cultures in most organisations and institutions are not composed of the working women who have to display such abilities. The assumption is not about personality as such, but about having, or aspiring to, the right kind of personality. In contrast to managerial assessment, the assessment of shop-floor workers has traditionally focused on psychometric tests of capacities and aptitudes rather than personality. Psychometric tests examine factors such as verbal, logical and mathematical reasoning, and are said to have high test–retest validity, in that they yield similar results over time for the same subjects, which is not necessarily the case with personality inventories. Both are tests of the ability to do the job, the difference being that it is assumed that only in the higher levels of organisational hierarchies does personality become a relevant factor. The utility of psychometric tests is in essence their cost-saving ability to predict who is capable of, or willing to be, trained. Hollway (1984: 50) also notes that where psychometric tests are used in assessment centres, the more objective information they yield is still contaminated by the subjective preferences of decision-makers, possibly on the basis of photographs and biographical details attached to assessment forms. It is again the pragmatic psychology of Taylorism that is at work here: as long as the person can do the job, who they are and what they are is of little importance. Even the personality of a manager is not important, as long as he or she has a 'managerial' personality. What is evident here is that from concerns with inherent types of personality, organisational use of personality has moved on to trait descriptions and on to the regulation of workplace behaviour. The difficulty here is that as explanation moves from the essential qualities of the person to what they do, the actual cause of their behaviour becomes just as contingent on situational context as in any personal characteristic and subject to far more in the way of intervening variables.

This is further evidenced in the development of rating scales for assessing and appraising job performance. Smith and Kendall developed the Behaviourally Anchored Rating Scale (BARS) in 1963 which replaced earlier trait-based performance ratings with scales based on dimensions of job performance produced by job evaluation. These in turn were superseded by Behaviour Observation Scales (BOS), which rely on assessments based on the frequency of occurrence on critical incidents such as 'Provides constructive feedback to the team'. This type of approach has since been applied to measuring the performance of whole organisations in Kaplan and Norton's (1992) 'Balanced Scorecard', which have even been touted as a type of universal strategic management system (1996). The interesting thing about such systems is that where their relative effectiveness is assessed, the best evidence seems to show that BOS-based systems are preferred because they yield more favourable effect in terms of changing attitudes (Tziner and Kopelman, 2002). Once again it is not who you are, but how you behave and the attitudes you exhibit that are the crucial factor.

For example, the principles and resources of OB are used in Knowledge Management (KM) in the same way as they are in the service of HRM, unsurprising since human resource practice is becoming more and more linked to the 'people track' of KM (see Chapter 16). In the same way that distinctive personalities are reduced to stereotypical measurable traits, knowledge and skill are reduced to putatively measurable competencies as in the use of BARS and BOS in performance appraisal. Competencies are being used in exactly the same way as personality traits, though what they represent is more an index of behavioural fit than cultural fit as with personality traits. Just as in selection testing where people show their commitment by choosing answers exhibiting the traits they feel present the image the organisation wants, then competencies become a *currency of development*, often the only route to a pay rise in an era of flattened hierarchies and mainly lateral mobility, through applying for better posts or a new job. This is a process of categorisation and just as perceptual categorisation involves filtering and selective attention (see Chapter 18), then KM strategies effectively filter, selectively attend to and then categorise and store the aspects of informal learning, creativity and culture that allow it to produce the SOPs which are one of KM's major outputs. This means that recruitment and selection processes are critical to KM just as they are to the HCW (see the Sieloff material on Hewlett Packard in Chapter 16). What makes this possible at both individual and organisational level is the production of salient social identities within the context of the group (see Chapter 24).

Other personality factors and characteristics employed in assessment include *locus of control, self-monitoring, self-efficacy* and *positive/negative affect*. Locus of control (Rotter, 1972) refers to whether we believe that we control events (internal) or events control us (external); likewise self-monitoring (Snyder and Gangestad, 1986) refers to how attentive we are to internal states (low) or to appropriate situational and interpersonal cues (high) in determining our behaviour. High self-efficacy (Bandura, 1977) is the extent to which we believe we can overcome obstacles and get things done, whereas positive and negative affects represent the extent to which we accentuate the positive and negative in ourselves. In managerial selection, assessment and development, the preference is for the person who demonstrates an internal locus of control, low self-monitoring, high self-efficacy and positive affect. Thus supplicants for managerial status are measured against what is effectively a stereotype of an 'ideal' manager, mainly attentive to the demands of managerial identity and practice. In personality and attitude assessment, as in stereotyping, projection and attribution, the assignment of categories on the basis of limited information can lead to damaging consequences.

Pathological characters?

Assigning a biologically-fixed nature to personality that can be assessed through the identification of types and traits can reinforce the notion that problems within an organisation are rooted within the pathological personality characteristics and behaviours of individuals, much as with the use of somatypes we noted above. Thus the interpersonal, social and organisational problems that arise can be blamed on bad attitudes and in turn on bad personalities. The end result is blaming bad personalities on genetic inheritance, and then we are one step from the attitude that says that to resolve the problems you need to remove the people who cause them. (See Chorover, 1979 and Henriques, 1984 for extended discussions of biological and cognitive determinism in social theory and practice.) At a less extreme level, a branch manager commenting on the traits appropriate to sales work in insurance delineates them in a sex-typed fashion which acts to render problematic the employment of women in this area:

> " I'm looking for whether they've got drive, initiative and are basically a self-starter. So *he* must want to get on, and get on by *his* own efforts. (Knights and Collinson, 1987: 156)

There is also an evident disjuncture between what managers want in employee personality, for example Type A or 'bubbly', and what employees feel you need to do the job, for example patience. Similarly managers often bemoan the interpersonal or soft skills of their employees though their manner seems often to require nothing more than simple compliance from their subordinates. Employers still use a debased version of trait theory in terms of talking about the 'character' of employees and use personality as if it was an uncontroversial concept. Lacking understanding of underlying psychological processes and ignorant of developments such as social identity theory (see Chapters 8, 24 and 25), it is hard to see how managerial conceptions of personality can ever reflect any realistic estimations of character. Likewise social theorists often use notions such as character loosely. For example, Richard Sennett in *The Corrosion of Character* (1998) contrasts the 'character' of 'Enrico', whose mundane janitorial working life was structured around self-sacrifice for his family, with his son 'Rico' who, though he has more interesting and remunerative work, has a necessarily short-term viewpoint lacking loyalty or commitment. Sennett uses character to mean 'moral character' which is being corroded by the emphasis on short-termism and flexibility in modern working life. The important point here is that the manifest personalities of both father and son are determined by situational contingency, the 'character' of their work, and not any inherent set of qualities or traits. Sennett also focuses on the character of *teamwork* and how teams instead of fostering a sense of community lead to the adoption of a team-player personality that is effectively a faked veneer of cooperation and commitment (see Chapters 24 and 25 for more on this).

Personality and identity

The focus on traits and types in OB is a function of their utility in making personality amenable to classification and manipulation. Yet personality to a great extent is simply the observable manifestation of social identity, which a person develops and constructs through negotiation and interaction with others. The salience of group membership for the individual means that they will exhibit a personality tailored to the situation in order to maintain that membership; according to Deaux (1993: 5) the integration of identity within the group can be viewed as a stable personality disposition. In this sense, personality cannot simply be a cluster of traits; it is a process. It is not something that can be measured in terms of the ways in which people tend to react. Personality is a proactive process in which people present to others the image that will most benefit them in the situation in which they are. This is reflected in the use of development profiling systems that ask you to outline your strengths, weaknesses and career-related goals, as well as how, and by when, you intend to achieve them. They use techniques such as 'domain mapping' and self-report questionnaires similar in style to the Occupational Personality Questionnaire from the Saville & Holdsworth consultancy firm. The OPQ is claimed to be a way for people to indicate their own perceptions of self, and such self-descriptions are validated on the basis that they relate well to expert descriptions of respondents. Such systems have the added utility of producing a public commitment from the respondent, as well as reinforcing individual responsibility in the same fashion as 'project-based working', as noted in the previous chapter.

The focus on 'self-report' and its links to disciplined and goal-oriented behaviour gives us insights into what testing and the panoply of related measures, for example assessment centres, are really about. The whole point is to sell yourself to a prospective or present employer on the basis of how well your personal agenda and goals line up with objectives at organisational, departmental and group/personal levels. This means that selection, gatekeeping and appraisal are more to do with the management of impressions than with the FMJ/FJM paradigm (see Chapter 17) assumed in HRM practice. The process of acquiring a personality, a social identity, is itself influenced by filling out personality inventories or going through an assessment centre. It necessitates putting over an impression of your personality that is appropriate rather than accurate. The personality exhibited in this situation would be a social identity, a mask appropriate to the task at hand and is achieved through *impression management*, which we will examine in more detail in Chapter 25.

Though the mask we present might be appropriate to our own reading of how to cope with a situation, it might not fit others' expectations of how we should react. Argyris (1967) examined the extent to which the demands of managerial and organisational practices were inconsistent with the drive towards greater independence, self-control and complexity in the maturing personality. For employees, especially at the lower levels of organisational hierarchies, the imperatives of managerial control and decision-making may lead to frustration of their desire to actively pursue meaningful goals and to the employment of defence mechanisms to protect their personal identity. These include regression to less mature behaviour, daydreaming, apathy and aggression, and may be interpreted as personality characteristics by others. This might lead to the kind of 'assumption trap' attributed to Theory X attitudes (see Chapter 21), prompting managers to be even more directive and coercive. Likewise our assessment of the personality we need to exhibit might be inappropriate to guide our conduct in face of unfamiliar cultural contexts. Jackson (1994) proposes a '3Cs' (context–content–conduct) model of the factors which need to be accounted for in linking our individual differences to our behaviour in social processes (see Figure 19.2). This model indicates that personality, like perception, is interdependent with our socialisation and intention. It is constructed in relation to what one is trying to achieve, to developing strategies to survive the circumstances one has to endure. It is a tool that allows individuals to manipulate their own environment, even at the same time that it allows others to manipulate them in organisations.

Summary and key points

The story of personality theory in developing from accounts based on types to traits to situationally contingent factors, is one we shall come across again and again in OB, for example in relation to leadership (see Chapter 20). However, in OB terms the important thing about personality is not actually personality but the behaviour we exhibit and whether it is acceptable in organisational terms. Categorisations of behaviour exist to serve the project of selecting for those who will publicly commit to organisational objectives and against those who won't or can't. A 'sound' personality in this sense is one that fits the expectations of cultural groupings in the organisation while bad or pathological personalities are those that do not exhibit compliance with organisational norms. This is rather like the definition of mental illness in Soviet Russia: since the state represents the natural social order, then to be a dissident you must be either mentally ill, a criminal or a traitor.

We explored briefly the links between personality, character and identity, finding further linkages to teamworking and impression management. The personality component of our identity indicates the types of influence to which we are open, but whether such influences actually have an effect on us is

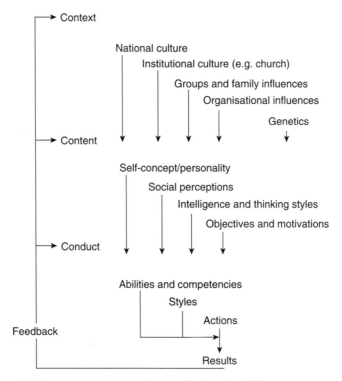

Figure 19.2 **The 3Cs model of context–content–conduct and individual differences**

Source: T. Jackson (1994) *Organisational Behaviour in Management*, Oxford: Butterworth-Heinemann, p. 42, with permission.

determined by whether we learn from them, and the extent to which that learning changes us. We need to learn in order to check on the validity of the identity we have secured for ourselves, and its appropriateness in our current context.

Further reading

Personality, like perception, enjoys fairly similar coverage in most OB texts, Furham and McKenna being good examples. For an in-depth treatment see Ryckman (2007) but for a good read on the evils of personality testing see Annie Murphy Paul's (2004) *Cult of Personality*. The further reading which we would most like to see is a good account linking personality and social identity which is not restricted to elaborations of field-dependency – go to it!

Furnham, A. (2005) *The Psychology of Behaviour at Work: The Individual in the Organisation* (2nd edn), Hove: Psychology Press.

McKenna, E. (2006) *Business Psychology and Organisational Behaviour* (4th edn), Hove: Psychology Press.

Paul, A. M. (2004) *The Cult of Personality: How Personality Tests Are Leading Us to Miseducate Our Children, Mismanage Our Companies, and Misunderstand Ourselves*, New York: Free Press.

Ryckman, R. M. (2007) *Theories of Personality*, Belmont, CA: Thomson/Wadsworth.

20 learning and change

> Given further acceleration, we can conclude that knowledge will grow increasingly perishable. Today's 'fact' becomes tomorrow's 'misinformation'. This is no argument against learning facts or data – far from it. But a society in which the individual constantly changes his job, his place of residence, his social ties and so forth, places an enormous premium on learning efficiency. (Toffler, 1970: 374)

Whether modern occupational patterns have changed to the extent that Toffler predicted over 30 years ago is debatable, but the focus on *learning* he forecast has most certainly come to pass. Toffler was perhaps most prophetic in asserting that we will have to 'learn how to learn' (1970: 374), a phrase that is by now familiar to many in educational and business organisations.

The aims of this chapter are to:

- give an account of how learning and associated socialisation processes have come to have such importance to the mainstream OB agenda.
- examine the basis for current managerial practices in systems of development profiling.
- explain the role of learning organisation initiatives as technologies of regulation aimed at facilitating change processes.
- locate the fundamental models and processes at the heart of the rather eclectic change literature.
- illustrate how the often ignored concept of stability is crucial to the understanding of change processes.

Learning and socialisation: seeing what to do

Our perceptual organisation enables us to comprehend our experience, but if we do not learn from it then our experience is of little use. The concepts and mechanisms of individual learning are of fundamental importance to understanding how we build up both unique identities and common behavioural patterns out of perceptual experience. Accounts of learning might then be expected to focus on how and where we acquire the behaviours appropriate and necessary to our social functioning and survival. In the psychological literature, this is usually presented in terms of models based variously on the *behaviourist*, *cognitive* and *social learning theory* approaches. Learning is commonly defined in relation to the individual in such terms as 'a relatively persistent change in an individual's possible behaviour due to experience' (Fontana, 1985: 64). The use of learning theory in organisational behaviour (OB), on the other hand, is tied to refining the processes by which individuals are socialised into the behaviour patterns required by organisations. Such *socialisation* is accomplished through prescriptions aimed at increasing the effectiveness of training programmes, and in team and cultural initiatives aimed at achieving organisational change.

Behaviourism

The behaviourist model focuses on *associative* and *instrumental* learning. Associative learning stemmed from separate strands of study of animal behaviour by Pavlov (1927) and Thorndike (1911). Pavlov's work was primarily on the association of *innate reflexes* and should really only be applied to involuntary behaviours, though reflexive actions, reminiscent of the 'mindless behaviour' we discussed in Chapter 18 on perception, happen all the time in everyday behaviour. For example, a bell or buzzer signalling the end of a tea-break can cause us to stop what we are doing and go back to work even if there is no supervisor present to tell us to do so. Even though this is not innate behaviour, we are still acting reflexively. Thorndike studied this association of *stimulus* and *response* in the learning of *conditioned reflexes*, for example charting how performance at a task improves with experience in a *learning curve*. The resulting model of *classical conditioning* can be applied to voluntary behaviour and proposes that we learn to behave in a certain fashion because we identify and associate that behaviour with a particular stimulus (classed as satisfying or positive reward or as aversive or negative reward or simply as punishment). Thus, if we go back to work when the buzzer sounds, we do this because we have identified the stimulus as signalling the danger of punishment for non-compliance and associate it with the behaviour of returning to work; we are thus conditioned to obey the buzzer. These approaches were later refined by Watson (1930), into *behaviourism*, a coherent theory of both animal and human behaviour.

Instrumental learning or *operant conditioning* extends the notion of classical conditioning and provides more explanation of why we learn, in that it focuses not just on the stimulus and response, but on the consequences that follow the behaviour. This process, pioneered by Thorndike and refined by Skinner (1971), focuses on the way in which the rewards and punishments which are the outcomes of a behaviour become associated with that behaviour. To extend the above example, if we do not go back to work when the buzzer sounds and get away with it, then we are rewarded by extending our rest period and by avoiding the associated punishment. Thus the likelihood of our doing the same thing in a similar situation is reinforced by the positive consequences of the behaviour.

These two mechanisms have been used at one time or another to explain the learning of just about every type of behaviour by the process of *shaping*, being repeatedly conditioned to close approximations of the desired behaviour. They do not, however, tell us very much about the mental processes which allow us to associate stimuli and behaviour or to expect and assess consequences, given that behaviourism does not generally regard mental processes as open to examination. The positive (reward) and negative (punishment) aspects of systematic conditioning in *reinforcement schedules* do, however, neatly fit into what we term the technologies of regulation which back up the processes of control in organisations. Such schedules vary the rate and ratio of positive or negative stimuli to achieve differing levels and rates of response, The incentives to work harder and the disincentives to social and collective interaction with other workers which a piecework system (a *fixed ratio* schedule) encourages present a good example of these techniques of control. McKenna (2000: 193–7) notes that the techniques of *organisational behaviour modification* which use conditioning and reinforcement principles to attempt to 'shape' the behaviour of workers (for example in areas such as safety practices and absenteeism) are mainly confined to 'highly controllable situations', the basic flaw in such techniques being that they ignore the 'interaction between situational and personal factors' which is 'encapsulated in social learning theory' (2000: 198).

The theoretical base of behaviourism does not really explain how we acquire new behaviours. It does not explain how someone would ignore the warning buzzer the first time, beyond doing it accidentally.

Theorists such as Chomsky (1959) have constructed damning critiques of behaviourism in terms of the inability of conditioning, reinforcement and shaping to explain phenomena such as the acquisition and use of language, particularly in respect of how we construct novel sentences. Chomsky, a linguist, is credited with successfully promoting the cognitive approach, assuming that mental states and thought should be the province of psychology, not just stimulus and response as Watson insisted.

Cognition and insight

Cognitive theory, was prefigured by the gestalt psychologist Kohler's work on the role of *imitation* and *insight* in animal learning, that is, how novel solutions to problems could be arrived at without the trial-and-error approach of Thorndike and the behaviourists. Another significant contribution came from Tolman (1948) who identified that although learning is *purposive* or *goal-oriented* (see Chapter 21), learning could be also be *latent*, that is, not yet reflected in behaviour. Although Tolman was a behaviourist, his work on how rats could learn mazes without reward showed that latent learning could be built up into *cognitive maps*, which were only accessed as needed and allow us to act on the basis of imperfect knowledge and expectation. This notion of mental mapping of location was later broadened into the notion of *cognitive schema*, which represent the mapping and organisation of knowledge about specific objects of any kind. For instance, with reference to our earlier example we could learn to ignore the buzzer in the right circumstances on the basis of what are known as 'TOTE' units. These Test–Operate–Test–Exit units (Miller *et al.*, 1960) represent the stages in which we learn a behaviour or a skill and process the information relating to it. The process involved is a simple *feedback* mechanism whereby we continuously monitor (test) the results of our actions (operations) until we successfully complete them (exit). TOTE unit's build up behaviours as part of sub-plans which feed into wider plans. Thus we might continually test out the limits of how far we can extend our tea-break as part of trying to increase our time away from work we dislike, or as part of attempts to annoy a hated supervisor, or even as a formally constituted plan to resist management controls. The importance of Miller's work is in establishing the importance of feedback in the dynamics of the learning process, although, as those of us who endure annual appraisal know, feedback of poor quality can turn learning into a chore rather than a dynamic opportunity.

The behaviours we learn can be built into schema, which allow for the role of anticipation and expectation in our responses, and through TOTE-like feedback loops simple behaviours can be built up into plans or scripts. The outcome of cognitive learning is that we can use learned knowledge through applying categories of particular behaviours in the context appropriate to specific activities. This is the process involved in the notion of *action regulation* (Hacker and Volpert, cited in Resch *et al.*, 1984), whereby all action is hierarchically organised into units representing sub-goals of the planned action. 'Actions are continually adjusted to changes in the environment' (Frese, 1982: 213), and are initially performed and learned at an *intellectual level* under conscious control. After time and practice they become more 'automatised' and are controlled at the level of *flexible action patterns*, which are the intermediary level of control and represent standardised scripts that can be somewhat modified in the face of situational change. At the final or *sensorimotor level*, actions become stereotyped, automatic responses. Thus when learning to drive we start out having to perform all actions consciously and often err in them. With practice we rehearse patterns of behaviour for changing gear, approaching junctions, and so on, to a standard sufficient to pass our driving test, though novel or unexpected situations can throw us back to the intellectual level. Eventually we get to the point where we can drive to work at speed, unconsciously negotiating all manner of obstacles, while at the same time rehearsing our arguments for an important meeting with our boss.

Thus when actions are learned to the sensorimotor level, the higher levels are made available for pursuing other goals and tasks. Of course in highly routinised work, although actions may be made at the sensori-motor level there is no concomitant 'freedom' to pursue personal goals. At the intellectual level such work only frees us to be frustrated or at best to daydream.

We can explain how we go about learning from the above perspectives, but it is more difficult to explain how we know what we need to learn, and what the appropriate behaviours are in any given situation. When we join an organisation, there are demands on us to learn certain things (how to do our work, 'correct' attitudes and behaviour) and we need to learn how to survive in a new and possibly unfamiliar environment. This process can occur in a formal fashion, as in induction programmes where we learn about the work itself and the rules and procedures that surround it. But more importantly it can proceed in an *informal* fashion, stemming not from training but from our interaction with those we work with, to explain which we need some recourse to *Social Learning Theory*.

Social learning and socialisation

Social learning theory combined elements of cognitive and behaviourist theory to produce a model of learning which focused on interaction. It deals directly with the psychological process of learning and explains novel behaviour on the basis of observing and imitating the behaviour of others, just as most people learn about work through observation and questioning of their workmates. These two aspects of the socialisation process are not separate, although they are conceptualised differently in organisational literature and are generally explained through psychosocial mechanisms rather than subjective experience. First there are the aspects of socialisation that deal directly with the psychological process of learning, notably the 'social learning' models characterised by Eysenck (1947) which focuses on inherited differences in a person's ability to build up conditioned responses, and by Bandura and Walters' (1963) model which focuses on how conditioned responses to external stimuli are mediated by internal psychological processes. Secondly, there are those aspects of socialisation dealing with the ways in which a person is tied to the demands of the groups to which they belong. These aspects are dealt with in *social identity theory* (SIT – Tajfel and Turner, 1979 1986; see also Chapters 20 and 21), though SIT itself does not have a formal theory of learning. That individuals learn in and from groups is a basic supposition of SIT, but the literature tends to assume effects rather than specify them. A typical line of reasoning here is that:

> The social identities in organizations serve as important drivers of performance. How people think as members of groups affects the outcomes of learning interventions. Therefore, social identity is a key input to or driver of learning and performance in organizations. (Korte, 2007: 166)

SIT therefore tends to be linked to the phenomenon of *Organisational Learning* (which we will discuss later) rather than individual learning.

The process through which we learn from observation in social learning theory is based, as in our perceptual processes, on the *selection*, *categorisation* and *transformation* of the stimuli provided through observation, and the subsequent *identification with* and imitation of, selected parts of the observed behaviour. This process, termed *modelling* by Bandura, goes further than mechanisms such as associative or instrumental learning, as it involves *self-reinforcement*, people generating their own rewards and reinforcements, and selecting behaviours in line with their own expectations and desired consequences. We do not slavishly imitate the behaviour of those about us, or even those appearing to act in the most appropriate fashions. We select those aspects of the activity we observe which we can usefully incorporate into our own repertoire of appropriately scripted behaviours. By modelling our behaviour in this fashion we avoid indulging in wasteful and possibly embarrassing attempts to fit ourselves to our surroundings by trial and error, while managing to exert some control and influence over our own activity. The combination of modelling and group-based socialisation can explain how we could be socialised into ignoring the buzzer and pushing the limits of how long we can take for a tea-break by imitation of and being encouraged by others who do so, the behaviour being appropriate to the group, but not approved by the organisation. Social learning theory establishes our behaviour as being not just purposive and goal-oriented, but also motivated by our desires, expectations and normative values.

Social learning has been effectively relied on for a long time in the default industrial training method known as the 'sitting with Nellie' approach, where the recruit works with an experienced operative to learn the skills necessary to the task. This semi-formal approach to training could, however, have unlooked-for informal consequences. The recruit may not only learn how to do the job, but may also 'learn the ropes', how to cope with work, utilise short-cuts, or learn to 'make-out' by manipulating bonus systems. A modern analogue of this approach is the practice of *mentoring* where 'entrants' or candidates for promotion are guided and counselled through their career development. Kram (1983) identifies stages of *initiation, cultivation, separation* and *redefinition* in this type of relationship, mentors effectively leading their charges to a stage where they can define their own relationship to the demands of their aspirational role or their 'career cycle'. As a formal learning process mentoring is fundamentally a gentler version of the process used to socialise army recruits, as identified by Wanous (1992: 232–4):

Stage 1: Environmental shock – disconfirm expectations, give boring ambiguous work so recruits cling to authority;
Stage 2: Engagement – strip away old identity by humiliating recruits/telling them they're worthless. Build anger and resentment;
Stage 3: Period of attainment – create new identity by implying inclusion. Give recruits credit for acquiring new skills and appropriate attitudes;
Stage 4: Period of termination – confidence and euphoria build. Plan for rest of army career.

This process of group bonding and isolation from the outside world and psychological and physical humiliation is taken even further in the example used by Corbett (1994: 13–16) to show how ostensibly 'normal' people can be trained as torturers by the military (psychopaths being too unreliable). Recruits undergo *incremental socialisation* by being gently introduced to the features of the job:

1 Recruits act as guards
2 Recruits carry food to prisoners in cells
3 Recruits ordered to deliver short beatings
4 Recruits supervise prisoners during prolonged forced standing
5 Recruits participate fully in torture.

Such incremental socialisation also requires the provision of rewards, though they need not be great, for example enough special treatment to make membership of the group seem important to the recruit. The rewards can be both actual and symbolic and in tying recruits to the salient features of the group can provide the impetus for the necessary condition of objectifying the victims as someone deserving torture. In the case reported by Corbett this is formally reinforced by seminars inculcating appropriate values and the use of demeaning language about victims, but it is easy to see how informal incremental learning of this sort could socialise people into a culture of bullying or racism in the workplace.

The importance of value systems or 'evaluative beliefs' to mentor/sponsor relationships is emphasised by Hosking and Morley (1991: 100–4) who note that as projects/organisations become larger, more reliance has to be placed on stable ideological belief structures. In other words, large organisations cannot rely on having enough reliable 'Nellies' to sit with and must rely more on the formalised expression of the cultural values of the organisation to guide socialisation. Hosking and Morley widen this discussion to the relations between scripted behaviour, cognitive dissonance, self-justification and rationalisation in building the networks supporting us in our work. This serves as a reminder that though we collaborate with others in our socialisation at work our learning is still instrumental, our self-interest guiding what is essentially a process of what we might term *self-socialisation* in support of our career and personal goals.

Roles

The modelling process guides us to the appropriate behaviours demanded of us in our organisational 'role'. The concept of 'role' has had too much interpretation for us give a full account (see Biddle, 1979 or Mullins, 1999: 470–6). However, for our present purposes, roles can be seen as sets of self-categorised, stereotyped and scripted behaviours enabling us to act in a contextually consistent manner. The effect of the *role expectations*, both formal and informal, placed on us by our work and peers are seen as so important to effective management that diagnostic instruments such as the Belbin Team Role Self Perception Inventory (1981) have been developed to aid people in effectively scripting their own differentiated roles in groups and teams (see Chapter 24). Through modelling, our behaviour can be influenced by that of those we select as *role models*, those whom we perceive to be acting in a 'correct' or desirable fashion. By building our own *behavioural repertoire* out of selected actions of role models we can fit our actions to those required by organisational culture. Thus close associations with role models can effectively form an informal mentoring relationship. We also utilise *negative role models* to define for us the types of behaviour we do not wish to imitate, generally based on those we perceive as acting in an inappropriate, socially disapproved or undesirable fashion. In other words, what individuals gain from the social learning process are guidelines and frameworks for action and self-evaluation in the production of an identity which can cope with and blend into its surroundings. Examples might be found in the way that newcomers are socialised into sexually-stereotyped occupations. For example, a branch manager explains that 'we try to keep people coming in at the bottom so that we can train them to our ways, get them used to the company' (Knights and Collinson, 1987: 161). The models that newcomers who want to fit in are most likely to emulate and compare themselves to are those who appear *situationally competent*, who fit the appropriate stereotypes and who hold the right attitudes, thus reproducing, for instance, the 'macho' image of the construction worker.

We need to emphasise once again though that socialisation through social learning does not simply transform an individual into an image of what an organisation requires, notwithstanding Handy's definition of socialisation in OB terms as 'the process by which an organisation seeks to make the individual more amenable to the prevalent mode of influence' (1976: 134). We certainly do learn to produce in ourselves normative characteristics and identities with consistent social meaning, but at the same time we acquire and produce distinctive characteristics, those defining our identities. Even though social learning enables us to take on a normative role, our observations can just as easily lead us to enhance those things about ourselves reinforcing our personal rather than social meaning. For example, the role models we use are not only those people with whom we are in immediate contact. In producing an identity we also use individuals and reference groups with whom we may have little or no interaction. We may base our social identity, the image we present, not only on those behaviours and models appropriate to our present context, but on those pertaining to roles and perceived identities to which we aspire. We may act in a way consistent with other workers, but at the same time adopt some behaviours which link us with superiors if we desire promotion, or perhaps the representatives of a professional or trade union organisation if we perceive enhanced meaning and identity as lying in that direction.

We referred above to social identity theory making assumptions about the influence of groups in learning: these assumptions extend to the distinction made between personal and social identity. SIT itself focuses on how social identities are constructed with the concomitant assumption that learning takes place within and from groups and while self-categorisation theory does focus on how the individual makes themselves part of the group, it still assumes that this is done on the group's terms. Thus though groups supply much of the *context of socialisation* and the fabric from which we construct social identities, we must be wary of attributing too much responsibility to groups as the *agents* of socialisation. To a great extent even allowing for the influence of groups, employees effectively *have to* socialise themselves if they are to identify with or at least exhibit normative values and behaviour, as following from our discussion in Chapter 18 it is the individual who is best at modifying and constructing their own attitudes and values even though external influences may shape them.

Skills, styles and experiential learning

As intimated earlier, much of the work on learning theory has been linked to increasing the effectiveness of formal training programmes, the key concepts here being the *transfer of learning*, the *acquisition of skills* and adapting training programmes to the '*learning curve*' of the trainee. (See McKenna, 2000: 571–2 for a useful discussion.) Learning transfer relates to the conditions under and extent to which stimuli can be generalised to new situations. Skill acquisition is generally approached through prescriptions about the nature of feedback to be given (developed, for example from Miller's TOTE model), and how learning tasks should be broken down into assimilable chunks prior to practising the integration of the whole task. Calculation of 'learning curves' tend to indicate that the rate of assimilation of learning tends to reach a plateau after a while, and that careful setting of objectives is needed to get the trainee to the next stage of his or her learning. This latter notion can be related to our earlier comments on action regulation, in that as action patterns are learned we need to go back to the intellectual level of learning before we can script new action patterns and get to the next stage of integrating the total activity into sensorimotor action. Where we have to learn consciously again, clear objectives become critical variables in our motivation to learn. (See the section on *goal-setting* in Chapter 21.)

Pressures to continually update employees' skills are becoming greater in this era of 'continuous professional development' (CPD) and quality standardisation in initiatives such as ISO9001 and Investors in People (IiP). This has consolidated the interest in management development circles on the notion of '*experiential learning*', derived from Kolb's (1976) work on the '*learning cycle*'. This suggests that learning takes place in four stages, all of which are necessary to effective learning:

1   Seeking concrete experiences related to goals.
2   Reflective observation and interpretation of experience.
3   Forming abstract concepts and generalisations related to goals.
4   Active experimentation on concepts, leading back to 1.

Kolb's evidence on management learning claims that personal preferences and learning goals will lead individuals to focus on particular stages of the cycle in learning styles which can be identified through use of the 'Learning Styles Inventory' (LSI). On this basis, Starkey (1996: 262) notes that 'In general managers tend to emphasise active experimentation over reflective observation. ... Theorists of management tend to stress reflective observation and abstract conceptualisation.' This is indicative of the fact that Kolb's learning styles actually relate to combinations of preferences for particular stages as follows:

- convergent (3 and 4)
- divergent (1 and 2)
- assimilation (2 and 3)
- accommodation (1 and 4).

Kolb (in Starkey, 1996: 279) then links these styles to a model of the problem-solving process so that the full process requires all four styles to be enacted. Style preferences are not simply related to personality characteristics, but to the context of, and the skills or strengths needed in, the learning situation. Thus managers would tend to an accommodation style which Kolb links to executing solutions and choosing models or goals. Management theorists on the other hand would tend to an assimilation style which Kolb links to problem selection and considering alternative solutions.

It is still the case that in much of the mainstream OB literature, learning styles are linked directly to personality traits in stages 1 to 4 above, rather than to Kolb's style typology. This can be seen in an often-cited application produced by Honey and Mumford (1982), who classify the stages themselves as styles:

- activist (1)
- reflector (2)
- theorist (3)
- pragmatist (4).

Honey and Mumford's styles are used more as predictive personality traits than as analytic or diagnostic categories, and are claimed to explain why 'given the same experience ... some people learn while others do not' (promotional brochure for Honey and Mumford's 'Learning Styles Questionnaire'). The probability is, of course, that given the same experience, what some people learn is that they do not want to assimilate the material their trainers are giving them. Though the cycle of experience and reflection is an integral part of the training processes which lie at the heart of much of modern education and HRM, when CPD becomes 'Compulsory Professional Development' as it now has for many professional associations worldwide, learning itself is in danger of becoming a chore which will promote either resistance or resigned acceptance to learning initiatives.

Learning and development

The predecessor of systems of continuous improvement and professional development was *staff development*, the theoretical base of which Miller and Verduin (1979) place in perceptual psychology, assuming attitudinal and behavioural changes to be dependent on changing perceptions, as argued in Chapter 18s. The element of *goal-setting* involved (see Chapter 21) made staff development the natural heir to Drucker's earlier *management by objectives* (MBO), but took the notion one stage further.

Instead of setting goals monitored by senior managers to ensure compatibility with organisational objectives, individuals were required to set goals compatible with their own aspirations and 'needs'. By emphasising the intra-organisational construction of individual goals, staff development provides an effective gloss over managerial strategies for transforming learning, motivation and identity into influence and productivity.

Self-report tools such as Personal Development Forms (PDFs) for profiling our work relationships have now become an integral part of organisational learning and development practices. They act as self-administered, continuously assessed, personality, attitude and aptitude inventories, providing feedback to both management and staff. They facilitate the moulding of operational identities through the integration of functional activities into social comparison processes and hierarchical relationships. Such profiling can be further reinforced by courses, trips and exchanges which act as rewards for correct behaviour, and the internalisation of group and organisational norms. Employers such as Ford Motors have, in the past, offered exchanges to production workers: they visit and work in plants employing new production processes and those which are said to have good productivity and industrial relations records. Return visits presumably imbue others with the values that have made particular plants successful and of course highlight workers' perceptions of their dispensability within the international division of labour. Exchanges can also produce social facilitation effects and rely on group conformity and peer pressure as in those of team-building exercises where members of the same group or organisation are required to dress similarly and/or indulge in activities designed to increase group identification (see Chapter 24).

What systems such as staff development and CPD are predicated on is the belief that individual change within processes of organisational change is facilitated by behavioural technologies such as the LSI, profiling systems and so on. CPD provides a rhetorical framework for managerial strategies transforming learning, motivation and identity into influence and productivity. In the same fashion, organisational change is facilitated by strategic approaches to learning which emphasise generating the 'right' *learning climate* in organisations. There are many forms of organisational learning initiative, but we wish to focus on phenomena of the learning organisation as it is founded on the links we wish to go on to make between learning and change.

Learning organisation

The literature on what has come to be known as the 'learning organisation' (LO) is characterised by themes of strategic and self-managed change as a way of dealing with environmental uncertainty. The notion, which can be traced back to the work of Argyris and Schön (1978) on *theories of action* in *organisational learning* and to the work of Lewis (1984) and others on *open learning* and computer-based training, is based on the recognition:

> that members of organisations must be equipped to create and sustain values, knowledge bases, processes, skills and systems which promote effective responses to change. This dictates the need for higher trust cultures, for responsive systems and knowledge workers who are capable of participating in making decisions and solving problems at point of discovery and without reliance on complex command and control systems. (West, 1994: 15)

Numerous writers including Senge, Lessem, Honey and Burgoyne have been involved in promoting the idea of a learning organisation, a phenomenon that John van Maanen of MIT has described as 'what

298 20

INTRODUCTION: REGULATING ORGANISATIONAL BEHAVIOUR ▪ PERCEPTION AND ATTITUDES: SEEING WHAT TO THINK ▪ MASKS FOR TASKS: PERSONALITY ▪ **LEARNING AND CHANGE** ▪ MOTIVATION: THE DRIVE FOR SATISFACTION ▪ LEADERSHIP: MIGHT OR MYTH? ▪

management in the twenty-first century will be about' (MCB University Press circular advertising *Learning Organisation* journal).

Research on learning in social psychology was in the main individually-based as indicated above, and the assimilation of such knowledge into a more collective notion such as the LO was difficult and only achieved at some cost. Analogies to individual learning used by leading organisational psychologists such as Argyris (1967) tended to rest on a physical/mental progression from infant passivity, dependency and submission to control, through to the maturity of reflection, foresight and responsibility for others. However, as Mathews notes (1994: 288), the concept of the learning organisation is distinct from the learning processes of individual employees. Thus people embody learning in their own minds, but organisations have no 'mind' except in a metaphorical sense. Organisations need to develop institutional structures embodied in organisational routines through which experience can be gathered and accumulated. Such organisational memory can be manifested informally through culture or formally through official records, minutes of meetings. and so on, though as we have seen in Chapter 16 the attempts to do this in Knowledge Management have shown the limits to this sort of formalisation and standardisation. The notion of *lifelong learning* has been touted around as an method of engaging employees, though as Crowther (2004: 125) notes:

> It is primarily a mode of social control that acts as a new disciplinary technology to make people more compliant and adaptable for work in the era of flexible capitalism … Lifelong learning diminishes the public sphere, undermines educational activity, introduces new mechanisms of self-surveillance and reinforces the view that failure to succeed is a personal responsibility. It is ultimately a 'deficit discourse', which locates the responsibility of economic and political failure at the level of the individual, rather than at the level of systemic problems.

Organisational learning versus learning organisations

The critique of the learning organisation literature presented above is not, however, the whole story. Much of the discussion of learning in organisations today comes under the heading of *organisational learning*, which like the learning organisation sounds on the surface like simple reification; organisations are not entities – therefore they cannot learn. However, as complex interactions of individuals and groups, and as flows of information and resources, organisations can be considered as 'communities of practice' (Brown and Duguid, 1991). As such they are arenas where both formal and informal learning takes place, where relevant knowledge is constructed, stored and transferred. How and whether organisational learning and learning organisations differ in relation to such a concept of organisation is seldom explored fully in mainstream texts.

Where differences are noted, they seem to centre on the formal/informal distinction as exemplified in the work of Jones and Hendry (1994). They associate organisational learning with traditional training regimes and HRM initiatives, and learning organisations with Pettigrew and Whipp's (1991) notion of *organisational capability*, which is more in line with informal socialisation and experiential learning as discussed earlier. The important point here is to what extent both are instances of *managed* versus *self-managed* learning (see Chapter 16). We know that significant numbers of people in modern organisations learn to appropriate information technologies to their own use, learning much more than is required of them in their work. Thus the development of capabilities by organisational members will proceed in a tacit manner even where no formal training is given.

In the light of such self-directed empowerment, McHugh, Groves and Alker (1998) note that in operational terms there appears to be little in learning organisation initiatives that provides any real commitment to HRM strategies of mobilising consent:

> " The linkage to strategy demands support for flexibility of organisation and open-ended intrinsic commitment, but for the learner the 'locus of control' is still exogenous in that learning must be shown to achieve objectives related to their task and role. (McHugh, Groves and Alker, 1998: 218)

Thus, although characterised by factors such as emphases on self-management, matrix-type structures, dedicated training support and flexibility in working practices (Sims, Fineman and Gabriel, 1993: 198), there is little practical difference between learning organisation initiatives and the content of traditional organisational learning. As such, the use of practices under these banners can also be viewed as yet another vehicle for achieving organisational change, or more accurately as Swieringa and Wierdsma (1992: 1) put it, for 'the changing of behaviour'.

This can be exemplified by reference to earlier notions of open learning via computer-assisted learning (CAL). Fuller and Saunders (1990: 32–3) note three basic rationales to open access learning: the *instrumental*, based on simple access to training opportunities; the *prescriptive*, based on empowerment of individuals and groups; and the *functional*, based on cost-effectiveness. They argue that the prescriptive approach (that closest to the ideal of the learning organisation) is 'likely to be inconsistent with company objectives' and 'inevitably constrained by commercial and organisational factors': in other words, it will be *managed learning*. The implication here is that learning organisation initiatives will be dependent on ad hoc instrumental opportunities and functional imperatives. Thus even a sincere attempt to promote a learning organisation will face a tendency to slide back into Jones and Hendry's organisational learning approach, all that is left of the learning organisation being the legitimating rhetoric of employee empowerment.

The idea of a learning organisation has by now become similar to the 'morally sustaining ideas' and 'socially integrating myths' through which Selznick characterises leadership (see Chapter 22). This is to be expected in that implementation of organisational learning can be firmly linked to that of 'new-wave' manufacturing techniques. Winfield and Kerrin (1994), in a survey of 60 Midlands manufacturers and a case study of Toyota in Derbyshire, note that the 'continuous improvement programmes' associated with organisational learning are deployed directly alongside TQM and JIT programmes. The introduction of such programmes is criticised for a lack of attention to 'human resource issues' (1994: 8), and learning systems and techniques complete the 'whole package' necessary for the effective utilisation of 'new' production practices. In a similar vein, Seely-Brown and Duguid (in Tsoukas, 1994c: 165–87) make important distinctions between 'espoused' and 'actual practice' in working and learning, Shrivastava (1983: 25) earlier noting a link between organisational learning and the development and introduction of new management information and control systems. The failed implementation of such systems was identified with a lack of concern by designers for existing socio-cultural norms and learning practices.

In its ties to the introduction of new working practices and disregard for subjective learning, the learning organisation would appear to devolve 'into a simple goal-setting exercise underwritten by an appeal to the superordinate goal of organisational survival' (McHugh, Groves and Alker, 1998: 218). As such it has little respect for the learning theory from which it claims descent, and is more properly seen as a tool of change and development practices, attempts to change behaviour and working practices through cultural initiatives, and more straightforward attitude change techniques. This is a reciprocal relationship in that the tools employed, for example Lewin's unfreezing–refreezing model, are essentially developments of learning theory, in this case the notion of the learning curve. The

300   20

INTRODUCTION: REGULATING ORGANISATIONAL BEHAVIOUR ▪ PERCEPTION AND ATTITUDES: SEEING WHAT TO THINK ▪ MASKS FOR TASKS: PERSONALITY ▪ **LEARNING AND CHANGE** ▪ MOTIVATION: THE DRIVE FOR SATISFACTION ▪ LEADERSHIP: MIGHT OR MYTH? ▪

identification of the individual's 'training needs', in systems such as development profiling, provide the mechanisms through which public commitment to change is acquired. That such technologies of regulation are seldom related to any real concern for individual development is evidenced by the argument that learning initiatives can be short-circuited by what Easterby-Smith characterises as an 'obsession with activity' (1992: 28), and Senge (1992: 38) as a concern with *performing rather than learning*. This bias towards productivity and 'bottom-line' definitions of growth once again confirms the paucity of claims to increase the motivational content of work and refocuses commitment as simple compliance (see Chapter 21).

The difficulties and self-defeating nature of linking strategic organisational demands to learning and motivational factors must in the end lead us to question the extent to which systematic control of such factors is ever possible. However, such systematic control is exactly what is sought in the study of how we learn to collaborate with organisational transformation through the planning and implementation of *change*.

Change

Models and processes

Most models of change are developments in one way or another of Lewin's and/or Leavitt's early models. Lewin's (1951) *force-field analysis* of *driving* and *restraining* forces has found widespread practical application in its *unfreeze–move–refreeze* model, which itself is also applicable to learning and attitude change. Newer models seldom do more than add new variables to the list of factors assumed to influence responses to change (see Martin, 1998: 589–91). Rather like the content theories of motivation we will discuss in Chapter 21, they tell us about the *what* of change but little about the *how*. When the how of change processes is discussed, it is generally in prescriptive terms and concerned with managerial responses or styles. While employee resistance is continually invoked as a barrier to change, the issue of managerial resistance is rarely mentioned, even though commentators such as Salaman and Butler (1994) cite managerial resistance to change as one of the reasons why 'managers won't learn' (34).

Other models such as that of French and Bell (1984) specifically develop Lewin as a mechanism for planning and evaluating change processes. Unfreezing here involves *preparing for change* by gaining trust and developing team awareness. The movement phase *evaluates* the current position, developing aims, objectives and action plans. *Implementation* can overlap the unfreezing phrase, where for French and colleagues the important courses of action consist of stabilisation and review of the situation.

Leavitt's (1965) people–task–technology–structure model is widely used to illustrate the interdependence of organisational variables in the process of managing change. Like the Lewin model, new variables such as strategy, environment or culture are routinely added to reflect current concerns (see Martin, 1998: 587, or Rollinson *et al.*, 1998: 612–13). Strangely, one of the few developments of Leavitt's model to highlight explicitly the role of the individual is the McKinsey 7-S framework of organisational analysis. Despite its genesis in the work of Peters and Waterman (1982) this model does highlight skills, staff and style as being of greater importance to change processes than strategy, systems and structure (shared values being the linking factor).

Collins (1998: chap. 4), in his review of sociological perspectives on change, produces a cogent critique of what he terms the *n-step* models of change abounding in the literature. N-step models act as programmatic, recipe-style guides to the change process much as the French model cited above, Collins giving a typical simplified example as follows (1998: 83):

1 Develop strategy
2 Confirm top-level support
3 Use project management approach
4 Communicate results.

These models are described as *undersocialised*, 'in that they fail to acknowledge change as a social activity, involving people from diverse social groups, who will tend to interpret issues in different, and often quite divergent ways' (1998: 82). Their rational, sequential and prescriptive nature (1998: 84) focuses mainly on the co-operative elements of organisation (1998: 87), where the 'futile resistance' of workers is centred around 'poor communications or deficiencies in worker psychology' (1998: 91). Opposition to 'new business realities' is ideologically recast as resistance by workers who are 'lacking the psychological make-up to deal with change' (1998: 92). Thus, according to Collins, real people are absent from n-step models (1998: 96) or appear to be 'docile, malleable and altruistic ... while managers appear to be strong, creative and decisive' (1998: 97). This illustrates why reading the change literature is such a frustrating experience. There are many models, innumerable prescriptions and case studies, but little that is truly informative. It also embodies a recurring tension between self-directed and imposed change. As Hollway notes in her commentary on Argyris's work on interpersonal skills training:

> How do you ensure change without imposing it? You convince the individual who is the object of the change that they are choosing it. This is what I mean by subjectification. Argyris calls it growth.
> (Hollway, 1991: 95)

An organisational capacity for change is often reduced to an individual's willingness to 'be motivated' or to 'accept ownership'. Such thinking neglects the complex mixture of identities and interests at work. As the extract above indicates, employees may reject or resent the 'subjectification' process. That is not to say that change does not or should not take place, merely that we need a deeper, more balanced understanding of it.

Staff and managers within public organisations are often trying to deal with change on many levels at once, trying to balance conflicting demands, trying to sustain a sense of personal worth and purpose within large and confusing organisations, to construct an identity out of the elements of professional, manager, citizen or activist that make sense of trying to feel good about what they do. They are working within the constraints of organisations that don't work well with creaking systems and not enough money. For many staff and managers, old realities exist. They do not experience change as transforming the everyday job, simply making it more difficult.

(Goss, 2001: 154)

Change and stability

What is often lacking in both theoretical models and real-world change processes is an awareness of the importance of continuity to individuals and groups involved in change. Alvin Toffler (1970: 342–3) argued that to cope successfully with change we need *zones of stability*. Toffler, who was one of the first advocates of managing rather than suppressing or adapting to change, identified factors such as close family ties and habits as 'patterns of relative constancy' (1970: 435) which provide us with what we would term a redoubt against the relentless pressure to change. However, in organisational terms, such zones of stability might represent the very factors managers and change models identify as sources of resistance to change. Thus we have a catch-22 in the fact that the implementation of change demonstrably lacks concern for the very factors that might make individuals tolerate it. It is often held that people prefer technological to cultural change, and in zones of stability we can see why: changes and uncertainty in the external environment, for example takeovers and rationalisation programmes, undermining zones of stability in a more distant and uncertain fashion than change in the technologies that you work with.

The management of change rather than the experience of change is the focus we find in mainstream OB. Hosking and Anderson (1992) cast doubts over this perspective, arguing that it produces an 'illusion of manageability'. They cite Ernecq on strategic interventions often being 'usurped by outcomes which were neither expected nor intended', and Crouch on his study on the 'myths of managing change', to the effect that:

> a common response to environmental change was for managers to initiate endogenous changes in their own organisations, which often result in pleasant feelings of coping with anxiety-provoking events. (Hosking and Anderson, 1992: 7)

Planned rational change

In a similar vein to the above, one senior manager in a case study company (Marks *et al.*, 1998) put it that the typical response to 'hitting the wall' is to reinvent the programme: a perspective driven by a problematic of 'change'. Mintzberg and Waters (in Tsoukas, 1994) also explore these issues in terms of whether change strategies are deliberate/conscious vs. emergent/unconscious and in the context of whether their outcomes are *realised* or *unrealised*. The unintended consequences of change programmes mean that it is the feedback or evaluation mechanisms built into the process that are actually most important in coping with or resisting internal or external pressures by accommodating or assimilating them. If there is a *strategy* to change here it appears to be a combination of a coping strategy (see Chapter 23) and an impression management strategy (see Chapter 25), being seen to do anything being more important than appearing to not be in control. Like being in love, being able to direct change programmes means never having to say you are sorry, as failure can be blamed on lax implementation.

Change as conceptualised by OB appears to be more a process of conscious attitudinal and behavioural adjustment and outcome evaluation than as presented by Ernecq and Mintzberg. Change processes are presented as value-neutral in much the same way as decision-making processes, political neutrality having an ideologically normative value for management (see Hosking and Anderson, 1992: 8–9). This reinforces the value to be had from cost and efficiency benefits, but ignores the problems raised by tensions between *stability* vs. *pressure to change* and *strategy* vs. *execution*, not to mention the tension between *autonomy* vs. *interdependence* ever present for groups and intervals. According to King and Anderson (1995: 86), what managers will increasingly demand in the future is 'evidence of rigorous evaluation of different intervention strategies'. Constant change programmes, coupled with the everyday experiential change to which individuals and groups are exposed, ought to put issues such as change fatigue to the fore as the focus of the study of change, though King and Anderson argue that managerial demands will lead instead to more research on factors such as teambuilding for innovation and creativity training. However, the undersocialised nature of planned rational change using n-step models like those identified by Collins (above) would tend to work against the potential success of such training as would their relative ignorance of constraints such as the size and growth characteristics of organisations, for example those identified by Greiner (1972) in terms of the crises suffered at differing stages of organisational growth.

Decision systems

The uncertainty of outcomes in planned change has led to the development of a huge number of analytic systems to aid in systematic planning and decision-making by managers, most of them again being derivations of Lewin's force field analysis or developments of cost–benefit calculations such as the more strategically oriented SWOT analysis used widely in marketing and corporate planning. The development of these systems, especially in the case of decision-making, started like personality theory with trait-based approaches which look at individual biases in decision-making styles in a manner similar to the use of Kolb's Learning Cycle by Honey and Mumford (see above). We would expect more contingent systems to develop and these by now have produced computer-based decision support systems that offer the optimisation of goal-planning and decision rules allowing for situational factors similar to the decision-tree methodology used in Vroom and Yetton's (1973) normative model of leadership (see Chapter 22). Another influential model of decision decision-making processes is Janis and Mann's (1977) conflict, commitment and choice model. This focuses on decisions of high salience to the self, for example relationship and career issues, and is further related to stress-coping behaviours (see Chapter 23). Individuals are said to be either optimistic or pessimistic that they can find a decision solution and to produce either adaptive or maladaptive outcomes. Adaptive, high-quality decisions are most likely to be reached through vigilance, carefully examining alternatives and weighing costs and benefits. Maladaptive, low-quality decisions are most likely to stem from *hyper-vigilance* (or panic) where decisions are made under time pressure and/or to reduce stress; *defensive avoidance* (or cop-out) making least-worst decisions, buck-passing or procrastinating or lastly *complacency*. Janis and Mann also look at the tactics used by decision-makers to bolster their own perceptions of their decisions; even when of low quality or not carried through, these tactics include minimising personal responsibility, surveillance by others and unfavourable circumstances.

What is still apparent with these models though is that, as with the study of personality (see Chapter 19), the concern is not for the uniqueness of the individual experience of the change or decision process but for consistent modes of response that can lead to predictive and/or prescriptive categories. Such categories are judged against outcomes and these in turn are judged against increasingly standardised sets of criteria, for example, 'benchmarking' against 'best practice'. Where models (such as Lewis, 1991) do attempt to account for subjective factors like individual feelings, skills and knowledge, they still tend to set personal factors against objective and task-related aspects of the change process. Thus they are still intended as tools to aid managers to 'imbue the person with the courage to confront his or her feelings about the change' (Rollinson *et al.*, 1998: 614–15).

Much as with the intent behind transformational leadership (see Chapter 22) change systems are about aiding managers to transform the attitude and behaviour of employees, that is, it is the interests of the change agent that are the focus, not those of the persons to be 'changed'. In the change literature as Buchanan and Badham (1999: 23) note, 'change champions' are often presented as heroic figures at the expense of the wider cast of characters. But while key individuals are important, this way of looking at things separates individuals from their context and neglects other participants. Though it is assumed that teams can be enlisted to aid in changing individual behaviour, other participants (for example professional or functional groupings) are often only brought into the picture as potential 'resistors to change', and on this basis Marks and colleagues (1998) argue that it might be more accurate to talk in terms of change agencies, as well as agents, since both positive and negative influences, or driving and restraining forces (in Lewin's terms) will influence the course of change. Change processes may in fact set off inter-professional conflicts as the various stakeholders compete to promote their sectional interests. So while change may be rationally planned and supported by decision-making systems, it is not just that it may have unintended consequences, but it may also have the consequences that depend on the effectiveness of the decisions made by competing parties with their own plans, strategy and set of legitimating cultural beliefs.

Change, socialisation and cultural capital

We have already noted the limits to culture as an agency of change (see Chapter 11), but culture does have a role in planned change, in the sense that successful change projects can be based on the formation and diffusion of *cultural capital*, although we should remember that this could also be the basis of successful resistance to change. Adapting the concept from Bourdieu (who uses it to explain comparative educational advantage), the spirits industry research referred to previously (Marks *et al.*, 1997; see also Chapter 7) found that United Distillers recruited managers who had experience of leading change programmes, rather than for their technical or sectoral experience. This infusion of managers constituted a key cultural resource. The change programme, Towards World Class (TWC), was conceived by the senior operational executive team and defined through 18 months in often gruelling meetings, facilitated by consultants. This constituted both a crucial learning period for senior operational managers and an intensive socialisation into the new expectations of United Distillers managers reminiscent of the military programmes discussed above (Wanous, 1992), though without, one assumes, the associated beating and humiliation. Six cross-functional project teams – Assets, Competencies, Standards, Service, Suppliers and Culture – acted as the foci of an integrated change effort, tied into matrix reporting. TWC became a vehicle that compelled managers at all levels to become embedded into networks whose triple purpose was improved performance, learning and innovation. The cultural capital accumulated by key agents at the beginning was diversified across plants and functions, TWC compelling managers to 'reinvent' themselves, delegating to wider layers and promoting changes in values. Thus, for the success of the intervention, managers here had to socialise themselves into becoming the change agency that could deliver the programme to the employees, having to learn to transform themselves so they could in turn transform the learning of others.

Summary and key points

The importance of learning and socialisation processes to the mainstream OB agenda lie not only in their underpinning of training but also in their role as technologies of regulation aimed at achieving individual transformation of identities and facilitating change processes. Initiatives such as the learning organisation attempt to associate strategic organisational demands with individual and group learning.

Change, then, being dependent on mechanisms of learning, seems to require the routine *unfreezing* or *creative destruction* of current attitudes and practices surrounding work. At the same time, there is no guarantee that this will not unfreeze the very values that led to identification with the organisation in the first place, even in the case of managers. Indeed many of the *systems of action* (Limerick *et al.*, 1994) which operate to recognise environmental discontinuities and overcome what Argyris (1976) termed *defensive routines*, are aimed at managers:

> Such routines 'enable managers and others to stay within the relative comfort zone of the current deep structure' (Argyris, 1976: 34) and it is the skills and feedback from the learning community which are proposed as the transformational trigger which can bring down such barriers to change. (McHugh, Groves and Alker, 1998: 210)

If 'deep structure' and defensive routines equate to Toffler's stability zones, then change through learning must be backed up by participation and support to succeed and may make change a speculative enterprise at best, unless creative and innovative learning opportunities are provided for all involved (see Thompson and McHugh, 2002, chap. 16). Unfortunately the factors most often employed in such endeavours represent the exercise of power through attempts to coercively change perceptions rather than by any mutual process. The difficulties of short-term attitude change masquerading as real learning or transformation are similar to the difficulties we will find in the next chapter where we again approach the notions of managerial and self-control through the use of an extended exemplar much as we utilised learning and change in this chapter. The project remains the same, but we move on to assess the extent to which psychological knowledge can deliver changes in employee behaviour in the direction of greater *commitment* to corporate objectives through the magic of *motivation*.

Further reading

On the basic psychological processes of learning McKenna is a good OB account and basic psychology texts can add any greater depth needed. For mainstream 'how to' resources on learning and development the CIPD website is a good place to start. The Alker and McHugh study (2000) on learning organisations has good links to HR strategy and Crowther (2004) is one of the few critical sources on the topic of lifelong learning and development, albeit a discourse-based account. On change we have not included diagrams of the classic Lewin and Leavitt models as these are available in many OB texts and from simple web searches. Goss gives a detailed account of change processes in the public sector and the Collins text, though a sociological account, has a classic debunking style and is very good on models of change. For a more psychological approach King and Anderson is still relevant and like the Marks and colleagues study we have referred to it provides useful links to innovation.

Alker, L. and McHugh, D. (2000) 'Human Resource Maintenance? Organisational Rationales for the Introduction of Employee Assistance Programmes', *Journal of Managerial Psychology*, 15. 4: 303–23.

Chartered Institute of Personnel and Development (CIPD) (2004) at – http://www.cipd.co.uk/default.cipd.

Collins, D. (1998) *Organisational Change: Sociological Perspectives*, London: Routledge.

Crowther, J. (2004) '"In and Against" Lifelong Learning: Flexibility and the Corrosion of Character', *International Journal of Lifelong Education*, 23. 2: 125–36.

Goss, S. (2001) *Making Local Government Work: Networks, Relationships and the Management of Change*, London: Palgrave.

King, N. and Anderson, N. (1995) *Innovation and Change in Organisations*, London: Routledge.

McKenna, E. (2006) *Business Psychology and Organisational Behaviour* (4th edn), Hove: Psychology Press.

Marks, A., Findlay, P., Hine, J., McKinlay, A. and Thompson, P. (1998) 'The Politics of Partnership: Innovation in Employment Relations in the Scottish Spirits Industry', *British Journal of Industrial Relations*, 36. 2: 209–26.

306 20

INTRODUCTION: REGULATING ORGANISATIONAL BEHAVIOUR ▪ PERCEPTION AND ATTITUDES: SEEING WHAT TO THINK ▪ MASKS FOR TASKS: PERSONALITY ▪ **LEARNING AND CHANGE** ▪ MOTIVATION: THE DRIVE FOR SATISFACTION ▪ LEADERSHIP: MIGHT OR MYTH? ▪

21 motivation: the drive for satisfaction

> Why is it that when a company wants people to direct their purchasing behaviour in a particular direction, they turn to advertising agencies for their expertise in *persuasion*, but when they want to direct their own employees' behaviour in a particular direction they call it *motivation*? (Hershey, 1993: 10)

In this chapter we explore the journey from the notions of instinctual drives governing our behaviour, through the content and processes of our motivations, to a final consideration of issues of identity and commitment in modern organisations. We begin by introducing the motif we employ throughout the chapter: the question of whether the abstract conceptions of motivation theory as found in mainstream organisational behaviour (OB) literature can be distinguished from the more pragmatic processes of influence and coercion.

The aims of this chapter are to:

- give an account of how the understanding of 'motivation' has been appropriated in the search for greater productivity.
- explore the assumed relationship between job satisfaction and performance.
- locate influence, power and domination in the functional utility of motivation models.
- query the uncritical use in mainstream OB of the concept of goals.
- demonstrate the role of motivation theory in the mobilisation of consent and commitment.

Motivation or motivating?

William F. Whyte, writing in 1956 on economic incentives and human relations, spoke of the 'Five M's of factory life: men, money, machines, morale and motivation' (1956: 1). The last of these, coupled with the aspects of satisfaction contained in the notion of morale, has driven the primary interests of organisational management in psychological knowledge. Motivation, according to Dawson (1986: 7), 'refers to the mainspring of behaviour; it explains why individuals choose to expend a degree of effort towards achieving particular goals'. It is explained in terms of biologically-based *needs* and *drives* and the selection of *goals* (content theories) and cognitively-oriented notions of *information processing* on the rewards, costs and preferences for particular outcomes of action (process theories). Knowledge of human motivation is linked to the service of organisational 'needs', in that motivation is understood in terms of the process of *social influence*. Even though Herzberg (1968) pointed out that in attempting to influence someone to work harder it is the manager who is motivated and not the worker, it is still the case that one of the principal concerns of organisational behaviour is to increase 'motivation' in the search for greater productivity.

Motivations are viewed as perceived predispositions to particular behaviours and outcomes, reflecting the things we want and the strategies we choose to achieve or obtain them. Originally they were explained in two ways. The first was in terms of instinctual drives which we are motivated to reduce: for example when we are thirsty we are driven to seek drink. Second, they were described in the mechanistic terminology of *stimulus–response*, when we seek out those things which satisfy or reward us and avoid those which punish or cost us. However, since motivation also concerns choice and hence intention, it is necessary to explain how such choices are made. This is explained within cognitively-oriented models that examine either the *content* of motivations, or the *process* through which they are expressed. The former examine what motivates people through concepts such as goals, needs and 'motivators', and is exemplified by the work of Maslow, Alderfer, McClelland and Herzberg. The latter examine how behaviours are selected, directed, initiated and maintained, as in the work of Porter and Lawler, Adams and also Vroom (see below).

Both types of theory are concerned with the notion that humans direct their behaviour towards goals. In the case of content theories the concern is with the source of the goals, while process theories focus on the decision-making process by which goals are selected and pursued. We must also consider motivation in terms of the process of social influence by which external agencies try to direct the selection and pursuit of desired goals by individuals. This aspect of motivation theory, into which both content and process theories are incorporated, is the practical focus of organisational behaviour as a whole, practitioners being concerned to understand the strengths and directions of human motivations in order to increase control over the performance of work-related behaviours.

An example of this is found in McGregor's (1960) conception of 'Theory X' and 'Theory Y', often presented as a need or content theory of motivation. Students, and some texts, often represent theories X and Y as showing that there are two types of people, those who dislike work and responsibility, focus on economic security and need to be coerced into effort (Theory X), and those who like work, will accept responsibility for their own effort and are capable of innovation (Theory Y). However, these theories are more properly understood as a continuum of managerial attitudes to workers, whereby Theory X views held by managers will produce an 'assumption trap' which leads to coercive behaviour on their part and thus a vicious circle leading to Theory X behaviour by employees. Likewise Theory Y assumptions should lead to Theory Y behaviour, though of course there would probably be no 'virtuous circle' here as it would eventually lead to the complete abdication of managerial control. The practical parallel here is in the fate of scientific management and the human relations movement. Both were assumed to increase motivation and performance, and both could be said to fail on the basis of ignoring the effects of the assumption traps they produced: scientific management via assumptions of coercion through economic rationality and the managerial appropriation of control and expertise, and human relations through the assumption that managers would give anything but lip-service to employee participation in decision-making.

Enriching the content

The goals to which we direct our behaviour constitute a formative influence in the identities we construct for ourselves. But this aspect of goal-related behaviour is not examined within organisational behaviour as a discipline, except to the extent that individual goals can be moulded or 'set' to fulfil organisational ends. The branch manager in an insurance company case provides relevant commentary:

> I'm looking for someone who will work with me. So I look for some one who I think I can mould to my own ways, but they must already have the necessary spark and drive. (Knights and Collinson, 1987: 154)

Identity and related goals are thus treated as external to the position of workers in the productive process, in that goals are usually related not to intentions but to biologically-derived drives, or more often, needs such as those identified by Maslow (1954). Maslow's typology of human needs has been discredited to the extent that the 'prepotency' of 'lower order' physiological needs (in other words, these needs must be fulfilled before 'higher order' social and psychological needs) is not supported, yet 'Maslow's hierarchy' is still given prominence in most OB and management development texts. The probable reason for this is that theories which actually tell us something about motivation are too complex and too dependent on contingent factors to have any simple predictive application in management practice. These 'needs' for food, shelter, affection, self-respect and individual growth are more accurately seen these days as operating on the basis of either *intrinsic*, *social* or *extrinsic* stimuli or rewards. Intrinsically-motivated persons are assumed to be influenced through their attachment to their work itself, through the enhancement of skill, responsibility, status or authority; socially-motivated persons through their social relations in the workplace to peers, colleagues and group membership. It is assumed that extrinsically-motivated persons will be influenced only by aspects of their work that facilitate their 'outside' interests such as pay levels, perks and increased leisure time. Though particular motivations may be more forceful for an individual at any one time, positive feedback from all three types of factor will have some bearing on how they direct their goal-related behaviour. We should note though that according to social identity theory (see Haslam, 2002: 71–2) whether rewards are seen as intrinsic or extrinsic depends to an extent on self-categorisation, that is, what is extrinsic in terms of personal identity could become intrinsic where group values are more salient; in fact we might argue that this has to happen in order for people to actually be able to identify with groups.

Content theories

Organisational behaviour texts almost always refer to Maslow and his 'hierarchy of needs' but very seldom consider the satisfaction of needs within the organisational environment beyond the extent to which they can be manipulated to increase productivity. They are once again seen as external to the place of the worker in the productive process. Those in positions of control in work organisations do not see themselves as being in the business of comprehensively supplying the needs that Maslow hypothesises. They exchange financial and sometimes material benefits for the labour of employees, but beyond a minimal concern that workers should be sufficiently satisfied with the conditions and rewards of work to improve performance, or at least to not disrupt production, little else is provided. Indeed McClelland's (1961) typology of needs as *affiliation*, *power* and *achievement* does not take the lower order needs into account at all, these being supplied through the *wage-effort bargain* (see Chapter 3).

The hypothesised need for 'self-actualisation' (based on the work of the therapist Carl Rogers) and individual growth has repeatedly been incorporated into prescriptive packages such as Herzberg's (1968) notion of 'job enrichment', which seeks to improve the content of work to the point where workers will be self-motivated to improve their performance. However, such initiatives tend to fail on the basis that no real improvement is made in factors relating to the conditions of work and the job context or environment. For example, in Nichols and Beynon's (1977) study of job enrichment at Chemco, managers were motivated to pursue the 'New Working Agreement' on the basis that they were convinced that they would get at what makes workers 'tick' and thus be able to coax more work from them. For most of the workers involved, all that came out of this was an inadequate system of job rotation which was worse than the system they had evolved for themselves. Hence managers in this study were easier to 'motivate' because the context of their work was adequate.

Herzberg himself recognised this in saying that job rotation constituted 'job enlargement' rather than enrichment, and this could result in no more than short-term improvements in productivity as it represented 'adding nothing to nothing' (1968: 263–4). Such prescriptions are still offered by organisational consultants and still bought by organisational management, however, possibly because even short-term improvements in productivity offer some kind of competitive edge in the market. Motivation, in the above example, is reduced to the status of things or techniques that will motivate, a manipulative rather than an explanatory concept. The outgrowth of Herzberg's notions in Hackman and Oldham's (1980) *Job Characteristics Model* links job redesign and enrichment to a diagnostic scheme which analyses work in terms of four variables (*skill variety*, *task identity*, *task significance* and *feedback*) indicative of the extent to which a job could or should be redesigned. Although this scheme is widely cited in the literature, Hollway (1991: 107) reports that it was not popular with managers in that its focus on the job rather than the individual did not fit the managerial ideology of the day.

The drive for satisfaction

The key concerns in these theories and related applications are to a great extent those that relate task performance to the concept of *job satisfaction*, which is difficult to define or measure in the first place. Thus the application of techniques based on the assumed relation between satisfaction and performance tends to ignore the operation of social, cultural, organisational and environmental factors which will all intervene to make a simple 'more satisfaction, more performance' relationship less likely. Argyle (1974) examined the relations between satisfaction and productivity, absenteeism and turnover, concluding that while absenteeism and turnover did have a direct relationship to levels of satisfaction, productivity did so for only highly skilled or intrinsically motivated workers and that even in these cases, individual differences were highly significant. (See Figure 21.1.)

It appeared that while, on average, people did work harder when satisfied, some people worked harder when less satisfied and some less hard when more satisfied. Working hard to make the time go faster in an unsatisfying job or just to forget about one's troubles is a familiar experience to many of us, and 'skiving' or systematic soldiering is a classic response to fragmented or meaningless work. The only aspirational

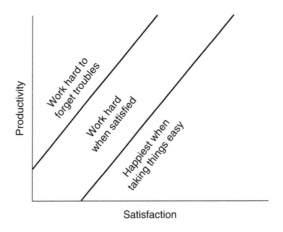

Figure 21.1 **The relation between productivity and performance**

Source: M. Argyle (1974) *The Social Psychology of Work*, Harmondsworth: Penguin, p. 239, with permission.

rewards available in such situations are those we can gain from controlling our own time and playing our own games (see discussion of Roy's work in 'Process theories', below).

Beyond these considerations, any meaningful view of the relation between job satisfaction and performance would have to recognise that alienated responses are rooted in the estrangement of workers from their creative capacities in the act of production, from ownership and control of the workplace, and from fellow workers. As the condition and responses derive, at least in part, from the basic structures of the capitalist labour process, changing them would require more than tinkering with peripheral aspects of work design. This does not mean that individuals will not report some sort of increased positive satisfactions. For example, Frese (1982) states that:

> much of the work on job satisfaction has tapped an attitude which could be labelled resigned job satisfaction. Because of the unavailability of other jobs and ways to change the job situation, a worker has reduced his aspiration level over time and has become resigned to his job. (Frese, 1982: 212)

Such feelings are directly related to powerlessness and lack of control over the job situation. Reduction of aspiration levels does not necessarily imply a lack of aspiration, however; it could simply mean resignation to progression as defined by the rules and procedures of the organisation, an acceptance of bureaucratic methods of control and the ideologies which underlie them. In Knights and Collinson's case study, for example, one of the female clerks who was continually discouraged from applying for a position as a sales inspector decided not to risk her position as senior clerk, and redefined her aspirations in terms of 'a woman's idea of going higher up within the company on the inside' (1987: 166). By considering the idea of progression into office management rather than sales, she has started the process of redefining her goals in line with the gendered job segregation fostered by the company.

People experiencing passive satisfaction with their lot rather than active satisfaction with their work may still be open to the types of influence exemplified by attempts at job enrichment or similar schemes. Herzberg's (1968) two-factor theory of motivation suggests that the intrinsic 'motivator' factors associated with job *content* and satisfaction are separate from the extrinsic 'hygiene' factors associated with job *context* and dissatisfaction. The content factors, such as *growth, responsibility, recognition, achievement* and *variety,* are similar to those assumed to motivate people who value intrinsic rewards and the status and esteem components of social rewards. The context factors, such as *salary, conditions, security, relationships* and possibly *policy* and *status*, are similar in effect to extrinsic and social rewards in that they make work either easier or more rewarding as they improve. Techniques such as job enrichment assume that if content and context factors are adequately met for individuals in organisations, then the motivation to work will be maintained. More importantly, they rely on the notion that people are passive recipients of organisational influences. If people do construct for themselves a passively resigned workplace identity, then the chances will increase that they will accept the redesign of their jobs on the basis that it will eventually improve their lot. The developments in flexible working practices and unitarist industrial relations in the 1980s may indicate that what was identified as a 'new realism' was nothing more than the kind of coping engendered by having to adopt a passive workplace identity in response to environmental constraints such as high unemployment.

Job context and content factors are seldom, if ever, met adequately for everyone within the work environment, so attempts to influence individual motivation levels will always run foul of factors they do not take account of. Thus in addition to active attempts to 'motivate' individuals, organisations take advantage of the socialising pressures of work to create a climate where people are open to these kinds of influence. However, attempts to motivate or socialise individuals into accepting the managerial direction tend to ignore the decision-making aspect of the process of becoming motivated. If motivation is indeed the 'mainspring of behaviour', then it refers not only to the selection of goals but also to the selection and development of the coping strategies and skills that individuals use to achieve those goals. Lee and Lawrence (1985) identify four factors that underpin all 'political' models of motivation that focus on decision-making:

- *Goals:* relating to values, interests and perceptions of individual opportunities and possibilities.
- *Strategies:* formulated to achieve goals or to react to threats to capacities to achieve them.
- *Coalitions:* exchanging commitment to group interests for support for goal strategies which cannot be achieved on an individual basis.
- *Power:* assessing success of goal strategies and membership of coalitions, arriving at estimates of personal power to affect events and revising goals in line with this.

The first three factors are dependent on the fourth, in that 'An individual's perception of his power will affect the goals he sets, the strategies he chooses and the nature of the coalitions he joins' (1985: 78). Likewise in the construction of identities, perceptions of a person's *situational power* (see Chapter 21) will determine the sources of meaning that are appropriate to the maintenance of a secure identity.

Motivation may be influenced by either interfering with, or facilitating, the individual's capacity to perceive, formulate or implement one or more of these factors. Organisational strategies that simply restrict the employees' capacity to act in these areas will, however, probably lead to individual and group attempts to circumvent them. Techniques aimed at the 'motivation' of groups and individuals may not in this sense achieve their aims. They may exacerbate the situations they were designed to ameliorate by reproducing or reinforcing existing areas of conflict, by reopening old issues or by introducing new topics of dispute.

Aimed at increasing production quality, overall productivity, workforce flexibility and job satisfaction, strategies aimed at enhancing group motivation depend on the production of workgroup identities consonant with the collective goals of management. These in the end can be sustained only to the extent that the organisation enables group members to maintain comparative material benefits and secure identities. This, however, has long-term implications for job security which are in direct contradiction to the aim of producing a flexible workforce responsive to the short-term demands for changes in product lines, working practices and manning levels. The threat of a reserve pool of unemployed labour is not sufficient to maintain the levels of commitment required by these programmes. Commitment based on the fear of losing one's job is only equivalent to the type of motivation achieved by holding a gun to someone's head. As soon as the threat is removed, so is the motivation. All that is achieved is an increase in the likelihood of retaliatory action.

In essence, then, the study of motivation in OB is the study of the processes of organisational influence and a study in the exercise of power and domination. No matter what the intent of consultants and practitioners in the area in terms of increasing job satisfaction and the elusive 'quality of working life', to management these techniques are effectively 'technologies of regulation' aimed at increasing control over behaviour and performance. Unfortunately, from a managerial point of view at least, in the long run such programmes cannot survive exposure to the contradictions inherent in trying to control subordinates who are actively attempting to control their own environment. Before moving on to consider process theories, we wish to reflect in more detail on the role of organisational behaviour and organisational psychology in motivational technologies of regulation. To do this we will consider Herzberg's (1968) pragmatic critique of motivational practices, which is still germane in modern OB.

The 'kick in the ass' (KITA) life cycle

> The problem arises when managements come to believe so firmly in their so-called motivation techniques and theories that they incorrectly attribute the behaviour they see with the attitude ('highly motivated') they impute with the source behind that behaviour. The very term 'motivation' in its shop-floor context, implies that workers are not intrinsically inclined to behave in the way their managers would want. (R. Hershey, 1993: 10)

Herzberg in *One More Time: How Do You Motivate Employees?* (1968) addresses the strategies available to the manager who answers the question: 'How do I get an employee to do what I want him to?' with the age-old response of 'Kick him!' (1986: 256). Herzberg raises the fundamental question of whether it is actually possible to motivate someone else, that whatever the external stimulus, motivation must come from within the person. He further used his analysis to examine his notion that most attempts to 'motivate' workers produce nothing more than short-term movement towards a reward or away from a punishment, and through this to argue that to produce self-motivating workers, jobs must be enriched. More interesting for our present purposes, though, is his analysis of the development of the techniques available to achieve these objectives, the so-called, *KITAs*. Herzberg argued that the basic technique of the kick, or *negative physical* KITA, failed due to the problems of image and retaliation associated with a regime of punishment. Psychologists naturally came to the rescue by uncovering 'infinite sources of psychological vulnerabilities and the appropriate methods to play tunes on them', that is, *negative psychological* KITA (1986: 257). As Weissman (2001) notes re General Electric in the 1990s, the practice of management by KITA is analogous to what Parker and Slaughter (1988) called *Management by Stress* (see Chapter 23) in its focus on cutting slack and in constantly pushing upwards the standard of what constitutes hard work:

> In this case, it is time to turn to the KITA approach. 'Maintaining a high level of tension through the KITA approach does maintain acceptable productivity levels,' the memo notes. 'It requires constant time and attention of the leader, because productivity will fall without that false tension being maintained.' A companion 1991 document focuses on team manager training. It contains a series of modules to make managers more effective. Module Four instructs supervisors that they have five obligations: to appoint the right people for positions; to make sure employees know their responsibilities; to properly train employees; to 'set standards for professional pride;' and to 'weed the garden.' 'When you have met your obligations to an individual,' Module Four states, 'and they continue to fail to live up to the job description or the Team's expectations, they must be terminated, or replaced.' The KITA approach is designed not only to squeeze workers' physical labor, but their mental labor and ideas, says Chris Townsend, political director for the United Electrical Workers, which represents GE workers. (Weissman, 2001)

Herzberg rejected this form of KITA as still being coercion, rather than motivation and still liable to produce hostility and resistance and moved on to consider *positive* KITA, both physical and psychological.

Positive KITA were mainly associated with rewards and thus rejected by Herzberg as bribery rather than motivation and as with the traditional range of rewards employed by management they were, as with many OB-related variables, subject to diminishing returns, getting less from workers as you give them more and more. Once again managers had to listen to the 'behavioural scientists who, more out of a humanist tradition than scientific study, criticised management for not knowing how to deal with people' (1986: 258). The self-replicating string of KITAs resulting from this collaboration gave us, according to Herzberg, *human relations, sensitivity training, communications* and *two-way communication, job participation* and *employee counselling.* If we extend the roll-call of positive KITAs we can include everything from Herzberg's own critical output in job enrichment to autonomous working, socio-technical systems, management by objectives and all the rest of the 'bag of schemes' routinely employed to increase motivation. That these offer no more than temporary influences towards greater commitment and goal consensus, rather than avenues towards self-generated motivation to work, is not important to management, as long as they give rise to short-term productivity gains. This reinforces the status of the products of OB as an integral part of the labour process itself. It is almost as if the techniques and approaches coming out of behavioural science have their own version of the marketing concept of the 'product life-cycle'. As soon as one KITA is reaching its diminishing level of marginal utility, the research and development process of critique and hypothesis testing gives rise to a new one. That all that is new about them is often only the name is unimportant, as long as the 'improved product' is sufficiently distinctive enough to carry out its function as an ideological cover story for yet another technology of regulation.

The attractions of KITAs to managers parallel their attitudes to new technologies. They have an intrinsic marketing advantage over their target audience in that if the competition has them, then they feel that they have to have them too. The similarity goes further, in that like new technologies, KITAs are often brought in by management who do not fully understand them or their possibly deleterious effects on cultures based on established procedures and working practices. Worse still, they only ever work effectively so long as management remain committed to resourcing them properly and do not use them as levers for unilaterally increasing levels of control and productivity.

Process theories

The content theories of motivation only ever really sought to explain motivation in terms of its directions, and lacked the sophistication to explain the strength of motivations. To be really useful in terms of selection or developmental training it is the relative force of motivation that needs to be measured; this being seen in 'process theories' such as exchange theory (Homans, 1961), equity theory (Adams, 1965) and expectancy theory (Vroom, 1964). Equity theory is based on notions of cognitive social comparison and exchange, expectancy theory on comparison of outcomes and preferences. These are reinforced by techniques that actively intervene in the selection and pursuit of goals and personal agendas such as goal-setting (see below), which are based on comparison and reinforcement of behavioural standards. All extend the basic notion of cognitive comparison to attempt greater levels of accuracy in prediction and control. Though in general empirical support for these theories is positive, expectancy theory in particular has been singled out for some criticism (see Arnold *et al.,* 1998: 252–4). Social information processing theory Salancik and Pfeffer (1978) manages to link aspects of content and process theories by incorporating the observational modelling of social learning theory (see Chapter 20) and focusing on how social cues taken from both others and ourselves inform self-attributions of our attitudes and behaviours. Social information-processing links learning and motivation to the social construction of needs and attitudes (including job satisfaction) and as such challenges the conception of needs as stable and hence predictable, but although at base a theory of job design, it is too complex for integration into straightforward managerial practices.

The effort to integrate 'human resources' more fully into the production process, typical of content theories, is similarly present in the usage of process theories of motivation. The difficulties in using motivation theories as a basis for 'people processing', can be seen in the application of the expectancy theory of Vroom (1964). This seeks to quantify and predict the strength of an individual's tendency to behave in a particular way as an assigned probability which is given by the *simplified expectancy equation* (see Thompson and McHugh, 1995: 301–4). On the surface, this appears to be a simple and powerful tool for predicting behaviour, but the assumptions made in such a measurement present a number of problems. The first is that expectancy theory provides a *rational-cognitive* explanation of individual behaviour. Can we assume that individuals make rational calculations based on their cognitive input in deciding whether to act in a particular way? Even assuming that this is the case, do these form the major determinant factor in their subsequent actions? These questions are sometimes posed in organisational behaviour texts, but no adequate account is generally given of whether such assumptions are warranted. The question is simply stated prior to a discussion of what can be done with expectancy theory in terms of understanding motivational goals, in order to influence and alter people's behaviour.

A further objection arises from those, including Langer (1981), who suggest that many of our behaviours, rather than being acted out in analytic, rational fashion, are carried out in what they term a 'mindless' manner. We follow unconscious 'scripts' analogous to sensorimotor learning (see Chapter 20) in much the same way as we do not consciously think of the complex series of actions we go through in making a cup of tea. Although we may consider the options open to us and the best way of going about a task, the underlying motivation may simply be that we are following the script which we have come to learn as appropriate to that situation. The work of Roy (1973) provides examples of how both labour and social interaction in the workplace can take on the attributes of ritual. Roy's monotonous and fatiguing work of 'mincing plastic sheets into small ovals, fingers and trapezoids' (1973: 208) was made 'relatively satisfying' in Baldamus' (1961) terms, by turning the production process into a series of 'games' which varied the colour, shape and ordering of the components turned out. The self-induced scripting of the work itself was accompanied by the breaking-up of the working day into 'times', such as 'peach', 'banana' and 'pickup time'. 'Times' were constructed around the ritualised social interactions and verbal interplay in the brief interruptions to production, which were repeated on a daily basis. Thus the behavioural scripts built up around eating, drinking and visits from outsiders reintroduced some level of meaning and interest for the machine operators into a deskilled labour process. Interest was further enhanced by the continuous repetition during work of 'serious' and 'kidding' verbal 'themes', centred around the characteristics and problems of the operators involved. In this sense, then, scripted behaviours become an effective, though not necessarily actively planned, mechanism for coping with the mundanity of working life.

A related problem for models of motivation is the narrow and over-deterministic series of accounts of experience that rational-cognitive theories of human behaviour produce. These accounts place the responsibility for action on individuals, rather than on the contexts in which they find themselves. By focusing on how information is embedded in social context, Salancik and Pfeffer's social information processing perspective goes some way to addressing the over-reliance on individual predispositions and rational decision-making processes. It can, for example, address the consequences of past choices and self-expectations but still tends to reinforce the view that the pathology of organisations is based on the irrational actions of individuals. In this view, the problems and uncertainties faced by organisations are caused by the self-serving behaviour of those who do not appreciate the 'big picture' of organisational life.

Even if the behaviour of individuals in organisations is largely carried out in the context of scripts which their socialisation into organisational life has taught them, they still bring to their working life an actively constructed identity which has been transformed within the organisation into an appropriate image. These behaviours and scripts do not exist in isolation. Even considering the possible outcomes of working harder on one particular task, as is done in expectancy calculations, this would involve an almost endless series of ramifications and secondary consequences. Thus to obtain a realistic prediction about how motivated a single individual would be to behave in a particular way, we would have to provide a basis of comparison. This would involve taking into account not only most of the behaviours applicable to a person's work and home life, but also those of similar individuals inside and outside the organisation. The project of fully understanding how people are motivated would from this perspective necessitate identifying and explaining all of the subjective and structural influences on their lives and those of the others surrounding them.

The relative lack of success of process theories in managerial terms is due to the very complexity that makes them more powerful in explanatory terms than content theories. Most management development texts still present content theories in the main because they are simple, easier to demonstrate, and they sound powerful, whereas cognitive/process theories suffer from the very fact that they are multifactorial and multivariate, with the implications that:

- there are too many factors which can affect the relations between effort, performance and outcomes
- too many value associations have to be made in assessing outcomes
- it is too difficult to place accurate values on variables
- models require assumptions of complex mental calculations which are hard to reproduce and demonstrate.

We will return to this theme below in considering new developments in motivation such as control and self-concept theories. At present, however, we wish to summarise and reflect on some of the problem aspects of the account we have given of motivation so far. In doing this we especially wish to query the uncritical use in mainstream OB (and by ourselves!) of the ubiquitous concept of *goals*.

The goals of motivation

Motivation as presented above lies at the heart of the explanatory project of organisational psychology, and as such can be used to reflect on the limits and contradictions of mainstream theories and practices. At one level, motivation is a classic case of Adorno's concept of '*identity thinking*' (Rose, 1978), where a concept is used as if it denoted instances of something, when it does not. For example, individuals are not 'motivated' to perform well at a particular task or 'satisfied' with their job when the underlying goal of their performance is to maintain a reasonable level of subsistence and not to lose their job. In this sense, OB and organisational psychology assume an identity between being motivated to do something and being constrained to do it by physical and social necessity. In Adorno's terms one can only make proper use of a theoretical concept or construct in the context of the 'theory of society' through which it is itself constructed.

In taking the situational contexts in which behaviour in organisations takes place largely as given, concepts such as goals in mainstream analyses are often reified, involving 'the conversion of concrete social relations of production into abstracted, quantitative measures' (Wexler, 1983: 66). Reification in this sense can be viewed as a dual process, and is productive of entitative relationships as identified by Hosking and Morley (1991, see Chapter 14 and below). First, the products of human thought and activity are treated as things in themselves; and second, socially produced concepts are treated as being intrinsic to individuals and organisations. In relation to the first part of this process, organisations are often treated as actual entities or organisms with their own needs, drives, goals and characteristics analogous to those of people, rather than as the continuously recreated products of human labour and organisational ingenuity. The second element of the reification process is illustrated by the content theories discussed above in their use of highly generalised typologies of needs such as that of Maslow (1954). These are developed into measurement packages that seek to typify the range of needs applying to individuals in order to establish the minimum conditions for their compliance with the goals of the organisation.

Thus the concept of motivation is applied to organisations themselves in that they are seen as having their own internally derived goals that can change to accommodate the environmental contingencies which the organisation is faced with. At the same time, individual goals are conceptualised as a subset of those organisational goals. For instance, the currently fashionable 'continuous development' programmes designed ostensibly to meet the 'training needs' of organisations, serve mainly to locate organisational problems at the individual rather than the structural level (see Chapters 15 and 18). Such systems could be seen simply as extensions of social facilitation though the medium of the technique of *goal-setting*.

Goal-setting

Goal-setting as a technique is said not only to be effective with scientists, managers, and blue-collar workers, and thus assumed to extend earlier techniques such as management by objectives in that it is claimed to work beyond supervisory and managerial grades; it is also claimed by Locke and Latham to be a core motivational technique (1984: 121) that can underpin job enrichment, behaviour modification or other processes. It operates through attention to levels of:

- commitment to goals
- acceptability of goals
- difficulty of goals
- specificity of goals
- participation in setting goals.

It is seen to affect the choice of goals, the effort put into them and the strategies selected in pursuing them. The outcomes are assumed to be thoroughly positive in managerial terms: human resources are fully utilised by directing attention and action; energy and effort are mobilised; persistence is increased and the development of appropriate task strategies are encouraged. It works by breaking down goal-related behaviour into simpler sub-routines in the way that scientific management does with physical operations, thereby reducing the stress of dealing with complex goals. Locke and Latham portray it as a tool which 'gets results', but when used improperly can result in 'conflict, feelings of failure, increased stress, dishonesty' (1984: 171).

Arnold *et al.* (1998: 259–620) give a useful account of the limits of goal-setting, noting that it 'could be criticised in its early days for being a technique rather than a theory' (1998: 261). Regardless of subsequent developments, goal-setting is still an example of the extension of technologies of regulation that replaces 'impractical models and theories' with 'a technological approach to using human resources effectively for the creation of industrial wealth' (Wellin, 1984: 4). These are essentially contingent strategies for increasing effectiveness, or 'a practical bag of tools for solving human problems in organisations' (1984: 183). However, it is probable that such strategies will probably never work as intended. Even if individual subjectivity can act, as Knights and Willmott (1985) argue, to separate people and blind them to their collective interests, it will still operate to motivate and enable them to circumvent technologies of regulation for their own purposes. You can in no way guarantee that staff will develop the goals set for them, only that they will develop goals, just as you cannot guarantee what staff will learn, only that they will.

Goals versus identity projects

Goals themselves have been queried as a useful concept, especially in Hosking and Morley's (1991: chap. 2) comments on top-down, *entitative* approaches to persons (that is, the characteristics, traits and behaviours of individuals) and groups in organisations, through topics such as motivation, attitudes, job design, leadership and group dynamics. These are essentially reified approaches that depend on assumptions of the independence of person and organisation. Hosking and Morley identify (1991: 72) the focus on goals in such approaches as a major sticking-point that pervades the organisational literature, and argue for an emphasis on projects rather than goals to explain the interlocking nature of personal and social processes. They illustrate this with the following example:

> Consider the projects of three academics. One has reached a certain point in his career and now actively is seeking promotion; another wishes to build a network of persons whose research interests are the same as hers; another wishes to get more favourable publicity for her subject. They join forces in organizing a conference; not one of them has resources sufficient for organizing the conference on their own; and each has different reasons (grounded in their different projects) for coordinating their actions in this way. (Hosking and Morley, 1991: 74, based on Weick, 1979)

The goals of these individuals may appear the same, but if something went wrong with the conference project, their differing personal agendas might make them respond quite differently. The important point here is that we need others to pursue our projects or *personal agendas* regardless of their congruence or divergence. This frees us somewhat from abstract concepts of goals and complex motivations, and may also help to explain why changing circumstances affect individual motivation differently. Hosking and Morley (1991: 29–32) refer to personal projects as a series of *conversations*, which have aspects that are variously, but not exclusively, *pragmatic*, *structuring* and *semantic*. These are said to define culture for groups, and are the arena in which individual and group subjectivity are constructed and transformed in organisations.

Though Hosking and Morley produce a powerful critique of goals as a motivational concept, there is a sense in which it comes too late, since goals are thoroughly pervasive in the literature and more importantly are embedded in common usage. Even if the goals of individuals are divergent and/or incongruent with organisational 'goals', they are still assumed to be necessary for organisations to exist at all. In other words, we utilise at least some implicit sense of shared goals or values and some notion of how goals are developed in motivational terms in much the same way as we utilise implicit personality theories (see Chapter 19). Goals are perhaps best viewed in the end as a variable in the process of setting our personal agendas and pursuing our personal projects (see 'Control theories' and 'Self-concepts' below). We might perhaps view personal agendas as more action-oriented than goals, related more to what you are doing or need to do than aspirations or strategic objectives and in this sense at least personal agendas may be the very things which interfere with goal-directed behaviour. It may be that the more important distinction is our freedom or ability to pursue personal agendas or goals versus our burden of obligations or our *role set*.

Motivation as an artefact

It appears, then, that the functional utility of motivation models is in establishing the minimum conditions under which workers can be *mobilised* to consent to the nature of work that is demanded of them. This is achieved through a narrow conceptualisation of motivation which is useful in engaging consent for working practices by actively manipulating perceptions of expectations, preferences, social and material rewards, and threats. What is effectively happening here is that extrinsic factors largely outside the control of the individual, such as pay and conditions, are being translated into intrinsic factors. These include those processes assumed to be under individual control, for instance satisfaction and motivation, thus making employees personally responsible for their own objective situation, much as we argue is the case in the attribution of stress. Seivers (1986) goes further by arguing that motivation is not an intrinsic factor of individual personality, but an artefact produced by the science of organisational behaviour; which acts as a surrogate for the meaning that people have lost from fragmented and dehumanised work:

> Motivation only became an issue – for management and organisation theories as well as for the organisation of work itself – when meaning was either lost or disappeared from work. ...In consequence, motivation theories have become surrogates for the search for meaning. (Seivers, 1986: 338–9)

That management has become such a great consumer of theories and techniques of motivation is in itself an indication that in much work there is little which can in itself act as a source of meaning and the basis for a secure identity. Attempts to introduce greater levels of participation, to 'humanise' work, to 'enrich' jobs, are in part a recognition that at least some level of commitment from workers is necessary to valorise capital efficiently. Attempts to 'motivate' are founded on the assumption that workers need to be led, as in Theory X, but their theoretical bases do not examine the corollary that they need to be influenced to co-operate because of their essential alienation from the productive process. However, the use of motivation as a manipulative concept implies not a lesser but a greater unitarism of outlook from management. The integration of individual and organisational 'goals' not only binds people ever closer to the productive process, but creates the climate where programmes such as TQM make them responsible for monitoring their own performance. The 'motivations' served are the managerial aims of greater unit productivity; the drive for more work and less waste, operating under the cover story of a consensus-based participation provided by motivational techniques which have not moved on much since the days of Herzberg and McGregor.

Motivation from the view in this section is a chimera, a hybrid concept that owes more to science and organisational necessity than to nature, human or otherwise. It is often linked to that other organisational chimera, the so-called 'psychological contract' (see Guest's 1998 review and critique), though the latter in fact conflates any number of theories of motivation and commitment, as well as only being evident when the contract is violated. The question is why do we need the psychological contract when we already have concepts like trust and loyalty and we know that the wage-effort bargain and the various forms of organisational commitment are all mediated by the factors in exchange, equity, expectancy, goal-setting theory, etc.? As we will see below, organisational psychology has moved on to specify even further the factors involved in motivation. This could in fact be the real reason for the psychological contract as a concept, that the broader concerns of sociologists, business theorists and consultants need a simple umbrella explanation, or possibly that they simply do not want to deal with motivational variables, much like managers with process theories. The explanatory power of the psychological contract has suffered further from association with similarly suspect notions of 'organisational citizenship' (see Brotherton,

1999: 44). Like the psychological contract, motivation seems to be noted more in the breach than its observance, and managers often appear to be better at demotivating workers than at enthusing them with the spirit of the enterprise. From short-term productivity initiatives based mainly on social facilitation, influence or coercion, we now have a huge ramshackle edifice which constantly reshapes and renames itself to accommodate the changing contexts of work.

Control theories

Whether motivation theory can move on to a more considered view of the social relations of production will depend to a great extent on whether theories can begin to incorporate both the objective and subjective dimensions of work. One attempt to do this is found in what is probably the most powerful development in motivation theory to appear in the last 15 years: Klein's *Integrated Control Theory of Work Motivation* (1989). What this theory manages to do is to integrate cognitive motivation theories, theories of scripted response, theories of attribution and of causal perception, for example Powers' (1973) *perceptual control theory* and Wiener's (1948) *cybernetic* hypothesis. These latter, combining information processing and the control of action through feedback, are similar to Miller's notion of TOTE units given in Chapter 20. The main elements of behavioural control theories are given below:

- cognitive
  - internal goals
  - information on current state
  - comparison of goals and state
- affective
  - perceived discrepancies
  - behavioural resolutions.

Klein's model (see Figure 21.2) is essentially a meta-theory aimed at accounting for the hypotheses generated by the various approaches it incorporates, and according to Klein (1989) it is consistent with the propositions of social learning, equity, expectancy and satisfaction theories. However, it also claims to focus more on individuals' self-regulation in response to external influences than on the effects of those influences, such as in providing goals and incentives, as is the case with most motivation theories.

If we imagine that many of these processes, for example the continuation of previous behaviour (1989: 7), might themselves be organised into hierarchical systems of goal-directed action, the theory's potential explanatory power becomes enormous. Since the model does acknowledge the influence of individual and situational factors such as ability, past experience, social comparison processes, situational constraints and reward structures, this theory offers some hope of reconciling cognitive/rational theories with approaches emphasising subjectivity and its construction, notwithstanding our comments on goals above. However, the propositions that Klein derives from control theory are still to be tested in any detail. Even so, as Klein demonstrates with his extended example of a salesperson trying to meet a quota, it does offer considerable insight into the dynamic processes of self-regulation in individual action and of how 'automatic and conscious processes operate simultaneously to initiate and direct behaviour' (1989: 168).

On the basis that Klein's model represents an even more sophisticated and multivariate theory than previous accounts of motivation, any predictions would have to view practical applications as still a long way off. A similar view on control and integration to Klein's is advocated by Brotherton (1999: 38–43).

320   21

INTRODUCTION: REGULATING ORGANISATIONAL BEHAVIOUR ■ PERCEPTION AND ATTITUDES: SEEING WHAT TO THINK ■ MASKS FOR TASKS: PERSONALITY ■ LEARNING AND CHANGE ■ **MOTIVATION: THE DRIVE FOR SATISFACTION** ■ LEADERSHIP: MIGHT OR MYTH? ■

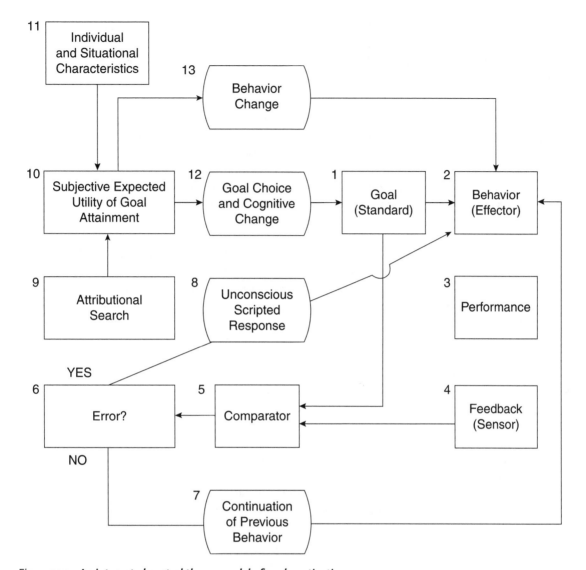

Figure 21.2 **An integrated control theory model of work motivation**

Source: H. J. Klein (1989) 'An Integrated Control Theory of Work Motivation', *Academy of Management Journal*, 14. 2: 1451, with permission.

This is Ford's *motivational systems theory* (1992), which seeks to integrate factors such as goals, emotions, personal agency and behavioural schemata in a fashion which, according to Brotherton, conceptualises motivation in a fashion that emphasises 'facilitation, not control, should be the guiding idea' (1999: 40). In support of Ford, Brotherton notes that 'Psychology makes a fundamental error if it adopts the proposition that managers need oversimple models of what are actually complex processes', but at the same time, 'there is too much pressure on managers already to have them accept the quick fix' (1999: 42–3). As such, it appears that managers are caught in a cleft stick, needing simple techniques to attempt continually to gain a competitive edge in motivational terms, but suffering the consequences of employing inadequate conceptualisations of workplace motivation. Brotherton argues that future shifts in values and training are key factors in being able to utilise more complex approaches. In the meantime, it is probable that the blunt instruments of Herzberg's KITAs will remain the dominant techniques to be employed and redeployed in the process of mobilising commitment.

Self-concept theory

Though models such as Klein's make a comprehensive attempt to integrate content and process theories, they are still open to the kind of critique put forward by those such as Shamir, who claims that:

> current motivational theories are restricted in certain respects due to their over reliance on individual–hedonistic assumptions and their over-emphasis on cognitive–calculative processes. (Shamir, 1991: 405)

According to Shamir, the kind of influence strategies employed by 'transformational leaders' (see Chapter 22), who try to 'persuade their followers to transcend their own interests for the sake of the team' (1991: 407), cannot be explained from the point of view of theories which highlight individual satisfaction. There have been past attempts to link content and process theories using self-concepts in order to give a more contingent appreciation of motivation. For example, *Self-discrepancy theory* (Higgins, 1987) takes notions of balance and examines how we negotiate between our

- actual self: how people believe they really are;
- ideal self: how people would ideally like themselves to be
- ought self: how people think they ought to be

to show how the struggle to maintain consistency between multiple selves in face of the vagaries of our beliefs, aspirations, self-perceptions and actual behaviours can produce dissonance effects and in the long term have negative effects on our self-esteem. However, self-discrepancy theory still focuses on satisfaction albeit in terms of delineating the possible constraints individuals face in being able to experience satisfaction. It is possible that the concept of *subjective expected utility*, as found in expectancy theory and incorporated by Klein, can go beyond a reliance on satisfaction through the mechanism of delayed gratification of rewards attached to superordinate goals. This could not, however, counter the second strand of Shamir's critique, in that process theories may have their greatest explanatory power in what Mischel (1973) characterised as strong situations where there are clear goals and expectancies tied to performance incentives. The inability to explain weak situations where there may be large variations in individual behaviour is tied to what Shamir argues is a tendency of content theories to 'emphasise easily and measurable and observable and relatively discrete behaviours' (1991: 408).

Shamir further asserts that motivation theories tend to embody limited concepts of intrinsic motivation and to exclude values and moral obligations. Such conceptions are said to ignore the fact that a task may have no intrinsically satisfying properties and yet might still be 'motivating due to its meaning for the individual, for instance in terms of the affirmation of his or her identity and collective affiliations' (1991: 409). Even where motivation theories do make strong distinctions between intrinsic and extrinsic motivation, Shamir notes that the task-oriented focus tends to 'neglect the symbolic and expressive aspects of human beings' (1991: 409). This is especially true of the notion of denotic motivation, which examines the possibility of a drive towards discharging one's moral obligations (from Schwartz, 1983, and Etzioni, 1988).

Shamir's self-concept theory of motivation attempts to produce both a theory of general work motivation (investing effort in the work role) and general job motivation (investing effort in your current job). It does not attempt to explain the motivation to perform specific tasks but, like Klein, Shamir integrates material from a number of sources, notably Bandura's (1986) social cognitive theory, 'structural symbolic interactionism' from Stryker (1980), and Gecas' (1986) self-concept theory. The assumptions driving the theory are given below:

1 'Humans are not only goal oriented but also self expressive.' They 'choose to spend time in situations that allow them to express their dispositions, attitudes and self-conceptions'.
2 'People are motivated to maintain and enhance their self esteem and self-worth.' This is reflected in that 'both competence standards and cultural values are internalised into the self concept in the form of evaluative standards.'
3 'People are also motivated to retain and increase their sense of self-consistency. ... In a sense, the self-concept is an ideology that people attempt to express and validate in their behaviour.'
4 Self-concepts are composed, in part, of identities. ... People derive meaning from being linked to social collectives through their identities', and may operate on an 'authenticity motive' (Gecas) to reflect their 'true identity' in their actions.
5 'Self-concept related behaviour is not always related to clear expectations or immediate and specific goals.' It may be motivated by faith and 'the imagined possibilities of the self'. (Shamir, 1991: 411–15)

Overall, general job motivation is seen as determined by the extent to which the person's self-concept is congruent with their current job and its situational context. Job-related identities are seen as central to the self-concept, though other identities (for example, national, ethnic and family) must be acknowledged (1991: 417). The theory is said to be most powerful in 'weak' situations (see above) where goals and the means for achieving them are unclear and there is no explicit linkage between performance and external rewards (1991: 416). However, Shamir does claim that the theory may be useful for explaining some 'strong' situations, for example, 'deviant, nonconforming behaviour such as whistle-blowing' (1991: 416), presumably on the basis that these activities have strong identity salience.

Control, self-concepts and identity
The need for such a synthesis of control and self-concept theories can be demonstrated through Jackson's (1994: 83) summary of the influence of cultural factors on motivation. Jackson argues that in international comparisons, process theories are more portable due to their focus on 'universals' of motivation and since 'static-content theories do not travel very well between cultures' (1994: 83). Self-concept theory might thus provide useful insights into how general work motivation is subject to cultural variation, while control theory can provide explanation of the 'universal' processes by which persons choose specific courses of action.

With self-concept theory, we can focus on the content and processes of motivation as inputs to situationally determined strategies that people adopt to enhance the identities they have constructed. People would not be 'intrinsically' or 'extrinsically' motivated, rather, they would take meaning from whatever sources are available and use it to enhance both the image they have of themselves and the images that others hold of them. In a work environment where possibilities for securing meaning were scarce, people might still be capable of taking meaning from the situation to the extent that they can gain some personal or collective control over their work. Strongly cohesive workgroup cultures might in this sense actually identify with working practices to the extent of feeling that they, and not management, 'own' them. Attempting to redefine working practices in such situations might only detract from the sources of meaning available in the workplace, and in essence, attack whatever portion of identity resides there. If this is the case, then compensations, even assuming they are designed to satisfy both intrinsically and extrinsically derived motivations, would probably not overcome hostility to changes and would make them difficult to implement. Whatever the case, it appears debatable that motivational interventions can actually manage to mobilise any real *commitment* to organisations, a contention we wish to explore in our final section.

Mobilising commitment

As far as the practical use of motivation theory at present is concerned, individual identity is essentially an *intervening variable* acting to complicate applications that attempt to mobilise worker commitment and make motivations difficult to assess with standardised test inventories such as interest questionnaires. But it is already the case that social identity measures are being used almost as predictive personality traits. For example, James and colleagues (1994) use measures such as self- and collective esteem, value differences, expressiveness and perceived prejudice in assessing the health of minority workers. The relative degrees of prediction and attempted control actually available to managers are illustrated by the model proposed by Myers and Myers (1982, in Jackson, 1994: 73) in Table 21.1 below.

It is evident that the processes described in control and self-concept theory operate mainly at Myers' 'psycho-social' level, where the possible degree of managerial control is said to be only moderate to low. As with Herzberg's commentary on motivational techniques and the Hershey quote that opens the chapter, the problem is an imperfect control of intrinsic motivational impulses which can only partially be corrected by the deployment of extrinsic rewards. To achieve systematic control over commitment, were this even possible, would require that psychosocial factors be regulated through social and organisational processes. However these must be considered in relation to effects of environmental variables (politico-legal, socio-cultural, market-economic, and so on), which even in relation to Leavitt's (1978) basic model of the interaction between people, task, technology and structure could be seen to produce a welter of mediating variables. Thus, the main burden of change initiatives, for example, falls on people rather than systems, as they are the factor over which management has the least reliable control.

Such structural and cultural pressures, ideologically legitimated by the 'need' to change tasks and technologies, coupled with the long-term failure to control intrinsic motivation, have produced the whole panoply of modern-day KITAs. Ranging from desperate attempts to reassert control over rewards in performance-related pay and share schemes, through group-based initiatives, to the bludgeon-like tools of restructuring and corporate culture, what success these initiatives have is not in producing general job and work motivation. It is merely the production of short-term movement towards increased effort on specific tasks. The only routes that appear to be left for increasing general motivation are in the control of meaning and of group-based socialisation into work roles (see Chapter 20) as the main psychosocial factors subject to external manipulation.

Internalisation of commitment

To achieve this form of change requires that practices which have evolved into scripted behaviours be 'unfrozen' in Lewin's (1947) terms, so that re-socialisation can take place. As scripts are based on the kinds of flexible action patterns and sensorimotor learning discussed in Chapter 20, what would be sought here is the constant re-engagement of the intellectual level of learning. Behaviour would not

Table 21.1 **Management control of motivating influences**

Factors	Examples	Degree of management control
Organisational	Nature of jobs	High
	Physical/technical environment	
	Reward system	
	Supervision	
	Available information	
	Organisational goals	
	Organisational structure	
Social	Reference groups	Moderate
	Peer groups	
	Work groups	
	Role-set	
Psycho-social	Needs	
	Perceived abilities	Moderate to low
	Aspirations	
	Personal objectives	
	Perceptual set	
Psycho-biological	Genetics	Nil
	Nurture	

Source: M. T. Myers and G. E. Myers (1982) *Managing by Communication: An Organisational Approach*, New York: McGraw Hill, reproduced in T. Jackson (1994) *Organisational Behaviour in International Management*, Oxford: Butterworth-Heinemann, p. 73, with permission.

be directed by learned patterns of experience, desire or collective obligation, but by adaptive behaviour in response to constant uncertainty. This situation is reflected in Hopwood's model (1974, cited in Johnson and Gill, 1993: 34–5) linking social and administrative controls. Social controls, such as group norms, aimed at regulating output, and administrative controls, such as reward systems, aimed at increasing productivity, require enactment through their internalisation as self-controls. Johnson and Gill (1993: 34–6) extend this by reference to Kelman's (1961) work on conformity and Kanter's (1968) comments on organisational identity. In Kelman's eyes, internalisation is one form of conformity whereby the individual adopts the norms and value structures of 'significant others' in the development of their 'internal moral imperatives'.

Compliance is conformity based on the motivation to gain rewards and avoid costs, which may be linked in organisational terms to Hopwood's administrative controls. Identification also involves 'significant others', but is conformity to the social influence they exert on the basis of our becoming emotionally attached to them, wishing to be like them or perhaps to be identified as one of the group or cultural community to which they belong. The role of compliance and identification is finally linked to the idea of internalised self-controls through Kanter's concepts of 'mortification' and 'surrender': the former involving the 'exchanging of a private identity for one provided by the organisation', and the latter the 'attachment of one's decision-making prerogative to a greater power' (Kanter, 1968, cited in Johnson and Gill, 1993: 35–6). The importance of this for Johnson and Gill is that:

> it draws our attention to the processes that can disengage the individual from prior social and ideological attachments by redirecting his or her beliefs and norms towards those that predominate in any organisational context – whatever those might be. (Johnson and Gill, 1993: 36)

This is linked to the development of organisational commitment through reference to Brown (1965) on the nature of conformity and moral development. Individuals are seen to initially obey external demands and sanctions and then to develop emotional attachments in 'everyday social interactions' that produce identification and eventual internalisation (1965: 36).

The dilemma here is that the context within which internalisation takes place is as important to the outcomes as the process itself. As Hosking and Morley (1991: 5) note, 'people are both products of their contexts and participants in the creation of those contexts'. Beyond the modelling processes social information processing (see above) identifies in the social construction of attitudes and motivations the relation between person and context is one of 'assimilation' by changing the context and 'accommodation' by changing oneself. Relationships of this kind would make attempts to promote the internalisation of controls appear to be a one-sided process. Accommodation and compliance would be the normative valuation for those instituting control systems, whereas assimilation and identification would be the desired outcomes for those subject to control. Since the opportunities for assimilation of context are limited for most employees, it is likely that any accommodation that takes place is rather a case of resigned acceptance more analogous to mortification than 'empowerment'.

Institutional commitment?

The concern noted by Hershey at the start of the chapter essentially devolves to an appeal for line managers and HRM practitioners to employ the techniques of persuasive communication used by advertisers to compensate for the lack of success of motivation theory and the managerial practices which made motivation theory necessary. This reflects the focus within the Myers model above on the extent of managerial influence at the psychosocial level being limited to training and communication. Commitment, on the other hand, implies both a condition of personal commitment to courses of action or belief as aspired to in the mainstream literature, and one of 'being committed'. This latter, in the sense of being locked into a system which is somehow beyond our control, is more representative of the critical literature on management. It presents organisations as institutions to which we are committed against our will and where persuasive *therapeutic* techniques are used on us in order to produce a good 'organisation person'.

This view harks back to Goffman's notion of a total institution in his 1961 book *Asylums*. Such institutions – exemplified by prisons, mental hospitals and so on – were seen to have extensive if not complete control over their inmates' lives, backed by systems enforcing their formal rules. This does not imply that inmates are passive recipients of control; both Goffman and later Becker (1963) noted that these institutions also embody informal rule systems enacted by both inmates and staff, which can work against the formal rules but which are necessary to the continued performance of their respective roles. The picture here is of total compliance with control, but of resistance to, and lack of internalisation of, control systems – almost the opposite of Kanter's notions of mortification and surrender as outlined above.

Kunda (1992) addresses the extent to which modern work organisations can be likened to total institutions in his case study of control and commitment in 'Tech', a high-tech US engineering company. On the surface, the resemblance to a total institution is slight, employment at Tech being economically rewarding and desirable and members being continually involved in 'reflective discourses' that openly embody irony, cynicism and humour. But at the same time there is a pull towards an escalation of commitment to the corporation, towards corporate definitions of reality, and continual pressure on the boundaries of personal privacy. The outcome, according to Kunda, is that 'people over time are submerged in a community of meaning that is to some extent monopolised by management: a total institution of sorts' (1992: 224). The self is not surrendered or captured in Kanter's terms, but the foundations on which the self is built are continually undermined as the authenticity of experience is continually appropriated by corporate ideology.

The effect of such an appropriation of meaning overlays rules of belief onto the systems of rules regulating behaviour, imperfect articulation between the two giving rise to manufactured uncertainty and insecurity. This insecurity is a classic precondition for the exercise of power through self-discipline as exemplified in Grey's (1994) study of professional accountants. The uncertainty produced by exhortations on the superiority of accountants, coupled with a secretive employment and promotion policy, led to constant self-surveillance. This was characterised by a search for 'signs of grace' signalled by formal indications such as salary, job ratings and allocations and informal signs such as working and social relationships with superiors. Where 'grace' is found this reinforces the self-confidence of the individual and hopefully engenders a self-fulfilling prophecy of success. Thus to gain, in Whyte's (1957: 404) terms, 'the peace of mind offered by the organisation' and to reduce levels of manufactured uncertainty does not require abject surrender to the formal restrictions or beliefs of the total institution. At the same time, though, it will require the same types of tacit collaboration and 'tactful' behaviour that Goffman saw as necessary to the continuation of organisational 'performances' and which we explore further in Chapter 25.

Summary and key points

We have sought here to show what motivation is *not* – that coercion and bribery are not motivation and suffer like most other motivational 'techniques' from diminishing returns in the short term – that the over-simplified concepts still utilised by managers and trainers simply cannot account for individual variation and situational contingency. Even though motivation and goals may be socially constructed artefacts, OB and Org. Psych. still seek to further integrate motivation with other theories such as attribution and theories of the self, and this effort is not wasted if our objective is actually to understand why people do the things they do, that is, how, why and in support of what *they* mobilise their commitment and consent. The problem for motivation theory in the workplace is its success in specifying the range and scope of the variables involved and in the face of this complexity managers falling back on KITAs and social theorists on the psychological contract and the like.

In consultancy and management development work we often hear managers complain that 'my workers are not motivated' and the stock response has become: 'No, only dead people aren't motivated, they're just not motivated to do what you want them to'. To a great extent, in this era of short-term contracts and demands for continuous development, we are now expected to be responsible for our own motivation to work. Now that we are not supposed to have a comfortable progression up a job ladder to mobilise our commitment, and the diminishing returns of reward and autonomy are recognised everywhere except in the case of CEO remuneration, organisations have been turning elsewhere for inspiration. The phenomenon we move on to in the next chapter is one regularly diagnosed as the source and solution of many organisational problems – *leadership*.

Further reading

OB textbooks are much of a muchness on this topic with Arnold and colleagues providing a more up-to-date account than most and Johnson and Gill's (1993) text is still good for linking motivation to issues of control. A good historical account focusing on the theorists and the origins of theory is found in Latham (2006), but the seminal work remains Herzberg's 1968 article for *Harvard Business Review* which is available as an expanded reprint and an e-book.

Arnold, J., Silvester, J., Patterson, F., Robertson, I., Cooper, C. and Burnes, B. (2004) *Work Psychology* (4th edn), Financial Times/Prentice Hall.

Herzberg, F. (2008) *'One More Time, How Do You Motivate Employees?'*, Harvard Business Review Classics, Cambridge, MA: Harvard Business Press.

Johnson, P. and Gill, J. (1993) *Management Control and Organisational Behaviour*, London: Paul Chapman.

Latham, G. P. (2006) *Work Motivation: History, Theory, Research, and Practice*, London: Sage.

22　leadership: might or myth?

> The best of all rulers is but a shadowy presence to his subjects.
> Next comes the ruler they love and praise;
> Next comes one they fear;
> Next comes one they despise (or – one with whom they take liberties) ...
> ... When his task is accomplished and his work done
> The people all say, 'It happened to us naturally'.
>
> > (attributed to Lao Tzu – 'The Old Master',
> > Tao Te Ching, Verse 17, around 500BC)

Is a ruler necessarily a leader and are leaders really at their best when we don't notice them, as the ancient Chinese proverb seems to say? For that matter, are managers necessarily leaders and does it make any difference whether they are or not? Most importantly, how do leaders get to be leaders and how do leaders maintain their position of leadership? Conventional wisdom holds that leadership is in some fashion a quality, an attribute or characteristic of the person that enables or entitles them to lead others. It is by querying this link between personality and leadership that we can start to see the processes which shape leaders and through which leaders attempt to shape the behaviour of others.

The aims of this chapter are to:

- give an account of the development of the theoretical conception of leadership from personal traits through to modern theories of networks and social identies
- show how changing conceptions of leadership have changed the duties and obligations of managers
- locate leadership as a role that is played in relation to social groups within the labour process
- show how leaders are interdependent with followers
- demonstrate the variability in leader behaviour and its role in perceptions of leaders and leadership.

Defining leadership

Leadership was defined by Buchanan and Huczynsci (1985: 389) as 'a social process in which one individual influences the behaviour of others without the use or threat of violence'. The assumption here seems to be that coercion is not leadership and yet, as with rule by fear, there are more ways to coerce people than by threatening them with violence. The historical study of leadership tended to focus on the habits, sayings and characteristics of those recognised as great leaders, hence the *Great Man* notion of leadership theory that is also referred to as the *Zeitgeist* (literally: 'Spirit of the Age') theory. According to this notion, leaders were born to lead and would rise to power and influence like the cream on the milk, or the scum on the pond, depending on whether you were a follower or a victim of their cause, a problem that still dogs us with modern political leaders. People could 'rise from the ranks' if they had the necessary qualities, but this view did tend to favour those already in positions of social dominance in that they would be better fed, housed, educated and have access to resources and social networks unavailable to others (that is, more 'henchmen'). However the search for what leaders had in common only managed to establish the range of variation possible in leaders, from the short, balding French Emperor to the handsome, gay Macedonian one. The one thing that is certain about this approach, however, is that there seemed to be no problem with those who used violence being recognised as leaders.

Since the 1900s, explanation in this area has tended to focus on personality traits, styles of leadership and more recently on situation-contingent styles and relations between leaders and group members. It is commonly assumed that the threat of violence is not relied upon today to maintain positions of leadership, though the continuing use of threats to, and sanctions on, financial and job security in organisations means that the 'social process' of leadership must be understood in its intimate relationship with the exercise of power (and possibly in the continued existence of bullying, sweatshops and slave labour). According to Fiedler (1967: 108), 'the acid test of leadership theory must be in its ability to improve organisational performance'. The study of leadership has then long been directly related to the improvement of management control strategies and to the refinement of the tactical options open to managers in the day-to-day practice of regulating workplace behaviour. This can be seen in the notion explored below that managers, in dealing with problems and subordinates in differing situations, can adopt various 'leadership styles'. In addition, leadership also serves as an almost perfect exemplar of how behavioural theory is incorporated into managerial discourse only up to the point where it becomes too complex for easy assimilation into ideology and practice, with the consequence that the managerial literature then tends to fall back on prescriptive generalities based on theory and research that has been long discredited or overtaken.

In a more considered definition, Katz and Kahn (1966, 1978) refer to leadership in terms of three sets of meanings that are often used simultaneously: first, there are the attributes of the *occupancy of a position* in a social structure; second, the *qualities or characteristics* of a particular person; and last, the *categories of behaviour* associated with a particular person. Occupancy of position essentially refers to the *position power* (see section on *'Contingent leadership'* below) of a person in an organisational hierarchy: for example, regardless of their characteristics, soldiers are to obey officers no matter who and what they are like. Characteristics and behaviours associate particular qualities with individuals in terms of their recognition as a leader by a particular group. Thus an officer may have the power to lead but may not be recognised as a leader.

Traits and characteristics

As with personality theory the failure of the search for predictive physical characteristics led to an effort to find common psychological factors in the *trait approach*. The ideas that particular traits can predict leadership ability and that leaders can be selected still hold fast in conventional wisdom, though in effect all this approach did was to further establish the wide range of possible characteristics that leaders can have. Stodgill's (1974/1976) review of research on traits did not bring up any reliable correlations between leadership ability and particular traits, and found that traits in general were ambiguous and ill-defined, for example the so-called 'helicopter ability' (Handy, 1980: 109), which is taken as the ability to 'rise above the situation and see the big picture'. Where we still see lists of leadership traits in the managerial literature, their most abiding feature is that they are generally more representative of those traits thought to be stereotypically male, such as dominance, aggressiveness and rationality, rather than traits stereotypically associated with women such as passivity, nurturance and emotionality. This emphasises the point that leadership qualities can function as a legitimising ideological support for the notion that it is the duty and obligation of the manager/leader to direct those not blessed by access to their particular sources of power. When viewed through the kind of assumptions made by managers in McGregor's 'Theory X' (see Chapter 21) and the managerial control imperative of scientific management, the continuing popularity of this largely discredited approach is completely understandable. Indeed Selznick (1957) identified leadership as partly founded on 'morally sustaining ideas' and 'socially integrating myths'. The former mobilise support for the notions of compromise and restraint underpinning management's search for meaning and security. The latter are the *superordinate goals*, that is, goals larger than those of the individual or group, which leaders appeal to in order to unite organisational members behind managerial strategies. An example of channelling perceptions towards superordinate organisational goals can be seen in the fashionable 'Japanese' management styles of the 1980s (discussed in Chapters 11 and 14) which used single-status canteens and dress- and workgroup-based discussion circles to lock both managers and workers into appearing to make the organisation successful for the good of all.

Possibly the most interesting pieces of evidence from the trait line of research were the somewhat disconfirmative findings on the acceptability of leaders to group members, which appear to show that groups prefer high-status members as leaders and that the characteristics of followers determine the acceptability of leadership characteristics (Stodgill, 1974/1976: 208–14). The most predictive factors in the characteristics of any given leader would then be their apparent status and the values, interests and personalities of their followers. What is indicated here is that leadership is a relationship with a group of followers or subordinates, a role and not a set of characteristics. However, this is not to say that the trait approach, or even the 'great man' approach has gone away, The UK government has recently pumped millions of pounds into leadership initiatives in both the public and private sectors based on a perceived lag behind France, Germany and the US. Figure 22.1 below shows the 'Leadership Qualities Framework' developed for the UK National Health Service (NHS, 2003) on the basis of 'analysis of the qualities which define effective leaders across the private and public sectors', focus groups and 50 in-depth structured interviews with Chief Executives and Directors. What it shows is a classic set of ambiguous and ill-defined 'qualities' which any high-school student could identify as possibly important in leadership situations. What it actually represents is the development of a competency model for Chief Executives and Directors against which their performance can be measured in a tick-box fashion similar to the Behaviour Anchored Rating Scales we talked of in Chapter 19.

Types, styles and roles

The outcome of work such as that of Likert at Michigan, and more significantly Stodgill's work at Ohio State, meant that rather than being limited to selecting people with leadership traits, it became more accepted that leaders could be trained in the form and style of their behaviours and relationships with their followers or subordinates. The Michigan work followed on from the work of Lewin, Lippitt and White (1939) which related three *types* of leadership to the emotional climate and hence the assumed effectiveness of work groups. This followed in the trait tradition in that the types are assumed to be universal or at least enduring attributes which can be described by trait clusters. The first of these types, *autocratic* leadership, continues the tradition of strong personal control and rule-bound relationships, while *democratic* leadership is less regulatory and emphasises collaboration and responsive relationships. This latter type can be firmly linked to the human relations tradition in OB and shifts the view of leadership away from duty and direction towards responsibility and co-ordination. The managerial assumptions

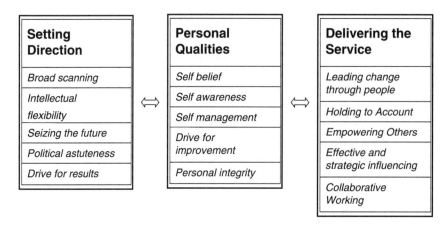

Setting Direction	Personal Qualities	Delivering the Service
Broad scanning	Self belief	Leading change through people
Intellectual flexibility	Self awareness	Holding to Account
Seizing the future	Self management	Empowering Others
Political astuteness	Drive for improvement	Effective and strategic influencing
Drive for results	Personal integrity	Collaborative Working

Figure 22.1 **The NHS 'Leadership Qualities Framework'**

Source: Adapted from NHS Institute for Innovation and Improvement (2006, 1).

here are perhaps best exemplified in McGregor's 'Theory Y' (see Chapter 21) and human relations in general, though interestingly Stodgill (1974/1976: 365) relates 'Theory Y' more closely to the third style, *laissez-faire* leadership. This third type did not provoke as much research effort as the first two, which is easily understood in that it is described as a type in which the leader 'fails' to accept the responsibilities of the position.

The Ohio work stepped away from the trait approach in describing leader behaviour as open to modification and not as an inherent attribute of a person. Two specific forms of behaviour were identified: *initiating structure*, aimed at defining roles, patterns of communication, organisation and action; and *consideration*, aimed at developing working relationships, trust and respect. The only essential difference between these and the autocratic and democratic styles was that any given leader could rate high or low on either or both forms of behaviour. Overall, these bodies of work led to research and training programmes aimed at changing the leadership climates of organisations and the behaviour of leaders – climate being found to have more enduring effects on behaviour than training. This led to assumptions about managerial behaviour shifting at the time towards the notion that it was the duty of managers to co-ordinate rather than direct effort.

Other work, such as that of Vroom and Mann (1960), found that style preferences depended more on the situation, autocratic styles being preferred where objectives centre on task accomplishment. Further developments in this direction appeared to show that autocratic styles were more acceptable in stressful or crisis situations, where the speed of decision-making may be more important than the quality of the decision. Stodgill's impressive review and summary of these approaches (1974/1976: 403–7) concluded that 'In view of the complexity of leader behaviour and the variety of situations in which it functions, a conditional and multivariate hypothesis seems more reasonable than a simplistic, bipolar view of the leader–follower relationship' (1974: 407). In general, then, no one form of leadership could be guaranteed to produce increases in group productivity.

The notion that leadership is a role performed in a group context was strengthened by work such as that of Benne and Sheats (1948) on group roles, Tuckman (1965) on group formation, Bavelas (1950) and Leavitt (1951) on communication networks and Bales (1950) on the interaction analysis of group performance. Though these bodies of work tend to suffer criticisms stemming from the artificiality of their methods, a synthesis of their general principles rather than their detailed prescriptions can provide useful insights into the processes by which leaders may emerge from newly formed groups. For example, Bales' work introduced the notion that a group may have a leadership structure rather than a leader as such, with an acknowledged leader and a 'second-in-command'.

This increases in importance when related to the often-disregarded notion of leadership 'acts', where leadership is seen as a series of acts or behaviours that can be performed by any member of a group regardless of status and power. Acts tend to fall into two major categories, as in Bales' group functions or Benne and Sheats' group roles, which are conceptually divided into *task maintenance* and *group maintenance*:

- *task maintenance acts* – preventing irrelevant behaviour, overcoming goal barriers and rewarding performance
- *group maintenance acts* – defusing tensions, offering support and encouraging and rewarding participation.

The consistent and competent performance of acts in these categories increases the likelihood of particular individuals emerging either as a leader or second-in-command of a group depending on their success and as either as a task- or group-oriented leader as they internalise the success of their actions.

The performance of leadership acts within the arena of group formation could be seen as an input to Tuckman's process of role differentiation in the group (see Chapter 24), and similarly as a mechanism by which members come to have differential access to and control of communication networks. In this sense an emerging leader would be the group member who most consistently performs leadership acts in the *forming* stage and influences the setting of interaction patterns in the group in the *norming* stage. From the development of Bales' work we also get a refinement of the notion that a group may effectively have two leaders. Since both task and group maintenance roles are necessary to group functioning, even where a formal leader is appointed to a group, the informal and subsidiary leadership role or 'second-in-command' would be occupied by the member most consistently performing leadership acts of the opposite type to the formal leader (in this case most probably the group maintenance or *socio-emotional* role).

Another strand of often-ignored work adding to this synthesis is Hollander's notion of *idiosyncrasy credit* (1964, also see Katz, 1982). Here the consistent compliance of a leader with the norms and expectations of a group, gains them 'credit' which subsequently permits them to deviate from group norms. Thus the consistent performance of leadership acts such as strong identification and high levels of interaction with the group allows the leader to act in an idiosyncratic fashion when necessary. This is a simple concept with great explanatory power, again viewing leadership as a specifically group-oriented role, but a role that emphasises the relationship with other group members and allows the leader to act outside the normal social and task maintenance processes of the group in order to serve its interests. A leader may have to represent the group outside of its own context, and help the group deal with new demands that do not fit its current norms or expectations. As such, the ability to act idiosyncratically and innovatively may be of benefit to the group as a whole. This concept could be extended to include the acceptability of leadership behaviours such as the selective reward and punishment of group members. As long as they have credit with their group, leaders can act in a manner that might not be acceptable to or from other members. When a leader is seen to act incompetently or deviates too far from group norms, 'credit' may pass to the member performing the subsidiary leadership role and shift the power relations in the group. Adding to the finding from Stodgill above that groups prefer high-status members as leaders, idiosyncrasy credit indicates that the status and legitimacy of leaders is in their reciprocal relations with the group, an idea which had been studied since the 1960s and became formalised when those such as Bennis (1993) and more importantly, Hollander (1992; 1995) took it further with the notion of *followership*, which we shall return to below.

Contingent leadership

Many other elements could be added to a synthesis of the kind introduced above, which though over-generalised does highlight the notion that leadership is a *process* in which power, influence and role definitions are conferred on or competed for by group members in the mundane performance of tasks and getting on with others. A major fault of such a synthesis is that it cannot easily account for situational and contextual variables, and in considering these factors alongside leader behaviour, leadership theory moved towards *contingency models*, best exemplified in Fiedler's (1967) theory of leadership effectiveness. This was based on his use of his *least-preferred co-worker scale* (LPC), with research based on real-world groups of many kinds from bomber crews to basketball teams. As a way of getting past stereotypical views of leaders, respondents were originally asked to rate their most and least preferred co-workers (MPC and LPC), though in effect it was found that the LPC rating accounted for the greatest variation in the contingent variables. Those rating LPCs positively were designated 'high LPC' and found to be less controlling and more group-oriented; those rating LPCs more negatively were designated 'low LPC' and tended to be more autocratic and task-centred. (For a discussion of this see McKenna, 2000, or Smith, 1991.)

Leadership effectiveness in Fiedler's model was seen as dependent on *situational favourableness*, which was in turn contingent on levels of:

- *task structure* – the more structured, defined and routine the more favourable
- *leader–member relations* – the more trust and liking for the leader the more favourable
- *leader's position power* – the more power to coerce, reward and punish the more favourable.

Of these factors, leader–member relations were assumed to be the most significant and in situations of mixed favourableness the high LPC, employee-centred leader was found to be most effective. In very favourable or very unfavourable situations the low LPC, task-centred leader was more effective. Additionally, Fiedler like Bales, also noted that groups might tend to have more than one leader, and in stable or mature group structures the best combination might be for a low LPC leader, with a high LPC second-in-command.

Many have cast Fiedler's conclusions into doubt, most particularly because in delineating situational variables it cannot at the same time deal adequately with the dynamic between group context and intra- and inter-group interpersonal relations. However, for our purposes the model does sit well with the notions that democratic leaders are preferred in most situations and that autocratic leaders will be more acceptable in crisis situations. What is less understandable in Fiedler's model is why the autocratic leader should be more effective in highly favourable situations. However, the notion that a leader's behaviour could be adjusted to fit the situation or that conditions could be adjusted to fit the leader remains a powerful influence in the field of study, offering as it does the idea that leadership is a variable that can be manipulated to achieve organisational objectives. Other models which extend the themes of situational and behavioural contingency are those of House and Mitchell (1974) and Vroom and Yetton (1973), which both bring in factors relating to the acceptability of leaders by subordinates. House's path–goal model is termed a *transactional* theory as it considers the balance of exchange between leaders and followers, accounting for follower attitudes and expectations. It gives four dimensions of leadership behaviour, subdividing the traditional autocratic–democratic split into *directive, achievement-oriented, supportive* and *participative*.

Vroom and Yetton's model extends the notion of leader–member relations to consider the quality of leader decisions and the information and skill requirements of subordinates. They give four styles similar to those of House and Mitchell: *autocratic, delegative, group dominated* and *consultative*. The achievement-oriented and delegative styles offer a partial explanation of Fiedler's finding that autocratic leaders could be more effective in highly favourable situations in that a mature, effective and cohesive group might prefer a leader who simply sets goals or delegates tasks and leaves them to get on with it. This form of leadership might represent the return of the laissez-faire leader to the extent that it is exemplified in the 'hands-off' approach often used with high skill or status groups such as research and design teams.

The style elements of leadership will also be significantly influenced by the ideological elements of organisational climate or culture. Purcell (1987) has summarised such effects on employee relations in a model of management style in which dimensions of individualism versus collectivism give rise to a range of behavioural and strategic options for managers. (See Rollinson, 1998: 693 and Figure 22.2 below.)

The Purcell model serves to remind us that the contingent nature of managerial behaviour is itself routinely exploited in the regulation of employees and that managerial labour itself has to be transformed in the face of situational contingencies.

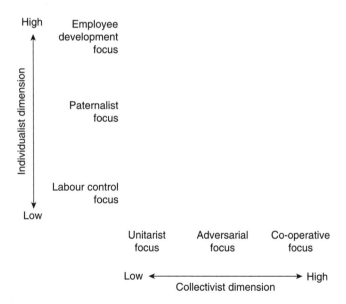

*Figure 22.2 **Purcell's scheme for mapping management styles***

Source: Reproduced from D. Rollinson, A. Broadfield and D. J. Edwards (1998) Organisational Behaviour and Analysis: An Integrated Approach, Harlow, Essex: Addison-Wesley. After J. Purcell (1987) 'Mapping Management Styles in Industrial Relations', *Journal of Management Studies*, 24. 5: 535–48. © Blackwell Publishers Ltd.

Transforming leadership

The Vroom and Yetton model is known as a 'normative' or 'prescriptive' model in that it specifies leader behaviours further than the four basic styles and links these to decision-making approaches to be used in relation to a range of individual or group problems and situations. The decision-tree methodology used to decide which approach is the most appropriate is still in use as a heuristic to explain how decisions might be reached, but has less practical applicability in that it is complex to use because the variables are difficult to map onto real situations and produce few non-obvious results. The increasing complexity of leadership theory and research was recognised in Stodgill's conclusions to his review (1974: 411–29), where he noted that directions for future research would best be pursued under a conditional or contingency model, but warned that studies would have to account for interactions between more than thirty variables encompassing combinations of leader, follower and group characteristics and outcome criteria such as follower satisfaction and leader acceptance, group productivity, motivation and cohesiveness. If we add intervening variables derived from context, structural factors and interaction processes, leadership becomes much less of a unitary, predictable phenomena. It moves closer to Selznick's 'socially integrating myth', the multiplicity of variables involved meaning that numerous strands of research have been sidelined in mainstream OB in favour of more prescriptive models linking leadership to organisational development and change. Good examples of these are Adair's functional model of '*action-centred leadership*' (1979) and McGregor Burns' (1978) '*transformational leadership*'. Adair's model focuses on developing the leader's awareness, understanding and skills in order to perform effectively and integrate the functions required by the task, team maintenance and individual needs of the group. Leadership here resides in the function and not in the person, and so is close to the notions of role-based leadership discussed earlier.

However, group processes are conceived non-developmentally and Adair's model mainly deals with how formally-appointed managers can be trained to be reflexive about the way that their behaviour affects group commitment and goals. Adair's model embodies some elements of transactional leadership and in its emphasis on achieving change can be linked to Burns' model, which highlights the leaders' need to transform their followers through a focus on their intrinsic or higher-order needs rather than on a particular style. This is essentially a form of motivational 'consciousness raising' which attempts to highlight for individuals how they can satisfy their needs and desires through commitment to group (and of course managerial) goals. Though presented as where 'leaders and followers raise each other to higher levels of morality and motivation' (1978: 20), it is effectively a group-based behavioural technology for turning self-gratification into a superordinate goal. It is unsurprising that this technique enjoyed great popularity in the 1980s with the focus on cultural change, and indeed both this and Adair's model have served as the basis for numerous leadership initiatives in the area of organisational and managerial development. Like the trait approach this strand of research continues today, the UK Government leadership initiatives discussed earlier include the 'Inspirational Leadership: Insight to Action tool' (DTI/Caret, 2005), which was designed to 'enable leaders to be clearer about their most natural leadership styles and strengths so that they can shape their roles and those of their team accordingly ... inspiring others to follow them'. Based on a survey of '2,600 workers across a range of UK companies about factors that would inspire them to follow a leader', this appears to appeal directly to the transformational leadership approach. In fact it simply adds an element of self-development profiling to a trait-based competency approach that is little different to the NHS 'Leadership Qualities Framework' (see Figure 22.1 above). Table 22.1 shows the attributes and elements the tool requires of 'inspirational leaders' and unsurprisingly they tell us little or nothing about the process of leadership, all they really do is tell us

Table 22.1 **Inspirational leadership**

The top six ranked attributes of 'inspirational leaders'	The six essential elements of 'inspirational leadership'
• Enabler	• Genuinely care about their people
• Team builder	• Involve everybody
• Social adaptability	• Show lots of appreciation
• Enthusiastic learner	• Ensure work is fun
• Reflective	• Show real trust
• Self-belief.	• Listen a lot

Source: Adapted from the 'Inspirational Leadership: Insight to Action tool' (DTI/Caret, 2003a, 2005b).

about how managers need to act to increase the chances of being perceived as a leader, that is, what kind of leadership acts to perform.

Charisma vs. self-control

The ambitions, if not the content, of the Inspirational Leadership tool, follow directly in the tradition of the development of Burns' transformational model by people such as Bass (1985) and Tichy and Devanna (1986) which brought back into the managerial literature on leadership the concept of *charismatic leadership*. This was put forward by Weber in the 1920s and had fallen so far out of favour by the 1970s that it rated only six lines and no index entry in Stodgill's opus:

> The *charismatic leader* operates with a staff of disciples, enthusiasts and possibly bodyguards. He tends to sponsor causes and revolutions and is supported by charismatic authority, resting on devotion to the sanctity, heroism or inspirational character of the leader and on the normative patterns revealed or ordained by him. (Stodgill, 1974/1976: 26)

Stodgill does note that Weber's ideas on legitimate authority and leadership were becoming more influential in the US at the time, but this most probably referred to interest in the transition from patrimonial to bureaucratic forms of leadership and authority. The portrayal of the charismatic leader and its discourse of sanctity and disciples is a classic 'morally sustaining idea' that underwrote many of the sermons on visionary leadership from the corporate culture merchants of the 1980s. Causes and cultural change, heroic identification and the idea that everyone can turn themselves into a winner if they will only believe were the stock-in-trade of Tom Peters and his numerous imitators; only the bodyguards were missing! Hollway's discussion of this phenomenon (1991: 140–4) notes that it attempted to reverse the trend of subsuming leadership into a management function or skill and reintroduced 'soft' human relations ideas into the harder world of professional management training, using the claim that such an approach was capable of capturing for management the 'intractable and intuitive side of the organisation' (1991: 143). Hollway further suggests that in the end rationalistic management practice would find it 'hard to embrace' this cultist version of people management principles. All the same, the 'socially integrating myth' aspect was useful to many organisations to the extent that rationalisation could easily be disguised as revolution. In terms of changing attitudes through culture, whipping up some enthusiasm, even if it is mainly engendered by fear of being on the downside of downsizing, can beget the minimum public commitment necessary to get people on your side for long enough to achieve your desired changes. Haslam (2001: 49) cites Meindl and others and others on charisma as integral to the 'romance of leadership' and Gemmill and Oakley (1992) to the effect that it is an 'alienating social myth', in that it acts to increase differntiation between leaders and followers and from our point of view to downplay their interdependence in the labour process.

Under the models discussed above, from House to Burns and beyond, the duties and obligations of management have shifted considerably. From directive and co-ordinating leadership we have moved to a model that is underwritten not so much by duties or obligations but rather by a desperate casting about for methods of controlling the motivation and commitment of workers. This is achieved mainly through strategies emphasising the manipulation of situations and the management of meaning. Leadership has come down to the management of employee self-control, a problem which Hollway claims has never been solved to the satisfaction of senior management (1991: 143). Johnson and Gill (1993) cite the work of Mantz and Sims (1989) as a major contribution to leadership strategies aimed at producing self-regulation in pursuit of the 'self-controlling organisation'. They suggest that *extrinsic control mechanisms* (that is, traditional controls, external to the individual) should be judged effective to the extent that they 'influence self-control mechanisms based on the internalisation of norms within individual organisational members' (1993: 121). The focus of leadership behaviour here is to encourage 'self-reinforcement, self-observation, evaluation and control; self-expectation and goal-setting and rehearsal and self-criticism' (1993: 131). This is not of course the 'abdication of responsibility' of the laissez-faire leader of old, but is more a recognition of the type of power that needs to be exercised to ensure the mobilisation of commitment necessary to labour processes embodying work intensification and reduced supervision. However, just as Hollway was dubious about the acceptability of such an approach to management, Johnson and Gill are also pessimistic about the advent of the self-controlling organisation, depending as it does on the 'democratisation of society in general and its institutions'. Of course it is always possible that in an attempt to maintain their cultural acceptability workers could present themselves as intrinsically motivated and committed to self-control when the real source of their commitment is greed, guilt or fear – followers just cannot be trusted!

Networking

We now return full circle to the notion that leadership is about legitimating the exercise of power at both the strategic and interpersonal levels. It is not simply the wielding of power, but an inherent component of the armoury of tacit and open skills employed in the negotiation and brokerage of individual and group hegemony. This is exemplified in the approach taken by Hosking and Morley (1991: chap. 9) who see leadership as 'a more or less skilful process of organising, achieved through negotiation, to achieve acceptable influence over the description and handling of issues within and between groups' (1991: 240).

Their critique of leadership in HRM and OB centres around the entitative approach (based on Meyer *et al.*, 1985) they see as endemic in these literatures. These are exemplified by the treatment of person and organisation as separate entities, persons being theorised independently of their contexts with the result that 'the concept of organisation is implicit and underdeveloped in the treatment of individuals and groups' (Hosking and Morley, 1991: 40). Because of this, leadership processes are under-emphasised in favour of a focus on leaders and their manipulations of others in pursuit of 'organisational goals' (1991: 241). Rather than talking about leaders and followers they speak of *participants* in relationships who perceive 'each other as achieving influence in different ways', with varying degrees of acceptability in particular contexts and in line with our earlier comments on leadership acts, that all participants may 'come to be expected to make contributions' (1991: 240). Hosking and Morley highlight the social construction of relational exchanges in terms of *social, cognitive* and *political* processes. They argue that cognitive processes need to be understood as 'sense making' rather than as instruments for diagnosing and selecting appropriate behaviours (1991: 247). The political processes and power should be viewed as mainly resident not in structural factors and interpersonal influence but in the 'quality of relationships' and 'the context of interdependence' (1991: 249). Finally they examine the cognitive and political aspects of the organising process of skilful leadership through the 'vehicles' of *networking*, negotiation and enabling.

The political quality of networks lies in their influence on commitments to shared understandings, lines of action and the projection of shared valuations. 'Networking' is the process of relationship-building by which persons build up 'organisational intelligence'. Leaders would be those who build enabling relations through negotiation with other participants (with networks of their own?) who can act as their 'eyes and ears' and on whom they can depend for specialised skills. Leaders' networks would probably be small and cohesive, as more diffuse networks might jeopardise the quality of relationships (1991: 252). Where networks may actually be most important is in sustaining and maintaining leadership. For example, the networks that support political leaders are what allow them to appear that they are in personal control of a country or government when of course no one person could possibly do everything necessary to maintain such control. In the case of powerful leaders who have more or less uncontested political control it is often only through attacking and removing their supporters and thus damaging their support networks that their opponents can effectively contest them, Margaret Thatcher and Tony Blair providing good examples of this.

We should note that for all that Hosking and Morley's work is detailed, dense with examples and carefully constructed to avoid the failings of mainstream OB, what they conclude is most akin to a more rational and contextually-grounded version of transformational leadership. Networking needs to take place in conditions of 'open-minded thinking' and participation, negotiation through 'acceptable influence' and enabling in respect of the valuations and projects of all participants and not just leader-derived goals (1991: 258). They speak of a 'culture of productivity' where 'all participants take responsibility for the relational processes through which they may help and be helped', a laudable aspiration which is ignorant of the constraints of ideological structures and defensive identities.

Attributing leadership

The authority claimed by managers may be based on the networks that support them but that power is claimed on the basis of the personal fitness of managers to lead, attributing their leadership abilities to their personal characteristics, rather than the situational favourableness that Fiedler identified. Such self-serving attributional bias (see Chapter 18) affects us all, but becomes crucial for managers in that it supports their legitimacy to both themselves and others. As is the case for any organisational member, managers work within a series of role and informational networks and under both myriad situational influences and, as noted by Lord and Maher (cited in Brotherton, 1999: 66), the cognitive context of perceptions of past behaviours and performances.

So personal meaning and influence for managers derive in large part from consistent performances of group roles, but it is also the case that anyone can perform group and task maintenance acts and that the type and form of these acts can and will vary between cultures. The expectations placed on managers with formal leadership roles might aid managerial labour by working to mask the visibility of such acts by others. In this sense power and legitimacy are dependent on the shaping of cultural meanings within groups in the direction of dispositional rather than situational attributions. These would enable perceptions of competence to be ascribed to specific individuals rather than to the group as a whole.

Returning to Hosking and Morley's view that leadership is contingent on the networks that can be activated and maintained by managers, we have also to note that networks can be seen as an example of what Feldman and Klich (1991: 76–7) identify as *inauthentic social relations*, the members of a network may appear to be acting togther in pursuit of a superordinate goal, but may as individuals simply be pursuing their own agendas. Thus the managerial influence and perceived competence that underwrite leadership may depend, both in their production and maintenance, on creating perceptions of co-operative behaviour, while the reality of the relationship is essentially self-serving (as we noted above in relation to presenting an image of motivation and self-control). According to Bolman and Deal:

> Leadership, therefore,is less a matter of action than appearance. And when leaders do make a difference in a more proactive sense, it is usually by enriching and updating the script for the organisational drama – by constructing new myths that alter beliefs and generate faith among members of their audience. (Bolman and Deal, 1994: 105)

Creating such perceptions will depend on the maintenance of an illusion of the non-interdependence of intra-group relationships, that is, that power and legitimacy is not based on the work of others and the support of networks. Such an illusion could be essentially derived from follower 'tact' (Goffman, 1971; see Chapter 25) in that continued group membership would necessitate the collaboration of group members in allowing others to produce consistent performances. Tact may break down in circumstances where there is a loss of perceived legitimacy and/or competence, activating self-serving bias so that group attributions would tend to shift towards situational factors, placing the competence of the group over that of the manager/leader role. Shifts of this kind are seen to occur in performance appraisal processes (Tennen and Affleck, 1990) whereas breakdowns in situational tact might again best be observed in organisational change interventions, where managers may have to place task maintenance over group maintenance factors. In a similar vein, variations have also been noted in the task/group orientation of both leaders and subordinates in terms of cross-cultural comparisons, for example, those of Hofstede (1980) and Misumi. and colleagues (1989), although once again we need to beware of the stereotypical characterisations embodied in such comparisons.

The implications of attributional theories of leadership show that those in leadership roles carry significant advantages in the social perception of their actions by others. For example if we believe that it is possible to affect events, then a 'leader' taking action will be more likely to be perceived as causing the event (Calder, 1977). Meindl and colleagues (1985; 1987) also note that when causes are not clear we are more likely to attribute leadership as the cause (though this might not be unilaterally favourable to leaders) and that organisational success was rated more favourably when attributed to leadership than when attributed to the situation (both cited in Jewell and Seigel, 1990: 432).

Social identity and followership

We noted earlier that one of Stodgill's 1974 findings was that the characteristics of followers determine the acceptability of leadership characteristics and that leader-member relations had been developed by Hollander (1992) into the notion of *followership*, which essentially concerns the role of the group member in supporting (or not!) the leadership role. Just as members of a network can support a leader through delegation and role differentiation, then followers can give varying levels of support to leaders by the extent to which they act as a committed 'team player', supporting others and listening to and following leader direction. Levels of support for a leader would vary as with, for example, Fiedler's situational variables and the context of the leader–follower relationship in terms of issues such as legitimacy and trust. It is also possible that followership actions could be seen as a case of followers themselves performing leadership acts in support of the group, rather than specifically in relation to a leader, as in the case of a second-in-command.

This study of followership is developed in what Hogg (2001) identifies as a social cognitive understanding of leadership in Hollander's (Hollander and Julian, 1969) *implicit leadership theory and* Lord and colleagues' (1984) *leadership categorisation theory.* In the managerial literature implicit leadership theory is often taken to represent some form of laissez-faire leadership characterised by low-profile, delegating leaders who provide direction but do not direct. More accurately implicit leadership concerns attributions made *of* leaders by others, for example the attribution of charisma or consistency, or as we noted earlier the attribution of male gender stereotypes. Similarly leader categorisation theory holds that leadership is subjectively determined by the preconceptions people hold about leader behaviour, though as Hogg (2001: 198) notes these preconceptions are 'a product of individual information processing, not a structural property of real groups'.

It is this notion of leader categorisation that links leadership to social identity theory and self-categorisation theory through the concept of leader *prototypicality*, which suggests for Hogg (2001: 201) that perceptions of evaluation and effectiveness depend on the extent to which the leader conforms to the *in-group prototype*, in terms of identification with and conformity to group norms or in Haslam's (2001: 45) terms both '*defining and being defined*' by the social categories salient to the group. The greater the prototypicality of the leader, the more socially attractive they are to the group and the more influence they have, leading to increased attributions of leader effectiveness (2001: 204). Where leaders exhibit highly prototypical behaviour over time this becomes more likely to be attributed to the personality of the leader, rather than simply to their position in the group (2001: 205). This could lead to categorisation of a leader as charismatic by both the group and themselves, which according to Hogg serves to reinforce status differences and heighten role differentiation, further separating the group into leader and followers. So from this perspective perceived characteristics such as charisma are more like self-fulfilling stereotypes than personal attributes.

Haslam's (2001) chapter on social identity and leadership produces a great deal of evidence on leader prototypicality as it relates to various issues in leadership, showing for example that prototypical leaders are more able to do as they see fit, while aprototypical leaders have to prove their *status* to the in-group, supporting the notion of idiosyncrasy credit. He also argues (2001: 48) that, 'without shared social identity there can be no leadership' and that charisma is, 'an emergent product of the self-categorisation process', which goes further to indicate that charisma is an *outcome of social relations* rather than a trait. Haslam does caution (2001: 49), like Hogg above, that prototypicality is not indicative of specific leader attributes and adds that neither does it indicate that relative levels of leadership attributes can be assumed to inherently fit different categories or types of leaders or leader behaviours. In examining the *emergence* of leaders he explains (2001: 50) that it is again not the qualities or type of the leader *per se* that count, but the extent that leader maximises the categorical differences between in-groups and out-groups, that is, 'us vs. them'. Leader *fairness* or even-handedness is shown to be less important than a leader's *affirmation of group identity* (2001: 52), in that, 'only when the leader had a history of standing up for the shared values of the group was the group prepared to stand up for him and *do the necessary work* for his vision to be realised'. Identity affirmation was also more important than, for example, *moral integrity* in predicting leader success (2001: 53). Haslam further notes that competition for the leadership role within groups is generally assumed to enhance group performance (2001: 54), which is common to conceptions of group development such as that of Tuckman (see Chapter 24) and hypothesises that where the group already has a salient group identity this process might do no more than increase interpersonal *rivalry* within the group. This was even more the case where leaders were *systematically selected* for or within a group rather than emerging from the group or randomly selected, experimental evidence (2001: 55) confirming that for groups with a strong identity random leader selection worked best but was perceived as unsatisfactory due to functional stereotypes held about leaders which again serve to differentiate between leaders and followers. Such stereotypes justify the differential treatment of leaders and followers and mean that, 'even where leadership does not exist, there are pressures to invent it' (2001: 55). The invented leader will be unlikely to be a maverick of any kind though (2001: 57) as not fitting the stereotype is obviously deleterious to the prototypicality that leaders trade on in their relations with subordinates.

From our viewpoint the most crucial implication of Haslam's arguments is that rather than the transformational leadership view that leaders change followers or at least their attitudes, from a social identity perspective effective leaders are those 'whose individuality is transformed by group membership in such a way that they come to articulate, embody and direct the social identity based interests that they share with other group members' (2001: 57). In other words we have come from leaders being 'born not made' to leaders being 'made not born', made not by the organisation, but by their self-typification of their relative success at being perceived as leaders by others in the social relationships they pursue at work.

Summary and key points

Leadership, like personality (see Chapter 19) has shown the classic developmental sequence of a psychological concept as new variables and mediating factors are found to affect it. This pattern of focusing in turn on broader to more specific concepts, that is:

Types>Traits>Behaviour>Style>Situation>Contingency

These will be found again in later chapters, but for now it is enough that as these patterns of evidence and analysis have developed, then so have the conceptions of the duties and obligations of managers. That leadership characteristics cannot account for leader behaviour means that leadership, if it is to be understood at all given the range of behaviour that can constitute it, is to be understood as at least *two* related roles which are played out in the contexts of groups and followers.

Of all the problem areas addressed by psychology in organisations, it is possibly the question of what constitutes leadership that has most influenced the construction of managerial identity. Groups are a tool (see Chapter 24), but it is the status of the manager as leader which most acts to mobilise the commitment of managers to endure the role conflicts which are the inheritance of their hierarchical position. The commitment of managers, who of necessity must buy into ideologies of control, is more or less taken for granted. It is primarily the assumed ability of managers to infuse motivation and commitment in others that is the common external measure of their fitness for leadership. Internal recognition of such fitness among managers themselves will nevertheless be mainly reflected in factors serving to buttress managerial identity against the contradictory role expectations placed on them by their status as managers and leaders. A crucial factor here is the extent to which managers can withstand and capitalise on these very pressures, and such resistance needs to be understood in terms of the topic we turn to next. This is a phenomenon which we all increasingly recognise in our lives and which is often borne as a badge of honour by managers, *stress*.

Further reading

As intimated earlier there is more rubbish written on leadership than on any topic other than creationism: try anything with a title like 'The leadership secrets of…' for a laugh and a lesson in how to aggregate self-aggrandising homilies into a book. In terms of OB texts Rollinson is good on management style and Haslam is as good as ever on leadership and social identity. An account which emphasises follower identity can be found in Lord and Brown (2004). The mother lode is still to be found in Stodgill's opus (available via JSTOR), though the Bass and Stodgill update is a good substitute.

Bass, B. and Stodgill, R. M. (1990) *Handbook of Leadership, A Survey of Theory and Research* (3rd edn), New York: Free Press.

Haslam, S. A. (2004) *Psychology in Organizations: The Social Identity Approach* (2nd edn), London: Sage.

Lord, R.G. and Brown, D.J. (2004) *Leadership Processes and Follower Self-Identity*, Mahwah, NJ: Lawrence Erlbaum Associates.

Rollinson, D. (2008) *Organisational Behaviour and Analysis: An Integrated Approach*, Harlow: Financial Times/Prentice-Hall.

Stodgill, R.M. (1974/1976) *Handbook of Leadership, A Survey of Theory and Research*, New York: Free Press.

putting the pressure on: stress, work, well-being and emotion

> There's a lot of tension now, and that makes people mean. We had more control before and less confusion. You could get things done. Every once in a while my head starts to throb. I can't take it. (Stock and bond transfer assistant cited in Zuboff, 1988: 143)

Stress is essentially an umbrella concept, which covers a number of psychological reactions to pressure put on the individual and we have expanded our brief outline of the physiological basis of stress before moving on to examine its management by organisations and individuals. More emphasis has been placed on issues of well-being and work-life balance though maintaining the focus on control and the individualisation of workplace problems. From a brief section on emotions and emotional labour at work in previous editions we have shifted our coverage to examine the nature of emotions as conceptualised in OB in more depth, partially as a counter to the rather loose and unitarist conceptions used in many modern accounts. To extend this analysis and partially to explore the commodification of emotions we also introduce a section on emotional intelligence.

The aims of this chapter are to:

- give an account of the processes through which stress factors in the individual have become integral to systems of management.
- show how the understanding of stress and stressors has informed the development of systems of measuring and managing stress.
- locate and explain the role of counselling and employee assistance programmes in managing employee welfare.
- demonstrate and illuminate how issues of well-being and work-life balance have influenced policy and practice.
- examine how the understanding of employee affect has moved from emotions as a form of labour to trait-based measures of competencies.

Stress: the force to adapt

Managerial work was one of the first areas to be associated with the negative effects of stress, especially through personality traits linked with supposedly high rates of coronary heart disease (Rosenman *et al.*, 1964, see 'Stress management' below). These are in turn associated with high levels of personal investment in work, as is generally assumed to be the case with those in managerial grades. It has since been established that stress-related illness is more likely to vary inversely than positively with organisational status, position and job-related skill (Cooper and Smith, 1985) though this has recently been queried (Chandola *et al.*, 2008, see below). Whatever the case the work intensification associated with JIT, lean production and teamworking has long been known as 'management by stress' (Parker and Slaughter, 1988; 1995) and there is still a great concern with stress and in ameliorating its possible effects on organisational effectiveness.

Stress is an all-pervasive phenomenon the effects of which are detectable from the biological level, through the psychological and the interpersonal levels, right up to socio-cultural systems of values, knowledge and technology, as recognised by C. D. Jenkins (1979). Hans Selye, a pioneer of stress research, identified two main forms of stress as early as the 1930s, *distress* (often termed strain), which is the negative form found in conventional wisdom, and *eustress*, which is the 'healthy, normal stress' that leads to positive feelings and possibly to what have been termed 'peak experiences'. These forms of stress are possibly better thought of as positive and negative consequences of what is termed *arousal*, or the level of drive or motivation we put into a task. This notion arose from the work of Yerkes and Dodson (1908; see Fisher, 1986: 94–6) on the relation between drive level and learning ability, the idealised results of which are summarised in Figure 23.1 below. What this does is to establish the consequences of the now familiar notion of too much stress (overload or *hyperstress*) and of too little stress (underload or *hypostress*) and that some level of stress is necessary to our basic functioning. It also takes the effects of eustress into account, though the notion of an optimal level of stress is flawed in the sense that it cannot be generated, only experienced, and of course you can have too much of a good thing.

These results were mainly generated from exposing animals to deprivation or painful stimuli and went on to distinguish two functions of arousal, the *cue* function, which serves to guide behaviour, and the *vigilance* function concerned with the amount of energy expended. The continuation of this line of research into the effects of various stimuli on performance has received both confirmation and qualification in work on humans, using incentives as well as negative stimuli. In general, three dimensions of arousal can

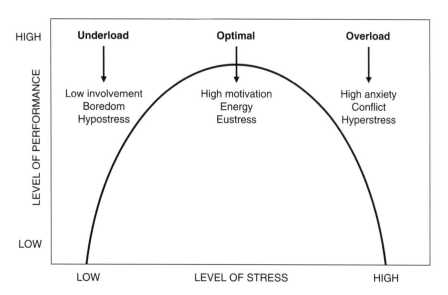

Figure 23.1 **Stress and performance**

be distinguished (Schonpflug, 1983, cited in Fisher, 1986: 109):

- *Arousal* – facilitating performance.
- *Interference* – trying to ignore the stimulus.
- *Compensatory effort* – putting extra effort into the task.

Thus, from the start, research into what we now term 'stress' has focused on the *facilitation* and *inhibition* of performance. Further, the definition of stress has been problematic both in terms of whether stress causes illness directly (*aetiological*) or indirectly (*non-aetiological*) and because of the range of stimuli and other factors often cited under the catch-all definition of stress, for example, anxiety, fear and frustration. Recently the aetiological view has received support from the findings of the longitudinal Whitehall II study (Chandola *et al.*, 2008) of 10,000 UK civil servants since 1985 which showed direct links between stress and coronary heart disease (CHD) among the under 50s regardless of worker status. The aetiology was linked mainly to poor regulation of heartbeat (vagal tone) and levels of the stress hormone cortisol, though typically for findings in this area the picture was blurred in that lifestyle was also implicated in terms of those under stress lacking the time to eat well and exercise.

Physiological stress

In 1936 Cannon was the first to make the important link between behavioural changes in individuals and physiological responses to stimuli that upset the organism's homeostatic balance of energy provision. In order to avoid or defend against threats, the organism's circulatory, muscular and digestive systems react similarly to what is commonly termed a 'fight or flight response'. It is now understood that heart and respiration rates increase, blood supplies to the skin and intestines are reduced while that to the muscles is increased, and hormones are released which both heighten arousal and promote the increased uptake of blood sugars to meet energy demands:

> However, it was Selye in 1956 who really promoted what we now know as stress-related illness in his identification of stress as 'the body's non-specific response to any demand that is placed on it, whether that demand is pleasant or not'. (From an interview with Selye: Cherry, 1978: 60)

Selye had been working since the 1930s on physiological stress in terms of his 'general adaptation syndrome', which identified three phases in the body's response to stressors. The first phase, the alarm response, is where a stressor is perceived and the physiological responses given above take place. The resistance phase is where the organism adapts to the particular stressor though at the same time becoming less resistant to other stressors. The final phase, exhaustion, is where the symptoms of stress-related illness develop (or the 'pathological end-state' according to Jenkins, 1979), where prolonged exposure or overload means that adaptation or resistance could not be maintained (Selye, in Clarke *et al.*, 1994: 398). The problem for the organism here is that the stress response is both cumulative and additive: small stresses or prolonged low-level stress adding up to a larger effect, and different stressors adding to the overall level of stress. The classic relation of stress to heart disease can be understood in relation to long-term increases in heart rate and blood pressure, and likewise the proneness when under stress to other illnesses such as bacteriological and viral infections through the long-term depression of the body's immune responses. Indeed this model can be used to explain a multitude of phenomena from 'cold spots' in haunted houses (reduced bloodflow to the skin when something scares us) to 'butterflies in the stomach' when apprehensive or in love (reduced bloodflow to, and contraction of, the intestines).

346 23

INTRODUCTION: REGULATING ORGANISATIONAL BEHAVIOUR ■ PERCEPTION AND ATTITUDES: SEEING WHAT TO THINK ■ MASKS FOR TASKS: PERSONALITY ■ LEARNING AND CHANGE ■ MOTIVATION: THE DRIVE FOR SATISFACTION ■ LEADERSHIP: MIGHT OR MYTH? ■

An interesting note here is that chemically the hormones released by the stress reaction are similar to various recreational drugs and over-exposure to them has similarly negative effects, up to and including addiction. Adrenaline (or epinephrine) produces similar effects to amphetamines or ecstasy, cortisol to the steroids commonly misused by bodybuilders and athletes, endorphins are natural opiates similar to heroin and the stress reaction produces other natural painkillers similar to the cannabinoids in marijuana. Breakdown products of chemicals produced in the stress reaction such as alkaloids can produce similar effects to hallucinogenic drugs.

What Selye's work was attempting to do was to distinguish the aetiological, causative factors in the stress reaction from our generalised responses, though Beech and colleagues (1982: 10) note that this has not been followed up by most researchers, who refer to both causes and responses as stress, further adding to the confusion as to what stress actually is. Likewise the distinction between eustress and distress is not followed up greatly in the modern stress literature, even though it provides the basis for the most important element of most contemporary models of stress and techniques for stress 'management'. This is that the outcome of the stress response in positive or negative terms is linked to cognitive appraisal, the perception, interpretation and attribution of the stressors concerned. What one person perceives as stressful may be pleasurable to another. We may change our interpretation of a stressor from something that causes us distress to something we might perhaps look upon as a challenge, or we might react differently to a stressor depending on our locus of control and on whether we attribute its cause internally or environmentally. On this basis individuals have differing thresholds for the recognition of stressors and the initiation of stress reactions, factors such as our levels of competency and skill moderating our perceptions of stressors. A problem here is that the effects of individual differences and context on perception of stressors are difficult to distinguish from other factors which moderate goal-directed effort. The results of frustration, for example, may interact with stress leading to both constructive (more effort, innovation, new goals) and disruptive (aggression, withdrawal) outcomes. Similarly factors associated with increased stress levels such as lack of job security and high status incongruity (Newell, 1995) could for some people be the very things that spur them into action and help them to cope with their perceived stress.

Cognitive appraisal, coping and role stress

The cognitive appraisal approach is most commonly identified with Lazarus (1966), who emphasised cognition over the previous medical and physiological approach. However, Lazarus, like Cannon, acknowledged that stress was a result of person–environment interactions and it was this factor which led to possibly the most popular modern approach to stress, promoted by the social psychologists Katz and Kahn (1966), which examines stress as a question of *person–environment fit*, that is, of whether a person's abilities match the demands of the job and whether their goals and aspirations matched the outcomes of their work. In Lazarus and Folkman's (1984) *transactional model* individual differences in cognitive appraisal of what is stressful centre around *primary appraisal* (- is it stressful?) and *secondary appraisal* (- can I cope with it? – are there alternatives?). Lazarus' work, along with that of others such as Moos and Billings (1982), goes on to characterise the psychological *coping strategies* we employ in dealing with stress. *Appraisal-focused* coping can be seen logical analysis and cognitive redefinition of stressors and in strategies of *avoidance* (or in Cannon's terms *flight*, which again is essentially similar to defence mechanisms such as *mental inhibition* or *disavowal*, see Chapter 19) Such strategies can help us to deal with stress, but stressors have the habit of reoccurring and we cannot analyse, redefine or avoid every source of stress in our lives. *Emotion-focused* coping (or *affective regulation*) tries to manage our internal responses to the stressor, as in the traditionally British 'stiff upper lip' (similar to *repression*, see Chapter 19), or in *resigned acceptance* (similar to *resigned job satisfaction*, see Chapter 21) or *emotional discharge* (catharsis). Affective regulation tends, however, to be a short-term strategy on the basis that subjective, emotional coping has diminishing returns in the face of objective problems. *Problem-focused coping* concerns trying to alleviate or manage the stressor itself through *guidance* or *counselling*, developing *alternative rewards* or by taking *direct action*. These categories of response describe almost the full range of modern approaches to managing stress, the question for most organisations being the cost-effectiveness of the approach. Combinations of emotion-focused coping, counselling and programmes based on *cross-resistance* (see *stress management* below) seem to be the preferred strategies, as individuals taking direct action and/or redesigning work to avoid stress are potentially disruptive and costly.

For Katz and Kahn, psychological stress in social situations was linked to how well a person's skills and abilities matched the expectations of their social roles. In the OB literature, expectations are routinely dealt with through the notion of role: the roles we wish to play ourselves, the roles others wish or expect us to play, and the roles set or demanded of us from our relations within work organisations. The total number of *role expectations* that impinge on any individual is referred to as a *role-set*, and can comprise contradictory demands from workmates, supervisors, management, customers or clients, and from what is today referred to as the *home/work interface* (see 'Well-being and work-life balance' below). Where the demands of a role or roles are unclear and norms and standards of social comparison are lacking, people may experience *role ambiguity*. The negative consequences of such ambiguity are evident in the importance given to clarity of roles and objectives in management development and employee learning initiatives. Where competing role expectations (for example, those that play a part in determining an individual's intra- and extra-organisational roles) cannot be fulfilled, we come into *role conflict* and such pressures may also originate in *role overload* or *underload*, where the demands of a role are greater or lesser than expected. French and Caplan (1972) further distinguished between *quantitative* and *qualitative* overload (too much or too difficult work) and underload (too little or too monotonous work). Role conflicts existing between expectations from the differing parts of a person's role-set are inevitable with the level of pressure that most of us are exposed to in or out of work these days, as people cannot always fulfil all the demands of their role-set. In addition, we may experience role conflicts between external role demands and personal values and beliefs, or between a person's gender, ethnic or skill identity and their treatment by other workers or management.

Stress management

Contemporary accounts of the stress 'process' in the work place often follow the *person–environment fit* notion of stress as 'resulting from a misfit between an individual and their particular environment' (Arnold, Cooper and Robertson, 1998: 422), where internal or external factors push individuals' adaptive capacities beyond their limit. This view has been widely popularised by Cooper and his many co-workers, who have found confirmation for their general model in studies covering a wide range of occupations and organisations. The model proposed by Cummings and Cooper (1979), a 'Cybernetic Framework for the Study of Occupational Stress', reprises many elements of the homeostatic medical model proposed by Cannon, as can be seen from the summary below:

• People attempt to keep their thoughts, emotions and relationships in a homeostatic balance or 'steady state'.

- For any individual the various elements of their physical and emotional makeup will have a balance he or she is comfortable with, or a 'range of stability'.
- Stressors are forces which push physical or psychological factors beyond their range of stability, producing strain and provoking behaviour which attempts to restore the balance or feeling of comfort.
- The various behaviours individuals use to maintain their state of balance constitute their 'coping strategies' or 'adjustment process'.
- Knowing that a stress might occur constitutes a threat to the individual and threat can itself produce strain. (See Cooper and Robertson, (1998), chap. 17)

Derivations of this model, typologies of sources of stressors and the forms of pathological end-state to be encountered, as in the Jenkins model above, have accounted for much of the modern stress literature. This tends to emphasise the amount of productivity lost due to stress, its inevitability and the benefits for the enterprise of managing stress. Costs are examined socially in terms of rates of heart disease, mental disorder and social dysfunction, and in the workplace through effects on job satisfaction, performance and absenteeism rates, and more recently in the costs of compensation claims and health insurance (see Arnold, Robertson and Cooper, 1998). Estimates vary on the cost of stress-related illness to industry, and figures vary in terms of how they are measured, but the Health and Safety Executive (UK) reported survey results in 2004–5 indicating that, 'over half a million workers were suffering from work-related stress, depression or anxiety caused or made worse by their current or past work', with rates of stress doubling since the rapid increase of the 1990s, though 'levelling out since 2000' (LRD, 2006: 5). The HSE further estimates 'almost 31 working days lost per year for each affected case', leading to 12.8 million working days lost per year at a cost of £400 million for UK employers and £3.7 billion in social costs. (LRD, 2006: 11). Figures such as these have led to an increasing concern with organisational programmes to promote employee well-being and to help individuals cope with work-related stress and conflicts over the home/work interface. The HSE (2005) has identified six primary sources of stress representing the main risk factors at work where stressors can have a negative impact on employee well-being:

1 **Demands** – such as workload, work patterns and the work environment.
2 **Control** – such as how much say the person has in the way they do their work.
3 **Support** – such as the encouragement, sponsorship and resources provided by the organisation, line management and colleagues.
4 **Relationships** – such as promoting positive working to avoid conflict and dealing with unacceptable behaviour.
5 **Role** – such as whether people understand their role within the organisation and whether the organisation ensures that they do not have conflicting roles.
6 **Change** – such as how organisational change (large or small) is managed and communicated in the organisation.

The HSE promotes these six areas as 'Management Standards' towards which organisations need to assess risks and set targets towards good practice in reducing stress and promoting *wellness* at work. The promotion of wellness goes back at least as far as the physical components of the ancient Greek notion of arête (virtue, excellence) and had more notorious manifestations such as the six million-strong People's Health Movement (Proctor, 1988: 228) linked to the Nazi eugenics programme. Modern examples of 'wellness' programmes such the 'Staywell' programme and Employee Advisory Resource of the Control

Data Corporation in the US typically offer 24-hour advice on assessing health risks, medical screening and health education to help people to change life and work styles in healthy directions (Lucas, 1986; McKenna, 2000). 'Companies have a major stake in promoting a healthier life style for employees, because of the potential benefits in reduced insurance costs, decreased absenteeism, improved productivity and better morale' (McKenna, 1987: 403). Ginn and Henry (2003: 26), in examining the importance of wellness programmes to strategic HRM, quality and commitment, cite Conrad's (1988) classification of four types of wellness programme:

1   *risk assessment* – tests and self report measures assessing risk levels of illnesses and lifestyle factors
2   *fitness promotion* – programmes to increase cardiovascular and muscular fitness and mental acuity and to reduce depression
3   *health education* – avoidance or care of disease and injury, nutritional counselling, smoking cessation and techniques such as relaxation and biofeedback
4   *demand management* – promoting self-care through *employee assistance programs* (see below), that is, referral programs for emotional or psychological problems, substance abuse or adjustment to work or home life.

Ginn and Henry (2003: 27) further assert that 'risk assessment programs seem to have universal applicability', while fitness, health education, and demand management programmes 'are a function of contingencies' based on employee demographics, as information and programmes relevant to one group may be irrelevant or unattractive to another, for example in terms of factors such as age or ethnicity. A brief web search will reveal the extent of the modern 'wellness industry' – from courses in 'managing integrated health and wellness' to 'corporate wellness tracking systems' and into realms beyond:

> Ashstar Wellness Programs are state-of-the-art 'personalized' detox-cleansing and Rejuvenation protocols specifically designed to help you meet the challenges of our modern Western Lifestyle. Balanced-Professional Programs run by Holistic Health Practitioners in a Relaxed Peaceful Tropical Beach Environment. (http://www.ashstar.net/, 12/12/07)

As much as we would like our bosses to be convinced that we all need such high-end wellness provision, participation in wellness programmes is not only limited by cost and situational power, to the extent that 'quite a large percentage of employees who took part in wellness programmes stopped doing the exercises and showed an inclination to return to their old lifestyles' (Ivancevich and Matteson, cited in McKenna, 2000: 629). It seems that even when provided gratis it takes more than good intentions to ignore our more pressing short-term concerns in favour of what are, for the individual, mainly long-term gains.

Wellness vs control

In contrast to the wellness view, the Labour Research Department (LRD) concluded that 'only a minority of organisations are tackling the problem directly' and that the main effort is towards management rather than prevention:

> Where they exist management 'stress control' programmes peddle individual victim-blaming approaches to stress problems that in reality can only be solved by changing workplace organisation and relations. (LRD, 1988: 2) …or claiming that stress is all down to pressures outside the workplace. (LRD, 2006: 23)

350   23

INTRODUCTION: REGULATING ORGANISATIONAL BEHAVIOUR ▪ PERCEPTION AND ATTITUDES: SEEING WHAT TO THINK ▪ MASKS FOR TASKS: PERSONALITY ▪ LEARNING AND CHANGE ▪ MOTIVATION: THE DRIVE FOR SATISFACTION ▪ LEADERSHIP: MIGHT OR MYTH? ▪

This view sees management as directly opposed to the kinds of standards the HSE above identifies as needed to achieve reductions of stress at work, through both the individualisation of organisational problems as personal pathological reactions and the rejection of any intra-organisational attribution of stressors. These are not only strategies for the *organisational avoidance of stress* as an issue as opposed to the rhetoric of organisational concern for employee well-being, but they are also strategies for the avoidance of managing the causes of stress (which is a legal requirement) in favour of a policy of managing the people who experience the stress. Such strategies are effectively demonstrated by the use of stress inventories in the diagnosis and 'treatment' of stress. Such inventories commonly rely on identifying the extent to which the individual fits the 'Type A' behavioural pattern which Rosenman and colleagues (1964) labelled *coronary-prone behaviour* owing to the correlation with increased rates of coronary heart disease (see Chapter 19 for more discussion). The inventories themselves are problematic, as indicated by Selye who claimed that 'all stress inventories in common use are somewhat flawed because they fail to give enough weight to individual differences' (Selye, in Cherry, 1978: 63). It is likely, however, that the mere use of a stress inventory does serve to educate and inform respondents as to the nature of their problems. In the main, attempts to modify Type A behaviour tend to concentrate not on relieving the source of the strain but on modifying behaviour through goal-setting and time-management techniques, so that the stress is in effect being actively managed though personal self-control. The result of this is a reduction of the strain felt by the individual into a managerial control variable determining fitness to the required organisational role.

This is further demonstrated by the differential focus on coping in mainstream accounts. Again the emphasis is not on dealing directly with the problem but with emotion-focused coping and what is termed *cross-resistance*. This latter is the notion that increasing adaptive capacities in one area, for example health and fitness, will increase resistance to other stressors, and is the foundation of many of the corporate wellness programmes discussed above. Emotion-focused coping is seen mainly in the popularity of relaxation training, and indirectly in what is possibly the most common corporate response to stress, *counselling*, though it is also used in techniques relying on stress *inoculation* (see below). Counselling is an indirect approach to stress, and at best is effected by '*cognitive redefinition*' of the 'problem' in much in the same way that psychoanalysis requires patients to redefine their identity and worldview within a framework that makes their difficulties understandable. There is nothing new here, of course. Baritz's interpretation of the Hawthorne study points out that research on employee counselling led some to the conclusion that 'workers did not have compelling objective problems' (1960: 201), as their grievances could be dealt with by allowing them to 'talk them out'. It is the ability of counselling to address, albeit on a superficial level, individual differences and subjectivity that makes it highly cost-effective in the stress management stakes, with the added benefit that it again persuades the individual that it is *his or her* problem. However, it is unlikely to actually remove the source of the experienced strain and does not necessarily increase adaptive capacities. The role of the organisation in producing unhealthy systems and conditions of work is in danger of being ignored. In its place we get systems reinforcing the self-attribution of stress and anxiety as personal problems to be coped with in the fulfilment of our various roles rather than structural issues to be contested. The modern focus of work in this area concentrates on the operation of employee assistance programmes, or EAPs, which manage the care of employees and also on peer-based and often union-run by *member assistance programmes,* or MAPs. Alker and McHugh (2000: 316) argue that EAPs are primarily introduced for instrumental reasons, dealing with the consequences of change and the introduction of new working practices, and that, 'there may at least be a "residual role" for welfare and/or counselling in modern HRM practice as evinced by reported difficulties in handling counselling' (for a discussion of counselling, EAPs and MAPs see Thompson and McHugh, 2002).

Other techniques such as relaxation training and its derivatives (including meditation and biofeedback) are also individual-centred and using exercises to reduce muscle tension and reduce stress through improved relaxation and identification of stress symptoms. Murphy and Sorenson (1988), in a quasi-experimental study of highway maintenance workers who were given either relaxation or biofeedback training, found that although the workers felt better both physiologically and mentally, the expected improvements in absenteeism and productivity were not manifested. What they did conclude, however, was that:

> Stress management may be most useful as an adjunct to organisational change interventions e.g. increased participation in decision-making, improved worker autonomy, task identity and feedback and implementation of flexible work schedules. (Murphy and Sorenson, 1988: 181)

To deal directly with stress and to effectively promote wellness requires problem-focused coping, where individuals or groups might actively design their own working environments and methods, negotiate their own roles or acquire new capacities. Such an approach, though highly effective in managing stress, would necessitate the vertical integration of control over work design and costs, and is consequently not highly popular.

Confronting and contesting stress

Though organisations may rely heavily on coping with stress through personal self-control, there is still a need for individuals to manage what may at time be severe and debilitating levels of stress. We noted above that most coping and wellness programmes rely mainly on cross-resistance and stress inoculation. The latter has become a proven procedure for the therapeutic treatment of individual stress (though it is often carried out in groups) through what is essentially a meticulous cognitive restructuring technique taking the level of involvement and effort in its processes even further than the kind of life-management strategies employed by the *Selection*, *Optimisation* and *Compensation* model (SOC – Baltes *et al.*, 1999, see 'Well-being' below for more on this). Meichenbaum (1996: 4–7), gives three phases to *Stress Inoculation Training* for coping with stressors:

- Education (or conceptualisation) phase – clients are:
  - educated about the transactional nature of stress and the role appraisal processes
  - encouraged to view perceived threats as problems-to-be-solved and to identify changeable aspects of their situations
  - taught how to –
    - 'fit' their problem- or emotion-focus to the perceived demands of the situation
    - break down global stressors into specific short, intermediate and long-term goals
- Rehearsal (or skills acquisition) phase –
  - coping skills are taught, practised, rehearsed and tailored to specific stressors
  - coping skills may include emotional self-regulation, self-soothing and acceptance, relaxation training, self-instructional training, cognitive restructuring, problem-solving, interpersonal communication skills training, attention diversion procedures, using social support systems and fostering meaning-related activities

- *Implementation* (or *application*) phase – follow-through or booster sessions provide opportunities for the clients to:
  - use techniques such as imagery and behavioural rehearsal, modelling, role playing, and graded exposure in the form of 'personal experiments'
  - help others with similar problems
  - identify high risk situations, warning signs and attribution & relapse prevention procedures
  - appropriate ownership by putting changes into their own words.
  (Adapted from Meichenbaum, 1996: 4–7)

The three phases here are, not surprisingly, analogous to Lewin's (1951) *unfreeze–move–refreeze* model of change (see Chapter 20), since most systems of attitudinal and behavioural change follow Lewin's stages to some extent. The critical factor here is the painstaking planning and implementation (and the associated costs) that go into such a programme. This goes far beyond what can be achieved by the counselling experienced with a call-centre EAP or the cross-resistance engendered by a corporate fitness programme. Stress inoculation training works, but requires levels of effort, commitment and longitudinal backup that has more in common with programmes aimed at recovering alcoholics than with what is commonly applied to stress at work.

In contrast to the stress management techniques outlined above, the Labour Research Department (LRD) has offered guidelines for dealing with stress on a collective basis, urging union members to research stress-related workplace issues which could be negotiated with management, and to communicate results to all members and appropriate officers and institutions. The negotiation strategy itself gives the following advice:

- Concentrate on one, preferably winnable, stress issue to gain confidence.
- Do not be afraid to consider a long-term strategy.
- Don't think of stress in isolation from other workplace hazards and issues. (Labour Research Department, 1988: 22)

Such collective attempts to alter conditions for the individual and the organisation are in direct contrast to the individual-centred methods which invoke the 'psychological fallacy' that 'since the organisation is made of individuals, we can change the organisation by changing its members' (Katz and Kahn, 1978: 391). As identified originally in the healthcare professions (e.g. Bailey, 1985) and since then in multinational corporations (Lansisalmi *et al.*, 2000), stress can both be experienced collectively and dealt with through collective coping strategies, the latter tending towards uniform learned responses to both stressors and the cultural meanings they convey, such as the systematic undervaluation of groups of employees. The LRD advice took the collective approach further in highlighting stress as an issue of workplace control, not only of job performance, but also of personal lifestyle in support of this. Wheeler and Lyon (1992: 48–9) cite commentators such as Steele and Handy as supporting the control view of stress in relation to worker assistance and health programmes and also Orlans on counselling often only dealing with problems at the individual level. Paradoxically, in its latest advice, the LRD (2006) has shifted its approach from one of high collective involvement to more standardised union-based responses centred on contesting employer responsibilities through risk assessment and negotiating stress policies. Such standardised responses, unless entirely successful in minimising or eliminating stressors, would not deliver the level of perceived individual or collective control that would truly help individuals cope with stress in the work and family domains in the same way as high-involvement techniques, such as SOC strategies and Stress Inoculation Training.

High job demands and loads can be perceived positively in situations of high control, but where control is low, high demand is associated with strain. For models of stress which go beyond individual-level approaches and account for perceived levels of control, we need to turn to work such as that of Karasek and Theorell (1990) or Fisher (1986). Karasek and Theorell link job strain to dimensions of *demand* from the situation, and the level of control, autonomy or *jurisdiction discretion* available to the individual in the workplace. The outcome of this is that in hierarchical, authoritarian conditions characterised by high demand and low jurisdiction, the best available coping response may be the reduction of effort (see Fisher, 1986: 157, 238), which raises the possibility that what appear to be wholly reactive responses such as Taylor's 'systematic soldiering' are actually coping strategies. Karasek and Theorell (1990) also give evidence that low levels of social support may exacerbate the relation between high demands and low control, while Wheeler and Lyon (1992: 47) note that Karasek's approach, 'effectively recognises the relationship between the subjective experience of stress and the social conditions which may give rise to it'. Fisher takes this a step further in examining coping responses to stressful conditions as strategic responses, the range of which are constrained by life experiences and personal style. The implication of this trend in research is that not only are work and organisational designs significant sources of strain, but our lack of control over them may also limit our adaptive capacities to cope with the stress produced, which is not exactly conducive to a healthy work-life balance.

Well-being and work-life balance

The capacity of wellness programmes and EAPs to deliver on employee well-being is constrained by not only their focus on individual coping and responsibility but also reliance on models emphasising person–environment fit. By focusing on individual characteristics and coping they tend to ignore that perceived distress or strain is determined by interactions with situational factors. Stress itself is not the modern focus of much work in this area but rather the concern is the problem of employee well-being. Individual well-being has been described by Ryff (1989) as dependent on such factors as *self acceptance, positive relations with others, autonomy* and *environmental mastery*, though this is a largely context-free model. The problem of contextualising well-being has been addressed by study of *work-life balance* (WLB), a notion that has obvious overtones of homeostatic models and which tends to set up work as a separate domain and not as part of life in itself. A better, though less fashionable term is *work–home interface* (sometimes *home–work* interface), which acknowledges the conceptual distinction of the domains but emphasises their interaction and possible interference rather than a striving to balance incompatible forces. We deal with work-life balance in Chapter 15 also, but there WLB is presented as an issue of work intensification and elasticity of work. Though acknowledging this, we deal here with a broader range of theoretical issues and models to further explicate the concept.

In contrast to models which assumed the *compartmentalisation* or *segmentation* of the home and work domains, Kanter (1977: 8) queried the 'myth of separate worlds' for home and family. The interactions of these domains have since been characterised by *compensation*, *spillover* and *conflict* theories:

- *Compensation theory* (see Staines, 1980) – assumes an inverse relationship between work and home life whereby disappointment or deprivation in one domain is compensated for by increased involvement in the other domain and/or in pursuing desirable experiences in the other, for example sports and hobbies outside work.

- *Spillover theory* (see Staines, 1980) – emphasises the similarities between domains and that factors in one domain 'spill over' into related areas in the other with either positive or negative effects, for example insecurity at work leading to anxiety at home. The congruence model though examining similar positive and negative relationships asserts that intervening variables such as genetics, personality, culture and behavioural styles are responsible for the apparent spillover.
- *Work-family conflict theories* – these relate mainly to role-based stressors (see Role Stress above), especially inter-role conflict as identified by Kahn and colleagues (1964). Conflict theories assume that personal resources are both scarce and fixed and that multiple roles and time conflicts from home and work will impair individual well-being.

The common factor here is the way that these theories address workfamily, work–life and work–home issues,that is, there is a prevailing assumption of a unidirectional influence of work to home, most especially in conflict theories. In addition there is an assumption that the influence is inherently of a negative nature and that work–home relations embody a gender bias mainly disadvantaging women, with the further implication that work–home relations are conducted among traditional nuclear families. The real issue here is one of the boundaries between work and home and the status and quality of the relationships enacted within those boundaries. Essentially these theories are still subsets of the transactional model (Lazarus and Folkman, above), which emphasise work to home relationships over the bi-directional nature of stress in the transactional model. Modern developments of the model see the domains of stress as outlined in Figure 23.2.

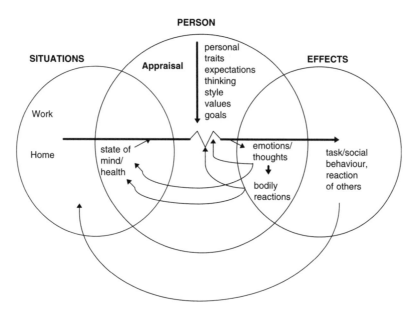

Figure 23.2 **A transactional model of stress**

Source: A. Ostell (1996), 'Managing Stress at Work' in C. Molander (ed.), *Human Resources at Work*, London: Chartwell-Bratt, with permission.

Here work and home are themselves subsets of the situational domain and felt strain in relationships experienced at work and home (e.g. married vs. unmarried; children vs. no children; level of social support, etc.) are mediated by feedback both internal and external to the person. Setting boundaries between work and home life has proved to be an increasingly difficult problem, Hochschild (1997) noting the *time blind* paradox where people spent more time at work to escape from the tensions caused at home by long working hours. In face of job insecurity and the erosion of employment protection and sickness benefits in the UK and US in recent years this problem has moved on to the extent that the term *presenteeism*, originally used in General Motor's 1980s Saturn project (Lawrence, 1985) to indicate a desire or motivation to go to work that needed to be rewarded, has by now come to mean going to work when one is not fit for duty (see Lewis and Cooper, 1996). Unfit workers can in turn spread illness to others, Goetzel and colleagues (2004) estimating that presenteeism actually costs the US economy more than absenteeism. Presenteeism, which is akin to Sturdy's (1987) notion of *shifting*, entails employees needing to be seen to prioritise work to get ahead (Simpson, 2000; R. Taylor, 2002) and to cope with increased workloads (Kodz *et al.*, 2002), Cooper (1994) linking the phenomenon to insecurity, job loss and coming into work when sick. At the same time though, as we note in Chapter 10, 'men used their additional capacity or willingness to stay late as a competitive weapon, recolonising management for themselves and criticising women who left "early"' (Simpson, 1998).

The problem of actually achieving a work-life balance for the individual employee is to a great extent the problem of being able to make choices (see Clutterbuck, 2003) about the allocation of time and effort and of course this is precisely what is being lost in many modern working environments. In the family domain, though arguing that there are few models showing how individuals successfully manage work–family conflict, Weise (2000) has found that childless couples using life-management strategies based on Baltes and colleagues (1999) *Selection, Optimisation* and *Compensation* (SOC) model, 'experienced lower work-family conflict' (reported in Weise *et al.*, 2002: 322–3):

> the SOC model postulates that *selection* (i.e., developing, elaborating, and committing oneself to personal goals) provides the basis for focusing resources on a delineated number of life domains in which to achieve one's goals (*optimization*; i.e., the acquisition, refinement, and application of goal-relevant skills or resources) or in which to maintain one's goals in the face of losses in goal-relevant means (i.e., *compensation*). (See Weise *et al.*, 2002: 322, or Lerner, 2001: 2, 24)

So while individuals and families can ameliorate stress through rigorous planning and decision-making activities, structural interventions such as the European Employment Strategy and Working Time Regulations vie with a situation where most families have parents working outside the home, greater numbers of women with young children are in work and the population in general is ageing with more people of working age caring for elderly or disabled relatives (see Chapter 14 for more on these issues with regard to the labour market). The answer, according to the stakeholders in the problem such as government, employers and the CIPD, is found in promoting 'family-friendly' policies such as flexible working hours and working from home, the CIPD (2004) reporting that flexible working hours are now offered by some 50 per cent of UK companies while 20 per cent of firms offer the ability to work from home. The problem with these broad figures though is reflected in the 2005 ACAS report on flexible working and work-life balance where they report that:

- Flexitime is mostly used for office-based staff below managerial level in the public sector and private sector service organisations
  - manufacturing companies are less likely to operate flexitime

- Flexitime arrangements are rare for:
  - shift workers –
    - e.g. newspaper production, public utilities, hospital and emergency services
    - shift working has spread to industries such as telephone sales and banking
- senior managers. (ACAS, 2005: 4, 15)

Other forms of flexible working such as job-sharing and compressed working weeks are available to some workers and of course there is the 'flexibility' of part-time (particularly for women), temporary and casual working which allows workers in manual and low-level service grades to exert some choice in working hours. Active against this is the spread of on-call working from the traditional areas of shift-working to support staff in the service sector. Eikhof and colleagues (2007: 327) conclude that flexible working hours schemes are offered by employers as work-life balance initiatives to allow them to appear employee-friendly while meeting business needs.

As regards working from home the figures are again blurred by categories such as teleworkers and mobile workers:

- Teleworkers spend all or part of their working week at a location remote from employers' workplaces
- Traditional mobile workers, for example sales representatives and delivery drivers, receive instructions and information via telephones, computers or fax machines at home or in their vehicles
- Managerial and professional staff spend working days away from their office base and also communicate via telephones, computers or fax machines from their home, car or other remote location
- Specialists or office support staff who carry out a range of duties from home or other remote locations and communicate via telephones, fax machines and computers. (ACAS, 2005: 24)

Likewise working from home is not an option for some categories of work or workers (e.g. carers or cleaners) and in relation to the rationale for homeworking Felstead and colleagues (2001: 29), based on the 1998 WERS (see Chapter 15) data, note that:

> despite the rhetoric, there is little evidence to suggest that the entitlement to work at home is associated with a more enlightened management attitude to work-life balance since such attitudes have little bearing on whether or not establishments offer this particular employment option.

For managers in particular the rhetoric of government initiatives such as 'Health Work and Well-being' are offset by continued exhortations along the lines of, 'So you'd like to know how to squeeze an extra hour out of a day? Wish you could master the art of being in two places at once?' (http://howdoyou. managers.org.uk), which act to reinforce the unidirectional nature of work–home relations via self-monitoring. Rana and Higginbottom (2002), for example, note the fear of possible damage to career prospects resulting from taking flexible work options.

As we noted earlier in this section we must not, in studying stress at work, forget the person who feels the strain created both in physical and emotional terms. Fineman claims that though organisations can be seen as 'emotional arenas', the persons within them are presented as 'emotionally anorexic', their emotions reduced to managerial control variables (see Table 23.1), 'the feelings of *being* organised, *doing* work and organising are hard to detect' (1993: 9). At the same time he asserts that stress has 'come out' as an issue, in that counselling is provided at least by some and also that there is a tacit acknowledgement that 'being sick or off work for reasons of stress is acceptable – up to a point' (1993: 219).

Table 23.1 **Translating affective terms**

Terms used in research	Formal definition	Colloquial terms
Affect	Umbrella a term encompassing a broad range of feelings that individuals experience, including feeling states, such as moods and discrete emotions, and traits, such as trait positive and negative affectivity (all defined below).	"I feel…" "She seems to be feeling…" "He is usually unemotional…"
Discrete Emotions	Emotions are focused on a specific target or cause – generally realized by the perceiver of the emotion; relatively intense and very short-lived. After initial intensity, can sometimes transform into a mood.	For example, love, anger, hate, fear, jealousy, happiness, sadness, grief, rage, aggravation, ecstasy, affection, joy, envy, fright, etc.
Moods	Generally take the form of a global positive (pleasant) or negative (unpleasant) feeling; tend to be diffuse – not focused on a specific cause – and often not realized by the perceiver of the mood; medium duration (from a few moments to as long as a few weeks or more).	Feeling good, bad, negative, positive, cheerful, down, pleasant, irritable, etc.
Dispositional (Trait) Affect	Overall personality tendency to respond to situations in stable, predictable ways. A person's "affective lens" on the world.	"No matter what, he's always _____." "She tends to be in a _____ mood all the time." "He is always so negative."
a) (Trait) Positive Affectivity	Individuals who tend to be cheerful and energetic, and who experience positive moods, such as pleasure or well-being, across a variety of situations as compared to people who tend to be low energy and sluggish or melancholy.	"She's always so energetic and upbeat!" "He's such a downer all the time!"
b) (Trait) Negative Affectivity	Individuals who tend to be distressed and upset, and have a negative view of self over time and across situations, as compared to people who are more calm, serene and relaxed.	"She is always so hostile in her approach." "Why is he always so anxious/nervous?" "I admire his steady calmness and serenity."
Emotional Intelligence	"The ability to monitor one's own and others' feelings and emotions, to discriminate among them, and to use this information to guide one's thinking and actions" (Salovey & Mayer, 1990: 189).	"My manager is terrible at expressing his emotions." "My teammate is great at knowing how everyone else on the team is feeling." "The CEO is brilliant at dealing with her employees' emotions – a real motivator!"

Continued

INTRODUCTION: REGULATING ORGANISATIONAL BEHAVIOUR ▪ PERCEPTION AND ATTITUDES: SEEING WHAT TO THINK ▪ MASKS FOR TASKS: PERSONALITY ▪ LEARNING AND CHANGE ▪ MOTIVATION: THE DRIVE FOR SATISFACTION ▪ LEADERSHIP: MIGHT OR MYTH? ▪

Table 23.1 **Continued**

Terms used in research	Formal definition	Colloquial terms
Emotional Regulation	Individuals' attempts to "influence which emotions they have, when they have them, and how they experience and express these emotions" (Gross, 1998a: 275).	"He handles his emotions really well, even under high pressure situations."
Emotional Labor	Requires an employee to "induce or suppress feeling in order to sustain the outward countenance that produces the proper state of mind in others" (Hochschild, 1983: 7).	She has to put on a smile when dealing with customers, because it's part of the job.
Emotional Contagion	Processes that allow the sharing or transferring of emotions from one individual to other group members; the tendency to mimic the nonverbal behavior of others, to "synchronize facial expressions, vocalizations, postures, and movements" with others, and in turn, to "converge emotionally" (Hatfield, Cacioppo, & Rapson, 1994).	"And when we feel good, it's contagious." (Advertising slogan from Southwest Airlines) "I don't know why, but every time I talk to him I feel really anxious afterwards." "Infectious enthusiasm."
Collective Affect	A "bottom-up" approach to collective affect emphasizes the affective composition of the various affective attributes of the group's members. That is, the degree to which individual level affective characteristics combine, often through emotional contagion, to form group level emotion or mood. A "top-down" approach to collective affect emphasizes the degree to which groups are characterized by emotion norms for feeling and expression.	"Our group has a _____ feel to it." "What a negative group!" "In our group showing positivity is very important."

Source: Reproduced from *Why Does Affect Matter in Organizations?* by Sigal G. Barsade and Donald E. Gibson, Academy of Management Perspectives February 2007, 36–59; http://www-management.wharton.upenn.edu/barsade/docs/Barsade_WhyAffectMattersAOM.pdf, with permission of the authors.

Emotions at work

Acknowledging the interacting emotional impact of work and non-work also means we have to acknowledge emotions themselves, which represent a class of phenomena that were for a long time regarded in OB as simple, attitudinal responses, though today emotions are seen as the key to maintaining work-life balance. Even as emotional or *affective* responses, emotions were only one component of attitudes (see Chapter 18) and often reduced to dichotomised positive vs. negative concepts representing feelings as good or bad, like or dislike, etc. In practical terms they were treated as straightforward mediating factors in variables such as satisfaction/dissatisfaction or at best as personality factors such as emotional stability in the Eysenck scale.

Alongside the resurgence of subjectivity as the 'missing subject' in OT, emotions have enjoyed greatly increased popularity both as a subject of study and object of analysis. Emotions did not, like identity, raise a fundamental problematic in methods and analysis and this has led to emotions being an umbrella concept covering a disparate range of concepts and approaches to their study. As with the study of stress this means that emotions can lack conceptual consistency, a problem which Barsade and Gibson (2007) have tried to address in producing Table 23.1 above which gives formal definitions and examples for 'affective terms'. What Barsade and Gibson do here is first to distinguish between affect, emotions and moods, secondly to delineate emotion as a trait and thirdly to attempt conceptually to separate the main areas of contemporary study of emotions. This latter effort is the most difficult of the three due to the overlap between notions such as emotional labour, regulation and intelligence.

Emotional labour

The psychological pressures on individuals have been well documented, not only in terms of pressures to mould behaviour and identity, but also in terms of the intrapsychic conflicts they can produce. Interpersonal conflicts and conflicts between role expectations are seen as causative factors in producing anxiety, stress and negative affect. The conflicts which fulfilling a role may induce are seen in Hochschild's (1983) notion of *emotional labour*. Hochschild characterises emotional labour as 'a covert resource, like money or knowledge, or physical labour, which companies need to make the job done' (1993: xii; see chaps 10 and 13 for more discussion). This was originally identified in occupations where individuals have to manage their emotions in order to serve the commercial purposes of the enterprise and to produce an appropriate emotional climate for the client. Other writers on emotional labour (see Fineman, 1993) have extended such notions to the full range of behaviour in work organisations and most recently to resistance (see Sturdy and Fineman, 2001 for a comprehensive discussion). It should be noted that emotional labour is about the valorisation of human capital; it is not a 'catch-all' phrase for anything to do with emotions and work (Fineman, 1993). Furthermore, Hochschild does make a differentiation between 'deep' and 'surface' labour, a construct that links emotional labour directly to the questions of identity and impression management discussed in Chapter 25. One possible caveat to the notion that emotional labour produces strain is reported by Barsade and Gibson in that, 'for many workers surface acting does not cause strain, particularly if workers are "faking in good faith" and believe the act they are putting on is a legitimate part of the work role' (2007: 41).

In such situations, where management attempts to mould the social identities of individuals and groups into images consonant with commercial demands, people can become estranged from their own feelings. As an interdependent process, emotional labour requires both the collaboration of the client and the adjustment of personal feelings to accommodate client demands. For the emotional labourer, identification with the job itself can lead to difficulties in making constant adjustments to situations, and considerable socio-emotional costs may be incurred. Work in the 'caring' professions, for example, requires that people identify closely with their work or clients, and also that they exercise self- and emotional control over their role-based work. This may bring them into conflict with the levels of commitment required in their work, in that they have to constrain emotional responses to an extent that has serious consequences for their mental health and social relationships.

In order to respond to conflicts between commitment and capacity to act, people may *burn out*. Storlie (1979) argues that this occurs where the individuals confront an intractable reality that cannot be changed, so that the only effective response is to change themselves. The end result is that they continue to 'go through the motions', but remove any emotional or identity investment they had in their work. This acts as a defence mechanism against the stresses that may result from the conflicts between their own tendencies and their role demands. Emotional labour can thus lead the individual into a removal of emotion, labour being reduced to mere activity. This may have some benefits to the employer, but for the employee such numbing of emotional response leads to a loss of a central source of meaning for them. (See Kunda, 1992: 198–204, for an extended discussion.)

Emotion work and emotional regulation

The control of labour in emotional terms has been explored in a number of case studies in the service sector, including a study of call centre work at Telebank by Callaghan and Thompson (2002). They use a distinction from Bolton (2000) which differentiates between *pecuniary* (according to reward) emotional labour, and *philanthropic* (according to endowment) emotional labour, which they illustrate in Telebank workers as follows: 'At the weekend, on a Saturday, you get old women or men phoning and they just want to talk. It's great, I love getting these calls.'

That such chats require emotional labour is evident, but these emotions are not directly part of the remunerated emotional labour enacted in normal dealings with clients, as in Hochschild's original conception. Rather, they are given as what Bolton terms a gift, which could also be given to others as an 'extra', even in formal organisational interactions. However, at the same time as such giving such emotional gifts, Telebank workers have to be aware of the other forms of labour they perform:

> " I'm quite happy to chat to them, but it's always in the back of your mind, got to watch my average handling time. I think you set a better example for the bank. (Callaghan and Thompson, 2002)

This example serves to illustrate the other two categories of emotional labour that Bolton distinguishes: these are *prescriptive* (according to organisational or professional rules of conduct) and *presentational* (according to general social rules) emotion management, reflecting the demands of the work itself (handling times) and those of the culture that surrounds it (identification with the image of the bank). Bolton observes that 'Hochschild's concept recognises that employees' private emotional systems have been appropriated by management as a renewable resource' (2000: 163), but makes her categorisations on the basis that Hochschild does not recognise emotional labour in the 'unmanaged spaces' in organisations. It is not the nature of emotional labour which changes in Bolton's formulation, but its range and scope in terms of what people have to do to their emotions in order to survive and cope with their work. Philanthropic emotional labour is especially important here, as it illustrates how part of emotion management actually contributes to employees being able to make space for the expression of their own identities, or possibly to just get a breather in the relentlessly computer-paced modern workplace. Overall Bolton produces a unitary conception of emotions which focuses more on the nature of responses and the prescriptive elements of emotional labour whereas more psychological typologies tend to focus more on what people do, that is, its presentational aspects.

A good example is the more utilitarian typology of emotional labour given by Mann (1999) in her discussion of what she terms the 'have a nice day' (HAND) culture endemic in the service sector. The HAND culture is of one what Mann claims are a number of scripted cultures which companies are 'frantically foisting' on their staff and customers (1999: 38). These scripted cultures and their associated display rules are discussed further in Chapter 21. The typology of emotional labour Mann puts forward is based on the work of Briner (1995) and reflects the fact that emotional display in work does not always match our own feelings, nor is it always in line with social and organisational expectations. On this basis emotional labour can be categorised as:

- *Emotional harmony*, where 'displayed emotion is the same as expected emotion and felt emotion'.
- *Emotional dissonance*, where 'displayed emotion is the same as expected emotion but different from felt emotion'.
- *Emotional deviance,* where 'displayed emotion is the same as felt emotion but different from expected emotion'. (Mann, 1999: 68–9)

Of these, *emotional dissonance* is the only area where true emotional labour is involved. In comparison with Bolton, all three of Mann's categories could be classed as pecuniary, whereas only emotional harmony could be philanthropic in organisational terms. Both harmony and dissonance would be both prescriptive and presentational, while emotional deviance would be neither, and might better be classed as a coping mechanism or low-level burnout. Mann has extended her work on emotional labour through the Mann Emotional Requirements Inventory (MERI published by Ward-Dutton), which claims to 'work out how much emotional labour you perform, on average, in your day-to-day working life' (Mann and Ward Dutton, 1999: 115).

Typologies such as Bolton's are trying to understand the boundaries between emotional work and emotional labour, while psychological typologies are more concerned with the broader dynamics of how emotions play out in workplace. What the kind of typologies put forward by Bolton and Mann have in common is that they represent the first step in the process of emotional labour being seen as a necessary skill in employees. As such, it might be operationalised into a technology of regulation to be accredited and appraised alongside all of the other explicit and tacit work skills appropriated as competencies by management and OB practitioners and this has begun to happen with the burgeoning popularity of *emotional intelligence* (see below) as a purportedly measurable competence or ability. The Mann inventory is at present a self-report technique, and we do not yet have to fill in 'emotional development forms' in our appraisals, but Callaghan and Thompson (2002) do give the example of the 'rapport training' given at Telebank which attempts to 'recognise and extract worker emotions'. Such regulation is itself problematic, however:

> The system of work makes building effective rapport difficult, workers are asked to produce both quantity and quality, to combine strength and stamina with emotional labour to deliver 180 second units of 'bubbly personality' one hundred and twenty times a day. (Callaghan and Thompson, 2002)

Even with rapport training, such pressure means that absenteeism is rife and that obtaining two years' work out of an employee is seen as a 'reasonable return on investment' for some call centre operators. Emotional work of whatever form appears to have the same problem of diminishing returns as emotional regulation does, as a mechanism for coping with stress (see section on 'Role stress' above). Under the conditions of work intensification inherent in much modern job design, emotional work has its own Catch-22 in that the more it is required, the more it can become a prelude to burnout. Although we have both emotion and stress management and management by stress and emotion, the difference is that to a large extent organisational concerns with stress are mainly reactive and concerned with the quantity of stress while concerns with emotion are regulatory and concerned with the quality of emotion. The exception to this, where emotions are burned out or expressed in socially unacceptable terms, for example aggression, show the limits of emotional regulation in that when emotions become pathological they are treated in the same manner as stress.

It is clear that emotional labour needs to be distinguished better from and contextualised within the other forms of labour we perform on ourselves and others in pursuit of organisational demands. McHugh (1997) identifies these other forms of managerial work as follows:

- *operational labour* – regulation of behaviour and discipline
- *emotional labour* – regulation of affective responses
- *intellectual labour* – regulation and construction of meanings and symbols
- *dramaturgical labour* – *regulation of impressions* and advocacy (similar to *aesthetic labour*: Nickson *et al.*, 2004)
- *attributional labour* – regulation and ascription of intent and commitment.

These categories need refinement and consideration of whether they apply to self-management in terms of non-managerial work, but they do serve to illustrate that it is not just our emotions that we control in our working lives. The latter two categories in particular are discussed further in Chapter 25, but for now we simply need to note that each of these forms of labour carries its concomitant stressors and contributes to the role conflicts we suffer. Emotional work and regulation each require self-monitoring of both actual and desired emotional states in regard to ourselves and others and the extent to which such monitoring is linked to our perceived social effectiveness is described by work related to emotional intelligence.

Emotional intelligence? – Wellness for the mind

Charles Darwin, in his treatise on the expression of emotion (1872), regarded emotions as equivalent to sensations, the difference being that the former are derived from internal rather than external stimuli. Emotions, in terms of observed facial expressions (i.e. attitudes) and behaviours were reactions to internal states that we did not necessarily have any knowledge of. This behavioural conception of emotion has evolved, like most other concepts in OB, into situationally and behaviourally contingent process models such as that demonstrated in the Salovey and Mayer (1990: 189) definition of emotional intelligence (EI) used (in Table 23.1) by Barsade and Gibson: 'The ability to monitor one's own and others' feelings and emotions, to discriminate among them, and to use this information to guide one's thinking and actions'. This conceptualises EI as a cognitive process and/or skill and is understood in terms of the appraisal, regulation and use of emotions in social settings. What this could also mean is that EI is in fact an emotional analogue or even a special case of *self-monitoring* (Snyder, 1979; 1987; see Chapter 18). Self-monitoring consists of *observing your own behaviours and adapting them to the situation* and if we replace 'behaviours' with 'emotions' in this statement (albeit a simplification of both concepts), we have a fair definition of EI. The only apparent difference, that EI includes the monitoring of others, is false in that being high or low in self-monitoring depends on the tendency to look for behavioural cues by monitoring others (high SM) or by relying on the monitoring of internal cues (low SM). Since Snyder (1979) identifies these cues in SM as including both *affective* states and attitudes we might question why we need a concept such as emotional intelligence in the first place.

The development of EI as a concept shows similarities to the development of concepts in the study of personality and leadership, going from *types>traits>behaviour>style>situation>contingency* in terms of the factors and variables that differing models are characterised by. In this sense EI as distinguished from self-monitoring may simply be an alternative conception of a fundamental concept or process as in the differing conceptions of leadership styles or contingency leadership (see Chapter 22). As such we might expect and do indeed find the same problems with EI as with personality and leadership concepts: trait categories are vague, stereotypical and of dubious reliability and/or validity; the expression of related characteristics or abilities is sensitive to context (see Chapter 19) and only predictable at extremes. Measures, especially self-report 'tests', are susceptible to motivational distortion or faking and liable to be culture-bound and insensitive to individual and situational differences, for example in diverse occupational communities. Even if we consider EI as a process, then monitoring, discriminating between and acting appropriately on our own or others' emotional states and reactions assumes that at some level EI embodies a rational process of categorisation and calculation. This is simply at odds with everyday experience in that generally speaking only false emotions are associated with rational choice, crocodile tears not being authentic emotions. In this sense then, EI is just a form of impression management (see Chapter 25), a concept which in turn is already highly associated with self-monitoring.

Landy (2005) credits Thorndike in the 1920s as originally proposing EI within his construct of social intelligence, even though social intelligence is, once again, a broader concept covering the understanding and management of others. Today the profligate use of such terms as emotional literacy, health, skill, and competency underwrite the vagueness of the concept and debates over the measurability of EI abilities and the predictability of EI traits are unlikely to be satisfactorily resolved when, as Landy argues:

> " It appears that emotional intelligence, as a concept related to occupational success, exists outside the typical scientific domain. Much of the data necessary for demonstrating the unique association between EI and work-related behavior appears to reside in proprietary databases, preventing rigorous tests of the measurement devices or of their unique predictive value. For those reasons, any claims for the value of EI in the work setting cannot be made under the scientific mantle. (2005: 411)

Similarly Zeidner and colleagues (2004: 371) note that with EI, 'the ratio of hyperbole to hard evidence is high, with over-reliance in the literature on expert opinion, anecdote, case studies, and unpublished proprietary surveys' – all of which contribute to the blurring and propagation of definitions and measures.

The confusions over the definition and status of EI stem mainly from there being two major models within which EI research is conducted, the Mayer-Salovey model we cite above is, according to Weinberger (2000: 215), an 'ability-model' while the other, coming from Goleman's highly popular but much criticised 1995 book, is a 'mixed-model', being 'broader and more inclusive'. Ability models restrict EI research to the validation of measurable variables in behavioural rating scales while mixed models are business-oriented and closer to social intelligence. The latter lead to definitions of EI such as, 'the awareness of and ability to manage one's emotions in a healthy and productive manner' (Allpsych Online, see Further Reading) or 'the ability to manage oneself and interact with others in mature and constructive ways' (Kinicki and Kreitner, 2008). We can immediately query why mixed models only conceptualise managing emotions towards positive outcomes when such value judgements flatly contradict the experience of those who have been subjected to the ministrations of bullies, manipulative bosses and their ilk. This dark side of EI is yet to be explored in any systematic fashion but what we can say is that just as conmen are skilled in impression management, bullies, etc. are either exhibiting high *emotional literacy* or at minimum are skilled in utilising *affective scripts* to manage the emotions *and behaviour* of others.

The dual conception of EI in academia and management is common to other concepts we have dealt with. For example, the attraction of mixed models of EI such as Goleman's may be that the social learning of scripts is easier to incorporate into managerial strategy and training than the rational calculation of ability models, much as with the attractions of content over process models in motivation (see Chapter 21). Further, at the same time as saying we can all learn EI, Goleman's conception also exhorts its predictive power (Mayer *et al.*, 2000) much as with Honey and Mumford's reduction of Kolb's Learning Cycle to a set of predictive traits (see Chapter 20), conveniently ignoring the contradiction between EI being represented as both a learned skill and a constellation of relatively fixed personality characteristics.

As we noted above, EI has become part of the process of operationalising emotional work and labour as a necessary skill in employees. Like stress, EI is well on its way to becoming an industry and developing the associated technologies of regulation to underwrite its prescriptive managerial narrative. As with stress and wellness we would expect the topics of *emotional well-being* (EWB) and *emotional balance* (or *emotional work-life balance*) to also become part of the business 'box of tricks' in this area. As research topics they are currently mainly limited to the health and educational psychology literatures, but we are already seeing EWB being linked to attributions of success in career management with the application of the SOC model (see Wiese *et al.*, 2002 above). As to the future, *spiritual intelligence* has its own lively debates among psychologists of religion over whether it is innate and/or measurable and the first stirrings of *ethical intelligence* are easy to find on the web. There are, however, no signs as yet of concepts of spiritual and ethical labour to fully fit them into the labour process, though we keenly look forward to debates over the difference between ethical intelligence and wisdom on one hand and spiritual intelligence and snake oil on the other.

Returning to the notion we introduced earlier of emotion as a component of attitude, we need to remind ourselves that treating emotion as conceptually distinct, measurable and susceptible to conscious manipulation may suffer the same problems as only looking at one component of an attitude – we may overestimate the correlation between attitude/emotion and subsequent behaviour. The implication for emotional management and regulation is that it is harder to succeed at managing emotions than EI proposes. People try to manage their own emotions, but do not always succeed, as most of us know in terms of having 'lost it' to some extent at some time. Likewise trying to manage the emotions of others can be one of the quickest ways to engender hostility and resistance and even being successful at it may still leave us in the position of the emotional blackmailer – using the management of emotions to perpetuate an abusive relationship.

Emotion, stress and control

The psychological and physiological pressures which impinge on us are generally seen these days as being manifested as stress, though in other times and using other terms they have been linked more to notions such as fatigue, anxiety, alienation and even to neurotic and psychotic disorders (see Thompson and McHugh, 2002; chap. 21). In fact, some commentators claim that stress is an artefact (see Briner and Reynolds, 1993 for an introduction to this debate), much in the same way that Seivers (see Chapter 21) claims motivation to be a product of the relations between psychologists and managers. Regardless of its status as a phenomenon, stress-related pressures and the individualisation of attributions of stress mean that we all face normative pressures, not the least of which centre around fitness to work. Such expectations form one basis of what is termed the *psychological contract* (Argyris, 1960; or see Schein, 1980: 22), and act as a form of normative control over the identities we are capable of constructing for ourselves in the workplace and thus are key to understanding how we deal with the pressures of both work and home.

Emotional labour and EI could be viewed as a simple extension of normative control, for example Hughes (2005: 610–11), in examining Goleman's conception of EI noting that 'EI can be understood as part of a broader neo-human relations movement that focuses attention on the emotional conditions of labour', where, 'character becomes a deployable human resource, one that is consumed and developed'. Hughes sees the outcome of this in an 'emotional customer service orientation' involving the 'corporate colonisation (Casey, 1995) of worker subjectivity and affect through the adoption of normative control strategies'. Hughes contrasts the view of EI as part of 'totalizing regimes of organizational domination' effectively subsuming identity and limiting resistance (2005: 614) with the possibility that increasing 'emotional honesty' in the workplace may enable 'new forms of resistance' (2005: 615). The focus here on character in relation to EI follows from the work of Sennett (1998; see Chapter 25 for further discussion):

> Sennett (1998) explores how the era of the post-Fordist flexible workplace has promoted a shift in the outlook of employees. Within this context, he proposes, the arrangement of work promotes an emphasis on short-termism that corrodes trust, loyalty, and genuine commitment. Social bonds in the workplace become weaker as fleeting ties of association have greater utility to employees than more stable and permanent connections.... The personal qualities of 'good work' no longer correspond to the qualities of 'good character'.... Where Sennett understands team-building and adapting to change as root causes of the corrosion of moral character, Goleman views these as fundamentally important talents and abilities crucial to success, as skills to be developed; the stuff of 'star performers' at work. (Hughes, 2005: 606, 607, 608)

EI then has the potential for cementing normative control both through providing appropriate emotional repertoires for adapting individual character to the team environment and through the individual adapting their character to the instrumental goals of the corporate ladder or the portfolio career, in support of their own or their family's lifestyle. However, in terms of work-life balance, the utility of EI to the organisation may also have the potential for creating situations where individuals face increased pressures from trying to be loyal to the organisation, the team, their self and their dependants. The tensions inherent in such circumstances have the potential to add new layers of concerns, contradictions and conflicts to already stressed employees and in terms of having to present different identities to different members of our role-set are also the basis of what Feldman and Klich (1991) term *inauthentic social relations*.

In practice, though EI is mainly a way of selling managers the idea that it is acceptable to directly manipulate people's emotions for instrumental purposes as well as demanding emotional labour from them, it is just what the hard-pressed modern manager thinks they need to do if they are to survive the stresses of their own high-commitment workplace. The manipulation of emotion implied in EI is simply another persuasive technique in the wider project of mobilising behaviour and consent in ourselves and others. As to the personal growth aspects of EI, as with our comments on wisdom above, it is about what is acting intelligently in the given circumstances and in the case of EI it is collaborating in managing your own and other's emotions in pursuit of corporate strategy.

Summary and key points

The problem with all forms of role-based stress as explanatory concepts is that they have the effect of portraying the phenomenon as natural and individually based, instead of a product of the historically produced conditions of work. Identities can, then, be reactively moulded as a coping response to situational stress factors, and in directions that reproduce the experience of subordination and domination in work in ourselves and others. The implications here are that in order for any stress 'management' programme to succeed, it has to change both attitudes and cultural factors in the workplace and become part of managerial strategies for moulding the identities of workers. It does appear that material on the moulding of identities in organisations tends to focus on professional, skilled and managerial workers. However, such concepts as emotional labour and the utility of 'wellness programmes' would indicate that organisations may routinely attempt to mould the identities of all levels of employees. At the same the kind of approaches coming from the Labour Research Department and the advent of MAPs do offer some hope that stress can be managed for the individual as well as the organisation.

If the negative consequences of stress are our bodies' way of telling us to slow down, then stress management is the organisation's way of telling us to keep up. Just as health and safety legislation recognises the concept of 'contributory negligence' in attributing the blame for accidents, stress management communicates the nature of power relations in the workplace by bringing home to us our negligence in not being 'fit for work'. This phenomenon now seems to extend to how well we fit our emotions to our occupational roles and identities, and we may be left with the view that work is just plain unhealthy in physiological and emotional terms. As such, we are probably as guilty as the mainstream literature in ignoring the eustress aspect of the stress paradigm in our lack of emphasis on positive arousal and feelings.

It is true that work can be a joy, but that is usually when our intellect and emotions are fully engaged in 'learning the ropes' of work that is rewarding in personal or material terms. Once anything becomes a chore, in that it is both unpleasant and compulsory, then the only 'eustressors' available to us may be based more in misbehaviour and bloody-minded resistance to control than in the work we once loved.

If stress and emotion are often treated reactively in organisations the area we move to next is possibly the one in which organisations have most aggressively pursued the use of OB knowledge in recent years. In the next chapter then, we explore the regulation of organisational behaviour through the nature and dynamics of *groups* or, to be more in line with modern usage, through *teams*.

Further reading

Regarding stress, if advice is what is wanted then the HSE and LRD produce excellent materials. OB texts tend to be fairly similar once again though the historical treatments in Cooper and Dewe (2004) and Jones and colleagues (2001) are both readable and comprehensive. On emotions the Barsade and Gibson paper we cite is a good antidote to a lot of the loosely conceptualised emotions-at-work literature, while the best advice on emotional intelligence is simply to avoid anything related to Goleman's work. Jack Mayer's annotated bibliography is a good guide to the development of the concept and has an entry on spiritual intelligence.

Allpsych Online, 'Emotional Intelligence'. http://allpsych.com/dictionary/dictionary2.html (27.10.09).

Barsade S. G. and Gibson, D. E. (2007) 'Why Does Affect Matter in Organizations?', *Academy of Management Perspectives*, February, 36–59. Available at: http://www-management.wharton.upenn.edu/barsade/docs/Barsade_WhyAffectMattersAOM.pdf.

Cooper, C. and Dewe, P. (2004) *Stress: A Brief History*, Oxford: Blackwell.

Jones, F., Bright, J. and Clow, A. (2001) *Stress: Myth, Research and Theory*, Harlow: Pearson Education.

Labour Research Department (2006) *Stress at Work*, LRD Booklets, April. Also see: http://www.lrd.org.uk/index.php

Mayer, J., Annotated bibliography on EI. Available at http://eqi.org/mayer.htm.

The Health and Safety Executive on stress at http://www.hse.gov.uk/stress/

368 23

INTRODUCTION: REGULATING ORGANISATIONAL BEHAVIOUR ▪ PERCEPTION AND ATTITUDES: SEEING WHAT TO THINK ▪ MASKS FOR TASKS: PERSONALITY ▪ LEARNING AND CHANGE ▪ MOTIVATION: THE DRIVE FOR SATISFACTION ▪ LEADERSHIP: MIGHT OR MYTH? ▪

24 from groups to teams

> In individuals, insanity is rare; but in groups, parties, nations, and epochs it is the rule. (Friedrich Nietzsche, *Beyond Good and Evil*, 1844–1900)

As we saw in Chapters 15, teams are at the forefront of contemporary work reform. Some of the management writers and organisational psychologists who once wrote about groups have now dusted down their material and applied it to teams, along with the possibility of reproducing the kind of difficulties Nietzsche alluded to. This chapter seeks to outline and evaluate that journey, considering the traditional behavioural literature on groups, before looking at the extent to which the equivalent writings on teamwork adds to, distracts from or distorts it.

The aims of this chapter are to:

- examine how the conception and definition of groups can produce false distinctions of their nature.
- give an account of how the processes of group formation and composition contribute to organisational socialisation and the effects of cohesiveness and polarisation on this process.
- show how groups and networks actively transform the identities of members and the impact of this on group resistance and conflict.
- locate and explain the importance of teamworking in re-engaging worker commitment.
- demonstrate how groups and teams are conflated in the HRM literature to produce false assumptions of mutuality and homogeneous commitment.

The authority of the group

Groups are defined in terms that vary according to the aspects of the topic that are being studied. However, a composite definition could describe a group as 'a collection or coalition of people who interact meaningfully in the pursuit of common goals or objectives and who have at least a tacit sense of agreed standards, values and common identity' (based on Schein, 1965, and Drake and Smith, 1973). Groups are often referred to as the 'building blocks' of organisations and are studied in terms of the roles and associated norms generated within them, their role and communication structures, their interpersonal dynamics and their relations to other organisational coalitions and interest groups. We live out much of our existence in the contexts of varying coalitions to which we are attached for a purpose, whether this is by individual design, accident or external determination. Groups in this sense are social and interpersonal tools, or even possibly technologies of action through which we achieve ends that are beyond our perceptions of personal power. At the same time, our activities are circumscribed by, and directed towards, whatever goals or ends the group exists to serve.

Defining groups

In organisations, groups tend to be formed around the divisions and stratifications inherent in structural and or social processes. Thus they can arise around and within sectional, divisional and hierarchical boundaries, and also out of the interactions of groups of peers, workmates or social interests. Any individual is likely to have allegiance to any number of such groups at the same time, even though they might not actually consider themselves to be a member of any particular group. In the same way our allegiances may change and shift without this registering in a conscious fashion. Numerous typologies of groups are in use, which classify them, for example, as *membership, affiliation* or *interest, formal* or *informal*. More useful classifications for the study of groups in the workplace examine them on the basis of levels of *skill* and *interaction*, closeness/type of *relationships*, and the levels of *control* the group has over factors such as *methods and pace of work, membership* and *adherence to norms*. The various typologies of groups are often used very loosely in the organisational literature and even more so in the HRM literature, which often assumes global effects of group membership that are not always true of all types of group. For example, typologies which give groups as *task* (sometimes *project*), *team and command* (sometimes *technological*) can be interpreted as classifying groups according to the levels of control that the group itself has over the factors given above. Task groups would have high levels of control and latitude for decision-making, command groups little or none.

Though the distinction between formal and informal groups is well-rehearsed in the literature, it is false in the sense that even the most rigidly constituted formal groups still have informal processes surrounding the interactions of members both within and without the group. By the same token, even loose informal coalitions have their behaviour formally constrained to some extent by evaluative standards such as norms. In reality this distinction should be restricted to whether the group has been formally or informally constituted and to levels of control as above. Hollway (1991: 70–1), for example, notes that the focus on the informal group in Mayo's Hawthorne studies did not lead to practices based on the informal interactions of friendship or social affiliation, but rather to the genesis of the training group, 'temporarily constituted of strangers in isolation and permanently under the control of the trainer' (1991: 71). Likewise, distinctions based on the closeness and type of relationships in the group, normally given as *primary* or *secondary* groups, are again misleading. The closer, mainly face-to-face interaction of primary groups such as families, teams or groups of colleagues working on a task is not of necessity any more influential than the more distant and impersonal secondary group such as a company, union, professional association or a public institution. There are certainly more opportunities for influence to be effective in the primary group, but secondary groups very often act as *reference groups*. These we use as a source of personal or group standards or as a basis for comparison; they can be significant in determining the social and organisational roles that we aspire to or are constrained by. As such, they may have greater effects on our individual norms or values than the groups to which we presently belong, and even be a source of conflict between our values and such groups.

Of particular importance within organisations are what Alderfer and Smith (1982) refer to as *identity groups*. These are a special case of interest groups that can cut across sectional and hierarchical divisions and generally originate outside organisational boundaries. In fact they can often be organisations themselves, professional associations, pressure groups and most notably unions. When they form a significant source of norms and values they can exert considerable influence on workplace attitudes and behaviour, often in a fashion counter to organisational objectives. As such, it is possible to see much of the culture/HRM movements of recent years as an attempt to undermine the influence of external identity groups and to shift the focus of reference back towards the employing organisation.

Group formation and composition

In terms of the definitions given above, a given collection of people is not immediately a group, and the process of group formation and maturation is seen as important in determining the eventual role relationships and the performance effectiveness of the group. The most often-cited model of group formation is Tuckman's (1965), in which four stages of *forming, storming, norming* and *performing* lead to effective teamwork; a fifth stage, *adjourning,* was added to cover temporary groups and committees (1977). This model has been adapted by Wanous and colleagues (see Cherrington, 1989: 390–2) to relate it to Feldman's notions on organisational socialisation as shown in Figure 24.1.

What this work establishes is that *group roles are a function of group processes* and are not necessarily dependent on the personalities of specific group members and though essentially a linear, sequential model, in practice groups may slip back to previous stages or cycle through the process repeatedly. As indicated in Chapter 22 on leadership, structural differentiation in groups was recognised as far back as Benne and Sheats' (1948) work on group roles which established not just the group-maintenance and task-maintenance roles implicated in leadership acts but also *self-centred* roles (see Table 24.1 below) involving acts which could actively hamper group development, pushing a group back into confrontation and conflict.

Many groups, of course, never actually reach the mature, collaborative stage, many groups falling apart in the earlier stages. Business students should be familiar with this as most of them will at some point have to deal with a case study where a mature group is disrupted by a new member or shift in circumstances. Further to this, if group cohesion (see 'Group cohesiveness and polarisation' below) does not develop, then the attractiveness of other social attachments might undermine the commitment of members to the purpose or task of the group. The command group described above has obvious barriers to ever being able to develop into the final stages owing to its formalised communication hierarchy. The way in which new members of organisations (for example, first-year students) may form many group attachments before finally settling into a particular friendship group illustrates how competition for particular group roles may lead prospective members to abandon the group rather than take up a role they are not prepared to play. Poole (1981; 1983a, b) has produced a less linear, *Multiple Sequence Model* of small group development which deals with the substance of interpersonal relations in groups by examining how groups shift between goal-directed processes (the *Task Track*), the current focus of activity or discussion

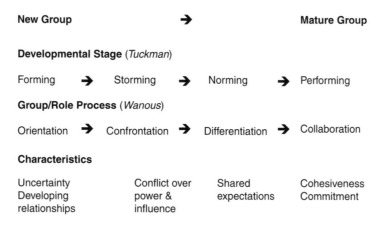

Figure 24.1 **Group development process**

Sources: Based on Robbins (1991: 276–8) and D. J. Cherrington (1989: 390–2).

Table 24.1   ***Benne and Sheats' Group Roles***

Group Task Roles
Coordinator
Orienter-summarizer
Evaluator-critic
Secretary-recorder

Group Building & Maintenance Roles
Supporter-encourager
Tension-releaser
Harmonizer
Compromiser
Standard setter

Self-Centered Roles
Blocker
Aggressor
Recognition seeker
Deserter
Dominator
Clown
Confessor

(*Topic Track*) and interpersonal relationships among group members (*Relation Track*). These three inter-dependent tracks, or *threads,* intertwine and interlock, shifting activities and attention between tracks and sometimes achieving a consensus on all three that unifies their efforts. Significantly Poole's model acknowledges the importance of *breakpoints* in shifting between tracks or from delays and disruptions as crucial in allowing a group to reflect on and possibly to redefine relationships, goals and tasks.

If individuals are to maintain group membership through the vagaries of stages, tracks and competing affiliations the group must exhibit some utility to the individual which Schein (1985: 150–2) identifies as rooted in their socio-psychological 'functions'. Thus they act to provide a sense of belonging and identity, affiliation with others, guidelines for behaviour, and as a possible means for altering the formal struc-tures of an organisation to suit group members better. An example of this is seen in Nichol and Beynon's (1977) 'Chemco' study (see Chapter 21) where a formal job rotation system was introduced under a job enrichment programme which only allowed workers to move from one routine job to another. Yet the workgroups had already organised an informal job rotation system which allowed members to rest while others covered for them.

The fact that the internal dynamics of groups impact on their effectiveness has led to group *composition* receiving a great deal of attention in management development circles. At its most basic this is reflected in the level of *homogeneity* vs. *heterogeneity* in groups (or *similarity* vs. *dissimilarity* of group members). More heterogeneous groups are assumed to be more effective due to the diverse range of abilities and information available to the group, but this comes at the cost of greater opportunities for in-group con-flict. Models of group and more especially of *team* (see *Groups vs. Teams* below) effectiveness have become increasingly complex in terms of the numbers of factors and variables they take into account (e.g. see

Hackman, 1987; or Salas *et al.*, 1992) and focus mainly on interactions of individual, group and task characteristics. The concern for composition, especially in relation to the skills necessary to produce a *balanced* team, has produced some of the most overtly manipulative technologies of regulation in the organisational behaviour (OB) bag of tricks. Best known are the Belbin *Self-Perception Inventory* (1981) and its typology of personality-based team roles, and the Margerison and McCann *Team Management Wheel* (1986), which links team roles to job functions. (See Furnham, 1997: 456–61, or McKenna, 2000: 341–7, for extended discussions.) Both of these have limited reliability and validity as tests, and the Belbin inventory in particular has attracted extensive criticism, not least because it is based 'on data obtained from training courses run for senior management' (Hosking and Morley, 1991: 197). According to Hosking and Morley (1991: 199) and Furnham (1997: 458), Belbin's work does, however, establish the importance of the leadership role, creativity, support for group members and open communication in effective teams. Hosking and Morley further note that 'Belbin's theory is most useful when firms lack systematic working procedures and rely too heavily on informal methods of communication' (1991: 199). At the same time, the contradictory nature of using inductively derived personality constructs to develop processes dependent on group interaction rather than individual characteristics (as noted above) is not acknowledged by users of the Belbin typology. This, along with difficulties in matching individuals to required roles (see McKenna, 2000: 345) is why this 'would be' technology of regulation is difficult to use outside training sessions and is mainly useful as a heuristic device for scripting managerial behaviour.

Group socialisation

Groups can also be highly effective mechanisms for making out, and directly instrumental for their member's capacity to control the wage–effort bargain, as research such as Burawoy's (1979) study shows. On the other hand, however, groups also have formal, instrumental functions for organisations as a whole, and by implication for the dominant power groupings within them. In this sense they are the basis for the distribution of work, the units of monitoring, control and data collection and an integral part of many organisational decision-making processes (Schein, 1985: 149–50). Groups and looser coalitions are also the arenas within which individuals secure identities, and of management attempts to regulate them. As identity groups, such as trade unions, professional or employers' associations, they set the contexts within which individuals and smaller groups compete for power over the structures and processes of organisations and for access to the material and psychic rewards they can supply.

In terms of making out, groups can also be viewed as sites of socialisation and as a major venue of attitudinal change, as indicated by Lewin's (1956) experimental research showing the greater impetus to attitude change in group versus individual techniques. The constructs that are of greater salience to individual meaning and social definition based on class, race, gender, or religion are communicated to us through the behaviours and beliefs we internalise (see Chapter 19) by participating in groups. The processes of socialisation through which the appropriate behaviours an organisation demands are developed are dependent on the operation of intra-group processes for their effectiveness. Thus individuals entering an organisation become attached, or are assigned, to particular groups, wherein they 'learn the ropes' of how to survive and what is expected of them. As direct influence and hierarchical control is a possible source of threat to identity, it is possible that such moulding into appropriate images could better be pursued through the influence of peers. This can be seen clearly from the examples of use of peer-group pressures as a form of social control in Japanese management techniques. Similarly, when using the 'sitting with Nellie' approach to job training, companies would be foolish not to ensure that 'Nellie' is someone whose own workplace identity is at least roughly compliant with managerial objectives.

Group cohesiveness and polarisation

The extent to which we are influenced or affected by the particular groups to which we belong is generally seen to be associated with the relative *cohesiveness* of different groups. Cohesiveness is both a function and consequence of the individual's attraction to a group. The motivation to remain a member stems from the individual's subjective expectations concerning the personal, social or material rewards to be gained, mediated by factors related to group composition, context and processes such as those shown in the simple table below.

Factors increasing cohesiveness	Factors decreasing cohesiveness
Homogeneity of members	Heterogeneity and clique formation
Agreement on group goals	Focus on individual goals
Limited group size	Increasing size of group
High level of in-group interaction	Lack of in-group communication
Isolation from out-groups	Interaction with out-groups
Inter-group competition	Intra-group competition
High levels of participation	High levels of coercion
Group rewards	Individual rewards

In addition to the above, practices such as initiations and group rituals can increase cohesiveness, as can contextual factors such as external threats to the group. The benefits of high cohesiveness are that it is assumed to increase levels of involvement, satisfaction and compliance with group goals while lowering absenteeism and turnover, though importantly cohesiveness is not necessarily seen to increase productivity or performance. For example, increased compliance with group goals does not mean that the group will be more compliant with organisational goals, much as with our comments on formal and informal groups above. Neither are the assumed benefits of cohesiveness unilateral since groups will also vary in relation to their norms regarding performance, self-esteem or status, groups with high norms reacting differently from groups low on these factors. Performance norms may in fact produce cohesiveness as a feedback effect, group cohesion developing as a consequence of the perceived success and effectiveness of high performance or productivity in groups. There is also no necessity that we have to calculate differential attractiveness and available rewards rationally, as we may become members of various groups simply as a result of following appropriate scripts for making out in various social situations. Calculations of advantage and disadvantage may only actually apply when we become self-reflexive about our membership of a particular group. Most of the time we will probably construct a social identity in line with the identity of the group, on the basis that it is appropriate to the behaviours the group carries out. When a group becomes something to cope with, rather than something that helps us to cope, we may reflect on the possibilities we have of rejecting one group membership for another. Alternatively we may try to redefine our own position in the group and thus our own identity within it, or even attempt to redirect the group itself and thus reconstruct group identity in line with our own interests.

A useful distinction is made by Janis (1972; see Hosking and Morley, 1991: 106–7 for a discussion) between *interpersonal* versus *task-based* cohesiveness, which respectively can produce an 'illusion of unanimity' among group members and feelings of commitment to task-based norms. High interpersonal cohesiveness may lead to people suppressing personal doubts and bowing to group consensus through self-censorship, high task-based cohesiveness to selective perception, and convergent thinking, especially in conditions where openness of expression is not encouraged. These are the kind of conditions under which Janis' (1972) notion of *Groupthink* occurs, where moral judgement and 'reality testing' (sometimes 'reality checking') are suspended, particularly in the face of high-risk decisions in high-status groups. Groupthink is said to be more likely in socially insulated, homogenous groups with dominant leadership and under high-stress conditions of possible failure and threats to self-esteem. A group in this situation is assumed to exercise self-censorship, producing an illusion of unanimity or invulnerability that leads to the stereotyping of and even moral crusades against out-groups. A good example of this was the decision of the Thatcher Government to prosecute in the 'Spycatcher' book affair, where concerns for secrecy and solidarity outweighed the opinion of the rest of the world that it could not win the case. The Challenger space shuttle disaster is another well-documented classic example (see Corbett, 1994) and the rhetoric behind the Bush administration's 'war on terror' coupled with the decisions to invade Iraq show just how serious the consequences of groupthink can be.

Groupthink is said to be a special case of Moscovici and Zavalloni's (1969) notion of *group polarisation*, where social comparison processes and persuasive arguments can lead to groups shifting towards higher risk or more caution in decision-making discussions. Haslam (2000: 149–55) provides an excellent overview of research in this area which queries the extent to which polarisation effects are universal and rooted in individuals rather than being the social products of particular groups. Further, an analysis from the social identity approach leads Haslam to agree with Fuller and Aldag (1998) that 'groupthink' as a concept has led to serious limitations in research on group-decision making. Coined by Janis to utilise the Orwellian metaphor of 'doublethink', groupthink applies a negative spin to psychological processes within groups, which can, according to Haslam (2000: 177):

- be psychologically efficient and creative
- be grounded in group members' social reality
- have the potential to be socially enriching.

Hosking and Morley (1991: 100–12) provide further insights into the relation between individual and group coping and group context, learning and cohesion. In a discussion of Janis and Mann's (1977) conflict, commitment and choice model in decision-making processes, they too conclude that psychological processes are not necessarily negative in their effects:

> Fortunately the process is not inevitable. ... If a cohesive group has norms and working procedures which require a 'primary commitment to open-minded scrutiny of new evidence and a willingness to admit errors' the tendency to cling to unsuccessful policies may be replaced by 'a careful reappraisal of the wisdom of past judgements'. (Hosking and Morley, 1991: 111, citing Janis and Mann, 1977: 18)

Much as stereotypes have a negative image but a vital psychological function, polarisation effects may have a vital part to play in all group-decision processes and may not be universally negative for group members or the wider organisation. Regardless of this, the perceived dangers posed by such effects to the efficacy of group decision-making (see Chapter 20) have prompted a great deal of research on methods to avoid them and to make decision processes more effective. The techniques evolved include classics such as brainstorming, the 'Delphi' technique, the use of 'devil's advocates' and even 'dialectical inquiry' (Sweiger *et al.*, 1986). Whether such techniques produce more creative or effective decisions is a moot point; their effect, however, is less ambiguous. What they are aimed at, along with the teamworking initiatives discussed below, is the translation of interpersonal into task-based cohesiveness, much as motivational techniques attempt to translate extrinsic into intrinsic factors (see Chapter 21). It would appear that from the point of view of organisational effectiveness, the interpersonal and political processes taking place in groups can become too powerful. The decision-making capacities they are often employed for may need to be restrained lest they lose sight of the 'common good' of the enterprise. It seems possible, then, that it is the efforts we make to adapt to the groups to which we belong that in the end make organisation and organisations possible. Further, the strength of group effects themselves has a role in the construction of the organisational 'need' for regulation and discipline.

Networking and group identity

The consequences for the individual of not adapting to the authority of the group can lie in physical or social sanctions from the group itself and/or in increased feelings of stress and anxiety. At the same time, just as group polarisation might produce positive effects, individuals can use groups actively to transform their personal and social identities. For example, the reflexiveness involved in raising consciousness of disadvantage in social groups can be the spur for responses to pressures that direct the use of groups as technologies of action. Thus interest groups can actively promote not only the material interests of members, but also their development of positive identities as mechanisms for making out. The patriarchal nature of power relations in organisations were contested throughout industry, commerce and the professions in the 1980s by women's groups that relied on their own systems of *networking* to counter the male cliques who controlled their destinies.

Such networks provided forums for ideas and information and heightened awareness of the position of women in organisations. Their capacity for social transformation was dependent not only on the extent and nature of the contacts they built up, but also on the extent to which they empowered women to develop strong individual and group identities. On this basis, such groups are often more than promotional or defensive interest groups, in that they act to foster the recognition and self-development of the capacities of all women. 'Our purpose is to help women to develop their potential – not to foster elitism' (North-West Women into Management, 1987).

The recognition of group identity by members and those outside group boundaries will be a major determinant of the kinds of responses groups can make to threats to their identity. In addition, the social components of our identities are highly dependent on the meanings we ascribe to objects, persons and events, and which we assimilate through our interaction with and accommodation to 'reference persons and groups' whose behaviour and attitudes have particular 'salience' for us. The importance of groups, according to Hosking and Morley, lies in the fact that 'social actions are inherently ambiguous' (1991: 98), and what we get from such persons and groups are systems of evaluative belief including attitudes and ideologies which:

> focus our attention on the need to justify our actions, so that they appear reasonable to members of our reference groups. This would generate modes of behaviour that are more consistent, more selective, and more characteristic of the person considered as a member of that group. (Hosking and Morley, 1991: 98)

The better-defined the identity of a group, the greater the value of the group to its members as a source of social support, comparison and evaluation. The more effective these processes are, the greater the range of external pressures which can be perceived as affecting the group, and thus the more likely that some kind of collective response will be demanded. Haslam (2000: 305) notes that 'identification with a group increases an individual's sensitivity to injustices against it'. Likewise, the stronger the identity of a particular group, the more the likelihood of other competing groups perceiving its members and their actions as sources of threat, and thus the more likely that competitors will take action which once more demands some form of response.

An important factor is the extent to which group identity is constructed around a salient and coherent set of values: for example, common instrumental strategies for maximising extrinsic rewards or the needs and desires of group members for affiliation and interaction. This is most visible in the contestation over control of the labour process between management and workers, but that conflict is also manifested within intergroup relations. Thompson and Bannon (1985) showed that the instrumental and anti-authoritarian attitudes of the better-paid 'high-flying' groups in their case study of telecommunications workers caused friction not only with management, but with lowly-rewarded and traditional craft workgroups. Each group identity was strengthened by the conflict, and the prime target of resentment was more often other workgroups, rather than management. Individual identities can of course suffer in intergroup struggles, but this is a measure of the extent to which group membership provides powerful means of resisting pressures from outside. The pressure to conform can outweigh the pressure to secure oneself against uncertainty and damage. Brown confirms the above example, arguing that intergroup conflicts act to strengthen group and intra-group identities, and when groups do resist management, 'the psychological satisfactions an individual may gain from his group membership may be more potent than the rewards (or threats) the management can hold out' (1980: 167). For management, the problem of how to disrupt, short-circuit or redirect group identities is central for securing organisation goals, mobilising consent, exerting influence and promoting 'motivation' and organisationally directed goals.

Group resistance and conflict

Group resistance needs to be considered in relation to groups as sites of socialisation and as technologies of action. Group reactions are often along the same lines as those available to individuals, but with the added facility of being able to join in cohesive coalitions where group identity can be secured or enhanced. Of course at the same time as such responses can enable us, they can also be utilised as the basis for managerial strategies for controlling workplace behaviour. Even when there is only a tacit, unacknowledged sense of group identity, the stereotyped judgements of power holders about particular groups may lead them to form *sub-cultural* units. They are likely to be based around resistance to managerial activities rather than in a coherent ideology of their own. Individual cohesion within such a group may be low, and resistance may not be co-ordinated in any sense. It may not even be visible as such, but manifested in jokes at the expense of superiors, general stubbornness and lack of co-operation (Nichols and Beynon, 1977). At this level, pressure on individual members may be no more than disapproval at not joining in or, at worst, definition as being somehow different. Over time, the benefits of belonging to such a group in terms of access to sources of meaning may cause it to coalesce into a true sub-culture with the ability to protect members against threats to identity.

Haslam (2000, chap. 7) explores a similar theme on social identity in intergroup negotiation and conflict management. He introduces a wide range of evidence to show that identification with sub-groups, for example same-sex groups, can be beneficial in negotiation and conflict situations. By bringing conflict out into the open, sub-groups have the potential to:

- explore issues fully (clear the air rather than paper over the cracks)
- identify parties' real concerns
- consider more options
- avoid false optimism
- enhance feelings of empowerment and justice. (Haslam, 2000: 205)

Such effects are dependent on the development of a superordinate social identity which 'frames subgroup differences' and provides social motivation to participants (Haslam, 2000: 205). This focus on superordinate identity reinforces the arguments in the section on cohesiveness and polarisation above, in that group processes are not necessarily of negative import. However, in the absence of a superordinate identity, conflict might escalate, and this where the skills of negotiators themselves come into play if the process is not to run out of control. Hosking and Morley discuss these skills at length (1991: 161–9), especially noting the importance of cognitive and political processes in avoiding unnecessary or unrealistic conflict. Cognitive processes 'help negotiators to match their intellectual capacities to the demands of the task', and reduce unnecessary obstacles to agreement. Political processes 'help negotiators to organize disagreement so that it is seen as a natural part of a business relationship', rather than requiring a 'defensive response' (1991: 167). Once again, we have a process whereby potential contestation of issues is appropriated in such a manner as to place the responsibility on individuals and groups, rather than on the organisation, informal processes being transformed into formal relationships.

Many informal organisational processes, including sub-cultural groupings, are generated within the free areas that groups and their members carve out for themselves within the division of labour. Whether formally or informally constituted, such groups have to in some fashion reduce the possible internal tensions that might develop out of any contradictory goals and identity concerns of their members. The internal dynamics of groups have been seen to consist largely of role-based mechanisms and processes directed at the maintenance of the group, and according to Breakwell, 'group dynamics are the most frequent sources of threats to identity. These threats need not be personalised: they are directed at the individual as a group member, a cipher in a social category, not as a personality' (1986: 128). The detailed operation of such processes will be group-specific. But like the actions of individuals, it will be oriented towards identity-securing strategies. Just as the construction of individual identities depends in part on competition with others for sources of meaning, the production of group identities depends on gaining access to symbols and resources or behaviour patterns which serve to distinguish the group from others. We will return to the issue of what distinguishes groups in behavioural terms after first exploring the area in which this issue is of most contemporary concern, *teamworking*.

Teamworking

'Teamworking is a central element of new forms of work organisation' (Cully *et al.*, 1999: 42), notions of the high commitment workplace (HCW – see Chapter 16) being critically dependent on the deployment of teams. As we saw in Chapter 15, there is little doubt that, in manufacturing at least, teams are replacing individuals as the basic unit of work organisation, and project teams are increasingly used as a means of co-ordinating managers and professionals. In terms of practices critical to the HCW according to the 2004 Work Employment Relations Survey (WERS) team working was more common than either multi-skilling or the use of problem-solving groups:

- Almost three-quarters (72 per cent) of workplaces having at least some core employees in formally-designated teams;
- Where team-working was in place, it was usually embedded among staff: four-fifths (80 per cent) of workplaces with team-working extended it to at least three-fifths of core employees;
- Two-thirds (66 per cent) of workplaces had trained at least some staff to be functionally flexible;
- Around one fifth (21 per cent) of workplaces had groups of non-managerial employees that met to solve specific problems or discuss aspects of performance or quality. (Based on Kersley *et al.*, 2007: 17–19)

What is it that managers and management writers see as particularly advantageous in teamwork? Much of the enthusiasm for teams and teamwork can be traced back to the fashions for reorganising production processes into semi-autonomous work groups in the 1970s and for Japanese working practices in the 1980s. Autonomous work groups, based on notions of job enrichment and redesign (see Chapter 21), gave employees some latitude of decision-making over operational matters, and integrated different levels of production-related skills into more flexible working on more 'natural' units of work. This effectively turned production-line assembly into a semblance of unit or small-batch production. Wall and colleagues (1986), in a long-term study of autonomous workgroups, identified the justifications underlying their implementation as being in their assumed effects in increasing intrinsic motivation to work. These included enhancing employee satisfaction (confirmed by the WERS 2004 data), improving group performance and reducing labour turnover, as well as suggested increases in organisational commitment and improvements in mental health.

The results of this study indicated that 'employees clearly appreciated the autonomous work system. On balance managers did too, though clearly there were costs in terms of personal stress arising from the difficulties involved in managing and maintaining the system' (1986: 298). Of the assumed effects, only intrinsic job satisfaction and productivity were significantly increased, along with reported perceptions of increased autonomy. Labour turnover actually increased, through increased dismissals of those who could not or would not fit in to the new systems. The enhanced productivity was not due to employees working any harder. If anything, their individual productivity was lower in comparison with those working on more traditional lines. Improvements largely flowed from reduced indirect labour costs, due to decreases in the need for direct supervision of the work groups. This organisational benefit can be seen as a gain at the expense of increased managerial effort, with greater responsibilities being generated in monitoring and managing the new system, though according to the 2004 WERS data the levels of actual autonomy allowed to teams was often limited:

> However, teams did not always have autonomy. In 83 per cent of workplaces with team-working, teams were given responsibility for specific products and services, and in 61 per cent they could jointly decide how work was done. However, in just 6 per cent they were allowed to appoint their own team leaders. (Kersley *et al.*, 2007: 17–18)

In part, then, companies have been persuaded of the 'bottom-line' advantages of teamwork: less a case of enhancing the quality of working life and more that of enabling greater flexibility, problem-solving and continuous improvement. Yet behind these technical rationales lie further assumptions that teams can reproduce much of the dynamics of groups, while turning the goals and outcomes in a managerial direction. In other words, team members can be persuaded to think like managers by delegating responsibilities that were once the preserve of management. Supporters of teams, largely from an OB tradition, see this positively in terms of group cohesion facilitating co-operative and productive units (Eby and Dobbins, 1997); critics present this more negatively as peer pressure, and self-surveillance as socialisation into corporate identities (Casey, 1996; Sewell, 1998). Both, however, seem to accept that teams are effective sites for socialisation and vehicles for normative integration (Findlay *et al.*, 2000b). Restated in the language of group theory, teams can be *sentient* as well as *task* groups. This is a distinction drawn by Miller and Rice (1967), with task groups being based on the human resources necessary for work activity, while sentient groups are those to which individuals are prepared to commit themselves and on which they depend for emotional support (see 'Groups versus teams' below).

Re-engaging the worker

Most of the interventions to which members of organisations are periodically subject are based around either simple social facilitation or attempts to re-engage the intellectual level of learning (see Chapter 16). In current terms, teamworking interventions are among the most common attempts to *re-engage* the worker. They are often necessary due to the legacy of downsizing and flattening of hierarchies, with their concomitant increases in spans of control. This means that managerial skills (and what might be termed the *organisational locus of control*) need to be driven downwards in the hierarchy in order that control can be maintained.

A particularly influential article that appears to provide support for the above arguments, albeit from a critical perspective, comes from Barker (1993). Barker offers evidence that the values of control systems appear to be internalised by some groups of workers in specific circumstances. This is exemplified in the concept of concertive control taken from Tompkins and Cheney (1985). This fourth form of control:

> represents a key shift in the locus of control from management to the workers themselves, who collaborate to develop the means of their own control. Workers achieve concertive control by a negotiated consensus on how to shape their behaviour according to a set of core values, such as those of a corporate vision statement. (Barker, 1993: 411)

Here, though, it is both the organisation and its members that are seen to adopt a 'new substantive rationality' and a 'new set of consensual values'. It would appear that this represents the translation of Hopwood's (see Chapter 21) administrative controls into social controls, and thus the achievement of accommodation, assimilation, identification and finally internalisation. Barker's case study was of ISE Communications, a small US manufacturing company which adopted a structure based on self-managed teams in the late 1980s. The structural changes in the company are detailed in Table 24.2.

The process by which concertive control came into being was first through the development of a value consensus based on the company 'vision statement', then the emergence of normative rules driven by the addition of new teams:

> Members of the old teams responded to these changing conditions by discursively turning their value consensus into normative rules that the new workers could readily understand and to which they could subject themselves. (Barker, 1993: 424)

The final stage was the formalisation of these rules into a system that resembled in some ways the old bureaucratic structure. The formalisation of abstract values into specific behavioural guidelines was seen to provide a sense of stability, and was not interpreted as the creation of a bureaucracy, in that though they represented a rational, rule-based system, the rules were formulated and enacted by the teams themselves. The teams were thus said to be 'their own masters and their own slaves' (1993: 433) and even though managing the concertive system produced a great deal of strain in team members, they were reluctant to give up their control of their working practices, uncommitted workers not lasting very long. Barker's conclusion is that in the end even a self-managed rational apparatus only serves to bind employees further to Weber's 'Iron Cage', resistance being at the cost of risking their human dignity by 'being made to feel unworthy as a "team-mate"' (1993: 436).

The self-managed responsibilities produced by the concertive system themselves begin to enact the construction of a rational apparatus, in that the formalisation of consensual values into rules could be seen as an adaptive mechanism to relieve the levels of stress induced by autonomous decision-making. Thus team members become, in Willmott's (1994) terms, 'responsible individuals' who seek the stability of a rational apparatus in that they 'are spared the anguish of choice because feelings of anxiety and guilt associated with this responsibility are contained within organisationally defined boundaries' (1994: 26). However, here it is the uncertainty produced by the move to self-management which unfreezes team members to the point where corporate ideals can be identified with, rather than the generalised uncertainty Willmott associates with the 'indeterminacy and finitude of human existence' (1994: 26).

The Barker study demonstrates that re-engagement of the intellectual level of learning (see Chapter 20) can be achieved through collective obligations that guide adaptive behaviour in response to manufactured uncertainty. But once again the identification here is not directly to administrative controls and managerial values. Identification with the corporate mission is dependent on the continued abdication and transfer by management of responsibility and control to social consensus. Management has changed the context of control by changing the structures through which it is enacted, but the extent to which this

Table 24.2 **Structure of ISE before and after the change of teams**

Before the change

1. Three levels of managerial herarchy between the vice president and the manufacturing workers.
2. Manufacturing assembly line organises the plant. Workers manufacture boards according to their individual place on the line.
3. Line and shift supervisors form the first managerial link.
4. Workers have little input into work-related decisions. Managers make all decisions and give all directions.
5. Management disciplines workers.
6. Management interviews and hires all new workers.

After the change

1. Managerial hierarchy extends directly from the manufacturing teams to the vice president.
2. Team work areas organise the plant. Teams are responsible for complete fabrication, testing and packaging of their assigned circuit boards.
3. Teams manage their own affairs, elect one person to co-ordinate information to them.
4. Team members make their own decisions within guidelines set by management and the company vision statement. Teams have shared responsibility for their own production.
5. Team members discipline themselves.
6. Team members interview, hire and fire their own members.

Source: J. R. Barker (1993) 'Tightening the Iron Cage: Concertive Control in Self-Managing Teams', *Administrative Science Quarterly*, 38: 417.

represents any real measure of internalisation, rather than simple compliance with a new locus of control, must be questioned. What this form of self-management achieves are constant self-monitoring and environmental scanning by the team, and learned changes in behaviour that are not necessarily accompanied by increases in either general or specific job motivation. As indicated in Chapter 21, what appears to be important here is not genuine motivation, but the mobilisation of commitment. Even this is not commitment to intrinsic values, but to the expenditure of effort in required directions. The mechanisms for accomplishing this may rest on appeals to values and the construction of meaning, but their aim is the attainment of strategically-directed change.

Team dimensions

There are, however, grounds for scepticism about how far teams are sentient and characterised by high levels of normative cohesion. Part of the problem is that both advocates and critics of teams tend to present them as a 'package' in which task functions, value-orientations and capacity for self-governance are all mutually reinforcing. Along with other recent commentators on teamwork (see Proctor and Mueller, 2000), we prefer the view that teams can take many different forms dependent on context, in part because teamwork has different components. A widely-used example of such an approach is the *team dimensions model* (Thompson and Wallace, 1996; Findlay *et al.*, 2000b). This uses a threefold distinction between the technical, governance and normative dimensions of teamwork. (See Figure 24.2 below.)

The technical dimension is at the heart of the current wave of managerial interest in teams, and is concerned with issues directly related to the actual tasks undertaken by team members (for example, problem-solving and flexibility). Teamwork must, however, also rest on changes in the normative (for example, socialisation of team members and changes in attitudes and behaviours), and governance dimensions

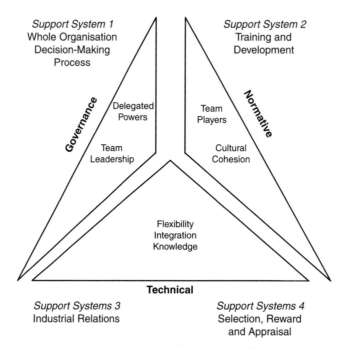

Figure 24.2 **The team dimensions model**

INTRODUCTION: REGULATING ORGANISATIONAL BEHAVIOUR ▪ PERCEPTION AND ATTITUDES: SEEING WHAT TO THINK ▪ MASKS FOR TASKS: PERSONALITY ▪ LEARNING AND CHANGE ▪ MOTIVATION: THE DRIVE FOR SATISFACTION ▪ LEADERSHIP: MIGHT OR MYTH? ▪

(management of teams including increased responsibilities and decision-making). In turn, the dimensions are influenced by wider support systems such as reward and industrial relations arrangements.

A multi-dimensional approach enables the variety of managerial objectives and configurations of actual practices to be identified and more adequately understood. Two such trends have been identified in earlier discussions of teamworking. First, the overwhelming rationale for the introduction of teams is instrumental and pragmatic, focusing on benefits in the technical sphere such as functional flexibility. Second, only a small number of teams have a high degree of autonomy. Companies tend to initiate only that degree of involvement in decision-making necessary for more effective use of workers' tacit knowledge and skills to improve efficiency. It follows that the precondition of an association between self-governance and positive normative behaviours, identified in parts of the OB and critical literatures, is not present or is underdeveloped in many contexts. There is no identifiable trend for teams acting like groups as effective sites for socialisation and normative integration, though this will vary considerably across and within particular companies and countries.

This is not to say that the normative dimension is absent or irrelevant. Even those organisations with limited, largely pragmatic objectives require that employees change some of their behaviours and attitudes in order to become better 'team players'. Emphasis may be put on co-operativeness, willingness to listen and learn, or acceptance of collective responsibility and avoidance of a 'blame culture'. Some companies therefore invest in soft skills training to back up these objectives, using teams as additional vehicles to spread awareness of business goals and conditions of competitiveness. In case studies in the Scottish spirits industry, Findlay and colleagues (2000a; 2000b) found that the two companies had some success in developing positive attitudes and normative competencies in areas such as communication. Team members were also more aware of business issues. However, they were far from simply internalising company values through teams. If anything, their experience militated against it. Awareness of business made many of them more critical of the gap between corporate rhetoric and shop-floor reality. Many team members felt disillusioned with teamwork, complaining of abuse of flexibility and intensification of work pressures. Most importantly, they were very aware of and sceptical towards any perceived attempt by the company to indulge in extensive socialisation through soft skills training or other means, labelling it 'brainwashing'. Interestingly, similar reactions have been picked up in other case studies (Pollert, 1996; McCabe, 2000). More generally, many studies have found that team sub-cultures continue to provide sources of dissatisfaction, resistance and distancing from managerial objectives (Robertson et al., 1992; Stephenson, 1994; Sharpe, 1996).

What the above discussion reveals is that the different dimensions of teamwork may not only vary, but also pull against each other. If, however, the purpose of a multi-dimensional model is to identify different configurations of practices, we have to allow for the possibility that there are indeed a small number of companies that have much more ambitious normative agendas. They may even be more successful in the resultant social engineering. Even if Barker *has* identified the conditions for concertive control in his case study, he gives little consideration to the extent to which it is typical or generalisable from what may be a highly specific context. Even companies with similar ambitious agendas of socialisation and self-surveillance have found that they may unravel under employee suspicion and resistance (McKinlay and P. Taylor, 1996).

Groups versus teams

This section attempts to reflect on and tie together some of the issues raised by our discussion of the compatibility of group and team dynamics. If groups are the building blocks of organisations and the ability of groups to modify individual behaviour is what in the end makes hierarchical organisation possible, then what of teams? Can we assume they have the same characteristics and psychological effects as groups, or are they a special case that is dependent on context for their specific functioning? Relating to the assumed effects of group membership, Brown (1992: 73) notes that the studies of the textile industry and coal mining associated with the Tavistock Institute in the 1950s recognised the difficulties of generalising conclusions on the benefits of reorganising groups on socio-technical principles. These difficulties are what led to the Miller and Rice (1967) distinction between task and sentient groups discussed above.

The task/sentient distinction parallels the classic formal/informal group differentiation with the added dimension of identifying the sentient/informal group more strongly with the classic psychological group. The problem is that the boundaries of task and sentient groups often do not coincide in temporal, spatial or organisational terms, and it may prove impossible to bring them into alignment. There is no necessity for task groups to exhibit the attributes of emotional closeness accruing to the sentient group although, as we noted above, teamworking initiatives often represent attempts to translate interpersonal into task-based cohesiveness. Even where such transformations apparently take place, it may result in resistance to change through attachment to existing structures and practices. Attitudes to participation, for example, are seen as determined by group membership rather than occupational category (Brown, 1992: 51). In addition to this, Haslam notes that:

> in most of the situations where researchers have drawn inferences about the behaviour of individuals in groups, their research has failed to study groups that are psychologically real and engaging for those individuals. (Haslam, 2002: 271)

The major focus of concern with groups in labour process analysis has tended to be on their role in the restriction of output and in the production of group solidarity. Beyond the recognition that there are internal dynamics that alter behaviour, the tendency has been to treat groups as simple aggregates rather than as negotiated collectives with their own logics of conflict, control and resistance. Overall, consent, commitment and compliance are conceptualised as individual relationships, mitigating against accurate interpretation of how related practices are reproduced as a social phenomenon and how the rules of consent are communicated.

The acknowledgement of groups as sites of resistance and concomitantly as bearers of sectional and cultural interests has over time tended to reinforce the conception of groups as conveyors and communicators of oppositional values. Studies such as Thompson and Bannon (1985) and Egri (1994) typify the parameters of this treatment. Thompson and Bannon exemplify the task group as the site of sectional contentions within a factory culture, while Egri examines organic versus traditional farming, treating groups as social movements contesting the cultural transformation of work organisation both within a particular industry and in society at large. Because of links between sectional interests and wider identity groups, such distinctions can only be made in the account of particular cases, but they are repeated constantly within the labour process and wider sociological literatures.

The labour process collections on skill and consent (Sturdy, Knights and Willmott, 1992) and on resistance and power (Jermier, Knights and Nord, 1994) provide many good examples, notably in the studies by Yarrow, Sturdy and Collinson. Yarrow's (1992) study of Appalachian coal-mining communities in particular highlights how concerns with 'group unity' and elementary notions of group socialisation are often incorporated into issues that mainly focus on gender competition and degradation of relative status (1992: 35–7). The hostility of male miners and managers to women coming into the mines during the 1970s is understood here in terms of male socialisation into the values of solidarity, competition, physical strength and courage. These produce psychological resistance to the degradation of status posed by women being able to do the work. But at the same time Yarrow reports that 'miners have typically made accommodations to maintain the unity of the crew' (1992: 36).

The most difficult thing to explain in this study is that there was any acceptance of women at all within groups where gender and class consciousness were so deeply embedded. But from the perspective of the working group, especially in a case such as this where Yarrow acknowledges that safety considerations acted to heighten the import of interpersonal dependence, it is understandable that women could quite quickly come to share in-group unity. In such highly cohesive groups where effective collaboration and communication is paramount, the group exercises a power of its own. This harks back to Minard's classic 1950s socio-psychological study where black and white mine workers lived segregated lives on the surface while co-operating and exhibiting group solidarity downshaft. The ability to demonstrate that members can effectively fulfil their role demands appears to outweigh other considerations during the performance of the task. In this sense the lack of preoccupation with group process leads to an under-theorising of why we might not exhibit resistance in the conditions of a particular labour process, which is surely as important to a holistic account as why we do!

If we now consider the converse of resistance as exemplified by worker commitment, Marchington's (1992) analysis of consent and co-operation in labour relations highlights how the lack of a group perspective might make labour process analysis itself dependent on rational-cognitive explanation. Marchington notes (1992: 158–9) how a conception of individual relationships in terms of hierarchical position fails to account for personal motivations and objectives such as the more basic prospect of 'doing a good job'. This is said to be central to much of our socialisation into work, and in support of this Marchington cites work as diverse as that of Peters (Peters and Austin, 1986), Nichols and Beynon (1977) and Knights and Collinson (1987), who raise the notion that workers often voice critical appraisals of managers based on their mistakes, lack of understanding, commitment, and failures to communicate.

The theme of groups as regulating mechanisms is more familiar in labour process analysis than is the theme of the group as a medium of individual and collective expression. The debate around the latter conception was raised by Whyte (1957) in his analysis of the relations between individuals and groups. Whyte recognised that the concept of 'groupness' was often incidental in many situations (1957: 50) but that even where people might not think of themselves as a group, for example in a committee, the aggregate could still function as a 'disciplining vehicle' in the production of acquiescence. Whyte was sceptical of the role of the group as a creative vehicle, however, and referred to the false collectivisation characterised by managerial attempts to treat formally constituted groups as if they embodied the attributes of what have been later termed as mature collaborative groups. The often unwarranted managerial assumptions made about the effects of cohesiveness on group behaviour and group effects on performance levels almost appear as a form of 'wishful groupthink' in the desire to reproduce the illusion of unanimity in task groups.

This is typical of the uncritical approach to groups and the 'common interests' of organisational members taken in the HRM and quality literatures, in other words, the instrumental and socio-psychological functions of groups are taken as unilateral phenomena, applicable to all group members regardless of personal agendas and identity projects. This is evidenced in the claims of Armstrong in 'HRM: Strategy and Action' (1992), where the eliciting of commitment in HRM practices is dependent on promotion of 'mutuality' of goals, influence, rewards and responsibility, which are said to produce benefits in terms of productivity and individual development.

The fallacy involved in such assumptions of mutuality and homogeneous commitment is essentially that teams and task groups might naturally develop the same levels of role differentiation and collaboration as a settled and cohesive psychological group might be expected to exhibit. The problem is that while psychological or sentient groups presuppose at least some level of interpersonally negotiated role differentiation, teams only presuppose a limited level of negotiated task differentiation, and task or command groups nothing more than prescribed task specialisation (see the section on 'Team dimensions' above). Unless teams or task groups are allowed the time and space for action, confrontation and autonomy that allow them to develop into sentient groups, the probable outcome will be no more than a heightened sense of domination within processes of control. The greater likelihood is, however, that teams will be broken up long before they can develop such dangerously high levels of confidence and awareness of their own capabilities and situational power. Managerial teams may of course be subjected to 'development' in the form of the Belbin inventory, or related techniques, to remind members of their scripted roles in task performance.

As with our discussion of motivation Chapter 21, we might posit the assumed similarities of groups and teams as another instance of Adorno's *identity thinking*. What we need are analytic tools that will allow us to gauge the extent to which teams and task groups do exhibit the psycho-social effects of groups. One such is found in Haslam's (2004) summary of his chapter on group productivity and effectiveness, where he concludes that a social identity approach has the following implications:

- Individuals in groups will tend to underperform when a relevant social identity is not salient or a group goal is prescribed by an outgroup.
- Labour will be divided more effectively if group members share a relevant social identity.
- Productivity on a group task will increase to the extent that group goals are congruent with a salient social identity.

These might be seen as the minimum conditions under which teams or task groups might be expected to exhibit any of the characteristics of sentient groups and any of the benefits which group working is assumed to have. The problem here is that much of what we have described as teamwork in this chapter precludes the congruence of social identity and group goals in anything but a prescribed fashion. Coupling work such as Haslam's with the team dimensions model might at least allow us to gauge the extent to which there is room for identity salience or superordinate identity in a teamworking system, and thus what chances there are of teams being able to perform like sentient groups. What we have to beware of is the tendency to emphasise the technical over the normative and governance dimensions of teams, as this constrains the extent to which identity salience can be generated within a team. Without cognisance of such constraints, teamworking becomes little more than another form of domination and control, and will suffer from the attempts of groups and their members to establish and secure identities that are psychologically real for them.

Summary and key points

Without groups and their transformational effects on individual behaviour we would not have organisations in the forms that they exist in today. More than any other topic in OB an understanding of the development and dynamics of and differentiations within and between groups is fundamental to any realistic analysis of systems of work and workplace relations. Socialisation into group roles is likewise crucial to analyses of leadership, decision-making and commitment.

The unitary conception of groups evident in the HRM literature in particular has led to teams likewise being assumed to have global effects on individual behaviour which cannot be assumed or relied on without knowledge of the development and contexts of the groups concerned. Groups and teams, then, are as much psychological constructs as they are social constructions, and the levels of mutuality and commitment they exhibit depend to a great extent on the salience of the social identities members can secure for themselves from the resources the group offers.

We organise ourselves into and within groups naturally and informally, which means that the translation of intrinsic group processes into extrinsic controls is in some ways *the* job of management. The dialectic between the shaping of identities and the forms of resistance and coping arising out of initiatives aimed at domination and control of people in groups is, for many of us, *the* experience of being organised. In the next chapter we move on to examine how the construction and maintenance of identities is implicated in the production of control and self-control in employees and managers alike and the contrivances through which such *identity work* is achieved.

Further reading

There are a host of managerialist texts on coaching teams and sport psychology is increasingly concerned with this area. In standard OB texts Furnham is a good place to start on groups, while if looking for a comprehensive treatment from a psychological perspective Levi's text is better on the distinction between groups and teams than most. Though not easily available these days it is worth hunting down Hosking and Morley from the library, not only for its focus on managerial teams but for its discussion of entitative perspectives in psychology which assume that groups (and organisations) are somehow separate from their environment and characterised by a unitary shared purpose. On cohesiveness and groupthink Haslam is yet again the place to go, especially Chapter 6 on Group Decision Making.

Furnham, A. (2005) *The Psychology of Behaviour at Work: The Individual in the Organisation*, Hove: Psychology Press.

Haslam, S. A. (2004) *Psychology in Organizations: The Social Identity Approach* (2nd edn), London: Sage.

Hosking, D. and Morley, I. (1991) *A Social Psychology of Organising: People, Processes and Contexts*, Hemel Hempstead: Harvester Wheatsheaf.

Levi, D. (2007) *Group Dynamics for Teams* (2nd edn), London: Sage Publications.

25 identity and identity work

> Social organization is both means and bar to control. The concrete physical and biological settings in which actions occur are crucial. It is thus the outcomes and contentions among identities which is what cumulates into social organisation. (Harrison White, 1992: 16)

In the first edition of this book, we sought to promote the study of identity and the 'identity work' of managers and employees for organisation analysis. At that time – the end of the 1980s – such issues were not prominent and certainly not much researched outside the realms of social psychology. Our goal was to bring some of the early critical thinking about identity that was emerging from labour process and other debates (Knights and Willmott, 1985) to what was known about issues such as roles, groups and stress in the OB literature. Picking up on themes in the rest of the book, identity was treated as a form of regulation. Shaping identities was important to employers because it was more likely to generate active consent to rules and controls than conventional bureaucratic methods. On the other hand, individuals and groups also seek to self-regulate their identities in search of stable, favourable outcomes. These negotiated transactions thus formed the basis of the 'identity work' described and discussed in the chapter.

Two decades later the situation is very different. Identity, in Europe at least, is arguably now the *most* written about topic in organisation and many other fields of study in the social sciences (Cornelissen, Haslam and Balmer, 2007). Given our original objectives, this is welcome, but it has come at a cost – identity tends to be over-sold as explanation and under-conceptualised as empirical object (Thompson and Marks, 2007). With respect to the former, this may be the fate of all fashionable concepts that become over-consumed and made to do too much work of explanation (Alvesson, 2007). As for its conceptualisation, this derives mainly in our view from its treatment by the dominant perspective – post-structuralism. Moving from the observation that identities are fluid and multiple social constructions rather than stable or enduring essences, post-structuralists assign to discourse the power to shape identities, whether they be individual or organisational (Collinson, 2003; Ainsworth and Hardy 2004). Organisational actors are not wholly passive, but their 'identity work' is limited primarily to positioning themselves within the interplay of discourses, choosing between 'subject positions'. The outcome is that the individual or other site of identity formation tends to be treated, in Thompson and Mark's term, as a blank slate to be textualised.

It is beyond our scope to give a detailed account and commentary on these new writings (see Webb, 2006). While we will make reference to ideas and debates, we want to remain close to our original objective of giving an account of identity work that reflects the assumptions about subjectivity at work we began Part III with – that employees are both subject to the actions of dominant power holders and subject of the pursuit of their own interests and identities. We want to restore a sense of the differences between the sources and sites of identity formation – self, group, organisation, occupation – and a sense of the tensions between them. In order to do this, we need to re-state and update a discussion of identity work, this time giving greater priority to perspectives from social psychology and other sources that, whatever their other flaws, facilitate a more rounded and complex picture than one which relies on discourse as medium and explanation.

The aims of this chapter are to:

- Give an account of identity and identity work that reflect the assumptions about subjectivity at work we have used throughout Part III.
- Show how identity is used in producing images appropriate to our social, cultural and work context.
- Explore how issues of gender and ethnic identity have today become organisational issue of Diversity.
- Examine the notion of organisational identity and its relation to the individual involvement of identities in the workplace.
- Indicate how situational power is implicated in both 'perceived behavioural control' and individual and collective resistance.
- Explore how identity work uses the organisation and illustrate through the personal and group identity work done by managers.

Explanations of identity

As intimated in Chapter 17, the journey of an individual into and through the world of work is constituted by the mainstream agenda in organisational behaviour (OB) as a fairly discrete set of common and basic processes through which individuals develop identities and the behavioral and emotional repertoires which support them. Through these processes, notably learning, perception and socialisation, the individual is seen to develop distinctive patterns of personality, motivation and affiliation which can be factored and compared to give organisations performance-related data. There has been much of use to learn from examining that journey, but as an account of the development of subjectivity and identity within an organisational context, it still has distinct limitations. It fails to adequately understand individual identity as a social reality through which we transact with our environment. At a more macro-level of analysis, the sociological stream of organisation theory is much more comfortable with notions of groups acting according to economically determined interests. But objective reality is perceptually filtered through *subjective constructions* which interpret and shape our whole world in terms of what we value about ourselves. Our focus on subjective identity lies in this process, because as individuals we guide our actions according to what will in our view best defend, enhance or substantiate our identities. Identity is thus a tool that we use to present ourselves in, and possibly transform ourselves into, images appropriate to our social, cultural and work context.

Unless personality and identity are exclusively genetically-determined phenomena, there can be little doubt that social contexts and pressures shape an individual's identity. In researching differential socio-emotional development in male and female children, Lewis (1975) found that parallel to the earliest distinguishable biological influences, there are differences in the treatment of the two sexes by adults and other children. Thus, though biological influences undoubtedly have some effects on personality in the same way that they have an influence on hair colour and general bodily characteristics, these effects cannot easily be differentiated from social or environmental influences.

According to Weigert *et al.* (1986: 31), 'identity is a definition that transforms a mere biological individual into a human person. It is a definition that emerges from and is sustained by the cultural meanings of social relationships activated in interaction'. To extend the above example, if someone dyes or changes their hairstyle, they have taken steps to place a self-directed social construction on the body they were born with. Considering the myriad identifications we make with role models, reference groups, ideological contructs and symbols we are taking for ourselves, identities, both *personal* (who we think we are) and *social* (who we want others to think we are), are produced out of what we select as attractive or appropriate out of the social values, expectations and fashions of our time. The tradition of sociological social psychology represented by Weigert and others tried to avoid any contradictions between notions of personal and social identity, taking the view that identity is a *social product* both bestowed on the individual by others and appropriated by individuals for themselves. It takes the form of a *typified self*, any of a number of self-produced categorisations of what is available to the individual within the various situations in which they participate (see self-categorisation below).

Shifting the focus from personal to social identity, we can see that we constantly represent our subjective selves to others in our social environment. In the way we dress, speak and behave we present a changing image of who we are. Identity is in this sense a *negotiated* construction. Depending on who we are dealing with, we present images intended to appear appropriate to both the situation and the expectations of others. Using a symbolic interactionist framework, Erving Goffman (1971, see 'Impression management' below) explored this conception of self within a dramaturgical metaphor, representing social identity as a performance analogous to that of an actor.

The image presented is not necessarily the 'real' self of the person but a situationally appropriate image sustained by the 'actors' and those observing and/or interacting with them. The students in a lecture theatre, even though they may not consider themselves socially or intellectually inferior to the lecturer, collaborate to enable the lecturer to present a consistent performance. They thus maintain an image of authority for the lecturer and one of subordination for themselves, that is, social identities consistent within the situation. They exercise '*tact*' in order to continue participating in the production of a performance that fits the perceived rules of the situation.

The interface between social and personal identity lies in this act of interpersonal negotiation. A social identity does not simply spring fully formed from the demands of the situation, but requires effort and practice from the individual and appropriate feedback from others. Thus the contexts from which we are able to construct unique subjective identities for ourselves consist mainly of 'rationalised' performances where we construct personal identity out of the strategies and responses we devise to deal with contingencies. The idea that we each possess a core identity relating to what we value about ourselves is examined in the *social learning* conception of identity (Miller, 1963). As a source of meaning, identity links us to others in the social structure through perceived similarities and processes of identification. As a definition or typification, identity sets us apart from others; it is the basis of social comparison, showing us the things and people which our particular personal meanings debar us from identifying with. Personal, subjective identity consists of the meanings and images we have found to represent us accurately in the past. Social identity, where it is different to the former, consists of the negotiated position between our personal identity and the meanings and images demanded of us in our current social context.

This leads us to a final aspect of identity as a linking concept between differing levels of explanation. We gain identities through interaction and association with the social and cultural groupings to which we belong. These groups provide us with points of reference and comparison out of which we can define ourselves, and through this route are in turn directly shaped by social structure. For this reason Miller (1963) saw identity as the foundation of the links between social structure and personality, and fundamental as such to the explanation of socialisation, motivation and psychological conflict. Likewise, the *social identity theory* of Tajfel and Turner (1979; 1986) links intergroup relations to social conflict and through *self-categorisation theory* (Turner, 1985) to the interpersonal dynamics of groups (see Chapters 17 and 21 on perception and groups). Our personal transactions with social structures are conducted in the great part through the organisations we belong to, work for, and with which we have to deal. Organisations attempt to socialise people into their particular workplace cultures and management attempts to influence individual motivation to its advantage. The amelioration of the psychological, interpersonal and group conflicts engendered by these activities is a major rationale for the involvement of social and behavioural scientists in organisations.

Redefining the agenda

To understand more adequately the individual's development towards an organisational participant who is active, yet acted upon, we need to further redefine some of the issues and agenda. For example, because so much of OB took the structures, workings and goals of organisational life for granted, it underestimated the degree to which the environment restricts sources of meaning for the securing of identities and imposes costs on individuals. The resources that individuals can bring to an identity project will depend on their *situational power* in the organisation (see below). Situational power does not depend simply on a person's place in an organisational hierarchy: a shop-floor worker can construct an identity just as, or even more, secure than that of someone with more position power. An individual's perception of his or her own situational power, whether at an interpersonal, group or organisational level, conditions how secure he or she feels, mediated by factors such as *self-monitoring*, *locus of control* and *self-efficacy* (see Chapters 17 and 18). These identities are not necessarily situation-specific, providing meaning and support outside the context they were constructed within, though there are of course limits. The 'organisation man', secure in his identification with organisational goals and objectives, may generalise associated attitudes and behaviours to situations where such an identity may be inappropriate.

The treatment of identity in mainstream psychology also neglected contextual issues in treating identity in an everyday fashion as being inherent in the person. Breakwell (1987: 95) argues that psychologists 'tend to treat identity as the origin of action'; they use it as a 'motivational variable', much as happened with emotions and as we saw in Chapter 23. In contrast, we see identity as the outcome of interaction within particular material contexts which act as constraints on available sources of meaning and on the process of identity construction and what is important here is how we use the organisation for our own purposes as opposed to how organisations and organisational discourses use us. The central limiting factor on available sources of meaning is the context of *intensified*, *fragmented* and *commodified* work. In an externally controlled environment, the most individuals can often hope for is to maintain or increase their situational power and material resources. Our relationships with, and our attribution of motives to, others are reduced to their instrumental function in the process of 'accumulation without regard to need' (Wexler, 1983: 122). Socio-psychological models of motivation continually reflect this, as in the rational calculations of personal advantage we are assumed to make in process models of motivation or in the mixed-models of emotional intelligence (see Chapters 21 and 23).

Diverse identities

The instrumentality of relationships also extends into the definition of gender identities in the workplace. As we saw in Chapter 10, writers such as Hearn and Parkin (1987) identify the *desexualised* nature of work organisations as reinforcing patriarchy and sexism. Instrumentality in the continuing forms of fragmented, Taylorised work relations defines masculinity and reproduces organisational work as a male concern:

> The workman is, potentially at least, nothing more than the doer of the task, without feelings and emotions. The ideal workman would appear to almost lose physical presence, or be a mere disembodied bearer of role, in effect part of a machine system. (Hearn and Parkin, 1987: 19)

Women workers have been and still are, excluded from the predominantly male culture of organisations, feminine gender identity being routinely suppressed or marginalised. Women managers especially are often required to adapt to masculine models of management, or risk being viewed as exceptions to women in general. Likewise domestic labour is not viewed as 'real' work in the fashion that paid work is; the identity construct of 'worker' is reserved for those carrying out the latter. Women's labour in organisations has often been an extension of domestic labour, as in the example of secretaries who act as 'office wives, protecting their charges from unnecessary interference and strain, making tea, buying presents, even cleaning their bosses' false teeth' (1987: 92). The expectations of and reactions to gender identities often appear contradictory or arbitrary, for example, why does it appear to be more acceptable to be a gay police chief than a gay footballer? In this case the contradiction can be understood in terms of formal support for and informal intolerance of gender identities, for example with a Police Service committed to eradicating institutional racism and gender discrimination as opposed to the casual vehemence of fans against players in a sport that does not yet allow women players in its top ranks.

Sexual, and racial, discrimination in labour markets was reinforced by stereotypical categorisations of women and black workers that portrayed them as 'naturally' inferior in various abilities or suited to only certain types of work. Notions such as women being better suited than men to boring, repetitive tasks served to legitimise restricted access to labour markets. Black workers in particular have been discriminated against in recruitment and selection processes on the basis of a stereotyped lack of acceptability in white workplace cultures. Jenkins (1986) notes that the causes of racism were often attributed to those who were discriminated against: 'managers do, in the main, see black workers as posing problems for their organisations. These problems were typically seen to be created by black workers, not by white racism' (1986: 114). Where institutions now attempt some amelioration of discrimination it is today carried out under the banner of *diversity training* (see Chapter 10 for a wider discussion); it is not so much social or business concerns that drive lower tolerance of discrimination but a fear of litigation and with public organisations a necessity to be seen to comply with legislation. *Diversity* itself is defined in terms of social identity theory by Nkomo and Cox (1999: 89) as, 'a mixture of people with different group identities within the same social system'. Nkomo and Cox (1999: 90) produce a useful conceptual map of approaches to identity and the effects of diversity in organisations, but they are focused on gender and minority (race in their terms) and as with subsequent institutional definitions (which generally add disability issues) do not take into account the diverse nature and skills of the disaffected, the maverick and the collectivist or even the 'Type B' personality. Diversity is thus for the 'deserving' minority and inextricably linked to organisational estimations of employee character and aspirations.

Where they are not simple compliance or even just lip service, attempts to 'manage' diversity appear to follow an HRM dominated, 'one size fits all' approach which fits with Giddens' (1990; 1991) *reflexive modernisation hypotheses* that managerial identity will become more gender-neutral and dominated by career-based concerns with self-marketing. In examining the 'career narratives' of managers, Wajcman and Martin (2002: 99) note that:

- What we have termed a market narrative was most commonly used by the managers in our study to understand and explain their career paths and to account for their likely future choices … this narrative provided a flexible, sustaining framework for managers to understand their careers and make career choices.
- Men and women place themselves as apparently ungendered market actors in their career stories and can adopt much the same career strategies in dealing with the new labour market.
- While these findings accord with the reflexive modernization picture of largely ungendered career identities along with a strong sense of individual autonomy, our research also shows that 'choice' means quite different things in the private world for men and women.
- Because the available private identities remain so deeply gendered, women face a negotiation of employment and domestic responsibilities which is different from that of men.

Yet questions also need to be raised about possible disjunctures between managerial and worker identities. Wajcman and Martin contrast their findings with Sennett's (1998) notion of the *corrosion of character* where:

> He argues that the possibility of sustained, predictable, usually lifetime, engagement with a workplace has been the bedrock of people's identities – their 'character' – since the advent of industrial societies. With its principle of 'no long term', the new capitalism has torn away the basis for the formation of sustaining identities, resulting in a growing malaise as people search in vain for a place to anchor a meaning for their lives. (Wajcman and Martin, 2002: 987)

Since most workers only have the ability to be instrumental in extrinsic terms, the flexibility afforded to managers will be harder to come by, making Sennett's view possibly more appropriate in the employee context. This is supported by Webb (2004: 719) who argues that it is increased instrumentalism on the part of employers rather than short-termism which is the more damaging and results in 'the experience of increased responsibility without meaningful discretion and authority'.

It is important to recognise here that threats to job security do not inevitably produce organisational domination. Consent has to be mobilised, because domination by coercion is often 'inefficient', requiring constant reinforcement of such pressures and extensive monitoring of reactions to them. As with motivation earlier, domination of the individual through self-limitation and constraint is far more effective. This is engendered through individual assimilation of, and accommodation to, dominant workplace cultures and ideologies. At its most visible level, this process can be seen in the internalisation of norms and accepted standards of behaviour that occurs in organisational and group socialisation (see Chapters 21 and 24). If consent is not present, pressures to shape ourselves in appropriate images may not be perceived as legitimate, and could promote active resistance. In Westwood's (1984) 'Stitchco' study, women participated in a patriarchal labour process which management viewed as 'harmonious' in its appeals to common, progressive goals and paternalistic values. The women, however, had a 'clear understanding that there were sides in industry and that these sides maintained an uneasy truce which was easily broken' (1984: 25). Westwood argues that the 'deprivation, pain and waste that black and white working class women live with on a daily basis' can be 'a spur to action rather than defeat'. Domination can thus become the source of identity projects empowering creativity and resourcefulness, sisterhood being the focus of resistance that does more than enable survival in a hostile environment.

Of course the contextual issues raised above are not necessarily simply sources of constraint. They may for some be the very factors which allow them to secure identities. Workers with worries over job security may find meaning in defining themselves through nationalist or traditionalist sentiments, giving expression to their fears through hostility to 'immigrant' workers or women who should remain at home. Likewise, hostility and resistance to organisational goals and practices may arise out of the conditions of exploitation, domination and alienation which render others submissive. It would appear that identities are constructed out of whatever meanings and symbolic resources are readily available, and are constrained by the individual's ability to sustain them. Thus the construction of identity is a continuous process that has to be understood in the context of the workplace, where it is maintained and reproduced on a daily basis.

Organisations and identities

If society is characterised by the involvement of individuals in organisational structures, then organisations are characterised by their attempts to *control the performance and behaviour* of the individuals of which they consist. It is this rule-bound control of individual behaviour that distinguishes organisational behaviour from other forms of social organisation. Home and family life, for example, are undoubtedly organised, and controls and sanctions are placed on the behaviour of family members. But this control is in no sense as systematic as that existing in even a small commercial organisation. On this basis, for work organisations of any type to maintain their present forms of authority, hierarchy and control, it becomes necessary to produce some kind of change in the types of regulation to which employees will consent (see Chapter 20).

However, organisations do not simply transform individual identities at work by some form of brainwashing. Neither do they simply depend on individuals' recognition of economic necessity to ensure their consent to the control of their performance in their work. The concept of 'economic man' is not adequate to explain workers' consent to change. Rules and procedures constraining work-related behaviour may conflict with attempts to secure stable and favourable identities. Alternatively, workers could construct viable identities out of the very rules which restrict them, becoming 'organisation men', or setting themselves up in opposition to their employers – or perhaps distancing themselves from the whole affair by concentrating on external interests. Whatever the survival and coping tactics employed by individuals, they may in time transform themselves into an image that functions in a way that is useful to the organisation they work for. Even the 'deviant' or militant worker may provide images of what the 'good' employee *should not be* (see Ackroyd and Thompson, 1999: 21–8, for a discussion), as well as providing a focus for the attribution of blame (see Chapter 17) rather than the appreciation of diversity.

The claims made by Sennett (see above) have parallels with post-structuralist notions that there is no fixed, stable identity and that identity is constructed from dominant discourses, rather than actual and symbolic resources which vary in their availability. According to Thompson and Marks (2007: 1) this is to assume 'a congruence between the identity "needs" of the organisation and the individual'. This may wrongly conflate the notion of organisational identity in terms of public image with the actions of organisational members who construct organisational identities in order to survive their daily workplace experience. We can identify personal, social, collective identities and organisational identities in individuals, but organisations do not have mechanisms for securing identities, just as they cannot learn or have needs or tacit knowledge.

Identity is thus a key basis of individual involvement in organisations and the basis for manipulation achieved through negotiated transactions between organisational strategies of control and individual strategies for securing identity, but to deny agency to individuals in constructing identities is to ignore the choices and calculations inherent in many of the psychological processes people must go through to perceive and utilise the resources they produce identities from. The consequences of this are not always positive for the organisation, and we all have to cope in a creative fashion with the constraints of work or unemployment. Strategies used for survival can become powerful tools for extending our own abilities and capacities. Those who try manipulating our behaviour must face the fact that they are interfering with the self-perceptions and judgements that make us what we are. If manipulation goes too far, it may do no more than encourage employee identities more resistant to organisational control. Feelings of being manipulated could reduce feelings of situational power and lead people to rely on resources that they may have been reluctant to access earlier – union meetings are always better attended when management has pulled yet another stupid stunt.

Identity work and situational power

Subjective experience in organisations consists of *lived relationships* bounded by social, organisational and workgroup cultures in the context of structural and ideological constraints. These form the three basic contexts within which individual identity is continually reproduced. Lived relationships are the subject-ive arena of identity construction. Even though our subjective 'now' is informed by our past experience and moulded by the pressures brought to bear on us, we still act as if we are independent and self-directed entities. Thus our everyday existence can continue as if it largely by-passes the influence of cultural and structural constraints on our behaviour. Thus *situational power* is central to the explanation of organisa-tional behaviour. This is recognised in what Azjen and Madden (1986) term 'perceived behavioural con-trol', which, according to Augoustinos and Walker (1995: 25), links behavioural attitudes and norms in the 'actor's perception of the ease or difficulty of performing the behaviours'. The extent to which we can control our behaviour and estimate our ability to act will determine the kind of strategies available for achieving our personal agendas or identity projects.

Social, organisational and workgroup cultures are, then, the arenas in which 'fitting behaviour' is moulded and regulated and in which we perform *identity work* (Goffman, 1971; Cohen and Taylor, 1978). Just as our perceptions of the world are simplified by the use of stereotypical categories, the activities we carry out in the workplace are simplified by the use of stereotyped categories of behaviour. These various cultural contexts also represent the medium of communication and translation of structural contexts to everyday existence. These are the limiting factors on identity construction in work and social life. They act to define possible sources of meaning and activity in hierarchical organisations and also provide the contextual limitations on what is acceptable practice for those who study, design and intervene in organ-isations. The element of self- and other regulation in identity work is acknowledged in post-structuralist accounts but is often accompanied by a caveat such as in Alvesson and Willmott (2002, cited in Sturdy *et al.*, 2006: 845) that identity work must also be conceptualised as interpretive activity, which 'refers to people being engaged in forming, repairing, maintaining, strengthening or revising' their personal con-structions or narratives (Sveningsson and Alvesson, 2003: 1165)'.

From a social identity theory perspective the main context of identity formation and the enactment of situational power is the group, but it is not simply by declaring oneself a member that a group identity is secured. Kaufman's study of *How Working-Class Individuals Construct Middle-Class Identities* (2003: 481) notes that, 'Self-avowals are not enough to achieve a desired social identity; rather, individuals must engage in the requisite identity-work activities in order to be successful in social transformation'. Neither is the strength of identification to be taken for granted, as may often be the case in post-structuralist accounts. Reflecting on social identity theory, Thompson and Marks (2007: 8) note that factors such as small group size and group heterogeneity increase identification. From this perspective, the act of self-categorisation itself is evidence that, 'individuals are more than inert receptors of organizational narratives'. Deaux and Martin, 2003) argue that social identification is driven mainly by status but mediated by identification with large-scale categorisations (e.g. race or religion), whereas interpersonal networks are more important drivers of collective identity.

Other factors mediating situational power such as individual and group concerns with job security, status, promotion, conflict and satisfaction, can be characterised under a number of related categories:

- the prediction and control of reality
- coping with uncertainty
- retaining autonomy and discretion
- maintaining or enhancing situational power.

The concern with uncertainty here returns us to the views of Knights and Willmott (1989) and Collinson (2003) which see insecurity and anxiety as the driving force behind an ultimately fruitless search for a secure and stable sense of self. Overall, these concerns represent the tensions created by trying to maintain and monitor the *strategies* through which we enact behaviours. An identity secure in the ability to control these tensions both forms a bulwark against threats and provides personal standards for social comparison and action. The strategies utilised by individuals and groups to secure or appropriate identity will thus seek to control sources of power and meaning. As a consequence, identity construction may threaten the organisation of work (Knights and Willmott, 1985; Weigert, 1986; Breakwell, 1987). At the same time we must recognise that in focusing on individual insecurity and threat, post-structuralist approaches neglect vital mediating factors, such as unions and professions, of an agency role in securing identities through offering collective resources; it is not after all for nothing that unions and professions are known as identity groups (see Chapter 20).

Organisational strategy, in trying to reduce uncertainty, is willing to allow room for the maintenance of worker identities insofar as they make the control of behaviour and production processes more effective. In implementing the introduction of computer numerically controlled (CNC) machine tools, firms such as Westland Helicopters allowed an element of manual input from operators on the basis that human intervention is necessary in automated processes because they are not absolutely error-free (Corbett, 1985a). The ubiquity of the modern systems analysts and the all-too-familiar IT help-line attests to the fact that in maintaining computer systems human skill and decision-making is still paramount. Such decisions allow operators to exert some levels of skill and discretion within labour processes that were once seen as increasing tendencies towards deskilling. Thus alongside gains in the reduction of uncertainty in the production process, there may also be benefits to organisations in reducing the level of threat to skilled identities implied by automation of processes and skills.

The greater the effort put into attempts to define employees' work lives, the greater the use of undefined areas by workers to develop 'informal work group cultures'. Cultures of this type can provide workers with a degree of autonomy and a basis for active resistance. By the same token, membership of sub-cultural groups in organisations may provide the same benefits to threatened identities as they do for sub-cultures in wider society: 'the threatened can regain self-esteem, generate positive distinctiveness and promote continuity' (Breakwell, 1986: 141). Although Breakwell argues that societal sub-cultures have virtually no impact on power structures, they are, she maintains, the focus of possible social concerns and the associated 'moral panics' (Cohen, 1973) that identify them as being 'scheduled for control'.

This is not to say that managers never recognise this tendency and take steps to short-circuit the development of informal groups that may become hostile to organisational goals. Drago and McDonough (1984: 67) quote from a management planning document that was part of a 'controlled participation experiment' at the General Food's Topeka plant: 'No power groups will exist within the organisation that create an anti-management posture.' In trying to predict and control reality, it is our subjective concepts and values that are most amenable to change, as we cannot on our own hope to change the structural framework of the organisations within which we work. Even for those with the power to effect change, there is still no absolute security of position or certainty that their actions will produce results fully in line with their projects. Thus, in coping with the uncertainties of organisational life most individuals are forced either into a strategy of accommodation which necessitates a gradual redefinition of self and subjective reality, or a strategy of assimilation which requires these to be subjected to the superordinate identity of the group.

Situational power is likewise implicated in individual and collective resistance to organisational controls. Resistance can be both a source of meaning and a pressure on the security of identity, founded on the perception by individuals of contradictions between the goals, ideologies, approved identities and required behaviours manifested in organisational settings. Leonard (1984: 116–18) identifies four sources of pressures leading to resistance, avoidance and dissent (see Thompson and McHugh 2002, for a wider discussion):

- Contradictory consciousness – results in reactions from deviance or theft to industrial sabotage or 'destructive' actions
- Unconscious resistance – results in reactions from anxiety and frustration to neurosis and psychosis
- The development of individual capacities – reducing alienation through personal activities either within or outside work
- Participation in collective action – enhancing situational power through collective strength and raising of consciousness.

The first two sources are about having one's self redefined by situational and structural pressures, that is, the condition of being subject to. The second two concern redefinitions of self that can counter subordination and are about being an active subject. All four reflect to various extents the forms of coping with stress noted by Moos and Billings (1982; see Chapter 23). What such pressures do *not* mean is that resistance is inevitable, even though it may be structured into the forms and processes of organisations. Where there are no overt conflicts, it is possibly easier for individuals to accept managerial definitions of reality; to become 'organisation people' and to gain meaning from their appointed roles. It must be remembered, however, that these responses are interdependent processes, which can be conceptually separated, but which are all part of the cycle of organisational control and resistance. In securing and maintaining a stable and meaningful identity, individuals are faced with the difficulty of presenting consistent images to the other people with whom they must deal. When threats arise, they are left with the choice to accommodate or resist. Both involve possibly substantial redefinitions of the identities they have secured. However, just as in the world of fashion or popular music, where people's creative and autonomous control over their own image and expression are eventually incorporated into commercial products, the smart company will incorporate the efforts of individuals to indulge in non-alienated activity into the organisation of the labour process. In the world of the work organisation, the 'revolt into style' may be transformed into the instrumental rewards of the suggestion box as we have already seen with the practices of Knowledge Management (see Chapter 16).

Impression management and scripting

Before discourse became the dominant explanatory framework, the management of identities had been explored in the tradition of Goffman's (1959) work on *impression management* (IM). Goffman focuses on the presentation of self and coping strategies within identity work, where meaning and status are sought by individuals in the ordering of interaction. The individual, like an actor on stage, attempts to maintain a consistent and believable performance for the audience: those who have a significant influence over the role they play. When used in this sense, identity is malleable and instrumentally defined. However active and manipulative such identities are, they are still dependent on the collaboration of others not to interfere with the performance. We know that the performance of an actor is not real. But according to Goffman we exercise '*tact*' to allow the performance to proceed, as in the case of a management 'pep-talk'.

Goffman's *dramaturgical* model (1959, especially chaps 3 and 7) established the basics of informal rules for interaction and the relations between personal and social identity. It makes the distinction between *frontstage* (the arena where the performance is carried out and interaction is primarily with the 'audience' or 'client') and *backstage* where the interaction is primarily with other 'actors' and the 'resources' for performance are created. Goffman essentially sees IM as a form of self-presentation and ongoing self-definition of what he called the *personal front*. It is this personal front which enables us to maintain *inauthentic social relations* (see Chapters 20 and 23) with others in order to advance our personal interests while still appearing to exercise normative self-control in both formal and informal groups. A similar notion to personal front used by Harré is that of *persona*, though this implies more of a conscious choice in selecting appropriate persona than Goffman would admit to. Thompson and Marks (2007: 10) contextualise the personal front within organisational identity by claiming that:

> The front acts as the vehicle of standardisation, allowing others to understand the individual on the basis of projected character traits with normative meanings. As a 'collective representation', the front establishes a proper 'setting,' 'appearance,' and 'manner' for the social role assumed by the actor, uniting interactive behaviour with the personal front. (Goffman, 1959: 27)

Schlenker (1980) had previously tried to reconcile the purposive and passive or reactive aspects of IM when he defined it as 'the conscious or unconscious attempt to control images that are presented in real or imagined social interactions' (cited in Russ, 1991: 220). We should, however, note the caveat that regardless of agency, in using IM, we do not necessarily use it as well as others or rely on it to the same extent; based apparently on our skill at self-monitoring (see Chapter 18): More recent developments of Goffman's work are noted by Thompson and Marks who argue they:

> have recently emerged in the form of role identity theory (e.g. Thoits and Virshup, 1997) and identity theory (Burke, 1980; Burke and Stets, 2001). Again, role identity theory acknowledges the function of individual interests, in that individuals are perceived as different to other group members with their own duties and resources, when transposed onto the group level, however, there is still the assumption

> that interests compete, so a negotiation processes is undertaken throughout which the maintenance of the group identity is seen of greater importance than the individual (or indeed, group) interests. (Thompson and Marks, 2007: 11; see also Deaux and Martin, 2003, for a discussion of integrating developments in identity theories)

Thoits and Virshup, 1997 claim that psychological theories of identity cope better than sociological ones with 'conflict between social structures and individuals, and attempts to explain social change' (cited in Deaux and Martin, 2003: 102). Thoits and Virshup refer to identity work as *identity performances*, linking such efforts more closely to IM than is generally the rule in social identity theory. In terms of more traditional OB approaches to IM Giacalone and Rosenfeld's excellent set of readings on *Applied Impression Management* (1991) discusses the widespread and significant implications of IM in areas such as organisational development, careers, appraisal, negotiation and conflict, gender and culture. They also provide useful summaries of the major models of IM. Leary and Kowalski (1991: 87–8) focus on the concepts of *impression motivation*, 'the desire of individuals to generate specific impressions in others' minds in order to maximise social and material outcomes, self-esteem, and/or cultivate a particular public identity', and of *impression construction*, 'the process of choosing the kind of impression to create and deciding exactly what behaviours would be effective in transmitting such an image'.

Tedeschi and Norman (1991: 105) conceptualise the IM process as a reward exchange where, 'each party is providing reinforcements to the other for his or her ultimate gain'. Baumeister (1991: 197) similarly views the goals of impression management as audience pleasing and constructing the ideal self, particular practices being mediated by normative and cultural pressures. Martinko (1995: 259–77) provides a detailed applied model that, while recognising 'many IM behaviours may be unconscious and unintentional', views IM 'as a systematic and purposive process of behaviour self-management that is both conscious and intentional'. The specific issues Martinko sees as being of future interest to IM are the extent to which IM behaviour is *plastic* or malleable or is conversely located in traits, and thus to what extent we can be trained in IM. Martinko also raises questions of ethics and credibility, individual, group and cultural differences and, perhaps most important of all, raises the relation of IM to self-monitoring as conceptualised by Snyder and Copeland (1985). The Martinko model is essentially prescriptive, but like many such models it acts better as a description of the processes involved than as practical guidance because of the multitude of variables involved.

The extent to which IM works in a practical sense is documented by Baron and Byrne (1997: 67–9), citing experimental studies which stress the importance of other-enhancement (for example, ingratiation; see below) as a key factor in gaining higher performance ratings at work. They also cite evidence (1997: 503–6) pertaining to IM in job interviews, especially with reference to effects of appearance, gender and the role of expectations in interviewer style and behaviour. Arnold and colleagues note the importance of IM as a set of skills in their commentary on Goffman's work (1998: 243–4). Examples of the type of skills and associated contexts involved are in interviewing, testing, communication and presentation. Such techniques are discussed in more detail by Feldman and Klich (1991: 69) who summarise them as:

- Ingratiation: flattery, agreement, doing favours
- Intimidation: veiled threats, appearing dangerous
- Self-promotion: embellishing accomplishments, overstating capabilities
- Exemplification: appearance of dedication or self-sacrifice
- Accounting: denying responsibility, assuaging problems
- Supplication: promoting sympathy, nurturance or allegiance from superiors.

Such *protective* impression management including excuses, apologies and damage control is seen as important by Rosenfeld, Giacolone and Riordan (1995), who cover its measurement and relations to HRM in some detail.

Kunda's study of 'Tech' (1992, chap. 5) also provides numerous and excellent examples of related forms of identity work. These include routine *identity displays* of behaviours which either embrace or distance the worker from organisational roles, and *artefactual displays*, for example, of signs and posters, in personal workspaces which supply the image of 'a strong individual surviving in a hard, competitive, often irrational world' (1992: 196). Artefactual displays are a particular form of *non-verbal communication*, which itself is a specific aspect of IM and includes Goffman's notion of *signing* in relation to the tactics and techniques we use to register impressions on others. Both types of display are seen as dramatic performances balancing the display of the successful organisational self with an image of ability to meet organisational concerns, giving oneself some space for manoeuvre.

Such performance may break down in the context of threats and constraints in the work environment, and we may be forced to respond with impressions and performances which are 'out of character' for the expected role. Kunda characterises these as *enlargement dramas*, where in formal or informal circumstances the routine order of role-playing is allowed temporarily to break down, and individuals are allowed to enlarge upon the selves they generally present, exhibiting attitudes or capabilities beyond their required roles. Such dramas are often associated with temporary or marginal members of organisations. Similarly, individuals may experience difficulty in coping with situations where their projected images are not adequate to achieving some measure of control or meaning. For example, Hochschild, in examining the supervision of emotional labour, cites the reaction of a flight attendant whose pay cheque had been mishandled: 'I can't take this all day and then come back here and take it from you! You know I get paid to take it from the passengers, but I don't get paid to take it from you' (1983: 18).

The IM element of Kunda's identity displays is analogous to the *display rules* noted by Mann (1999, see below). These rules are generally organisation-specific, but they can be related to the scripted cultures such as the 'have a nice day' (HAND) culture which, she argues, are spreading out from the service sector. The HAND culture is characterised by the *fast-food server* script which is used by waitresses, shop assistants, receptionists and flight attendants to guide IM and emotional labour to encourage customers to come back. The rules are not, however, homogenous across cultures, the rule about smiling, for example, being contrary to expectations in Japan and some Muslim cultures, though in some Mediterranean cultures such as Greece they are even stronger than in the US/UK (1999: 24–6). The 'have a rotten day' culture, on the other hand, though again familiar from Hochschild's conception of emotional labour, is characterised by the *debt collector* script, where people such as bouncers, security staff and police use displays of anger, irritation or disapproval 'to discourage re-use of the service' (1999: 45). The final script Mann notes is the *lawyer* script characteristic of the 'have a cool day' culture used in many professional and social settings to mask emotions. Doctors, managers and politicians might use this script, which emphasises lack of warmth and emotion, in order to maintain an image of 'detached concern' (1999: 43). The importance of these scripted cultures is both in their integration of IM and emotional labour, and in the extent to which learning them is crucial to the development of careers and the professional identities associated with them. This reaches its zenith in the notion of *personal branding* (Peters, 1997) where the commodification of the self is recommended as the route to career success and requires the careful packaging of identity in IM terms (see Lair, Sullivan and Cheney, 2005 for a further discussion). However, career development is in effect a misnomer for many undertaking routine work in modern occupations. Scripted impression management effectively is the job and the employees are often carrying out *dramaturgical labour* (McHugh, 1997), involving both regulation of their impressions and advocacy for the organisation. Within such strictures, identity work in contexts such as call centres must be carried out in whatever spaces a scripted culture leaves to them. (Callaghan and Thompson, 2002).

Identity working: strategies for organisational survival

With the capacity to redefine meanings and manage impressions, human beings are capable of creating their own self-fulfilling prophecies and self-attributed judgements, shifting the ground on which they stand to justify both success and failure. Indeed strategies of this kind could in one sense be said never to fail entirely. In counterpoint to strategies which lead to negative consequences for the individual, there are forms of making out which can lead more unambiguously to social recognition, approval and self-justified identities. For example, pressure to define identity in line with assumed leadership qualities can lead to subjectively supportive behaviours and self-perceptions. The failure of others to recognise an individual as a leader, or attempts to undermine their leadership, might lead to perceived contradictions with the leader's self-justified role. These could be handled by more autocratic attempts at control, justified by attributions of deviant characteristics to those causing the disturbance. Conversely, if strategies to cope with the situation fail and put the identity of the ostensible leader at risk, he or she could distance him or herself from the role on the basis that dealing with such people was impossible or not worth the effort.

Such strategies are by no means restricted to leadership roles, nor are they simply abstract categories of identity work, but basic strategies of *domination* and *distancing* (Knights and Willmott, 1985) which allow managers or others to ignore the fact that their power is dependent on the compliance of their colleagues or subordinates. Compliance in this sense is related to Rotter's (1972) notion of internal and external *loci of control*. People who feel that they are externally controlled may also put themselves into a state of *learned helplessness*, where the tendency to comply becomes part of the way individuals define themselves (Seligman, 1975).

At the same time, distancing is also one of the main patterns of identity work identified by Cohen and Taylor (1978), whose focus is not on power and interdependence, but rather on 'escape attempts'. Escape from, or resistance to, the mundanity and unpleasantness of everyday life is in this sense crucial to our subjectively 'making out'. However, the strategies they see as employed in identity work can still have relevance to the understanding of how making out is incorporated into the social relations of production. Cohen and Taylor start out at the level of the 'regularities which we happily accept as part of life' (1978: 26). These regularities are not necessarily tedious behavioural repetition, but are scripts to which we *unreflexively accommodate* as a method of managing the 'paramount reality' of our objective world. Scripts in this sense are more than the 'mindless' behaviour posited by Langer or the 'sensorimotor' activity posited by Hacker and Volpert (see Chapter 20).

The habitual dependence on scripts referred to by Cohen and Taylor can be a defence against uncertainty, as well as providing meaning through their very regularity. However, our capacity for self-reflection allows us to create a *zone for self* or *identity domain* (1978: 32), which enables us to distance ourselves from those who appear to be committed to the scripts by which they live. The capacity to be self-reflexive can effectively remove the need actually to do anything about the conditions of our existence, because we critically separate ourselves from them in our thoughts. At the same time we often deprecate those we see as not having our own level of critical self-awareness, defining them as something less than ourselves. The paradox here is our fellow workers are likely to have the same thoughts about ourselves, since they do not see our thoughts, only our regulated actions and routine behavioural displays.

A concomitant capacity with which self-reflexiveness endows us is the release of the *escape into fantasy* where we can alter the conditions of our life to our own satisfaction. This form of escape is akin to the strategy of unconscious resistance identified by Leonard. Leonard's identification of these escapes with position in the organisational hierarchy can now be understood, in that fantasy is free. Cohen and Taylor also note socially institutionalised routes of escape which are seen as legitimate self-expression, where 'assertions of meaninglessness of the activity are virtually taboo' (1978: 95). These *activity enclaves* give us free areas in our lives, where, in the terminology of Seve and Leonard, we can develop 'personal concrete capacities'. Such socially approved escapes from work or the lack of it include hobbies, games, sports, holidays and the attractions of mass culture.

On the other hand, there are less socially approved activity enclaves which are often viewed as self-obsessive or destructive. 'Preoccupations' with sex, gambling, drugs and even dependence on therapy are examples of this form of escape. They are, however, only different to other forms in terms of the social, legal and historical contexts in which they are carried out. Again self-reflexiveness carries its own internal contradictions. Distancing ourselves from the roles we play is, in the end, another limited and passive strategy which tends to confirm existing organisational structures, separating the individual from the possibilities inherent in social relations.

Finally, to escape from this vicious spiral of making out through reconstruction of identity concerns, Cohen and Taylor identify the strategy of *self-conscious reinvestment*. Individuals become recommitted to aspects of the very regularities – language, rituals, clothing – from which they are escaping. Within work organisations this represents the return to the fold, making something of one's life, or the rescue of career. All of these means of psychic escape can be utilised to further managerial control, either by employees' dependence on the financial and social supports necessary to pursue them or, in the case of reinvestment, the cleaving-back to the very structures of control themselves. For those who run organisations, the problem is to monitor and control the identity work of employees to ensure that they do not overstep the bounds of the acceptable. For the employee, the problem is to discover the appropriate mode of escape, enjoyment and making out for the subjective and objective conditions pertaining at the time. Indeed in the introduction to the second edition of *Escape Attempts* Cohen and Taylor, after trying manfully to come to terms with the post-structuralist appropriation of individual agency and rejection of any paramount reality, conclude that:

> We think now that we should have shown more appreciation of the comic/heroic diversity of people's search for something outside of paramount reality, more recognition of folk wisdom, more sensitivity to the idea that the very activity of 'attempting' to escape is an imaginative way to understand more about the limitations of our world. We would feel less constrained now to explain away the resultant diversity, inventiveness and messiness by appealing to what Rorty calls the 'aesthetic priesthood's' attempt to escape from time and chance. (Cohen and Taylor, 1992: 28)

This recalls our earlier comments that what is important in identity work is how we use the organisation as much as how organisations use us and nowhere is this better exemplified than in the area of managerial identity work.

Managerial labour and identity work

Managerial education outside organisations is based on reinforcing the ideological identity work required of managers. The content of managerial education is effectively directed at making concrete the notion that systematic control over complex and variable processes is possible. For managers, the expected rewards in financial and career mobility terms are bought through a process of personal and group identity work. This increases self-perceived competence at handling the contingent uncertainties of organisational life, with the concomitant organisational gains of increased effort and commitment in overcoming goal barriers. Management education can be a means of reinforcing self-image and confidence. In Sturdy and colleagues' terms, the MBA thus becomes: 'a means for acquiring appropriate language fluency in management and the self-confidence to gain legitimacy and social privilege in senior management' (2006: 841), a form of, 'therapeutic language training' (2006, 855).

The form and content of control processes are influenced by the responses of managerial groups to pressures on the identities produced in their role as agents of capital. Mobilising their consent to expose themselves to the threats and pressures of management roles has its own particular place in the labour process. It also underpins the mobilisation of consent of production workers to comply with that supervision:

> Managers, though suffering from frustration and a perceived lack of strategic control, provide operational and systemic flexibility in organisations through their labour...it is the buffering provided by managerial labour between strategic policies and productive labour itself that is necessary to provide the continuance of structured forms of organising work. (McHugh, 1997: 2)

We saw in Chapter 7 that changes in the managerial labour process have often fragmented and diminished the power of individual managers (Tuelings, 1986). This will depend, of course, on the position and situational power of the managers involved, but it does point to the fact that managerial work has its own levels of alienation and fragmentation. If this is so, then dominant organisational groups will also expend effort and devise strategies to secure and defend their identities. Hochschild (1993: xi), for example, notes that managers are involved in emotional labour in regulating both their own feelings and those of others. This dual responsibility can have mixed effects, Sturdy and colleagues (2006: 845) noting that:

> Sennett (1998) for example, has highlighted the fragility and fragmentation of management identities in conditions of flexibility, downsizing and changing management culture – 'How can a human being develop a narrative of identity and life history in a society composed of episodes and fragments'. (1998: 26; see also Heery and Salmon, 2000; Webb, 2004)

In delineating forms of managerial work, McHugh (1997) (see Chapter 23) argues that managers, as well as being involved in operational, emotional, intellectual and dramaturgical practices, perform attributional labour in regulating and ascribing intent and commitment to themselves and their subordinates. Causal judgement in attributional terms (see Chapter 18) is thus claimed to be a significant factor in managerial versions of impression management and identity work, especially in processes such as performance appraisal and locating the pathology of organisational problems. The implication here is that managerial activity may be derived more from attributions about causes of events than from simple responses to circumstances. As such, there may be a managerial bias to dispositional attributions in defining performance objectives for employees, and an environmental bias in defining such objectives for themselves. At the same time McHugh (1997: 8) cites Leavitt and Bahrami (1988: 65) to the extent that 'managers are both blessed and cursed by that tendency to ascribe causality, because the causality – either way – is often ascribed to them rather than to other aspects of the situation'.

Effective managerial identity work can thus utilise worker resistance and associated damage to productivity and profitability as an ideological justification for managers' own strategies to enhance identity.

At the same time, managerial responsibility for shaping the identities and emotions of employees can threaten managers' own identities and emotions. As we discussed in Chapter 11, managers make considerable emotional investments in the design and outcomes of culture change programmes. Yet those programmes tend to be predicated on unrealistic expectations that employees will 'buy into' or 'take ownership' of the objectives and practices. When that does not happen, it is managers who have to carry the 'culture burden' (Thompson and Findlay, 1999). They are caught in the middle between selling the message to the troops and explaining why it is not working to the board. Their identity as effective change agents can be secured only by taking responsibility for redoubling efforts to 'communicate effectively', or alternatively becoming cynical about and partially disengaging from the change process itself.

Managers, may then misbehave in ways that serve their interests at the expense of the organisation, Ackroyd and Thompson (1999; see Chapter 8) present an analysis of how acting contrary to organisational interests through various categories of misbehaviour produces managerial practice. They look at the factors influencing managerial decisions about and responses to misbehaviour (1999: 81) and the kinds of managerial strategy these are typically related to (1999: 88). Especially important here is the concept of 'controlled autonomy', which is what HRM policies pursue but seldom achieve because of the barriers placed on change, including those of managerial identity. Ackroyd and Thompson offer a useful account of how the dynamics of control act to produce and amplify misbehaviour, adding detail to classic concepts such as the 'vicious spirals' associated with McGregor's Theory X and Y (see Chapter 21. Though this is schematic and stylised, it does offer insights into the process of control, rather than using control as an abstract determinant concept like authority or power. It also raises the notion of two effects that intensify the 'impulse to control' (1999: 95–6). The first, the measurement effect, is the area in which classic organisational psychology serves managerial strategy in producing technologies of regulation, and is resonant of our arguments on personality testing in Chapter 15. The second, the innovation effect, where 'increased managerial attention will cause behavioural innovation' (1999: 95), can be related to the idea of 'engaging the intellect' we raised in Chapter 20. Thus processes of surveillance, environmental scanning and self-monitoring produce new behaviours and practices to identify, subvert and constrain them. Ackroyd and Thompson thus provide linkages from managerial labour and identity work to specific psychological processes such as learning, group dynamics and attribution.

Summary and key points

Identity work is conscious and unconscious, individual and collective, competitive and collaborative. It is the vehicle of self-expression and enactment, and at the same time binds us to systems of ideological self-legitimation through which we accede to systems of control, both internal and external. The networks we access and the roles we are expected to take on in the workplace provide the scripts, our interactions and negotiations with others the arena in which we act them out. It appears that what we strive towards in producing consistent role performances and in maintaining a secure identity is a situation where we do not have to negotiate who and what we are with others, where our concerns, actions and status are automatically legitimate. In this sense, identity work is the medium through which we express power over ourselves, others and situations.

We buy into systems of control in order to increase our situational power, and at the same time we resist pressures to make us completely controlled by our role and the demands of others. In many ways identity work is the primary work of organising, if not of organisations themselves. As such, it must also be the primary work of those who structure the processes of organising towards corporate ends. One appeal of management, beyond the extrinsic rewards, is that just being a manager automatically affirms and protects identity, at the expense of diminishing the manager's capacity to resist the role demands the position confers. The manager as a communicator of role demands has in effect committed him- or herself to controlling the identity work of others, which in turn commits him or her to one or another form of response to such pressures.

It is through identity work that the conditions of being a subject and of being subject gain substance for managers and workers alike. The negotiation and pursuit of identity concerns and projects make up the drama of everyday organisational experience. As we have seen, the psychological processes underwriting that drama cannot give an adequate account of it in purely mechanistic terms. Neither, though, can interpretative or structural accounts afford to ignore the influence those processes have on us in our journey to becoming fully-fledged participants in the modern work organisation.

Further reading

Ostensibly there should be a myriad of further readings on this topic, the problem being that the very amount of work now extant on identity tends to confuse the issue, especially in terms of the alternative readings available in post-structuralist accounts. For example, the collection by Pullen, Beech and Sims (2007) has the worthy and the obfuscating in equal measure in Part 1, though Part 2 on methods is a very good resource for anyone interested in researching identity. The approach we have taken in this edition is informed in detail by Thompson and Marks' (2007) ILPC paper on the 'Blank Slate'; to follow up on the issues raised there see Webb's (2006) sociological text and Leidner's (2006) paper. Knippenberg and Schie's (2000) paper provides a useful psychological perspective though in socio-psychological terms it is still worthwhile to go back to Breakwell's (1992) text, which is still available. If you want a rewarding read in the area then go back to Goffman's *Presentation of Self* which is still a staple for social psychology students. And last but not least, Cohen and Taylor's *Escape Attempts* is a much more wide-ranging exposition than the narrow focus we have portrayed here.

Breakwell, G.M. (1992) *Social Psychology of Identity and the Self Concept*, Guildford: Surrey University Press in association with Academic Press.

Cohen, S. and Taylor, L. (1992) *Escape Attempts: The Theory and Practice of Resistance to Everyday Life* (2nd edn), London and New York: Routledge.

Goffman, E (1959) *The Presentation of Self in Everyday Life*, Garden City, NY: Doubleday.

Knippenberg, D.V. and Schie, E.C.M.V (2000) 'Foci and Correlates of Organisational Identification', *Journal of Occupational and Organisational Psychology*, 73: 137–47.

Leidner, R. (2006) 'Identity and Work', in M. Korczynski, R. Hodson and P. Edwards (eds.), *Social Theory at Work*, Oxford: Oxford University Press, 424–63.

Pullen, A., Beech, N. and Sims, D. (2007) *Exploring Identity: Concepts and Methods*, London: Palgrave Macmillan.

Thompson, P. and Marks, A. (2007) 'Beyond the Blank Slate: Towards an Understanding of the Formation of Identities and Interests in the Employment Relationship', International Labour Process Conference.

Webb, J. (2006) *Organisations, Identities and the Self*, London: Palgrave Macmillan.

part IV

theorising organisation

Introduction: the story so far

In Chapter 1 we set out some broad principles or ways of seeing organisations and society that inform a critical approach, and that have guided our efforts in this book. These include the need to be reflexive in not taking organisational processes for granted, to locate theory and practice in their historical and comparative contexts, and for explanations to be multi-dimensional. We have tried to utilise an approach that can explain the embeddedness of organisational action. Throughout the book we have been highly resistant to any variety of deterministic, 'one best way', or single, overarching explanations for complex processes. Yet clearly action is not random. The reciprocal interaction of different structures and agencies still produces specific patterns and these need to be theorised.

In earlier chapters we have, of course, discussed theory, whether that is Weber's account of bureaucracy, a labour process analysis of control, or population ecology explanations of organisation–environment relations. So what is different here? Many of the theories we have looked at are specific to particular issues, such as the resource dependency theory of power. Others, such as institutional theories of convergence and diversity, have broader application but are still specific to the organisational sphere. The purpose here is to dig a little deeper and look at the resources provided by more general social science theories.

So what is the state of play? When concluding his entertaining 'short and glorious history of organisation theory', Perrow (1973) hit an optimistic note. The forces of light (human relations) and darkness (scientific management and other mechanistic perspectives) had fought each other to a standstill. Out of the debris, all schools of thought agreed that organisations should be understood as complex, open systems in which environmental variables, including technology, explained most of the variation within and between industries. Solutions based on better interpersonal relations, good leadership and job redesign had no scientific basis. Changing the structure of rewards or authority remained the most effective route to success: 'after manipulating these variables, sit back and wait for two or three months for them to take hold. This is complicated and hardly as dramatic as many of the solutions being peddled, but I think the weight of organisational theory is in its favour' (1973: 27).

Looking back, this optimism looks decidedly odd. As Reed had earlier commented, 'contemporary students of organisation find themselves at a historical juncture and in a social context where all the old ideological "certainties" and technical "fixes" that once underpinned their "discipline" are under attack and seemingly on the retreat' (1997: 32). Nor is this new. The field had begun to fragment and become more contested within a decade of Perrow's original musings, and such trends accelerated thereafter. Those differences and conflicts have evolved in recent years, away from the original interpretive and Marxian critiques of the system's orthodoxy to contemporary challenges posed by postmodernism. We hope in previous chapters to have captured some of the ebb and flow of such debate. But as an introductory text, we could not let the shadow of grand theory fall too heavily across the pages. Part IV pulls in the other direction, though nothing too ambitious is attempted. Instead, the emphasis is put on examining more of the theoretical resources that underpin organisational research and analysis, reflecting back on some of the substantive issues we have dealt with elsewhere.

Later in Part IV we turn our attention to examining the relations between theories, and between theory and practice. In doing so, we evaluate the usefulness of treating general theories as competing paradigms, an approach pioneered by Burrell and Morgan (1979). A paradigm is a conceptual map that draws on basic differences in the philosophy of science and social theory to enable us to see the world (and the place of organisations within it) in a distinctive way. Particular groups of theorists develop common conceptual languages that are different from and hostile to other paradigms. Parker and G. McHugh comment that:

> For Burrell and Morgan, paradigms are incommensurable belief systems that contain the core assumptions to which a research community adheres. Along with Kuhn (1970), they argue that these are not merely 'opinions' on a particular matter but the ontological and epistemological grounds on which theorists build their particular conceptions of a discipline. (Parker and G. McHugh, 1991: 451)

Leaving aside the controversial 'incommensurability' question for the time being, ontology refers to the assumptions we make about what we know and the nature of reality, while epistemology concerns assumptions about how we know things, the grounds of knowledge that influence that often underpin the methodological choices researchers make. While, as will become clear, we are unsympathetic to the idea that organisational analysis is or should be driven by a never-ending paradigm war, subsequent chapters do show that theoretical conflicts do inter-cut between ontological and epistemological questions. We shall try and guide the reader through these troubled and complex waters.

The aims of Part IV are to:

- Briefly outline some of the core theoretical resources that underpin mainstream management writing about work and organisation.
- Give a more detailed account, comparison and evaluation of critical alternatives to the mainstream, from social action/interpretive approaches and critical social psychologies, to labour process and radical Weberian perspectives, and postmodernism and post-structuralism.
- Enable how concrete issues, such as control strategies and McDonaldisation of service work can be better understood through the theoretical resources that generated the concepts and research.
- Examine the implications of critical approaches for relations between theories and between theories and practice, and to make a case for a pluralistic, problem-solving and practice-oriented approach to analysing work and organisation.

26 resources for orthodoxy

If one were to examine the contents of some of the leading organisation theory journals, particularly in Europe, a quite different picture of orthodoxy would emerge from that described in this chapter. Such journals abound with postmodern and other critical perspectives. What, then, is the justification for regarding systems theory and its related ways of thinking as orthodoxy? It is in part historical: this was constructed as the mainstream. It is also geographic: North America remains dominated by what one of its leading defenders describes as a 'functionalist-positivist' approach (Donaldson, 1996). Most of all, it is about the unique relationships that organisational analysis has with a practitioner community. Mainstream approaches continue to provide theoretical resources that range from standard academic research to simple 'how to do it' manuals. If we were to take a narrower version of management theory, it would be accurate to say that practice has drawn unevenly on two basic traditions: a rational, mechanistic one that came to the fore with Taylor and scientific management, and a stream of more normative, organic thinking that is particularly associated with human relations (Barley and Kunda, 1992). But management thinking, on the surface at least, draws lightly on theory. What are the deeper roots and means of explanation?

Weber, bureaucracy and rationality

We outlined Weber's views in some detail in Chapter 3, and his writings on bureaucracy reappear in a variety of contexts. Yet his intellectual legacy is, as we shall see, not straightforward, for it is claimed by both mainstream and critical traditions. The basis of the former claim is not difficult to identify. Donaldson affirms that 'much of Organisation Theory derives from Weber's (1968) work on authority and bureaucracy' (1985: 6). If, as one of its advocates asserts, mainstream theory 'has as its central problematic the design of efficient organisations' (Hinings, 1988: 2), Weber's model of bureaucracy remains the template. Donaldson goes on to argue that 'Organisation Theory seems to be distinguishable as a body of thought by a concern for internal characteristics such as differentiation, standardisation, specialisation, integration, coordination and the like' (1985: 118). Weber's characterisations of functional specialisation, hierarchy, depersonalisation, formal rules and the like tend to be projected as general laws, though open systems ideas of transacting with the environment have added in arguments concerning the key contemporary and determinant variable: size, technology or any other factor.

Weber also provides orthodoxy with the theoretical sinew of rationality. Rationalisation was a theory of the transition from traditional to modern societies. For Weber, social stability was established through acceptance of authority as a form of control which people regarded as legitimate. Previous societies had been dominated by limited forms of authority based on charisma (personal qualities of leaders), or tradition (established rights and customs of dominant groups). Weber's theory went beyond economic life. Rationalisation was held to encompass processes as diverse as law, politics, religion and scientific method itself. All were becoming governed by impersonal objectives, procedures and knowledge, embodied in structures and processes which confront 'individuals as something external to them' (Brubaker, 1984: 9). The modern world is thus characterised above all by the spread of this *formal* rationality. Its elements provide a framework for coping with uncertainty, In this sense, mainstream theory draws on the idea that rational calculation makes the world more purposeful and manageable (Clegg, 1990: 32–3).

More specifically we saw in Chapter 3 that Weber believed that the rational organisation of labour required its disciplined subordination to management and organisational goals. In this Taylor was a resource. Weber saw in his schemas for the potentially 'scientific' character of management, echoes of the themes of rationality and formal control. Paralleling Weber's work, Taylor saw management by 'scientific' methods as a move away from traditional authority, where owners and managers attempted to control by inefficient, personal means. Orthodoxy also sustains its conservatism through Weber's emphasis on the market embodying rationality because it was the classic example of a disenchanted, impersonal realm dominated by the calculation of advantage, without intrusion of moral considerations (Holton and Turner, 1989: 179). Alternatives were dismissed: 'More and more the material fate of the masses depends upon the steady and correct functioning of the increasingly bureaucratic organisations of private capitalism. The idea of eliminating these organisations becomes more and more utopian' (Weber, 1984: 36).

However, Donaldson and other mainstream writers fail adequately to acknowledge that for Weber rationalisation was a morally and politically problematic development. Weber makes important distinctions between types of rationality, notably *formal* and *substantive*. The former refers only to the constraining features of structure and the calculability of techniques and procedures: 'What makes modern capitalism rational is not its ends but the unprecedented extent to which actions of its economic agents are calculated' (Sayer, 1991: 96). In contrast, substantive rationality emphasises the dominance of norms and values in the choice of means to ends (Ritzer, 1996: 576). The key point is that while formal techniques are of a specific type, such values and ends inevitably differ. Thus space is opened up for recognition of contested rationalities between groups and individuals. Indeed Weber acknowledged that the formal and substantive were always potentially in conflict, frequently making pessimistic comments about human needs being subordinated to the former. The formally rational, such as the pursuit of profit by merging and 'asset stripping' companies, may be substantively irrational in terms of its social consequences. For example, downsized companies may improve short-run profitability but find that they have lost the tacit and organisational knowledge necessary for long-term efficiency and innovation. In this sense Weber does make some separation of rationality and efficiency, not only for the above reason, but because there could in principle be different views of what constitutes either category. For example, workers' co-operatives and private ownership could both be regarded as efficient on the basis of different value criteria.

These kind of points form part of the basis of a defence of Weber by some writers (such as Albrow, 1992) against the normal way his ideas are used in mainstream theory. But though this has some validity, it is not clear how significant it is. Aside from the fact that Weber is not always clear about the separation and its consequences (see Storey, 1983: 26–34), from the viewpoint of evaluating mainstream perspectives as a whole, most theorists influenced by Weber have acted as if rationality and efficiency are the same thing. As a result they have tended to be rather uncritical of existing organisations. Reed notes:

> The causal link which he is thought to have identified between rational bureaucracy and technical efficiency provided a substantive focus and theoretical bone of contention from which a general theory of organisations, based on a systems frame of reference, could be constructed in the course of the 1950s. (Reed, 1985: 17)

Weber's model of bureaucracy has of course been endlessly refined and renewed. Some neo-Weberians have sought to offset its simplicities by developing alternative designs within bureaucracy, such as those influenced by contingency models (Fischer and Sirriani, 1984: 9). Others, such as Blau and Gouldner, have built from the distinction between formal and substantive rationality in order to uncover the neglected aspects of the functioning of bureaucratic organisations, their empirical research revealing two key processes. First are the inefficiencies arising from the following of impersonal rules, such as the displacement of the original goals by obsession with narrow interest and ritual by the office holder. Second is the dependence of bureaucratic organisations on informal, innovative behaviour and consensual human relations. These writers have greater affinities with social action theory, which we will examine later. We will also return to examine the alternative, radical structuralist reading of Weber in the next chapter.

Durkheim, human relations and social needs

The other 'founding father' of sociology to have a significant impact on organisational analysis has been Durkheim, though there is a marked contrast to Weber. Durkheim's contribution to understanding the transition to modernity centres on the significance of the *division of labour* in sustaining the social solidarity necessary for the survival of the 'organism' of society or enterprise. Writing in the late nineteenth century, he observed that the more complex division of labour in industrial, urban society was undermining traditional values and social order of a 'mechanical' kind held together by faith in a common morality. But at the same time it was laying the basis for a more effective integration of individuals in society, which was labelled 'organic solidarity'. This advanced industrial, technological division of labour was inevitably based on specialisation, hierarchy and functional interdependence between tasks and occupations. Durkheim recognised that the new arrangements and formal structures contained sources of social disorganisation, conflict and harmful individualism, summed up in the term *anomie*. Any effective division of labour could therefore take root and bind people together only when it was sustained by new social values, by moral communities such as professional or occupational groups, and when workers had an understanding of their place within the overall scheme of production.

This kind of formulation was later interpreted through mainstream theory in terms of the permanent tension between the technical and formal needs of the organisation and the social needs of those who worked in it. It was therefore management's role not just to organise the former, but to carry out running repairs on the latter. This necessitated paying specific attention to the *informal* side of the organisation, particularly to the primary groups to which people belonged, such as workgroups. In the 1920s and 1930s this theme was taken up and popularised by Elton Mayo, who had identified problems arising from the breakdown of traditional skills and values associated with the rise of mass production. Researchers could help management to reintegrate the worker by identifying social needs and relating them to common values that led to identification with the company. Human relations analysis also drew from a Durkheimean framework, when it 'defined the anomic consequences of capitalism as abnormal, as a deviation from the ideal circumstances of organic solidarity' (P. Hamilton, 1980: 70).

Barnard (1938) extended the original analysis with emphasis on how large-scale organisations could become 'co-operative social systems', based on specialised competencies and common goals. He more clearly defined the role of the executive and the specialised managerial function in terms of defining and communicating goals, and securing workforce effort. A key feature of the human relations approach is the social engineering role given to management through maintaining equilibrium and integrating the parts of the organisation. The vehicle is not formal structures of co-ordination and command, but values, informal practices and the 'logic of sentiment'. Though a subordinate aspect of organisational analysis for considerable periods, as we saw in Chapter 11, it reappeared within a new socio-economic context and new management writings on corporate culture such as Peters and Waterman's *In Search of Excellence*

(1982). Attention is being focused once again on employees' social needs, the human side of the enterprise, and on creating and sustaining unity through common cultures. In one of the more theoretical pieces, Ouchi and Johnson (1978) draw directly on a Durkheimean framework which sees a modern division of labour involving a loss of moral community and mutual obligation, with a decline in the role of the family, Church and other institutions. Durkheim believed that the necessary function of social control and cohesion could be played by professions and occupational groups, a theme echoed later by Mayo. Ouchi and Johnson argue that Japanese work organisations have provided the necessary primary relations. Ray (1986) extends the analysis by pointing out that the corporation is expected to take on the functions embodied in Durkheim's realm of the sacred. Hence the emphasis is both on faith in the firm and binding rites and rituals.

Interestingly, the emphasis on corporate culture clashes with some central features of Durkheim's perspective that depended on the existence of professions and other intermediary groups to generate moral communities. For Durkheim, the modern individual must be equipped to question moral systems, not just to need to identify with the collective or its symbols (Dahler-Larsen, 1994: 10). In addition, Durkheim provided a critique of market rationality, which tends to foster excessive egoism and acquisitive individualism. This is just one example of a growing trend in social theory to see a diferent, more critical legacy from Durkheim's work (Pearce, 1989; Starkey, 1992; Lincoln and Guillot, 2006). But, even more so than Weber, it remains the case that this is not how Durkheim has been used as a resource for orthodoxy.

Systems theory

The roots of systems thinking go back a very long way. As we saw in Chapter 2, engineering 'systematisers' were a driving force in the construction of early management theory and practice. Human and non-human entities were seen as interchangeable and manipulable (Shenhav, 1999: 19). While such thinking was limited as theory, its focus on organisations as purposeful, interdependent systems resembles the basic organic analogy used by Durkheim and others, in which all social systems have to adapt to the environment to survive. In such biological analogies, system parts (or sub-systems) are interconnected, and each is functional to the viability of the organisation, for example by generating binding social values. This became a theme of *functionalist* social theory (Parsons, 1951) which regards social systems as self-regulating bodies, tending towards a state of equilibrium and order. This has long had an influence in organisational theory. In their description and theorisation of the Hawthorne experiments, Roethlisberger and Dickson (1964) talked of industrial organisation in terms of functioning social systems striving for equilibrium under the influence of environmental factors (Reed, 1998: 37). Donaldson (1985: 29) argues that there *is* movement within equilibrium, but it is a process of internal adjustment between the sub-systems and to the environment over time, normally triggered by external change such as those in technologies or markets. Nevertheless any breakdown of order tends to be treated as pathological, and the non-rational elements confined to the informal organisation.

The classical theories, including scientific management and human relations, can be conceived as *closed system* perspectives, previously discussed in Chapter 3. By treating the organisation as a structure of manipulable parts that could be regulated internally, it appeared as if a rational means–ends relationship could be optimised. It was a question of re-balancing the human and technical, or formal and informal components, when one changed more rapidly than the other (Brown, 1992: 45). This can again be related to functionalist analysis, whose primary assumption is that the components of the structure must be integrated to ensure system survival. Change is likely to occur when 'the functional contributions of a given structural arrangement are exceeded by dysfunctions associated with the arrangement' (Tolbert and Zucker, 1996: 176).

The focus of manipulating the parts, as we know, shifted to an *open systems* approach – organisations coping with uncertainty through exchange and transaction – with *contingency theory*, with its emphasis on 'designing organisations rationally so that their internal coherence and external match to their environments are both maximised' (Tsoukas, 1994c: 4), the most popular variant. As Donaldson (1996: 63) notes, 'Fit is the underlying key'. While, as we saw in Chapter 5, contingency theorists identify a range of factors that might couple structure and environment, the common theory is structural adaptation to regain fit. In other words, there is a positive performance outcome of a fit between each contingency and one or more aspect of organisational structure. If an organisation moves into misfit, a new phase of structural adaptation begins to regain the desired relationship. Despite such transactions, mainstream organisational analysis has increasingly presented itself as divorced from broader theory. One of Donaldson's (1985) central arguments is that organisations can be studied as an independent realm. If the outside world comes into it, it is as the 'environment', a backcloth against which it is possible to specify relationships between contingencies, structure and performance. As Willmott observes, the various factors in this environment 'must be registered and controlled if strategic adjustments are to be successfully achieved. There is minimal consideration of the relevance of social theory ... for the study of organisations' (1990: 45).

Woodward, one of the most noted contingency theorists, sums up the intellectual confidence felt by those pursuing this approach from the 1950s onwards:

> " Even more important from the point of view of ultimate theory building is the fact that various schools of thought are beginning to see themselves as concerned with the study of systems ... the starting point is the identification of a system and the subsequent questions asked are very much the same: what are the objectives and strategic parts of the system under review and how are these parts interrelated and interdependent? One result is that those concerned with the study of organisation are beginning to develop a common language, on whatever discipline their work is based. (Quoted in Eldridge and Crombie, 1974: 93)

Donaldson (1996) accurately observes that the systems-contingency approach became the dominant paradigm and there was a considerable period of doing 'normal science' (a term taken from Kuhn), and designating the testing of evidence and replication of studies within a particular framework. He argues that though challenged by critics, such as Child's concept of strategic choice (see Chapter 5) and by institutional theory (see Chapter 6), structural contingency theory has provided effective refutations or can cope with the addition of new variables. It is certainly true that most of the organisation theory done during the 1950s and 1960s can be contained under the heading 'systems rationalism' (Barley and Kunda, 1992). While not all its components could be described in terms of systems theory, operations research, decision-making theory and process theories of motivation shared an emphasis on controlling organisations through managing the boundaries between sub-units and the interface between inputs and outputs. In such theorising 'employees were largely absent' (Barley and Kunda, 1992: 380), which is another way of saying that agency had been squeezed out of the picture.

However, not all of the challenges are easily absorbed. Take the rise of institutional theory (see Lounsbury and Ventresca, 2003). It is true that a key emphasis is on the symbolic properties of systems. Successful adaptation to the environment in terms of legitimacy and resources depends significantly on fit with dominant institutional and state-influenced practices (such as employment policies) and social norms (Meyer and Rowan, 1977). While in one sense this is adding culture as an adaptive variable, institutional theory challenged the way in which efficiency and rationality were understood in the systems approach. As Tolbert and Zucker (1996) observe, organisations and particular structures could survive despite relatively limited efficiency, and rational decision-making is normatively bounded. Institutional theories (which we discussed mainly in Chapter 6) move beyond open system approaches by considering, 'how different kinds of "environments" might be structurally connected to varying kinds of organisations such that their nature could be expected to differ systematically in contrasting situations' (Whitley, 2003: 484). The varieties of capitalism perspective is one example. Despite these advances, such approaches often did not move far enough beyond the determinism in systems theory. Institutionalisation was too often characterised by habitualised action, largely taken for granted by the actor.

Meanwhile, Donaldson (2005) continues to affirm the system's faith, but even he seems to accept that there is a certain exhaustion reached in contingency and related approaches. In a contribution to a symposium in *The Journal of Management Inquiry* (Schwarz *et al.*, 2007), he argues for a new approach – statistico-organisational theory – that prioritises methodological principles over substantive organisational theories. The belief that methods in general and a very particular one in practice have sufficient explanatory power to adequately engage with the complexities of organisational life is unlikely to persuade non-adherents that his favoured orthodoxy can contain and absorb critique. If we examine the theoretical developments since the 1970s, the problem of determinism has been the key factor. Donaldson (1998) is open about the unwillingness or inability to offer explanations at the level of the human actor, preferring to talk of systems imperatives constraining managerial action to a high degree, influencing only the timing of structural change; but he underestimates the significance of a failure to do so. Individual behaviour is seen as 'determined by and reacting to structural constraints that provide organisational life with an overall stability and control' (Astley and Van de Ven, quoted in Mills and Murgatroyd, 1991: 5). The new wave of theorising was set to react against these images of orderly entities and passive people.

27 critical alternatives

A lot of academic water has passed under many theoretical bridges since early editions of this book. The most significant, for the purposes of this chapter, has been the rise of Critical Management Studies, widely abbreviated to CMS. This now has a well-established bi-annual conference in the UK, a formally recognised Interest Group of the American Academy of Management Group (from 2002), as well as its own listserv and sympathetic journals such as *Organization*. It will soon have its own prestigious Handbook (Alvesson, Bridgman and Willmott, 2009). What all this reflects and now shapes is the availability of a much greater variety and depth of critical resources available. Given that, as the most authoritative overview of the field notes, 'Overall, CMS has been strongest in the area of work organization' (Adler, Forbes, and Willmott, 2007: 34), this growth is doubly welcome for territories covered by our book. As that review also recognises, the more CMS has grown in scale and scope, the more it has become a somewhat heterogeneous catch-all that shares some common themes. However, we can broadly distinguish between two versions of CMS: a broad tent whose theoretical resources are pluralistic, albeit divided between structural-materialist and postmodern (as in Adler, Forbes and Willmott, 2007) and a smaller tent in which the favoured approaches are clearly postmodern and post-structuralist (see Fournier and Grey, 2000). *Work Organisations* would be firmly in the former tent, but not in the latter. We try to give some sense of why in this chapter, but our discussion of critical resources is necessarily different to that covered by the CMS debates, because of the specific work and organisation territories covered in the book.

Social action theory

The most significant sign of a major alternative to mainstream perspectives emerged with an attack on the dominant systems theory by Silverman (1970). He brought together elements of an approach described as the *action frame of reference*, or social action theory. It was not new, drawing on the phenomenological writings of Schutz (1967) and Berger and Luckman (1967). In fact its methods can partly be traced back to Weber's conception of a social science, rather than his writings on bureaucracy. For Weber, such a science begins from interpreting social action, and the subjective meanings and purposes attached to it. This rests on a distinction between the natural and social worlds, but retains an attempt to situate individual action within material structures. Donaldson recognises another, 'interpretative' Weber, and remarks that the approach works by 'gaining insights into the subjective world of actors and constructing a model of motivated actions of the typical actor in a particular social setting' (1985: 107). His complaint is merely that those who take this up ignore the 'structural', deterministic Weber.

In renewing an action perspective, Berger and Luckman popularised the concept of *social construction of reality*. Rather than conceiving of people as products of systems and institutions, they view them as 'actors' who create these patterns through their own meaningful activity. However, it was accepted that the products of their action, for example organisational structures, appear to them as exterior 'things' with an independent existence. Social construction was one of the aspects of a dialectical approach discussed in Chapter 1, and it puts a necessary stress on the possibility of change through purposeful reflection and action.

Silverman was able to apply these kind of ideas more specifically to organisations, considering them as social constructs produced and reproduced through their members' activities. This was largely neglected in systems theory, which regards organisations as part of the natural world governed by laws concerning their structures and effects on behaviour. Hence, as we have argued, they have reified organisations and taken their basic features for granted. Silverman did not ignore structure, recognising that *roles*, as systematic patterns of expectations, were developed in the interplay between organisations and their environments. His study was largely theoretical, but built on others that were of a more empirical nature, utilising the concept of organisations as *negotiated orders* (see Day and Day, 1977). By the early 1960s Strauss and colleagues (1963) had been analysing the negotiated order in hospitals, while other notable studies included those concerned with police and legal practices (Bittner, 1967; Cicourel, 1968), and welfare agencies (Zimmerman, 1971). Another influence on this tradition was Goffman (1971), who focused on the detailed dynamics or dramas of social interaction, such as impression management and presentation of self. We discussed the importance of some of these ideas for an understanding of aspects of identity work in Chapter 25. A recurring theme of such ideas applied to the workplace was that controls exercised through rules in formal organisations were inevitably incomplete and unsuccessful. Any degree of effective co-ordination and co-operation is dependent on constant reworking of rules and goals, and formal and informal negotiation processes involving all participants. The subsequent customs and practices in any workplace act as a constraint on management.

The critique developed through action theory challenged the consensual and objective images of organisations that were often based on 'favoured' managerial definitions. By focusing on the realities of multiple goals and competing groups, dimensions of organisational life, such as work patterns and practices, could be demystified. It also shed light on why organisations do not operate as they are supposed to. As we saw in Chapter 3, this latter emphasis tied into empirical work by *neo-Weberians* who were also concerned with the bending of bureaucratic rules through the value-systems of employees (Blau, 1955; Gouldner, 1955). Indeed, Silverman utilises some of these studies extensively. He notes, for example, how Gouldner shows that industrial relations in a gypsum mine had been based on an 'indulgency pattern': implicit rules rooted in give and take rather than formal codes. When management attempted to introduce changes that clashed with the established values and practices and reasserted formal rules, it generated grievances and strike activity.

In organisation theory as such, the action perspective made its impact through Child's (1972) concept of strategic choice, which was directed against the environmental determinism of contingency theory, and was discussed in detail in Chapter 5. The theoretical significance is drawn out by Brown: 'This criticism emphasises "agency" as against "structure", that is the role of actors – managers, workers, or whoever – in choosing to pursue certain goals and/or follow certain lines of action albeit within constraints set by the actions of others and the context within which they are placed' (1992: 36).

Meanwhile, during the 1970s Silverman and other writers shifted the action approach in the more 'radical' direction of *ethnomethodology*. Though 'translated' as people-centred, it is actually only concerned with the production of a common-sense world and eschews any attempt at analysis of causation which would impose external categories. Nor is it concerned with the relation between ideas and interests, or social and organisational structures present in the Weberian tradition. It restricts itself to accounting for the processes through which members construct their everyday life. Structures tend to be viewed at best as temporary patterns created by interpersonal action and based on available stocks of knowledge. While some useful material on the 'organisational work' of reinterpreting these stocks of knowledge and routine practices was generated (Silverman and Jones, 1976), it soon became difficult to locate any notion of *organisation* in the traditional sense. Phenomena such as power or control, which are expressed through relatively durable structures beyond specific situations and face-to-face interactions and meanings, are simply outside its frame of reference.

Though taken to extremes in ethnomethodology, these weaknesses were inherent in action theory. In Silverman's earlier work he argued, contrary to contingency theory, that technological and market structures were meaningful only in terms of the understandings and attachments of participants. Though structures require the involvement of actors in their reproduction, something like a product or labour market does have a structural existence partly independent from how particular individuals think or act – as anyone who has lost their job, or a fortune on the stock exchange, will testify. Concepts such as 'role' that were used to link subjective action and structure are useful but not substantial enough to carry the burden of explaining organisational behaviour. The more disconnected action theory became from wider concerns, the more it became 'buried in an obsessive concern for the minutiae of "everyday life" as exemplified in the intricacies of organisational routines' (Reed, 1985: 48). This is linked to a further problem limiting its capacity to act as a critical resource. Despite the emphasis on empirical studies, as we raised earlier and as Silverman has admitted, the approach is aimed at providing a method of analysis, rather than a theory of organisations. Nevertheless, Silverman and social action theory continue to be a focus for discussion (Hassard and Parker, 1994) and influence (Tsoukas, 1994c). Empirical studies utilising a negotiated order framework have been undertaken in the last decade with respect to kitchen workers (Fine, 1996) and environmental inspectors (Fineman, 1998).

Social action theory is also a resource for critical psychology, in this case because of the stress on the inter-subjective nature of social behaviour as a form of negotiated order. The useful contribution of social action theories is, first, in the methodological emphasis maintained in rooting their work in accounts of subjective experience; and second, in the linking of accounts of how subjectivity is constructed to structures of control, culture and ideology in organisations. In relation to organisational psychology they represent that part of the domain of analysis characterised by subjective, partly rational action processes based on phenomenological, social constructionist models. They provide a link to the ethnomethodological tradition in sociology and to symbolic interactionism that has been influential in both sociology and social psychology.

Symbolic interactionism, following from Mead (1934), has long been the area where an interface between sociological and socio-psychological conceptions of identity has existed. The construction of identity and the social milieu within which individual identity exists is, in this model, dependent on interaction with others and through others with the self. Subjectivity, then, is mainly a product of inter-subjective processes and is constructed through the negotiation of social rules and conventions. The social production of subjectivity, though acknowledged, is addressed through an understanding of how the formal and informal processes of culture and ideology impinge upon individual functioning. This phenomenological emphasis on situated meaning in the construction of subjectivity is a necessary methodological focus in providing a reflexive account of organisational behaviour, and informs much of our account of the securing and reproduction of identity in Chapter 25. However, most of the academics who were attracted to such a view now gravitate towards the postmodernist or post-structuralist version of the 'social construction of reality' (which we examine later in the chapter). For example, a recent commentator on Goffman complained that few theorists have systematically used his work in the last 25 years (Manning, 2008: 677). For less sympathetic critical theorists, the social action approach is felt to lack a framework for understanding the social order that conditions action inside the organisation.

Radical structuralism

To escape the limits of an action approach, theory must move beyond how organisations and their environments are subjectively constituted to some kind of structural explanation of the dynamics of organisational development within capitalist societies. This section examines some of the resources that can be found for that purpose by reworking and extending the concepts provided by Marx and Weber. Following Burrell and Morgan (1979), we use the common heading of radical structuralism to signify that such theorising begins from an account of the structural framework of organisational behaviour, but is directed towards a critical explanation of the processes of regulation and change.

Marx and LPT

Marx had little to say about issues of administrative or even political organisation, and even less about the specific question of bureaucracy. As Goldman and Van Houten note, 'Systematic study of the sociology of organisations is almost absent in the classical and modern Marxist traditions' (1977: 110). Those wishing to generate a discussion from Marx have had to rely on fragments of a critique of the Prussian bureaucracy and writings on the Paris Commune of 1871 as a model of the possibility of elimination of bureaucracy through a fully democratic administrative system (Marx, 1984). When he made observations about bureaucracy, they were very Weberian, with references to systematic division of labour, hierarchies of knowledge and mechanisms of formal behaviour (Sayer, 1991: 78). Marxist theory has tended to focus on the dynamics and contradictions of capitalism as a whole, and issues concerning the distribution of the surplus product, neglecting changes in productive processes, organisational forms and occupational structures. Some Marxist concepts have been influential, if often misunderstood, notably his account of the alienation of labour; but they have remained unconnected to any systematic organisational analysis.

However, during the last three decades Marxist-influenced theory and research has had a profound effect on all of the disciplines concerned with work and organisation (see Hyman, 2006 for a good overview). This trend worries Donaldson (1985: 127), who argues that 'Marxism is a theory of society therefore it cannot be a theory of organisation'. Clegg (1988: 10) makes the apposite response that applying the same criteria to Weber would place his work on bureaucracy outside the level appropriate to organisation theory. There is a different point to be made. It is not the full apparatus of Marxist theory of history and society that has been influential, but a narrower set of ideas, though these are still central to his account of the working of capitalist production. That vehicle has been *labour process theory* (LPT), set in motion by Braverman's (1974) reworking of Marx's analysis of capitalist production (for a full account of labour process debates see Thompson, 1989; Thompson and Smith, 2000). We discussed this mainly in Chapter 8 as the framework for an explanation of control. Here we examine the deeper theoretical context.

Though more obviously influential in industrial sociology, LPT has provided conceptual tools observable in a wide range of critical organisation writers. Among the first were Clegg and Dunkerley, who began *Organization, Class and Control* (1980) by defining the theoretical object of organisational analysis: 'For this volume we have proposed as such an object the concept of organisation as control of the labour process' (1980: 1). What enables such an argument to be made? Marx may not have been interested in an understanding of organisations *per se*, but he was centrally concerned with issues of work and its organisation. By this we mean a combined emphasis on work organisations as the site of key economic processes and contradictions, and the meeting place of capital and labour; as well as organisation of work in terms of questions including the division of labour, relations of authority and control, and the distribution of rewards.

Donaldson also rightly observed that 'To qualify as distinctly neo-Marxian one would need to show the connection between work life in the organisation and change at the societal level' (1985: 128). Now there are a variety of ways in organisation analysis to demonstrate and discuss such connections, including new structuralism that draws on institutional theories (Lounsbury and Ventresca, 2003). However, connections between work relations and political economy are a strength of LPT, which Donaldson misses because the 'Marxism' he attacks is an earlier, much more general and less successful application to the sphere of work organisation. Marx defined the form of a society and economy in a manner strongly conditioned by an understanding of work relationships. Each mode of production gives rise to class relations, which under capitalism are based on the sale and purchase of labour power. The partial antagonism between capital and labour as collective classes arises from the exploitation and appropriation of the surplus labour by capital, based on its ownership and control of production. This is a far cry from the notion of fair exchange implied in mainstream theory. Work relations therefore cannot be analysed in general, but only as they are shaped by the demands of a specific system of production. As we explained in Chapter 8, the central characteristic of this process is the nature of labour as an active and indeterminate commodity. In other words, when it is purchased by capital, the outcomes remain mere potential. The goal of profitable production may be thwarted by workers asserting their own needs and self-organisation. In many ways this is a more sophisticated account of what industrial relations and other disciplines call the *wage–effort bargain*, the exchange of effort for reward, which has at its core the employment relationship (Edwards and Scullion, 1982).

The above processes cannot be understood within the confines of one organisational unit. Competition between enterprises and the conflict within the employment relationship create an accumulation process that compels capital constantly to reorganise production. Certain general features of work organisation and organisation of work tend to follow:

1   Employers need to exercise control over labour, both at the level of general directive powers and over working conditions and tasks. At the same time it is necessary to motivate employees and gain some level of consent and co-operation. Meeting these diverse and sometimes contradictory needs is the function of management systems and agents.
2   There are constant competitive pressures to cheapen the costs of production, notably labour. This may take place through deskilling, relocation of plant, work intensification or some other means; though it is subject to constraints, including worker resistance and market variations.
3   Control and cost reduction structure the division of labour, involving the design of work and division of tasks and people to give the most effective control and profitability. This is sustained by hierarchical structures and the shaping of appropriate forms of science and technology.

Let us restate this and spell out the consequences with more specific reference to organisations:

1   Work organisations are distinct from other organisations and can only be properly understood by locating the labour process within more general trends in the accumulation of capital. This 'political economy' is a bigger picture than the mainstream conception of 'the environment', but takes into account not just global patterns of ownership and competition, but how markets are shaped institutionally at regional, national and local level.
2   'Organisations are structures of control' (Salaman, 1981: 143). This involves more than control over uncertainty, monitoring objectives or means of getting work done. They are administrative apparatuses

concerned with control over productive activity in order to maximise the surplus. Managerial agency, though inherently variable and multi-layered, develops in this context.

3   In advanced capitalist societies large-scale organisations are strategic units acting as mechanisms which integrate economic, political, administrative and ideological structures (Burrell, 1980: 99).

4   Organisational structures and processes; including management and worker organisation, control and reward systems and job design, therefore are shaped by power relations and involve political issues, decisions and choices.

5   Organisations do not embody any universal rationality, but rather contested rationalities arising from the partly antagonistic relation of capital and labour, as well as from other conflicts, notably that of gender relations. Organisational change will reflect the subsequent dialectic of control and resistance.

This is not merely a question of the 'seamy side' of otherwise excellent organisations, as Gareth Morgan appears to believe (1986: 316–17). Relations of exploitation and domination are integral to capitalist and other class-divided forms of work organisation. Nevertheless the underlying principles of the relations between organisations and capitalist society are conceptualised at a very general level. Reference to class pertains to relations between capital and labour as workplace actors, with any connections to societal changes being conditional and requiring a broader frame of analysis. Similarly, while radical structuralism shares a language of structural imperatives with systems theory, it does not try to identify specific causal relations between forms of work organisation and environmental variables. Within labour process theory, there are no laws or functional imperatives concerning *specific* forms of control, organisational structures, management strategies or job designs. While structural imperatives shape and constrain the parameters of action, all these and other matters are empirical questions to be determined by research and the unfolding of real events.

It is true that a reading of Braverman's (1974) emphasis on deskilling and Taylorism as dominant tendencies can give the impression of determinism. However, second-wave and subsequent LPT has made a considerable effort to give a more complex account of structure and agency, in part by identifying a variety of levels of influence on action, including global, state and sector: 'the objective is to examine structures and actors at different *levels*, without reducing the workplace to a mirror expression of these processes, or providing over-arching schemas of determination such as the deskilling thesis, post-Fordism or control schemas from earlier labour process research' (Thompson, Smith and Ackroyd, 2000: 1153).

In more general terms, such thinking parallels frameworks such as Giddens' (1984) concept of *structuration* (though see Layder, 1987 and Whittington, 1991b for criticisms). Structures are conceived of as sets of formal and informal rules that generate common expectations and sanctions, and resources consisting of material goods and services that affect life chances. But these are conceived of not as 'external' forces, but as things on which people draw in their social interactions. Structures become both the medium and outcome of that interaction. Action is conceived more precisely as agency. Agents deploy a range of causal powers, sometimes on behalf of others who command greater resources, sometimes to bend and break rules, but always purposeful and reflexive.

We can illustrate this way of thinking about the reciprocal interaction of structure and agency through the example of the role of management. As we saw in Chapter 7, there is a tendency in mainstream literature, particularly of the popular variety, to see managers as free-floating individuals, always able to shape the destiny of their organisation. To conceive of managers as an agency of others, as a set of activities locked into structural constraints, goes against the grain. Yet that is the nature of the relations between ownership and control in a capitalist economy. This view, taken in the book, is often caricatured. Weir refers to 'the vulgar Marxist rhetoric of the inevitable polarisation of organisation between the two fundamental classes of bourgeoisie and proletariat. The managers are simply a muddle in the middle according to this way of thinking' (1993: 16). Or try Watson talking about the managers at ZTC: 'They were indeed interested in control, but it was control over their own circumstances. ... Managers were not seeking control on behalf of other groups' (1994: 85). Such explanation is all agency and no structure. Yes, managers are individuals with their own identities and values, struggling to make sense of their world and fight their corner within it. That makes a difference, but what they may seek and what they can do are often two different things, as Watson's own fascinating case makes clear. Managers are an agency of control, but the interesting questions start there, because that has to be achieved in the messy reality of particular firms with particular employees, in particular economies, governed by particular parties. A sense of management as agency is not about any simple functional necessities but, as Armstrong's work demonstrates (see Chapter 8), it is about the struggles of different professional or occupational groups to become the key core group in the workings of the enterprise. Any account of contemporary organisation must be at least *capable of* illuminating all levels, from the broader institutional constraints, through the sectional conflicts and down to real flesh and blood individuals.

The renewal of Marxist and LPT has generated or influenced a tremendous amount of historical and contemporary research at a more 'micro'-level. These share features of rich description of everyday working life with ethnomethodological and negotiated order frameworks, but seek to situate such action within a broader structural context. (See Thompson and Warhurst, 1998 for a recent collection of articles.) The selective and qualified use of Marx suggested here and by other theorists has inevitably led to accusations that LPT is no longer Marxist (Cohen, 1987; Rowlinson and Hassard, 2000). This may be true, though authentic affinity with Marxism is of concern to only those who zealously guard orthodoxy and the sacred text. Even more importantly, even if the resource provided by LPT is valuable, there are still many gaps in explanations of key organisational processes. Some of this can no doubt be remedied by further research, but it is important to recognise the limits inherent in the perspective. It sets organisations specifically in the context of capitalist production, which is both strength and weakness. Among the gaps are the following:

1   Though the labour process is the core of productive activity, it does not encompass all aspects. Any theory of the role of organisations in capitalist society must deal with the *full circuit of capital* (Kelly, 1985; Nichols, 1986), including its realisation through the sale of commodities on the market, financial issues and the prior purchase of labour (see Chapter 8 for a full discussion of this). It would be very misleading for any critical theory to proceed on the assumption that organisational processes and managerial activities were based solely on the control of labour, neglecting factors such as sales and marketing, financial controls, supply of components and product quality. Even the employment relationship, though intimately connected to the labour process, is constituted on a far wider basis (Littler, 1982). Institutions such as the state and the family, plus different cultural values and patterns in a given society, shape the distinctive character of employment relationships, as can be seen by observing examples from Japan or farm work. LPT is thus only a partial contribution to such analyses, though paradoxically it is in some ways ideally suited to organisation studies, given that the dominant managerial theories are also overwhelmingly concerned with 'the labour problem'.

2   Not all work organisations are based on commodity production, or are capitalist in character. Those in health, education or other parts of the public sector are, at least for the moment, concerned with

services for use, not profit. It is possible to construct a labour process or Marxist-oriented analysis which shows the links between the various types of public and private sector within the totality of capitalist society (Johnson, 1972; Heydebrand, 1977; Cousins, 1987). But it remains the case that not all organisational processes or forms of work activity can be understood solely through a theory whose categories are geared to explaining capitalist production, despite distorted attempts to do so, such as Bellaby and Orribor's (1977) analysis of the health service.

3   Non-profit-making organisations in capitalist societies, and forms of administration and enterprise in 'socialist' ones such as those in China and formerly in the Soviet bloc countries, also show evidence of bureaucracy, power hierarchies and work fragmentation: 'contemporary socialist societies appear to be at least as bureaucratic and with as much of a self-perpetuating bureaucracy as capitalist ones' (Dunkerley and Salaman, 1986: 87). This suggests that the dynamic of bureaucratisation is partly independent of capital–labour relations, and that critical theory requires concepts that enable us to focus on that problem.

4   While LPT is good at elaborating the connections between capitalism in general and work organisation, it has not been as successful at delineating relationships with particular forms of capitalist political economy. In practice, LPT has tended to rely on institutional theories such as those expressed in varieties of capitalism perspectives (see Chapter 6; and Coates, 2000).

For these and other reasons, as Hyman (2006: 52) observes, Marxist and labour process analysis on its own is insufficient and needs to be complemented by theoretical resources that add something, but are broadly compatible. So, what might that be? Depending on the issues, this might be feminist or institutional theories. But the most obvious way of correcting many of the points above is to draw on the tradition of radical Weberian analysis. On the one hand, his work points to the distinctive ethos and 'regime values' of bureaucratic public administration, a reflection largely of the political environment within which it operates (du Gay, 2000: 7). On the other, Weber provides a broader account of bureaucratic rationalisation that is a necessary part of explaining its spread beyond market relations. For example, he perceptively predicted that state socialist systems would be more bureaucratic than capitalism, because of the absence of countervailing power structures between the state and markets. In a command economy, the power of bureaucratised management would increase, as would the dictatorship of the official (Sayer, 1991: 145–6).

Radical Weberianism
The relevance of a left Weberianism has been largely ignored. Though some defenders of orthodoxy such as Donaldson recognise a radical Weber, many critical theorists, particularly those of a Marxist persuasion, have been hostile to the Weberian tradition (Marcuse, 1971; Johnson, 1980). Their objections relate to many of the points raised elsewhere in this book. This includes the tendency to argue that there is a bureaucratic imperative obliterating organisational differences within and between societies; that there is an inherent rationality of technique; and the identification of rationality with capitalism and the market. Also there are genuine limits to Weber's own categories, for example the emphasis on the bureaucratic hierarchy of offices has less relevance to shop-floor employees. Nevertheless there are radical Weberian perspectives, and critical writers who aim at some kind of synthesis of key aspects of Marx and Weber's analysis of work organisations (Salaman, 1979; 1981; Littler, 1982; Ray and Reed, 1994a). They rightly point to common concerns with control and domination by management and bureaucratic élites: 'For both Marx and Weber the major elements of the structure of modern large-scale organisations stem from the efforts of those who own, manage and design the organisation, to achieve control over the members'

(Salaman, 1979: 20–1). Despite this, mainstream accounts excluded domination from their reading of Weber (Shenhav, 1999: 8).

From a radical viewpoint, Weber's insights allow us to focus on a number of key areas. Work organisations operate on different levels, and in some of these, formal control procedures are important. Power is frequently constructed and legitimised through 'rationalisation', particularly through the expertise associated with science and technology, and what Weber described as 'control based on knowledge'. Even where analyses differ in focus and content, they are often complementary. Weber recognised that control rested on the 'complete appropriation' of all the material means of production by owners. Whereas Marx provides insights from an analysis of the consequences of the private ownership of the means of production, Weber identified the problem of concentration of power through the *means of administration*:

> The bureaucratic structure goes hand in hand with the concentration of the material means of management in the hands of the master. This concentration occurs, for instance, in a well-known and typical fashion, in the development of big capitalist enterprises, which find their essential characteristics in this process. A corresponding process occurs in public organisations. (Weber, 1984: 33)

In addition, both attempt to explain organisational dynamics within wider social and political structures rather than as independent, isolated phenomena, subject to their own 'laws'; though clearly the analysis of structural contexts differs. Marx's account of alienated labour and Weber's emphasis on the 'iron cage of industrial labour' share a concern for the fragmented and dehumanised nature of work. Weber saw that maximum formal rationality favoured economically powerful groups and their ability to use superior resources to dictate terms and conditions in what may appear as a freely-made contract of legal equality (Brubaker, 1984: 42–3). Social tensions and sectional conflicts between different interest groups were therefore inevitable.

Overlaps are less surprising than they appear. Both theorists shared a similar view of the necessity for modernity to sweep away the traditional social relations based on conceptions of natural order, personalised power and patriarchy. Capitalism was a flawed but dynamic system compelled constantly to revolutionise production and all social spheres. The difference, as Sayer observes, was that for Marx, 'what makes modernity modern is, first and foremost, capitalism itself' (1991: 12). In contrast, for Weber, 'capitalism is but one theatre among others where the drama of rationality is played out' (1991: 134). Weber was surely right in this, but, as we shall see later, wrong in some of the ways he understood the relationship between capitalism, rationalisation and modernity.

Key aspects of work organisation are not reducible to capitalism and its imperatives. As Littler (1982) points out, Weberian categories are especially important in understanding the employment relationship, and the career structure of employees in particular. Bureaucratic procedures and rules are relevant to the analysis of processes such as recruitment, reward and promotion. On a broader canvas, modern states and enterprises involve complex functions, management of competing interests, and performance of problematic tasks according to observable rules and norms. Some of these processes are created by and reflect specific relations of production, as in layers of supervision whose sole function is labour control and discipline. Certain functions may be artificially expanded, and new ones absorbed by bureaucrats themselves as a form of self-preservation. But as Polan notes, bureaucratic forms are a necessary object of analysis in their own right: 'Only as a result of conceding to the bureaucracy its genuine, legitimate and distinct functions can one begin to determine the boundaries of its powers and construct political control procedures that may successfully police those boundaries' (1984: 71).

Part of this legitimacy, as du Gay (2000: 4) demonstrates, is to recognise that attributes of the 'good bureaucrat' – adherence to procedure, expertise, impersonality and hierarchy – constitute 'a positive moral and ethical achievement in its own right' with respect to the particular requirements of equitable treatment of citizens and workers by public administration. For these and other reasons, radical Weberian analysis can act as a corrective to some of the more utopian aspects of the Marxist tradition in which bureaucracy and efficiency are simply reduced to specific class interests. This utopianism is reinforced by giving alternative socialist production relations a utopian capacity to avoid bureaucratisation altogether in a model of 'total democracy', based on:

> the election of everyone above the level of ordinary worker, with no fixed hierarchy and [no one] having the right to give commands (except insofar as this right is temporarily delegated, with the commands always subject to the review of the group as a whole). Moreover, instead of a plethora of rules and an illusory focus on bureaucratically defined expertise…regulations are reduced to a minimum, freedom is maximised, and everyone becomes technically competent to do the work. (Clawson, 1980: 16–17)

More realistic radical models emphasise feasible levels of task-sharing, egalitarian reward systems, democratic controls and participation and co-operative cultures (see Sirriani, 1984; Rothschild and Allen Whitt, 1986; K. Ramsay and Parker, 1992). This would result in what might be described as a *minimal bureaucracy*. Only by recognising certain necessary and distinct functions for bureaucracy can we begin to control and transform them. Clegg and Higgins comment that such arrangements:

> will neither eliminate rules nor the division of labour; in this sense it will not eliminate bureaucracy at all. To presume to do so would be chimerical. What we will achieve is a form of bureaucracy – administration by office and rules – which is not premised on hierarchy, but on collectivity; not on authoritarianism but on democracy; a new ideal type of a bureaucratic, democratic and collectivist organisation. (Clegg and Higgins, 1987: 217)

Radical Weberian perspectives are, however, divided on how much scope there is to modify and democratise hierarchical organisations. Orthodox Weberian analysis, by treating rationalisation and bureaucracy as independent, inexorable forces, risks losing sight of the specificity that location within particular modes of production or market systems creates. This insight is the central dividing line between one strand of radical Weberians and orthodox interpretations, for it brings with it a rejection of Weber's fatalism about the relations between bureaucracy and industrial societies. Radical Weberians believe that bureaucracy is not necessarily universal or inevitable, but rather a pervasive tendency that takes specific forms and therefore can and must be countered. Like some contemporary labour process theorists, there is more emphasis on bureaucratic control as a *management strategy* (Edwards, 1979; Burawoy, 1979; Clawson, 1980). Though not unique to any system of production, bureaucracy has to be explained through its relations with that wider formation. Capitalist social relations are the primary influence on the imperative to appropriate the means of production from workers, though the outcomes are shaped by processes of bureaucratic rationalisation.

A second strand of radical Weberianism retains the traditional pessimism, but combines it with a powerful critique of the negative effects of rationalisation. This is particularly associated with the influential work of George Ritzer, discussed earlier, particularly in Chapter 15. In *The McDonaldization of Society* (1993), Ritzer attributes these insights solely to the modern application of Weber's idea of formal rationality, with its characteristicly differentiated, dehumanised and disenchanted forms of work and life. Elsewhere, however, he notes that, 'This discussion of the exploitation of customers (and workers) in McDonaldized settings serves to bring together the two great theories in the history of sociology – Weber's theory of rationalisation and Marx's theory of capitalist expansion and exploitation' (Ritzer, 1998: 73). He also acknowledges that his descriptions of the growth of routinised, deskilled 'McJobs' parallels Braverman's analysis of the degradation of labour, while adding an emphasis on service work, the involvement of customers and broader commercial trends not present in labour process theory.

This and other studies of the bureaucratisation of services are radical both as a powerful antidote to fashionable post-bureaucratic discourses, and as a critique of the irrational excesses that happen when formal rationality is taken to dehumanising extremes. Ritzer therefore reminds us of the distinction between formal and substantive rationality that is lost in mainstream readings of Weber. However, he also inherits and reproduces the weaknesses of a purely Weberian approach, notably its pessimistic fatalism. Rejecting the Marxian idea that there is a core of creative labour that can resist the rationalised and exploitative character of work, 'McDonaldization becomes the kind of iron cage described by Weber from which there is no escape and, worse, not even any interest in escaping' (Ritzer, 1998: 67). All we are allowed to do is 'rage' against the destructive, anti-social character of McDonaldised systems, mitigating their worst excesses through personal gestures in the sphere of consumption (1996: 304–5). This kind of dystopian radicalism brings to mind many of the contemporary applications of Foucault (see Chapters 8 and 9). This is not surprising because both frameworks remove labour as an active agency, or at least one that is capable of substantial dissent and resistance. Indeed, O'Neill (1986) argues that one can trace the idea of disciplinary society, with its imagery of loyal workers and committed citizens in prison, factories, hospitals and school, directly from Weber to Foucault. Ray and Reed also draw parallels with the Foucauldian nightmare of total control, this time facilitated by *self*-discipline:

> The supervisory 'gaze' of the foreman, guard, clerk and teacher gives way to the more unobtrusive, subtle and indirect forms of surveillance and control which are no long dependent on rules or visible human intervention, but rely on the automatic and continuous disciplining of thought and behaviour. (1994b: 178)

Amongst such panoptic scenarios discussed in other chapters is teamworking and, in a 'discursive and representational' reading of Weber that links him to Foucault and Nietzsche, Sewell and Barker (2006) re-package their well-known teamwork as studies in self-discipline in precisely that way.

Whether these links are credible or not, as Smart (1999) and other essays in his edited collection make clear, Ritzer neglects and underestimates the varieties of consumer, worker and ecological resistance to McDonaldisation. This is merely one of the reasons why Ritzer's claims for the supposed inexorability of rationalisation are one-sided and unconvincing. Much of the evidence for the 'inevitable expansion' of McDonaldisation is other fast food operations. When it strays from that territory, we get fleeting and fragmentary examples from dumbed-down newspapers, assembly-line pornography, and bureaucratised birth and death (1996: 294–302). Yet, as he later admits, counter-examples, even within the same processes, can easily be identified. The central problem is twofold. First, while fast food is an important sector, it cannot be used as the *template* for economic development in a globalising economy. Paradoxically, while Ritzer *does* add useful insights, his thesis is at its strongest when it is describing classic labour process concerns such as fragmented work and the separation of conception and execution through scripted service interactions. When moving onto a broader terrain, he is constrained by both his largely American focus of experience and the separation of rationalisation and capitalism we identified earlier. Locating the former within the latter would reveal that fast food is only one template of rationalisation. Not only does labour act as a constraint to rationalisation, but also national and regional patterns of competition produce diverse market rationalities and competing models of production.

Smart suggests that Ritzer fails to make sufficient distinction between fast food and formal rationality on the one hand, and rationalisation and commodification on the other. Much of the expansion of standardised products and services can be explained predominantly by the 'relentless pursuit of capital accumulation' into new global markets (1999: 4). Kellner (1999) makes a similar warning against excessive dependence on Weber, and calls for a synthesis with Marxian analysis in order to comprehend the combined instrumental rational of production and consumption. A thesis with a bit more Marx and a little less Weber also has the additional benefit that economic rationalisation need not be presented as the 'irrationality of rationality', but as the normal pursuit of profit within the capitalist mode of production (Smart, 1999: 16).

These weaknesses should not detract from the achievements of even a pessimistic Weberian analysis. As we argued in Chapters 13 and 14, there is a strong case that a modified and updated Weberian analysis of bureaucracy and rationalisation remains indispensable for an understanding of contemporary work organisation. With the relevant elements derived from a Marxist tradition, they emphasise both the continuity in social relations and the capacity of bureaucratic forms to change and adapt in new conditions within capitalist society. Structuralist theories, radical or otherwise, have traditionally been stronger explaining the constraints on human action than the way that individuals experience and deal with them. In principle, theoretical resources from within social and work psychology should be able to help fill that and other gaps.

Critical social psychologies

Mainstream theory has long included a psychological component, but has tended to treat people in organisations as 'psychologically determined entities' with abstractedly and individually defined needs. In addition the 'sciences' of organisational behaviour have managed to produce better ways of manipulating the identities and behaviour of employees, but have not succeeded in addressing the problems that make such manipulation necessary. A redefinition of the traditional agenda of organisational psychology requires that individual, group and organisational behaviour be placed in a wider context, particularly the social relations of production and gender relations. Specifically, this would account for subjective experience, while avoiding the over-utilisation of rational-cognitive explanations which focus on the individual determinants and constraints of purposive activity. Given these requirements and the limitations of existing perspectives, it is understandable that over time we have seen the development of a variety of critical social psychologies. This label covers a multiplicity of radical viewpoints which have utilised concepts from mainstream Western social psychology, Marxist and humanist perspectives and Freudian theory.

Social psychology has historically encompassed a wide variety of critical traditions differing mainly in their concerns for internal critique of methodology and content, as opposed to a broader critique of the socio-cultural relations of the knowledge they produce (Wexler, 1983). From work such as that of Moscovici (1972), Gergen (1973) and Rosnow (1981), we gain a focus on the methodological limitations of social psychology and its lack of relevance to social issues. These are essentially calls for reform, which in their understanding of social relations in terms of relatively fixed characteristics and roles follows the liberal tradition of social emancipation through individual transformation. There have been specific developments in these kinds of 'internal' critique that go further than the mainstream in addressing issues of the socio-cultural relations of knowledge. Though still disparate in perspective, these approaches place an emphasis on factors such as social networks, cognition and identity, albeit with the more prosaic aims of reforming the discipline rather than the subject or the client. This is exemplified in Hollway's (1991) proposals on a movement towards a work psychology reflexive of the relations of knowledge, power and practice, and also in Hosking and Morley's (1991) cognitive/political psychology of organising. Hosking and Morley (1991: 40–2) critique the top-down, entitative approaches (based on Meyer, 1985) that have dominated OB and HRM literatures. These are essentially reified perspectives relying on assumptions of the independence of person and organisation rather on their interdependence. Entitative approaches to persons focus on characteristics, traits and behaviours of individuals, while they treat organisations as entities in their own right with their own values and goals. Wider developments in social cognition are exemplified in Augoustinos and Walker's (1995) attempts to integrate American individualism with the more ideological concerns for identity found in European social psychology, emphasising linkages between individual and collective processes. Though neither radical in comparison to Armistead and others, nor expressly critical, these approaches represent a shift in line with that from micro- towards macro-organisation behaviour, as identified by Nord and Fox (1996; see Chapter 15). Nord and Fox reviewed the linkages between organisation studies and psychological factors and processes. They found that the focus on the individual in organisational psychology has gradually moved away from the essentialist view of the individual found in approaches emphasising personality, motivation attitudes and so on. The shift has been towards 'sociology, literature, communications and other disciplines consistent with a more macro conceptual orientation' (1996: 170).

An obvious starting point for external critique would be Marxism. Such contributions to psychology, in their understanding of subjectivity at work, begin with the concept of alienation, the estrangement of creative capacities which means that 'work is external to the worker, that it is not part of his nature, and that, consequently, he does not fulfil himself in his work but denies himself' (Marx, 1963: 124–5). The reference to a 'human nature' is not to an eternal set of values or behaviours such as aggression or jealousy beloved of reactionary thinkers, but rather to certain characteristics which distinguish man's species-being, such as the capacity for purposeful and reflective action.

Alienation is given specific and concrete form by its location in the capitalist labour process; individual needs and capacities are subordinated to the requirements of capital accumulation, with the psychological consequence that the worker feels a stranger in his or her work. Management, though, still needs to engage the subjectivity and tacit skills of the workforce at some level to ensure profitable production, for example through quality circles. The problem with constructing a critical psychology from Marxism is that there are no adequate tools for understanding how alienated social relations are subjectively experienced and acted on by the individual. Marxism tends to deal with individuals only as bearers of economic categories such as labour and capital, and many social scientists influenced by Marxism have explicitly rejected any psychological explanation, as with Clegg and Dunkerley's (1980) work. It is certainly necessary to have an account of the material structures which shape our experiences and personalities. But this does not mean that people are simply 'bearers' or that attitudes and behaviour can be 'read- off' from material circumstances (Leonard, 1984: 25). A purely structural analysis, even where it allows for human action and resistance, fails to get sufficiently inside those routine everyday experiences in which people react, adapt, modify and consent to work relations.

Knights and Collinson (1987) argued that Marxist and labour process literatures tend to produce critiques of social structures and institutions that take as given the behavioural practices reproducing our concerns with identity. Such structures are both consequences of, and give rise to, the behavioural routines through which we generate secure identities for ourselves. Without accounts of identity, then, analysis of structures and the power relations and strategies through which they are maintained will always be incomplete. 'The absence of this social psychology from LPT means that it is unable to recognise how individuals ... seek security either through controlling, and/or subordinating themselves to, others', (Knights and Collinson, 1987: 171). The dearth of an analysis of identity helps explain why Marxists have had a tendency to try a forced marriage with Freudianism. This led to the appropriation of ideas such as that of the unconscious and the dynamic model of personality (Schneider, 1975; Deleuze and Guattari, 1977), though for some this was always an attempt to reconcile the irreconcilable (N. O'Neill, 1985). The limited resources with orthodox Marxism have led academics seeking better ways to address issues of subjectivity and identity to postmodernism and post-structuralism.

For example, drawing on Foucauldian notions of power-knowledge discourses, psychological knowledge is assumed to provide both theoretical legitimacy and technical assistance to projects aimed at the control and utilisation of the 'human resource' in a rational-efficient manner. The 'real' psychology here is simply in the name: once you internalise the discourse constructing people as human resources, the rest is just window dressing. Such observations draw on a longer tradition of critique, such as the 'anything goes' methodology of Feyerabend (1975) and tradition of the Frankfurt School. The common theme in the latter, for example in the work of Horkheimer, Adorno, Marcuse and latterly Habermas, was the examination of the role of ideologies in the production of our knowledge of the social contexts in which we exist. This enabled a self-reflexive critique of how social psychology both operates to uphold the current social order, and at the same time works against the possibility of a socially-transforming discipline. However desirable and probably necessary, a psychology based on this variant of critical theory will probably not provide a great deal of competition to current practices in terms of their influence on and role on organisational strategies and strategies.

This limitation is reproduced in more recent critiques influenced by postmodernism. In line with the project of reviewing and 'reconnecting' the current state of critical social psychology, the contributors to the Ibanez and Ininguez (1997) text raise questions and produce much in the way of methodological speculation, but in the end come no closer to any real integration. What we find is largely an iterative debate over realism versus relativism and their respective takes on social construction and political/ideological action. Indeed Spears (1997: 4) notes that the putative 'critical' paradigm in social psychology could not, in its 'isolated critique', challenge the 'paper mills of positivism' in terms of the production of practices. Criticism, when elevated to an emancipatory practice in itself, cannot compete with the packaged solutions and prescriptions of the mainstream, reducing further the chance that alternative conceptual frameworks will lead to effective practices.

The more recent developments in post-structuralist and postmodern critique in social psychology, heavily influenced by Potter and Wetherall's (1987) *Discourse and Social Psychology*, are themselves as varied as anything that has gone before, but as with, for example, Tuffin (2005) generally begin from a critique of experimentalism. In the end it is the lack of engagement with the traditional topics of social psychology that is most disappointing here. There is more concern for meta-theory and pseudo-methodologies such as 'critical polytextualism' (see Potter, 1997) than for critical evaluation of what mainstream and radical approaches might have to offer. What we have here is a desire for critique that at best does no harm and indeed is not capable of doing any, in that it is indecipherable to any but its acolytes. Much of critical social psychology has lost the desire to be critical of anything but itself and its own roots, reducing both structural and cognitive accounts to mere objects of self-reflexive literary criticism. It is perhaps unfair to comment on and criticise postmodern contributions to psychology before we have considered those theoretical resources more generally. It is to that task we now turn.

The postmodern challenge to rationality

Postmodernism is the least cohesive of the general social theories we have examined in this part of the book, the term being loosely applied to an overlapping set of ideas about society and knowledge deriving from French social theorists such as Baudrillard, Lyotard and Derrida, which have become increasingly influential in organisation theory in recent years (Clegg, 1990; Parker, 1992; Hassard and Parker, 1993). It lays claim to be the most radical break from orthodoxy, but the orthodoxy is different from the systems and related ideas we have talked about so far. Anything with 'post' automatically specifies its opposite, so the orthodoxy must be *modernism*. This may appear puzzling: after all, existing social theories have not traditionally been defined by that label. But an illustration of the changed way of thinking is that for Clegg (1990: 2), having shuffled off his Marxist coil, organisation theory is a 'creature' of modernity. Similarly, Gergen (1992: 211–12) includes almost the full range of organisational and behavioural theories in the 'modernist' camp.

So, what is modernity? In some usages, it designates a type of society or epoch (the ontological dimension); at its simplest, industrialism in which the dominant feature is the large-scale, hierarchical bureaucracy concerned with rationality and planning throughout social and economic life. Willmott sums up the argument thus: 'Its ideal is the expertly designed, perfectly ordered and controlled world in which all ambivalence and indeterminacy are attenuated, if not wholly eliminated' (1992: 70). But within such conceptions we see the seeds of another designation, modernism as a way of thinking, a way of representing knowledge about society and organisations (the epistemological dimension). Above all, it is held to be characterised by a concern for developing the 'grand narrative', a coherent story about the development of the social and natural world, revealed through the application of reason and science (Cooper and Burrell, 1988). Modernism is thus equated with positivism, the pursuit of objective truths through a 'logico-scientific mode of knowing' in which events are explained in terms of general laws and clear cause and effect relations (Czarniawska, 1999).

Post-modernists develop a dual challenge in both these dimensions of what society is (ontology) and how we should look at it (epistemology). We have already outlined the basis of the former in Chapters 12 and 13. Rapid social change, the shift from a society based on production to one based on information and consumption, the emergence of segmented markets dominated by more discerning consumers, and turbulent environments are all said to be requiring diversity and flexibility from work organisations, which are then able to release workers from their bureaucratic iron cage. For many postmodernists, particularly those influenced by Foucault, that does not mean no cage. As we have seen elsewhere, there is considerable emphasis on panoptic (self)discipline and in a neat twist, Gabriel (2005) shifts the metaphor to one of a glass cage. Proceeding from postmodern assertion that we have moved to a society based on consumption, Gabriel argues that the glass cage is characterised by the power of its spectacle and symbols, as well as its requirement for performance based on emotional displays and appearances. Employees and consumers are trapped by the illusion of choice, glamorous image and brand identity. Even Ritzer buys into the partial re-enchantment of work and life through cyber-malls and other 'cathedrals of consumption', though pulls back from the full postmodern line in recognising that, 'The mass production of such things is virtually guaranteed to undermine their enchanted qualities. This is a fundamental dilemma facing the new means of consumption' (2001: 129).

Though it is not their exclusive property, postmodernists concerned with the workplace tend to embrace the notion of the post-bureaucratic organisation in which the old specialised division of labour and centralised control no longer holds sway (see Palmer and Hardy, 2000). In turn, social theorists with a broader societal remit use this tenuous evidence of 'debureaucratisation' and 'reprofessionalisation' to sustain a broader vision of postmodernisation (Crook, Paluski and Waters, 1992). We have made an extensive critique of such claims in Chapter 12, so for most of this section we will concentrate on the other, epistemological, dimension of post-modernism. Arguably, this discussion is directed at the issues that post-modern thinking is having greatest influence on in organisation and management theory. For example, Fournier and Grey's (2000) useful and influential account of postmodern influences on 'critical management studies' confirms the view that critical scholarship is moving away from challenging what society and organisations look like, towards alternative ways of seeing. (See Thompson, 2001 for a discussion of this.)

At the heart of this is the postmodern rejection of the grand narrative. The search for the coherent story (Braverman's theory of the degradation of the labour process in the twentieth century), or the total picture (Weber's account of the interrelated processes of rationalisation) is both pointless, because of the fragmentation of economic and cultural life, and dangerous, because such 'totalising claims' submerge diverse voices and the multiplicity of 'local' phenomena. Difference, incoherence and fluidity are preferable and more realistic because meaning cannot be fixed; it is what we make it through language that constructs, rather reflects, reality. One variant of this kind of thinking can be seen in Baudrillard and his concept of *hyperreality*. In a media-saturated world which thrives on spectacle and encourages politicians to employ 'spin-doctors' to put a twist on events before and after they happen, it becomes impossible to distinguish between the real and fictive. We cannot refer to distortion of reality, because there are too many realities for anything to be measured against. Similarly, Alvesson and Deetz (1996) argue that, as society becomes more fragmented and hyperreal, discourses multiply, reality becomes virtual and any forces that stabilise identity are lost. To return to Baudrillard, his most (in)famous claim was that during the Gulf conflict, it was impossible to know whether any events had taken place. This was literally a war of words in which all our information was second-hand, simulated and structured through media manipulation (for a critique see Norris, 1992).

While some post-modernists seek a softer version that 'recognises the ontological existence of the social world, however precarious and fluid' (Palmer and Hardy, 2000: 265), the core view remains that there is no way of distinguishing between representation and reality, with 'truth' becoming merely a product of language games. We have Derrida's 'nothing exists outside the text', taken as the interplay of different discourses (Hassard, 1994: 9). In this context, the task of the social theorist is not to construct the authentic explanation, but to *deconstruct* texts in order to reveal the contradictions, origins, instabilities and gaps. For example, this process of rereading may uncover the silences on gender issues in the classics of 'malestream' organisation theory (Calás and Smircich, 1992). While such treatment is 'exposed' to public gaze, it may be regarded as inevitable, for discourse always bears the imprint of the social identity of its producers. This notion – labelled 'perspectivism' – adds a further layer to the conception of multiple viewpoints and realities. In one sense it is an absolute relativism, moving beyond a contingent explanation for being unable to access the real (because it is too fragmented) to an all-purpose one ('truth' is merely the will to power). The outcome is, nevertheless the same – truth claims cannot be adjudicated: 'all knowledge is self-referential, coherent only in terms of its own discourse, since there exist no meta-justification agencies, no higher external authority, by reference to which claims to knowledge may be judged' (Coleman, 1991: 26).

In our previous discussions in this book, an emphasis on the primacy of language and discourse emerged most strongly in Chapter 9, through an examination of the ideas of Foucault and post-structuralism on power. Here, power is not a thing possessed by sovereign agents, but operates through discourses that produce knowledge and disciplinary practices which define and constrain the identities of workers, consumers and citizens. Power is indeed a complex and multi-dimensional phenomena. However, as we argued in that chapter, the danger is that any subject of action is lost in the interplay of discourses (Newton, 1994). This is part of a wider problem of post-structuralist analysis, that promotes an 'agentless' conception of discursive formation in which the role of specific agents – individual and/or collective – and forms of agency is simply reduced to that of nodal points in the intersection of various discourses' (Reed, 1998: 195). Perhaps the best known illustration in organisation theory of the abandonment of the search for the truth lying beneath the surface of social relations is Morgan's *Images of Organisation* (1986). Morgan does not just analyse organisational life in terms of a series of metaphors – the machine, the psychic prison, the tool of domination – but treats those images as of equal validity. Despite representing contradictory 'claims', they are all 'true' in their own terms; their 'cognitive power and empirical veracity can only be assessed in terms of the purposes for which they are constructed and used ... reality is what you make of it' (Reed, 1990b: 36).

Also influential in applications of post-modern and post-structural epistemology is the shift of concern from analyses of control and rules to the construction of organisational life through cultural and symbolic resources, as we saw in Chapter 13. Alvesson and Deetz argue that as economic activity shifts from manufacturing to services, issues of corporate culture and identity rise up the managerial agenda, and that 'Objects for management control are decreasingly labour power and behaviour and increasingly the mindpower and subjectivities of employees' (1996: 192). In a period where lean production and downsizing have been the primary means of corporate rationalisation, this judgement looks particularly misplaced. But it also reveals the tension between post-modernism as epoch and epistemology. Logically, an approach that rejects narrative and totalising pictures should be hostile to or uninterested in an alternative conception of society. Alvesson and Deetz are sensitive to the problem of 'proclaiming a new postmodern epoch', given weak empirical indicators and the danger of relabelling old ideas. At the same time, and within two paragraphs, they cannot resist justifying their claims of shifting managerial practices by reference to 'new social conditions' (1996: 192). Such writing is unfortunately typical of a new form of cultural historicism in which the source of evolutionary development is no longer technological and economic imperatives, but the management of values and engineering of the soul (Reed: 1996b). As Reed goes on to note, the appeal of cultural historicism is primarily ideological: it provides a new vocabulary of motive for organisational change in circumstances where old managerial and corporatist rationales lack legitimacy.

There is, admittedly, a difference between those theorists such as Clegg who have been quite happy to use conventional tools of rational enquiry to develop accounts of post-modernity, and those such as Cooper and Burrell (1988: 106) who, in their own words, prefer the discursive 'production of organisation' to the 'organisation of production'. But the distinction is not as clear-cut as it seems. Continuities and commonalities arise in a variety of ways. In both dimensions there is a shared language of fragmentation and fracturing of the theoretical and practical order (Reed, 1991: 125). This imagery is taken from the origins of post-modernism as a perspective in art and culture, where eclecticism, stylistic promiscuity, paradox and mixing of modes replace hierarchical judgements of value and distinctions between high art and popular culture (Featherstone, 1988). They are also linked by a rejection of the 'false promises' of rational design, the idea that knowledge should offer methodologies for defining the most rational means of controlling complex, large-scale organisations (Hassard, 1994: 4). Finally and most importantly, there is the inconvenient and much observed fact that post-modernism is itself a meta-narrative (Boyne and Rattsani, 1990: 39–40). The need to create pictures of reality is inescapable in the illustrative and conceptual acts of theorising, and there is ample evidence that writers such as Lyotard, Morgan and Baudrillard draw on post-industrialism, information society and other models which take as their starting point some kind of epochal break. (For a critique, see Thompson, 1993.) Even those who have most resolutely avoided any engagement with the empirical cannot resist reference to 'the changing conditions of modern life', to justify their calls for conceptual shifts in the body of organisation theory, or in this case the theory of the organisational body (Dale and Burrell, 2000: 25).

In practice, then, the post-bureaucratic organisation located in the post-modern epoch is a rival narrative to those traditions deriving from Marx and Weber. As we saw in Chapter 14, the evidence for any substantial presence for such a mode of organising is either absent or misunderstood. Post-modern theorists appear to see little problem in sharing the agenda and language of popular management texts on such issues. (See Clegg and Hardy, 1996: 11.) Organisations may not be the 'tightly-coupled' rational machines beloved of systems theory, but when Hassard argues that 'Above all, we should seek to explode the myth of robust structural relations through establishing the fragile character of organisational life' (1994: 16), this is merely standing orthodoxy on its head, rather then a realistic picture of the modern firm.

Just as there is considerable continuity in capitalist relations of production and in rationalisation processes, large-scale organisations are considerably more durable and able to marshal powerful resources than post-modernists allow. In attacking the second edition of this book, along with the work of Salaman, Dale and Burrell (2000: 20–4) object to any reference to organisations as regular, patterned activities and corporate entities with powers over and above their members. It remains our view that power converts ambiguity into order, though the latter is not synonymous with the equilibrium of systems theory, because it is always contested and disrupted. New forms of theorising are in danger of moving so far away from rationality that they are unable to conceptualise *organisation* at all, particularly at a macro-level. At its most post-structuralist extreme, it is argued that organisation has no autonomous, stable or structural status outside the text that constitutes it (Westwood and Linstead, 2001). In their overview of CMS, Adler, Forbes and Willmott (2007: 32) describe that position slightly differently: 'Any attempt to control or fix the meaning of any word – including words like management or organization – is inherently precarious since reality is always in excess of what is signified by any particular set of signifiers. Poststructuralists in CMS celebrate this excess and strive to widen and deepen its scope and influence, seeing it as potentially subversive and emancipatory'.

Even when not reaching the outer limits of epistemological excess, as Reed (1996a: 42) notes, postmodernism, reinforced by post-industrial images of decentred, fragmented economies, has retreated into local aspects and small pictures of organisational life. Willmott makes a similar point when observing that a focus on local diversities, for example in the work of Clegg, can distract from the broader 'patterning of process of economic and organisational development' (1995: 41). This is not just a question of the nature of contemporary structure and agency, but of the equally flawed alternative ways of seeing. As Reed comments:

> The theoretical glue once provided by an assumed epistemological commitment to rational analysis of 'organised rationality' has given way under the pressure exerted by a cacophony of voices which celebrate the reality of multiple and contested organisational rationalities which cannot be assessed or evaluated in any coherent way. (Reed, 1993: 181)

It is true, as we have continually stressed in this book, that there are conflicting ends and means pursued by rival organisational actors, and a diversity of organising logics and institutional settings. But contested practical rationalities need to be understood on rational grounds. How can we debate the *character* of organisational life if we cannot compare and evaluate theoretical claims or Morgan's 'images'? If these remain self-contained, self-referential discourses, as Reed notes elsewhere (1991: 38), organisation theory just becomes a supermarket where metaphors or other means of representation are purchased according to preference and power.

In all this critique, we should not lose sight of the observation that discourse is an entirely legitimate object of analysis and can reveal important insights about the way that work and life are organised. Similarly, deconstruction can be a useful tool for discovering what has been put in and left out of texts. However, there has been an increasing and dangerous tendency in organisation studies to treat management strategy, corporate culture, Taylorism, Fordism and so on, only or even primarily as discourses. When presented to us as texts, the subsequent deconstructions and rereadings are sometimes illuminating, but at the cost of confinement to the world of inter-textuality. The interplay of agency and structures has a real material existence. In his critique of post-modernism, Tsoukas persuasively illustrates the point:

> It is because actions are not taken and voices not uttered in a vacuum that *not* all accounts are equally valid. No matter how much I shout at my bank manager he is not likely to lend me money if I am unemployed. This is not a figment of my imagination. Others also tell me they have had similar experience. (Tsoukas, 1992: 644)

There is, in other words, an extra-discursive realm of material structures that may constrain discursive practices and enable others. Studying *just* discourse is itself a constraint on our explanatory power. This is not a book about philosophies of science, but we will return to some questions of evidence and truth claims in the discussion of paradigm incommensurability in the next and final chapter.

28 theory, knowledge and practice

In previous chapters we have tried to set out the main general resources available for theorising about work organisations. Our own prime resources have been labour process theory, radical Weberianism and elements of critical social psychology. It would be difficult to argue that these and other components of a critical approach could, or even should, be easily or adequately synthesised into a unified and coherent explanation of work organisations.

However, despite differences and sometimes flatly opposed explanations, they can be drawn on as a resource for understanding the complexity of issues involved. In part, this is because there is some common ground. Referring to action theory and the more radical structuralist perspectives, Dunkerley and Salaman observe: 'Both seek to undermine the notion of inevitability in organisational structure; both seek to insert active human beings and groups and their values and interests into the complex processes which give rise to organisational structures' (1986: 93). Complementarity is often more feasible than synthesis, for example when labour process and radical Weberian analyses illuminate power and control through the discussion of means of production and of administration.

This rather pragmatic view of theorising will be opposed by those who believe that theories can and must operate from within hermetically sealed boxes. For one of the assumptions made by Burrell and Morgan (1979) about the paradigms with which we began the chapter is that they are incommensurable. In other words, their differences about knowledge and the world are so basic that theory can only be developed within each framework, which would then do battle with the others. As paradigms frame and define relevant interpretation, 'any observations that do not seem to fit in a particular approach belong in some other paradigm' (Ackroyd, 1994: 278). Ackroyd is rightly sceptical about the origins and consequences of the mentality of paradigm closure. Yet it is difficult for paradigms to 'speak' to one another, when they not only make different 'reality assumptions', but develop highly distinctive 'languages' of their own. It is, in fact, one of life's little ironies that many of those who believe most strongly in the constitutive power of language cannot write a sentence that can be understood without a dictionary, a gin and tonic and a great deal of patience. The problem of theoretical communication is compounded by the very different national traditions in organisation theory, as accounts of the past and present in North America (Aldrich, 1992) and Francophone analysis (Chanlat, 1994) reveal.

Paradigm diversity or closure?

The paradigm wars have, however, moved on, with Clegg and Hardy observing that we now have a 'three-cornered debate' (1996: 5). The first position – incommensurability – is less popular than it was. This may be that the main defensive rationale for closure – that it would provide a space for alternative perspectives outside the functionalist-positivist orthodoxy – is less of an issue now that a variety of critical theories compete robustly in the lecture hall and through the pages of journals. Nevertheless, some paradigm warriors, notably Jackson and Carter (1991, 2000), continue to argue that communication is impossible because of the unique character of each paradigm, and dangerous given the 'intellectual imperialism' of the still-powerful orthodox voices. Such fears have been fed by some of those on the opposite side of the (non-existent) bridge. Pfeffer (1993) reasserts the need for paradigm consensus. Though there is an obvious pre-existing belief that knowledge is produced in a cumulative, developmental manner, capable of leading to agreement on methods, research questions and outcomes, Pfeffer's main worry is that organisational analysis will lose any influence it has unless it can demonstrate a degree of integration and unity that are the hallmarks of any 'mature science' (see also Donaldson, 1998).

Given the highly contested nature of organisational theory, such pleas will undoubtedly fall on deaf ears. Yet it is interesting to note that on both sides the arguments appear to be driven as much by expediency as by principle. A more positive pragmatism can be seen in a third and increasingly influential camp: those who assert the need for paradigm diversity, or multi-paradigm thinking. Gareth Morgan has certainly shifted his stance in this way and now talks about the need to 'harness the possibilities which they offer' (1990: 27). A multi-paradigm perspective is primarily influenced by post-modernists trying to draw back from extreme relativism and seek greater dialogue. In part this may reflect the diverse and multifaceted nature of reality which no single approach can grasp (Schultz and Hatch, 1996). Similarly, Kamoche argues that unless human resource management is analysed from within each paradigm, we may be 'ignoring the insights that other perspectives have been shown to yield' (1991: 13). A more concrete version of the same thing is offered by Hassard (1991), who interprets empirical data on the fire service in the UK through the paradigmatic 'eyes' of each of Burrell and Morgan's original quartet.

Such arguments are superficially attractive. Who, after all, could be against dialogue, or resist the call for greater 'democracy' in organisation theory (Hassard, 1991: 296)? In addition, there is no doubt that such exercises are fruitful individual exercises in collective and individual learning. But, as Parker and McHugh (1991) observed of Hassard's effort, the ability to hop between languages is not the same as demonstrating its analytical usefulness. The practice of multiple paradigm analysis tends to be closure by any other name, for each speaks from behind its own walls. Indeed, Hassard (1988) treats meta-theories as distinct language games in which we can be trained. The normal purpose of dialogue is to resolve issues or move beyond disagreements. This is difficult for post-modernists given their denial of any grounds against which to make judgements. It may be true, as Kamoche says, that paradigms generate different insights, but what if those insights are based on competing claims, for instance about the relative weight of hard and soft HRM in contemporary workplace practice? The relativist twist that everything is of equal value merely adds to the problem, and is open to the same objections that were raised by Reed of Morgan's use of metaphors: that we end up taking products down from the shelf as uncritical consumers, rather than promoting rigorous debate and research.

With these observations in mind, it seems to us that multi-paradigm or perspective approaches do not fully address the limits of incommensurability. To express a concern for the limits of multi-paradigm thinking is not to say that it is impossible or unnecessary for theories and theorists to engage with one another. This may not be as difficult as it appears. It is possible to have reservations about the strategic exchange theory of Watson (1994) or the discourse analysis of Pringle (1989), but still find their books to be exciting and revealing accounts of managerial and secretarial work. Sometimes it is necessary to get behind the different languages and explore whether writers are saying substantively similar things. As Ackroyd (1992, 1994) reminds us, a lot of the best research is not led by a commitment to paradigms, or is stimulated by 'boundary exchanges' between them. Ritzer (1975) also refers to the capacity of the classical sociological theories to bridge paradigms. Some differences can be put down to the level of analysis.

It is perfectly legitimate to have a more structural or a more micro-emphasis on management or some other aspect of organisational life, or to creatively combine micro and macro. The key is not to analytically close off the possibilities of 'seeing' the other dimension, and to ensure that observations made about action and structure at different levels – workgroup, organisational, societal – are compatible with one another (Ackroyd, 2000). A multi-dimensional approach was one of the principles of good analysis set out in Chapter 1. It is possible to argue that such dimensions are sometimes most effectively addressed by different perspectives. Kellner (1999: 194) says that 'McDonaldization is a many-sided phenomenon and the more perspectives that we can bring to its analysis the better grasp of the phenomenon one will have'. This 'more the better' outlook may be overdoing it, but Kellner does persuasively argue that post-modern concepts can successfully be deployed to explain a later development of McDonaldisation, when a modernist emphasis on mass production was complemented by a set of practices around consumption and management of global identities. But it's also about *levels* of analysis. Post-modernists may be right that the world has become more fragmented, but increased complexity means that social scientists have to find better ways to make conceptual and methodological connections: 'to move beyond single units of analysis and to understand organisations at multiple levels – building theory across individual and work groups, establishments, firms and institutions...' (Ackroyd *et al.*, 2006: 14). In this book, the intersections between the sociological/structural and psychological dimensions of action have been a central theme. Different modes of analysis are needed to deal with the complexities and levels of human behaviour. People are constituted as individual subjects at the level of their identities, emotions and self-directed actions, but that process is informed by the same 'structural' phenomena that shape managerial strategies or job design, such as the social relations of production between capital, labour or gender.

To return to the general theme, our view is that there is an implicit fourth position in the paradigm wars: one that rejects incommensurability, but sees grounds, not only for dialogue, but for some kind of knowledge progression within a social-science framework. Reed (1993) notes that the pendulum has swung back from post-modern excesses towards recognition of historical continuities, narrative patterns and accumulated knowledge and procedures. Such a position admittedly leaves some of the most difficult problems unresolved. Theoretical pluralism is certainly here to stay, and that is welcome. However, the sharp theoretical disagreements will remain, not so much because of different paradigms, but because of rival claims being made about organisations and society. Ultimately the key problem is not paradigm, but reality incommensurability. For example, organisations, or at least particular types, cannot be at the same time becoming more and less bureaucratic. That might seem obvious, but the current fashion for relativism makes it difficult to take the issue any further. In other words, as we noted earlier, under the influence of post-modernism, a large number of scholars of organisation believe that it is impossible to either make truth claims or resolve them: 'Any interpretation is temporary, and specific to the discourse within which it is produced ... the postmodern argument liberates me: my discourse is as valid as any other' (Coleman, 1991: 26–7).

In order to sustain this kind of thinking, post-modernism tends to treat science purely as 'conversation', whose logic of enquiry is rhetorical (Czarniawska, 1999: 10). Much of the force of this argument comes from a reading of the philosopher of science, Thomas Kuhn (1970), referred to at the start of this part of the book with reference to the idea of paradigms. He challenged the accepted, positivist view that science was based on the linear, patient, disinterested collection of facts, leading to hypotheses that were then tested or 'falsified' until the truth was discovered. In the process of discovery, the protagonists are not merely comparing findings to the real world, but making judgements about what is acceptable in their own professional domain. Science, then, is not wholly rational, and is shaped by ideologies and power.

Given the undeniably greater ideological influences on subjects such as management and organisation studies, post-modernists were now able to argue that 'a plurality of legitimate and competing perspectives is to be expected in all sciences, but especially in the social ones' (Burrell, 1996: 648). This reading of Kuhn is, however, debatable. Kuhn argued that though observation and experiment drastically restrict the range of admissible belief, progress takes place in the state of knowledge, and that the distinction between the scientific and non-scientific is real. In short, scientific judgements involve the comparison of paradigms both with nature and with each other. Science may not be wholly rational, but it has a rational core.

This does *not* mean that the ability to make definitive statements about the natural world transfers to the social. The difference between the two is, after all, the starting point of a critique of positivism that is shared by most organisational theorists. But having misrepresented science, post-modernists go on to do the same thing with social explanation. This is done primarily by constructing stereotypical oppositions. As Ackroyd and Fleetwood note:

> Here we arrive at the commonly held position that there are two basic perspectives on offer: either the world is objectively and unproblematically available and capable of being known by the systematic application of the empirical techniques common to positivism, or it is not knowable objectively at all; and in the place of claims to objectivity, we find that what is known is merely the product of discourses. (Ackroyd and Fleetwood, 2000: 3–4)

Our knowledge is inherently constrained and shaped by the social process of its production, but there is an alternative, middle ground between positivism and relativism. As a philosophy of science, *critical realism* accepts that social structures and the meanings actors attribute to their situation have to be recognised in the way we construct explanations. However, entities such as labour markets and gender relations exist independently of our perceptions and investigations of them (Bhaskar, 1989; Collier, 1994; Archer, 1995; Danermark *et al.*, 2002; Reed, 2008). As Ackroyd and Fleetwood (2000) argue, the ontological question, 'what exists?' is often confused with the epistemological one, 'how can we know what exists?' Hence, as our knowledge is bound up with our conceptions, the misleading conclusion is drawn that all that exists is our concepts or discourse. The difficulties of establishing absolute certainty should not be used to assert that we can make *no* 'truth claims'. In his defence of post-modern epistemology, Newton asks, 'How can we be sure that we have found "the real"?' (1996: 22). The short answer is that we cannot be totally sure, but that is a far cry from not knowing anything: realists 'want to hold that better and worse forms of knowledge exist and that there are reliable procedures for producing knowledge of things and events' (Ackroyd and Fleetwood, 2000: 3–4).

There cannot be an exact correspondence between reality and our representations of it, but good research aims to grasp the real with as much accuracy and complexity as is feasible. In other words, while what we know is inherently incomplete, we require a capacity to generate generalisable knowledge and to identify trends, if not laws; and we need empirical work that can help distinguish between the rhetorics of the powerful and the realities of power. For example, we know that the vast majority of studies of empowerment demonstrate, through a variety of quantitative and qualitative methodologies, a massive gap between managerial claims of delegated decision-making and workplace outcomes. Similarly, and to return to an issue raised earlier, while politicians and generals devise forms of representation that make events such as the Gulf and Balkan wars difficult to grasp, as time unfolds and practices unravel, knowledge of what really happened on the ground does emerge into the public domain and becomes accepted as real (see Norris, 1992). Not only can we attempt to distinguish between representation and reality, it is fundamental to a healthy social science and democratic polity that we seek to do so.

When it is fashionable for social science to problematise everything, the focus is always on what we don't know rather than what we do. Whether organisational theory embraces critical realism or not, the question of addressing the real is inescapable. As we demonstrated in an earlier chapter, many post-modernists deny that it is possible to make truth claims, yet litter their discussions of contemporary organisational life with references to 'new realities', though often with quotation marks to indicate ironic distance. In other words, such theorists presuppose access to the real in order to make claims about the post-modern world (Kellner, 1988). If truth claims are inevitable, we need to have transparent, shared ways of discussing and resolving them, however partial and limited they may be. Post-modern epistemology may be 'liberating' for the individual theorist; but it is not very useful for the body of organisational theory. However, the uses of knowledge are themselves disputed and contested. This seems a useful point to move towards a broader consideration of relations between management, theory and knowledge.

Management and theory

If we examine the interaction between theories and practices described in previous chapters, no mechanical and few direct relationships can be found. As with the approach to theorising by academics, organisational theories are a resource for practitioners, mostly, of course, employers and managers. Taylor and Mayo, for example, were great synthesisers of ideas and practices in a way that management found useful, not just as a guide to action but as a way of clarifying and legitimating their role. Yet theorists, and Taylor was a prime case, frequently rail against companies that do not swallow their whole package but rather apply them selectively. As Chandler (1977: 277) observes, 'No factory owner ... adopted the system without modifying it'. This should come as no surprise. Employers and managers are pragmatists and, with some exceptions such as the Quaker-owned companies in the UK, seldom show any intrinsic interest in ideas in themselves, but rather for their 'use value' or, as one senior manager is quoted as saying in Gowler and Legge (1983: 213), 'There's no good ideas until there's cash in the till'.

This is one of the main reasons why, as Watson (1986: 2) correctly notes, there will never be a full and generally acceptable organisational or management theory. But it is not merely a case of a plurality of competing perspectives. The *partiality* of such theories is inherent in their use in control and legitimation processes. It is in the nature of theories of and for management that they give incomplete pictures. The perspectives and accompanying prescriptions only address aspects of the basic contradictions in capitalist and hierarchical work organisation. Therefore, at one level both theorists and practitioners respond within a continuum that has Taylor's minimum interaction model at one end and varieties of human relations at the other. Employers, of course, would like it both ways. Bendix gives an example of a management journal in 1910 calling for 'absolute authority as well as the willing co-operation of the workers' (1956: 272).

To some extent they can do this by *combining* theories and practices within the continuum. So we saw in Chapter 3 that human relations did not challenge Taylorism on its own terrain of job design and structures, but rather sought to deal with its negative effects and blind spots. That story of combination to deal with different dimensions of organisational experience is repeated through every period and sector. It is, of course, the case that management is not only trying to deal with the contradictory aspects of utilising human labour. Variations in strategy and practice reflect broader problems, such as harmonising different functions and sites of decision-making. But the resultant difficulties in managing the contradictions are similar: different routes to partial success and failure, as Hyman noted in Chapter 8.

It would be wrong to give the impression that the choice and use of theories are solely internal matters. This would reinforce the erroneous view that organisational theories are a historical sequence of 'models of man', the new naturally replacing the old as grateful managers learn to recognise the more sophisticated account of human needs and behaviour. Ideological conditions are influential, as evidenced by the spillover of entrepreneurial values from the political to the managerial sphere. Selectivity is also conditioned by *circumstances*, involving a number of key 'macro' and 'micro' dimensions. At the broadest level, organisational theories interact with the political economy of broad phases of capital accumulation. Taylorism and classical management perspectives emerged at a time when the scale and complexity of organisations and of markets were undergoing a fundamental change. The globalisation of markets and intensified competition, particularly from Japan, stimulated major shifts in management thinking in the more recent period. At a micro-level, the choices made by particular companies reflect even more complex factors. In particular, the *sector*, with its specific product market and labour market, technological framework and political context, is a vital consideration. Each country, too, has its own unique configuration of intellectual, social and economic conditions mediating the form and content of organisational change.

But just as there are global markets for products, so there are increasingly for ideas. This process is enhanced by the spread of pop-management and the global consulting firms that frequently inform them, as the success of the excellence genre and subsequent fads is testament to. Unfortunately it reinforces the tendency for academics to form alliances with sections of management around particular perspectives or techniques as solve-all solutions. So much ideological investment is made in the process that the chosen vehicle can seldom meet the burden placed on it: hence burnout, cynicism and later fortunate loss of memory, until, that is, a new solution comes along! But why do managers so often become locked in this fatal embrace? The production and consumption of managerial knowledge has been an underdeveloped area, but there is a literature that is trying to address such issues (Huczynski, 1993; Thompson and O'Connell Davidson, 1994; Abrahamson, 1996; Furusten, 1999; Fincham and Clark, 2002; Clark 2004). Part of the explanation is that, as an interest group, management requires a means of defining and expanding its activities. Referring to the spread of interest in corporate culture, Thackray comments, 'Culture is particularly seductive because it appears to open up a new frontier of managerial activism' (1986: 86). This option is particularly attractive to the personnel or human resource teams of large corporations, as is knowledge management to IT departments (see Chapter 16). Such examples remind us that the adoption of theories and practices is also likely to be affected by the internal fissures within the managerial labour process. With the demise of the great practitioner-theorists such as Taylor and Fayol, and the growth of more specialised academic production, management is also in a more *dependent* position.

But the attraction is also a reflection of the fact that the meaning of management is inseparable from the management of meaning (Gowler and Legge, 1983). Organisational theories become part of a language and a sub-culture through which management tries to understand itself and legitimate its activities to others, even when those ideological resources are used in a contradictory and rhetorical way. The essence of these points is that regardless of the social influences, organisational and management theory has a level of autonomy and its own rhythm of development. Regardless of the cycles of interest in ideas and proneness to fads and fashions, theories have their own very real effects. And as they are grappling with genuine problems it is possible to draw positive lessons, even for those of us who want to take the process of organisational change much further.

Beyond criticism?

Some time ago, Lex Donaldson described a new generation of radical commentators as demonstrating 'a supreme indifference in the fate of actual people in real organisations. … If there was a genuine interest, then this would indeed lead to wanting to know how to make organisations better' (1989: 250). More recently, another heavyweight mainstream theorist, William Starbuck, made a similar observation that organisational analysis has lost its 'external mission' and 'until organization theorists test their theories by suggesting ways to improve organizations, their research will remain a version of historical analysis' (2003: 449). They have a point (or points), but spoil it by arguing that betterment requires a science with predictive powers and the systematic elimination of ambiguity in casual explanation. In other words, to do the right thing, theorists would have to enter into the closed paradigm of positivist-functionalism.

Nevertheless, critical scholars have had a problem about practice. In the 1960s and 1970s the view of management and rationality as neutral technique was replaced by an equally unhelpful hostility that failed to distinguish between particular forms of authority expressed through existing structures and systems, and the necessity for co-ordination and control of resources. Or, as Landry and colleagues put it:

> There is a vital distinction to be made between 'management' and those people who hold manager-ial positions, and 'management' as an assortment of integrative functions which are necessary in any complex organisation – planning, harmonising related processes, ensuring appropriate flows of information, matching resources to production needs, marketing, financial control, linking output to demand, etc. (Landry *et al.*, 1985: 61)

This is part of an excellent dissection of the weaknesses of many community and other organisations in the radical movements in this period. Frequently they rejected any form of specialised division of labour, skills and expertise, and formal structures of decision-making, in favour of informal methods and rotation of all responsibilities. The result was seldom democratic or efficient. Even those collective and democratic forms of organisation, such as worker co-operatives, that have proved more durable have also remained small in number and relatively marginal in importance.

For these and other reasons, we now have something of a paradox: interest in critical perspectives on management and organisation has increased in inverse proportion to the actual existence of any practical alternatives. This could be problematic in that a critique of theoretical and practical orthodoxy that simply knocks everything down is limited and dangerous. To paraphrase Gouldner's comment for other purposes, critical social scientists have too often been morticians who bury people's hopes. We believe that it is important for critical theory not just to proclaim the limits of existing organisational forms and practices. Those constraints arising from dominant relations of wealth, power and control are real enough, as observation of the very partial progress of empowerment programmes or employee participation illustrates. But solely 'negative learning' implies an essence to work organisation under capitalism that denies it any significance.

The search for profitability involves innovations in technology, co-ordination of resources and utilisation of people's skills and knowledge that offer positive lessons relevant to any more democratic and egalitarian social order at work. This is not the same as the orthodox Marxist view, expressed by the founders of the Soviet Union, that a socialist society simply 'adds on' the techniques of capitalist work organisation to new property relations. Those techniques rather have to be added to, rethought and resituated in a new context of a more democratic and egalitarian economy. For job enrichment or teamworking, however flawed, are also indicators of the great potential of human labour to create more efficient and satisfying forms of work. To argue that all this is mere superficial window dressing is to fly in the face of the reality that we all find some work situations more creative and rewarding than others.

A further reason for not regarding the worlds of today and tomorrow as wholly sealed off from one another is that there is much to learn from the existing practices of employees. As Brecher (1978) rightly says, there is a massive 'hidden history of the workplace' which needs to be recognised and uncovered.

That history is based on the self-organisation of workers trying to resist and transform work relations. Admittedly that was easier to see when craft labour was dominant and many workers genuinely felt that they could run the factories better than their bosses. Old-style movements for workers' control are no longer feasible in a world of transnationals, global production and semi-skilled labour. But there remains a wealth of untapped experience and knowledge in employees' informal job-controls and patterns of organisation (see Ackroyd and Thompson, 1999), as well as in progressive practice in the public sector (Goss, 2001).

Finally, we need to note that what Donaldson identified as armchair theorising has been given greater intellectual weight by the increased influence of post-modernism. It has become more difficult to move beyond criticism in circumstances where more and more academics have abandoned belief in 'narratives of progress' or progress through any type of rational action or design. While the official domain statement of the CMS Interest Group in the American Academy of Management tries hard to specify a practical critique (P. Adler, Forbes and Willmott, 2007), many adherents of CMS are ambivalent. In the previously referred to article on CMS, Fournier and Grey (2000) argue that a stance against performative intent is one of its three defining boundaries. Performativity is taken to be that which is aimed at contributing to the effectiveness of management practice. It is no good banging on about reflexivity all the time, if all we are doing is reflecting on our own academic practices, no matter how fascinating they appear (not).

In effect, given the nature of existing organisations and the post-modern rejection of progress, the distaste for performativity can quickly slip into *any* practice. So, Fournier and Grey make a distinction between legitimately invoking notions of power, inequality and control, and the illegitimate invocation of efficiency, effectiveness and profitability. Yet why is this illegitimate in itself? In any feasible economic relations, some organisations or practices will be more effective and efficient than others, though how this is measured and what action follows from it will always be open to dispute.

Productivity matters to employees as well as managers. It is reasonable to argue that HRM or equal opportunity can be positive for efficiency, as long as this is not the only criterion on which progressive practices are advocated. While a reflexive attitude is a feature of any critical approach, hyper-reflexivity in which everything is deconstructed or problematised, while solving nothing, is ultimately arid and self-defeating. There are still practices and a world to remake.

part IV: further reading

Theory is not an easy sell and the way that it's often written about, particularly in organisational analysis, makes that task even harder. The edited collection from Korczynski and colleagues (2005) has some excellent contributions, but others severely try the reader's patience. That volume is primarily sociological. McAuley and collagues' (2006) textbook is one of the more accessible on organisation theory, while Westwood and Clegg's (2003) volume organises contributions into debates in a lively way. The current fashion is to collect theory and research in hefty Handbooks. It's not high theory, but as in Part II we've drawn extensively on Ackroyd and colleagues (2005). The new *Handbook of Critical Management Studies* from Alvesson and colleagues (2009) will give plenty of attention to the more post-modern side of the debates. It is certainly worth taking a look at P. Adler and colleagues' (2007) overview of CMS, which also has a useful list of sources, as well as the earlier Grey and Willmott (2005) reader. A lot of intellectual energy has been expended in recent years debating meta-theoretical, philosophy of science issues. Though important, these can be even harder to follow. If you've the stomach for it, take a look at the exchanges in *Journal of Management Studies* between the critical realist Mike Reed and post-structuralist opponents Alessia Contu and Hugh Willmott. Reed is a leading organisation theorist of a Weberian orientation. His edited collection on new Weberian perspectives (Ray and Reed, 1994a) is excellent. A similar exchange was organised by Tsoukas (2007) in *Organization Studies* on CMS and labour process theory between Adler, Thompson, Knights and Willmott, Delbridge, and Vallas. Finally, while its on HRM and employment relations rather than organisations, the volume on theory published by the Industrial Relations Association (Kaufman, 2004) is often very good and accessible (the Introduction can be downloaded at http://digitalcommons.ilr.cornell.edu/books/16/)

Ackroyd, S., Batt, R., Thompson, P. and Tolbert, P. (eds) (2005) *The Oxford Handbook of Work and Organization*, Oxford: Oxford University Press.

Adler, P., Forbes, L. and Willmott, H. (2007) 'Critical Management Studies', *The Academy of Management Annals, Volume 1, Chapter Three* (and see http://www.criticalmanagement.org/publications/working. htm).

Alvesson, M., Bridgman, T. and Willmott, H. (eds) (2009) *The Oxford Handbook of Critical Management Studies*, Oxford: Oxford University Press.

Contu, A. and Willmott, H. (2005) 'You Spin Me Round: The Critical Realist Turn in Management and Organization Studies', *Journal of Management Studies*, 42. 8: 1645–62.

Grey, C. and Willmott, H. C. (eds) (2005) *Critical Management Studies: A Reader*, Oxford: Oxford University Press.

Kaufman, B. E. (ed.) (2004) *Theory and the Employment Relationship*, Industrial Relations Research Association, Cornell: ILR Press.

Korczynski, M., Hodson, R. and Edwards, P. (eds) (2005) *Social Theory at Work*, Oxford: Oxford University Press.

McAuley, J., Johnson, P. and Duberley, J. (2006) *Organization Theory: Challenges and Perspectives*, London: Pearson Higher Education.

Ray, L.J. and Reed, M. (eds) (1994a) *Organizing Modernity: New Weberian Perspectives on Work, Organization and Society*, London: Routledge.

Reed, M. (2005b) 'Reflections on the Realist Turn in Organisation and Management Studies', *Journal of Management Studies*, 42. 8: 1621–44.

Reed, M. (2005c) 'Doing the Loco-Motion: Response to Contu and Willmott's Commentary on "The Realist Turn in Organization and Management Studies"', *Journal of Management Studies*, 42. 8: 1663–73.

Tsoukas, H. (2007) 'Forum on "The Future of Critical Management Studies"', *Organization Studies*, 28. 9: 1309–84.

Westwood, R.I. and Clegg, S. (2003) *Debating Organization: Point-counterpoint in Organization Studies*, London: Blackwell Publishing.

references

Abrahamson, E. (1996) 'Management Fashion', *Academy of Management Review* 21. 1: 254–85.

Abrahamsson, L. (2007) 'Exploring Construction of Gendered Identities at Work', in S. Billett, T. Fenwick and M. Somerville (eds), *Work, Subjectivity and Learning*, Bonn: Springer.

ACAS (1988) *Labour Flexibility in Britain: The 1987 ACAS Survey*, ACAS Occasional Paper 41, London: ACAS.

ACAS (2005) *Advisory Booklet on Flexible Workingand Worklife Balance*, available at: http://www.acas.org.uk/media/pdf/q/4/B09_1.pdf

Acker, J. (1990) 'Hierarchies, Jobs, Bodies: A Theory of Gendered Organizations', *Gender and Society*, 5: 390–407.

Acker, J. and Van Houten, D. R. (1992) 'Differential Recruitment and Control: The Sex Structuring of Organizations', in A. J. Mills and P. Tancred (eds), *Gendering Organisational Analysis*, London: Sage.

Acker, S. (1992) 'Gendering Organisational Theory', in A. J. Mills and P. Tancred (eds) *Gendering Organisational Analysis*, London: Sage.

Ackers, P. and Black, J. (1991) 'Paternalist Capitalism: An Organisation in Transition', in M. Cross and G. Payne (eds), *Work and the Enterprise Culture*, London: Falmer.

Ackroyd, S. (1992) 'Paradigms Lost: Paradise Gained? Notes on the Discovery of Meta-Theory in Organisational Analysis', in M. Reed and M. Hughes (eds), *Rethinking Organisation: New Directions in Organisation and Analysis*, London: Sage.

Ackroyd, S. (1994) 'Recreating Common Ground: Elements for Post-Paradigmatic Theories of Organisation', in J. Hassard and M. Parker (eds), *Towards a New Theory of Organizations*, London: Routledge.

Ackroyd, S. (1995) 'On the Structure and Dynamics of some Small, UK-Based Information Technology Firms', *Journal of Management Studies*, 32. 2: 141–61.

Ackroyd, S. (2000) 'Organisational Constitution and Societal Structuration', in S. Ackroyd and S. Fleetwood (eds), *Realist Perspectives in Management and Organisation*, London: Routledge.

Ackroyd, S. (2002) *The Organization of Business*, Oxford: Oxford University Press.

Ackroyd, S. (2005) 'Organising and Organisations', in S. Ackroyd, R. Batt, P. Thompson and P. Tolbert (eds) *A Handbook of Work and Organization*, Oxford: Oxford University Press.

Ackroyd, S. (2006) 'Aspects of Flexible Economic Systems: Some Recent Developments in the UK Economy', in *Facets of Flexibility*, E.J. Skorstad and H. Ramsdal (eds), Oslo: Ostfold University Press.

Ackroyd, S. (2008) 'Organisational Conflict', in Cooper, C.L. and Clegg, S.R. (eds), *Handbook of Organisational Behaviour*, London: Sage.

Ackroyd, S., Batt, R., Thompson, P. and Tolbert, P. (2005) 'Texts and Times: Mapping the Changing Study of Work and Organizations', in Ackroyd, S., Batt, R., Thompson, P. and Tolbert, P. (eds) *The Oxford Handbook of Work and Organization*, Oxford: Oxford University Press.

Ackroyd, S., Burrell, G., Hughes, S. and Whitaker, A. (1987) 'The Japanisation of British Industry', *Industrial Relations Journal*, Spring 1988, 9. 1.

Ackroyd, S. and Crowdy, P. A. (1990) 'Can Culture be Managed? Working with "Raw" Material: The Case of English Slaughtermen', *Personnel Review*, 19. 5: 12–13.

Ackroyd, S. and Fleetwood, S. (eds) (2000) *Realist Perspectives in Management and Organisation*, London: Routledge.

Ackroyd, S. and Lawrenson, D. (1996) 'Knowledge Work and Organisational Transformation: Analysing Contemporary Change in the Social Use of Expertise', in R. Fincham (ed.) *New Relationships in the Organised Professions*, Aldershot: Ashgate.

Ackroyd, S. and Proctor, S. (1998) 'British Manufacturing Organisation and Workplace Industrial Relations: Some Attributes of the New Flexible Firm', *British Journal of Industrial Relations*, 36. 2: 163–83.

Ackroyd, S. and Thompson, P. (1999) *Organisational Misbehaviour*, London: Sage.

Adair, J. (1979) *Action-Centred Leadership*, London: Gower.

Adams, J. L. (1979) *Conceptual Blockbusting* (2nd edn), New York: W. W. Norton.

Adams, J. S. (1965) 'Injustice in Social Exchange', in L. Berkovitz (ed.), *Advances in Experimental Social Psychology*, vol. 2, New York: Academic Press.

Adams, T. and Demaiter, E. (2008) 'Skill, Education and Credentials in the New Economy', *Work, Employment and Society*, 22. 2: 351–62.

Adkins, L. (1992) 'Sexual Work and the Employment of Women in the Service Industries', in A. Witz and M. Savage (eds), *Gender and Bureaucracy*, Oxford: Blackwell.

Adkins, L. and Lury, C. (1994) 'The Cultural and the Sexual and the Gendering of the Labour Market', paper presented to the BSA Conference on Sexualities in their Social Context, University of Central Lancashire, March.

Adler, N. and Bartholomew, S. (1992) 'Managing Globally Competent People', *Academy of Management Executive*, 6. 3: 52–65.

Adler, N. J. (1994) 'Competitive Frontiers: Women Managing across Borders', in N. J. Adler and D. N. Izraeli (eds), *Competitive Frontiers: Women Managers in a Global Economy*, Oxford: Blackwell.

Adler, N. J. and Izraeli, D. N. (1988) *Women in Management Worldwide*, Armonk, NY: M. E. Sharpe.

Adler, P. (1997) 'Work Organisation: From Taylorism to Teamwork', *Perspectives on Work*, 1. 3: 61–5.

Adler, P. (2001) 'Market, Hierarchy, and Trust: The Knowledge Economy and the Future of Capitalism', *Organization Science*, 12. 2: 215–34.

Adler, P. and Borys, B. (1996) 'Two Types of Bureaucracy: Enabling and Coercive', *Administrative Science Quarterly*, 41: 61–89.

Adler, P., Forbes, L. and Willmott, H. (2007) *Critical Management Studies*, The Academy of Management Annals, vol. 1, chap 3 (and see http://www.criticalmanagement.org/publications/working.htm).

Adler, P., Kwon, S.-W. and Heckscher, C. (2008) 'The Evolving Organization of Professional Work', *Organization Science*, 19. 2: 359–76.

Adler, P. S. (1993) 'Time-and-Motion Regained', *Harvard Business Review*, Jan.–Feb.: 97–107.

Adler, P. S. (1995) 'Democratic Taylorism: The Toyota Production System at NUMMI', in S. Babson (ed.), *Lean Work: Empowerment and Exploitation in the Global Auto Industry*, Detroit, MI: Wayne State University Press.

Aglietta, M. (1979) *A Theory of Capitalist Regulation*, London: New Left Books.

Ainsworth, S. and Hardy, C. (2004) 'Discourse and Identities', in D. Grant, C. Hardy, C. Oswick and L. Putnam (eds), *Handbook of Organizational Discourse,* London: Sage.

Ajzen, I. (1988) *Attitudes, Personality and Behaviour*, Milton Keynes: Open University Press.

Ajzen, I. and Fishbein, M. (1980) *Understanding Attitudes and Predicting Social Behaviour*, Englewood Cliffs, NJ: Prentice Hall.

Albrow, M. (1973) 'The Study of Organizations – Objectivity or Bias?' in G. Salaman and K. Thompson (eds), *People and Organizations*, Harlow: Longman.

Albrow, M. (1992) 'Sine Ira et Studio – or Do Organizations Have Feelings?', *Organisation Studies*, 13. 3: 313–29.

Alderfer, C. P. and Smith, K. K. (1982) 'Studying Intergroup Relations Embedded in Organizations', *Administrative Science Quarterly*, 27: 35–65.

Aldrich, H. and Ruef, N. (2006) *Organizations Evolving*, London: Sage.

Aldrich, H. E. (1979) *Organizations and Environments*, Englewood Cliffs, NJ: Prentice Hall.

Aldrich, H. E. (1992) 'Incommensurable Paradigms? Vital Signs from Three Perspectives', in M. Reed and M. Hughes (eds), *Rethinking Organisation: New Directions in Organisation and Analysis*, London: Sage.

Aldrich, H. E. and Pfeffer, J. (1976) 'Environments and Organizations', in A. Inkeles *et al.* (eds) *Annual Review of Sociology 2*, Palo Alto: Annual Reviews.

Aldrich, H. E. and Stabler, U. (1987) 'Organisational Transformation and Trends in US Employment Relations', paper presented to the Labour Process Conference, Aston-UMIST.

Alker, L. and McHugh, D. (2000) 'Human Resource Maintenance? Organisational Rationales for the Introduction of Employee Assistance Programmes', *Journal of Managerial Psychology*, 15. 4: 303–23.

Allen, J. and Henry, N. (1994) 'Fragments of Industry and Employment: Contract Service Work and the Shift towards Precarious Employment', paper presented to the Conference on Work, Employment and Society in the 1990s, September, University of Kent.

Allen, S. and Workowtiz, C. (1987) *Homeworking: Myths and Realities*, London: Macmillan.

Allport, F. H. (1991) *Pattern and Growth in Personality*, London: Holt, Rinehart & Winston.

Alvesson, M. (1985) 'A Critical Framework for Organisational Analysis', *Organisation Studies*, 6. 2: 117–38.

Alvesson, M. (1988) 'Management, Corporate Culture and Corporatism at the Company Level: A Case Study', *Economic and Industrial Democracy*, 13. 12: 347–67.

Alvesson, M. (2007) Shakers, Strugglers, Story-tellers, Surfers and Others, Paper presented to Research Workshop, University of New South Wales, March.

Alvesson, M. and Billing, Y. (1992) 'Gender and Organisations: Towards a Differentiated Understanding', *Organisation Studies*, 13. 12: 73–102.

Alvesson, M. and Billing, Y. (1997) *Understanding Gender and Organisations*, London: Sage.

Alvesson, M., Bridgman, T. and Willmott, H. (eds) (2009) *The Oxford Handbook of Critical Management Studies*, Oxford: Oxford University Press.

Alvesson, M. and Deetz, S. (1996) 'Critical Theory and Postmodern Approaches to Organisational Studies', in S. Clegg, C. Hardy and W. Nord (eds) *Handbook of Organisation Studies*, London: Sage.

Alvesson, M. and Kärreman, D. (2004) 'Interfaces of Control. Technocratic and Socio-ideological Control in a Global Management Consultancy Firm', *Accounting, Organization and Society* 29: 423–44.

Alvesson, M. and Thompson, P. (2005) 'Post-Bureaucracy?', in S. Ackroyd, R. Batt, P. Thompson, and P. Tolbert, (eds) *A Handbook of Work and Organization*, Oxford: Oxford University Press.

Alvesson, M. and Willmott, H. (1992) 'Critical Theory and Management Studies', in M. Alvesson and H. Willmott (eds) *Critical Management Studies*, London: Sage.

Alvesson, M. and Willmott, H. (2002) 'Identity Regulation as Organizational Control – Producing the Appropriate Individual', *Journal of Management Studies*, 39(5): 619–44.

American Psychiatric Association (1994) *Diagnostic and Statistical Manual of Mental Disorders* (4th edn), Washington, DC: Author.

Amin, A. (1989) 'A Model of the Small Firm in Italy', in E. Goodman and J. Bamford (eds), *Small Firms and Industrial Districts in Italy*, New York: Routledge.

Amin, A. (1991) 'Flexible Specialisation and Small Firms in Italy: Myths and Realities', in A. Pollert (ed.), *Farewell to Flexibility?* Oxford: Blackwell.

Amsden, A. H. (1992) *Asia's Next Giant: South Korea and Late Industrialisation*, Oxford: Oxford University Press.

Anderson, N. R. and King, N. (1993) 'Innovation in Organizations', in C. L. Cooper and I. T. Robertson (eds), *International Review of Industrial and Organisational Psychology*, vol. 8, Chichester: Wiley.

Anderson, P. (2009) 'Intermediate Occupations and the Conceptual and Empirical Limitations of the Hourglass Economy Thesis', *Work, Employment and Society*.

Andreff, W. (1984) 'The International Centralisation of Capital and the Reordering of Work Capitalism', *Capital and Class*, 22: 58–80.

Anker, R. (1997) 'Theories of Occupational Segregation by Sex: An Overview', *International Labour Review*, 1366. 7: 315–40.

Anthony, P. D. (1990) 'The Paradox of the Management of Culture or "He Who Leads is Lost"', *Personnel Review*, 19. 4: 3–8.

Anxo D. and Niklasson, H (2006) The Swedish Model in Torrent Times: Decline or Renaissace? *International Review*, 145. 4: 379–412.

Appelbaum, E., Bailey, T., Berg, P. and Kalleberg, A. L. (2000) *Manufacturing Advantage: Why High Performance Work Systems Pay Off*, Ithaca, NY: Cornell University Press.

Appelbaum, E. and Batt, R. (1994) *The New American Workplace: Transforming Work Systems in the United States*, Ithaca, N.Y.: ILR Press.

Applebaum, E. and Berg, P. (1999) 'Hierarchical Organization and Horizontal Coordination: Evidence from a Worker Survey', in M. Blair and T. Kochan (eds.), *The New Relationship: Human Capital in the American Corporation*, Washington, DC: Brookings Institution.

Archer, M. (1995) *Realist Social Theory: The Morphogenetic Approach*, Cambridge: Cambridge University Press.

Archibald, W. P. (1978) *Social Psychology as Political Economy*, Toronto: McGraw-Hill Ryerson.

Argyle, M. (1974) *The Social Psychology of Work*, Harmondsworth: Penguin.

Argyris, A. (1967) 'Today's Problems with Tomorrow's Organizations', *Journal of Management Studies*, 4. 1: 31–55.

Argyris, C. (1960) *Understanding Organisational Behaviour*, Homewood, IL: Dorsey Press.

Argyris, C. (1976) 'Leadership, Learning and Changing the Status Quo', *Organizational Dynamics* (Winter): 29–43.

Argyris, C. and Schön, D. A. (1978) *Organisational Learning: A Theory of Action Perspective*, Reading, MA: Addison-Wesley.

Arias, M. E. (1993) 'MNCs, Organisational Models, and Local Firms in Developing Countries: The case of the Pharmaceutical Industry in Ecuador', paper presented to the 11th EGOS Colloquium, Paris.

Armistead, N. (1974) *Reconstructing Social Psychology*, Baltimore: Penguin.

Armstrong, M. (1987) 'Human Resource Management: A Case of the Emperor's New Clothes?' *Personnel Management*, 19. 8: 30–5.

Armstrong, M. (1992) *Human Resource Management: Strategy and Action*, London: Kogan Page.

Armstrong, P. (1984) 'Competition between the Organisational Professions and the Evolution of Management Control Strategies', in K. Thompson (ed.), *Work, Employment and Unemployment*, Milton Keynes: Open University Press.

Armstrong, P. (1986) 'Management Control Strategies and Inter-Professional Competition: The Cases of Accountancy and Personnel Management', in D. Knights and H. Willmott (eds), *Managing the Labour Process*, Aldershot: Gower.

Armstrong, P. (1987a) The Divorce of Productive and Unproductive Management', paper presented to the Labour Process Conference, Aston-UMIST.

Armstrong, P. (1987b) 'Engineers, Management and Trust', *Work, Employment and Society*, 1. 4: 421–40.

Armstrong, P. (1988) 'The Personnel Profession in the Age of Management Accountancy', *Personnel Review*, 17. 1: 25–31.

Armstrong, P. (1989) 'Management, Labour Process and Agency', *Work, Employment and Society*, 3. 3: 307–22.

Armstrong, P. (1991) 'The Influence of Michel Foucault on Historical Research in Accounting: An Assessment', paper presented to the Academy of Accounting Historians Research Methodology Conference, University of Mississippi, December.

Armstrong, P., Marginson, P., Edwards, P. and Purcell, J. (1994) 'Divisionalisation, Trade Unionism and Corporate Control: Findings from the Second Company-Level Industrial Relations Survey', paper presented to the 12th Annual International Labour Process Conference, Aston.

Arnold, J., Cooper, C. and Robertson, I. T. (1998) *Work Psychology: Understanding Human Behaviour in the Workplace*, London: Financial Times/Pitman.

Arnold, J., Robertson, I. T. and Cooper, C. (1991) *Work Psychology: Understanding Human Behaviour in the Workplace*, London: Pitman.

Aronoff, J. and Wilson, J. P. (1985) *Personality in the Social Process*, Hillsdale, NJ: LEA.

Aronson, E. (1972) *The Social Animal*, San Francisco: W. H. Freeman.

Asch, S. E., Block, H. and Hertzmann, M. (1938) 'Studies in the Principles of Judgements of Attitudes: I. Two Basic Principles of Judgement', *Journal of Psychology*, 5: 219–51.

Ashkenas, R., Ulrich, D., Jick, T. and Kerr, S. (1995) *The Boundaryless Organization, Breaking the Chains of Organizational Structure*, San Francisco: Jossey-Bass.

Atkinson, J. (1984) 'Manpower Strategies for Flexible Organizations', *Personnel Management*, August.

Atkinson, J. (1985) *IMS Report no. 89*, Institute of Management Studies, Sussex: Falmer.

Atkinson, J. and Gregory, D. (1986) 'A Flexible Future: Britain's Dual Labour Force', *Marxism Today*, April: 12–17.

Auer, P. (2006) 'Protected Mobility for Employment and Decent Work', *Journal of Industrial Relations*, 48. 1: 21–40.

Augoustinos, M. and Walker, I. (1995) *Social Cognition: An Integrated Approach*, London: Sage.

Azjen, I. and Madden, T. J. (1986) 'Prediction of Goal-Related Behaviour: Attitudes, Intentions, and Perceived Behavioural Control', *Journal of Experimental Social Psychology*, 22: 453–74.

Bachrach, P. and Baratz, M. S. (1962) 'Two Faces of Power', *American Political Science Review*, 56: 947–52.

Bacharach, S. B., Bamberger, P. A. and Sonnenstuhl, W. J. (1996) 'MAP's: Labor-Based Peer Assistance in the Workplace', *Industrial Relations*, 35. 2: 261–75.

Bachrach, S. B. and Lawler, E. J. (1980) *Power and Politics in Organizations*, London: Jossey-Bass.

Bachrach, P. and Baratz, M. S. (1982) 'Two Faces of Power', *American Political Science Review*, 56: 947–52.

Badham, R. (1997) 'Towards an Ethnography of Politics', unpublished paper, University of Wollongong.

Bailey, R.D. (1985) *Coping with Stress in Caring*, Oxford: Blackwell.

Bain, P. and Taylor, P. (2000) 'Entrapped by the Electronic Panopticon? Worker Resistance in Call Centres', *New Technology, Work and Employment*, 15. 1: 2–18.

Baines, S. (1999) 'Servicing the Media: Freelancing, Teleworking and "Enterprising" Careers', *New Technology, Work and Employment*, 14. 1: 18–31.

Baldamus, W. (1961) *Efficiency and Effort: An Analysis of Industrial Administration*, London: Tavistock.

Baldock, R. (1999) *The Last Days of the Giants?* London: Wiley.

Baldry, C., Bain P., Taylor P., Hyman J., Scholarios, D., Marks, A., Watson, A., Gilbert, K., Gall, G. and Bunzel, D. (2007) *The Meaning of Work in the New Economy*, Basingstoke: Palgrave Macmillan.

Bales, R. F. (1950) *Interaction Process Analysis: A Method for the Study of Small Groups*, Reading, MA: Addison-Wesley.

Baltes, P. B., Baltes, M. M., Freund, A. M. and Lang, F. (1999). *The Measurement of Selection, Optimization, and Compensation (SOC) by Self-Report: Technical Report 1999*. Berlin, Germany: Max Planck Institute for Human Development.

Bandura, A. (1977) *Social Learning Theory*, Englewood Cliffs, NJ: Prentice Hall.

Bandura, A. (1986) *Social Foundations of Thought and Action: A Social Cognitive Theory*, Englewood Cliffs, NJ: Prentice Hall.

Bandura, A. and Walters, R. H. (1963) *Social Learning and Personality Development*, New York: Holt, Rinehart & Winston.

Bannister, D. (1966) 'Psychology as an Exercise in Paradox', *Bulletin of the British Psychological Society*, 63: 21–6.

Banton, R., Clifford, P., Frosh, S., Lousada, J. and Rosenthall, J. (1985) *The Politics of Mental Health*, London: Macmillan.

Barham, K. and Rassam, C. (eds) (1989) *Shaping the Corporate Future: Leading Executives Share their Vision and Strategies*, London: Unwin Hyman.

Baritz, L. (1960) *The Servants of Power*, Middletown, CT: Wesleyan University Press.

Barkan, J. (2004) *The Corporation*, London: Constable.

Barker, J. R. (1993) 'Tightening the Iron Cage: Concertive Control in Self-Managing Teams', *Administrative Science Quarterly*, 38: 408–37.

Barker, J. R. (1999) *The Discipline of Teamwork: Participation and Concertive Control*, London: Sage.

Barker, R. and Roberts, H. (1993) 'The Uses of the Concept of Power', in D. Morgan and L. Stanley (eds), *Debates in Sociology*, Manchester: Manchester University Press.

Barley, S. (1996) *The New World of Work*, pamphlet, British–North American Committee: London.

Barley, S. (2005) 'What We Know (and Mostly Don't Know) about Technical Work', in S. Ackroyd, R. Batt, P. Thompson and P. Tolbert (eds), *Oxford Handbook of Work and Organization*, Oxford: Oxford University Press.

Barley, S. and Kunda, G. (2004) *Gurus, Hired Guns, and Warm Bodies: Itinerant Experts in a Knowledge Economy*, Princeton, NJ: Princeton University Press.

Barley, S. R. and Kunda, G. (1992) 'Design and Devotion: Surges of Rational and Normative Ideologies of Control in Managerial Discourse', *Administrative Science Quarterly*, 37: 363–99.

Barnard, C. (1938) *The Functions of the Executive*, Cambridge, MA: Harvard University Press.

Baron, R. A. and Byrne, D. (1997) *Social Psychology* (8th edn), Needham Heights, MA: Allyn & Bacon.

Barry, K.M. (2007) *Femininity in Flight: A History of Flight Attendants*, Durham, NC: Duke University Press.

Barsade, S. G. and Gibson, D. E. (2007) 'Why Does Affect Matter in Organizations?', *Academy of Management Perspectives*, February, 36–59. Available at: http://www.management.wharton.upenn.edu/barsade/docs/Barsade_WhyAffectMattersAOM.pdf.

Bartlett, C. and Goshal, S. (1990a) *Managing across Borders*, Boston: Harvard University Press.

Bartlett, C. and Goshal, S. (1990b) 'The Multinational Corporation as an International Network', *Academy of Management Review*, 4: 603–25.

Bartlett, C. and Goshal, S. (1992) 'What is a Global Manager?', *Harvard Business Review*, Sept.–Oct.: 124–32.

Bass, B. M. (1985) *Leadership and Performance beyond Expectations*, New York: Free Press.

Basset, P. (1989) 'All Together Now', *Marxism Today*, June: 44–7.

Batt, R. (1999) 'Work Organisation, Technology and Performance in Customer Service and Sales', *Industrial and Labour Relations Review*, 52. 4: 539–64.

Batt, R. and Doellgast, V. (2005) 'Groups, Teams and the Division of Labour: Interdisciplinary Perspectives on the Organization of Work', in S. Ackroyd, R. Batt, P. Thompson and P. Tolbert (eds), *Oxford Handbook of Work and Organization*, Oxford: Oxford University Press.

Bauer, T. K. (2004) High Performance Workplace Practices and Job Satisfaction: Evidence from Europe, IZA Discussion Paper No. 1265, August. Available at SSRN: http://ssrn.com/abstract=582304./

Baum, J. A. C. (1995) 'The Changing Basis of Competition in Organisational Populations: The Manhattan Hotel Industry 1898–1990', *Social Forces*, 74: 177–205.

Bauman, Z. (1998) *Work, Consumerism and the New Poor*, Cambridge: Polity.

Bavelas, A. (1950) 'Communication Patterns in Task-Oriented Groups', *Journal of the Acoustical Society of America*, 22: 725–30.

BBC NEWS (2007) 'How Do Telephone Lie Detectors Work?', http://news.bbc.co.uk/1/hi/magazine/6983359.stm, accessed 7/09/07.

Beck, U. (1992) *Risk Society: Towards a New Modernity*, London: Sage.

Beck, U. (2000) *The Brave New World of Work*, Cambridge: Polity.

Becker, G. (1985) 'Human Capital, Effort and the Sexual Division of Labour', *Journal of Labor Economics*, 3. 2: 33–58.

Becker, H. S., Geer, B., Hughes, E. C. and Strauss, A. (1963) *Boys in White*, Chicago: University of Chicago Press.

Beech, H. R., Burns, L. E. and Sheffield, B. F. (1982) *A Behavioural Approach to the Management of Stress: A Practical Guide to Techniques*, Chichester: Wiley.

Beer, M., Spector, B., Lawrence, P., Quin Mills, D. and Walton, R. (1985) *Human Resource Management: A General Manager's Perspective*, Glencoe, IL: Free Press.

Beirne, M., Ramsay, H. and Pantelli, N. (1998) 'Developments in Computing Work: Control and Contradiction in the Software Labour Process', in P. Thompson and C. Warhurst (eds), *Workplaces of the Future*, London: Macmillan.

Belbin, M. (1981) *Management Teams*, London: Heinemann.

Bell, D. (1960) *The End of Ideology*, New York: Collier Macmillan.

Bell, D. (1973) *The Coming of Post-Industrial Society*, Harmondsworth: Penguin.

Bellaby, P. and Orribor, P. (1977) 'The Growth of Trade Union Consciousness among General Hospital Nurses', *Sociological Review*, 25: 801–22.

Bellamy Foster, J. (2007) 'The Financialization of Capitalism', *Monthly Review*, 58. 11: 8–10.

Benders, J. (2005) 'Teamworking: Partial Participation', in J. Hyman, P. Thompson and B. Harley (eds), *Participation and Democracy at Work: Essays in Honour of Harvie Ramsay*, Basingstoke: Palgrave Macmillan.

Benders, J. and Huigen, F. (1999) On *the Incidence of Group Work: Results from a European Survey*, EPOC Report, Dublin

Bendix, R. (1956) *Work and Authority in Industry*, New York: Harper & Row.

Beneria, L. (1995) 'Response: The Dynamics of Globalization', *Labor and Working Class History*, 47: 45–52.

Benne, K. D. and Sheats, P. (1948) 'Functional Roles of Group Members', *Journal of Social Science*, Spring: 41–9.

Bennis, W. (1993) *An Invented Life: Reflections on Leadership and Change*, Reading, MA: Addison-Wesley Publishing Co.

Benson, J. K. (1977) 'Innovation and Crisis in Organisational Analysis', in J. K. Benson (ed.), *Organisational Analysis:Critique and Innovation*, London: Sage.

Berg, M. (1985) *The Age of Manufactures*, London: Fontana.

Berger, P. L. and Luckman, T. (1967) *The Social Construction of Reality*, London: Allen Lane.

Berggren, C. (1993) 'Lean Production: The End of History?', *Work, Employment and Society*, 7. 2: 163–88.

Berggren, C. (1996) 'ABB: Local Presence and Cross-Border Learning within a Multi-national', in J. Storey (ed.), *Blackwell Cases in Human Resource Management and Change*, Oxford: Blackwell.

Berkeley Thomas, A. (1993) *Controversies in Management*, London: Routledge.

Berle, A. A. and Means, G. C. (1935) *The Modern Corporation and Private Property*, New York: Macmillan.

Berridge, J. Cooper, C. L. and Highley-Marchington, C. (1997) *Employee Assistance Programmes and Workplace Counselling*, New York: Wiley.

Best, M. (1990) *The New Competition: Institutions of Industrial Restructuring*, Cambridge, MA: Harvard University Press.

Beynon, H. (1975) *Working for Ford*, Wakefield: E. P. Publishing.

Beynon, H. (1987) 'Dealing with Icebergs: Organisation, Production and Motivation in the 1990s', *Work, Employment and Society*, 1. 2: 247–59.

Bhaskar, R. (1989) *Reclaiming Reality*, London: Verso.

Biddle, B. J. (1979) *Role Theory: Expectations, Identities and Behaviours*, London: Academic Press.

Biewener, J. (1997) 'Downsizing and the New American Workplace: Rethinking the High Performance Paradigm', *Review of Radical Political Economics*, 29. 4: 1–22.

Biggart, N. W. (1989) *Charismatic Capitalism: Direct Selling Organizations in America*, London: University of Chicago Press.

Birchall, D. and Lyons, L. (1995) *Creating Tomorrow's Organisation*, London: Financial Times/Pitman.

Bittner, E. (1967) 'The Police on Skid Row: A Study of Peace Keeping', *American Sociological Review*, 32. 5: 699–715.

Bittner, E. (1973) 'The Concept of Organisation', in G. Salaman and K. Thompson (eds), *People and Organizations*, Harlow: Longman.

Blackler, F. (1982) 'Organisational Psychology', in S. Canter and D. Canter (eds), *Psychology in Practice: Perspectives in Professional Psychology*, Chichester: Wiley.

Blackler, F. (1995) 'Knowledge, Knowledge Work and Organizations: An Overview and Interpretation', *Organisation Studies*, 16. 6: 1021–46.

Blackler, F. and Shimmin, S. (1984) *Applying Psychology in Organizations*, London: Methuen.

Blair, H., Taylor, S. G. and Randle, K. (1998) 'A Pernicious Panacea: A Critical Evaluation of Business Process Re-engineering', *New Technology, Work and Employment*, 13. 2: 116–27.

Blakemore, K. and Black, R. (1996) *Understanding Equal Opportunities Policies*, London: Prentice Hall/Harvester Wheatsheaf.

Blau, G., Linnehan, F., Brooks, A. and Hoover, D. K. (1993) 'Vocational Behaviour 1990–1992: Personnel Practices, Organisational Behaviour, Workplace Behaviour and Industrial/Organisational, Measurement Issues', *Journal of Vocational Behaviour*, 43: 133–97.

Blau, P. M. (1955) *The Dynamics of Bureaucracy*, Chicago: University of Chicago Press.

Blau, P. M. (1964) *Exchange and Power in Social Life*, New York: Wiley.

Blau, P. M. (1970) 'A Formal Theory of Differentiation in Organizations', *American Sociological Review*, 35: 201–18.

Blau, P. M. and Schoenherr, R. A. (1971) *The Structure of Organizations*, New York: Basic Books.

Blau, P. M. and Scott, W. (1963) *Formal Organizations: A Comparative Approach*, London: Routledge & Kegan Paul.

Blauner, R. (1964) *Alienation and Freedom*, Chicago: University of Chicago Press.

Blinkhorn, S. and Johnson, C. (1990) 'The Insignificance of Personality Testing', *Nature*, 348. 20/27 December: 671–2.

Blinkhorn, S. and Johnson, C. (1991) 'Personality Tests: The Great Debate', *Personnel Management*, September: 38–9.

Bluestone, B. and Bluestone, I. (1992) *Negotiating the Future: A Labor Perspective on American Business*, New York: Basic Books.

Bluementritt, R. and Johnston, R. (1999) Towards a Strategy for Knowledge Management, *Technology Analysis and Strategic Management*, 11: 287–300.

Blyton, P. and Turnbull, P. (1992) *Reassessing Human Resource Management*, London: Sage.

Blyton, P. and Turnbull, P. (1998) *The Dynamics of Employee Relations* (2nd edn), London: Macmillan.

Boddy, D. and Buchanan, D. (1992) *Take the Lead: Interpersonal Skills for Project Managers*, London: Prentice Hall.

Bok, M. and Simmons, L. (2009) 'Working But Poor: Experiences in the American Low-Wage Labour Market', in Bolton, S. and Houlihan, M. (eds), *Work Matters: Critical Reflections on Contemporary Work*, Basingstoke: Palgrave Macmillan.

Bolman, L. G. and Deal, T. E. (1994) 'The Organisation as Theater', in H. Tsoukas (ed.), *New Thinking in Organisational Behaviour*, London: Butterworth and Heinemann.

Bologh, R. (1990) *Love or Greatness: Max Weber and Masculine Thinking: A Feminist Inquiry*, London: Unwin Hyman.

Bolton, S. (2000) 'Emotion Here, Emotion There, Emotional Organisations Everywhere', *Critical Perspectives on Accounting*, 11: 155–71.

Bolton, S. (2005) *Emotion Management*, Basingstoke: Palgrave Macmillan.

Bolton, S. and Houlihan, M. (eds) (2009) *Work Matters: Critical Reflections on Contemporary Work*, Basingstoke: Palgrave Macmillan.

Bordieu, P. (1977) *Towards a Theory of Action*, Cambridge: Cambridge University Press.

Bordieu, P. (1994) 'Structures, Habitus and Practices', in *Polity Reader in Social Theory*, Cambridge: Polity.

Boreham, P. (1980) 'The Dialectic of Theory and Control: Capitalist Crisis and the Organisation of Labour', in D. Dunkerley and G. Salaman (eds), *Control and Ideology in Organizations*, Milton Keynes: Open University Press.

Boreham, P. (1992) 'The Myth of Post-Fordist Management: Work Organisation and Employee Discretion in Seven Countries', *Employee Relations*, 14. 2: 13–24.

Boreham, P., Parker, R., Thompson, P. and Hall, R. (2008) *New Technology@Work*, London: Routledge.

Bouchikhi, H. and Kimberly, J.R. (2007) *The Soul of the Corporation, How to Manage the Identity of Your Company*, Wharton School Publishing.

Boulding, K. (1953) *The Organisational Revolution*, New York: Harper & Brothers.

Bowles, M. L. and Coates, G. (1993) 'Image and Substance: The Management of Performance as Rhetoric or Reality?', *Personnel Review*: 3–21.

Boxall, P. and Purcell, J. (2003) *Strategy and Human Resource Management*, Basingstoke: Palgrave Macmillan.

Boyer, R. and Drache, D. (eds) (1996) *States against Markets: The Limits to Globalisation*, London: Routledge.

Boyne, R. and Rattsani, A. (eds) (1990) *Postmodernism and Society*, London: Macmillan.

Bradley, H. (1986) 'Work, Home and the Restructuring of Jobs', in K. Purcell, S. Wood, A. Watson and S. Allen (eds), *The Changing Experience of Employment, Restructuring and Recession*, London: Macmillan.

Bradley, H. (1996) *Fractured Identities: Changing Patterns of Inequality*, Oxford: Polity.

Bradley H. (1997) 'Gender and Changes in Employment: Feminization and Its Effects', in R.K. Brown (ed.), *The Changing Shape of Work*, New York: St Martin's Press.

Bramble, T. (1988) 'The Flexibility Debate: Industrial Relations and the New Management Production Practices', *Labour and Industry*, 1. 2: 187–209.

Bramble, T., Parry, K. and O'Brien, E. (1996) 'Middle Management in an Era of Corporate Restructuring: A Case Study of Retailing', *Labour and Industry*, 7. 2: 79–102.

Brannan, M.J. (2005) 'Once More With Feeling: Ethnographic Reflections on the Medication of Tensions in a Small Team of Call Centre Workers', *Gender Work and Organization*, 12. 5: 420–39.

Brannen, P. (1983) *Authority and Participation in Industry*, London: Batsford.

Braverman, H. (1974) *Labor and Monopoly Capital: The Degradation of Work in the Twentieth Century*, New York: Monthly Review Press.

Brazier, M., Lovercy, J., Moran, M. and Potton, M. (1993) 'Falling From a Tightrope: Doctors and Lawyers between the Market and the State', *Political Studies*, 92: 197–213.

Breakwell, G. M. (1986) *Coping with Threatened Identities*, London: Methuen.

Breakwell, G. M. (1987) 'Identity', in H. Beloff and A. M. Colman (eds), *Psychology Survey 1987*, Leicester: British Psychological Society.

Brecher, J. (1978) 'Uncovering the Hidden History of the American Workplace', *Review of Radical Political Economics*, Winter, 10. 4: 1–23.

Brenner, O. C., Tomkiewicz, J. and Schien, V. E. (1989) 'The Relationship between Sex Role Stereotypes and Requisite Management Characteristics Revisited', *Academy of Management Journal*, 32. 3: 662–9.

Brewis, J. and Kerfoot, D. (1994) 'Selling Our "Selves"? Sexual Harassment and the Intimate Violations of the Workplace', paper presented to the BSA Conference Sexualities in their Social Context, University of Central Lancashire, March.

Briggs, P. (1987) 'The Japanese at Work: Illusions of the Ideal', paper presented to the Conference on Japanisation of British Industry, UMIST, also in *Industrial Relations Journal*, Spring 1988, 19. 1.

Briner, R. B. (1995) 'The experience and expression of emotion at work', *Proceedings of the British Psychological Society Occupational Psychology Conference*, 229–334.

Briner, R. B. and Reynolds, S. (1993) 'Bad Theory and Bad Practice In Occupational Stress', *Occupational Psychologist*, 19: 8–13.

Broad, G. (1987) 'Beyond Quality Circles: A Critical Review of Employee Participation in Japanese Industry', paper presented to the Conference on Japanisation of British Industry, UMIST.

Brooks, A. and Wee, L. (2008) 'Reflexivity and the Transformation of Gender Identity: Reviewing the Potential for Change in a Cosmopolitan City', *Sociology*, 42. 3: 503–21.

Brotherton, C. (1999) *Social Psychology and Management: Issues for a Changing Society*, Milton Keynes: Open University Press.

Brown, A. and Keep, E. (1999) *Review of Vocational Education and Training Research in the United Kingdom*, Warwick: SKOPE, University of Warwick.

Brown, G. (1977) *Sabotage*, Nottingham: Spokesman.

Brown, H. (1980) 'Work Groups', in G. Salaman and K. Thompson (eds), *Control and Ideology in Organizations*, Milton Keynes: Open University Press.

Brown, J. S. and Duguid, S. (1991) 'Organizational Learning and Communities of Practice: Towards a Unified View of Working, Learning and Innovation', *Organization Science*, 2. 1: 40–57.

Brown, P. and Hesketh, A. (2004) *The Mismanagement of Talent: Employability and Jobs in the Knowledge Economy*, Oxford: Oxford University Press.

Brown, R. (1965) *Social Psychology*, London: Collier-Macmillan.

Brown, R. (1992) *Understanding Organizations: Theoretical Perspectives in Industrial Sociology*, London: Routledge.

Browne, K. R. (1998) *Divided Labour: An Evolutionary View of Women at Work*, London: Weidenfeld & Nicolson.

Brubaker, R. (1984) *The Limits of Rationality: An Essay on the Social and Moral Thought of Max Weber*, London: Allen & Unwin.

Bruner, J. S. (1957) 'On Perceptual Readiness', *Psychological Review*, 64, 123–52.

Bruner, J. S. (1968) *Towards a Theory of Instruction*, New York: Norton.

Bryman, A. (1984) 'Organisation Studies and the Concept of Rationality', *Journal of Management Studies*, 21: 394–404.

Bryman, A. (1993) 'The Nature of Organisation Structure: Constraint and Choice', in D. Morgan and L. Stanley (eds), *Debates in Sociology*, Manchester: Manchester University Press.

Buchanan, D. (1986) 'Management Objectives in Technical Change', in D. Knights and H. Willmott (eds), *Managing the Labour Process*, Aldershot: Gower.

Buchanan, D. (2000) 'An Eager and Enduring Embrace: The Ongoing Rediscovery of Teamworking as a Management Idea', in S. Proctor and F. Mueller (eds), *Teamworking*, London: Macmillan.

Buchanan, D. and Badham, R. (1999) *Power, Politics and Organisational Change: Winning the Turf Game*, London: Sage.

Buchanan, D. and Badham, R. (2008) *Power, Politics and Organizational Change: Winning the Turf Game* (2nd edn), London: Sage.

Buchanan, D. and Huczynski, A. (1985) *Organisational Behaviour: An Introductory Text*, London: Prentice Hall International.

Buford, B. (1991) *Among the Thugs*, London: Secker.

Burawoy, M. (1979) *Manufacturing Consent: Changes in the Labour Process Under Monopoly Capitalism*, Chicago: University of Chicago Press.

Burawoy, M. (1985) *The Politics of Production*, London: Verso.

Burchell, B. (2002) 'The Prevalence and Redistribution of Job Insecurity and Work Intensification', in B. Burchell, D. Ladipo, and F. Wilkinson, (eds), *Job Insecurity and Work Intensification*, London: Routledge.

Burchell, B. J., Day, D., Hudson, M., Ladipo, D., Mankelow, R., Nolan, J. P., Reed, H., Wichert, I. C. and Wilkinson, F. (1999) *Job Insecurity and Work Intensification*, London: Joseph Rowntree Foundation.

Burchell, S., Clubb, C. and Hopwood, A. (1985) 'Accounting in its Social Context: Towards a History of Value-Added in the United Kingdom', *Accounting, Organizations and Society*, 10. 4: 381–413.

Burgess, J. and Strachan, G. (1999) 'The Expansion in Non-Standard Employment in Australia and the Extension of Employers' Control', in A. Felstead and N. Jewson (eds), *Global Trends in Flexible Labour*, London: Macmillan.

Burgess, S. and Rees, H. (1996) 'Job Tenure in Britain 1975–92', *Economic Journal*, 106. 435: 334–44.

Burgoyne, J. G. (1993) 'The Competence Movement: Issues, Stakeholders and Prospects', *Personnel Review*, 22. 6: 6–13.

Burke, R. J. (1997) 'Are Families Damaging to Careers?' *Women in Management Review*, 12. 8: 320–4.

Burnham, J. (1945) *The Managerial Revolution*, Harmondsworth: Penguin.

Burns, J. M. (1978) *Leadership*, New York: Harper & Row.

Burns, T. (1982) *A Comparative Study of Administrative Structure and Organisational Processes in Selected Areas of the National Health Service* (SSRC Report, HRP 6725), London: Social Science Research Council.

Burns, T. and Stalker, G. M. (1961) *The Management of Innovation*, London: Tavistock.

Burrell, G. (1980) 'Radical Organisation Theory', in D. Dunkerley and G. Salaman (eds), *The International Yearbook of Organisation Studies 1979*, London: Routledge & Kegan Paul.

Burrell, G. (1988) 'Modernism, Post Modernism and Organisational Analysis: The Contribution of Michel Foucault', *Organisation Studies*, 9. 2: 221–35.

Burrell, G. (1992) 'Sex and Organizations', in A. J. Mills and P. Tancred (eds), *Gendering Organisational Analysis*, London: Sage.

Burrell, G. (1994) 'Foreword' to H. Tsoukas (ed.), *New Thinking in Organisational Behaviour*, London: Butterworth and Heinemann.

Burrell, G. (1996) 'Normal Science, Paradigms, Metaphors, Discourses and Genealogies of Analysis', in S. Clegg, C. Hardy and W. Nord (eds), *Handbook of Organisation Studies*, London: Sage.

Burrell, G. and Morgan, G. (1979) *Sociological Paradigms and Organisational Analysis*, London: Heinemann.

CAITS (1986) *Flexibility, Who Needs It?*, London: CAITS.

Calás, M. and Smircich, L. (1992) 'Rewriting Gender into Organisation Theorising: Directions from Feminist Perspectives', in M. Reed and M. Hughes (eds), *Rethinking Organisation: New Directions in Organisation and Analysis*, London: Sage.

Calás, M. B. and Smircich, L. (1996) 'From the "Woman's" Point of View: Feminist Approaches to Organisation Studies', in S. Clegg and C. Hardy (eds), *Handbook on Organisations*, London: Sage.

Calder, B. J. (1977) 'An Attribution Theory of Leadership', in B. M. Staw and G. R. Salancik (eds), *New Directions in Organisational Behaviour*, Chicago: St Clair.

Callaghan, G. and Thompson, P. (2001) 'Edwards Revisited: Technical Control and Worker Agency in Call Centres', *Economic and Industrial Democracy*, 22: 13–37.

Callaghan, G. and Thompson, P. (2002) 'We Recruit Attitude: The Selection and Shaping of Call Centre Labour', *Journal of Management Studies*, 39. 2: 233–254.

Callan Hunt, G. (1992) 'Men and Women in Nontraditional Jobs: An Exploratory Study of Men in the Pink Ghetto', *Association of Management*, August.

Callinicos, A. (1989) *Against Postmodernism: A Marxist Critique*, Cambridge: Polity.

Campbell, A. and Currie, B. (1987) 'Skills and Strategies in Design Engineering', paper presented to the Conference on the Labour Process, Aston-UMIST.

Campbell, G. (1994) 'The Languages of Workplace Reform', paper presented to the 12th International Labour Process Conference, Aston.

Campbell, J. P. and Dunnette, M. D. (1968) 'Effectiveness of T-Group Experiences in Managerial Training and Development', *Psychological Bulletin*, 70: 73–104.

Cappelli, P. (1995) 'Rethinking Employment', *British Journal of Industrial Relations*, 33. 4: 563–602.

Cappelli, P. (2001) 'Assessing the Decline of Internal Labor Markets', in I. Berg, and A/ Kalleberg (eds), *Sourcebook of Labor Markets: Evolving Structures and Processes*, New York: Plenum.

Carchedi, G. (1977) *On the Economic Identification of the Middle Classes*, London: Routledge & Kegan Paul.

Carey, A. (1967) 'The Hawthorne Studies: A Radical Criticism', *American Sociological Review*, 32: 403–16.

Carroll, G.R. and Hannan, M. T. (2000) *The Demography of Corporations and Industries*, Princeton, NJ: Princeton University Press.

Carter, P. and Jeffs, P. (1992) 'The Hidden Curriculum: Sexuality in Professional Education', in P. Carter, T. Jeffs and M. Smith (eds), *Changing Social Work and Welfare*, Milton Keynes: Open University Press.

Carter, R. (1985) *Capitalism, Class Conflict and the New Middle Class*, London: Routledge & Kegan Paul.

Casey, B. (1991) 'Survey Evidence on Trends in "Non-Standard" Employment', in A. Pollert (ed.), *Farewell to Flexibility?*, Oxford: Blackwell.

Casey, C. (1995) *Work, Self and Society*, London: Routledge.

Casey, C. (1996) 'Corporate Transformations: Designer Culture, Designer Employees and "Post-Occupational" Solidarity', *Organization*, 3. 3: 317–39.

Castells, M. (1996) *The Rise of the Network Society: The Information Age – Economy*, Oxford: Blackwell.

Castells, M. (2000) *The Rise of the Network Society: The Information Age: Economy, Society and Culture Vol. I* (2nd edn), Oxford, UK: Blackwell.

Castells, M. (2001) *The Internet Galaxy: Reflections on the Internet, Business and Society*, Oxford: Oxford University Press.

Cattell, J. M., Eber, H. W. and Tatsuoka, M. M. (1970) *Handbook for the 16PF*, Colombia: IPAT.

Caulkin, C. (1999) 'No Room at the Top for Women', *The Observer*, 12 December.

Caulkin, S. (2003) 'The Boss We Love to Hate', *The Observer*, 6 July.

Cave, K. (1997) 'Close to the Core: Zero-Hours Working Surveyed', *Flexible Employment*, 2. 3: 21–3.

Cavendish, R. (1982) *Women on the Line*, London: Routledge & Kegan Paul.

Chandler, A. (1962) *Strategy and Structure: Chapters in the History of the Industrial Enterprise'* Cambridge, MA: MIT Press.

Chandler, A. (1977) *The Visible Hand*, Cambridge, MA: Harvard University Press.

Chandler, A. D. (1990) *Scale and Scope: the Dynamics of Industrial Capitalism*, Cambridge, MA: Harvard University Press.

Chandola, T., Britton, A., Brunner, E., Hemingway, H., Malik, M., Kumari, M., Badrick, E., Kivimaki, M. and Marmot, M. (2008) 'Work Stress and Coronary Heart Disease: What Are the Mechanisms?', *European Heart Journal*, March; 29: 640–8.

Change Partnership (1999) *The Changing Culture of Leadership: Women Leaders' Voices*, London: Tavistock Institute.

Chanlat, J.-F. (1994) 'Francophone Organisational Analysis (1950–1990): An Overview', *Organisation Studies*, 15. 1: 47–80.

Chartered Institute of Personnel and Development (2004) *Flexible Working and Paternity Leave*. Survey report. London: CIPD: available at: http://www.cipd.co.uk/subjects/wrkgtime/flexwking/paternityflexwork.htm

Chartered Institute of Personnel and Development (2005) *Managing Change: the Role of the Psychological Contract*, Change Agenda. London: CIPD.

Chartered Institute of Personnel and Development (2007) *Employee Engagement Survey 2006*, London: CIPD.

Chell, E. (1993) *The Psychology of Behaviour in Organisations* (2nd edn), Basingstoke: Macmillan.

Cheng, C. (ed.) (1996) *Masculinities in Organizations*, London: Sage.

Cherrington, D. J. (1989) *Organizational Behaviour: The Management of Individual and Organisational Performance*, Boston, MA: Allyn & Bacon.

Cherry, E. C. (1953) 'Some Experiments on the Recognition of Speech, with One and with Two Ears', *Journal of Acoustic Society of America*, 25, 975–9.

Cherry, L. (1978) 'On the Real Benefits of Eustress', *Psychology Today*, March: 60–70.

Child, J. (1969) *British Management Thought*, London: Allen & Unwin.

Child, J. (1972) 'Organisation Structure, Environment and Performance: The Role of Strategic Choice', *Sociology*, 6. 1: 1–22.

Child, J. (1984) *Organisation: A Guide to Problems and Practice* (2nd edn), London: Harper & Row.

Child, J. (1985) 'Managerial Strategies, New Technology and the Labour Process', in D. Knights, H. Wilmott and D. Collinson (eds), *Job Redesign: Critical Perspectives on the Labour Process*, London: Gower.

Child, J. (1987) 'Organisational Design for Advanced Manufacturing Technology', in T. D. Wall, C. W. Clegg and N. J. Kemp (eds), *The Human Side of Advanced Manufacturing Technology*, Chichester: Wiley.

Child, J. (1997) 'Strategic Choice in the Analysis of Action, Structure, Organizations and Environment: Retrospect and Prospect', *Organization Studies*, 18. 1: 43–76.

Child, J., Fores, M., Glover, I. and Lawrence, P. (1983) 'Professionalism and Work Organisation: A Reply to Kevin McCormack', *Sociology*, 20. 4: 607–14.

Child, J. and Rodrigues, S. (1993) 'The Role of Social Identity in the International Transfer of Knowledge through Business Ventures', paper presented to the 11th EGOS Colloquium, Paris, July.

Child, J. and Smith, C. (1987) 'The Context and Process of Organisational Transformations – Cadbury Limited in its Sector', *Journal of Management Studies*, 24. 6: 565–93.

Chorover, S. L. (1979) *From Genesis to Genocide: Meaning of Human Nature and the Power of Behaviour Control*, Cambridge, MA: MIT Press.

Christopherson, C. (2004) 'The Divergent Worlds of New Media: How Policy Shapes Work in the Creative Economy', *Review of Policy Research*, 21. 4: 543–58.

Cialdini, R. B. (1988) *Influence: Science and Practice* (2nd edn), London: Harper Collins.

Cialdini, R. (2001) *Influence: Science and Practice* (4th edn), New York: Allyn & Bacon.

Cicourel, A. V. (1968) *The Social Organisation of Social Justice*, New York: Free Press.

Clairmonte, F. and Cavanagh, J. (1981) *The World in their Web: The Dynamics of Textile Multinationals*, London: Zed.

Clark, D. D. and Hoyle, R. (1988) 'A Theoretical Solution to the Problem of Personality–Situational Interaction', *Personality and Individual Differences*, 9: 133–8.

Clark, H., Chandler, J. and Barry, J. (1994) *Organisations and Identities*, London: Chapman & Hall.

Clark, T. (2004) 'The Fashion of Management Fashion: A Surge Too Far?' *Organization*, 11.2: 297–306.

Clarke, S. (1990) 'The Crisis of Fordism or the Crisis of Social Democracy?', *Telos*, 83: 71–98.

Clarke, T. and Clegg, S. (1998) *Changing Paradigms: The Transformation of Management Knowledge for the 21st Century*, London: Harper Collins Business.

Clarke, J. and Newman, J. (1997) *The Managerial State; Power, Politics and Ideology in the Remaking of Social Welfare*, London: Sage.

Clawson, D. (1980) *Bureaucracy and the Labour Process: The Transformation of US Industry, 1860–1920*, New York: Monthly Review Press.

Clegg, S. (1977) 'Power, Organisation Theory, Marx and Critique', in S. Clegg and D. Dunkerley (eds), *Critical Issues in Organizations*, London: Routledge & Kegan Paul.

Clegg, S. (1988) 'The Good, the Bad and the Ugly', *Organisation Studies*, 9. 1: 7–13.

Clegg, S. (1989) *Frameworks of Power*, London: Sage.

Clegg, S. (1990) *Modern Organizations: Organisation Studies in the Postmodern World*, London: Sage.

Clegg, S., Boreham, P. and Dow, G. (1987) *Class, Politics and the Economy*, London: Routledge & Kegan Paul.

Clegg, S. and Dunkerley, D. (eds) (1977) *Critical Issues in Organizations*, London: Routledge & Kegan Paul.

Clegg, S. and Dunkerley, D. (1980) *Organisation, Class and Control*, London: Routledge & Kegan Paul.

Clegg, S. R. and Hardy, C. (1996) 'Introduction: Organisations, Organisation, Organising', in *Handbook on Organisations*, London: Sage.

Clegg, S. and Higgins, G. (1987) 'Against the Current: Organisational Sociology and Socialism', *Organisation Studies*, 8. 3: 201–21.

Clegg, S., Rhodes, C. and Kornberger, M. (2007) 'Desperately Seeking Legitimacy: Organizational Identity and Emerging Industries', *Organization Studies*, 28, 4: 495–513.

Clutterbuck, D. (ed.) (1985) *New Patterns of Work*, Aldershot: Gower.

Clutterbuck, D. (2003) *Managing Work-Life Balance. A Guide for HR in Achieving Organisational and Individual Change*, CIPD, London.

Coates, D. (2000) *Models of Capitalism*, Cambridge: Polity Press.

Coats, D. (2009) 'The Sunlit Uplands or Bleak House? Just How Good are Today's Workplaces?', in Bolton, S. and Houlihan, M. (eds), (2009) *Work Matters: Critical Reflections on Contemporary Work*, Basingstoke: Palgrave Macmillan.

Cochrane, A. and Dicker, R. (1979) 'The Regeneration of British Industry: Jobs and the Inner City', in Community Development Project, *The State and the Local Economy*, Newcastle.

Cockburn, C. (1983) *Brothers: Male Dominance and Technological Change*, London: Pluto.

Cockburn, C. (1985) *Machineries of Dominance: Men, Women and Technical Know-How*, London: Pluto.

Cockburn, C. (1990) 'Men's Power in Organizations: "Equal Opportunities" Intervenes', in D. Morgan (ed.), *Man, Masculinities and Social Theory*, London: Unwin Hyman.

Cockburn, C. (1991) *In the Way of Women: Men's Resistance to Sex Equality in Organizations*, London: Macmillan.

Cohen, S. (1973) *Folk Devils and Moral Panics*, London: Paladin.

Cohen, S. (1987) 'A Labour Process to Nowhere?', *New Left Review*, 107: 34–50.

Cohen, S. and Taylor, L. (1978) *Escape Attempts: The Theory and Practice of Resistance to Everyday Life*, Harmondsworth: Pelican.

Cohen, S. and Taylor, L. (1992) *Escape Attempts: The Theory and Practice of Resistance to Everyday Life* (2nd edn), London and New York: Routledge.

Coleman, G. (1991) *Investigating Organisations: A Feminist Approach*, Bristol: SAUS.

Colgan, F. and Ledwith, S. (1996) 'Women as Change Agents', in S. Ledwith and F. Colgan (eds), *Women in Organisations: Challenging Gender Politics*, London: Macmillan.

Collier, A. (1994) *Critical Realism*, London: Verso.

Collins, D. (1998) *Organisational Change: Sociological Perspectives*, London: Routledge.

Collins, R. (1986) *Weberian Sociological Theory*, Cambridge: Cambridge University Press.

Collinson, D. (1992) *Managing the Shopfloor: Subjectivity, Masculinity and Workplace Culture*, Berlin: De Gruyter.

Collinson, D. (1994) 'Strategies of Resistance: Power, Knowledge and Subjectivity in the Workplace', in J. Jermier, W. Nord and D. Knights (eds), *Resistance and Power in the Workplace*, London: Routledge.

Collinson, D. (2003) 'Identities and Insecurities: Selves at Work', *Organization*, 10. 3: 385–409.

Collinson, D. and Ackroyd, P. (2005) 'Resistance, Misbehaviour, Dissent', in S. Ackroyd, S., R. Batt, R., P. Thompson, and P. Tolbert, P. (eds), *A Handbook of Work and Organization*, Oxford: Oxford University Press.

Collinson, D. and Collinson, M. (1989) 'Sexuality in the Workplace: The Domination of Men's Sexuality', in J. Hearn, D. L. Sheppard, P. Tancred-Sheriff and G. Burrell (eds), *The Sexuality of Organisation*, London: Sage.

Collinson, D. and Collinson, M. (1994) ' "It's Only Dick": The Sexual Harassment of Women Managers in Insurance Sales', *Work, Employment and Society*, 10. 1: 29–56.

Collinson, D. and Collinson, M. (1997) ' "Delayering Managers": Time–Space Surveillance and its Gendered Effects', *Organization*, 4, 3: 375–411.

Collinson, D. and Hearn, J. (1994) 'Naming Men as Men: Implications for Work, Organisation and Management', *Gender, Work and Organizations*, 1. 1: 2–22.

Collinson, D., Knights, D. and Collinson, M. (1990) *Managing to Discriminate*, London: Routledge.

Competition Commission (2000) *Supermarkets: A Report on the Supply of Groceries from Multiple Stores in the UK*, London: Competition Commission.

Competition Commission (2008) *The Supply of Groceries in the UK: Market Investigation*, London: Competition Commission.

Conley, H. (2008) 'The Nightmare of Temporary Work: A Comment on Fevre', *Work, Employment and Society*, 22. 4: pp. 731–36.

Content and Inspirational Leadership Tool, (2005) © DTI and Caret 2005. Software © PSL 2005, available at: http://www.berr.gov.uk/files/file33117.pdf – december – accessed 21-08-07.

Considine, M. (1996) 'Market Bureaucracy? Exploring the Contending Rationalities of Contemporary Administrative Regimes', *Labour and Industry*, 7. 1: 1–28.

Control Data Corporation (1985) 'Telecommuting', in D. Clutterbuck (ed.), *New Patterns of Work*, Aldershot: Gower.

Contu, A and Willmott, H. (2005) 'You Spin Me Round: The Critical Realist Turn in Management and Organization Studies', *Journal of Management Studies*, 42. 1: 622–45.

Cooper, C. L. (1994) 'The Costs of Healthy Work Organizations', in C.L. Cooper and S. Williams (eds), *Creating Healthy Work Organizations*, Wiley, Chichester.

Cooper, C. L. (1984) 'What's New in . . . Stress', *Personnel Management*, June: 40–4.

Cooper, C. and Dewe, P. (2004) *Stress: A Brief History*, Oxford: Blackwell.

Cooper, C. L. and Smith, M. J. (1985) *Job Stress and Blue Collar Work*, Chichester: Wiley.

Cooper, D. (1994) 'Productive, Relational and Everywhere? Conceptualising Power and Resistance within Foucauldian Feminism', *Sociology*, 28. 2: 435–54.

Cooper, R. and Burrell, G. (1988) 'Modernism, Postmodernism and Organisational Analysis: An Introduction', *Organisation Studies*, 9. 2: 91–112.

Coopey, J. and Hartley, J. (1991) 'Reconsidering the Case for Organisational Commitment', *Human Resource Management Journal*, 1. 3: 18–32.

Corbett, J. M. (1985a) 'The Design of Machine-Tool Technology and Work: Technical Science and Technical Choice', unpublished draft, Sheffield: MRC/ESRC Social and Applied Psychology Unit.

Corbett, J. M. (1985b) 'Prospective Work Design of a Human-Centred CNC Lathe', *Behaviour and Information Technology*, 14. 1: 201–14.

Corbett, J. M. (1994) *Critical Cases in Organisational Behaviour*, London: Macmillan.

Coriat, B. (1980) 'The Restructuring of the Assembly Line: A New Economy of Time and Control', *Capital and Class*, 11: 34–43.

Cornforth, C. (1988) 'Patterns of Cooperative Management: Revising the Degeneration Thesis', paper presented to a Conference on New Forms of Ownership and Management, Cardiff Business School.

Courpasson, D. (2000) 'Managerial Strategies of Domination: Power in Soft Bureaucracies', *Organization Studies*, 21. 1: 141–61

Cousins, C. (1987) *Controlling Social Welfare: A Sociology of State Welfare Work and Organisation*, Brighton: Wheatsheaf.

Cousins, C. (1999) 'Changing Regulatory Frameworks and Non-Standard Employment: A Comparison of Germany, Spain, Sweden and the UK', in A. Felstead and N. Jewson (eds), *Global Trends in Flexible Labour*, London: Macmillan.

Coventry, Liverpool, Newcastle and N. Tyneside Trades Councils (1981) *State Intervention in Industry: A Workers' Inquiry*, Newcastle: Spokeman.

Coyle, D. (1997) *The Weightless World*, Oxford: Capstone Publishing.

Cressey, P. and Cousins, C. (1986) 'The Labour Process in the State Welfare Sector', in D. Knights and H. Willmott (eds), *Managing the Labour Process*, Aldershot: Gower.

Cressey, P. and Jones, B. (1991) 'A New Convergence?', *Work, Employment and Society*, 5. 1: 493–5.

Cressey, P. and MacInnes, J. (1980) 'Voting for Ford: Industrial Democracy and the Control of Labour', *Capital and Class*, 11: 5–37.

Crompton, R. (1997) *Women and Work in Modern Britain*, Oxford: Oxford University Press.

Crompton, R. (with N. Feuvre) (1996) 'Paid Employment and the System of Gender Relations', *Sociology*, 30. 3: 427–46.

Crompton, R. and Jones, G. (1984) *White Collar Proletariat*, London: Macmillan.

Crook, S., Paluski, J. and Waters, M. (1992) *Postmodernization*, London: Sage.

Cross, M. (1985) 'Flexible Manning', in D. Clutterbuck (ed.), *New Patterns of Work*, Aldershot: Gower.

Crouch, C. (1999) 'The Skills Creation Triangle out of Balance', *Renewal*, 7. 4: 60–71.

Crouch, C., Finegold, D. and Sako, M. (1999) *Are Skills the Answer? The Political Economy of Skill Creation in Advanced Industrial Countries*, Oxford: Oxford University Press.

Crowther, S. and Garrahan, P. (1987) 'Invitation to Sunderland: Corporate Power and the Local Economy', paper presented to the Conference on Japanisation of British Industry, UMIST.

Cully, M., O'Reilly, A., Millward, D., Forth, N., Woodland, S., Dix, G. and Bryson, A. (1998) *The 1998 Workplace Employee Relations Survey: First Findings*, Department of Trade and Industry, London: HMSO.

Cummings, T. and Blumberg, M. (1987) 'Advanced Manufacturing Technology and Work Design', in T. D. Wall, C. W. Clegg and N. J. Kemp (eds), *The Human Side of Advanced Manufacturing Technology*, Chichester: Wiley.

Cummings, T. and Cooper, C. L. (1979) 'A Cybernetic Framework for the Study of Occupational Stress', *Human Relations*, 32: 395–419.

Cutcher-Gershenfeld, J., Nitta, M., Barrett, B., Belhedi, M., Bullard, J., Coutchie, C., Inaba, T., Ishino, I., Lee, S., Lin, W.-J., Mothersell, W. and Rabine, S. (1994) 'Japanese Team-Based Work Systems in North America: Explaining the Diversity', *California Management Review*, 37. 1: 42–63.

Cutler, T. (1992) 'Numbers in a Time of Dearth: The Use of Performance Indicators to "Manage" Higher Education', paper presented to the 10th International Labour Process Conference, Aston.

Cyert, R.M. and March, J.G. (1963) *A Behavioural Theory of the Firm*, Englewood Cliffs, NJ: Prentice Hall.

Czarniawska, B. (1999) *Writing Management: Organisation Theory as a Literary Genre*, Oxford: Oxford University Press.

Dahl, R. (1957) 'The Concept of Power', *Behavioural Science*, 2: 201–15.

Dahl, R. (1958) 'A Critique of the Ruling Elite Model', *American Political Science Review*, 52.

Dahler-Larsen, P. (1994) 'Corporate Culture and Morality: Durkheim-Inspired Reflections on the Limits of Corporate Culture', *Journal of Management Studies*, 31. 1: 1–18.

Dahrendorf, R. (1959) *Class and Class Conflict in Industrial Society*, London: Routledge & Kegan Paul.

Dale, K. and Burrell, G. (2000) 'What Shape Are We in? Organisation Theory and the Organized Body', in J. Hassard, R. Holliday and H. Willmott (eds), *Body and Organisation*, London: Sage.

Dandeker, C. (1990) *Surveillance, Power and Modernity: Bureaucracy and Discipline from 1700 to the Present Day*, Cambridge: Polity.

Danermark, B., Ekstrom, M., Jakobsen, L. and Karlsson, J. (2002). *Explaining Society: Critical Realism in the Social Sciences*, London: Routledge.

Danford, A. (1997) 'Teamworking and Labour Regulation: A Case Study of Shop-Floor Disempowerment', paper presented to the 15th International Labour Process Conference, March, Edinburgh.

Danford, A. (1998) *Japanese Management Techniques and British Workers*, London: Mansell.

Danford, A. (2003) 'Workers, Unions and the High Performance Workplace', *Work, Employment and Society*, 17. 3: 569–73.

Daniel, W. W. and McIntosh, N. (1972) *The Right to Manage?*, London: MacDonald.

Daniel, W. W. and Millward, N. (1983) *Workplace Industrial Relations in Britain*, London: Heinemann.

Dankbaar, B. (1988) 'New Production Concepts, Management Strategies and the Quality of Work', *Work, Employment and Society*, 2. 1: 25–50.

Darwin, C. R. (1872) *The Expression of the Emotions in Man and Animals*, London: John Murray.

Davidson, M. and Cooper, C. (1992) *Shattering the Glass Ceiling*, London: Paul Chapman.

Davis, K. (1991) 'Critical Sociology and Gender Relations', in K. Davis, M. Leijenaar and J. Oldersma (eds), *The Gender of Power*, London: Sage.

Davis, K., Leijenaar, M. and Oldersma, J. (eds) (1991) *The Gender of Power*, London: Sage.

Dawson, P. and Webb, J. (1989) 'New Production Arrangements: The Totally Flexible Cage?', *Work, Employment and Society*, 3. 2: 221–38.

Dawson, S. (1986) *Analysing Organizations* (2nd edn, 1992), London: Macmillan.

Day, R. A. and Day, J. V. (1977) 'A Review of the Current State of Negotiated Order Theory: An Appreciation and a Critique', *Sociological Quarterly*, 18, Winter: 126–42.

De Cindio, F., De Michaelis, G. and Simone, C. (1988) 'Computer-Based Tools in the Language/Action Perspective', in R. Speth (ed.), *Research into Networks and Distributed Applications*, Amsterdam: North Holland.

de los Reyes, P. (2000) 'Diversity at Work: Paradoxes, Possibilities and Problems in the Swedish Discourse on Diversity', *Economic and Industrial Democracy*, 21: 253–66.

De Vroey, M. (1975) 'The Separation of Ownership and Control in Large Corporations', *Review of Radical Political Economics*, 7. 2: 1–10.

Deal, T. and Kennedy, A. (1988) *Corporate Cultures: The Rites and Rituals of Corporate Life*, Harmondsworth: Penguin.

Deal, T. and Kennedy, A. (1999) *The New Corporate Cultures: Revitalizing the Workplace after Downsizing, Mergers and Reengineering*, New York: Texere.

Deaux, K. (1993) 'Reconstructing Social Identity', *Personality and Social Psychology Bulletin*, 19. 4. 4–12

Deaux, K. and Emswiller, T. (1974) 'Explanations of Successful Performance on Sex-Linked Tasks: What is Skill for the Male is Luck for the Female', *Journal of Personality and Social Psychology*, 24: 30–85.

Deaux, K. and Martin, D. (2003) 'Interpersonal Networks and Social Categories: Specifying Levels of Context in Identity Processes', *Social Psychology Quarterly*, 66. 2: 101–117.

Deery, S. and Kinnie, N. (2002) 'Call Centres and Beyond: A Thematic Evaluation', *Human Resource Management Journal*, 12: 3–13.

Deery, S., Iverson, R. and Walsh, J. (2000) 'Work Relationships in Telephone Call Centres: Understanding Emotional Exhaustion and Employee Withdrawal', paper to International Industrial Relations Association Conference, Tokyo, May–June.

Deetz, S. (1992) 'Disciplinary Power in the Modern Corporation', in M. Alvesson and H. Willmott (eds), *Critical Management Studies*, London: Sage.

Dejoy, D. M. (1994) 'Managing Safety in the Workplace: An Attribution Theory Analysis Model', *Journal of Safety Research*, 25. 1: 3–17.

Delamarter, R. T. (1988) *Big Blue: IBM's Use and Abuse of Power*, London: Pan.

Delbridge, R. (1998) *Life on the Line in Contemporary Manufacturing*, Oxford: Oxford University Press.

Delbridge, R., Lowe, J. and Oliver, N. (2000) 'Worker Autonomy in Lean Teams: Evidence from the World Automotive Components Industry', in S. Proctor and F. Mueller (eds), *Teamworking*, London: Macmillan.

Delbridge, R., Turnbull, P. and Wilkinson, B. (1992) 'Pushing Back the Frontiers: Management Control and Work Intensification under JIT/TQM Regimes', *New Technology, Work and Employment*, 7: 97–106.

Deleuze, G. and Guattari, F. (1977) *Anti-Oedipus: Capitalism and Schizophrenia*, New York: Viking.

Dent, M. (1993) 'Professionalism, Educated Labour and the State: Hospital Medicine and the New Managerialism', *Sociological Review*, 41. 2: 244–73.

Despres, C. and Hiltrop, J-M. (1995) 'Human Resource Management in the Knowledge Age: Current Practice and Perspectives in the Future', *Employee Relations*, 17. 1: 9–23.

Deutsch, M. and Gerard, H. B. (1955) 'A Study of Normative and Informational Social Influences upon Individual Judgement', *Journal of Abnormal and Social Psychology*, 51: 629–36.

Devanna, M. A., Fornbrun, C. J. and Tichy, N. M. (1984) 'A Framework for Strategic Human Resource Management', in C. J. Fornbrun, N. M. Tichy and M. A. Devanna (eds), *Strategic Human Resource Management*, New York: Wiley.

Dews, P. (1987) *Logics of Disintegration*, London: Verso.

Dex, S. (1985) *The Sexual Division of Work*, Brighton: Wheatsheaf.

Di Maggio, P. and Powell, W. (1983) 'The Iron Cage Revisited: Institutional Isomorphism and Collective Rationality in Organizations', *American Sociological Review*, 48: 147–60.

Di Tomaso, N. (1989) 'Sexuality in the Workplace: Discrimination and Harassment', in J. Hearn, D. L. Sheppard, P. Tancred-Sheriff and G. Burrell (eds), *The Sexuality of Organisation*, London: Sage.

Dicken, P. (1992) *Global Shift*, London: Paul Chapman.

Dicken, P. (2007) *Global Shift: Mapping the Changing Contours of the World Economy* (5th edn), London : Sage Publications; New York : Guilford Press.

Dickens, P. and Savage, M. (1988) 'The Japanisation of British Industry? Instances from a High Growth Area', *Industrial Relations Journal*, Spring, 19. 1.

Dickson, T. *et al.* (1988) 'Big Blue and the Unions: IBM, Individualism and Trade Union Strategy', *Work, Employment and Society*, 2. 4: 506–20.

Dill, W. R. (1962) 'The Impact of Environment on Organisation Development', in S. Mailick and E. H. Van Ness (eds), *Concepts and Issues in Administrative Behaviour*, Englewood Cliffs, NJ: Prentice Hall.

Ditton, J. (1974) 'The Fiddling Salesman: Connivance at Corruption', *New Society*, 28 Nov.

Domhoff, G. (1967) *Who Rules America?*, Englewood Cliffs, NJ: Prentice Hall.

Donaldson, L. (1985) *In Defence of Organisation Theory: A Reply to the Critics*, Cambridge: Cambridge University Press.

Donaldson, L. (1989) 'Reflections in Organisational Analysis', *Australian Journal of Management*, 14. 2: 243–54.

Donaldson, L. (1996) 'The Normal Science of Contingency Theory', in S. Clegg, C. Hardy and W. Nord (eds), *Handbook of Organisation Studies*, London: Sage.

Donaldson, L. (1998) 'The Myth of Paradigm Incommensurability in Management Studies: Comments by an Integrationist', *Organisation*, 5. 2: 267–72.

Donaldson, L. (2001) *The Contingency Theory of Organizations*, Thousand Oaks, CA: Sage.

Donaldson, L. (2003) 'Organizational Theory as a Positive Science', in H. Tsoukas and C. Knudsen (eds), *The Oxford Handbook of Organization Theory: Meta-theoretical Perspectives*, Oxford: Oxford University Press.

Donaldson, L. (2005) 'Following the Scientific Method: How I Became a Committed Functionalist and Positivist', Vita Contemplativa, *Organization Studies*, 26. 7: 1071–88.

Donaldson, L. (2007) 'Statistico-organizational Theory', contribution to G. M. Schwarz, S. Clegg, T. G. Cummings, L. Donaldson and J. B. Miner, "We See Dead People? The State of Organization Science", *Journal of Management Inquiry*, 16. 4: 300–17.

Donovan, Lord (Chairman) (1968) *Report on the Royal Commission on Trade Unions and Employers' Associations*, London: HMSO.

Doogan, K. (2001) 'Insecurity and Long-Term Employment', *Work, Employment, and Society*, 15. 3: 419–41.

Doogan, K. (2005) 'Long-Term Employment and the Restructuring of the Labour Market in Europe', *Time and Society*, 14. 1: 65–87.

Doogan, K. (2008) 'Dematerialisation and the Transformation of Work, Paper to International Labour Process Conference, March, Dublin.

Doray, B. (1988) *A Rational Madness: From Taylorism to Fordism*, London: Free Association.

Drago, R. and McDonough, T. (1984) 'Capitalist Shopfloor Initiatives, Restructuring and Organising in the '80s', *Review of Radical Political Economics*, 716. 4: 52–77.

Drake, R. I. and Smith, P. J. (1973) *Behavioural Science in Industry*, London: McGraw-Hill.

Drucker, P. (1955) *The Practice of Management*, New York: Harper & Row.

Drucker, P. (1959) *Landmarks of Tomorrow*, New York: Harper & Row.

Drucker, P. (1968) *The Age of Discontinuity*, New York: Harper & Row.

Drucker, P. (1977) *People and Performance*, London: Heinemann.

Drucker, P. (1979) *Management*, London: Pan.

Drucker, P. (1981) *Managing in Turbulent Times*, London: Pan.

Drucker, P. (1992) 'The New Society of Organizations, *Harvard Business Review*, Sept.–Oct.: 95–104.

Drummond, H. (1996) *Power: Creating It, Using It*, London: Kogan Page.

Due Billing, Y. (1994) 'Gender and Bureaucracies: A Critique of Ferguson's "The Feminist Case against Bureaucracy"', *Gender Work and Organization*, 1. 4: 173–93.

du Gay, P. (1991a) 'The Cult[ure] of the Customer', *Journal of Management Studies*, 29. 5: 615–33.

du Gay, P. (1991b) 'Enterprise Culture and the Ideology of Excellence', *New Formations*, 13: 45–61.

du Gay, P. (1992) 'Numbers and Souls: Retailing and the De-Differentiation of Economy and Culture', paper presented to the Employment Research Unit Annual Conference, Cardiff Business School, September.

du Gay, P. (1996) *Consumption and Identity at Work*, London: Sage.

du Gay, P. (2000) *In Praise of Bureaucracy*, London: Sage.

Duenas, G. (1993) 'The Importance of Intercultural Learning in the International Transfer of Managerial and Organisational Knowledge', paper presented to the 11th EGOS Colloquium, Paris, July.

Dumaine, B. (1990) 'Who Needs a Boss?' *Fortune*, 7 May: 40–7.

Dunford, R. and McGraw, P. (1987) 'Quality Circles or Quality Circus? Labour Process Theory and the Operation of Quality Circle Programmes', paper presented at the Conference on the Labour Process, Aston–UMIST.

Dunkerley, D. and Salaman, G. (eds) (1980a) *The International Yearbook of Organisation Studies 1979*, London: Routledge & Kegan Paul.

Dunkerley, D. and Salaman, G. (eds) (1980b) *The International Yearbook of Organisation Studies 1980*, London: Routledge & Kegan Paul.

Dunkerley, D. and Salaman, G. (eds) (1982) *The International Yearbook of Organisation Studies 1981*, London: Routledge & Kegan Paul.

Dunkerley, D. and Salaman, G. (1986) 'Organizations and Bureaucracy', in M. Haralambos (ed.) *Developments in Sociology vol. 2*, Ormskirk: Causeway.

Dunning, J. H. (1986) *Japanese Participation in British Industry*, London: Croom Helm.

Durand, J-P. (2007) The *Invisible Chain: Constraints and Opportunities in the New World of Employment*, Basingstoke: Palgrave.

Easterby-Smith, M. (1992) 'Creating a Learning Organisation', *Personnel Review*, 19. 5: 24–8.

Easterby-Smith, M., Thorpe, R. and Lowe, A. (1991) *Management Research: An Introduction*, London: Sage.

Eby, L. T. and Dobbins, G. H. (1997) 'Collectivistic Orientation in Teams: An Individual and Group Level Analysis', *Journal of Organizational Behaviour*, 18: 275–95.

Eccles, R. G. and Nohria, N. (1992) *Beyond the Hype: Rediscovering the Essence of Management*, Boston, Mass.: Harvard Business School Press.

Economic Progress Report (1986) 'A More Flexible Labour Market', no. 182, HM Treasury.

Edquist, C. and Jacobsson, S. (1988) *Flexible Automation: The Global Diffusion of New Technology in the Engineering Industry*, Berkeley, CA: University of California Press.

Edwardes, M. (1978) *The Dark Side of History: Magic in the Making of Man*, St Albans: Granada.

Edwards, P.K. (1986) *Conflict at Work: A Materialist Analysis of Workplace Relations*, Oxford: Blackwell.

Edwards, P. K. (1990) 'Understanding Conflict in the Labour Process: The Logic and Autonomy of Struggle', in D. Knights and H. Willmott (eds), *Labour Process Theory*, London: Macmillan.

Edwards, P., Armstrong, P., Marginson, P. and Purcell, J. (1996) 'Towards the Transnational Company?', in R. Crompton, D. Gallie and K. Purcell (eds), *Corporate Restructuring and Labour Markets*, London: Routledge.

Edwards, P. K. and Scullion, H. (1982) *The Social Organisation of Industrial Conflict: Control and Resistance in the Workplace*, Oxford: Blackwell.

Edwards, R. (1979) *Contested Terrain: The Transformation of the Workplace in the Twentieth Century*, London: Heinemann.

Edwards, R., Reich, M. and Gordon, D. M. (1975) *Labour Market Segmentation*, Lexington, MA: D. C. Heath.

Egan, G. (1994) *Working the Shadow Side: A Guide to Positive Behind-the-Scenes Management*, San Francisco: Jossey-Bass.

Egri, C. P. (1994) 'Working with Nature: Organic Farming and Other Forms of Resistance to Industrialised Agriculture', in J. Jermier, D. Knights and W. Nord (eds), *Resistance and Power in Organisations*, London: Routledge.

Ehrenreich, B. (2001) *Nickel and Dimed: Undercover in Low-Wage USA*, London: Granta Books.

Ehrenreich, B. and Ehrenreich, J. (1979) 'The Professional-Managerial Class', in P. Walker (ed.), *Between Labour and Capital*, Brighton: Harvester.

Eikhof, D. R., Warhurst, C. and Haunschild, A. (2007) 'Introduction: What Work? What Life? What Balance?', *Employee Relations*, 29. 4: 325–33.

Eiser, J. R. (1986) *Social Psychology: Attitudes, Cognition and Social Behaviour*, Cambridge: Cambridge University Press.

Elbaum, B. and Lazonick, W. (eds) (1986) *The Decline of the British Economy*, Oxford: Clarendon.

Eldridge, J. E. T. and Crombie, A. D. (1974) *A Sociology of Organizations*, London: Allen & Unwin.

Elger, T. (1987) 'Flexible Futures? New Technology and the Contemporary Transformation of Work', *Work, Employment and Society*, 1. 4: 528–40.

Elger, T. (1990) 'Technical Innovation and Work Reorganization in British Manufacturing in the 1980s', *Work, Employment and Society* special issue, May: 67–101.

Elger, T. (1991) 'Task Flexibility and Intensification of Labour in UK Manufacturing in the 1980s', in A. Pollert (ed.), *Farewell to Flexibility?* Oxford: Blackwell.

Elger, T. and Burnham, P. (2001) 'Labour, Globalization and the "Competition State"', *Competition and Change*, 5. 2: 1–23.

Elger, T. and Smith, C. (1994) 'Global Japanisation? Convergence and Competition in the Organisation of the Labour Process', in T. Elger and C. Smith (eds), *Global Japanisation*, London: Routledge.

Elias, J. and Scarbrough. H. (2004) 'Evaluating Human capital: An Exploratory Study of Management Practice', *Human Resource Management Journal*, 14. 4: 21–40.

Elizur, D. (1991) 'Work and Non-work Relations: The Conical Structure of Work and Home Life Relationship', *Journal of Organizational Behavior*, 12, 313–22. available at: http://findarticles.com/p/articles/mi_qa3702/is_200204/ai_n9033726/pg_1.

Elliot, D. (1980) 'The Organisation as a System', in G. Salaman and K. Thompson (eds), *Control and Ideology in Organizations*, Milton Keynes: Open University Press.

Elliot, K. and Lawrence. P. (1985) *Introducing Management*, Harmondsworth: Penguin.

Eros, F. (1974) 'Review of L. Garai's *Personality Dynamics and Social Existence*', *European Journal of Social Psychology*, 4. 3: 369–79.

Esland, G. (1980) 'Professions and Professionalism', in G. Esland and G. Salaman (eds), *The Politics of Work and Occupations*, Milton Keynes: Open University Press.

Esland, G. and Salaman, G. (eds) (1980) *The Politics of Work and Occupations*, Milton Keynes: Open University Press.

Etzioni, A. (1961) *A Comparative Analysis of Complex Organizations*, New York: Free Press.

Etzioni, A. (1988) *The Moral Dimension: Towards a New Economics*, New York: Plenum.

McKenna, E. F. (2006) *Business Psychology and Organisational Behaviour*, Hove: Psychology Press.

Everingham, C., Stevenson, D. and Warner-Smith, P. (2007) '"Things are Getting Better All the Time"? Challenging the Narrative of Women's Progress from a Generational Perspective', *Work, Employment and Society*, 41. 3: 410–37.

Eysenck, H. J. (1947) *Dimensions of Personality*, London: Routledge & Kegan Paul.

Eysenck, H. J. and Wilson, G. (1975) *Know Your Own Personality*, Harmondsworth: Penguin.

Farnham, D. and Horton, S. (eds) (1993) *Managing the New Public Services*, London: Macmillan.

Farnham, D. and Horton, S. (1993) 'The New Public Service Managerialism: An Assessment', in D. Farnham and S. Horton (eds), *Managing the New Public Services*, London: Macmillan.

Featherstone, M. (1988) 'In Pursuit of the Postmodern: An Introduction', *Theory, Culture and Society*, 5: 195–215.

Feldman, D. C. and Klich, N. R. (1991) 'Impression Management and Career Strategies', in R. A. Giacolone and P. Rosenfeld (eds), *Applied Impression Management: How Image-Making Affects Managerial Decisions*, Newbury Park, CA: Sage.

Felstead, A. (1994) *Corporate Paradox: Power and Control in Business Franchise*, London: Routledge.

Felstead, A. and Jewson, N. (1999a) 'Flexible Labour and Non-Standard Employment: An Agenda of Issues', in A. Felstead and N. Jewson (eds), *Global Trends in Flexible Labour*, London: Macmillan.

Felstead, A. and Jewson, N. (eds) (1999b) *Global Trends in Flexible Labour*, London: Macmillan.

Felstead, A., Jewson, N., Phizacklea, A. and Walters, S. (2001) 'Blurring the Home/Work Boundary: Profiling Employers Who Allow Working at Home', *ESRC Future of Work Programme*, Working Paper No 15, May.

Feng, H., Froud, J., Johal, S., Haslam, C. and Williams, K. (2001) 'A New Business Model? The Capital Market and the New Economy', *Economy and Society*, 30. 4: 467–503.

Ferguson, K. (1984) *The Feminist Case against Bureaucracy*, Philadelphia: Temple University Press.

Ferner, A. and Edwards, P. (1995) 'Power and the Diffusion of Organisational Change within Multinationals', *European Journal of Industrial Relations*, 1. 2: 229–57.

Fernie, S. and Metcalf, D. (1997) '(Not) Hanging on the Telephone: Payment Systems in the New Sweatshops', *Centre for Economic Performance*, London: London School of Economics.

Festinger, L. (1954) 'A Theory of Social Comparison Processes', *Human Relations*, 7: 117–40.

Festinger, L. (1957) *A Theory of Cognitive Dissonance*, Palo Alto, CA: Stanford University Press.

Festinger, L. and Carlsmith, J. M. (1959) 'Cognitive Consequences of Forced Compliance', *Journal of Abnormal and Social Psychology*, 58: 203–11.

Fevre, R. (1986) 'Contract Work in the Recession', in K. Purcell, S. Wood, A. Watson and S. Allen (eds), *The Changing Experience of Employment, Restructuring and Recession*, London: Macmillan.

Fevre, R. (2007) 'Employment Insecurity and Social Theory: The Power of Nightmares', *Work, Employment and Society*, 21. 5: 17–535.

Feyerabend, P. (1975) *Against Method: An Outline of an Anarchistic Theory of Knowledge*, London: NLB.

Fiedler, F. E. (1967) *A Theory of Leadership Effectiveness*, New York: McGraw-Hill.

Fiedler, F. E. (1978) 'Situational Control: A Dynamic Theory of Leadership', in B. King, S. Steufert and F. Fiedler (eds), *Managerial Control and Organisational Democracy*, Washington, DC: Winston and Wiley.

Filby, M. (1992) 'The Figures, the Personality and the Bums: Service Work and Sexuality', *Work Employment and Society*, 6. 1: 23–42.

Fincham, R. and Clark, T. (2002) *Critical Consulting: New Perspectives on the Management Advice Industry*, Oxford: Blackwell.

Findlay, P., Marks, A., McKinlay, A. and Thompson, P. (2000a) 'Flexible if it Suits Them: The Use and Abuse of Teamwork Skills', in F. Mueller and S. Proctor (eds), *Teamwork*, London: Macmillan.

Findlay, P., Marks, A., McKinlay, A. and Thompson, P. (2000b) 'In Search of Perfect People: Teamwork and Team Players in Scottish Spirits Industry', *Human Relations*, 53. 12: 1549–74.

Fine, G. A. (1996) *Kitchens: The Culture of Restaurant Work*, London: University of California Press.

Finegold, D. (1999) 'Creating Self-Sustaining High-Skill Ecosystems', *Oxford Review of Economics*, 15. 1: 60–81.

Fineman, S. (ed.) (1993) *Emotion in Organizations*, London: Sage.

Fineman, S. (1998) 'Street Level Bureaucrats and the Social Construction of Environmental Control', *Organisation Studies*, 19. 6: 953–74.

Finlay, P. (1985) 'Control', in K. Elliot and P. Lawrence (eds), *Introducing Management*, Harmondsworth: Penguin.

Finn, D. (1986) *Training without Jobs*, London: Macmillan.

Fischer, F. and Sirriani, C. (eds) (1984) *Critical Studies in Organisation and Bureaucracy*, Philadelphia: Temple University Press.

Fisher, D. (1993) *Communication in Organizations* (2nd edn), St Paul, MN: West Publishing.

Fisher, S. (1986) *Stress and Strategy*, London: Lawrence Erlbaum.

Fiske, S. T. and Taylor, S. E. (1991) *Social Cognition* (2nd edn), New York: McGraw-Hill.

Fleishman, E. A. (1974) 'Leadership Climate, Human Relations Training and Supervisory Behaviour', in E. A. Fleishman and A. R. Bass (eds), *Studies in Personnel and Industrial Psychology*, New York: Dorsey. Fligstein, N. (1990) *The Transformation of Corporate Control*, Cambridge, MA: Harvard University Press.

Fleming, P. (2001) 'Beyond the Panopticon?', *Ephemera*, 1. 2: 190–4.

Fleming, P. (2005) 'Workers Playtime: Boundaries and Cynicism in a "Culture of Fun" Program', *The Journal of Applied Behavioral Science*, 41. 3: 285–303.

Fleming, P. and Spicer, A. (2002) 'Working at a Cynical Distance: Implications for Power, Subjectivity and Resistance', *Organization*, 10: 157–79.

Florida, R. and Kenney, M. (1991) 'Organisation vs. Culture: Japanese Automotive Transplants in the US', *Industrial Relations Journal*, 2. 2: 181–96.

Fontana, D. (1985) 'Learning and Teaching', in C. L. Cooper and P. Makin (eds), *Psychology and Managers*, London: BPS and Macmillan.

Ford, M. E. (1992) *Motivating Humans, Goals, Emotions and Personal Agency Beliefs*, Newbury Park, CA: Sage.

Fores, M. and Glover, I. (1976) 'The Real Work of Executives', *Management Today*, Sept.

Fores, M., Glover, I. and Lawrence, P. (1992) 'Management Thought, the American Legacy and the Future of European Labour Processes in 1992', paper presented to the 10th International Labour Process Conference, Aston.

Forsgren, M. (1990) *Managing the Internationalisation Process: The Swedish Case*, London: Routledge.

Foucault, M. (1972) *The Archaeology of Knowledge*, London: Tavistock.

Foucault, M. (1977) *Discipline and Punish: The Birth of the Prison*, Harmondsworth: Penguin.

Foucault, M. (1984) *The History of Sexuality: An Introduction*, Harmondsworth: Peregrine.

Fournier, V. and Grey, C. (2000) 'At the Critical Moment: Conditions and Prospects for Critical Management Studies', *Human Relations*, 53. 1: 7–32.

Fowler, A. (1985) 'Getting into Organisational Restructuring', *Personnel Management*, 17. 2: 24–7.

Fox, A. (1974) *Beyond Contract: Work, Power and Trust Relations*, London: Faber and Faber.

Fox, A. (1980) 'The Meaning of Work', in G. Esland and G. Salaman (eds), *The Politics of Work and Occupations*, Milton Keynes: Open University Press.

Francis, A. (1986) *New Technology at Work*, Oxford: Oxford University Press.

Frank, T. (2000) *One Market Under God: Extreme Capitalism, Market Populism and the End of Economic Democracy*, New York: Secker and Warburg.

Fraser, N. (1989) *Unruly Practices: Power, Discourse and Gender in Contemporary Social Theory*, Cambridge: Polity.

Fraser, J.A. (2001) *White Collar Sweatshop: The Deterioration of Work and its Rewards in Corporate America*, New York: W.W. Norton & Co.

Freedman, D. (1992) 'Is Management Still a Science?', *Harvard Business Review*, Nov.–Dec.: 26–37.

Freedman, M. (1984) 'The Search for Shelters', in K. Thompson (ed.), *Work, Employment and Unemployment*, Milton Keynes: Open University Press.

French, W. L. and Bell, C. H. (1984) *Organization Development: Behavioral Science Interventions for Organization Improvement*, 3rd edn. Englewood Cliffs, NJ: Prentice Hall.

French, J. R. P. and Caplan, R. D. (1972) 'Organizational Stress and Individual Strain', in Morrow, A. (ed.), *The Failure of Success*, New York, AMOCOM, pp. 30–66.

French, J. R. P. and Raven, B. H. (1959) 'The Social Bases of Power', in D. Cartwright (ed.), *Studies in Social Power*, Ann Arbor: University of Michigan Press.

Frenkel, S., Korczynski, M., Donohue, L. and Shire, K. (1995) 'Re-Constituting Work', *Work, Employment and Society*, 9. 4: 773–96.

Frenkel, S., Korczynski, M., Shire, K. and Tam, M. (1999) *On the Front Line: Pattern of Work Organisation in Three Advanced Societies*, Ithaca, NY: Cornell University Press.

Frese, M. (1982) 'Occupational Socialisation and Psychological Development: An Underdeveloped Research Perspective in Industrial Psychology', *Journal of Occupational Psychology*, 55: 209–24.

Freud, A. (1937) *The Ego and the Mechanisms of Defence*. London: Hogarth Press and Institute of Psycho-Analysis.

Freud, S. (1927) *The Ego and the Id*, Hogarth Press and Institute of Psycho-analysis, London.

Fridenson, P. (1978) 'Corporate Policy, Rationalisation and the Labour Force: French Experiences in International Comparison, 1900–29', paper presented to the Nuffield Deskilling Conference.

Friedman, A. (1977) *Industry and Labour: Class Struggle at Work Monopoly Capitalism*, London: Macmillan.

Friedman, A. (1987) 'The Means of Management Control and Labour Process Theory: A Critical Note on Storey', *Sociology*, 21. 2: 287–94.

Friedman, A. (1990) 'Managerial Strategies and the Labour Process', in D. Knights and H. Willmott (eds), *Labour Process Theory*, London: Macmillan.

Friedman, M. and Rosenman, R.H. (1974) *Type A Behavior and Your Heart*, New York: Fawcett.

Frost, P. J., Moore, L. F., Louis, M. R., Lundberg, C. C. and Martin, J. (eds) (1985) *Organisational Culture*, Beverley Hills/London: Sage.

Froud, J., Johal, S., Leaver, A. and Williams, K. (2006) *Financialization and Strategy: Narratives and Numbers*, London: Routledge.

Fucini, J. and Fucini, S. (1990) *Working for the Japanese: Inside Mazda's American Auto Plant*, New York: Free Press.

Fuller, A. and Saunders, M. (1990) 'The Paradox of Open Learning at Work', *Personnel Review*, 19. 5: 29–33.

Fuller, L. and Smith, V. A. (1991) 'Consumers' Reports: Management by Customers in a Changing Economy', *Work, Employment and Society*, 5. 1: 1–16.

Fuller, S. R. and Aldag, R. J. (1998) 'Organizational Tonypandy: Lessons from a Quarter Century of the Groupthink Phenomenon', *Organizational Behaviour and Human Decision Processes*, 2. 3: 163–4.

Furnham, A. (1990) 'Faking Personality Questionnaires: Fabricating Different Profiles for Different Purposes', *Current Psychology: Research and Reviews*, 9. 1: 46–55.

Furnham, A. (1997) *The Psychology of Behaviour at Work: The Individual in the Organisation*, Hove: Psychology Press.

Furusten, S. (1999) *Popular Management Books*, London: Routledge.

Gabriel, Y. (1988) *Working Lives in Catering*, London: Routledge.

Gabriel, Y. (2005) Glass Cages and Glass Palaces: Images of Organizations in Image-Conscious Times'. *Organization*, 12. 1: 9–27.

Galbraith, J. K. (1967) *The New Industrial State*, Harmondsworth: Penguin.

Garnsey, E., Rubery, E. J. and Wilkinson, F. (1985) 'Labour Market Structure and Workforce Divisions', Unit 8 of Open University Course *Work and Society*, Milton Keynes: Open University Press.

Garrahan, P. and Stewart, P. (1992) *The Nissan Enigma: Flexibility at Work in a Local Economy*, London: Mansett.

Garrahan, P. and Stewart, P. (1993) 'Working Leaner but Smarter, or Meaner and Harder?: New Management Practices and the Recomposition of Employee Attitudes – The Case of the Auto Industry in Britain', paper presented to the American Sociological Association 88th Annual Meeting, Miami Beach, Florida.

Gatta, M. (2009) 'Balancing Trays And Smiles: What Restaurant Servers Teach Us About Hard Work In the Service Economy', in S. Bolton and M. Houlihan (eds). *Work Matters: Critical Reflections on Contemporary Work*, Basingstoke: Palgrave Macmillan.

Geary, R. (1985) *Policing Industrial Disputes: 1893–1985*, London: Methuen.

Gecas, V. (1986) 'The Motivational Significance of Self-Concept for Socialisation Theory', in E. J. Lawler (ed.), *Advances in Group Processes*, vol. 3, Greenwich, CT: JAI.

Gennard, J. and Kelly, J. (2001) *Power and Influence in the Boardroom: The Role of the Personnel/HR Director*, London: Routledge.

George, M. and Levie, H. (1984) *Japanese Competition and the British Workplace*, London: CAITS.

Geras, N. (1983) *Marx and Human Nature: Refutation of a Legend*, London: Verso.

Gergen, K. (1992) 'Organisation Theory in the Postmodern Era', in M. Reed and M. Hughes (eds), *Rethinking Organisation: New Directions in Organisation and Analysis*, London: Sage.

Gergen, K. J. (1973) 'Social Psychology as History', *Journal of Personality and Psychology*, 26. 2: 302–20.

Gerhardi, S. (1996) 'Gendered Organisational Cultures: Narratives of Women Travellers in a Male World', *Gender, Work and Organisation*, 3. 4: 187–201.

Gereffi, G. (1994) 'The Organization of Buyer-Driven Global Commodity Chains: How US Retailers Shape Overseas Production Networks', in G. Gereffi and M. Korzeniewicz (eds), *Commodity Chains and Global Capitalism*, London: Greenwood Press.

Gereffi, G. (1996) 'Global Commodity Chains: New Forms of Coordination and Control among Nations and Firms in International Industries', *Competition and Change* 1. 4: 427–39.

Gereffi, G., Humphrey, J. and Sturgeon, T. (2005) 'The Governance of Global Value Chains', *Review of International Political Economy*, 12. 1: 78–104.

Gherardi, S. (2003) 'Feminist Theory and Organization Theory: A Dialogue on New Bases', in H. Tsoukas and C. Knudsen (eds), *The Oxford Handbook of Organization Theory*, Oxford: Oxford University Press.

Giacolone, R. A. and Greenberg, J. (eds) (1997) *Antisocial Behaviour in Organizations*, London: Sage.

Giacolone, R. A. and Rosenfeld, P. (eds) (1991) *Applied Impression Management: How Image-Making Affects Managerial Decisions*, Newbury Park, CA: Sage.

Giddens, A. (1982) 'From Marx to Nietzsche? Neo Conservatism, Foucault and Problems in Contemporary Political Theory', in *Profiles and Critiques in Social Theory*, London: Macmillan.

Giddens, A. (1984) *The Constitution of Society*, Cambridge: Polity.

Giddens, A. (1990) *The Consequences of Modernity*, Cambridge: Polity Press.

Giddens, A. (1991) *Modernity and Self Identity: Self and Society in the Late Modern Age*, Stanford: Stanford University Press.

Gilbert, D. T. and Malone, P. S. (1995). 'The Correspondence Bias', *Psychological Bulletin*, 117: 21–38.

Giles, E. and Starkey, K. (1987) 'From Fordism to Japanisation: Organisational Change at Ford, Rank Xerox and Fuji Xerox', paper presented to the Conference on Japanisation of British Industry, UMIST.

Gill, C. (1985) *Work, Unemployment and the New Technology*, Cambridge: Polity.

Gill, J. and Johnson, P. (1991) *Research Methods for Managers*, London: Paul Chapman.

Gill, R. and Grint, K. (1996) *The Gender–Technology Relation*, London: Taylor & Francis.

Ginn, G.O. and Henry, J.L. (2003) Wellness programmes in the context of Strat HRM, *Hospital Topics*, 001185868, Winter, 81. 1: 23–8.

Giordano, L. (1985) 'Beyond Taylorism: Computerisation and QWL Programs in the Production Process', paper presented to the Conference on the Labour Process, Aston-UMIST, also published in D. Knights and H. Willmott (eds) (1988) *New Technology and the Labour Process*, London: Macmillan.

Glenn, E. K. and Feldberg, R. L. (1979) 'Proletarianising Office Work', in A. Zimbalist (ed.), *Case Studies on the Labour Process*, New York: Monthly Review Press.

Glover, I., Kelly, M. and Roslander, R. (1986) 'The Coming Proletarianisation of the British Accountant?' paper presented to the Conference on the Labour Process, Aston-UMIST.

Glucksman, M. (1990) *Women Assemble: Women Workers and the New Industries in Inter-War Britain*, London: Routledge.

Glucksmann, M. A. (1995) 'Why "Work"? Gender and the Total Organisation of Labour,' *Gender, Work and Organization*, 2. 2: 63–75.

Goetzel, R. Z., Long, S. R., Ozminkowski, R. J., Hawkins, K., Wang, S. and Lynch, W. (2004) 'Health, Absence, Disability, and Presenteeism; Cost Estimates of Certain Physical and Mental Health Conditions Affecting U.S. Employers', *Journal of Occupational and Environmental Medicine*, April, 46. 4: 398–412.

Goffmann, E. (1959) *The Presentation of Self in Everyday Life*, New York: Doubleday Anchor.

Goffman, E. (1961) *Asylums*, New York: Doubleday.

Goffman, E. (1971) *The Presentation of Self in Everyday Life*, Harmondsworth: Pelican.

Goldin, L. and Applebaum, E. (1992) 'What was Driving the 1982–88 Boom in Temporary Employment? Preferences of Workers of Decisions and Power of Employers', *Journal of Economy and Society*, 51.

Goldman, P. and Van Houten, D. R. (1977) 'Managerial Strategies and the Worker: A Marxist Analysis of Bureaucracy', in J. K. Benson (ed.), *Organisational Analysis: Critique and Innovation*, London: Sage.

Goldman, P. and Van Houten, D. R. (1980) 'Uncertainty, Conflict and Labor Relations in the Modern Firm 1: Productivity and Capitalism's Human Face', *Economic and Industrial Democracy*, 1: 63–98.

Goldsmith, W. and Clutterbuck, D. (1985) *The Winning Streak*, Harmondsworth: Penguin.

Goleman, D. (1995) *Emotional Intelligence*, New York: Bantam Books.

Goodrich, C. (1975) *The Frontier of Control*, London: Pluto.

Gordon, D. (1988) 'The Global Economy: New Edifice or Crumbling Foundations?' *New Left Review*, 168. March–April: 24–65.

Gordon, D. M., Edwards, R. and Reich, M. (1982) *Segmented Work, Divided Workers*, Cambridge: Cambridge University Press.

Goss, S. (2001) *Making Local Government Work: Networks, Relationships and the Management of Change*, London: Palgrave.

Gouldner, A. (1955) *Wildcat Strike*, London: Routledge & Kegan Paul.

Gouldner, A. W. (1954) *Patterns of Industrial Bureaucracy*, New York: Free Press.

Gourlay, S. (2001) 'Knowledge Management and HRD', *Human Resource Development International*, 4. 1, March 2001: 27–46.

Gowler, D. and Legge, K. (1983) 'The Meaning of Management and the Management of Meaning: A View From Social Anthropology', in M. J. Earl (ed.), *Perspectives on Management: A Multidisciplinary Analysis*, Oxford: Oxford University Press.

Granovetter, M. (1985) 'Economic Action and Social Structure: The Problem of Embeddedness', *American Journal of Sociology*, 91. 3: 481–510.

Granovetter, M. (1994) 'Problems of Explanation in Economic Sociology', in N. Nohria and R. G. Eccles (eds), *Networks and Organizations*, Boston, MA: Harvard Business School Press.

Grant, W. (1983) 'Representing Capital', in R. King (ed.), *Capital and Politics*, London: Routledge & Kegan Paul.

Green, E. and Cassell, C. (1994) 'Women Managers, Gendered Cultural Processes and Organisational Change', paper presented to the 12th Annual International Labour Process Conference, Aston University, March.

Green F. (2001) 'It's Been a Hard Day's Night: The Concentration and Intensification of Work in Late Twentieth-Century Britain', *British Journal of Industrial Relations*, 39. 1: 53–80.

Green F (2006) *Demanding Work: The Paradox of Job Quality in the Affluent Economy*, Princeton, NJ: Princeton University Press.

Greenbaum, J. (1979) *In the Name of Efficiency*, Philadelphia: Temple University Press.

Greenbaum, J. (1998) 'The Times They are A'Changing: Dividing and Recombining Labour through Computing Systems', in P. Thompson and C. Warhurst (eds), *Workplaces of the Future*, London: Macmillan.

Greenslade, M. (1994) 'Managing Diversity: Lessons from the United States', *Personnel Management*, December: 28–33.

Grenier, G. J. (1988) *Inhuman Relations: Quality Circles and Anti-Unionism in American Industry*, Philadelphia: Temple University Press.

Grey, C. (1994) 'Organisational Calvinism: Insecurity and Power in a Professional Labour Process', paper presented to the 12th Annual International Labour Process Conference, Aston, March.

Grey, C. (2005) *A Very Short, Fairly Interesting and Reasonably Cheap Book about Studying Organizations*, London: Sage.

Grey, C. and Mitev, N. (1995) 'Re-Engineering Organizations: A Critical Appraisal', *Personnel Review*, 24. 1: 1–18.

Grey, C. and Willmott, H. C. (eds) (2005) *Critical Management Studies: A Reader*, Oxford: Oxford University Press.

Grieco, M. and Whipp, R. (1985) 'Women and Control in the Workplace: Gender and Control in the Workplace', in D. Knights and H. Willmott (eds), *Job Redesign: Critical Perspectives on the Labour Process*, Aldershot: Gower.

Griffin, S. (1984) *Women and Nature: The Roaring inside Her*, London: Women's Press.

Grimshaw, J. (1986) *Feminist Philosophers*, Brighton: Wheatsheaf.

Grint, K. (1995) *Management: A Sociological Introduction*, Oxford: Polity.

Grint, K. and Gill, R. (eds) (1996) *The Gender–Technology Relation: Contemporary Theory and Research*, London: Taylor & Francis.

Gronhaug, K. and Falkenberg, J. (1994) 'Success Attributions within and across Organizations', *Journal of European Industrial Training*, 18. 11: 22–9.

Grossman, R. (1979) 'Women's Place in the Integrated Service', *Radical America*, 14. 1: 29–48.

Guest, D. (1998) 'Human Resource Management, Trade Unions and Industrial Relations', in C. Mabey, G. Salaman and J. Storey (eds), *Strategic Human Resource Management*, London: Sage.

Guest, D. E. (1987) 'Human Resource Management and Industrial Relations', *Journal of Management Studies*, 24. 5: 503–21.

Guest, D. E. (1989) 'Personnel and HRM: Can You Tell the Difference?' *Personnel Management*, January: 48–51.

Guest, D. E. (1990) 'Human Resource Management and the American Dream', *Journal of Management Studies*, 27. 4: 377–97.

Guest, D. E. (1992) 'Right Enough to be Dangerously Wrong: An Analysis of the In Search of Excellence Phenomenon', in G. Salaman (ed.), *Human Resource Strategies*, London: Sage.

Guest, D. E. (1999a) 'Human Resource Management: When Reality Confronts Theory', paper presented to a conference of the Netherlands HRM Network, Rotterdam, November.

Guest, D. E. (1999b) 'Human Resource Management: The Workers' Verdict', *Human Resource Management Journal*, 9. 3: 5–25.

Gummeson, E. (1991) *Qualitative Methods in Management Research*, London: Sage.

Gutek, B. (1985) *Sex and the Workplace*, London: Jossey-Bass.

Habermas, J. (1971) *Toward a Rational Society*, London: Heinemann.

Habermas, J. (1987) *The Philosophical Discourses of Modernity*, Cambridge: Polity.

Hacker, W., Volpert, W. and Von Cranach, M. (eds) (1982) *Cognitive and Motivational Aspects of Action*, Amsterdam: North Holland.

Hackman, J. R. and Oldman, G. R. (1980) *Work Redesign*, Reading, MA: Addison-Wesley.

Hackman, J. R. (1987) 'The Design of Work Groups', in J.W. Lorsch (ed.), *The Handbook of Organizational Behavior*, Englewood Cliffs, NJ: Prentice-Hall, pp.315–42.

Hakim, C. (1990) 'Core and Periphery in Employees' Workforce Strategies: Evidence from the 1987 ELUS Survey', *Work, Employment and Society*, 4. 2: 157–88.

Hakim, C. (1995) 'Five Feminist Myths about Women's Employment', *British Journal of Sociology*, 46. 3: 429–55.

Hakim, C. (1996) *Key Issues in Women's Employment: Female Heterogeneity and the Polarisation of Women's Employment*, London: Athlone.

Hakim, C. (2004) *Key Issues in Women's Work: Female Diversity and the Polarisation of Women's Employment*, London: Glasshouse Press.

Hales, C. P. (1986) 'What do Managers Do? A Critical Review of the Evidence', *Journal of Management Studies*, 23. 1: 88–115.

Hales, C. P. (1988) 'Management Processes, Management Divisions of Labour and Managerial Work: Towards a Synthesis', paper presented to the Conference on the Labour Process, Aston-UMIST.

Hales, C. (1993) *Managing through Organisation*, London: Routledge.

Hales, C. (2000) 'Management and Empowerment Programmes', *Work, Employment and Society*, 14. 3: 501–19.

Hales, C. (2002), 'Bureaucracy-lite' and Continuities in Managerial Work', *British Journal of Management*, 13. 2: 51–66

Halford, S., Savage, M. and Witz, A. (1997) *Gender, Careers and Organisations*, London: Macmillan.

Hall, P. A. (1986) 'The State and Economic Decline', in B. Elbaum and W. Lazonick (eds), *The Decline of the British Economy*, Oxford: Clarendon.

Hall, R. H. (1977) *Organizations: Structure and Process* (2nd edn), Englewood Cliffs, NJ: Prentice Hall.

Hallet, S. (1988) 'Privatisation and the Restructuring of a Public Utility: A Case Study of BT's Corporate Strategy and Structure', paper presented to the Conference on New Forms of Ownership and Management, Cardiff Business School.

Hallier, J. (2004) 'Embellishing the Past: Middle Manager Identity and Informality in the Implementation of New Technology', *New Technology, Work and Employment*, 19, 1: 43–62.

Hallier, J. and James, P. (1997) 'Middle Managers and the Employee Psychological Contract: Agency, Protection and Advancement', *Journal of Management Studies*, 34. 5: 703–28.

Hamel, G. and Prahalad, C. K. (1996) 'Competing in the New Economy: Managing out of Bounds', *Strategic Management Journal*, 17: 237–42.

Hamilton, G. G. and Biggart, N. W. (1988) 'Market, Culture and Authority: A Comparative Analysis of Management and Organisation in the Far East', in C. Winship and S. Rosen (eds), 'Organizations and Institutions', *American Journal of Sociology*, 94, supplement, Chicago: University of Chicago Press.

Hamilton, P. (1980) 'Social Theory and the Problematic Concept of Work', in G. Esland and G. Salaman (eds), *The Politics of Work and Occupations*, Milton Keynes: Open University Press.

Hammer, M. and Champy, J. (1993) *Re-engineering the Corporation*, London: Nicholas Brealey.

Hammond, K. (2005) 'Why We Hate HR', *Fast Company* 97: 40–1.

Hammond, V. and Barham, K. (1987) *Management for the Future: Report on the Literature Search*, Herts: Ashridge Management College.

Hampden-Turner, C. and Trompenaars, F. (1993) *The Seven Cultures of Capitalism*, New York: Doubleday.

Handy, C. (1976; 1980; 1985) *Understanding Organizations*, Harmondsworth: Penguin.

Handy, C. (1984) *The Future of Work*, London: Blackwell.

Handy, C. (1989) *The Age of Unreason*, London: Business Books.

Handy, C. (1994) *The Empty Raincoat*, London: Hutchinson.

Handy, C. (1995) *The Future of Work*, W. H. Smith Contemporary Papers 8.

Hannan, M. T. and Carroll, G. R. (1992) *Dynamics of Organisational Populations: Density, Competition and Legitimation*, New York: Oxford University Press.

Hannan, M. T., Carroll, G. R., Dundon, E. A. and Torres, J. C. (1995) 'Organisational Evolution in a Multinational Context: Entries of Automobile Manufactures in Belgium, Britain, France, Germany and Italy', *American Sociological Review*, 60: 509–28.

Hannan, M. T. and Freeman, J. H. (1977) 'The Population Ecology of Organizations', *American Journal of Sociology*, 82: 929–64.

Hardt, M. and Negri, A. (2000) *Empire*, Cambridge, MA: Harvard University Press.

Hardy, C. (1996) 'Understanding Power: Bringing about Strategic Change', *British Journal of Management*, 7, special issue: S3–16.

Hardy, C. (1998) 'The Power Behind Empowerment: Implications for Research and Practice', *Human Relations*, 51. 4: 451–82.

Harley, B. (1998) 'The Myth of Empowerment: Work Organisation, Hierarchy and Employee Autonomy in Contemporary Australian Workplaces', Department of Management Working Paper, University of Melbourne.

Harley, B. (2001) 'Team Membership and the Experience of Work in Britain: An Analysis of the WERS98 Data', *Work, Employment and Society*, 15: 721–42.

Harley, B. (2005) 'Hope or Hype? High Performance Work Systems', in J. Hyman, P. Thompson and B. Harley (eds), *Participation and Democracy at Work: Essays in Honour of Harvie Ramsay*, Basingstoke: Palgrave.

Harris, R. (1987) *Power and Powerlessness in Industry: An Analysis of the Social Relations of Production*, London: Tavistock.

Harrison, B. (1994) *Lean and Mean: The Changing Landscape of Corporate Power in the Age of Flexibility*, New York: Basic Books.

Harrison, E. and Marchington, M. (1992) 'Corporate Culture and Management Control: Understanding Customer Care', paper presented to the Employment Research Unit Annual Conference, Cardiff Business School, September.

Harrison, R. G. (1984) 'Reasserting the Radical Potential of OD', *Personnel Review*, 13. 2: 12–18.

Hartley, J. F. and Stephenson, G. M. (eds) (1992) *Employment Relations*, Oxford: Blackwell.

Harvey, D. (1989) *The Condition of Postmodernity*, Cambridge, MA: Blackwell.

Haslam, S. A. (2000) *Psychology in Organizations: The Social Identity Approach*, London: Sage.

Hassard, J. (1988) 'Overcoming Hermeticism in Organization Theory: An Alternative to Paradigm Incommensurability', *Human Relations*, 41. 3: 247–59.

Hassard, J. (1991) 'Multiple Paradigms and Organisational Analysis: A Case Study', *Organisation Studies*, 12. 2: 275–99.

Hassard, J. (1994) 'Postmodern Organisational Analysis: Towards a Conceptual Framework', *Journal of Management Studies*, 31. 3: 1–22.

Hassard, J., Holliday, R. and Willmott, H. (2000) 'Introduction', in J. Hassard, R. Holliday and H. Willmott (eds), *Body and Organisation*, London: Sage.

Hassard, J. and Parker, M. (1993) *Postmodernism and Organizations*, London: Sage.

Hassard, J. and Parker, M. (eds) (1994) *Towards a New Theory of Organizations*, London: Routledge.

Hassard, J. and Pym, D. (eds) (1990) *The Theory and Philosophy of Organizations*, London: Routledge.

Hawkins, K. (1978) *The Management of Industrial Relations*, Harmondsworth: Penguin.

Hearn, J. (1992) *Men in the Public Eye*, London: Routledge.

Hearn, J. and Parkin, W. (1987) *Sex at Work: The Power and Paradox of Organisation Sexuality*, Brighton: Wheatsheaf.

Hearn, J. and Parkin, W. (1992) 'Gender and Organizations: A Selective Review and a Critique of a Neglected Area', in A. J. Mills and P. Tancred (eds), *Gendering Organisation Analysis*, London: Sage.

Hearn, J., Sheppard, D. L., Tancred-Sheriff, P. and Burrell, G. (eds) (1989) *The Sexuality of Organisation*, London: Sage.

Heckscher, C. (1995) *White Collar Blues: Management Loyalties in an Age of Corporate Restructuring*, New York: Basic Books.

Heckscher, C. (1997) 'The Changing Social Contract for White Collar Workers', *Perspectives on Work*, 1. 1: 18–21.

Heckscher, C. and Donnellon, A. (eds) (1994) *The Post-Bureaucratic Organisation*, London: Sage.

Heider, F. (1946) 'Attitudes and Cognitive Organisation', *Journal of Psychology*, 21: 107–12.

Heider, F. (1958) *The Psychology of Interpersonal Relations*, New York: Wiley.

Held, D. (1984) 'Central Perspectives on the Modern State', in D. Held (ed.), *States and Societies*, Oxford: Martin Robertson.

Henderson, G. (1993) 'Industrial Policy for Britain: Lessons From the East', *Renewal*, 1. 2: 32–42.

Henderson, J. (1989) *The Globalisation of High Technology Production*, London: Routledge.

Henderson, J. (1992) 'Global Economic Integration, Business Systems and States in East Asian European Development', paper presented to the First European Conference of Sociology, Vienna, August.

Hendry, C., Pettigrew, A. and Sparrow, P. (1988) 'Changing Patterns Of Human Resource Management', *Personnel Management*, Nov.

Henriques, J., Hollway, W. and Urwin, C. (eds) (1984) *Changing the Subject: Psychology, Social Regulation and Subjectivity*, London: Methuen.

Henwood, D. (1996) 'Work and its Future', *Left Business Observer*, 72, internet edn.

Henwood, D. (2003) *After the New Economy*, New York: The New Press.

Heery, E. and Salmon, J. (eds) (2000) *The Insecure Workforce*, London: Routledge.

Herriot, P. and Pemberton, C. (1994) *Competitive Advantage through Diversity*, London: Sage.

Hershey, R. (1993) 'A Practitioner's View of Motivation', *Journal of Managerial Psychology*, 8. 3: 10–13.

Herzberg, F. (1966) *Work and the Nature of Man*, Cleveland, OH: World Publishing.

Herzberg, F. (1968) 'One More Time, How Do You Motivate Employees?' in S. J. Carroll, F. T. Paine and J. B. Miner (eds), (1977) *The Management Process* (2nd edn), New York: Macmillan.

Herzberg, F. (2008) '*One More Time, How Do You Motivate Employees?*', Harvard Business Review Classics, Cambridge, MA: Harvard Business Press.

Herzberg, F., Mauser, B. and Snyderman, B. (eds) (1959) *The Motivation to Work*, New York: Wiley.

Heydebrand, W. (1977) 'Organisational Contradictions in Public Bureaucracies; Toward a Marxian Theory of Organisations', in J. K. Benson (ed.), *Organisational Analysis: Critique and Innovation*, Contemporary Social Science Issues 37, London: Sage.

Heydebrand, W. (1989) 'New Organisational Forms', *Work and Occupations*, 16. 3: 323–57.

Hickson, D. J. (1971) 'A Strategic Contingencies Theory of Interorganizational Power', *Administrative Science Quarterly*, 16: 216–29.

Hickson, D. J. (1973) 'A Convergence in Organisation Theory', in G. Salaman and K. Thompson (eds), *People and Organizations*, Harlow: Longman.

Hickson, D. J. (1990) 'Politics Permeates', in D. Wilson and R. Rosenfeld (eds), *Managing Organizations: Texts, Readings and Cases,* Maidenhead: McGraw-Hill.

Hickson, D. J., Lee, C. R., Schneck, R. E. and Pennings, J. M. (1973) 'A Strategic Contingencies Theory of Intraorganizational Power', in G. Salaman and K. Thompson (eds), *People and Organizations*, Harlow: Longman.

Hickson, D. J. and McCullough, A. F. (1980) 'Power in Organizations', in G. Salaman and K. Thompson (eds), *Control and Ideology in Organizations*, Milton Keynes: Open University Press.

Higgins, E. T. (1987) 'Self-discrepancy: A Theory Relating Self and Affect', *Psychological Review.* July, 94. 3: 319–40.

Hildreth, P. M. and Kimble, C. (2002) 'The Duality of Knowledge', *Information Research*, 8. 1, October.

Hill, S. (1991) 'Why Quality Circles Failed but Total Quality Management Might Succeed', *British Journal of Industrial Relations*, 29. 4: 541–68.

Hill, S., Martin, R., and Harris, M. (2000) 'Decentralization, Integration and the Post-Bureaucratic Organization: The Case of R & D', *Journal of Management Studies*, 37. 4: 563–85.

Hilmer, F. G. and Donaldson, L. (1996) *Management Redeemed: Debunking the Fads that Undermine Corporate Performance*, Sydney: Free Press.

Hindess, B. (1982) 'Power, Interests and the Outcome of Struggles', *Sociology*, 23: 535–58.

Hinings, B. (1988) 'Defending Organisation Theory: A British View from North America', *Organisation Studies*, 9. 1: 2–7.

Hirst, P. and Thompson, G. (1992) 'The Problem of Globalisation: International Economic Relations, National Economic Management and the Formation of Trading Blocs', *Economy and Society*, 21. 4: 359–95.

Hirst, P. and Thompson, G. (1996) *Globalisation in Question*, Oxford: Polity.

Hirst, P. and Zeitlin, J. (1991) 'Flexible Specialisation Versus Post-Fordism: Theory, Evidence and Policy Implications', *Economy and Society*, 20. 1: 1–56.

Hitt, M. A., Middlemist, R. D. and Mathis, R. L. *et al.* (1986) *Management Concepts and Effective Practice*, St Paul, MN: West Publishing.

Hobsbawm, E. J. (1975) *The Age of Capital: 1845–1875*, London: Weidenfeld & Nicolson.

Hochschild, A. (1997) *The Time Blind: When Work Becomes Home and Home Becomes Work*, New York: Holt.

Hochschild, A. R. (1983) *The Managed Heart: Commercialisation of Human Feeling*, London: University of California Press.

Hochschild, A. R. (1993) 'Preface' to S. Fineman (ed.), *Emotion in Organizations*, London: Sage.

Hochschild, A. (2003) *The Commercialization of Intimate Life: Notes From Home And Work*, San Francisco and Los Angeles: University of California Press.

Hodson, R. (1995) 'Worker Resistance: An Underdeveloped Concept in the Sociology of Work', *Economic and Industrial Democracy*, 16: 79–110.

Hodson, R. (2001) *Dignity at Work*, Cambridge: Cambridge University Press.

Hodges, B. H. (1974) 'Effect of Valence on Relative Weighting in Impression Formation', *Journal of Personality and Social Psychology*, 30, 378–81.

Hofstede, G. (1980) *Cultures Consequences: International Differences in Work Related Values*, Beverly Hills, CA: Sage.

Hofstede, G. (1986) 'Review of E. H. Schein, Organisational Culture and Leadership: A Dynamic View', *Organisation Studies*, 7. 2.

Hofstede, G. (1990) 'The Cultural Relativity of Organisational Practices and Theories', in D. Wilson and R. Rosenfeld (eds), *Managing Organizations: Texts, Readings and Cases,* Maidenhead: McGraw-Hill.

Hofstede, G. (1991) *Cultures and Organisations: Software of the Mind*, Maidenhead: McGraw-Hill.

Hofstede, G. and Søndergaard, M. (1993) 'Transfer of Management Ideas to Eastern European Business Organisations', paper presented to the 11th EGOS Colloquium, Paris.

Hogg, M. A. (2001) 'Social Identification, Group Prototypicality, and Emergent Leadership' in Hogg, A. and Terry, D. J. (eds), *Social Identity Processes in Organizational Contexts*, Hove: Psychology Press.

Hogg, M. A. and Abrams, D. (1990) 'Social Motivation, Self-Esteem and Social Identity', in D. Abrams and M. A. Hogg (eds), *Social, Identity Theory: Constructive and Critical advances*, Hemel Hempstead: Harvester Wheatsheaf.

Hogg, A. and Terry, D. J. (eds.) (2001) *Social Identity Processes in Organizational Contexts*, Sussex: Psychology Press.

Holland, S. (1975) *The Socialist Challenge*, London: Quartet.

Hollander. E. P. (1992) 'Leadership, Followership, Self, and Others', *Leadership Quarterly*, 3. 2: 43–54.

Hollander, E. P. (1964) *Leaders, Groups and Influence*, New York: Oxford University Press.

Hollander. E. P. and Julian, J. W. (1969) 'Contemporary Trends in the Analysis of Leadership Processes', *Psychological Bulletin*, 71, 387–97.

Holloway, J. (1987) 'The Red Rose of Nissan', *Capital and Class*, 32: 142–64.

Hollway, W. (1984) 'Fitting Work: Psychological Assessment in Organizations', in J. Henriques, W. Hollway and C. Urwin (eds), *Changing the Subject: Psychology, Social Regulation and Subjectivity*, London: Methuen.

Hollway, W. (1991) *Work Psychology and Organisational Behaviour: Managing the Individual at Work*, London: Sage.

Holton, R. J. and Turner, B. S. (1989) *Max Weber on Economy and Society*, London: Routledge.

Homans, G. C. (1961) *Social Behaviour: Its Elementary Forms*, London: Routledge & Kegan Paul.

Honey, P. and Mumford, A. (1982) *Manual of Learning Styles*, Maidenhead: Honey.

Hope, V. and Hendry, J. (1995) 'Corporate Culture: Is it Relevant for the Organisations of the 1990s?', *Human Resource Management Journal*, 5. 4: 61–73.

Höpfl, H. (1992) 'The Challenge of Change: The Theory and Practice of Organisational Transformations', paper presented to the Employment Research Unit Annual Conference, Cardiff Business School, September.

Höpfl, H., Smith, S. and Spencer, S. (1992) 'Values and Variations: The Conflicts between Culture Change and Job Cuts', *Personnel Review*, 21. 1: 24–38.

Hopkins, B. (2009) 'Inequality Street? Working Life in a British Chocolate Factory', in S. Bolton, and M. Houlihan (eds), *Work Matters: Critical Reflections on Contemporary Work*, Basingstoke: Palgrave Macmillan.

Hopper, T., Cooper, D., Lowe, T., Capps, T. and Mouritsen, J. (1986) 'Management Control and Worker Resistance in the National Coal Board: Financial Controls in the Labour Process', in D. Knights and H. Willmott (eds), *Managing the Labour Process*, Aldershot: Gower.

Hopwood, A. (1974) *Accounting and Human Behaviour*, London: Prentice Hall.

Horne, J. H. and Lupton, T. (1965) 'The Work Activities of Middle Managers', *Journal of Management Studies*, 2. 1: 14–33.

Hosking, D. and Morley, I. (1991) *A Social Psychology of Organising: People, Processes and Contexts*, Hemel Hempstead: Harvester Wheatsheaf.

Hosking, D. M. and Anderson, N. (1992) *Organisational Change and Innovation: Psychological Perspectives and Practices in Europe*, London: Sage.

Houlihan, M. (2002) 'Tensions and Variations in Call Centre Management Strategies', *Human Resource Management Journal*, 12. 4: 67–85.

House, R. J. and Mitchell, T. R. (1974) 'A Path-Goal Theory of Leadership', *Journal of Contemporary Business*, Autumn: 81–98.

Houseman, S.N., Kalleberg, A. L. and Erickcek, G.A. (2003) 'The Role of Temporary Help Employment in Tight Labor Markets', *Industrial and Labor Relations Review*, 57. 1: 105–27.

Howard, S. (1985) 'Big Blue's Big Family', *International Labour Reports*, March–April.

Howarth, N. and Hughes, S. (2000) 'Internationalisation, Industrial Relations Theory International Relations', *Journal of Industrial Relations*, 42. 2: 195–213.

HSE (2005) *Tackling stress: The Management Standards approach*, HSE, London: available at: http://www.hse.gov.uk/pubns/indg406.pdf

Huczynski, A. A. (1993) *Management Gurus*, London: Routledge.

Huczynski, A. and Buchanan, D. (2000) *Organizational Behaviour: An Introductory Text*, London: Financial Times/ Prentice Hall.

Hull, R. (2000) 'Knowledge Management and the Conduct of Expert Labour', in C. Prichard, R. Hull, M. Chumer and H. Willmott (eds), *Managing Knowledge: Critical Investigations of Work and Learning*, London: Macmillan.

Hunter, L. and MacInnes, J. (1992) 'Employers and Labour Flexibility: Evidence from the Case Studies', *Employment Gazette*, June: 307–15.

Huselid, M. (1995) 'The Impact of Human Resource Management Practices on Turnover, Production and Corporate Financial Performance', *Academy of Management Journal*, 38: 635–72.

Hutton, W. (1992) *The State We're In*, London: Cape.

Huws, U. (2003) *The Making of a Cybertariat*, New York: Monthly Review Press.

Huxley, A. (1954) *The Doors of Perception*, London: Chatto & Windus.

Hyman, R. (1981) 'Whatever Happened to Industrial Sociology?', in D. Dunkerley and G. Salaman (eds), *The International Yearbook of Organisation Studies 1980*, London: Routledge & Kegan Paul.

Hyman, R. (1986) 'Trade Unions and the Law: Papering Over the Cracks?', *Capital and Class*, 31: 93–114.

Hyman, R. (1987) 'Strategy or Structure: Capital, Labour and Control', *Work, Employment and Society*, 1. 1: 25–55.

Hyman, R. (1988) 'Flexible Specialisation: Miracle or Myth?' in R. Hyman and W. Streek (eds), *Trade Unions, Technology and Industrial Democracy*, Oxford: Blackwell.

Hyman, R. (1991) 'Plus ça Change? The Theory of Production and the Production of Theory', in A. Pollert (ed.), *Farewell to Flexibility?* Oxford: Oxford University Press.

Hyman, R. (2006) 'Marxist Thought and the Analysis of Work', in M. Korczynski, R. Hodson and P. Edwards (eds), *Social Theory at Work*, Oxford: Oxford University Press.

Ibanez, T. and Ininguez, L. (eds) (1997) *Critical Social Psychology*, London: Sage.

Hyman, J., Scholarios, D. and Baldry, C. (2005) 'Getting On or Getting By? Employee Flexibility and Coping Strategies for Home and Work', *Work, Employment & Society*, 19. 4: 705–25.

Ibarra, H. (1993) 'Personal Networks of Women and Minorities in Management: A Conceptual Framework', *Academy of Management Review*, 18: 56–87.

Ibarra, H. (1995) 'Race, Opportunity and Diversity of Social Circles in Managerial Networks', *Academy of Management Journal*, 38: 673–703.

Ichinowski, C., Kochan, T., Levine, D., Olsen, C. and Strauss, G. (1996) 'What Works at Work: Overview and Assessment', *Industrial Relations*, 35. 3: 299–333.

Ignacio García-Pérez, J. and Muñoz-Bullón, F. (2005) 'Temporary Help Agencies and Occupational Mobility', *Oxford Bulletin of Economics and Statistics*, 67 2: 163–80.

IHSM Consultants (1994) *Creative Career Paths in the NHS, Report no. 1: Top Managers*, London: Department of Health.

Inkson, K. (1993) 'Do Careers Exist? Studies of Managerial Job Change in the 90s', paper presented to the ANZAM Conference, Deakin University.

Institute of Management (1994) *The 1994 National Management Salary Survey*, London: Institute of Management.

Institute of Management (1995) *Survival of the Fittest: A Survey of Manager's Experience of and Attitudes to Work in the Post-Recession Economy*, London: Institute of Management.

Institute of Management (1996) *Are Managers under Stress? A Survey of Management Morale*, London: Institute of Management.

IPM Digest (1986) 'Flexibility: In Search of a Definition', *IPM Digest*, no. 253: August.

Israel, J. and Tajfel, H. (eds) (1972) *The Context of Social Psychology: A Critical Assessment*, London: Academic Press.

Itoh, M. (1984) 'Labour Control in Small Groups', *Radical America*, 18. 2, 3.

Izraeli, D. N. and Adler, N. J. (1994) 'Competitive Frontiers: Women Managers in a Global Economy', in N. J. Adler and D. N. Izraeli (eds), *Competitive Frontiers: Women Managers in a Global Economy*, Oxford: Blackwell.

Jackall, R. (1988) *Moral Mazes: The World of Corporate Managers*, Oxford: Oxford University Press.

Jackson, N. and Carter, P. (1991) 'In Defence of Paradigm Commensurability', *Organisation Studies*, 12. 1: 109–27.

Jackson, N. and Carter, P. (2000) *Rethinking Organisational Behaviour*, Harlow: Financial Times/Prentice Hall.

Jackson, P. (ed.) (1999) *Virtual Working: Social and Organisational Dynamics*, London: Routledge.

Jackson, T. (1994) *Organisational Behaviour in International Management*, Oxford: Butterworth-Heinemann.

Jacoby, S. (2005) *The Embedded Corporation: Corporate Governance and Employment Relations in Japan and the United States*, Princeton University Press.

Jacques, E. (1990) 'In Praise of Hierarchy', *Harvard Business Review*, Jan.–Feb.: 127–134.

Jacques, R. (1996) *Manufacturing the Employee: Management Knowledge From the 19th to the 21st Centuries*, London: Sage.

James, K., Lovato, C., Khoo, G. *et al.* (1994) 'Social Identity Correlations of Minority Worker's Health', *Academy of Management Journal*, 37. 2, April: 383–96.

Janis, I. L. (1972) *Victims of Groupthink: A Psychological Study of Foreign Policy Decisions and Fiascoes*, Boston, MA: Houghton Mifflin.

Janis, I. L. and Mann, L. (1977) *Decision Making: A Psychological Analysis of Conflict, Choice and Commitment*, New York: Free Press.

Jeffreys, S. (1990) *Anticlimax*, London: Women's Press.

Jenkins, A. (1994) 'Teams: From Ideology to Analysis', *Organisation Studies*, 15. 6: 849–60.

Jenkins, C. D. (1979) 'Psychosocial Modifiers of Response to Stress', *Journal of Human Stress*, 5. 4: 3–15.

Jenkins, R. (1982) 'Management, Recruitment Procedures and Black Workers', *Working Papers on Ethnic Relations*, no. 18, Birmingham Research Unit on Ethnic Relations.

Jenkins, R. (1984) 'Divisions over the International Division of Labour', *Capital and Class*, 34: 28–57.

Jenkins, R. (1986) *Racism and Recruitment: Managers, Organisations and Equal Opportunities in the Labour Market*, Cambridge: Cambridge University Press.

Jenkins, S. and Delbridge., R. (2007) 'Disconnected Workplaces: Interests and Identities in the "High Performance" Factory', in S. Bolton and M. Houlihan (eds), *Searching for the Human in Human Resource Management*, Basingstoke: Palgrave Press.

Jermier, J., Knights, D. and Nord, W. R. (eds) (1994) *Resistance and Power in Organisations*, London: Routledge.

Jessop, B. (1992) 'Towards the Schumpetarian Welfare State: Global Capitalism and Structural Competitiveness', unpublished paper.

Jewell, L. N. and Seigel, M. (1990) *Contemporary Industrial/Organisational Psychology* (2nd edn), St Paul, MN: West Publishing.

Jewson, N. and Mason, N. (1986) 'The Theory and Practice of Equal Opportunity Policies: Liberal and Radical Approaches', *Sociological Review*, 34: 307–34.

Johns, G. (1993) 'Constraints on the Adoption of Psychology-Based Personnel Practices: Lessons from Organisational Innovation', *Personnel Psychology*, 46: 569–92.

Johnson, I. and Moore, K. (1986) *The Tapestry Makers: Life and Work at Lee's Tapestry Works*, Birkenhead: Merseyside Docklands Community Project.

Johnson, P. and Gill, J. (1993) *Management Control and Organisational Behaviour*, London: Paul Chapman.

Johnson, T. (1972) *Professions and Power*, London: Macmillan.

Johnson, T. (1980) 'Work and Power', in G. Esland and G. Salaman (eds), *The Politics of Work and Occupations*, Milton Keynes: Open University Press.

Johnston, L. (1986) *Marxism, Class Analysis and Socialist Pluralism*, London: Allen & Unwin.

Jones, A. M. and Hendry, C. (1994) 'The Learning Organisation: Adult Learning and Organisational Transformation', *British Journal of Management*, 5. 2: 153–62.

Jones, A. N. and Cooper, C. L. (1980) *Combating Managerial Obsolescence*, Westport, CT: Greenwood.

Jones, B. (1991) 'A New Convergence?', *Work, Employment and Society*, 5. 1: 493–5.

Jones, B. (1997) *Forcing the Factory of the Future: Cybernation and Societal Institutions*, Cambridge: Cambridge University Press.

Jones, B. (1998) 'Whatever Happened to the Automatic Factory? A New Perspective on the Mutations of Fordism', paper presented to the Work, Employment and Society Conference, University of Cambridge, September.

Jones, C., Nickson, D. and Taylor, G. (1997) 'Whatever It Takes? Managing Empowered Workers and the Service Encounter in an International Hotel Chain', *Work, Employment and Society*, 11. 3: 541–54.

Jones, C., Thompson, P. and Nickson, D. (1998) 'Not Part of the Family? The Limits to Managing the Corporate Way in International Hotel Chains', *International Journal of Human Resource Management*, 9. 6: 1048–63.

Jones, F., Bright, J. and Clow, A. (2001) *Stress: Myth, Research and Theory*, Harlow: Pearson Education.

Jones, G. (1978) 'Ideological Responses to Deskilling of Managerial Work', paper presented to the Conference on Deskilling, Nuffield.

Jones, O. (1994) 'Professionalism and Work Study: An Alternative Perspective on Subjectivity and the Labour Process', paper presented to the 12th International Labour Process Conference, Aston.

Jones, O. (1997) 'Changing the Balance? Taylorism, TQM and Work Organisation', *New Technology, Work and Employment*, 12. 1: 13–24.

Jowett, G. S. and O'Donnell, V. O. (1992) *Propaganda and Persuasion* (2nd edn), Newbury Park, CA: Sage.

Joyce, P. (1980) *Work, Society and Politics*, London: Methuen.

Jürgens, U., Naumnann, K. and Rupp, J. (2000) 'Shareholder Value in an Adverse Environment: The German Case', *Economy and Society*, 29.1: 54–79.

Kahle, L. R. (1984) *Attitudes and Social Adaptation*, Oxford: Pergamon.

Kamata, S. (1982) *Japan in the Passing Lane*, London: Pantheon.

Kamin, L. (1979) *The Science and Politics of IQ*, Harmondsworth: Penguin.

Kamoche, K. (1991) 'Human Resource Management: A Multiparadigmatic Analysis', *Personnel Review*, 20. 4: 3–14.

Kamoche, K. (1994) 'A Critique and a Proposed Reformulation of Strategic Human Resource Management', *Human Resource Management Journal*, 4. 4: 29–47.

Kandola, R. and Fullerton, J. (1994) *Managing the Mosaic: Diversity in Action*, London: Institute of Personnel Development.

Kanigel, R. (1997) *The One Best Way: Frederick Winslow Taylor and the Enigma of Efficiency*, New York: Penguin.

Kanter, R. M. (1968) 'Commitment and Social Organisation: A Study of Commitment in Utopian Communities', *American Sociological Review*, 33. 4: 499–517.

Kanter, R. M. (1977) *Work and Family in the United States: A Critical Review and Agenda for Research and Policy*, New York: Russell Sage Foundation.

Kanter, R. M. (1984) *The Change Masters*, London: Unwin.

Kanter, R. M. (1993) *Men and Women of the Corporation* (2nd edn), New York: Basic Books.

Kaplan, R. S. and Norton, D. P. (1992) 'The Balanced Scorecard: Measures that Drive Performance', *Harvard Business Review*, Jan.–Feb.: 71–80.

Kaplan, R. S. and Norton D. P. (1996) 'Using the Balanced Scorecard as a Strategic Management System', *Harvard Business Review*, Jan.–Feb.: 75–85.

Karasek, R. and Theorell, T. (1990) *Healthy Work: Stress, Productivity and the Reconstruction of Working Life*, New York: Basic Books.

Karmel, B. (ed.) (1980) *Point and Counterpoint in Organizations*, Hinsdale, IL: Dryden.

Kärreman, D., Sveningsson, S. and Alvesson, M. (2002) 'The Return of the Machine Bureaucracy? Management Control and Knowledge Work'. *International Studies of Management and Organizations*, 32. 2: 70–92.

Katz, D. and Kahn, T. (1970) 'Open Systems Theory', in O. Grusky and G. A. Miller (eds), *The Sociology of Organizations: Basic Studies*, New York: Free Press.

Katz, D. and Kahn, R. L. (1966) *The Social Psychology of Organisations* (1978, 2nd edn), New York: Wiley.

Katz, F. E. (1968) *Autonomy and Organizations: The Limits of Social Control*, New York: Random House.

Katz, G. (1982) 'Previous Conformity, Status, and the Rejection of the Deviant', *Small Group Behaviour*, 13: 402–14.

Katz, H. (2005) 'Industrial Relations and Work', in S. Ackroyd, R. Batt, P. Thompson and P. Tolbert (eds), *The Oxford Handbook of Work and Organization*, Oxford: Oxford University Press.

Kaufman, P. (2003) Learning to *Not* Labor: How Working-Class Individuals Construct Middle-Class Identities, *Sociological Quarterly*, 44. 3, June: 481–504.

Keenoy, T. (1992) 'Constructing Control', in J. F. Hartley and G. M. Stephenson (eds), *Employment Relations*, Oxford: Blackwell.

Keep, E. (2000) 'Creating a Knowledge Economy: Definitions, Challenges and Opportunities', paper presented to the Progress Conference, The 21st Century Challenge, London: September.

Keep, E. and Mayhew, K. (1999) 'Towards the Knowledge-Driven Economy: Some Policy Issues', *Renewal*, 7. 4: 50–59, 60–71.

Keith, B. and Collinson, D. (1994) 'Policing Gender: Barriers to Change in the Police', paper presented to the 12th Annual International Labour Process Conference, Aston University, March.

Kelley, H. (1971) 'The Warm–Cold Variable in First Impressions of Persons', *Journal of Personality*, 18: 431–39.

Kellner, D. (1988) 'Postmodernism as Social Theory: Some Challenges and Problems', *Theory, Culture and Society*, 5: 239–63.

Kellner, D. (1999) 'Theorising/Resisting McDonaldization: A Multiperspectivist Approach', in B. Smart, *Resisting McDonaldization*, London: Sage.

Kelly, A. and Brannick, T. (1987) 'Personnel Practices and Strong Organisational Cultures in Ireland', paper presented at Conference on Japanisation of British Industry, UMIST.

Kelly, G. A. (1955) *The Psychology of Personal Constructs* (2 vols), New York: Norton.

Kelly, J. E. (1982) *Scientific Management, Job Design and Work Performance*, London: Academic Press.

Kelly, J. E. (1985) 'Management's Redesign of Work', in D. Knights, H. Willmott and D. Collinson (eds), *Job Redesign: Critical Perspectives on the Labour Process*, Aldershot: Gower.

Kelly, K. (1994) *Out of Control: The Rise of Neo-Biological Civilisation*, Reading, Mass.: Addison-Wesley.

Kelly, K. (1999) *New Rules for the New Economy*, London: Fourth Estate.

Kelly, J. (2005) 'Labour Movements and Mobilization', in S. Ackroyd, R. Batt, P. Thompson and Pamela Tolbert (eds), *The Oxford Handbook of Work and Organization*, Oxford, Oxford University Press.

Kelman, H. (1961) 'The Processes of Opinion Change', *Public Opinion*, 25: 57–78.

Keltner, J. W. (1973) *Elements of Interpersonal Communication*, Belmont, CA: Wadsworth.

Kent, R. L. and Martinko, M. J. (1995a) 'The Measurement of Attributions in Organizational Research', in M. J. Martinko (ed.), *Attribution Theory: An Organizational Perspective*, Delray Beach, FL: St Lucie Press, pp. 17–34.

Kent, R. L. and Martinko, M. J. (1995b) 'The Development and Evaluation of a Scale to Measure Organizational Attribution Style', in M. J. Martinko (ed.), *Attribution Theory: An Organizational Perspective*, Delray Beach, FL: St Lucie Press, 53–75.

Kerfoot, D. and Knights, D. (1994) 'Empowering the "Quality Worker": The Seduction and Contradiction of the Total Quality Phenomenon', in A. Wilkinson and H. Willmott (eds), *Making Quality Critical*, London: Routledge & Kegan Paul.

Kerr, C., Dunlop, J. J., Harbison, F. H. and Mayers, C. A. (1960) *Industrialism and Industrial Man*, Cambridge, MA: Harvard University Press.

Kersley, B., Alpin, C., Forth, J., Bryson, A., Bewley, H., Dix, G. and Oxenbridge, S. (2005) *Inside the Workplace: First Findings from the 2004 Workplace Employment Relations Survey*, London: DTI.

Kessler, I., Purcell, J. and Shapiro, J.C. (2000) 'New Forms of Employment Relations in the Public Services', *Industrial Relations Journal*, 31. 1: 17–34.

Kets de Vries, M. R. F. and Miller, D. (1984) *The Neurotic Organisation: Diagnosing and Changing Counterproductive Styles of Management*, San Francisco: Jossey-Bass.

Khandwalla, P. N. (1974) 'Viable and Effective Organisational Design of Firms', *Academy of Management Journal*: Sept.: 481–95.

Kieser, A. (1993) 'Review of Geert Hofstede, "Cultures and Organizations: Software of the Mind"', *Organisation Studies*, 14. 1: 85–8.

Kimmel, M. S. (1993) 'What do Men Want?' *Harvard Business Review*, Nov.–Dec.: 50–63.

King, N. and Anderson, N. (1995) *Innovation and Change in Organisations*, London: Routledge.

Kipnis, D. and Schmidt, S. M. (1988) 'Upward Influence Styles: Relationship with Performance Evaluations, Salary and Stress', *Administrative Science Quarterly*, 33: 528–42.

Kirton, G. and Greene, A.-M. (2000) *The Dynamics of Managing Diversity: A Critical Approach*, Oxford: Butterworth Heinemann.

Kitschelt, W. (1992) 'Industrial Governance Structures, Innovation Strategies and the Case of Japan: Sectoral or Cross-National Comparison?' *International Organisation*, 45. 4: 163–88.

Klandermans, B. and Oegma, D. (1992) 'Potentials, Networks, Motivations and Barriers: Steps Toward Participation in Social Movements', *American Sociological Review*, 52: 519–31.

Klein, H. J. (1989) 'An Integrated Control Theory Model of Work Motivation', *Academy of Management Journal*, 14. 2: 150–72.

Knights, D. and Collinson, D. (1987) 'Shop Floor Culture and the Problem of Managerial Control', in J. McGoldrick (ed.), *Business Case File in Behavioural Science*, London: Van Nystrand.

Knights, D. and McCabe, D. (2000) 'Bewitched, Bothered and Bewildered: The Meaning and Experience of Teamworking for Employees in an Automobile Company', *Human Relations*, 53. 11: 1481–517.

Knights, D. and Morgan, G. (1990) 'The Concept of Strategy in Sociology: A Note of Dissent', *Sociology*, 24: 475–83.

Knights, D. and Willmott, H. (1985) 'Power and Identity in Theory and Practice', *Sociological Review*, 33. 1: 22–46.

Knights, D. and Willmott, H. (eds) (1986a) *Gender and the Labour Process*, Aldershot: Gower.

Knights, D. and Willmott, H. (eds) (1986b) *Managing the Labour Process*, Aldershot: Gower.

Knights, D. and Willmott, H. (eds) (1988) *New Technology and the Labour Process*, London: Macmillan.

Knights, D. and Willmott, H. (1989) 'Power and Subjectivity at Work: From Degradation to Subjugation in Social Relations', *Sociology*, 23. 4: 535–58.

Knights, D. and Willmott, H. (eds) (1990) *Labour Process Theory*, London: Macmillan.

Knights, D. and Willmott, H. (eds) (2000) *The Reengineering Revolution*, London: Sage.

Knights, D. and Willmott, H. (2006) *Introducing Organizational Behaviour and Management*, London: Thomson Learning.

Knights, D., Willmott, H. and Collinson, D. (eds) (1985) *Job Redesign: Critical Perspectives on the Labour Process*, London: Gower.

Knoke, D. (1990) *Political Networks: The Structural Perspective*, New York: Cambridge University Press.

Koch, M. (2004) 'Labour Market Regulation after Fordism; Five Countries Compared', in P. Littlewood, I. Glorieux, and I. Jönsson (eds), *The Future of Work in Europe*, Aldershot: Ashgate

Kochan, T. (2006) 'Social Legitimacy of the Human Resource Management Profession: a U.S. Perspective', in P. Boxall, J. Purcell and P. Wright (eds), *Oxford Handbook of Human Resource Management*, Oxford: Oxford University Press.

Kochan, T., Katz, H. C. and McKersie, R. B. (1986) *The Transformation of American Industrial Relations*, New York: Basic Books.

Kochan, T. and Osterman, P. (1994) *The Mutual Gains Enterprise*, Boston, MA: Harvard Business School Press.

Kodz, J., Harper, H. and Dench, S. (2002) *Work-Life Balance: Beyond the Rhetoric*, Report 384, Institute for Employment Studies, March.

Köhler, W. (1925) *The Mentality of Apes*, London: Kegan Paul, Trench, Trubner & Co.

Kohn, M. L. and Schooler, C. (1983) *Work and Personality: An Inquiry into the Effects of Social Stratification*, Norwood, NJ: Ablex.

Kolb, D. A. (1976) *The Learning Style Inventory: Technical Manual*, Boston, MA: MacBer.

Komter, A. (1991) 'Gender, Power and Feminist Theory', in K. Davis, M. Leijenaar and J. Oldersma (eds), *The Gender of Power*, London: Sage.

Kondo, G. (1990) *Craftinvg Selves*, Chicago: University of Chicago Press.

Konzelmann, S., Wilkinson, F. and Mankelow. R. (2007) 'Work Intensification and Employment Insecurity in Professional Work', Centre for Business Research, University of Cambridge, Working Paper No. 345.

Korte, R. F. (2007) 'A Review of Social Identity Theory with Implications for Training and Development', *Journal of European Industrial Training*, 31. 3: 166–80.

Kotter, J. (1982) *The General Manager*, New York: Free Press.

Kouzmin, A. (1980) 'Control in Organisational Analysis: The Lost Politics', in D. Dunkerley and G. Salaman (eds), *The International Yearbook of Organisation Studies 1979*, London: Routledge & Kegan Paul.

Kraft, P. (1999) 'To Control and Inspire: US Management in the Age of Computer Information Systems and Global Production', in M. Wardell, T. L. Steiger and P. Meiksens (eds), *Rethinking the Labor Process*, Albany: State University of New York Press.

Kraft, P. and Dubnoff, S. (1986) 'Job Characteristics in Computer Software', *Industrial Relations* (USA), 25. 2: 179–95.

Kram, K. E. (1983) 'Phases of the Mentor Relationship', *Academy of Management Journal*, 26: 608–35.

Krugman, P. (1999) *The Return of Depression Economics*, London: Allen Lane.

Kuhn, T. (1970) *The Structure of Scientific Revolutions* (2nd edn), Chicago: University of Chicago Press.

Kumar, K. (1996) *From Post-Industrial to Post-Modern Society*, Oxford: Blackwell.

Kunda, G. (1992) *Engineering Culture: Control and Commitment in a High Tech Corporation*, Philadelphia: Temple University Press.

Kunda, G. and Ailon-Souday, G. (2005) 'Management, Markets and Ideologies Design and Devotion Revisited', in S. Ackroyd, R. Batt, P. Thompson and P. Tolbert (eds), *The Oxford Handbook of Work and Organization*, Oxford: Oxford University Press

Kyotani, E. (1999) 'New Managerial Strategies of Japanese Corporations', in A. Felstead and N. Jewson (eds), *Global Trends in Flexible Labour*, London: Macmillan.

Labour Research Department (1986a) *Flexibility Examined, Bargaining Report*, London: LRD.

Labour Research Department (1986b) *Franchising – Who Really Benefits?* August, London: LRD.

Labour Research Department (1988) *Stress at Work: The Trade Union Response*, London: LRD.

Labour Research Department (2006) *Stress at work*, LRD Booklets, April.

Lair, D. J., Sullivan, K. and Cheney, G. (2005) 'Marketization and the Recasting of the Professional Self: The Rhetoric and Ethics of Personal Branding', *Management Communication Quarterly*, 18. 3: 307–43.

Landes, D. S. (1969) *The Unbound Prometheus*, Cambridge: Cambridge University Press.

Landry, C., Morley, D., Southwood, R. and Wright, P. (1985) *What a Way to Run a Railroad: An Analysis of Radical Failure*, London: Comedia.

Landy, F. J. (2005) 'Some Historical and Scientific Issues Related to Research on Emotional Intelligence', *Journal of Organizational Behavior*, 26. 4: 411–24.

Lane, C. (1991) 'Industrial Reorganisation in Europe', *Work, Employment and Society*, 5. 4: 515–39.

Langer, E. J. (1981) 'Rethinking the Role of Thought in Social Interaction', in J. H. Harvey, W. Ickes and R. F. Kidd (eds), *New Directions in Attribution Research*, vol. 2, New York: Erlbaum.

Lansisalmi, H., Peiro, J. M. and Kivimaki, M. (2000) 'Collective Stress and Coping in the Cof Organizational Culture', *European Journal of Work and Organizational Psychology*, 9. 4: 527–59.

Larsen, K. S. (1980) *Social Psychology: Crisis or Failure?*, Monmouth, OR: Institute for Theoretical History.

Lasch, C. (1985) *The Minimal Self: Psychic Survival in Troubled Times*, London: Picador.

Lash, S. and Urry, J. (1987) *The End of Organized Capitalism*, Cambridge: Polity.

Lawler, E., Mohrman, I. and Ledford, G. E. (1995) *Creating High Performance Organizations*, San Francisco: Jossey-Bass.

Lawlor, E. E. (1976) 'Control Systems in Organizations', in H. D. Dunnette (ed.), *Handbook of Industrial and Organisational Psychology*, Chicago: Rand McNally.

Lawrence, F. (2004) 'Wanted: Workers Who are Flexible, Cheap and Expendable', *The Guardian*, 9 February.

Lawrence, J. F. (1985) Saturn Project: An Experiment in Togetherness, *Los Angeles Times*, 10 November.

Lawrence, P. R. and Lorsch, J. W. (1967) *Organisation and Environment*, Cambridge, MA: Harvard University Press.

Lawrence, T.B. and Philips, N. (2002) 'Understanding Cultural Industries', *Journal of Management Inquiry*, 11. 4: 430–41.

Layder, D. (1987) 'Key Issues in Structuration Theory: Some Critical Remarks', *Current Perspectives in Social Theory*, 8: 25–46.

Layton, E. T. (1969) 'Science, Business and the American Engineer', in R. Perruci and J. E. Gersth (eds), *The Engineer and the Social System*, New York: Wiley.

Lazarus, R. S. (1966) *Psychological Stress and the Coping Process*, New York: McGraw-Hill.

Lazarus. R.S., and Folkman, S. (1984). *Stress, Appraisal and Coping*. New York: Springer Publishing Company Inc.

Lazonick, W. and O'Sullivan, M. (2000) 'Maximising Shareholder Value: a New Ideology for Corporate Governance', *Economy and Society*, 29. 1: 13–35.

Leadbetter, C. (1999) *Living on Thin Air: The New Economy*, London: Viking.

Lerner, R. (2001) *Concepts and Theories of Human Development*, Mahwah, NJ: Lawrence Erlbaum Associates.

Leavitt, H. J. (1951) 'Some Effects of Certain Communication Patterns on Group Performance', *Journal of Abnormal and Social Psychology*, 46: 38–50.

Leavitt, H. J. (1965) 'Applied Organisational Change in Industry: Structural, Technological and Humanistic Approaches', in J. G. March (ed.), *Handbook of Organizations*, Chicago: Rand McNally.

Leavitt, H. J. (1978) *Managerial Psychology* (4th edn), Chicago: UCP.

Leavitt, H. J. and Bahrami, H. (1988) *Managerial Psychology: Managing Behaviour in Organizations* (5th edn), Chicago: University of Chicago Press.

Ledwith, S. and Colgan, F. (eds) (1996) *Women in Organisations: Challenging Gender Politics*, London: Macmillan.

Lee, B. (1985) 'Internal Politics', in K. Elliot and P. Lawrence (eds), *Introducing Management*, Harmondsworth: Penguin.

Lee, R. and Lawrence, P. (1985) *Organisational Behaviour: Psychology at Work*, London: Hutchinson.

Leflaive, X. (1996) 'Organisations as Structures of Domination', *Organisation Studies*, 17. 1: 23–47.

Legge, K. (1978) *Power, Innovation and Problem-Solving in Management*, London: Hutchinson.

Legge, K. (1989) 'Human Resource Management: A Critical Analysis', in J. Storey (ed.), *New Perspectives in Human Resource Management*, London: Routledge.

Legge, K. (1995) *Human Resource Management: The Rhetorics, the Realities*, London: Macmillan.

Legge, K. (2005) 'Human Resource Management', in S. Ackroyd, R. Batt, P. Thompson and P. Tolbert (eds), *The Oxford Handbook of Work and Organization*, Oxford: Oxford University Press

Lehman, C. and Tinker, T. (1985) 'The Not-So-Great Society: The Role of Business Literature on Reshuffling Johnson's New Deal', paper presented to the Conference on the Labour Process, Aston-UMIST.

Leidner, R. (1993) *Fast Food, Fast Talk: Service Work and the Routinization of Everyday Life*, Berkeley: University of California Press.

Leidner, R. (2006) 'Identity and Work', in M. Korczynski, R. Hodson and P. Edwards (eds), *Social Theory at Work*, Oxford: Oxford University Press.

Leinberger, P. and Tucker, B. (1991) *The New Individualists: The Generation After the Organization Man*, New York: Harper Collins.

Leonard, P. (1984) *Personality and Ideology: Towards a Materialist Understanding of the Individual*, London: Macmillan.

Lessem, R. (1985) 'The Enabling Company', in D. Clutterbuck (ed.), *New Patterns of Work*, Aldershot: Gower.

Lessem, R. (1986) *The Roots of Excellence*, London: Fontana.

Leverment, Y., Ackers, P. and Preston, D. (1998) 'Professionals in the NHS: A Case Study of Business Process Re-engineering', *New Technology, Work and Employment*, 13. 2: 129–39.

Levitt, T. (1991) 'The Globalization of Markets', in C. A. Montgomery and M. E. Porter (eds), *Strategy Seeking and Securing Competitive Advantage*, Boston, MA: Harvard Business School Press.

Lewin, K, Lippitt, R. and White, R. K. (1939) 'Patterns of Aggressive Behaviour in Experimentally Created Social Climates', *Journal of Social Psychology*, 10: 271–301.

Lewin, K. (1947) 'Frontiers in Group Dynamics', *Human Relations*, 1: 5–41.

Lewin, K. (1951) *Field Theory in Social Science*, New York: Harper & Row.

Lewin, K. (1956) 'Studies in Group Decision', in D. Cartwright and A. Zander (eds) *Group Dynamics: Research and Theory* (2nd edn), Evanston, IL: Row Peterson.

Lewis, M. (1975) 'Early Sex Differences in the Human: Studies of Socioemotional Development', *Archives of Sexual Behaviour*, 4. 4: 329–35.

Lewis, P. and Simpson, R. (2007) 'Gender and Emotions: Introduction', in P. Lewis and R. Simpson, *Gendering Emotions in Organizations*, Basingstoke: Palgrave Macmillan.

Lewis, R. (ed.) (1984) *Open Learning in Action: Case Studies, Open Learning Guide 1*, London: Council for Educational Technology.

Lewis, R. A. (1991) 'Models for Managing Change', *Management Development Review*, 4. 5: 3–6.

Lewis, S. and Cooper, Cary L. (1996) 'Balancing the Work and Family Interface: A European Perspective', *Human Resource Management Review*, 5: 289–305.

Liff, S. (1997) 'Two Routes to Managing Diversity: Individual Differences or Social Group Characteristics?' *Employee Relations*, 19. 1: 11–26.

Liff, S. (1999) 'Diversity and Equal Opportunities: Room for a Constructive Compromise?', *Human Resource Management Journal*, 19. 1: 65–75.

Likert, R. (1961) *New Patterns of Management*, New York: McGraw-Hill.

Limerick, D., Passfield, R. and Cunnington, B. (1994) 'Transformational Change: Towards an Action Learning Organisation', *The Learning Organisation*, 1. 2: 29–40.

Lincoln, J. and Guillot, D. (2006) 'A Durkheimean View of Organizational Culture', in M. Korczynski, R. Hodson and P. Edwards (eds), *Social Theory at Work*, Oxford: Oxford University Press.

Lindblom, C. E. (1959) 'The Science of Muddling Through', *Public Administration Review*, 19: 79–88.

Linnehan, F. and Konrad, A. (1999) 'Diluting Diversity: Implications for Inter-Group Inequality in Organizations', *Journal of Management Inquiry*, 8. 4: 399–414.

Linstead, A. and Catlow, G. (2004) 'Dilemmas beyond the Glass Ceiling: The Performances of Senior Women Managers in the National Health Service', in M. Dent, J. Chandler and J. Barry (eds), *Questioning the New Public Management*, London: Blackwell.

Linstead, S. and Grafton Small, R. G. (1992) 'On Reading Organisation Culture', *Organisation Studies*, 13. 3: 331–45.

Lipietz, A. (1982) 'Towards Global Fordism?' *New Left Review*, 132: 33–47.

Lippman, W. (1922) *Social Opinion*, New York: Harcourt Brace.

Littler, C. R. (1980) 'Internal Contract and the Transition to Modern Work Systems', in D. Dunkerley and G. Salaman (eds), *The International Yearbook of Organisation Studies 1979*, London: Routledge & Kegan Paul.

Littler, C. R. (1982) *The Development of the Labour Process in Capitalist Societies*, London: Heinemann.

Littler, C. R., Bramble, B. and McDonald, J. (1994) *Organisational Restructuring: Downsizing, Delayering and Managing Change at Work*, Canberra: Commonwealth of Australia.

Littler, C. R. and Salaman, G. (1982) 'Bravermania and Beyond', *Sociology*, 132: 33–47.

Littlewood , P., Ignace, G. and Jonsson, I. (2004) 'To Work Or Not To Work Changing Constraints and Opportunities in Western Europe', in P. Littlewood, I. Glorieux, and I. Jönsson (eds), *The Future of Work in Europe*, Aldershot: Ashgate.

Littwak, E. (1999) *Turbo Capitalism*, London: Orion Books.

Livingstone, D. W. and Scholtz, A. (2006) 'Contradictions of Labour Processes and Worker's Use of Skills in Advanced Capitalist Economies' in V. Shalla and W. Clement (eds), *Work in Tumultuous Times*, Montreal: McGill.

Lloyd, C. and Payne, J. (2006) 'Goodbye to All That? A Critical Re-evaluation of the Role of the High Performance Work Organization within the UK Skills Debate', *Work, Employment and Society*, 20. 1: 51–165.

Lloyd, M. (1993) 'The (F)utility of a Feminist Turn to Foucault', *Economy and Society*, 22. 4: 437–60.

Locke, E. and Latham, G. P. (1984) *Goal Setting: A Motivational Technique that Works!* London: Prentice Hall.

Lockett, M. (1988) 'Culture and the Problems of Chinese Management', *Organisation Studies*, 9. 4: 484–97.

Lodge, D. (1990) *Nice Work*, Harmondsworth: Penguin.

Lounsbury, M. and Ventresca, M.J. (2003) 'The New Structuralism in Organization Theory', *Organization*, 10. 1: 457–80.

Loveridge, R. (1982) 'Business Strategy and Community Culture', in D. Dunkerley and G. Salaman (eds), *The International Yearbook of Organisation Studies 1979*, London: Routledge & Kegan Paul.

Lucas, M. (1986) *How to Survive the 9–5*, Thames: Methuen.

Lukes, S. (1974) *Power: A Radical View*, London: Macmillan.

Lukes, S. (2005) *Power: A Radical View* (2nd edn), Basingstoke: Palgrave Macmillan.

Lupton, T. and Gowler, D. (1969) *Selecting a Wage Payment System*, London: Kogan Page.

Luthans, F. (1981) *Organisation Behaviour* (3rd edn), New York: McGraw-Hill.

Mabey, C., Salaman, G. and Storey, J. (1998) 'Strategic Human Resource Management: The Theory of Practice and the Practice of Theory', in C. Mabey, G. Salaman and J. Storey (eds), *Strategic Human Resource Management*, London: Sage.

McArdle, L., Proctor, S. J., Rawlinson, M., Hassard, J. and Forrester, P. (1994) 'Total Quality Management and Participation: Employee Involvement or the Enhancement of Exploitation?', in A. Wilkinson and H. Willmott (eds), *Making Quality Critical*, London: Routledge.

McAuley, J., Johnson, P. and Duberley, J. (2006) *Organization Theory: Challenges and Perspectives*, London: Pearson Higher Education.

McCabe, D. (2000) 'The Team Dream: The Meaning and Experience of Teamworking for Employees in an Automobile Manufacturing Company', in S. Proctor and F. Mueller (eds), *Teamworking*, London: Macmillan.

McCann, D. (1988) *'How to Influence Others at Work'*, London: Heinemann.

McCann, L., Hassard, J. and Morris, J. (2008) 'Normalised Intensity – The New Labour Process of Middle Management', in *Journal of Management Studies*, 45. 2: 343–71.

McClelland, D. (1961) *The Achieving Society*, New York: Van Nostrand.

Maccoby, M. (1977) *The Gamesman*, New York: Simon & Schuster.

McCullough, A. and Shannon, M. (1977) 'Organisation and Protection', in S. Clegg and D. Dunkerley (eds), *Critical Issues and Organizations*, London: Routledge & Kegan Paul.

MacDuffie, J. P. (1995) 'Human Resource Bundles and Manufacturing Performance: Organisational Logic and Flexible Production Systems in the World Auto Industry', *Industrial and Labor Relations Review*, 48: 197–221.

McGill, M., Slocum, J. and Lei, D. (1992) 'Management Practices in Learning Organisations', *Organisational Dynamics* (Summer): 5–17.

McGregor, D. (1960) *The Human Side of the Enterprise*, New York: Harper & Row.

McHugh, D. (1997) 'Self-Serving Bias: The Attribution of Cause as a Significant Form of Managerial Labour', paper presented to the 15th International Labour Process Conference, Edinburgh University, March.

McHugh, D., Groves, D. and Alker, A. (1994) 'Cultural Heuristics and Behavioural Change: What do We Learn from a Learning Organisation?' paper presented to the Conference on the Strategic Direction of HRM, Nottingham-Trent University, December.

McHugh, D., Groves, D. and Alker, A. (1998) 'Self-Managed Learning and Behavioural Change: What do we Learn from a Learning Organisation?', *The Learning Organisation*, 5. 5: 209–20.

MacInnes, J. (1987) *Thatcherism at Work*, Milton Keynes: Open University Press.

McKenna, E. (1987) *Psychology in Business: Theory and Applications*, London: Lawrence Erlbaum.

McKenna, E. (1994) *Business Psychology and Organisational Behaviour: A Student's Handbook*, Hove: Lawrence Erlbaum.

McKenna, E, (2000) *Business Psychology and Organisational Behaviour* (3rd edn), Hove: Psychology Press.

McKinlay, A. (1999) 'Recasting the Visible Hand? Strategy, Structure and Process in UK Manufacturing, c. 1970–97', *Contemporary British History*, 13. 3: 148–63.

McKinlay, A. (2000) 'The Bearable Lightness of Control: Organisational Reflexivity and the Politics of Knowledge Management', in C. Prichard, R. Hull, M. Chumer and H. Willmott (eds), *Managing Knowledge: Critical Investigations of Work and Learning*, London: Macmillan.

McKinlay, A. (2002) 'The Limits of Knowledge Management', *New Technology, Work and Employment*, 17. 2: 76–88.

McKinlay, A. (2005) 'Knowledge Management', in S. Ackroyd, R. Batt, P. Thompson and P. Tolbert (eds), *The Oxford Handbook of Work and Organization*, Oxford: Oxford University Press.

McKinlay, A. (2006) 'Managing Foucault: Genealogies of Management', *Management and Organisational History*, 1. 1: 87–100.

McKinlay, A. and Taylor, P. (1996) 'Power, Surveillance and Resistance: Inside the Factory of the Future', in P. Ackers, C. Smith and P. Smith (eds), *The New Workplace and Trade Unionism*, London: Routledge.

MacKinnon, C. A. (1979) *Sexual Harassment of Working Women*, New Haven, CT: Yale University Press.

McLellan, D. (1973) *Karl Marx: His Life and Thought*, London: Macmillan.

McSweeney, B. (2003) 'Hofstede's Model of National Cultural Differences and their Consequences: A Triumph of Faith – A Failure of Analysis', *Human Relations*, 55. 1: 89–118.

McSweeney, B. (2006) 'Are We Living in a Post-Bureaucratic Epoch?', *Journal of Organizational Change Management*, 19. 1: 22–37.

Maddock, S. and Parkin, D. (1993) 'Gender Cultures, Women's Choices and Strategies at Work', *Women in Management Review*, 8. 2: 3–9.

Maguire, M. (1986) 'Recruitment as a Means of Control', in K. Purcell, S. Wood, A. Watson and S. Allen (eds), *The Changing Experience of Employment, Restructuring and Recession*, London: Macmillan.

Manderscheid, R. and Henderson, M. (eds) (2002) *Mental Health, United States*, U.S. Department of Health and Human Services Substance Abuse and Mental Health Services Administration, Center for Mental Health Services, Maryland.

Mangum, G. L. and Mangum, S. L. (1986) 'Temporary Work: The Flip Side of Job Security', *International Journal of Manpower*, 7. 1: 12–20.

Mann, S. (1999) *Hiding What We Feel, Faking What We Don't: Understanding the Role of Your Emotions at Work*, Shaftesbury: Element.

Manning, P. K. (2008) 'Goffman on Organizations', *Organization Studies*, 29. 5: 677–99.

Manz, C. C. and Sims, H. P. (1989) *SuperLeadership: Leading Others to Lead Themselves*, New York: Prentice Hall.

March, J. G. and Simon, H. A. (1958) *Organizations*, New York: Wiley.

Marchington, M. (1992) 'Managing Labour Relations in a Competitive Environment', in A. Sturdy, D. Knights and H. Willmott (eds), *Skill and Consent*, London: Routledge.

Marchington, M. (2005) 'Employee Involvement: Patterns and Explanations', in J. Hyman, P. Thompson and B. Harley (eds), *Participation and Democracy at Work: Essays in Honour of Harvie Ramsay*, Basingstoke: Palgrave.

Marchington, M., Grimshaw, D., Rubery, J. and Willmott, H. (eds) (2005) *Fragmenting Work: Blurring Organizational Boundaries and Disordering Hierarchies*, Oxford: Oxford University Press.

Marchington, M. and Parker, P. (1987) 'Japanisation: A Lack of Chemical Reaction?', paper presented to the Conference on Japanisation of British Industry, UMIST.

Marchington, M. and Vincent, S. (2004) 'Analysing the Influence of Institutional, Organizational and Interpersonal Forces in Shaping Inter-Organizational Relations'. *Journal of Management Studies*, 41. 6: 1029–56.

Marchington, M. and Wilkinson, A. (1998) 'Direct Participation', in K. Sisson and S. Bach (eds), *Personnel Management in Britain* (3rd edn), Oxford: Blackwell.

Marchington, M., Wilkinson, M., Ackers, P. and Goodman, J. (1993) 'The Influence of Managerial Relations on Waves of Employee Involvement', *British Journal of Industrial Relations*, 31. 4: 553–76.

Marcuse, H. (1971) 'Industrialisation and Capitalism', in O. Stammer (ed.), *Max Weber and Sociology Today*, Oxford: Blackwell.

Marginson, P. (1991) 'Change and Continuity in the Employment Structures of Large Companies', in A. Pollert (ed.), *Farewell to Flexibility?*, Oxford: Blackwell.

Marginson, P., Armstrong, P., Edwards, P. and Purcell, J. (1995) 'Extending Beyond Borders: Mutinational Companies and the International Management of Labour', *International Journal of Human Resource Management*, 6. 3: 702–19.

Marglin, S. A. (1974) 'What do Bosses Do? The Origins and Functions of Hierarchy in Capitalist Production', *Review of Radical Political Economics*, 6: 60–102.

Marks, A., Findlay, P., Hine, J., McKinlay, A. and Thompson, P. (1997) 'Handmaid's Tale or Midwives of Change? HR Managers and Organisational Innovation', *Journal of Strategic Change*, 6: 469–80.

Marks, A., Findlay, P., Hine, J., McKinlay, A. and Thompson, P. (1998) 'The Politics of Partnership: Innovation in Employment Relations in the Scottish Spirits Industry', *British Journal of Industrial Relations*, 36. 2: 209–26.

Mars, G. (1983) *Cheats at Work: An Anthology of Workplace Crime*, London: Unwin.

Marsden, R. (1993) 'The Politics of Organisational Analysis', *Organisation Studies*, 14. 1: 93–124.

Martin, J. (1990) 'Deconstructing Organisational Taboos: The Suppression of Gender Conflict in Organisations', *Organisational Science*, 1: 1–21.

Martin, J. (1992) *Cultures in Organisations: Three Perspectives*, New York: Oxford University Press.

Martin, J. (1998) *Organisational Behaviour*, London: International Thomson Business Press.

Martin, J. and Siehl, C. (1983) 'Organisational Culture and Counterculture: An Uneasy Symbiosis', *Organisational Dynamics*, Autumn: 52–64.

Martin, P. (1993) 'Feminist Practice in Organizations', in E. Fagenson (ed.), *Women in Management: Trends, Issues and Challenges in Management Diversity*, Newbury Park, CA: Sage.

Martin, P. and Nicholls, D. (1987) *Creating a Committed Workforce*, London: Institute of Personnel Management.

Martinez, Lucio, M. and Stewart, P. (1997) 'The Paradox of Contemporary Labour Process Theory: The Rediscovery of Labour and the Decline of Collectivism', *Capital and Class*, 62: 49–77.

Martinez Lucio, M. and Weston, S. (1992) 'Human Resource Management and Trade Union Responses: Bringing the Politics of the Workplace Back into the Debate', in P. Blyton and P. Turnbull (eds), *Reassessing Human Resource Management*, London: Sage.

Martinko, M. (ed.) (2004) *Attribution Theory in the Organizational Sciences: Theoretical and Empirical Contributions*, Charlotte, NC: Information Age Publishing.

Martinko, M. J. (ed.) (1995) *Attribution Theory: An Organisational Perspective*, Delray Beach, FL: St Lucie.

Marx, K. (1963) *Early Writings*, trans. T. B. Bottomore, New York, NY: McGraw-Hill.

Marx, K. (1984) 'The Spirit of Bureaucracy and Beyond Bureaucracy: The Paris Commune', in F. Fischer and C. Sirriani (eds), *Critical Studies in Organisation and Bureaucracy*, Philadelphia: Temple University Press.

Maslow, A. H. (1954) *Motivation and Human Personality*, New York: Harper & Row.

Masreliez-Steen, G. (1989) *Male and Female Management*, Sweden: Kontura Group.

Mather, C. (1987) 'Disposable Workers', *New Internationalist*, July.

Mathews, J. (1993) 'Organisational Innovation: Competing Models of Productive Efficiency', paper presented to the Fifth APROS International Colloquium, Honolulu, Hawaii.

Mathews, J. (1994) *Catching the Wave: Workplace Reform in Australia*, New York: ILR.

Maurice, M., Sorge, A. and Warner, M. (1980) 'Societal Differences in Organising Manufacturing Units', *Organisation Studies*, 1. 1: 63–91.

May, T. (1999) 'Banana Time to Just-in-Time: Power and Resistance at Work', *Sociology*, 33. 4: 767–83.

Mayer, J. D., Salovey, P., and Caruso, D. R. (2000) 'Models of Emotional Intelligence', in R. J. Sternberg (ed.), *Handbook of Human Intelligence* (2nd edn), New York: Cambridge University Press. pp. 396–420.

Mayo, E. (1946) *Human Problems of an Industrial Civilisation*, New York: Macmillan.

Mead, G. H. (1934) *Mind, Self and Society*, Chicago: Chicago University Press.

Mechanic, D. (1962) 'Sources of Power of Lower Participants in Complex Organizations', *Administrative Science Quarterly*, 7: 349–64.

Meek, V. L. (1988) 'Organisational Culture: Origins and Weaknesses', *Organisation Studies*, 9. 4: 453–73.

Meichenbaum, D. (1996) 'Stress Inoculation Training for Coping with Stressors', *The Clinical Psychologist*, 49: 4–7, available at – http://www.apa.org/divisions/div12/rev_est/sit_stress.html

Meindl, J. R. and Ehrlich, S. B. (1987) 'The Romance of Leadership and the Evaluation of Organisational Performance', *Academy of Management Journal*, 30: 91–109.

Meindl, J. B., Ehrlich, S. B. and Dukerich, J. M. (1985) 'The Romance of Leadership', *Administrative Science Quarterly*, 30: 78–102.

Melling, J. (1982) 'Men in the Middle or Men on the Margin', in D. Dunkerley and G. Salaman (eds), *The International Yearbook of Organisation Studies 1981*, London: Routledge & Kegan Paul.

Merton, R. K. (1949) *Social Theory and Social Structure*, Glencoe, IL: Free Press.

Meyer, J. W. and Rowan, B. (1977) 'Institutionalised Organizations: Formal Structure as Myth and Ceremony', *American Journal of Sociology*, 83. 2: 340–63.

Meyer, J. W. and Scott, R. W. (1983) *Organisational Environments: Ritual and Rationality*, Beverley Hills, CA: Sage.

Meyer, M., Stevenson, W. and Webster, S. (1985) *Limits to Bureaucratic Growth*, New York: Walter De Gruyter.

Meyer, P. B. (1986) 'General Motors' Saturn Plant: A Quantum Leap in Technology and its Implications for Labour and Community Organizations', *Capital and Class*, 30: 73–96.

Miliband, R. (1969) *The State in Capitalist Society*, London: Weidenfeld & Nicolson.

Milkman, R. (1997) *Farewell to the Factory: Auto Workers in the Late Twentieth Century*, Berkeley, CA: University of California Press.

Milkman, R. (1998) 'The New American Workplace: High Road or Low Road?' in P. Thompson and C. Warhurst (eds), *Workplaces of the Future*, London: Macmillan.

Miller, D. R. (1963) 'The Study of Social Relationships: Situations, Identities and Social Interaction', in S. Koch (ed.), *Psychology: A Study of a Science*, vol. 5, New York: McGraw-Hill.

Miller, D. T. and Ross, M. (1975) 'Self-serving Biases in the Attribution of Causality: Fact or Fiction?', *Psychological Bulletin*, 82: 213–25.

Miller, E. J. and Rice, A. K. (1967) *Systems of Organisation: The Control of Task and Sentient Boundaries*, London: Tavistock.

Miller, G. A., Galanter, E. and Pribram, K. H. (1960) *Plans and the Structure of Behaviour*, London: Holt.

Miller, H. G. and Verduin, J. R. (1979) *The Adult Educator: A Handbook for Staff Development*, Houston: Gulf.

Miller, L. J. (2006) *Reluctant Capitalists: Bookselling and the Culture of Consumption*, Chicago: University of Chicago Press.

Miller, N. E. and Dollard, J. (1953) *Social Learning and Imitation*, New Haven, CT: Yale University Press.

Miller, P. and O'Leary, T. (1987) 'The Entrepreneurial Order', paper presented to the Conference on the Labour Process, Aston-UMIST.

Miller, P. M. (1989) 'Strategic HRM: What it Is and What it Isn't', *Personnel Management*, February.

Mills, A. J. (1991) 'Organisational Discourse and the Gendering of Identity', paper presented to the Conference on towards a New Theory of Organisations, University of Keele.

Mills, A. J. and Murgatroyd, S. J. (1991) *Organisational Rules: A Framework for Understanding Organisations*, Milton Keynes: Open University Press.

Mills, A. J. and Tancred, P. (eds) (1992) *Gendering Organisational Analysis*, London: Sage.

Mills, C. W. (1959) *The Power Elite*, Oxford: Oxford University Press.

Millward, N. (1994) *The New Industrial Relations?*, London: Policy Studies Institute.

Millward, N., Bryson, A. and Forth, J. (2000) *All Change at Work: British Employment Relations 1980–1988, As Portrayed by the Workplace Industrial Relations Survey Series*, London: Routledge.

Millward, T., Stevens, M., Smart, D. and Hawkes, W. R. (1992) *Workplace Industrial Relations in Transition, The ED/ESRC/PS1/ACAS Surveys*, Aldershot: Dartmouth.

Mintzberg, H. (1973) *The Nature of Managerial Work*, New York: Harper & Row.

Mintzberg, H. (1983) *Structure in Fives: Designing Effective Organizations*, Englewood Cliffs, NJ: Prentice Hall.

Mirchandani, K. (1999) 'Re-Forming Organisations: Contributions of Teleworking Employees', in P. J. Jackson (ed.), *Virtual Working*, London: Routledge.

Mischel, W. (1973) 'Towards a Cognitive Social Learning Reconception of Personality', *Psychological Review*, 80: 200–13.

Mitter, S. (1986) *Common Fate, Common Bond: Women in the Global Economy*, London: Pluto.

Montgomery, D. (1976) 'Workers' Control of Machine Production in the Nineteenth Century', *Labor History*, 17. 4: 486–509.

Moos, R. H. and Billings, A. G. (1982) 'Conceptualizing and Measuring Coping Resources and Processes', in L. Goldberger and S. Bresnitz (eds), *Handbook of Stress: Theoretical and Clinical Aspects*, New York: The Free Press, pp. 212–30.

Morgan, D. and Stanley, L. (eds) (1993) *Debates in Sociology*, Manchester: Manchester University Press.

Morgan, G. (1986) *Images of Organisation*, London: Sage. Morgan, G. (1990b) *Organizations in Society*, London: Sage.

Morgan, G. (1990a) 'Paradigm Diversity in Organisational Research', in J. Hassard and D. Pym (eds), *The Theory and Philosophy of Organizations*, London: Routledge.

Morgan, G. (1990b) *Organizations in Society*, London: Sage.

Morgan, G. (2005) 'Understanding Multinational Corporations, in S. Ackroyd, R. Batt, P. Thompson and P. Tolbert (eds), *The Oxford Handbook of Work and Organization*, Oxford: Oxford University Press.

Morgan, G. and Hooper, D. (1987) 'Corporate Strategy, Ownership and Control', *Sociology*, 21. 4: 609–27.

Morgan, K. and Sayer, A. (1984) 'A "Modern" Industry in a "Mature" Region: The Re-Making of Management–Labour Relations', working paper, Urban and Regional Studies, University of Sussex.

Morishima, M. (1995) 'Embedding HRM in a Social Context', *British Journal of Industrial Relations*, 33. 4: 617–40.

Morris, J. (1987) 'The Who, Why, and Where of Japanese Manufacturing Investment in the UK', paper presented to the Conference on Japanisation of British Industry, UMIST.

Moscovici, S. (1972) 'Society and Theory in Social Psychology', in J. Israel and H. Tajfel (eds), *The Context of Social Psychology: A Critical Assessment*, London: Academic Press.

Moscovici, S. and Zavalloni, M. (1969) 'The Group as a Polarizer of Attitudes', *Journal of Personality and Social Psychology*, 12: 125–35.

Mueller, F. (1994a) 'Societal Effect, Organisational Effect Globalisation', *Organisation Studies*, 15. 3: 407–28.

Mueller, F. (1994b) 'Teams Between Hierarchy and Commitment: Change Strategies and the "Internal Environment"', *Journal of Management Studies*, 31. 3: 383–403.

Mueller, F. (1996) 'Internationalisation of Markets and the Externalisation of Hierarchy in MNCS', paper presented to the Conference on Globalisation of Production and Regulation of Labour, Warwick.

Muffels, R. and Luijkx, R. (2008) 'Labour Market Flexibility and Employment Security of Male Employees in Europe', *Work, Employment and Society*, 22. 2: 221–42.

Mulgan, G. (1989) 'The Power of the Weak', in S. Hall and M. Jacques (eds), *New Times*, London: Lawrence & Wishart.

Mulholland, K. (1998) ' "Survivors" versus "Moves and Shakers": The Reconstitution of Management and Careers in the Privatised Utilities', in P. Thompson and C. Warhurst (eds), *The Future Workplace*, London: Macmillan.

Mullins, L. (1985) *Management and Organisation Behaviour*, London: Pitman.

Mullins, L. J. (1999) *Management and Organisational Behaviour* (5th edn), London: Financial Times/Pitman.

Mullins, L. (2005) *Management and Organisational Behaviour* (7th edn), Harlow: Pearson Education Ltd, UK.

Munk, N. (1998) 'The *New Organization Man*', *Fortune* 137. 5: 62–74.

Munro, R. (1994) 'Governing the New Province of Quality: Autonomy, Accounting and the Dissemination of Accountability', in A. Wilkinson and H. Willmott (eds), *Making Quality Critical*, London: Routledge & Kegan Paul.

Murakami, T. (1997) 'The Autonomy of Teams in the Car Industry: A Cross-National Comparison', *Work, Employment and Society*, 11. 4: 749–58.

Murphy, L. R. and Sorenson, S. (1988) 'Employee Behaviours before and after Stress Management', *Journal of Organisational Behaviour*, 9: 173–82.

Murray, F. (1983) 'The Decentralisation of Production and the Decline of the Mass-Collective Worker', *Capital and Class*, 19: 74–9.

Murray, F. (1987) 'Flexible Specialisation and the Third Italy', *Capital and Class*, 33: 84–95.

Murray, P. and Wickham, J. (1985) 'Women Workers and Bureaucratic Control in Irish Electronic Factories', in H. Newby (ed.), *Restructuring Capital, Reorganisation in Industrial Society*, London: Macmillan.

Murray, R. (1985) 'Benetton Britain', *Marxism Today*, November.

Mutch, A. (2002). 'Actors and Networks or Agents and Structures: Towards a Realist View of Information Systems', *Organization*, 9, 3: 477–96.

Myers, C. S. (1926) *Industrial Psychology in Great Britain*, London: Jonathan Cape.

Myers, C. S. (ed.) (1929) *Industrial Psychology*, London: Thornton Butterworth.

Myers, M. T. and Myers, G. E. (1982) *Managing by Communication: An Organisational Approach*, New York: McGraw-Hill.

Nadworny, M. (1955) *Scientific Management and the Unions*, Cambridge: MA: Harvard University Press.

Naisbitt, J. and Aburdene, P. (1985) *Reinventing the Corporation*, London: MacDonald.

Nandhakumar, J. (1999) 'Virtual Teams and Lost Proximity: Consequences on Trust Relationships', in P. J. Jackson (ed.), *Virtual Working*, London: Routledge.

NEDO (1986) *Changing Working Patterns*, report prepared by the Institute for Manpower Studies for the National Economic Development Office in Association with the Department of Employment, London: NEDO.

Neimark, M. and Tinker, T. (1986) 'On Rediscovering Marx: Dissolving Agency–Structure in Dialectical Unity', paper presented to the Conference on the Labour Process, Aston-UMIST.

Nelson, D. (1975) *Managers and Workers: Origins of the New Factory System in the United States 1880–1920*, Madison: University of Wisconsin Press.

Newell, H. and Dopson, S. (1996) 'Muddle in the Middle: Organisational Restructuring and Middle Management', *Personnel Review*, 25. 4: 4–20.

Newell, S. (1995) *The Healthy Organization*, London: Routledge.

Newsome, K., Commander, J. and Thompson, P. (2007) Power Dynamics and Labour Process Change in the Scottish Supermarket Supply Chain, Paper to International Labour process Conference, March, Amsterdam.

Newsome, K., Thompson, P. and Commander, J. (2009) 'The Forgotten Factories: Supermarket Suppliers and Dignity at Work in the Contemporary Economy', in S. Bolton, S. and M. Houlihan (eds), (2009) *Work Matters: Critical Reflections on Contemporary Work*, Basingstoke: Palgrave Macmillan.

Newton, T. (1994) 'Resocialising the Subject? A Re-Reading of Grey's "Career as a Project of the Self"', *Sociology*, 30. 1, 137–144.

Newton, T. (1996) 'Postmodernism and Action', *Organisation*, 3. 1: 7–29.

Newton, T. (1998) 'Theorising Subjectivity in Organizations: The Failure of Foucauldian Studies?' *Organization Studies*, 19. 3: 415–57.

Newton, T. and Findlay, P. (1996) 'Playing God? The Performance of Appraisal', *Human Resource Management Journal*, 6. 3: 42–58.

Newton, T., with Handy, J. and Fineman, S. (1995) *'Managing' Stress: Power and Emotion at Work*, London: Sage.

Ng, C. W. and Fosh, P. (2000) 'Prospects for Women Workers at East Asia Air: Sky's the Limit or Rough Climb through Thick Clouds?' paper presented to the Employment Relations Research Unit Conference, Cardiff Business School.

Nichols, T. (1986) *The British Worker Question*, London: Routledge & Kegan Paul.

Nichols, T. and Beynon, H. (1977) *Living with Capitalism*, London: Routledge & Kegan Paul.

Nickson, D., Warhurst C., Witz, A. and Cullen, A. M. (2001) 'The Importance of Being Aesthetic: Work, Employment and Service Organisations', in A. Sturdy, I. Grugulis and H. Willmott (eds), *Customer Service*, London: Palgrave.

Nickson, D., Warhurst, C. and Dutton, E. (2004) Aesthetic Labour and the Policy-Making Agenda: Time for a Reappraisal of Skills?, *SKOPE Research Paper*, No.48 Summer: available at: http://www.hrmguide.co.uk/general/looking_good.htm

Nickson, D., Warhurst, C. and Dutton, E. (2005) 'The Importance of Attitude and Appearance in the Service Encounter in Retail and Hospitality', *Managing Service Quality*, 15. 2: 195–208.

Nkomo, S. M. and Cox, T. Jr (1999) 'Diverse Identities in Organisations', in S. Clegg, C. Hardy and W. R. Nord (eds), *Managing Organizations: Current Issues*, Sage, London, pp. 88–103.

Noble, D. (1979) 'Social Change in Machine Design', in A. Zimbalist (ed.), *Case Studies in the Labour Process*, London: Monthly Review Press.

Nohria, N. (1992) 'Is a Network Perspective a Useful Way of Studying Organizations?', in N. Nohria and R. G. Eccles (eds), *Networks and Organizations*, Boston, MA: Harvard Business School Press.

Nohria, N. and Eccles, R. G. (eds) (1992) *Networks and Organizations*, Boston, Mass.: Harvard Business School Press.

Nolan, P. and Wood, S. (2003) Mapping the Future of Work, *Special Edition of British Journal of Industrial Relations*, 41. 2: 165–74.

Nonaka, I. (1996) 'The Knowledge-Creating Company', in K. Starkey (ed.), *How Organizations Learn: Strategy, Structure, Process and Leadership*, London: Routledge, pp. 18–31.

Nonaka, I. and Takeuchi, H. (1995) *The Knowledge Creating Company*, Oxford: Oxford University Press.

Noon, M. (2007) 'The Fatal Flaws of Diversity and the Business Case for Ethnic Minorities', *Work, Employment and Society*, 21. 4: 773–84.

Nord, W. R. and Fox, S. (1996) 'The Individual in Organisational Studies: The Great Disappearing Act', in S. Clegg, C. Hardy and W. Nord (eds), *Handbook of Organisation Studies*, London: Sage.

Norris, C. (1992) *Uncritical Theory: Postmodernism, Intellectuals and the Gulf War*, London: Lawrence & Wishart.

North-West Women Into Management (1987) Newsletter, Manchester: June.

Nyland, C. (1987) 'Scientific Management and Planning', *Capital and Class*, 33: 55–83.

Ó Riain, S. (1998) 'Networking for a Living: Irish Software Developers in the Global Workplace', paper presented to the Work Difference and Social Change Conference, Binghamton, May.

O'Brien, G. E. (1992) 'Changing Meanings of Work', in J. F. Hartley and G. M. Stephenson (eds), *Employment Relations*, Oxford: Blackwell: pp. 44–66.

O'Connell Davidson, J. (1993) *Privatisation and Employment Relations: The Case of the Water Industry*, London: Mansell.

O'Connell Davidson, J. (1994a) 'On Power, Prostitution and Pilchards: The Self-Employed Prostitute and Her Clients', paper presented to the 12th Annual International Labour Process Conference, Aston University, March.

O'Connell Davidson, J. (1994b) 'What Do Franchisers Do? Control and Commercialisation in Milk Distribution', *Work, Employment and Society*, 8. 1: 23–44.

O'Donnell, M. (1996) 'Into the Mystic: Cultural Change and TQM Teams in the NSW Public Sector', *Journal of Industrial Relations* (Australia), 38. 2: 241–63.

O'Driscoll, M. (1996) 'The Interface between Job and Off-Job Roles: Enhancement and Conflict', *International Review of Industrial and Organizational Psychology*, 11.

OECD (1977) *The Development of Industrial Relations Systems: Some Implications of the Japanese Experience*: Paris: OECD.

OECD (2002) *Economic Outlook No. 72*, Paris: OECD.

Ogbonna, E. (1992a) 'Managing Organisational Culture: Fantasy or Reality?' *Human Resource Management*, 3. 2: 42–54.

Ogbonna, E. (1992b) 'Organisation Culture and Human Resource Management: Dilemmas and Contradictions', in P. Blyton and P. Turnbull (eds), *Reassessing Human Resource Management*, London: Sage.

Ogbonna, E. and Wilkinson, B. (1988) 'Corporate Strategy and Corporate Culture: The View from the Checkout', *Personnel Review*, 19. 4: 9–15.

Ohmae, K. (1990) *The Borderless World*. New York: Harper Business.

Oldersma, J. and Davis, K. (1991) 'Introduction', in K. Davis, M. Leijenaar and J. Oldersma (eds), *The Gender of Power*, London: Sage.

Olins, W. (1996) *The New Guide to Identity: How to Create and Sustain Change through Managing Identity*, London: Gower.

Oliver, J. (1993) 'A Degree of Uncertainty', *Management Today*, June.

O'Meara, D. P. (1994) 'Personality Tests Raise Questions of Legality and Effectiveness', *HR Magazine*, Jan.

O'Neill, J. (1986) 'The Disciplinary Society: From Weber to Foucault', *British Journal of Sociology*, 37. 1: 42–60.

O'Neill, N. (1985) 'Marxism and Psychology', in M. Shaw (ed.), *Marxist Sociology Revisited*, London: Macmillan.

O'Reilly, C. A. and Chatman, J. A. (1996) 'Culture as Social Control: Corporations, Cults and Commitment', in B. M. Staws and L. L. Cummings (eds), *Research in Organisational Behaviour*, 18: 157–200, Greenwich, Conn.: JAI.

O'Reilly, J. (1992) 'Where Do You Draw the Line? Functional Flexibility, Training and Skill in Britain and France', *Work, Employment and Society*, 6. 3: 369–96.

Osterman, P. (1994) 'How Common is Workplace Transformation and How Can We Explain Who Adopts it?' *Industrial and Labor Relations Review*, Jan.: 175–88.

Ouchi, W. G. (1981) *Theory Z*, Reading, MA: Addison-Wesley.

Ouchi, W. G. and Johnson, J. B. (1978) 'Types of Organisational Control and their Relationship to Emotional Well Being', *Administrative Science Quarterly*, 23, June: 293–317.

Palmer, B. (1975) 'Class Conception and Conflict', *Review of Radical Political Economics*, 17. 2: 31–49.

Palmer, I. and Hardy, C. (2000) *Thinking about Management*, London: Sage.

Parent-Thirion, A., Fernández Macías, E., Hurley, J. and Vermeylen, G. (2007) *Fourth European Working Conditions Survey*, European Foundation for the Improvement of Living and Working Conditions, Dublin.

Parker, I. (1997) 'The Unconscious State of Social Psychology', in T. Ibanez and L. Ininguez (eds), *Critical Social Psychology*, London: Sage.

Parker, I. and Spears, R. (eds) (1996) *Psychology and Society: Radical Theory and Practice*, London: Pluto.

Parker, M. (1985) *Inside the Circle: A Union Guide to QWL*, Boston: Labour Notes.

Parker, M. (1992) 'Post-Modern Organizations or Post-Modern Organisation Theory?' *Organisation Studies*, 13. 1: 1–17.

Parker, M. (1998a) 'Capitalism, Subjectivity and Ethics: Debating Labour Process Analysis', *Organisation Studies*, 20. 1: 25–45.

Parker, M. (1998b) 'Organisational Culture and the Disciplines of Organisation: The Career of a Concept', paper presented to the International Labour Process Conference, UMIST.

Parker, M. (1999) *Organisation Culture and Identity*, London: Sage.

Parker, M. and Jary, D. (1994) 'Academic Subjectivity and the New Managerialism', paper presented to the 13th International Labour Process Conference, Aston.

Parker, M. and McHugh, G. (1991) 'Five Texts in Search of An Author: A Response to John Hassard's "Multiple Paradigms and Organisational Analysis: A Case Study"', *Organisation Studies*, 12. 3: 451–6.

Parker, M. and Slaughter, J. (1988a) Management by Stress, *Technology Review*, Or see http://multinationalmonitor. org/hyper/issues/1990/01/slaughter.html

Parker, M. and Slaughter, J. (1988b) *Choosing Sides: Unions and the Team Concept, Labor Notes*, Boston, MA: South End Press.

Parker, M. and Slaughter, J. (1995) 'Unions and Management', in S. Babson, (ed.), *Lean Work: Empowerment and Exploitation in the Global Automotive Industry*, Detroit, MI: Wayne State University Press

Parsons, T. (1951) *The Social System*, New York: Collier Macmillan.

Parsons, T. (1956) 'Suggestions for a Sociological Approach to the Theory of Organizations', *Administrative Science Quarterly*, 1: 63–85, 225–39.

Parsons, T. (1960) *Structure and Process in Modern Societies*, Chicago: Free Press.

Pascale, R. (1990) *Managing on the Edge*, Harmondsworth: Penguin.

Pascale, R. T. and Athos, A. G. (1982) *The Art of Japanese Management*, Harmondsworth: Penguin.

Pashler, H.E. (1998) *The Psychology of Attention*, Boston, Mass.: MIT Press.

Pavlov, I. P. (1927) *Conditioned Reflexes: An Investigation of the Physiological Activity of the Cerebral Cortex*, transl. and ed. G. V. Anrep, London: Oxford University Press.

Pearce, F. (1989) *The Radical Durkheim*, London: Unwin Hyman.

Pearson, R. (1986) 'Female Workers in the First and Third Worlds: The "Greening" of Women's Labour', in K. Purcell, S. Wood, A. Watson and S. Allen (eds), *The Changing Experience of Employment, Restructuring and Recession*, London: Macmillan.

Penn, R. (1985) *Skilled Workers in the Class Structure*, Cambridge: Cambridge University Press.

Penn, R. (1986) 'Socialisation into Skilled Identities: An Analysis of a Neglected Phenomenon', paper presented to the Conference on the Labour Process, Aston–UMIST.

Perlmutter, H. V. (1969) 'The Tortuous Evolution of the Multinational Corporation', *Columbia Journal of World Business*, Jan.–Feb.: 9–18.

Perloff, R. M. (1993) *The Dynamics of Persuasion*, Hillsdale, NJ: Lawrence Erlbaum.

Perrons, D. (2000) 'Living with Risk: Labour Market Transformation, Employment Policies and Social Reproduction in the UK', *Economic and Industrial Democracy*, 21: 283–310.

Perrow, C. (1961) 'The Analysis of Goals in Complex Organisations', *American Sociological Review*, 26: 854–66.

Perrow, C. (1972) *Complex Organizations: A Critical Essay*, Glenview, IL: Scott Foreman.

Perrow, C. (1973) 'The Short and Glorious History of Organisational Theory', *Organisational Dynamics*, Summer: 2–15.

Perrow, C. (1979) *Complex Organizations: A Critical Essay* (2nd edn), Glenview, IL: Scott Foreman.

Perrow, C. (1986) *Complex Organizations: A Critical Essay* (3rd edn), Glenview, IL: Scott Foreman.

Perrow, C. (1992) 'Small Firm Networks', in N. Nohria and R. G. Eccles (eds), *Networks and Organizations*, Boston, MA: Harvard Business School Press.

Peters, T. (1989) *Thriving on Chaos*, London: Pan.

Peters, T. (1992) *Liberation Management: Necessary Disorganisation for the Nanosecond Nineties*, New York: Alfred Knopf.

Peters, T. (1997) *The Brand Called You*, available at http://www.transformingmlm.com/resources/Brandcalledyou.pdf.

Peters, T. J. and Austin, N. (1986) *A Passion for Excellence*, New York: Random House.

Peters, T. J. and Waterman, R. H. (1982) *In Search of Excellence: Lessons from America's Best-Run Companies*, New York: Harper & Row.

Pettigrew, A. (1973) *The Politics of Organisational Decision-Making*, London: Tavistock.

Pettigrew, A. (1985) *The Awakening Giant: Continuity and Change at Imperial Chemical Industries*, Oxford: Blackwell.

Pettigrew, A. and Whipp, R. (1991) *Managing Change for Competitive Success*, Oxford: Blackwell.

Pettinger, L. (2004) 'Brand Culture and Branded Workers: Service Work and Aesthetic Labour in Fashion Retail', *Consumption, Markets and Culture*, 7. 2: 165–84.

Pettinger, L. (2006) 'On the Materiality of Service Work', *The Sociological Review*, 54. 1: 48–65.

Petty, R. E. and Cacioppo, J. T. (1981) *Attitudes and Persuasion: Classic and Contemporary Approaches*, Iowa: Wm. C. Brown.

Pfeffer, J. (1981a) 'Management as Symbolic Action', *Research in Organisational Behaviour*, 3: 1–52.

Pfeffer, J. (1982) *Organizations and Organization Theory*, Boston, MA: Pitman.

Pfeffer, J. (1987) 'A Resource Dependence Model of Intercorporate Relations', in M. S. Mizruchi and M. Schwartz (eds), *Intercorporate Relations: The Structural Analysis of Business*, Cambridge: Cambridge University Press.

Pfeffer, J. (1992) *Managing with Power: Politics and Influence in Organizations*, Boston, MA: Harvard Business School Press.

Pfeffer, J. (1993) 'Barriers to the Development of Organisational Science: Paradigm Development as a Dependent Variable', *Academy of Management Review*, 18: 599–620.

Pfeffer, J. (1994) Competitive Advantage through People: Unleashing the Power of the Work Force, Cambridge, MA: Harvard University Press.

Pfeffer, J. (1997) *New Directions for Organisational Theory: Problems and Practices*, Oxford: Oxford University Press.

Pfeffer, J. (1998) *The Human Equation: Building Profits by Putting People First*, Boston: Harvard Business School Press.

Pheysey, D. (1993) *Organisational Cultures: Types and Transformations*, London: Routledge.

Philpot. J. (2000) 'Behind the Buzzword: The New Economy', *Economic Report* 14, London: Employment Policy Institute.

Phizacklea, A. (1987) 'Minority Women and Economic Restructuring: The Case of Britain and the Federal Republic of Germany', *Work, Employment and Society*, 1. 3: 309–25.

Pierson, C. (1984) 'New Theories of State and Civil Society', *Sociology*, 18. 4: 563–71.

Pink, D. (2001) *Free Agent Nation*, New York: Warner Business.

Piore, M. J. (1986) 'Perspectives on Labour Market Flexibility', *Industrial Relations*, 25. 2: 146–66.

Piore, M. J. and Sabel, C. F. (1984) *The Second Industrial Divide: Possibilities for Prosperity*, New York: Basic Books.

Pitelis, C. (1993) 'Transnationals, International Organisation and Deindustrialisation', *Organisation Studies*, 14. 4: 527–48.

Poggio, B. (2000) 'Between Bytes and Bricks: Gender Cultures in Work Contexts', *Economic and Industrial Democracy*, 21: 381–402.

Polan, A. J. (1984) *Lenin and the End of Politics*, London: Methuen.

Polanyi, M. (1958) *Personal Knowledge: Towards a Post-critical Philosophy*, Chicago, IL: University of Chicago Press.

Pollard, S. (1965) *The Genesis of Modern Management*, London: Edward Arnold.

Pollert, A. (1981) *Girls, Wives, Factory Lives*, London: Macmillan.

Pollert, A. (1988a) 'Dismantling Flexibility', *Capital and Class*, 34, Spring: 42–75.

Pollert, A. (1988b) 'The Flexible Firm: Fixation or Fact?' *Work, Employment and Society*, 2. 3: 281–316.

Pollert, A. (ed.) (1991a) *Farewell to Flexibility?* Oxford: Oxford University Press.

Pollert, A. (1991b) 'The Orthodoxy of Flexibility', in A. Pollert (ed.), *Farewell to Flexibility?* Oxford: Oxford University Press.

Pollert, A. (1996) 'Teamwork on the Assembly Line: Contradiction and the Dynamics of Union Resiliance', in P. Ackers, S. Smith and P. Smith (eds), *The New Workplace and Trade Unionism*, London: Routledge.

Pollert, A. (2009) 'The Reality of Vulnerability among Britain's Non-Unionised Workers with Problems at Work', in S. Bolton, and M. Houlihan, *Work Matters: Critical Reflections on Contemporary Work*, Basingstoke: Palgrave Macmillan.

Poole, M. and Mansfield, R. (1992) 'Managers' Attitudes to Human Resource Management', in P. Blyton and P. Turnbull (eds) *Reassessing Human Resource Management*, London: Sage.

Poole, M. S. (1981) 'Decision Development in Small Groups I', *Communication Monographs*, 48: 1–24.

Poole, M. S. (1983a) 'Decision Development in Small Groups II', *Communication Monographs*, 50: 206–32.

Poole, M. S. (1983b) 'Decision Development in Small Groups III', *Communication Monographs*, 50: 321–41.

Poole, M. S. and Roth, J. (1989) 'Decision Development in Small Groups V', *Human Communication Research*, 15: 549–89.

Porter, M. (1980) *Competitive Strategy*, New York: Free Press.

Porter, M. E. (1990) *The Competitive Advantage of Nations*, London: Macmillan.

Potter, I. (1997) 'Discourse and Critical Social Psychology', in T. Ibanez and L. Ininugez (eds), *Critical Social Psychology*, London: Sage.

Potter, J. and Wetherall, M. (1987) *Discourse and Social Psychology*, London: Sage.

Potterfield, T. A. (1999) *The Business of Employee Empowerment: Democracy, Ideology and the Workplace*, Westport, CT: Quorum.

Poulantzas, N. (1975) *Classes in Contemporary Capitalism*, London: New Left Books.

Powell, W.J. (1990) 'Neither Market Nor Hierarchy: Network Forms of Organization', *Research in Organizational Behavior*, 12, s: 295–336.

Powers, W. T. (1973) *Behavior: The Control of Perception*, New York: Aldine deGruyter.

Prethus, R. (1962) *The Organisational Society*, London: Macmillan.

Prichard, C. (1998) 'Identity Work – Moving the "Theory of the Subject" From "Division to Depth" in Labour Process Analysis', paper presented to the 16th Annual International Labour Process Conference, Manchester School of Management, April.

Pringle, R. (1989) *Secretaries Talk: Sexuality, Power and Work*, London: Verso.

Proctor, A. J., Rowlinson, M., McArdle, L., Hassard, J. and Forrester, P. (1994) 'Flexibility, Politics and Strategy: In Defence of the Model of the Flexible Firm', *Work, Employment and Society*, 8. 2: 221–42.

Proctor, R. (1988) *Racial Hygiene: Medicine under the Nazis*, Cambridge, MA: Harvard University Press.

Proctor, S. (2005) 'Organizations and Organized Systems: From Direct Control to Flexibility', in Ackroyd, S., Batt, R., Thompson, P. and Tolbert, P. (eds.), *The Oxford Handbook of Work and Organization*, Oxford University Press.

Proctor, S. and Mueller, F. (2000) 'Teamworking: Strategy, Systems and Culture', in S. Proctor and F. Mueller (eds), *Teamworking*, London: Macmillan.

Pugh, D. S. (ed.) (1971) *Organisation Theory*, Harmondsworth: Penguin.

Pugh, D. S. and Hickson, D. J. (1973) 'The Comparative Study of Organizations', in G. Salaman and K. Thompson (eds), *People and Organizations*, Harlow: Longman.

Pugh, D. S. and Hickson, D. J. (1976) *Organisation Structure in its Context: The Aston Programme 1*, London: Saxon House.

Pugh, D. S., Hickson, D. J. and Hinings, C. R. (1968) 'Dimensions of Organisation Structure', *Administrative Science Quarterly*, 13: 65–103.

Pugh, D. S., Hickson, D. J. and Hinings, C. R. (1969) 'An Empirical Taxonomy of Structures of Work Organizations', *Administrative Science Quarterly*, 14.

Pugh, D. S., Hickson, D. J., Hinings, C. R., MacDonald, K. M., Turner, C. and Lapton, T. (1963) 'A Conceptual Scheme for Organisational Analysis', *Administrative Science Quarterly*, 8. 3: 289–315.

Purcell, J. (1987) 'Mapping Management Styles in Industrial Relations', *Journal of Management Studies*, 24. 5: 535–48.

Purcell, J. (1991) 'The Impact of Corporate Strategy on Human Resource Management', in J. Storey (ed.), *New Perspectives in Human Resource Management*, London: Routledge.

Purcell, J. and Sissons, K. (1983) 'A Strategy for Management Control in Industrial Relations', in J. Purcell and R. Smith (eds), *The Control of Work*, London: Macmillan.

Purcell, K., Hogarth, K. and Simm, C. (1999) *Whose Flexibility?*, London: Joseph Rowntree Foundation.

Purcell, K., Wood, S., Watson, A. and Allen, S. (eds) (1986) *The Changing Experience of Employment, Restructuring and Recession*, London: Macmillan.

Putnam, L. L. and Mumby, D. K. (1993) 'Organizations, Emotion and the Myth of Rationality', in S. Fineman (ed.), *Emotions in Organisations*, London: Sage.

Quattrone, G. A. (1982) 'Behavioral Consequences of Attributional Bias', *Social Cognition*, 1: 358–78.

Quinn Mills, D. (1993) *Rebirth of the Corporation*, New York: Wiley.

Rabinow, P. (ed.) (1991) *The Foucault Reader*, Harmondsworth: Peregrine.

Rainbird, H. (1991) 'The Self-Employed: Small Entrepreneurs or Disguised Wage Labourers?' in A. Pollert (ed.), *Farewell to Flexibility?* Oxford: Blackwell.

Rainnie, A. (1988) *Employment Relations in the Small Firm*, London: Routledge & Kegan Paul.

Rajan, A. (1999) *Employment: Bridging the Gap between Rhetoric and Reality*, London: Centre for Research in Employment and Technology in Europe.

Ramazanoglu, C. (1987) 'Sex and Violence in Academic Life or You Can't Keep a Good Man Down', in J. Hammer and M. Maynard (eds), *Women, Violence and Social Control, Explorations in Sociology* no. 23, London: Macmillan.

Ramsay, H. (1983) 'Evolution or Cycle? Worker Participation in the 1980s', in C. Crouch and F. Heller (eds), *Organisational Democracy and Political Processes*, London: Pitman.

Ramsay, H. (1985) 'What is Participation For: A Critical Evaluation of "Labour Process" Analyses of Job Reform', in D. Knights, H. Willmott and D. Collinson (eds), *Job Redesign: Critical Perspectives on the Labour Process*, London: Gower.

Ramsay, H. (1991) 'Reinventing the Wheel? A Review of the Development and Performance of Employee Involvement', *Human Resource Management Journal*, 1. 4: 1–22.

Ramsay, H. and Scholarios, D. (1998) 'Women and Workplace Democracy: An Attitude Problem?' unpublished paper, University of Strathclyde.

Ramsay, H., Scholarios, D. and Harley, B. (2000) 'Employees and High-Performance Work Systems: Testing Inside the Black Box', *British Journal of Industrial Relations*, 38. 4: 501–31.

Ramsay, H. and Scholarios, D. (2005) 'Organisational Participation and Women – An Attitude Problem?', in P. Thompson, J. Hyman and B. Harley (eds), *Participation and Democracy at Work: Essays in Honour of Harvie Ramsay*, Basingstoke: Palgrave Macmillan.

Ramsay, K. and Parker, M. (1992) 'Gender, Bureaucracy and Organisational Culture', in A. Witz and M. Savage (eds) *Gender and Bureaucracy*, Oxford: Blackwell.

Rana, E. and Higginbottom, K. (2002) 'Work-Life Balance Ghettoised', *People Management*, 8. 19, Sept: 8.

Randle, K. (1995) 'The Whitecoated Worker: Professional Autonomy in a Period of Change', paper presented to the 13th Annual International Labour Process Conference, University of Central Lancashire, Preston.

Randle, K. and Rainnie, A. (1994) 'Control, Contradiction and Complexity in a Pharmaceutical Research Company', paper presented to the 12th International Labour Process Conference, Aston.

Randolph, W. A. (1995) 'The Empowerment Effort that Came Undone', *Harvard Business Review*, Jan.–Feb.: 20–31.

Ray, C. A. (1986) 'Corporate Culture: the Last Frontier of Control?' *Journal of Management Studies*, 23. 3: 287–97.

Ray, L. J. and Reed, M. (1994a) *Organizing Modernity: New Weberian Perspectives on Work, Organization and Society*, London: Routledge.

Ray, L. J. and Reed, M.(1994b) 'Max Weber and the Dilemmas of Modernity', in L. J. Ray, and M. Reed, M. (eds), *Organizing Modernity: New Weberian Perspectives on Work, Organization and Society*, London: Routledge.

Reed, M. (1984) 'Management as a Social Practice', *Journal of Management Studies*, 21. 3: 273–85.

Reed, M. (1985) *Redirections in Organizational Analysis*, London: Tavistock.

Reed, M. (1990a) 'The Labour Process Perspective on Management Organisation: A Critique and Reformulation', in J. Hassard and D. Pym (eds), *The Theory and Philosophy of Organizations*, London: Routledge.

Reed, M. (1990b) 'From Paradigm to Images: The Paradigm Warrior Turns Post-Modernist Guru', *Personnel Review*, 19. 3: 35–40.

Reed, M. (1991) 'Scripting Scenarios for a New Organisation Theory and Practice', *Work, Employment and Society*, 5. 1: 119–32.

Reed, M. (1992a) 'Experts, Professions and Organizations in Late Modernity', paper presented to the Employment Research Unit Conference, Cardiff Business School.

Reed, M. (1992b) *The Sociology of Organisations*, London: Harvester.

Reed, M. (1993) 'Organizations and Modernity: Continuity and Discontinuity in Organisation Theory', in J. Hassard and M. Parker (eds), *Postmodernism and Organizations*, London: Sage.

Reed, M. (1996a) 'Organisational Theorising: A Historically Contested Terrain', in S. Clegg, C. Hardy and W. Nord (eds), *Handbook of Organisation Studies*, London: Sage.

Reed, M. (1996b) 'Rediscovering Hegel: The "New Historicism" in Organisation and Management Studies', *Journal of Management Studies*, 33. 2: 139–58.

Reed, M. (1997) 'In Praise of Duality and Dualism: Rethinking Agency and Structure in Organisational Analysis', *Organisation Studies*, 18. 1: 21–42.

Reed, M. (1998) 'Organizational Analysis as Discourse Analysis: A Critique', in D. Grant, T. Keenoy and C. Oswick (eds), *Discourse and Organization*, London: Sage.

Reed, M. (2005a) 'Beyond the Iron Cage: Bureaucracy and Democracy in the Knowledge Economy and Society', in P. Du Gay (ed.), *The Values of Bureaucracy*, Oxford: Oxford University Press.

Reed, M. (2005b) 'Reflections on the Realist Turn in Organisation and Management Studies', *Journal of Management Studies*, 42. 8: 1621–44.

Reed, M. (2005c) 'Doing the Loco-Motion: Response to Contu and Willmott's Commentary on the "Realist Turn in Organization and Management Studies"', *Journal of Management Studies*, 42. 8: 1663–73.

Reed, M. (2006) 'Organisational Theorising: A Historically Contested Terrain', in S. Clegg, C. Hardy, T. Lawrence and W. Nord (eds), *The Sage Handbook of Organisation Studies*, London: Sage.

Reed, M. (2008) 'Exploring Plato's Cave: Critical Realism in the Study of Organization and Management', in D. Barry and H. Hansen (eds), *The Sage Handbook New Approaches in Management and Organization*, London: Sage.

Reed, M. and Hughes, M. (eds) (1992) *Rethinking Organisation: New Directions in Organisation and Analysis*, London: Sage.

Rees, T. (1992) *Women and the Labour Market*, London: Routledge.

Reich, R. (1991) 'Who is Them?', *Harvard Business Review*, March–April. 77–88.

Reich, R. (1993) *The Work of Nations*, London: Simon & Schuster.

Reicher, S. (1997) 'Laying the Ground for a Common Critical Psychology', in T. Ibanez and L. Ininugez (eds), *Critical Social Psychology*, London: Sage.

Reid, S. (2007) 'Developing a Taxonomy of Professional Software Work as a Framework for Understanding Work Intensity and Work Intensification', International Labour Process Conference, Amsterdam, March.

Resch, M., Hacker, W., Leitner, K. and Krogoll, T. (1984) 'Regulation Requirements and Regulation Barriers: Two Aspects of Industrial Work', in M. Thomas (ed.), *Design of Work in Automated Manufacturing Systems*, Oxford: Pergamon.

Reynolds, Katherine J. and Turner, John C. (2001) 'Prejudice as a Group Process: The Role of Social Identity', in Martha Augoustinos and Katherine J. Reynolds (eds), *Understanding Prejudice, Racism, and Social Conflict*, London: Sage, pp. 159–78.

Rhinesmith, S. (1991) 'Going Global from the Inside Out', *Training and Development*, 45: 42–7.

Rifkin, J. (1995) *The End of Work: The Decline of the Global Labour Force and the Dawn of the Post-Market Era*, New York: G. P. Putnam.

Rifkin, J. (1999), *The Biotech Century*, New York: Tarcher Putnam.

Rifkin, J. (2000) *Age of Access: The New Culture of Hypercapitalism*, New York: J.P. Tarcher.

Ritzer, G. (1993) *The McDonaldization of Society*, London: Pine Forge.

Ritzer, G. (1975) *Sociology: A Multiple Paradigm Science*, Boston, MA: Allyn & Bacon.

Ritzer, G. (1996) 'The McDonaldization Thesis: Is Expansion Inevitable?' *International Sociology*, 11. 3: 291–308.

Ritzer, G. (1996) *Sociological Theory* (4th edn), New York: McGraw-Hill.

Ritzer, G. (1998) 'McJobs: McDonaldization and its Relationship to the Labour Process', in G. Ritzer (ed.), *The McDonaldization Thesis*, London: Sage.

Ritzer, G. (2001) *Explorations in the Sociology of Consumption*, London: Sage.

Robbins, T. (2001) *Labor's Loneliest Battles: New Survey Finds Union Self-Help Programs Point Way in Addiction Struggles*, Village Voice 23–29 May, available at: http://www.villagevoice.com/news/0121,robbins,24936,5.html (5, 1, 08).

Robertson, D., Rinehart, J. and Huxley, C. (1992) 'Team Concept: A Case Study of Japanese Production Management in a Unionised Canadian Auto Plant', paper presented to the 10th International Labour Process Conference, Aston.

Robinson, G. and Dechant, K. (1997) 'Building a Business Case for Diversity', *Academy of Management Executive*, 11. 3: 21–31.

Robinson, P. (1999) 'Explaining the Relationship between Flexible Employment and Labour Market Regulation', in A. Felstead and N. Jewson (eds), *Global Trends in Flexible Labour*, London: Macmillan.

Roeber, J. (1975) *Social Change at Work*, London: Duckworth.

Roethlisberger, F. G. and Dickson, W. J. (1939/1964) *Management and the Worker*, Science Editions, New York: Wiley.

Roethlisberger, F. G. and Dickson, W. J. (1984) 'Human Relations and the Informal Organisation', in F. Fischer and C. Sirriani (eds), *Management and the Worker*, New York: Wiley.

Roffe, I. (1999) 'Innovation and Creativity in Organisations: A Review of the Implications for Training and Development', *Journal of European Industrial Training*, 23. 4/5: 224–41.

Rogers, C. (1969) *Freedom To Learn: Studies of the Person*, Columbus, OH: Charles Merrill.

Rollinson, D., Broadfield, A. and Edwards, D. J. (1998) *Organisational Behaviour and Analysis: An Integrated Approach*, Harlow: Addison-Wesley.

Roper, M. (1994) *Masculinity and the British Organisation Man since 1945*, Oxford: Oxford University Press.

Rose, G. (1978) *The Melancholy Science: An Introduction to the Thought of Theodore W. Adorno*, London: Macmillan.

Rose, M. (1975, 1986) *Industrial Behaviour*, Harmondsworth: Penguin.

Rose, M. and Jones, B. (1985) 'Managerial Strategy and Trade Union Responses in Work Reorganization Schemes at Establishment Level', in D. Knights, H. Wilmott and D. Collinson (eds), *Job Redesign: Critical Perspectives on the Labour Process*, London: Gower.

Rose, N. (1989) 'Individualising Psychology', in J. Shotter and K. J. Gergen (eds), *Texts of Identity*, London: Sage, 99–118.

Rose, N. (1990) *Governing the Soul: The Shaping of the Private Self*, London: Routledge.

Rosenberg, S. and Lapidus, J. (1999) 'Contingent and Non-Standard Work in the United States: Towards a More Poorly Compensated, Insecure Workforce', in A. Felstead and N. Jewson (eds), *Global Trends in Flexible Labour*, London: Macmillan.

Rosener, J. (1990) 'Ways Women Lead', *Harvard Business Review*, Nov.–Dec.: 119–25.

Rosenfeld, P., Giacolone, R. A. and Riordan, C. A. (1995) *Impression Management in Organizations*, London: Routledge.

Rosenman, R. H., Friedman, M. and Strauss, R. (1964) 'A Predictive Study of CHD', *Journal of the American Medical Association*, 189: 15–22.

Rosenthal, P., Hill, S. and Peccei, R. (1997) 'Checking out Service: Evaluating Excellence, HRM and TQM in Retailing', *Work, Employment and Society*, 11. 3: 481–503.

Rosier, M. (1997) 'Postmodernism, Postmodernity and Social Psychology', in T. Ibanez and L. Ininugez (eds), *Critical Social Psychology*, London: Sage.

Rosnow, R. L. (1981) *Paradigms in Transition: The Methodology of Social Enquiry*, New York: Oxford University Press.

Ross, L. (1977) 'The Intuitive Psychologist and his Shortcomings: Distortions in the Attribution Process', in L. Berkowitz (ed.), *Advances in Experimental Social Psychology*, vol. 10, New York: Academic Press, pp. 173–220.

Rothschild, J. and Allen Whitt, J. (1986) *The Cooperative Workplace: Potentials and Dilemmas or Organisational Democracy and Participation*, Cambridge: Cambridge University Press.

Rothwell, S. (1987) 'Selection and Training for Advanced Manufacturing Technology', in T. D. Wall, C.W. Clegg and N. J. Kemp (eds), *The Human Side of Advanced Manufacturing Technology*, Chichester: Wiley.

Rothwell, W. J. and Kazanas, H. C. (1986) 'The Attitude Survey as an Approach to Human Resource Strategic Planning', *Journal of Managerial Psychology*, 2: 15–18.

Rotter, J. B. (1972) 'Generalised Expectancies for Internal versus External Control of Reinforcement', in J. B. Rotter, J. E. Chance and E. J. Phare (eds), *Applications of a Social Learning Theory of Personality*, New York: Holt, Rinehart & Winston.

Rowlinson, M. (1997) *Organisations and Institutions*, London: Macmillan.

Rowlinson, M. and Hassard, J. (2000) 'Marxist Political Economy, Revolutionary Politics and Labour Process Theory', *International Studies of Management and Organisation*, 30. 4: 85–111.

Roy, D. F. (1973) 'Banana Time, Job Satisfaction and Informal Interaction', in G. Salaman and K. Thompson (eds), *People and Organizations*, Harlow : Longman.

Royal, C. and O'Donnell, L. (2005) 'Embedding Human Capital Analysis in the Investment Process: A Human Resources Challenge', *Asia Pacific Journal of Human Resources* 43. 1: 117–36.

RSA Inquiry (1994) *Tomorrow's Company: The Role of Business in a Changing World*, London: Royal Society of Arts.

Rubery, J., Smith, M. and Fagan, C. (1999) *Women's Employment in Europe: Trends and Prospects*, London: Routledge.

Rubery, J. (2005) 'Labour Markets', in S. Ackroyd, R. Batt, P. Thompson, and P. Tolbert (eds), *A Handbook of Work and Organization*, Oxford: Oxford University Press.

Rubery, J., Earnshaw, J., Marchington, M., Cooke, F.L. and Vincent, S. (2005) 'Changing Organisational Forms and the Employment Relationship', in G. Salaman, J. Storey and J. Billsberry (eds), *Strategic Human Resource Management: Theory and Practice*, London: Sage.

Rueschemeyer, D. (1986) *Power and the Division of Labour*, London: Polity.

Rugman, A. (2000) *The End of Globalization*, London: Random House.

Rugman, A. (2005) *The Regional Multinationals*, Cambridge, U.K.: Cambridge University Press.

Ruigrok, W. *et al.* (1999) 'Corporate Restructuring and New Forms of Organizing: Evidence from Europe', *Management International Review*, 39. 2: 41–64.

Russ, G. S. (1991) 'Symbolic Communication and Image Management in Organizations', in R. A. Giacolone and P. Rosenfeld (eds), *Applied Impression Management: How Image-Making Affects Managerial Decisions*, CA: Sage.

Ryan, R. (1992) 'Flexibility in New Zealand Workplaces: A Study of Northern Employers', *New Zealand Journal of Industrial Relations*, 17: 129–47.

Ryff, C. D. U. (1989) 'Happiness is Everything, or Is It? Explorations on the Meaning of Psychological Well-being', *Journal of Personality and Social Psychology*, 57. 6, Dec.: 1069–81.

Sabel, C. (1991) 'Mobius Strip Organizations and Open Labour Markets: Some Consequences of the Reintegration of Conception and Execution in a Volatile Economy', in J. Coleman and P. Bourdieu (eds), *Social Theory for a Changing Society*, Boulder, CO: Westview.

Sabel, C. F. (1982) *Work and Politics and the Division of Labour in Industry*, Cambridge: Cambridge University Press.

Salaman, G. (1979) *Work Organizations: Resistance and Control*, London: Longman.

Salaman, G. (1981) *Class and the Corporation*, London: Fontana.

Salaman, G. (1986) *Working*, London: Tavistock.

Salaman and Butler (1994) 'Why Managers Won't Learn', in C. Mabey, and P. Iles (eds), *Managing Learning*, London: Routledge with the Open University.

Salaman, G. and Thompson, K. (eds) (1973) *People and Organizations*, Harlow: Longman.

Salaman, G. and Thompson, K. (eds) (1980) *Control and Ideology in Organizations*, Milton Keynes: Open University Press.

Salancik, G. R. and Pfeffer, J. (1978) 'A Social Information Processing Approach to Job Attitudes and Task Design', *Administrative Science Quarterly*, 23: 224–53.

Salas, E., Dickinson, T. U., Converse, S. A., Tannenbaum, S. I. (1992) 'Toward an Understanding of Team Performance and Training', in R.W. Swezey and E. Salas (eds), *Teams: Their Training and Performance*, Norwood, NJ: Ablex, pp. 3–29.

Salovey, P. and Mayer, J. (1990) 'Emotional Intelligence', *Imagination, Cognition and Personality*, 9: 185–211.

Salverda, W., Van Kalveran, M. and M. van der Meer (eds) (2008) *Low-Wage Work in the Netherlands, Russell Sage Foundation Case Studies of Job Quality in Advanced Economies*, New York: Russell Sage Foundation.

Sandberg, A. (1993) 'Volvo Human-Centred Work Organisation: The End of the Road?' *New Technology, Work and Employment*, 8. 2: 82–7.

Sandberg, A. (ed.) (1995) *Enriching Production*, Aldershot, Avebury.

Sandelands, L. E. and Srivatsan, V. (1993) 'The Problem of Experience in the Study of Organizations', *Organisation Studies*, 14. 1: 1–22.

Sargent, A. G. (1983) *The Androgynous Manager*, New York: AMACOM.

Saunders, C. S. (1981) 'Management Information Systems, Communication and Depart-mental Power: An Integrative Model', *Academy of Management Review*, 6: 431–42.

Sayer, A. (1986) 'New Developments in Manufacturing: the Just-in-Time System', *Capital and Class*, 30: 43–72.

Sayer, A. and Ray, L. (eds) (1999) *Culture and Economy after the Cultural Turn*, London: Sage.

Sayer, D. (1991) *Capitalism and Modernity: An Excursus on Marx and Weber*, London: Routledge.

Sayles, C. R. (1958) *Behaviour of Industrial Work Groups*, New York: Wiley.

Scarborough, H. (2003), 'Knowledge Management, HRM and the Innovation Process', *International Journal of Manpower*, 24. 5: 501–16.

Scarbrough, H., and Burrell, G. (1996) 'The Axeman Cometh: The Changing Roles and Knowledges of Middle Managers', in S. Clegg and G Palmer (eds), *The Politics of Management Knowledge*, London: Sage.

Scarbrough, H. and Swan, J. (2001) 'Explaining the Diffusion of Knowledge Management: The Role of Fashion', *British Journal of Management*, 12: 3–12.

Schein, E. H. (1965) *Organisational Psychology*, Englewood Cliffs, N.J.: Prentice Hall (also 1980, 3rd edn.).

Schein, E. H. (1985) *Organisational Culture and Leadership: A Dynamic View*, San Francisco: Jossey-Bass.

Schienstock, G. (1991) *The Brave New World of the Multinational Corporation*, 10th EGOS Colloquium, Vienna.

Schiffrin, A. (2001) *The Business of Books: How the International Conglomerates Took Over Publishing and Changed the Way We Read*, London: Verso.

Schiller, D. (1999) *Digital Capitalism Networking the Global Market System*, Boston, MA: MIT Press.

Schlenker, B. R. (1980) *Impression Management*, Monterey: Brooks/Cole.

Schneider, M. (1975) *Neurosis and Civilisation: A Marxist/Freudian Synthesis*, New York: Seabury.

Schneider, S. C. and Barsoux, J.-L. (1997) *Managing across Cultures*, London: Prentice Hall.

Schoenfeld, G. (2005) *Work-Life Balance: An MBA Alumni Report*, GMAC ® Research Reports, RR-05-09 13 October, available at: http://www.gmac.com/NR/rdonlyres/1BD3593C-5450-4A76-8CEA-8FE1BEAEE263/0/RR0509_WorkLifeBalance.pdf.

Schor, J. B. (1993) *The Overworked American: The Unexpected Decline of Leisure*, New York: Basic Books.

Schultz, M. and Hatch, M.-J. (1996) 'Living with Multiple Paradigms: The Case of Paradigm Interplay in Organisational Culture Studies', *Academy of Management Review*, 21: 529–57.

Schumann, M. (2000) 'The Development of Industrial Labour: New Inconsistencies', *Economic and Industrial Democracy*, 21: 97–106.

Schutz, A. (1967) *The Phenomenology of the Social World*, Evanston, IL: North Western University Press.

Schwartz, H. S. (1983) 'A Theory of Denotic Work Motivation', *Journal of Applied Behavioural Science*, 14: 204–14.

Scott, A. (1994) *Willing Slaves? British Workers under Human Resource Management*, Cambridge: Cambridge University Press.

Scott, J. (1979) *Corporations, Classes and Capitalism*, London: Hutchinson.

Scott, J. (1985) 'Ownership, Management and Strategic Control', in K. Elliot and P. Lawrence (eds), *Introducing Management*, Harmondsworth: Penguin.

Seivers, B. (1986) 'Beyond the Surrogate of Motivation', *Organisation Studies*, 7. 4: 335–351.

Seligman, M. E. P. (1975) *Helplessness*, San Francisco: Freeman.

Selznick, P. (1949) *TVA and the Grass Roots*, Berkeley, CA: University of California Press.

Selznick, P. (1957) *Leadership in Administration*, Evanston, IL: Row Peterson.

Senge, P. M. (1992) 'Building Learning Organisations: The Real Message of the Quality Movement', *Journal for Quality and Participation*, March.

Sennett, R. (1998) *The Corrosion of Character: The Personal Consequences of Work in the New Capitalism*, London: W. W. Norton.

Seve, L. (1978) *Man in Marxist Theory and the Psychology of Personality*, Sussex: Harvester.

Sewell, G. (1998) 'The Discipline of Teams: The Control of Team-Based Industrial Work Through Electronic and Peer Surveillance', *Administrative Science Quarterly*, 43: 406–69.

Sewell, G. and Barker, J. (2006) 'Max Weber and the Irony of Bureaucracy', in M. Korczynski, R. Hodson and P. Edwards (eds), *Social Theory at Work*, Oxford: Oxford University Press.

Sewell, G. and Wilkinson, B. (1992) '"Someone to Watch over Me": Surveillance, Discipline and the Just-in-Time Labour Process', *Sociology*, 26. 2: 271–89.

Sieloff, C. G. (1999) 'If only HP Knew What HP Knows', *Journal of Knowledge Management*, 3. 1: 47–53.

Shaiken, H., Herzenberg, S. and Kuhn, S. (1986) 'The Work Process under More Flexible Production', *Industrial Relations*, 125. 2: 167–83.

Shamir, B. (1991) 'Meaning, Self and Motivation in Organisations', *Organisation Studies*, 12. 3: 405–24.

Sharpe, D. (1996) 'Changing Managerial Control Strategies and Subcultural Processes: An Ethnographic Study on the Hano Assembly Line', paper presented to the 14th Annual Labour Process Conference, Aston.

Sharpe, R. (1998) 'Globalisation: The Next Tactic in the 50-Year Struggle of Labour and Capital in Software Production', paper presented to the Work Difference and Social Change Conference, Binghamton, May.

Shaw, M. (1990) 'Strategy and Social Process: Military Context and Sociological Analysis', *Sociology*, 24. 3: 465–73.

Shenhav, Y. (1999) *Manufacturing Rationality: The Engineering Foundations of the Managerial Revolution*, Oxford: Oxford University Press.

Sheppard, D. (1989) 'Organizations, Power and Sexuality: The Image and Self-Image of Women Managers', in J. Hearn, D. L. Sheppard, P. Tancred-Sheriff and G. Burrell (eds), *The Sexuality of Organisation*, London: Sage.

Shotter, J. and Gergen, K. J. (1989) *Texts of Identity*, London: Sage.

Shrivastava, P. (1983) 'A Typology of Organisational Learning Systems', *Journal of Management Studies*, 20. 1: 7–28.

Shutt, J. (1985) 'Tory Enterprise Zones and the Labour Movement', *Capital and Class*, 23: 19–44.

Silver, J. (1987) 'The Ideology of Excellence: Management and Neo-Conservatism', *Studies in Political Economy*, 24, Autumn: 105–29.

Silverman, D. (1970) *The Theory of Organizations*, London: Heinemann.

Silverman, D. and Jones, J. (1976) *Organisational Work: The Language of Grading and the Grading of Language*, London: Macmillan.

Silvia, P. J. (2006) *Exploring the Psychology of Interest*, New York: Oxford University Press.

Simon, H. A. (1960) *Administrative Behaviour*, New York: Macmillan.

Simpson, R. (1997) 'Have Times Changed? Career Barriers and the Token Women Manager', *British Journal of Management*, 8, special issue, June: S121–30.

Simpson, R. (1998) 'Presenteeism, Power and Organisational Change: Long Hours as a Career Barrier and the Impact on the Working Lives of Women Managers', *British Journal of Management*, 9, special issue, Sept.: S37–50.

Simpson, R. (2000) 'Presenteeism and the Impact of Long Hours on Managers', in D. Winstanley and J. Woodall (eds), *Ethical Issues in Contemporary Human Resource Management*, London: Macmillan, pp. 156–71.

Simpson, R. (2004) 'Masculinity at Work: The Experiences of Men in Female Dominated Occupations', *Work, Employment and Society*, 18. 2: 349–68.

Simpson, R. and Lewis, P. (2005) 'An Investigation of Silence and a Scrutiny of Transparency: Re-Examining Gender in Organization Literature through the Concepts of Voice and Visibility', *Human Relations*, 58. 10: 1253–75.

Simpson, R. and Lewis, P. (2007) *Voice, Visibility and the Gendering of Organizations*, Basingstoke: Palgrave Macmillan.

Sims, D., Fineman, S. and Gabriel, Y. (1993) *Organising and Organisations: An Introduction*, London: Sage.

Sirriani, C. (1984) 'Participation, Equality and Opportunity: Towards a Pluralist Organisational Model', in F. Fischer and C. Sirriani (eds), *Critical Studies in Organisation and Bureaucracy*, Philadelphia: Temple University Press.

Sisson, J. (1990) 'Introducing the Human Resource Management Journal', *Human Resource Management Journal*, 1. 1: 1–11.

Sisson, K. (1997) *New Forms in Work Organisation: Can Europe Realise its Potential?* Dublin: European Foundation for the Improvement of Living and Working Conditions.

Sisson, K. and Marginson, P. (1995) 'Management: Systems, Structure and Strategy', in P. K. Edwards (ed.), *Industrial Relations: Theory and Practice in Britain*, Oxford: Blackwell.

Skinner, B.F. (1959) Review of Verbal Behavior, *Language* 35, no. 1 (January–March): 26–57.

Skinner, B. F. (1971) *Beyond Freedom and Dignity*, New York: Knopf.

Sklair, L. (2001) *The Transnational Capitalist Class*, London: Blackwell.

Slaughter, J. (1987) 'The Team Concept in the US Auto Industry: Implications for Unions', paper presented to the Conference on Japanisation, UMIST.

Smart, B. (1985) *Michel Foucault*, London: Tavistock.

Smart, B. (1992) *Modern Conditions, Postmodern Controversies*, Oxford: Polity.

Smart, B. (1999) 'Resisting McDonaldization: Theory, Process and Critique', in B. Smart, *Resisting McDonaldization*, London: Sage.

Smircich, L. (1983) 'Concepts of Culture and Organisational Analysis', *Administrative Science Quarterly*, 28: 339–58.

Smith, C. (1987) 'Flexible Specialisation and Earlier Critiques of Mass Production', paper presented to the Conference on the Labour Process, Aston-UMIST.

Smith, C. (1991) 'From 1960s' Automation to Flexible Specialisation: A Déjà Vu of Technological Panaceas', in A. Pollert (ed.), *Farewell to Flexibility?*, Oxford: Blackwell.

Smith, C. (2005) 'Beyond Convergence and Divergence: Explaining Variations in Organizational Practices and Forms', in S. Ackroyd, R. Batt, P. Thompson and P. Tolbert (eds), *The Oxford Handbook of Work and Organization*, Oxford: Oxford University Press.

Smith, C. and Elger, T. (eds) (1994) *Global Japanisation? The Transnational Transformation of the Labour Process*, London: Routledge.

Smith, C., Valesechhi, R., Muller, F. and Gabe, J. (2008) 'Knowledge and the Discourse of Labour Process Transformation', *Work, Employment and Society*, 22. 4: 581–99.

Smith, C. and McKinlay, A. (2009) 'Creative Industries and Labour Process Analysis', in C. Smith and A. McKinlay (eds), *Creative Labour*, Basingstoke: Palgrave.

Smith, C. and Meiskens, P. (1995) 'System, Society and Dominance in Cross-National Organisational Analysis', *Work, Employment and Society*, 9. 2: 241–67.

Smith, C. and Thompson, P. (1992) *Labour in Transition: The Labour Process in Eastern Europe and China*, London: Routledge.

Smith, C., Valsechhi, R., Muller, F. and Gabe, J. (2008) 'Knowledge and the Discourse of Labour Process Transformation: Nurses and the Case of NHS Direct for England', *Work, Employment and Society*, 22. 4: 581–99.

Smith, D. (1987) 'The Japanese Example in South West Birmingham', paper presented to the Conference on Japanisation of British Industry, UMIST.

Smith, P. C. and Kendall, L. M. (1963) 'Retranslation of Epectations: An Approach to the Construction of Unambiguous Anchors for Rating Scales', *Journal of Applied Psychology*, 47: 149–55.

Smith, V. (1990) *Managing in the Corporate Interest: Control and Resistance in an American Bank*, Berkeley, CA: University of California Press.

Snyder, M. (1979) 'Self-Monitoring Processes', in L. Berkowitz (ed.), *Advances in Experimental Social Psychology*, vol. 12, New York: Academic Press, pp. 85–125.

Snyder, M. (1987) *Public Appearances/Private Realities: The Psychology of Self-Monitoring*, San Francisco: Freeman.

Snyder, M. and Gangestad, S. (1986) 'On the Nature of Self-Monitoring: Matters of Assess-ment, Matters of Validity', *Journal of Personality and Social Psychology*, 51: 123–39.

Solvell, O., and Zander, I. (1995) 'Organization of the Dynamic Multinational Enterprise: The Home-Based and the Heterarchical MNE', *International Studies of Management and Organization*, 25. 1–2: 17–38.

Søndergaard, M. (1994) 'Hofstede's Consequences: A Study of Reviews, Citations and Replications', *Organisation Studies*, 15. 3: 447–56.

Sorge, A., Hartmann, G., Warner, M. and Nicholas, I. (1983) *Microelectronics and Manpower in Manufacturing*, Aldershot: Gower.

Soskice, D. and Hall, P (2001) (eds) *Varieties of Capitalism: The Institutional Foundations of Comparative Advantage*, Oxford: Oxford University Press.

Sparrow, P. R. and Hiltrop, J.-M. (1998) 'Redefining the Field of European Human Resource Management: A Battle between National Mindsets and Forces of Business Tradition', in C. Mabey, G. Salaman and J. Storey (eds), *Strategic Human Resource Management*, London: Sage.

Spears, R. (1997) 'Introduction', to T. Ibanez and L. Iniguez (eds), *Critical Social Psychology*, London: Sage.

Spicer, A. and Bohm, S. (2007) 'Moving Management: Theorizing Struggles against the Hegemony of Management', *Organization Studies*, 28. 11: 1667–69.

Springer, R. (1999) 'The End of New Production Concepts? Rationalization and Labour Policy in the German Auto Industry', *Economic and Industrial Democracy*, 20: 117–45.

Staber, U. and Aldrich, H. (1987) 'Organisational Transformation and Trends in US Employment Relations', paper presented to the Conference on the Labour Process, Aston-UMIST.

Staines, G.L.S. (1980) Spillover Versus Compensation: A Review of the Literature on the Relationship between Work and Nonwork, *Human Relations*, 33. 2: 111–29.

Stainton-Rogers, R. and Stainton-Rogers, W. (1997) 'Going Critical?', in T. Ibanez and L. Ininguez (eds), *Critical Social Psychology*, London: Sage.

Standing, G. (1986) *Unemployment and Labour Market Flexibility:The United Kingdom*, Geneva: International Labour Office.

Standing, G. (1999) *Global Labour Flexibiity: Seeking Distributive Justice*, Basingstoke: Palgrave Macmillan.

Stanko, E. (1988) 'Keeping Women in and Out of Line: Sexual Harassment and Occupational Segregation', in S. Walby (ed.), *Gender Segregation at Work*, Milton Keynes: Open University Press.

Starbuck, W.H. (2003) 'Shouldn't Organization Theory Emerge From Adolescence?', *Organization*, 10. 3: 439–52.

Starkey, K. (1992) 'Durkheim and Organisational Analysis: Two Legacies', *Organisation Studies*, 13. 4: 627–42.

Starkey, K. (ed.), (1996), *How Organizations Learn: Strategy, Structure, Process and Leadership*, London : Routledge.

Steers, R. M. and Porter, L. W. (1987) *Motivation and Work Behaviour*, New York: McGraw-Hill.

Steffy, B. D. and Grimes, A. J. (1992) 'Personnel/Organisation Psychology: A Critique of the Discipline', in M. Alvesson and H. Willmott (eds), *Critical Management Studies*, London: Sage.

Steiner, T. and Miner, B. (1978) *Management Policy and Strategy*, West Drayton: Collier-Macmillan.

Stephenson, C. (1994) 'Problem Solving in a Lean Production Scenario', paper presented to the 12th Annual Labour Process Conference, Aston.

Stewart, E. (1967) *The Reality of Management*, London: Pan.

Stewart, E. (1976) *Contrasts in Management*, Maidenhead: McGraw-Hill.

Stodgill, R. M. (1948) 'Personal Factors Associated with Leadership: A Review of the Literature', *Journal of Psychology*, 25: 35–7.

Stodgill, R. M. (1974/1976) *Handbook of Leadership*, New York: Free Press.

Stone, K. (1973) 'The Origins of Job Structures in the Steel Industry', *Radical America*, 7. 6: 19–66.

Storey, J. (1983) *Managerial Prerogative and the Question of Control*, London: Routledge & Kegan Paul.

Storey, J. (1985) 'The Means of Management Control', *Sociology*, 19. 2: 193–211.

Storey, J. (ed.) (1989) *New Perspectives on Human Resource Management*, London: Routledge.

Storey, J. (1992) *Developments in the Management of Human Resources*, Oxford: Blackwell.

Storey, J. (ed.) (1995) *Human Resource Management: A Critical Text*, London: Routledge.

Storey, J., Mabey, C. and Thomson, A. (1997) 'What a Difference a Decade Makes', *People Management*, 12 June: 28–30.

Storlie, F. J. (1979) 'Burnout: The Elaboration of a Concept', *American Journal of Nursing*, December: 2108–11.

Strauss, A., Schatzman, L., Erlich, D., Bucher, R. and Sabshim, M. (1963) 'The Hospital and its Negotiated Order', in E. Friedson (ed.), *The Hospital in Modern Society*, New York: Macmillan.

Streek, W. (1987) 'The Uncertainties of Management in the Management of Uncertainty: Employers, Labour Relations and Industrial Adjustment in the 1980s', *Work, Employment and Society*, 1. 3: 281–308.

Stringer, P. (ed.) (1982) *Confronting Social Issues: Applications of Social Psychology*, vol. 2, London: Academic Press.

Stryker, S. (1980) *Symbolic Interactionism: A Social Structural Version*, Menlo Park, CA: Benjamin/Cummings.

Sturdy, A. (1987) 'Coping with the Pressure of Work', paper presented to the Conference on the Labour Process, Aston-UMIST.

Sturdy, A., Brocklehurst, M., Winstanley, D. and Littlejohns, M. (2006) 'Management as a (Self) Confidence Trick: Management Ideas, Education and Identity Work', *Organization*, 13. 6, 1 November: 841–60.

Sturdy, A. and Fineman, S. (2001) 'Struggles for the Control of Affect: Resistance as Politics of Emotion', in Sturdy, I. Grugulis and H. Willmott (eds), *Customer Service: Empowerment and Entrapment*, Basingstoke: Palgrave Macmillan.

Sturdy, A., Grugulis, I. and Willmott, H. (eds) (2001) *Servicing Consumers: Critical Studies of Consumer Service*, London: Palgrave.

Sturdy, A., Knights, D. and Willmott, H. (eds) (1992) *Skill and Consent: Contemporary Studies in the Labour Process*, London: Routledge.

Sturdy, A. and Korczynski, M. (2005) 'In the Name of the Customer? Service Work and Participation', in J. Hyman, P. Thompson and B. Harley (eds), *Participation and Democracy at Work: Essays in Honour of Harvie Ramsay*, Basingstoke: Palgrave.

Supple, B. (1991) 'Scale and Scope: Alfred Chandler and the Dynamics of Industrial Capitalism', *Economic History Review*, 44. 3: 500–14.

Sussman, L. (1991) 'Managers: on the Defensive', *Business Horizons*, Jan.–Feb.: 83.

Sveningsson, S. and Alvesson, M. (2003) 'Managing Managerial Identities: Organizational Fragmentation, Discourse and Identity Struggle', *Human Relations*, 56. 10: 1163–94.

Sweiger, D. M., Sandburg, W. R. and Ragan, J. W. (1986) 'Group Approaches for Improving Strategic Decision Making: A Comparative Analysis of Dialectical Inquiry, Devil's Advocacy and Consensus', *Academy of Management Journal*, 29: 149–59.

Swieringa, J. and Wierdsma, A. (1992) *Becoming a Learning Organisation*, Wokingham: Addison-Wesley.

Symons, G. (1992) 'The Glass Ceiling is Constructed over the Gendered Office', *Women in Management Review*, 7: 18–22.

Taber, T. D. (1991) 'Triangulating Job Attitudes with Interpretative and Positivist Measurement Methods', *Personnel Psychology*, 44. 3: 577–600.

Tailby, S. and Turnbull, P. (1987) 'Learning to Manage Just-in-Time', *Personnel Management*, January: 7–10.

Tajfel, H. (1982) *Social Identity and Intergroup Relations*, Cambridge: Cambridge University Press.

Tajfel, H. and Turner, J. C. (1979) 'An Integrative Theory of Intergroup Conflict', in W. G. Austin and S. Worschel (eds), *The Social Psychology of Intergroup Relations*, Monterey, CA: Brooks-Cole.

Tajfel, H. and Turner, J. C. (1986) 'The Social Identity Theory of Intergroup Relations', in W. G. Austin and S. Worschel (eds), *The Social Psychology of Intergroup Relations*, Monterey, CA: Brooks-Cole.

Tapscott, D. and Williams. A.D. (2007) *Wikinomics: How Mass Collaboration Changes Everything*, New York: Atlantic Books.

Taylor, F. W. (1947) *Scientific Management*, New York: Harper & Row.

Taylor, P. and Bain, P. (1998). 'An Assembly Line in the Head: The Call Centre Labour Process', *Industrial Relations Journal*, 30. 2: 101–17.

Taylor, P. and Bain, P. (2003) 'Subterranean Worksick Blues: Humour as Subversion in Two Call Centres', *Organization Studies*, 24. 9: 1487–1509.

Taylor, P. and Bain, P. (2006) 'India Calling to the Far Away Towns: the Call Centre Labour Process and Globalisation', in *Work, Employment and Society*, 19. 2: 261–82.

Taylor, R. (2002) *Britain's World of Work*, Myths and Realities (ESRC), available at: www.leeds.ac.uk/esrcfutureofwork/.

Taylor, R. (2006) *Sweden's New Social Democratic Model*, London: Compass.

Taylor, S. (1998) 'Emotional Labour and the New Workplace', in P. Thompson and C. Warhurst (eds), *Workplaces of the Future*, London: Macmillan.

Taylor, W. (1991) 'The Logic of Global Business: An Interview with ABB's Percy Barnevik', *Harvard Business Review*, March–April: 91–105.

Taylor, W. (1994) 'Control in an Age of Chaos', *Harvard Business Review*, Nov.–Dec.: 64–76.

Teasdale, P. (2000) 'What Can We Say about the Future of Work Using Statistics that Describe the Past?' paper presented to the 15th Annual Employment Research Unit Conference, Cardiff Business School, September.

Tedeschi, J. T., Schlenker, B. R. and Bonoma, T. V. (1971) 'Cognitive Dissonance: Private Ratiocination or Public Spectacle?', *American Psychologist*, 26: 685–95.

Tengblad, S. (2006) 'Is there a "New Managerial Work"? A Comparison with Henry Mintzberg's Classic Study 30 Years on', *Journal of Management Studies*, 43. 7: 1437–61.

Tennen, H. and Affleck, G. (1990) 'Blaming Others for Threatening Events' *Psychological Bulletin*, 108: 209–32.

Teulings, A. (1986) 'Managerial Labour Processes in Organised Capitalism: The Power of Corporate Management and the Powerlessness of the Manager', in D. Knights and H. Willmott (eds), *Managing the Labour Process*, Aldershot: Gower.

Thackray, J. (1986) 'The Corporate Culture Rage', *Management Today*, Feb.: 67–70.

Thackray, J. (1988) 'Flattening the White Collar', *Personnel Management*, August.

Thackray, J. (1993) 'Fads, Fixes and Fictions', *Management Today*, June: 41–3.

Thomas, A. and Kitzinger, C. (eds) (1997) *Sexual Harassment: Contemporary Feminist Perspectives*, Milton Keynes: Open University Press.

Thomas, R. J. (1988) 'What is Human Resource Management?' *Work, Employment and Society*, 2. 3: 392–402.

Thomas, R. and Davies, A. (2005) 'Theorizing the Micro-politics of Resistance: New Public Management and Managerial Identities in the UK Public Services', *Organization Studies*, 26. 5: 683–706.

Thompson, E. P. (1967) 'Time, Work Discipline and Industrial Capitalism', *Past and Present*, 38: 55–97.

Thompson, G. (2005) 'Interfirm Relations as Networks', in S. Ackroyd, R. Batt, P. Thompson, and P. Tolbert (eds.) *A Handbook of Work and Organization*, Oxford: Oxford University Press.

Thompson, J. D. (1967) *Organizations in Action*, New York: McGraw-Hill.

Thompson, J. D. and McEwan, W. J. (1973) 'Organisational Goals and Environments', in G. Salaman and K. Thompson (eds), *People and Organisations*, Harlow: Longman.

Thompson, P. (1984) 'The New Vocationalism: The Trojan Horse of the MSC', *Social Science Teacher*, 13. 2.

Thompson, P. (1988) 'The End of Bureaucracy? New Developments in Work and Organisation', in M. Haralambos (ed.), *Developments in Sociology*, vol. 5, Ormskirk: Causeway.

Thompson, P. (1989) *The Nature of Work: An Introduction to Debates on the Labour Process*, London: Macmillan.

Thompson, P. (1993) 'Fatal Distraction: Postmodernism and Organisation Theory', in J. Hassard and M. Parker, *Postmodernism and Organisations*, London: Sage.

Thompson, P. (1994) 'Corporate Culture: Myths and Realities, West and East', paper presented to the Conference on Convergence versus Divergence: the Case of Corporate Culture, Dunaújváros, Hungary.

Thompson, P. (2001) 'Progress, Practice and Profits: How Critical is Critical Management Studies?', paper presented to the 19th International Labour Process Conference, Royal Holloway.

Thompson, P. (2003a) 'Disconnected Capitalism: or Why Employers Can't Keep their Side of the Bargain', *Work, Employment and Society*, 17. 2: 359–78.

Thompson, P. (2003b) 'Fantasy Island: A Labour Process Critique of the "Age of Surveillance"', *Surveillance and Society*, 1. 2: 138–51.

Thompson, P. (2007) 'Making Capital: Strategic Dilemmas for HRM', in S. Bolton and M. Houlihan (eds), *Searching for the Human in Human Resource Management*, Basingstoke: Palgrave Press.

Thompson, P. and Ackroyd, S. (1995) 'All Quiet on the Workplace Front: A Critique of Recent Trends in British Industrial Sociology', *Sociology*, 29. 4: 615–33.

Thompson, P. and Bannon, E. (1985) *Working the System: The Shop Floor and New Technology*, London: Pluto.

Thompson, P. and Findlay, T. (1999) 'Changing the People: Social Engineering in the Contemporary Workplace', in A. Sayer and L. Ray (eds), *Culture and Economy after the Cultural Turn*, London: Sage.

Thompson, P., Flecker, J. and Wallace, T. (1995) 'Back to Convergence? Globalisation and Societal Effects on Work Organisation', in T. Boje (ed.), *The Welfare State and the Labour Market in a Changing Europe*, New York: M. E. Sharpe.

Thompson, P. and Harley, B. (2007) 'HRM and the Worker: Labour Process Perspectives', in P. Boxall, J. Purcell and P. Wright (eds), *The Oxford Handbook of Human Resource Management*, Oxford: Oxford University Press.

Thompson, P. and McHugh, D. (2002) *Work Organisations* (3rd edn), Basingstoke: Palgrave Macmillan.

Thompson, P., Jones, C., Nickson, D. and Wallace, T. (1998) 'Internationalisation and Integration: A Comparison of Manufacturing and Service Firms', *Competition and Change*, 3. 4: 387–416.

Thompson, P. and McHugh, D. (1995) *Work Organisations: A Critical Introduction*, Basingstoke: Palgrave Macmillan.

Thompson, P. and Marks, A. (2007) 'Beyond the Blank Slate: Towards an Understanding of the Formation of Identities and Interests in the Employment Relationship', International Labour Process Conference.

Thompson, P. and O'Connell Davidson, J. (1994) 'The Continuity of Discontinuity: Management Rhetoric in Turbulent Times', paper presented to the Conference on The Strategic Direction of Human Resource Management, Nottingham Trent University, December.

Thompson, P. and Sederblad, P. (1994) 'The Swedish Model of Work Organization', in C. Smith and T. Elger (eds.) *Global Japanisation*, London: Routledge.

Thompson, P. and Smith, C. (1998) 'Beyond the Capitalist Labour Process: Workplace Change, the State and Globalization', *Critical Sociology*, 24. 3: 193–215.

Thompson, P. and Smith, C. (2000) 'Follow the Redbrick Road: Reflections on Pathways in and out of the Labour Process Debate', *International Studies of Management and Organization*, 3. 4: 40–67.

Thompson, P., Smith, C. and Ackroyd, S. (2000) 'If Ethics is the Answer, You've Been Asking the Wrong Questions: A Reply to Martin Parker', *Organisation Studies*, 21. 6: 1149–58.

Thompson, P., van den Broek, D. and Callaghan, G. (2004) 'Teams without Teamwork: Explaining the Call Centre Paradox', *Economic and Industrial Democracy*, 25. 2: 197–218.

Thompson, P. and Wallace, T. (1996) 'Redesigning Production Through Teamworking', *International Journal of Operations and Production Management*, special issue on *Lean Production and Work Organisation*, 16. 2: 103–18.

Thompson, P. and Warhurst, C. (eds.) (1998) *Workplaces of the Future*, Basingstoke: Palgrave Macmillan.

Thompson, P., Wallace, T. and Flecker, J. (1992) 'The Urge to Merge: Organisational Change in the Merger and Acquisition Process', *International Journal of Human Resource Management*, 3. 2: 285–306.

Thompson, P., Wallace, T., Flecker, J. and Ahlstrand, R. (1994) 'It Ain't What You Do It's the Way that You Do It', paper presented to the 13th Annual International Labour Process Conference, Aston.

Thompson, P., Warhurst, C. and Callaghan, G. (2000) 'Human Capital or Capitalising on Humanity? Knowledge and Skills in Interactive Service Work', in C. Prichard, M. Chumer and R. Hull (eds), *Managing Knowledge: Critical Discussions of Work and Learning*, Basingstoke: Macmillan.

Thorndike, E. L. (1911) *Animal Intelligence*, New York: Macmillan

Thurley, K. and Wood, S. (1983) *Industrial Relations and Management Strategy*, Cambridge: Cambridge University Press.

Titchener, E. B. (2005) *A Beginner's Psychology*, Adamant Media Corporation (facsimile reprint of a 1922 edition by the Macmillan Company, New York).

Tichy, N. and Devanna, M. A. (1986) *Transformational Leadership*, London: Wiley.

Tichy, N., Fombrun, C. and Devanna, M. A. (1982) 'Strategic Human Resource Management', *Sloan Management Review*: 47–61.

Tierney, M. (1996) 'Negotiating a Software Career: Informal Work Practices and "The Lads" in a Software Installation', in K. Grint and R. Gill (eds), *The Gender-Technology Relation: Contemporary Theory and Research*, London: Taylor & Francis.

Toffler, A. (1970) *Future Shock*, New York: Bantam.

Tolbert, P. S. and Zucker, L. G. (1996) 'The Institutionalization of Institutional Theory', in S. Clegg, C. Hardy and W. Nord (eds), *Handbook of Organization Studies*, London: Sage.

Tolman, E.C. (1948) 'Cognitive Maps in Rats and Men', *Psychological Review*, 55: 189–208

Tomlinson, J. (1982) *The Unequal Struggle? British Socialism and the Capitalist Enterprise*, London: Methuen.

Tompkins, P. K. and Cheney, G. (1985) 'Communication and Unobtrusive Control in Contemporary Organizations', in R. D. McPhee and P. K. Tompkins (eds), *Organizational Communication: Traditional Themes and New Directions*, Beverly Hills, CA: Sage.

Torrington, D. (1989) 'Human Resource Management and the Personnel Function', in J. Storey (ed.), *New Perspectives on Human Resource Management*, London: Routledge.

Towers, B. (1987) 'Managing Labour Flexibility', *Industrial Relations Journal*, 18. 2: 79–83.

Townley, B. (1990) 'Foucault, Power/Knowledge and its Relevance for HRM', paper presented to the Employment Research Unit Annual Conference, Cardiff Business School, September.

Townley, B. (1993) 'Performance Appraisal and the Emergence of Management', *Journal of Management Studies*, 30. 2: 27–44.

Toynbee, P. (2003) *Hard Work. Life in Low Pay Britain*, London: Bloomsbury.

Tran, V. (1998) 'The Role of the Emotional Climate in Learning Organisations', *The Learning Organisation*, 5. 2: 99–103.

Triandis. H. C. (ed.) (1980) *Handbook of Cross-Cultural Psychology*, vol. 5, Boston, MA/London: Allyn & Bacon.

Trist, E. L. and Bamforth, K. W. (1951) 'Some Social and Psychological Consequences of the Longwall Method of Coal-Getting', *Human Relations*, 4. 1: 3–38.

Trist, E. L., Higgin, G. W., Murray, H. and Pollock, A. B. (1963) *Organisational Choice*, London: Tavistock.

Tsoukas, H. (1992) 'Postmodernism, Reflexive Rationalism and Organisational Studies: A Reply to Martin Parker', *Organisation Studies*, 13. 4: 643–49.

Tsoukas, H. (1994a) 'Socio-Economic Systems and Organisational Management: an Institutional Perspective on the Socialist Firm', *Organisation Studies*, 15. 1: 21–45.

Tsoukas, H. (1994b) 'What is Management? An Outline of a Metatheory', *British Journal of Management*, 5: 289–301.

Tsoukas, H. (1994c) 'From Social Engineering to Reflective Action in Organisational Behaviour', in H. Tsoukas (ed.), *New Thinking in Organizational Behaviour*, London: Butterworth-Heinemann.

Tuckman, A. (1994) 'Ideology, Quality and TQM', in A. Wilkinson and H. Willmott (eds), *Making Quality Critical*, London: Routledge & Kegan Paul.

Tuckman, B. W. (1965) 'Developmental Sequences in Small Groups', *Psychological Bulletin*, 63: 384–99.

Tuffin, K. (2005) *Understanding Critical Social Psychology*, Sage, London.

Turnbull, P. J. (1986) 'The Japanisation of British Industrial Relations at Lucas', *Industrial Relations Journal*, 17. 3: 193–206.

Turnbull, P (1988) 'The Limits to Japanisation: Just-in-Time, Labour Relations and the UK Automotive Industry', *New Technology, Work and Employment*, 3. 1: 7–20.

Turner, J. C. (1985) 'Social Categorization and the Self-Concept: A Social-Cognitive Theory of Group Behaviour', in E. J. Lawler (ed.), *Advances in Group Process: Theory and Research*, vol. 2, Greenwich, CT: JAI.

Turner, L. and Auer, P. (1994) 'A Diversity of New Work Organisation: Human-Centred, Lean and In-between', *Industrielle Beziehungen*, 1. 1: 39–61.

Tyler, M. and Taylor, S. (1997) ' "Come Fly with Us": Emotional Labour and the Commodification of Sexual Difference in the Airline Industry', paper presented to the 15th International Labour Process Conference, Edinburgh. A version of this paper was published in *Work, Employment and Society*, 14. 1: 77–95.

Tziner, A. and Kopelman, R. E. (2002) 'Is there a Preferred Performance Rating Format? A Non-psychometric Perspective', *Applied Psychology*, 51(3): 479–503, July. NHS Leadership Qualities (July 2003) available at: http://www.nhsleadershipqualities.nhs.uk/Portals/0/Technical_Research_Paper_Summary.pdf -, accessed 20.08-07.

Ursell, G. and Blyton, P. (1988) *State, Capital and Labour*, London: Macmillan.

Urwick, L. and Brech, E. F. I. (1949) *The Making of Scientific Management, vol. 1: Thirteen Pioneers*, London: Pitman.

Van Maanen, J. (1992) 'Drinking Our Troubles Away', in D. M. Kolb and J. M. Bartunek (eds), *Hidden Conflict in Organisations: Uncovering Behind the Scenes Disputes*, London: Sage.

Van Strien, P. J. (1982) 'In Search of an Emancipatory Social Psychology', in P. Stringer (ed.), *Confronting Social Issues: Applications of Social Psychology*, vol. 2, London: Academic Press.

Vargish, T. (1994) 'The Value of Humanities in Executive Development', in H. Tsoukas (ed.), *New Thinking in Organisational Behaviour*, London: Butterworth-Heinemann.

Vitols, S. (2001) 'Varieties of Corporate Governance: Comparing Germany and the UK', in P. A. Hall and D. Soskice (eds), *Varieties of Capitalism: The Institutional Foundations of Comparative Advantage.* Oxford: Oxford University Press.

Vroom, V. H. (1964) *Work and Motivation,* New York: Wiley.

Vroom, V. and Mann, F. C. (1960) 'Leader Authoritarianism and Employee Attitudes', *Personnel Psychology*, 13: 125–40.

Vroom, V. H. and Yetton, P. W. (1973) *Leadership and Decision Making*, Pittsburgh: University of Pittsburgh Press.

Wainwright, H. (1987) 'The Friendly Mask of "Flexibility"', *New Statesman*, 11 December.

Wajcman, J. (1996a) 'Desperately Seeking Difference: Is Management Style Gendered?' *British Journal of Industrial Relations*, 34. 3: 333–49.

Wajcman, J. (1996b) 'Women and Men Managers: Careers and Equal Opportunities', in R. Crompton, D. Gallie and K. Purcell (eds), *Changing Forms of Employment: Occupations, Skills and Gender*, London: Routledge.

Wajcman, J. (1998) *Managing Like a Man: Women and Men in Corporate Management*, Oxford: Polity and Blackwell.

Walby, S. (1986) *Patriarchy at Work*, Cambridge: Polity.

Walker, C. R. and Guest, R. H. (1952) *Man on the Assembly Line*, Cambridge, MA: Harvard University Press.

Wall, T. D., Clegg, C. W. and Kemp, N. J. (eds) (1987) *The Human Side of Advanced Manufacturing Technology*, Chichester: Wiley.

Wall, T. D., Kemp, N. J., Jackson, P. R. and Clegg, C. W. (1986) 'Outcomes of Autonomous Workgroups: A Long-Term Field Experiment', *Academy of Management Journal*, 29: 280–304.

Wallace, C. (1993) 'Reflections on the Concept of "Strategy"', in D. Morgan and L. Stanley (eds), *Debates in Sociology*, Manchester: Manchester University Press.

Walton, R. E. (1985) 'Towards a Strategy of Eliciting Employee Commitment Based on Policies of Mutuality', in R. E. Walton and P. R. Lawrence (eds), *Human Resource Management, Trends and Challenges*, Boston, MA: Harvard University School Press.

Walzer, M. (1985) 'The Politics of Michel Foucault', in D. Hoy (ed.), *Foucault: A Critical Reader*, Oxford: Blackwell.

Wanous, J. P. (1992) *Organization Entry: Recruitment, Selection, Orientation & Socialization of Newcomers*, Reading, MA: Addison-Wesley: 182–3.

Wardell, M. (1986) 'Labor and the Labor Process', paper presented to the Labour Process Conference, Aston-UMIST.

Warhurst, C. (1997) 'Political Economy and the Social Organisation of Economic Activity: A Synthesis of Neo-Institutional and Labour Process Analyses', *Competition and Change*, 2: 213–46.

Warhurst, C. and Nickson, D. (2007) 'Employee Experience of Aesthetic Labour in Retail and Hospitality', *Work, Employment and Society*, 21, 1: 103–20.

Warhurst, C., Nickson, D. and Shaw, E. (1998) 'A Future for Globalization? International Business Organisation in the Next Century', *Research in International Business and International Relations*, 7: 247–71.

Warhurst, C. and Thompson, P. (1998) 'Hands, Hearts and Minds: Changing Work and Workers at the End of the Century', in P. Thompson and C. Warhurst (eds), *Workplaces of the Future*, London: Macmillan: 1–24.

Warhurst, C. and Thompson, P. (2006) 'Mapping Knowledge in Work: Proxies or Practices?', *Work Employment and Society*, 20. 4: 787–800.

Warhurst, C. Thompson, P. and Nickson, D. (2008) 'Labor Process Theory: Putting the Materialism Back into the Meaning of Service Work', in C. MacDonald and M. Korczynski (eds), *Critical Perspectives on Service Work*, London: Routledge.

Waterman, R. H. (1988) *The Renewal Factor*, London: Bantam.

Watson, J. B. (1930) *Behaviourism* (2nd edn), New York: Norton.

Watson, T. (1980) 'Understanding Organizations: The Practicalities of Sociological Theory', in D. Dunkerley and G. Salaman (eds), *The International Yearbook of Organisation Studies 1980*, London: Routledge & Kegan Paul.

Watson, T. (1986) *Management, Organisation and Employment Strategy: New Directions in Theory and Practice*, London: Routledge & Kegan Paul.

Watson, T. (1994) *In Search of Management: Culture, Chaos and Control in Managerial Work*, London: Routledge.

Wanous, J.P. (1992) *Organizational Entry: Recruitment, Selection, Orientation & Socialization of Newcomers*, Reading, MA, Addison-Wesley, pp. 182–3.

Webb, J. (1996) 'Vocabularies of Motive and the "New" Management', *Work, Employment and Society*, 10. 2: 251–77.

Webb, J. (1997) 'The Politics of Equal Opportunity', *Gender, Work and Organisation*, 4. 3: 159–69.

Webb, J. (2004) 'Organizations, Self-Identities and the New Economy', *Sociology*, 38. 4: 719–38.

Webb, J. (2006) *Organisations, Identities and the Self*, Basingstoke: Palgrave Macmillan.

Webber, A. (1993) 'What's So New about the New Economy?' *Harvard Business Review*, Jan.–Feb.: 24–42.

Weber, M. (1968) *Economy and Society*, New York: Bedminster.

Weber, M. (1984) 'Bureaucracy', in F. Fischer and C. Sirriani (eds), *Critical Studies in Organisation and Bureaucracy*, Philadelphia: Temple University Press.

Webster, F. (2002) *Theories of the Information Society* (2nd edn), London: Routledge.

Webster, F. and Robins, K. (1993) 'I'll be Watching You: Comment on Sewell and Wilkinson', *Sociology*, 27. 2: 243–52.

Webster, J. (1996) *Shaping Women's Work: Gender, Employment and Information Technology*, London: Longman.

Weick, K. (1987) 'Organisational Culture as a Source of High Reliability', *California Management Review*, 39. 2: 112–27.

Weigert, A. J., Smith Teitge, J. and Teitge, D. W. (1986) *Society and Identity: Towards a Sociological Psychology*, New York: Cambridge University Press.

Weightman, J. (1999) *Introducing Organisational Behaviour*, Harlow: Longman.

Weir, D. (1993) 'Why Isn't There any Good Management Research?' *British Academy of Management Newsletter*, no. 15, June.

Weissman, R. (2001) 'The Case against GE: Global Management By Stress', *The Multinational Monitor*, 22. 7/8, July/August – available at: http://multinationalmonitor.org/mm2001/01july-august/julyaug01corp2.html.

Weitz, S. (1977) *Sex Roles: Biological, Psychological and Social Foundations*, New York: Oxford University Press.

Wellin, M. (1984) *Behaviour Technology: A New Approach to Managing People at Work*, Aldershot: Gower.

Westergaard-Neilson, N. (2008) *Low-Wage Work in Denmark: Russell Sage Foundation Case Studies of Job Quality in Advanced Economies*, New York: Russell Sage Foundation.

West, M. A. (1997) *Developing Creativity in Oerganizations*, Leicester: British Psychological Society.

West, P. (1994) 'The Concept of the Learning Organisation', *Journal of European Industrial Training*, 18. 1: 15–21, MCB University Press.

Westwood, R. I. and Clegg, S. (2003) *Debating Organization: Point-counterpoint in Organization Studies*, London: Blackwell Publishing

Westwood, S. (1984) *All Day, Every Day: Factory and Family in the Making of Women's Lives*, London: Pluto.

Westwood, S. and Linstead, S. (2001) *The Language of Organization*, London: Sage.

Wexler, P. (1983) *Critical Social Psychology*, Boston, MA: Routledge & Kegan Paul.

Wheeler, S. and Lyon, D. (1992) 'Employee Benefits for the Employer's Benefit: How Companies Respond to Stress', *Personnel Review*, 21. 7: 47–65.

Whipp, R. (1996) 'Creative Deconstruction: Strategy and Organisations', in S. Clegg, C. Hardy and W. Nord (eds), *Handbook of Organisation Studies*, London: Sage.

Whitaker, A. (1986) 'Managerial Strategy and Industrial Relations: A Case Study of Plant Relocation', *Journal of Management Studies*, 23. 6: 657–78.

White, H. C. (1992) *Identity and Control*, Princeton, NJ: Princeton University Press.

White, M., Hill, S., Mills, C. and Smeaton, D. (2004) *Managing to Change? British Workplaces and the Future of Work*, Basingstoke: Palgrave.

Whitehead, T. N. (1936) *Leadership in a Free Society*, Cambridge, MA: Harvard University Press.

Whitehead, T. N. (1938) *The Industrial Worker*, London: Oxford University Press.

Whitley, R. (1984) 'The Fragmented State of Management Studies', *Journal of Management Studies*, 21. 3: 331–48.

Whitley, R. (1987) 'Taking Firms Seriously as Economic Actors: Towards a Sociology of Firm Behaviour', *Organisation Studies*, 8. 2: 125–47.

Whitley, R. (1992a) *Business Systems in East Asia*, London: Sage.

Whitley, R. (1992b) *European Business Systems: Firms and Markets in Their National Contexts*, London: Sage.

Whitley, R. (1994) 'The Internationalisation of Firms and Markets', *Organisation*, 1. 1: 101–24.

Whitley, R. (1999) *Divergent Capitalism: The Social Structuring and Change of Business Systems*, Oxford: Oxford University Press.

Whittington, R. (1988) 'Environmental Structure and Theories of Strategic Choice', *Journal of Management Studies*, 25. 6: 521–36.

Whittington, R. (1991a) 'The Fragmentation of Industrial R&D', in A. Pollert (ed.), *Farewell to Flexibility?*, Oxford: London.

Whittington, R. (1991b) 'Putting Giddens into Action: Evolving Accounts of Managerial Agency', paper presented to the Conference, Towards a New Theory of Organizations, University of Keele.

Whyte, W. H. (1956) *The Organisation Man* (new edn, 2002), New York: Simon & Schuster.

Wichert, I. (2002) 'Job Insecurity and Work Intensification: The Effects on Health and Well-Being', in B. Burchell, D. Ladipo and F. Wilkinson (eds), *Job Insecurity and Work Intensification*, London: Routledge.

Wickens, P. (1987) *The Road to Nissan*, London: Macmillan.

Wickens, P. D. (1992) 'Lean Production and Beyond: The System, its Critics and the Future', *Human Resource Management Journal*, 3. 4: 75–89.

Wiener, N. (1948) *Cybernetics: Control and Communication in the Animal and the Machine*, Cambridge, MA: MIT Press.

Wiese, B. S. (2000). *Berufliche und familïare Zielstrukturen* (Work-related and family-related goal Structures). Münster, Germany: Waxmann.

Wiese, B. S., Freund, A. M. and Baltes, P. B. (2002) 'Subjective Career Success and Emotional Well-Being: Longitudinal Predictive Power of Selection, Optimization, and Compensation', *Journal of Vocational Behavior*, 60. 3, June: 321–35.

Wilkinson, A. (1992) 'The Other Side of Quality: Soft Issues and the Human Resource Dimension', *Total Quality Management*, 3. 3: 323–9.

Wilkinson, A., Godfrey, G. and Marchington, M. (1997) 'Bouquets, Brickbats and Blinkers: Total Quality Management and Employee Involvement in Practice', *Organisation Studies*, 18. 5: 799–819.

Wilkinson, A., Marchington, M. and Goodman, J. (1992) 'Total Quality Management and Employee Involvement', *Human Resource Management Journal*, 2. 4: 1–20.

Wilkinson, A. and Willmott, H. (1994) 'Introduction', in A. Wilkinson and H. Willmott (eds), *Making Quality Critical*, London: Routledge & Kegan Paul.

Wilkinson, B. (1983a) *The Shopfloor Politics of New Technology*, London: Heinemann.

Wilkinson, B. (1983b) 'Technical Change and Work Organisation', *Industrial Relations Journal*, 14. 2: 221–48.

Wilkinson, B. (1986) 'Human Resources in Singapore's Second Industrial Revolution', *Industrial Relations Journal*, 17. 2: 99–114.

Williams, C. (2007) *Rethinking the Future of Work: Directions and Visions*, Basingstoke: Palgrave.

Williams, K., Cutler, T., Williams, J. and Haslam, C. (1987) 'The End of Mass Production?' *Economy and Society*, 16. 3: 405–39.

Williams, K., Haslam, C., Williams J. and Cutler, T. with Adcroft, A. and Juhal, S. (1992a) 'Against Lean Production', *Economy and Society*, 21. 3: 321–54.

Williams, K., Haslam, C., Williams J. and Cutler, T. (1992b) 'Ford-v-"Fordism": The Beginning of Mass Production', *Work, Employment and Society*, 6. 1: 517–48.

Williams, R. (1988) 'The Development of Models of Technology and Work Organisation with Information and Communication Technologies', paper presented to the Conference on the Labour Process, Aston-UMIST.

Williamson, O. (1975) *Markets and Hierarchies*, New York: Free Press.

Williamson, O. (1981) 'The Economics of Organisation', *American Journal of Sociology*, 87: 548–77.

Willis, P. (1977) *Learning to Labour*, Farnborough: Saxon House.

Willmott, H. (1984) 'Images and Ideals of Managerial Work', *Journal of Management Studies*, 21. 3: 349–68.

Willmott, H. (1987) 'Studying Managerial Work: A Critique and a Proposal', *Journal of Management Studies*, 24. 3: 249–70.

Willmott, H. (1989) 'Subjectivity and the Dialectics of Praxis: Opening up the Core of Labour Process Analysis', in D. Knights and H. Willmott (eds), *Labour Process Theory*, London: Macmillan.

Willmott, H. (1990) 'Beyond Paradigmatic Closure in Organisational Enquiry', in J. Hassard and D. Pym (eds), *The Theory and Philosophy of Organizations*, London: Routledge.

Willmott, H. (1992) 'Postmodernism and Excellence: The De-differentiation of Economy and Culture', *Journal of Organisational Change*, 5. 1: 69–79.

Willmott, H. (1993a) 'Strength is Ignorance; Slavery is Freedom: Managing Culture in Modern Organisation', *Journal of Management Studies*, 30. 5: 515–52.

Willmott, H. (1993b) 'Managing the Academics: Commodification and Control in the Development of University Education in the UK', unpublished paper.

Willmott, H. (1994) 'Theorising Agency: Power and Subjectivity in Organisation Studies', in J. Hassard and M. Parker (eds), *Towards a New Theory of Organizations*, London: Routledge.

Willmott, H. (1995) 'What Has Been Happening in Organisation Theory and Does it Matter?' *Personnel Review*, 24. 8: 33–53.

Wilson, E. (ed.) (2001) *Organisational Behaviour Reassessed: The Impact of Gender*, London: Sage.

Wilson, F. and Thompson, P. (2001) 'Sexual Harassment as an Exercise of Power', *Gender, Work and Organizations*, 8. 1: 61–83.

Wilson, F. M. (1995) *Organisational Behaviour and Gender*, London: McGraw-Hill.

Wilson, G. (1997) 'Biology, Sex Roles and Work', in *Liberating Women from Modern Feminism*, London: Institute of Economic Affairs.

Wilson, T. (2001) *Re: Knowledge Management Teaching*, Jiscmail archives at http://www.jiscmail.ac.uk/cgi-bin/wa.exe?A2=indo112&L=know-org&P=R224&I=-3.

Wilson, T. (2002) 'The Nonsense of 'Knowledge Management', *Information Research*, 8. 1, October, available at – http://informationr.net/ir/8-1/paper144.html.

Winfield, I. J. and Kerrin, M. (1994) 'Catalyst for Organisational Learning: The Case of Toyota Motor Manufacturing UK Ltd', *The Learning Organisation*, 1. 3: 4–9, MCB University Press.

Wise, S. and Stanley, L. (1990) 'Sexual Harassment, Sexual Conduct and Gender in Social Work Settings', in *Social Work and Social Welfare Handbook*, Milton Keynes: Open University Press.

Witz, A. (1986) 'Patriarchy and the Labour Market: Occupational Controls and the Medical Division of Labour', in D. Knights and H. Willmott (eds), *Managing the Labour Process*, Aldershot: Gower.

Witz, A. (1992) *Professions and Patriarchy*, London: Routledge.

Witz, A., Halford, S. and Savage, M. (1994) 'Organized Bodies: Gender, Sexuality, Bodies and Organizational Culture', paper presented to the BSA Conference, Sexualities in their Social Context, University of Central Lancashire, March.

Witz, A. and Savage, M. (1992) 'The Gender of Organizations', in M. Savage and A. Witz (eds) *Gender and Bureaucracy*, Oxford: Blackwell.

Witz, A. and Savage, M. (eds) (1992) *Gender and Bureaucracy*, Oxford: Blackwell.

Witz, A., Warhurst, C. and Nickson, D. (2003) 'The Labour of Aesthetics and the Aesthetics of Organization', *Organization*, 10. 1: 33–54.

Wolkowitz, C. (2006) *Bodies at Work*, London: Sage

Womack, J., Jones, D. and Roos, D. (1990) *The Machine that Changed the World*, New York: Macmillan.

Wood, S. (1979) 'A Reappraisal of the Contingency Approach to Organisation', *Journal of Management Studies*, 16. 3: 334–54.

Wood, S. (ed.) (1982) *The Degradation of Work: Skill, Deskilling and the Labour Process*, London: Hutchinson.

Wood, S. (1986) 'The Cooperative Labour Strategy in the US Auto Industry', *Economic and Industrial Democracy*, 7. 4: 415–48.

Wood, S. (ed.) (1989a) *The Transformation of Work?* London: Hutchinson.

Wood. S. (1989b) 'The Japanese Management Model', unpublished paper.

Wood, S. and Albanese, M. T. (1995) 'Can We Speak of High Commitment Management on the Shop Floor?', *Journal of Management Studies*, 32: 215–45.

Wood, S. and de Menzes, L. (1998) 'High Commitment Management in the UK', *Human Relations*, 51: 485–515.

Woodward, J. (1958) *Management and Technology*, London: HMSO.

Woodward, J. (1965) *Industrial Organisation: Theory and Practice*, London: Oxford University Press.

Woolf, J. (1977) 'Women in Organisations', in S. Clegg and D. Dunkerley (eds), *Critical Issues in Organisations*, London: Routledge & Kegan Paul.

Wray, D. (1994) 'Paternalism and its Discontents: A Case Study', paper presented to the 12th International Labour Process Conference, Aston.

Wright, C. and Lund, J. (1996) 'Best-Practice Taylorism: "Yankee Speed-Up" in Australian Grocery Distribution', *Journal of Industrial Relations*, 38. 2: 196–212.

Wright, C. and Lund, J. (1998) '"Under the Clock": Trade Union Responses to Computer-ised Control in US and Australian Grocery Warehousing', *New Technology, Work and Employment*, 13. 1: 3–15.

Wright, S. (1994) 'Culture in Anthropology and Organisational Studies', in S. Wright (ed.), *Anthropology of Organizations*, London: Routledge.

Yakhlef, A. and Salzer-Morling, M. (2000) 'Intellectual Capital: Managing by Numbers', in C. Prichard, R. Hull, M. Chumer and H. Willmott (eds), *Managing Knowledge: Critical Investigations of Work and Learning*, London: Macmillan.

Yarrow, M. (1992) 'Class and Gender in the Developing Consciousness of Appalachian Coal-Miners', in A. Sturdy, D. Knights and H. Willmott (eds), *Skill and Consent*, London: Routledge.

Yates, D. (1986) 'Is Dual Labour Market Theory Dead? The Changing Organisation of Work: The Employer's Perspective', paper presented at the Conference on the Labour Process, Aston-UMIST.

Zeitlin, M. (1974) 'Corporate Ownership and Control: The Large Corporation and the Capitalist Class', *American Journal of Sociology*, 79. 5: 1073–119.

Zimbalist, A. (ed.) (1979) *Case Studies on the Labour Process*, New York: Monthly Review Press.

Zimbardo, P. G., Ebbesen, E. B. and Maslach, C. (1977) *Influencing Attitudes and Changing Behaviour* (2nd edn), Reading, MA: Addison-Wesley.

Zimmerman, D. (1971) 'The Practicalities of Rule Use', in J. Douglas (ed.), *Understanding Everyday Life*, London: Routledge & Kegan Paul.

Zuboff, S. (1988) *In the Age of the Smart Machine: The Future of Work and Power*, Oxford: Heinemann.

Zummato, R. (1988) 'Organisational Adaptation: Some Implications of Organisational Ecology for Strategic Choice', *Journal of Management Studies*, 25. 2: 105–20.

name index

Waterman, R. H. 105
Watson, T. 12, 91, 94, 95, 96, 111, 125, 126, 173, 291, 421, 435, 438
Webb, J. 155, 175, 388, 393, 403, 405
Webber, A. 195, 337
Weber, M. 4, 14, 16, 17, 19, 28, 34, 35, 36, 38, 39, 40, 41, 75, 124, 127, 128, 131, 140, 182, 222, 381, 407, 409, 410, 411, 415, 418, 422, 423, 424, 425, 426, 430, 432
Webster, F. 140, 148, 191
Webster, M. F. and Robbins, K. 132, 181
Weick, K. 168, 169, 255, 318
Weigert, A. J. 390, 396
Weigert, A. J. et al. 389
Weightman, J. 259
Weiner, N. 320
Weir, D. 421
Weise, B. 356, 365
Weissman, R. 313
Weldon, F. 144
Wellin, M. 317
Wenger, E. 242, 286
West, P. 298
Westwood, R.I. and Clegg, S. 442, 443
Westwood, R.I. and Linstead, S. 432
Westwood, S. 148, 167, 393
Wexler, P. 316, 391, 426
Wheeler, S. and Lyon, D. 353, 354
Whipp, R. 112
Whitaker, A. 66
White, M. et al. 206, 209, 212, 213, 219, 231, 251
Whitehead, T. 45, 50
Whitley, R. 68, 77, 78, 79, 81, 84, 87, 88, 91, 101, 414
Whittington, R. 65, 210
Whyte, W. H. 4, 158, 159, 174, 177, 307, 385
Wickens, P. 218, 220
Wilkinson, A. 64, 109
Wilkinson, A. and Willmott, H. 39, 220
Wilkinson, A., Godfrey, W. and Marchington, M. 171, 225, 226
Williams, C. 191

Williams, K. et al. 32, 81, 184, 186, 220
Williams, R. 187, 197
Williamson, O. 36, 37, 67, 133
Willis, P. 167
Willmott, H. 91, 123, 131, 160, 167, 168, 170, 172, 176, 177, 228, 381, 413, 432, 442
Wilson, F.M. and Thompson, P. 137, 149
Wilson, F.M. 140
Wilson, G. 142, 144
Wilson, T. 233, 237, 238, 239, 240, 241, 243, 246
Winfield, I. J. and Kerrin, M. 300
Winstanley, D. 109
Wise, S. and Stanley, L. 150, 152, 153
Witz, A. 112, 156
Witz, A. and Savage, M. 139, 143, 144, 157
Witz, A. et al. 222
Witz, A. Warhurst, C. and Nickson, D. 150, 157
Witz, A., Halford, D. and Savage, M. 150, 152, 153
Wolkowitz, C. 130, 150, 153, 157
Womack, J. et al. 81, 196
Womack, J., Roos, D. and Jones, D. 217
Wood, S. 60, 63, 65, 109, 185, 199, 221, 222, 225, 226
Wood, S. and De Menzes, L. 218
Woodward, J. 60, 61, 413
Woolf, J. 14
Wray, D. 165
Wright Mills, C. 5
Wright, C. and Lund, J. 39, 220
Wright, E. O. 167, 171

Yakhlef, A. and Sulzer-Morling, M. 189
Yarrow, M. 384, 385
Yates, D. 208

Zeitlin, M. 106
Zimbalist, A. 109
Zimbardo, P. G. et al. 277, 278
Zimmerman, D. 416
Zuboff, S. 97, 115, 116, 136, 344

subject index

values,   7–10, 21, 45–9, 55, 75–7, 124, 144–7, 218, 305, 322–3,
    369–70, 380–4, 410–12, 421–2, 427
  role of in organisations   58–76, 260–9, 374–8
  and motivation 294–8, 301, 305
Volvo 216, 225
  see also groups

Weberian theory   13, 35–7, 92, 149, 195, 416–18
  neo-Weberianism   38–40, 143, 354–7
  radical Weberianism   408, 422–8, 434, 442
WERS surveys   217–18, 224–5, 250, 357, 378–9
Work-life balance, boundaries   143, 230–1, 344, 348, 354–7,
    365–6